A DOCUMENTARY HISTORY
of RELIGION *in* AMERICA

Since 1877

A DOCUMENTARY HISTORY
of RELIGION *in* AMERICA

Since 1877

THIRD EDITION

Edited by

Edwin S. Gaustad

with revisions by

Mark A. Noll

WILLIAM B. EERDMANS PUBLISHING COMPANY
GRAND RAPIDS, MICHIGAN / CAMBRIDGE, U.K.

Library of Congress Cataloging-in-Publication Data

A Documentary history of religion in America /
    edited by Edwin S. Gaustad and Mark A. Noll. — 3rd ed.
     p.   cm.
    Includes bibliographical references and indexes.
    Contents: [1] To 1877 — [2] Since 1877.
    ISBN 0-8028-2229-0 (v. 1). — ISBN 0-8028-2230-4 (v. 2)
    1. United States — Religion — Sources. I. Gaustad, Edwin S. (Edwin Scott)
    BL2525.D63   1993
    200'.973 — dc20   93-25309
                                           CIP

For Evan Scott

Contents

Preface to the Third Edition   xix

Preface to the Second Edition   xx

Preface to the First Edition   xxi

Illustrations   xxiii

Acknowledgments   xxvi

CHAPTER SEVEN

A New Religious Landscape   1

  1. Bound for the Promised Land   6

    The Ocean's Bounty   6

     Europe   6

     Asia   10

    Roman Catholicism   13

     Education   13

     Ethnicity   17

     Liberty   21

    Judaism   24

     Education   24

     Organization   29

  2. Women's Work?   35

    Pulpit   35

    Society   39

    Academy   43

3. **The West**   47

    Western Indians   47

       Pierre Jean De Smet and the Sioux   47

       Sheldon Jackson, John Brady, and Alaska's Natives   50

    "Western Orthodoxy": Russia in America   52

       Russian Orthodoxy in Alaska   52

       Russian Orthodoxy in Western America   56

    "Western" Orient: Asia in Hawaii   58

4. **A New World — Abroad and at Home**   61

    Empire or Republic: Spanish-American War   61

       For Republic   61

       For Empire   62

       "The Philippine Question"   64

    A New Enthusiasm for Mission   67

       Missionary Review of the World   67

       Women Missionary Mobilization   69

    World's Parliament of Religions   71

       Hinduism   71

       Buddhism   73

       Islam   76

    The Uses of Diversity   78

       Census of 1890   78

       African-American Expansion   79

       American Dream   80

    Suggested Reading   84

CHAPTER EIGHT

Religion and Society Engaged   87

1. **Love and Justice**   93

    Redeeming the City   93

       Josiah Strong   93

       Washington Gladden   94

       John Lancaster Spalding   97

       Samuel S. Mayerberg   98

In His Steps 102
Redeeming the Factory 104
Frederic Dan Huntington 104
James Cardinal Gibbons 106
Walter Rauschenbusch 109
Pastoral Letter, 1920 111
Commission on Social Justice, 1928 112
Redeeming the Land 114
Walter Rauschenbusch 114
Edward McGlynn 117
Richard T. Ely 119
George D. Herron 121
John A. Ryan 122

2. War and Peace 125
Ploughshares to Swords: World War I 125
"To Love Is to Hate" 125
The Madness of Men 128
"The Lessons of War" 131
Peace and Disarmament 132
Church Peace Union 132
Kirby Page and the Churches 134
Frank Buchman and Moral Re-Armament 138

3. Evangelization of the World 142
Protestant Empire Revived 142
John R. Mott 142
Robert E. Speer 144
E. Stanley Jones 147
American Catholicism's New Era 148
Missionary Conference, 1908 148
Maryknoll, 1911 152
The Disinherited Abroad 155
Black Baptists, 1903 155
Mormons, 1904 158
Persecuted Witnesses, 1934 162

Missions Reevaluated 164
W. H. P. Faunce 164
William E. Hocking 165

4. New Structures 168
Comforting the Afflicted 168
Salvation Army 168
The "Y" Movement 172
Society of St. Vincent de Paul 174
Jewish Welfare Board 176
Gathering the Divided 178
Federal Council and Christian Cooperation 178
National Catholicism 180
Cooperative Judaism 181
Drying Out the Republic 183
Billy Sunday 183
Anti-Saloon League 185
Suggested Reading 188

CHAPTER NINE
Worlds Within and Beyond 193

1. Private Religion 199
Inspirational Reading: Lives of Jesus 199
The Greatest Story Ever Told 199
The Nazarene 202
The Robe 204
Bible Reading and Daily Meditation 206
Advice to Catholic Girls 206
A Protestant "Book of Hours" 209
The Inner Life 211
Prayer 211
Mysticism 212
Contemplation 214
One Day in Seven 217
"Remember the Sabbath Day" 217

"And on the First Day of the Week . . ."   219
Popular Preaching   221
    G. Campbell Morgan   221
    George W. Truett   222
    Francis J. McConnell   223
    Henry S. Coffin   225

2. **New Thought and New Thoughts**   **227**
    Theosophy and New Thought   227
       H. P. Blavatsky   227
       Warren Felt Evans   230
       Ralph Waldo Trine   232
    Institutions of New Thought   234
       Christian Science   234
       Unity School of Christianity   237
       Church of Religious Science   239
    Peace and Prosperity   242
       Acres of Diamonds   242
       You Can Win   243
    Psychology and Religion   245
       Emmanuel Movement   245
       Physicians of the Soul   247
       What Spiritual Healing Is   250

3. **Society Out of Joint**   **252**
    Unsafe for Democracy   252
       American Protective Association and Immigration   252
       The Klan's Americanism   256
       Rum and Rome   263
    Unsure of Capitalism   268
       Economic Disaster   268
       Christian Love   272
       Political Realism   275

4. **World Out of Time**   **278**
    Revivalism   278
       Dwight L. Moody   278

Sam Jones   281
Billy Sunday   282
Millennialism   284
Jehovah's Witnesses   284
Foursquare Gospel   286
Dispensationalism   288
Holiness and Pentecostalism   291
Doctrine   291
Experience   294
Cure of Souls   297
Suggested Reading   298

CHAPTER TEN

Religion and the Life of the Mind   303

1. Philosophy and Religion   308
   William James   308
   Josiah Royce   312
   Alfred North Whitehead   314
   John Dewey   317
   George Santayana   319

2. Science and Religion   322
   Confrontation   322
   John W. Draper   322
   John Wesley Powell   324
   T. DeWitt Talmage   327
   James Cardinal Gibbons   330
   Mediation   333
   Joseph Le Conte   333
   James McCosh   336
   B. B. Warfield   338
   John Augustine Zahm   341
   Litigation: The Scopes Trial   343
   Clarence Darrow   344
   William Jennings Bryan   346

Kirtley F. Mather 348

Bryan 350

3. **Studying and Reading the Bible** 353

Text and Context 353

"Bibles with the Bible" 353

Origins of the New Testament 356

"A Jewish Interpretation" 358

"The New Approach" 360

Reactions and Results 364

Protestant Trials 364

Catholic Concerns 370

Biblical Societies and Studies 372

New Bible Translations 377

Bible Translations Explained 377

Bible Translations Illustrated 386

4. **Modernism/Fundamentalism** 391

Roman Catholicism 391

Battle of the Bishops 391

Rome Speaks — and Is Spoken To 396

Protestantism 401

Christianity and Liberalism 401

The Faith of Modernism 404

Judaism 406

Reform Platforms 406

Conservative Approaches 412

5. **Theological Aftermath** 419

Neo-Orthodoxy 419

H. Richard Niebuhr 419

Paul Tillich 422

Neo-Thomism 426

The French Philosophers 426

An American Perspective 431

Neo-Fundamentalism: Evangelical Responsibility 432

Suggested Reading 436

CHAPTER ELEVEN
Consensus and Conflict   **439**

1. The World and Its Wars   446
   Legacy of World War II   446
      Hiroshima   446
      Holocaust   449
   Zionism and the State of Israel   452
      "Let Sovereignty Be Granted"   452
      "Zionism in America"   454
      "Fighting for Israel"   457
      "After Zionism"   458
   Fighting Communism: Hot Wars and Cold   463
      Cold War   463
      Vietnam   465
      Cold War Ended   470
   War in the Gulf   473
      Desert Storm, 1991   473
      Iraqi Freedom, 2003   478

2. Society and Its Conflicts, 1950s and 1960s   484
   Communism and the Churches   484
      "Reds and Our Churches"   484
      "I Protest"   487
   Civil Rights and the Churches   490
      Martin Luther King, Jr.   490
      Black Manifesto, 1969   494
      Response to Racism and Manifesto   496
   Politics and Religion — 1960s   498
      "A Roman Catholic for President?"   498
      "It Is My Job to Face It . . ."   501
   Moral Responsibility and Religion   504
      The Great Society   504
      The Betrayed Society   506

3. The Nation and Its Churches   509

   The Ecumenical Age   509

     National Council and World Council   509

     Consultation on Church Union/Churches Uniting in Christ   514

     The Lausanne Covenant   516

   Strife in the Denominations   523

     The Lutheran Church–Missouri Synod   523

     The Southern Baptist Convention   528

   Vatican II and Beyond   535

     "Pope John's 'Revolution'"   535

     Liturgical Renewal   539

     Religious Liberty   543

     Ecumenism Outlined   547

     Ecumenism Practiced   549

   Eastern Orthodoxy and American Culture   552

     Ethnicity and Religion   552

     Elusive Unity   555

     At the Start of a New Century   557

4. Revival and Retreat   559

   Postwar Revivalism: Billy Graham   559

   Theological Retreat   563

     Peace and Positive Thoughts   563

     The Death of God   566

     Religious Humanism   568

   Suggested Reading   569

CHAPTER TWELVE

E Pluribus . . . Unum?   575

  1. Pluralism Plus   584

   The Far East and the Near East in America   584

     Buddhism   584

     Islam   590

   Fatal Movements   596

     Jonestown   596

  Branch Davidians   600

  Neopaganism: The Circle   603

2. **Liberation/Alienation**   **608**

  African-Americans   608

   Liberation Theology   608

   Muslim Theology   610

  Hispanics   613

   Unity in Pluralism   613

   A Pastoral Plan   616

   Hispanic Evangelicals   618

  Native Americans   620

   Indian Religious Freedom Act, 1978 620

   Ecclesiastical Support   621

  Women   623

   Judaism   623

   Mormonism   628

   Roman Catholicism   631

   Conservatives   634

3. **Litigation/Division**   **638**

  Education   638

   Prayer and Meditation   638

   A Conservative Court and Separation 640

   Equal Access as "Free Exercise" 642

  Religious Freedom Restoration   649

   Religious Freedom Constrained 649

   Religious Freedom Restoration Act 651

   Judicial Setback   653

  Contraception and Abortion   655

   Contraception: Humanae Vitae   655

   Abortion: The Courts, 1973, 1989, 1992 660

   Abortion: The Churches, 1984, 1985, 1987, 1996 666

  Homosexuality and the Churches   672

4. Religion and the Public Order 679

Religious Dimensions of Public Life 679

Religious Belief and Public Morality 679

A Reformulated "Christian America"? 682

Religion and the Ballot, 1996 685

Religion and the Ballot, 2000 687

Presidents 690

Jimmy Carter 690

Ronald Reagan 694

Bill Clinton 696

George W. Bush 700

September 11, 2001 701

5. Into the New Millennium 709

Institutional Religion 709

Promise Keepers 709

The Black Church 711

Willow Creek 714

Drawing Boundaries 717

Lakota Nation 717

Jewish Students at Yale 720

Y2K and Beyond 723

Trauma within Catholicism 728

Crisis 728

Voice of the Faithful 731

Theology in the New Century 734

Mormons 734

Mestizaje 736

Suggested Reading 740

Index 747

Preface to the Third Edition

The scholarship of Edwin Gaustad that lay behind earlier editions of this documentary history was as impeccable for that purpose as it has been for all of his other major interpretations of American religion. As reviser, I have tried to do the minimum of necessary refurbishing in order to preserve the cohesion and breadth of those earlier editions. That refurbishing has meant an update of the bibliographical essays for the twelve chapters, a new set of documents for the dozen or so years since the second edition was prepared, and a few additions to reflect recent scholarly concerns. Those additions include a little more on the Civil War as a religious event, a few more documents reporting religious developments among women and people of color, and one or two new contributions related to research interests of my own. By way of compensation a few documents from the second edition have been dropped, but Professor Gaustad's major, and even secondary, emphases still prevail. The conceptualization, organization, and flow of this edition remain his. I have been privileged to lend a hand in updating this work for what I hope will be another generation of readers as grateful as I have been for Ed Gaustad's discerning guidance through the past. I am also pleased to acknowledge the great help I have received from my research assistant, Luke Harlow.

Mark A. Noll

Preface to the Second Edition

As noted in the preface to the first edition, the story of American religion is "still being told." Since that is the case, much notice had to be given to aspects of that ongoing story not covered in the first edition, now a decade old. These changes will be most apparent in Chapter Twelve, but newer developments have also been introduced elsewhere.

As in Volume One, permit me also here to express appreciation for the warm reception that the *Documentary* has received. I also wish once again to thank James D. LeShana for his able assistance in bibliographical matters.

E. S. G.

Preface to the First Edition

As in the case of Volume One *(To the Civil War)*, this second and concluding volume enables the reader to be his or her own historian. Using the many original sources here provided, the reader can construct a narrative, offer an analysis, arrive at an individually tailored synthesis. On the other hand, one may — in somewhat more relaxed fashion — simply enjoy the plethora of voices, now and then taking sides (or issue) with those who vigorously defend a given point of view.

Few of the documents that follow stand outside the stream of America's religious history. Most are written or spoken or hurled by persons planted firmly within that stream, by those drawing from the water's source and vitally concerned about its future direction. Disinterested documents are, in other words, the exception and not the rule. Which is just as well, for a large volume given over to authors who cared neither one way nor another about the outcome would make for a very dull book. Partisan voices have more flavor, if not always a perfect balance of piquancy and spice. An editorial aim has been to offer enough balance in introductions, documents, and suggested readings to set a table sufficient for virtually any taste. Naturally, it is never possible to empty the entire storehouse at any one time, however desirable in theory that might appear to be. In the long run, it is probably better to know that men and women have cared (and cared deeply) about a wide range of "faith and order" options than to know that every affirmation has its alternative or even its negation.

An explicit intent of Volume One, to be faithful to America's religious pluralism, persists in Volume Two. At times, however, the task has been not so much to be faithful to pluralism as to avoid being drowned by it. That is, one could concentrate so heavily on giving every novelty its due, granting to every marginal group its moment on center stage, that the major traditions, the large constituencies, the long-lived denominations would be shoved aside. The effort, especially in the twentieth century, has been to avoid both extremes: neither wholly ignoring the new and small nor wholly ignoring the old and large.

Of course, both reader and editor must know that no single simple principle explains every inclusion or justifies each omission.

Finally, here as before, personal exultation or exasperation has been preferred over the cool and generally clumsy prose of the committee. Rabbi Samuel Mayerberg's fight against municipal corruption in Kansas City or Pastor Washington Gladden's similar battle in Columbus, Ohio, make better reading than any Report on Measures for Consideration and Possible Adoption by the City Council. And candidate Alfred Smith's personal plea in Oklahoma during a tough presidential campaign may tell us more about American religion than any heavy-handed analysis of the Origins and Expressions of Protestant Nativism in Selected Communities of Pre-Depression United States.

The courtesy of publishers and journal editors is acknowledged elsewhere. Here I express sincerest appreciation to the University of California, Riverside, for intramural grants; to graduate student Jim German for tireless and efficient sleuthing in pursuit of elusive documents; and to Eerdmans editor Charles Van Hof for alert, discerning, and even good-humored direction of both volumes of this Documentary History. The nation's religious history is a full one: a drama with an enormous cast of characters, a story still being told.

E. S. G.

Illustrations

Fiesta of Santiago, Chimayo, New Mexico   cover
courtesy Maryknoll Missionaries, photo by M. Sandoval

Ellis Island, 1907   21

New York City, 1900   33

Lucretia Mott   45

Nez Perce Woman's Missionary Society   48

Pierre Jean De Smet, S.J.   49

Russian Orthodox cathedral, Sitka, Alaska   54

Russian Orthodox deputation from the Soviet Union   57

Buddhist Temple, Hawaii   60

Cardinal Gibbons with President McKinley and Admiral Dewey   65

Zen Buddhist meditation   75

El Rancho de Las Golondrinas, La Cienaga, New Mexico   81

Washington Gladden   95

James Cardinal Gibbons   108

Walter Rauschenbusch   115

Child laborers   118

John A. Ryan   123

World War I ambulance   129

China Bible School   145

Maryknoll missionary, Chile   153

Maryknoll missionary, Japan   154

Joseph Smith, Anthon Lund, and John Winder   160

Salvation Army coal distribution   170

Suffragette picketing the White House, 1918   187

Sharecropper, 1939   208

Synagogue service, 1944   210

Thomas Merton with the Dalai Lama   215

New York Herald cartoon — Sunday blue laws   219

Christian Science sanitarium, San Francisco   236

Ku Klux Klan parade   258

Ku Klux Klan pamphlet   262

Catholic Worker Movement House of Hospitality   273

Moody and Sankey revival   280

Aimee Semple McPherson   287

Storefront Holiness church   293

Speaking in tongues   295

E. J. Pace cartoon   328

Lyman Abbott   340

William Jennings Bryan and wife   351

E. J. Pace cartoon   362

Gutenberg Bible commemorative stamp   379

Patrick Skehan and New American Bible   381

John Ireland   393

Yeshiva University   414

Traditionalist synagogue   416

Paul Tillich   424

Survivors at Nagasaki, 1945   447

Munich synagogue, 1930s   451

Vietnam protest, 1967   469

G. Bromley Oxnam   488

Martin Luther King   492

James Forman   496

Emblem of the National Council of Churches   511

World Council of Churches Assembly, 1954 513

Pope John XXIII and Brooks Hays 537

Traditional Catholic mass 541

John Courtney Murray, S.J. 545

Greek Orthodox church, California 554

Billy Graham and President Richard Nixon 561

President Bill Clinton 582

Zen Buddhist meditation 586

Buddhist Temple, Los Angeles 588

Buddhist Temple, interior 588

Muslims at prayer 592

Islamic Center, Los Angeles 592

American Muslims 595

Jim Jones 598

Martin Luther King and Malcolm X 611

Requiem Mass, Santa Fe, New Mexico 614

Father Ksistaki-Poka 622

Rabbi Sally Priesand 625

Ordination of three Episcopal women 629

Ordination of Bishop Barbara Harris 633

Antiabortion protest, 1978 668

Proposition 22 meeting 675

Pope John Paul II and President Jimmy Carter 692

Terror evangelism 703

Promise Keepers meeting 710

Left Behind still 726

Acknowledgments

Publishers and Periodicals

With much gratitude I acknowledge the helpfulness of publishers, editors, and private individuals who have agreed to the use of materials under their control.

Abingdon Press. © 1968 Walter Rauschenbusch, *The Righteousness of the Kingdom.*

American Mercury. J. B. Matthews in Vol. 77 (July, 1953).

American Sociological Association. Nancy T. Ammerman, "Lessons from Waco," (American Sociological Association) *Footnotes* 22:1 (1994):3.

Asch, Moses. Sholern Asch, *The Nazarene* (1939).

Atlantic Monthly. H. P. Van Dusen in Vol. 154 (August, 1934).

Augsburg Fortress Press. *Justification by Faith: Lutherans and Catholics in Dialogue,* VII, ed. H. George Anderson, T. Austin Murphy, and Joseph A. Burgess (Minneapolis: Fortress, 1985), pp. 15-16, 73-74. © 1990 John H. Tietjen, *Memoir in Exile.*

Baker Books. Robert D. Preus, "Foreword," to Kurt E. Marquart, *Anatomy of an Explosion: A Theological Analysis of the Missouri Synod Conflict* (Grand Rapids: Baker, 1977), pp. 3-5. Robert G. Clouse, Robert N. Hosack, and Richard V. Pierard, *The New Millennium Manual: A Once and Future Guide* (Grand Rapids: Baker, 1999), pp. 187-88.

Billy Graham Evangelistic Association. *Christianism vs. Communism* (Minneapolis: Billy Graham Evangelistic Association, 1951), pp. 1, 3-4.

Bloch Publishing Co. S. S. Mayerburg, *Chronicle of an American Crusader* (1944).

Center for Migration Studies. S. J. LaGumina, *The Immigrants Speak* (1979).

Christian Century. James L. Guth, John C. Green, Corwin E. Smidt, and Lyman A. Kellstedt, "Partisan Religion," Copyright 2001 *Christian Century.* Reprinted by permission from the March 21-28, 2001, issue of the *Christian Century.* Interview with Juan Williams, "This Far by Faith: The Power of the Black Church," copyright 2003 *Christian Century.* Reprinted by permission from the May 31, 2003, issue of the *Christian Century.*

Christian Century Foundation. Billy Graham in Vol. 77 (Feb. 17, 1960).

Christianity Today. Carl Henry in July 8 and July 22, 1957, issues. "The Lausanne Covenant," *Christianity Today,* August 16, 1974, pp. 22-23; used by permission. George Brushaber, "War Cry," *Christianity Today,* Jan. 14, 1991, p. 14.

Commentary. Hillel Halkin, "After Zionism: Reflections on Israel and the Diaspora," reprinted from *Commentary,* June 1997, by permission. All rights reserved.

Joan Daves. © 1963 Martin Luther King, Jr., excerpt from "I Have a Dream."

Mrs. Virginia Douglas Dawson. Lloyd C. Douglas, *The Robe* (1942).

Dial Press. © 1971 T. C. Wheeler, *The Immigrant Experience.*

Doubleday & Co. © 1981 Sonia Johnson, *From Housewife to Heretic.* © 1949 Fulton Oursler, *The Greatest Story Ever Told.* © 1947 Fulton J. Sheen, *Peace of Soul.*

Edwin Mellen Press. © 1988 Rebecca Moore, *In Defense of People's Temple.*

Eerdmans. Richard V. Pierard, "We Are the People — The Revolution in East Germany," *Reformed Journal,* January 1990, pp. 8, 9-10, 11. Roger Ruston, "The War of Religions and the Religion of War," in Brian Wicker, ed., *Studying War — No More? From Just War to Just Peace* (Grand Rapids: Eerdmans, 1994), pp. 13-31.

Fr. Virgilio P. Elizondo. "A Galilean Christology," in *The Future Is Mestizo,* rev. ed. (University Press of Colorado, 2000).

Farrar, Straus & Giroux, Inc. Thomas Merton, *Seasons of Celebration,* © 1950, 1958, 1962, 1964, 1965 by the Abbey of Gethsemani. Xavier Rynne, *Letters from Vatican City,* © 1963 by the publisher.

First Things. John Green, Lyman Kellstedt, James Guth, and Corwin Smidt, "Who Elected Clinton: A Collision of Values," *First Things,* Aug./Sept. 1997, pp. 35, 37-38. Richard John Neuhaus, "Civil Religion or Public Philosophy," *First Things,* Dec. 2000, pp. 69-73.

Focus on the Family. Randy Phillips, "Seize the Moment," in *Seven Promises of a Promise Keeper* (Colorado Springs: Focus on the Family, 1994), p. 8.

Forward Movement Publications (412 Sycamore St., Cincinnati). *Reports from Four Meetings* (n.d.).

Harcourt Brace Jovanovich, Inc. Thomas Merton, *The Sign of Jonas* (1953), © Abbey of Our Lady of Gethsemani, renewed 1981 by Trustees of the Merton Legacy Fund.

HarperCollins. © 1929, 1956 Reinhold Niebuhr, *Leaves from the Notebook of a Tamed Cynic.* © 1932 Laymen's Foreign Missions Inquiry, *Re-Thinking Missions.* Anton T. Boisen, *The Exploration of the Inner World,* © Willer, Clark & Co. © 1970 James H. Cone, *A Black Theology of Liberation.* © 1963 Martin Luther King, Jr., *Why We Can't Wait.* Dorothy Day, *The Long Loneliness,* © 1952 by the publisher. E. J. Goodspeed, *As I Remember,* © 1953 by the publisher. G. B. Oxnam, *I Protest,* © 1954 by the publisher. © 1977 James E. Adams, *Preus of Missouri and the Great Lutheran Civil War.*

Hodder & Stoughton. "Preface," *The Holy Bible: New International Version, Inclusive Language Edition* (London: Hodder & Stoughton, 1996), pp. vii-viii.

Horizon Press. © 1955 T. Friedman and R. Gordis, *Jewish Life in America.*

Jewish Publication Society of America. C. H. Voss, ed., *Stephen Wise* (1969). Blu Greenberg, *On Women and Judaism* (1981). "Preface," *Tanakh: A New Translation of the Holy Scriptures According to the Traditional Hebrew Text* (Philadelphia: Jewish Publication Society, 5746/1985), pp. xv, xvii, xviii, xix-xxi. *Tanakh: A New Translation of the Holy Scriptures According to the Traditional Hebrew Text* (Philadelphia: Jewish Publication Society, 5746/1985), pp. 1131-32.

Jewish Theological Seminary of America (Melton Research Center for Jewish Education). Nahum Sarna, *Understanding Genesis* (1966).

Little, Brown, and Company. The Investigative Staff of the *Boston Globe, Betrayal: The Crisis in the Catholic Church* (Boston: Little, Brown, 2003), pp. 205-7, 215-16.

McGraw Hill Book Co., © 1981. Kenneth Wooden, *Children of Jonestown.*

Macmillan Publishing Co. H. F. Ward, *Our Economic Morality and the Ethic of Jesus,* © 1929 by the publisher, © 1957 by the author. Rufus Jones, *Pathways to the Reality of God,* © 1931 by the publisher, © 1959 by Mary H. Jones. A. N. Whitehead, *Process and Reality,* © 1929 by the publisher, © 1957 by Evelyn Whitehead. H. R. Niebuhr, *The Meaning of Revelation,* © 1941 by the publisher, © 1969 by Florence Niebuhr, C. M. Niebuhr, R. R. Niebuhr. © 1957 Walter J. Ong, *Frontiers of American Catholicism.*

Methodist Church (Board of Church and Society). *Concern,* Vol. 7 (Dec. 1, 1965).

Multnomah Press. Ronald Reagan, Speech on March 8, 1983, Appendix III, in *Winning the New Civil War,* by Robert P. Dugan, Jr. (Portland, OR: Multnomah, 1991), pp. 215, 222-26.

Thomas Nelson and Sons. W. A. Irwin, in *An Introduction to the Revised Standard Version of the Old Testament* (New York: Thomas Nelson & Sons, 1952), pp. 12-14. *The Holy Bible: Revised Standard Version* (New York: Thomas Nelson & Sons, 1952), pp. 4-5).

New York Review of Books. © 1984 Mario Cuomo, "Religious Belief and Public Morality."

New York Times. © Special Report, September 8, 1928. Samuel G. Freedman, "Yeshivish at Yale," *New York Times Magazine,* May 24, 1998, pp. 32-35. "Bush Remarks on Shuttle: 'Destruction and Tragedy'," *New York Times,* Feb. 2, 2003, p. 32.

Oxford University Press. "Hsi Lai Temple, Buddhism Coming to the West (1997)," in Thomas A. Tweed and Stephen Prothero, eds., *Asian Religions in America: A Documentary History* (New York: Oxford, 1999), pp. 331-334. "Bernard Glassman and Rick Fields, 'Recipes for Social Change' (1996)," in Tweed and Prothero, *Asian Religions in America,* pp. 285-288.

Random House, Inc. Etienne Gilson, *The Philosopher and Theology* (1962). *The Autobiography of Malcolm X* (1964). Sam J. Ervin, Jr., *The Whole Truth* (1980). Jimmy Carter, *Living Faith* (2nd ed., New York: Random House, 1998), pp. 161-68.

Religious News Service. "A conversation with Willow Creek's Bill Hybels" by Adelle M. Banks. Copyright 1997 Religion News Service. Used by permission.

Religious Humanism. W. S. Fisk in Vol. 1 (Winter, 1967).

Fleming H. Revell Co. © 1946, 1974. C. S. Macfarland, *Pioneers for Peace Through Religion.*

Rutgers University Press. Christel Manning, *God Gave Us the Right: Conservative Catholic, Evangelical Protestant, and Orthodox Jewish Women Grapple with Feminism* (New Brunswick: Rutgers University Press, 1999), pp. 167-68, 192-95.

Schocken Books. © 1978 Emil L. Fackenheim, *The Jewish Return into History.* Arthur Hertzberg, *Being Jewish in America,* © 1979 by the publisher.

Charles Scribner's Sons. Reinhold Niebuhr, *Reflections on the End of an Era,* © 1934 by the publisher, 1962 by the author.

Sheed and Ward (Andrews and McMeel, Inc.). R. S. Lecky and H. E. Wright, eds., *Black Manifesto* (1969). C. E. Curran and R. E. Hunt, eds., *Dissent In and For the Church* (1969).

Simon & Schuster. © 1970, 1971 C. H. Voss, ed., *A Summons Unto All Men.* © 1979 Rosemary Radford Ruether and Eleanor McLaughlin, eds., *Women of Spirit.*

Sojourners. Jim Wallis, "Hearts & Minds," *Sojourners,* May-June 2003, 7-8. Reprinted with permission from *Sojourners.* (800) 714-7474, www.sojo.net.

St. Vladimir's Theological Quarterly. John H. Erickson, "Orthodox Theology in a Changing World," *St. Vladimir's Theological Quarterly* 46 (2002): 307-08, 310-11.

Time. Nancy Gibbs, "A First Thick Shock of War." © 1991 TIME Inc. reprinted by permission.

Tyndale Publishers. *The Living Bible: Paraphrased* (Wheaton, IL: Tyndale House, 1971), p. 748. Tim LaHaye and Jerry B. Jenkins, *Left Behind: A Novel of the Earth's Last Days* (Wheaton, IL: Tyndale, 1995), pp. 16-19.

Union of American Hebrew Congregations. Julian Morgenstern, *The Book of Genesis* (1965 [1919]).

United States Catholic Conference. © 1987, 1989 *National Pastoral Plan for Hispanic Ministry.* All used by permission.

Unity. Charles Fillmore in Vol. 106 (June, 1947).

University of Chicago Press. Paul Tillich, *Systematic Theology,* Vol. I (1951); © 1951 by the publisher. Josiah Royce, *Problem of Christianity* (1968 [1913]), © 1918 by Macmillan Co., 1968 by the publisher.

University of Pennsylvania Press. Jacques Maritain in *Religion in the Modern World* (1941).

University of Tennessee Press. Timothy George, "Toward an Evangelical Future," in *Southern Baptists Observed,* ed. Nancy Tatom Ammerman (Knoxville: University of Tennessee Press, 1993), pp. 276-77.

University of Washington Press. H. S. Lucas, *Dutch Immigrant Memoirs,* Vol. 2 (1955).

Upper Room. Meditation, April 2, 1935, © The Upper Room, P.O. Box 189, Nashville, TN 37202.

Watch Tower Tract and Bible Society. Excerpt from *1974 Yearbook.*

Westminster Press. © 1967 William Hamilton in J. L. Ice and J. J. Carey, *The Death of God.*

Westview Press. John F. Wilson and Donald L. Drakeman, eds., *Church and State in American History: Key Documents, Decisions, and Commentary from the Past Three Centuries,* 3rd ed. (Boulder, CO: Westview, 2003), pp. 256-58, 259-63.

Wilson Quarterly (Hoover Institution Press). Nathan Glazer in Vol. 5 (Autumn, 1981).

Yale University Press. John Dewey, *A Common Faith* (1934).

Zondervan. *Holy Bible: New International Version* (Grand Rapids: Zondervan, 1978), pp. 511-12.

Websites

R. Albert Mohler, Jr., "Thoughts and Adventures," 21 March 2003, http://www.sbts.edu/mohler/ThoughtsPrint.php?article=03_21_2003 (27 May 2003).

Shahid Athar, "Personal Reflections on the Iraq War," http://www.islamfortoday.com/athar20.htm (27 May 2003).

Omar Siddiqui, "You are With Us or You are Dead," *MSA Link,* Spring 2003, p. 8; http://www.msa-national.org/publications/msalink/Link_Mar03.pdf (27 May 2003).

"What is CUIC?" http://www.eden.edu/cuic/whatiscuic/whatiscuic.htm (May 27, 2003).

2000 Baptist Faith and Message, http://www.sbc.net/bfm/bfm2000.asp (14 May 2003).

Jerry Rankin, "Does It Matter What Missionaries Believe?" http://www.baptist2baptist
.net/papers/rankinresponse.asp (28 May 2003).

Jim Denison, "Jim Denison writes to Pastors and Baptist Leaders," http://www.bgct.org/
bgctroot/officeloader.cfm?contentuuid=6DFE0E3E-EBF6-4EC0-
98D43D0FBBDD1E8F&deptid=9 (28 May 2003).

"We're All Americans . . . But, Which One of Us is a Muslim?" *Islam in America* Council
on American-Islamic Relations Advertisement Series 1 (2003), http://www
.americanmuslims .info/ads/0216.pdf (27 May 2003).

"Religious Accommodations Task Force," *MSA Link,* Spring 2003, 3, http://www.msa-
national.org/publications/msalink/Link_Mar03.pdf (27 May 2003).

Muqtedar Khan, "A Memo to American Muslims," http://www.islamfortoday.com/
khan01.htm (27 May 2003).

"Circle Sanctuary's Purpose and Work," http://www.circlesanctuary.org/aboutcircle/activ-
ities.htm (27 May 2003).

Selena Fox, "Circle of Goddesses," *Circle Magazine,* Spring 2002, pp. 30-31, http://
www.circlesanctuary.org/circle/articles/circlecraft/CircleOfGoddesses.html   (27
May 2003).

Religious Freedom Restoration Act of 1993, http://www.welcomehome.org/rainbow/nfs-
regs/rfra-act.html (April 14, 2003).

Syllabus: *City of Boerne v. Flores, Archbishop of San Antonio,* 25 June 1997, http://
supct.law.cornell.edu/supct/html/95-2074.ZS.html (May 14, 2003).

Reconciling Ministries Network, "Why Become a Reconciling Congregation," http://
www.rmnetwork.org/papers/resource3.pdf (30 May 2003).

The Confessing Movement, "Tract Number Three: Our Doctrinal Standards and Sexuality," http://www.confessingumc.org/tract3.html (30 May 2003).

"Text: President Clinton's Speech at Ministers' Leadership Conference," http://
www.washingtonpost.com/wp-srv/onpolitics/elections/clinton081000.htm   (29
May 2003).

"Billy Graham's Message: National Day of Prayer and Remembrance," http://www
.billygraham.org/newsevents/ndprbgmessage.asp (17 Sept. 2001).

Ted Olsen, "As the World Prays, Falwell and Robertson Blame ACLU, Gays, and Others for
'Deserved' Attack," *Christianity Today Weblog,* http://www.christianitytoday.com/
ct/2001/137/52.0.html (27 May 2003).

Kyabje Gelek Rinpoche, "On Love and Compassion in the Wake of the Terrorist Attacks,"
http://www.imdiversity.com/villages/asian/Article_Detail.asp?Article_ID=7994 (27
May 2003).

Shahid Athar, "The Future of American Muslims after September 11," http://www
.islamfortoday.com/athar09.htm (27 May 2003).

"Declaration of War Against Exploiters of Lakota Spirituality," 1993, http://puffin.creigh-
ton.edu/lakota/war.html (29 May 2003).

The three documents are from the Voice of the Faithful website, http://www.votf.org (5
June 2003).

"The Living Christ: The Testimony of the Apostles, the Church of Jesus Christ of Latter-
day Saints." LDS Home Page, http://www.ids.org/library/the_liv_chr.html (7 Apr.
2000).

SEVEN

A New Religious Landscape

"Reconstruction" of the break-away Southern states ended formally in 1877. After the disputed Hayes (Republican)-Tilden (Democrat) presidential election of that year, Democrats gave Rutherford B. Hayes the electoral votes necessary to extend Republican control of the White House. In return, Republicans agreed to pull the last Federal troops out of the South and, in effect, to return political control of that part of the nation to an all-white Democratic Party. Among the power elites of the nation, there was no stomach for the intense struggle it would have taken to ensure African Americans the full rights of citizenship. The nation was hurrying on; whatever the moral cost, the Americans who controlled public life thought it was time to get over the Civil War.

Of course the profound antagonisms that had surfaced in the war could not be done away with so easily. African Americans especially continued to suffer when attention was turned away from the effort to guarantee full civil rights for all. Their situation would also have an immediate impact on American religion, since the failure to achieve social equality was matched by a great boom in the establishment of black churches. In turn, these churches have continued to play a major role for African American communities to the present day. From the 1950s, the values they nourished began to make an obvious impact on the nation's history as a whole.

Long before the Civil Rights Movement of that later era, however, the shape of the nation's religious life was being drastically transformed. The older, well-established Protestant churches and the newer strength of the Catholic church no longer made up the entirety of the nation's organized religion. A great surge of immigration after the Civil War brought increased numbers of Jews to the United States, and soon there would be significant American populations of Muslims, Buddhists, and others from the furthest corners of the world. Yet changes worked in the history of American religion by immigration were only a few of the many new directions, new movements, new spaces, new challenges, and new constituencies that came to play important parts in religious history during the last quarter of the nineteenth century and into the daunting years of a new century.

Bound for the Promised Land

For all the blood that had soaked into the battlefields of Antietam, Gettysburg, and Petersburg, the ultimate healing came in the form of many transfusions of new blood. In the half-century following the Civil War, hundreds, then thousands, then millions of new immigrants arrived. From 1865 to 1915, about twenty-five million hopefuls reached America's shores. They came from western and northern Europe, from eastern and southern Europe, and even from Russia and the Far East. A pervasively Protestant America watched Roman Catholicism, already by 1850 the largest single denomination, grow by giant increments as new national groups arrived in wholesale lots. For its own part, this large church found the sudden surge in membership both enheartening and overwhelming. How to feed and house? to educate or mollify? to maintain in harmony as part of the one universal and apostolic Church? In New York City, for example, Archbishop John Hughes grappled with problems that daunted, even before the numbers swelled — and swelled.

In that same half-century (1865-1915), Judaism mushroomed from a modest and predominantly German minority to a large and visible presence. As with Roman Catholicism, the numerical growth among Jews brought with it a wondrous variety in liturgy, political attitude, and national origin. Most of the new arrivals reveled in the discovery that "in this great glorious and free country," as Solomon Schechter declared in 1904, "we Jews need not sacrifice a single iota of our Torah; and, in the enjoyment of absolute equality with our fellow citizens, we can live to carry out those ideals for which our ancestors so often had to die."

Women's Work?

One group of fellow citizens in the half-century after 1865 felt that equality continued to elude them. The emancipation of women, like the emancipation of the slaves, required reform of both Constitution and conscience. Not until 1920 did women win the right to vote, and more than half a century after that, full Constitutional equality remained ambiguous at best. The late nineteenth century, however, did see religious doors being opened more widely to women. Women entered pulpits, led reforms, edited and translated the Bible, although none of this was accomplished without stern opposition. Arguments — whether for or against the broader participation of women — came from history and tradition, from biblical direction and social need, from common sense and common hope. Little common ground could be found, however, between those who on the one hand held that "woman is not designed by God . . . to all the franchises in society to which the male is entitled," and those who on the other hand concluded that "the masculine and feminine elements, exactly equal and balancing each other, are as essential to the maintenance of the equilibrium of the universe as positive and negative electricity. . . ." Depending on the perspective of the antagonists, cosmic equilibrium in the 1880s and 1890s was either being badly upset or more nearly achieved.

The West

The nation's effective dominion over a vast continent, interrupted by a costly war, resumed its reach in the postwar period. Religious forces continued then, as they had earlier, to be instruments of civilizing and of Christianizing, those two processes being seen as complementary if not synonymous. Once the Mississippi River had been crossed, the lands to be reached were of greater expanse, the Indians to be instructed of profounder distrust. Roman Catholic Pierre Jean De Smet and Presbyterian Sheldon Jackson left St. Louis and kept walking westward and northward, Jackson continuing all the way to Alaska. Neither Catholics nor Presbyterians, however, managed to send the first missionaries into Alaska; that priority belonged to the Russian Orthodox Church. Well before the Civil War, that ancient church had entered the American West — not by crossing mountains, plains, and rivers, but the Pacific Ocean itself. Writing in 1840, Father John Veniaminov, Orthodoxy's most famous missionary to "Russian America," described with pleasure "the dissemination and consolidation of Christ's Faith in one of the most remote territories of our Society, where through God's pleasure I had the opportunity of spending many years." Also before the Civil War, mainland American missionaries had penetrated another outpost of empire: the Sandwich or Hawaiian Islands. After that war, Japanese emigrating to Hawaii filled those islands with a faith even more ancient than Russian Orthodoxy: namely, Buddhism. By this means, the Asiatic East was moving toward the American West at the same time that Atlantic seaboard easterners migrated toward the Pacific West. In the nineteenth century, East and West did meet; the twain were joined, even if they failed to become one.

A New World — Abroad and at Home

These important contacts in Alaska and the Pacific, however, were by no means the limit of American involvement with the world beyond its continental borders. Near the end of the nineteenth century, the Spanish-American War drew eyes to other places over seas, even as it raised issues of American destiny and American morality. Clergymen like Henry Van Dyke wondered aloud: "Have we set the Cubans free or have we lost our faith in freedom?" The "Philippine Question" concerned not only the balance of Protestant and Catholic additions to the empire, but also the question of the "white man's burden" with respect to the "weaker races" (to use the language of another Protestant clergyman, Thomas Dixon, in his popular and prejudiced 1902 novel, *The Leopard's Spots*). It is one thing to export our creed of human rights, freedom, and opportunity, said Roman Catholic John Spalding; it is quite another to thrust this or any other creed "down unwilling throats at the point of a bayonet."

More Americans were becoming aware of foreign lands through missionary labors than even through the exciting traumas of warfare. By the 1880s multiplying efforts by Protestants to carry the Christian message to other parts of the world had been underway for seventy years. Missionary interest and enthusiasm continued to rise in tandem with the nation's rising population, political power, and gross domestic product. Yet no simple equation could ever be drawn concerning such aspects of expanding national might and the volunteers who left American shores for expressly religious purposes. Perhaps the most obvious trait of those volunteers in the late nineteenth century was the leadership that women were assuming in the enterprise.

In 1893 East and West met with more deliberate intent in mid-America's great metropolis of Chicago. The occasion, the World Parliament of Religions, emerged as a sort of "side exhibit" of Chicago's Columbian Exposition of that year. But this side exhibit, brainchild of Congregationalist John Henry Barrows, appeared to the religiously minded to be as striking as the main show, and perhaps even more instructive. Now not only Buddhism but Hinduism, Confucianism, Shinto, and Islam had their own spokesmen. If Americans had heard anything at all of these religions, they had heard from Christian missionaries; now, a differing point of view made itself known. Judaism had its spokeswomen, Catholicism — both Greek and Roman — its apologists, Protestantism its participants as well as its sometimes anxious observers. And apart from the adherents of specific institutional forms of religion, many came to probe that slippery entity called "religion." The Parliament stood as an augury of the nation's future: pluralistic, adventuresome in dialogue, defensive in structure, persuaded that somehow men and women of goodwill could play a role in promoting peace on earth.

Yet confronted with diversity so flamboyant, so indelible, some wondered if this coat of many colors was religion's most impressive garment as it moved forward to solve humanity's problems or to offer solace for problems that had no solution. If, moreover, one looked at the world of religions in broadest terms — Hindu, Buddhist, Moslem, Christian, etc. — did this not suggest that those large divisions ought to present a united front to a restless world? Could not badly divided Christendom, for example, put its own house in order, the better to compete against other religious options, now seen as genuine and alive?

If Parliament dramatized diversity in religion, the Eleventh Census (1890) documented it so far as the United States was concerned. The Christian faith seemed a fractious, brawling collection of competing sects, too busy distinguishing themselves from their fellows to worry about the advances of Buddhism or Islam. "The external divisions of Christendom," said Lutheran seminary president Francis Pieper in 1893, "are a most deplorable state of things . . . contrary to the will of God." And the Methodist layman who had conducted the religious census, H. K. Carroll, thought that, at the very least, denominational families ought to be able to overcome their minor differences. Yet many others, like leaders of resurgent African-American denominations thought otherwise.

By the dawn of the twentieth century, the United States was a showplace of religious freedom. Some feared, however, that it might turn out to be the graveyard of sect, schism, and separation, of religious faith reduced to the most casual choice, the most insignificant option. Before many decades had passed, the nation's churches and synagogues might, like Samson without his hair, "become weak" and "not know that the Lord had left" them. Should that occur, the theological and ecclesiastical reconstructions and reaffirmations of the nineteenth century could be judged only as failures.

1. Bound for the Promised Land

The Ocean's Bounty

Europe

In the half-century between the end of one war and the beginning of another (1865-1914), the sources of European immigration tended to shift from northern and western Europe to the eastern and southern portions of that continent. The comparable shift, in religious terms, was away from Protestantism toward Roman Catholicism and Judaism. Nonetheless, the Protestant stream did not altogether cease. The following three excerpts reflect the flow from: (1) Russia (Mennonite); (2) Holland (Reformed); and (3) Norway (Lutheran). The Dutch recollection is provided by Lucy Klooster (d. 1941), a life-long resident of a Reformed community in Michigan, while the Norwegian account comes from Eugene Boe, a Minnesota native and later professional writer living in New York City.

1.

Eugene Schuyler, U.S. Legation, St. Petersburgh, to Hamilton Fish, No. 168, March 30, 1872.

I have the honor to enclose you a copy of a letter I have received from Mr. [Timothy] Smith, the Consul at Odessa, on the subject of the contemplated emigra-

---

[Sources: (1) *Mennonite Quarterly Review*, 24 (Oct., 1950), 338-39. (2) Lucy Klooster, in H. S. Lucas, *Dutch Immigrant Memoirs and Related Writings* (Seattle: University of Washington Press,

tion of the Mennonite colonies in the South of Russia to America, and also a copy of my answer thereto.

The Mennonites first came to Russia from Prussia in 1789 in answer to an invitation of Catherine II who gave them land, means with which to establish themselves and temporary relief from taxes and contributions, and promised them religious freedom and exemption for ever from every form of military service. They settled in the South of Russia, in what is now the Government of Taurid, on a tract of land between the rivers Dnieper, Molotschna and Tokmak, and in 1855 numbered some 17,000 souls (male).

The Mennonites are good agriculturists but are particularly noted for their plantations of fruit, forest and mulberry trees. This culture they have followed with great success on steppes that were formerly perfectly bare.

The Mennonites are intelligent, industrious and persevering, and in addition very clean, orderly, moral, temperate and economical. As may be judged from their application they are excessively religious. Petzholdt in his travels in 1855 says, that it is his "firm conviction that Russia can not show any more diligent and more useful citizens." There are schools in every village and education is universal amongst them.

The details of the Law of Universal Compulsory Military Service[1] have not yet been decided on, but it is not proposed to exempt any individuals or classes of the community from its operation.

I do not think it would be possible to find in Europe any better emigrant than these Mennonites, and should the whole colony go to the United States they would rapidly develop into good and useful citizens.

As I have stated in my letter to Mr. Smith, it is a crime for Russian subjects to emigrate, and a crime to induce them to emigrate without permission. If therefore it is thought desirable that these people should go to the United States, it will probably be necessary for our Government to assist them in obtaining from the Imperial authorities the requisite permission to emigrate. I desire also to call your attention to the question of the Mennonites as to whether any aid in money can be given them for their expenses.

2.

The sound of wagon wheels grinding steadily over dusty trails, bumping over corduroy roads, splashing into mudholes became quite common in this part of

---

1955), II, pp. 280-81. (3) Eugene Boe, in Thomas C. Wheeler, *The Immigrant Experience* (New York: Dial Press, 1971), pp. 68, 70.]

1. It was this Russian law, promising exemption to none, which prompted the pacifist Mennonites to seek refuge elsewhere.

Northern Michigan in the early 1880's. The occupants of such a wagon might have been a young man and woman seated upon two or three boxes containing all their worldly goods. A few hours before they very likely had arrived by train at Traverse City or Mancelona. Weary and worn by the many days' journey from the Netherlands and a several days' train trip from New York City, how good it would have seemed to have rested for a day or two! Why had they come? Money was scarce and land here was very cheap. Should they stay down in the Dutch settlements farther south, the only work for many of them might be that of hired help to other farmers. On the other hand, perhaps some relative or friend had come up to this territory before them and had written in glowing terms of the country, the springs, and the lakes. . . .

By the year 1886 several clearings had been made and new families were moving in quite regularly. They felt one handicap greatly, the distance to church. Many families walked the four or five miles to the church in Atwood, for on Sunday, if at all possible, they must be in the House of the Lord. Feeling the need of weekday services, in which they might present to Him their prayers and petitions, a new type of meeting was begun, upon which we may surely believe God looked with gladness of heart. Many of the settlers of the community, Dutch and English alike, gathered at the little schoolhouse on the corner every Thursday evening and despite handicaps of language and difference of denomination, together brought their prayers and petitions before the throne of Grace. This is the way an attendant, who lives in Kalamazoo, describes it: We had good times in those olden days when that good man of God, Martin van der Schouw, led in prayer — meetings to the glory of God. After reading and explaining a portion of Scripture he led us in prayer. Then everybody who wanted to pray or testify could do so. The audience in the old schoolhouse consisted of Reformed, Christian Reformed, Methodists, Presbyterians, etc., but they were united around the Cross of Calvary. The road to the meeting place was not so smooth as it is these days. We drove in ox wagons, came over drifting logs, through marsh and swamp. It happened some nights that there were more mosquitoes in the schoolhouse than people, but I for one must confess, that afterwards we could say, "It was good for us to be there, for the Lord was in our midst."

As the Dutch settlers arrived in the community, the talk of organizing a church became common. More children were coming, and the walk was almost too much for them. How wonderful it would be to have a church in the community which would make possible regular Sunday services for all the members of the family. Finally, in 1889 the request for organization was made and heard by the Grand River Classis and on September 10, . . . eight families joined together as a nucleus of the church. . . .

3.

The settlements [in Minnesota] were all homogeneous and self-contained. The immigrant invasion of that part of the country was overwhelmingly Scandinavian, but the separate components of Scandinavia did not become a melting pot in the New World. A township like Aastad remained exclusively Norwegian. The Swedes and Danes and Finns kept to themselves in communities that had names like Swedish Grove and Dane Prairie and Finlandia. The different groups could have made themselves understood to one another and might have found they had much in common. But these exchanges did not occur.

Even those first settlers who eventually left their farms to live in town — as did my grandparents after thirty-four years — managed to reestablish this separateness in a new community. The county seat, Fergus Falls [Otter Tail County], in the early 1900s was a polyglot village of Poles, Germans, Irish, Scotsmen, New England Yankees, and Dutch, as well as Scandinavians. But the various Scandinavian populations touched no other group but themselves. Each had its own Lutheran churches, newspapers, and social fraternities, with little or no cross-pollination. My grandfather and my grandmother lived more than sixty and eighty years, respectively, in this country, but there's no evidence they had more than glancing contact with anyone who was not Norwegian. . . .

They could still articulate the twenty-third Psalm and believe it. "The Lord is my shepherd, I shall not want. . . ." Even when poverty, disease, or death overtook them, they could see divine purpose being fulfilled. They must thank God, for God governed best. He sent them suffering and tribulations only to test their faith.

Their faith was their abiding comfort, and that faith alone enabled them to endure the perversities of fate. This time on earth was but a preparation for the heavenly home which would be their eternal abode. While they struggled through this mortal phase, a welcome was being prepared for their arrival in heaven. Ultimately they would assemble with God in the eternal mansion, where they would find everlasting joy and contentment in beholding God's face.

In the years before the first church was built, the little colony of settlers gathered each Sunday in one another's dugouts. The host would read a passage from the Bible and give his interpretation of it. Then there would be prayers and hymns. When the group came to my grandparents' hut, there was always the singing of . . . [a] favorite hymn, "Den Store Kvede Flok" ("The Big White Flock," signifying angels).

As years passed, the growing community had the services of a *klokker*. The *klokker* was not an ordained minister but a kind of peddler of spiritual wares who carried the Good Word from farm to farm. He knew the Bible, he could give sermons, and he had the authority to baptize.

The coming of the *klokker* was a great event. This was God's emissary on earth. Nothing was too good for him. The devoutness and hospitality of the family must shine forth so that God would receive a good report of them. They might be living on *grot* (a mixture of flour and water) and eggs, but one of the laying chickens must be killed to feed the *klokker*. Taking his leave, he would often say, "I'll be at your house next Friday if not Providentially detained." The coy reference suggested that at any moment God might see fit to recall him for some heavenly mission. But the *klokker's* gift for survival on this planet proved quite as remarkable as that of his flock's.

Asia

By the middle of the nineteenth century, Chinese emigrants began in large numbers to leave the hunger and wars of their homeland for the United States. With an annual emigration to the West Coast of some fifteen to twenty thousand Chinese, their numbers had risen to over three million by 1882 when the nation took steps to halt further emigration from China. Despite strong anti-Oriental prejudices and open wonderment at the cultural-religious-racial peculiarities of the Chinese, America's churches did launch missionary efforts among these "heathen." The first excerpt indicates the concern of a Chinese Baptist concerning evangelization; the second tells of the experience in San Francisco's Chinatown of newly converted Chinese Methodists.

1.

Letter of Missionary Fung Chak

[*Portland, Oregon*]

There is much, very much to do, but who shall perform the labor? When shall there be workers, and when shall there be means to carry on the work for the Chinese on this Coast? There are many here, and many more on the way to this country; but where, and how, and by whom are they to hear the Gospel?

The Chinese, in coming to America, meet with all its vices, but very few of its virtues. They see the worst side of all classes and very little of the better. The Baptists have so far accomplished very little for the Chinese on this Coast, but the need of work to be done is oh, how great! In Oregon, Washington Territory, and Idaho Territory, there are now thousands of Chinese. I have no means at

---

[Sources: (1) *Baptist Home Missions in North America: 1832-1882* (New York: Baptist Home Mission Rooms, 1883), pp. 98-99. (2) Jade Snow Wang in Thomas C. Wheeler, *The Immigrant Experience* (New York: Dial Press, 1971), pp. 113-14.]

hand of knowing accurately just how many there are, but there is no place for them to hear the Gospel with the exception of Portland. There are thousands of Chinese now employed on the construction of the railroad. Seattle is another centre in Washington Territory from whence many Chinese separate into the surrounding country.

But what can we do? We can only with aching hearts see these thousands of precious souls sinking into hell, with never a hand to save or a voice to warn. Oh, is there no money for the Chinese, however much there may be for others?

Must they be despised and hated themselves, and also the salvation of their souls utterly ignored? The Chinese are generally willing to hear the Gospel, and will gather and listen attentively to its preaching; but we have no wealthy converts yet, and so we cannot by ourselves carry on any great work, or employ missionaries. We are deeply grateful for the assistance that has been granted us by the Board thus far, and we pray that such assistance may be continued in time to come. Portland is a centre through which all the travel of Oregon and the upper country passes, so that not only many of the resident Chinese hear the Gospel here, but many who go out to work in various directions are also to a greater or less extent benefited. We trust and pray that the Board will fully sustain the mission here. We feel that the mission here must be sustained. The Chinese must not be wholly left without the Gospel. Whatever may be, do not think of helping the Chinese less. Think of thousands of souls without the Gospel, without one voice to warn them from the vortexes that yawn on every side to engulf them, and drag them down to endless ruin.

If such work is neglected not only are souls lost, but there is a reaction against those who refuse them the Gospel, by creating darkness where there should be light. It can hardly be realized in the East, what a strong arm of the work in China is the work on this Coast.

We have converts in China, while many have been to China and returned to this country.

There are also many who have heard the Gospel through this mission, and though they are not yet openly Christians, yet an impression has been made that can never be wholly effaced, and ideas have been introduced that will never be forgotten. Yet, comparatively, we can reach but a few of the many.

There is an immediate necessity for the appointment of another missionary; there should be two — one to look after the work in Washington Territory, making his home at Seattle, while the Chinese on the railroad and in the towns springing up in eastern Oregon, Washington and Idaho Territories, should have someone to tell them of the better way. The mission at Salem should not be allowed to come to nought. One of our mission scholars has had a little school at Astoria since last Summer. The scholars have paid room rent, bought some books, etc., but they are in nowise able to sustain a mission, and the effort must sooner or later be discontinued. Thus there seems opportunity to extend the work for the Chinese, if means could be granted for that purpose; and we trust the Board will in the future find it possible to more fully improve this needy and important field,

With great respect and Christian regards, I am, truly your Brother in the Lord Jesus Christ,

FUNG CHAK

2.

On Sundays, we never failed to attend the Methodist Church, as my father's belief in the providence of God strengthened with the years, and his wife and family shared that faith.[2] My father's faith in God was unwavering and unshakable. (Some day, we were to hear his will, which he wrote in Chinese, and which began, "I believe in God, Jehovah. . . .") I have no statistics on the percentage of Christians in Chinatown at that time, but I am sure they were a minority. Our Methodist branch could not have had more than a hundred adult members, with less than fifty regular Sunday attendants. Many of Daddy's contemporaries scoffed at or ridiculed Christians as "do-gooders" who never gambled, when Mah-Jongg games were Chinatown's favorite pastime. Father used to chase lottery peddlers away from his factory; cards were never allowed in our home. I suppose that for him, the Christian faith at first comforted him far from his loved ones. Secondly, it promised him individual worth and salvation, when all his life in China had been devoted only to his family's continuity and glorification. Third, to this practical man who was virtually self-taught in all his occupations, Christianity suggested action on behalf of others in the community, while Confucianism was more concerned with regulating personal relationships. Daddy seldom hesitated to stick his neck out if he thought social action or justice were involved. For instance, he was on the founding board of the Chinese YMCA and fought for its present location, though he was criticized for its being on a hill, for being near the YWCA, for including a swimming pool.

Group singing and community worship in a church must have been dramatically different from the lonely worship of Chinese ancestral tablets at home. He listened to weekly sermons, expounding new ideas or reiterating old ones, and sometimes they were translated from the English spoken by visiting pastors. His daughters learned to sing in the choir and were permitted to join escorted church visits to Western churches — their only contact with a "safe" organization outside of Chinatown.

If my father had one addiction, it was to reading. He eagerly awaited the delivery of each evening's Chinese newspaper — for there had been none where

2. The father as a young man left southern Canton for San Francisco in 1903.

he came from. His black leather-bound Testaments, translated into Chinese, were worn from constant reference. Before our Sunday morning departure for Sunday School, he conducted his own lessons at our dining table. No meal was tasted before we heard his thankful grace.

Roman Catholicism

Education

Among the alluring promises that America extended to its new arrivals was that of a free and public education — surer and safer than bread or shelter, as immigrant Mary Antin had written. But for Roman Catholics, the promise contained a joker. That "free and public" education possessed a distinctly Protestant cast. Given that circumstance, some Catholics wondered if public monies could not also be used to support an education with a distinctly Catholic cast. Archbishop John Hughes (1797-1864) thought that a not unreasonable request, but his battle in New York was lost. The only alternative remaining, the Catholic hierarchy concluded, was to provide — at whatever cost — a separate and private system of education for the thousands of Catholic children already in America and for the thousands arriving annually upon its shores. Two documents shed light on this important development: (1) Hughes's strong protest in 1840 against a system unfair and unworthy "of our just and glorious constitution"; and (2) a Pastoral Letter of 1884 revealing the depth of both conviction and commitment of the nation's Catholic leadership.

1.

Besides the introduction of the Holy Scriptures without note or comment, with the prevailing theory that from these even children are to get their notions of religion, contrary to our principles, there were in the class-books of those schools false (as we believe) historical statements respecting the men and things of past times, calculated to fill the minds of our children with errors of fact, and

---

[Sources: (1) John R. G. Hassard, *Life of the Most Reverend John Hughes . . .* (New York: D. Appleton & Co., 1866), pp. 230-32. (2) Peter Guilday, ed., *The National Pastorals of the American Hierarchy, 1792-1919* (Washington: National Catholic Welfare Conference, 1923), pp. 244-47.]

at the same time to excite in them prejudice against the religion of their parents and guardians. These passages were not considered as sectarian, inasmuch as they had been selected as mere reading lessons, and were not in *favor* of any particular sect, but merely *against* the Catholics. We feel it is unjust that such passages should be taught at all in schools, to the support of which we are contributors as well as others. But that such books should be put into the hands of *our own* children, and that in part at our own expense, was in our opinion unjust, unnatural, and at all events to us intolerable. Accordingly, through very great additional sacrifices, we have been obliged to provide schools, under our churches and elsewhere, in which to educate our children as our conscientious duty required. This we have done to the number of some thousands for several years past, during all of which time we have been obliged to pay taxes; and we feel it unjust and oppressive that while we educate our children, as well we contend as they would be at the public schools, we are denied our portion of the school fund, simply because we at the same time endeavor to train them up in principles of virtue and religion. This we feel to be unjust and unequal. For we pay taxes in proportion to our numbers, as other citizens. We are supposed to be from one hundred and fifty to two hundred thousand in the State. And although most of us are poor, still the poorest man among us is obliged to pay taxes, from the sweat of his brow, in the rent of his room or little tenement. Is it not, then, hard and unjust that such a man cannot have the benefit of education for his child without sacrificing the rights of his religion and conscience? He sends his child to a school under the protection of his Church, in which these rights will be secure. But he has to support this school also. In Ireland he was compelled to support a church hostile to his religion, and here he is compelled to support schools in which his religion fares but little better, and to support his own school besides.

Is this state of things, fellow-citizens, and especially Americans, is this state of things worthy of *you*, worthy of our country, worthy of our just and glorious constitution? Put yourself in the poor man's place, and say whether you would not despise him if he did not labor by every lawful means to emancipate himself from this bondage. He has to pay double taxation for the education of his child, one to the misinterpreted law of the land, and another to his conscience. He sees his child going to school with perhaps only the fragment of a worn-out book, thinly clad, and its bare feet on the frozen pavement, whereas, if he had his rights he could improve the clothing, he could get better books, and have his child better taught than it is possible in actual circumstances.

Nothing can be more false than some statements of our motives which have been put forth against us.

It has been asserted that we seek our share of the school funds for the support and advance of our religion.

We beg to assure you with respect, that we would scorn to support or advance our religion at any other than our own expense. But we are unwilling to pay taxes for the purpose of destroying our religion in the minds of our children. This points out the sole difference between what we seek and what some narrow-minded or misinformed journals have accused us of seeking.

If the public schools could have been constituted on a principle which would have secured a perfect NEUTRALITY of influence on the subject of religion, then we should have no reason to complain. But this has not been done, and we respectfully submit that it is impossible. The cold indifference with which it is required that all religion shall be treated in those schools — the Scriptures without note or comment — the selection of passages, as reading lessons, from Protestants and prejudiced authors, on points in which our creed is supposed to be involved — the comments of the teacher, of which the commissioners cannot be cognizant — the school libraries, stuffed with sectarian works against us — form against our religion a combination of influences prejudicial to our religion, and to whose action it would be criminal in us to expose our children at such an age.

2.

Few, if any, will deny that a sound civilization must depend upon sound popular education. But education, in order to be sound and to produce beneficial results, must develop what is best in man, and make him not only clever but good. A one-sided education will develop a one-sided life; and such a life will surely topple over, and so will every social system that is built up of such lives. True civilization requires that not only the physical and intellectual, but also the moral and religious, well-being of the people should be promoted, and at least with equal care. Take away religion from a people, and morality would soon follow; morality gone, even their physical condition will ere long degenerate into corruption which breeds decrepitude, while their intellectual attainments would only serve as a light to guide them to deeper depths of vice and ruin. This has been so often demonstrated in the history of the past, and is, in fact, so self-evident, that one is amazed to find any difference of opinion about it. A civilization without religion, would be a civilization of "the struggle for existence, and the survival of the fittest," in which cunning and strength would become the substitutes for principle, virtue, conscience and duty. As a matter of fact, there never has been a civilization worthy of the name without religion; and from the facts of history the laws of human nature can easily be inferred.

Hence education, in order to foster civilization, must foster religion. Now the three great educational agencies are the home, the Church, and the school. These mould men and shape society. Therefore each of them, to do its part well, must foster religion. But many, unfortunately, while avowing that religion should be the light and the atmosphere of the home and of the Church, are content to see it excluded from the school, and even advocate as the best school system that which necessarily excludes religion. Few surely will deny that childhood and youth are the periods of life when the character ought especially to be subjected to religious influences. Nor can we ignore the palpable fact that the school is an important factor in the forming of childhood and youth, — so important that its influence often outweighs that of home and Church. It cannot, therefore, be desirable or advantageous that religion should be excluded from the school. On the contrary, it ought there to be one of the chief agencies for moulding the young life to all that is true and virtuous, and holy. To shut religion out of the school, and keep it for home and the Church, is, logically, to train up a generation that will consider religion good for home and the Church, but not for the practical business of real life. But a more false and pernicious notion could not be imagined. Religion, in order to elevate a people, should inspire their whole life and rule their relations with one another. A life is not dwarfed, but ennobled by being lived in the presence of God. Therefore the school, which principally gives the knowledge fitting for practical life, ought to be pre-eminently under the holy influence of religion. From the shelter of home and school, the youth must soon go out into the busy ways of trade or traffic or professional practice. In all these, the principles of religion should animate and direct him. But he cannot expect to learn these principles in the work-shop or the office or the counting-room. Therefore let him be well and thoroughly imbued with them by the joint influences of home and school, before he is launched out on the dangerous sea of life.

All denominations of Christians are now awaking to this great truth, which the Catholic Church has never ceased to maintain. Reason and experience are forcing them to recognize that the only practical way to secure a Christian people, is to give the youth a Christian education. The avowed enemies of Christianity in some European countries are banishing religion from the schools, in order gradually to eliminate it from among the people. In this they are logical, and we may well profit by the lesson. Hence the cry for Christian education is going up from all religious bodies throughout the land. And this is no narrowness and "sectarianism" on their part; it is an honest and logical endeavor to preserve Christian truth and morality among the people by fostering religion in the young. Nor is it any antagonism to the State; on the contrary, it is an honest endeavor to give to the State better citizens, by making them better Christians. The friends of Christian education do not condemn the State for not imparting religious instruction in the public schools as they are now organized; because they well know it does not lie within the province of the State to teach religion. They simply follow their conscience by sending their children to denominational schools, where religion can have its rightful place and influence.

Two objects therefore, dear brethren, we have in view, to multiply our schools, and to perfect them. We must multiply them, till every Catholic child in the land shall have within its reach the means of education. There is still much to do ere this be attained. There are still thousands of Catholic children in the United States deprived of the benefit of a Catholic school. Pastors and parents should not rest till this defect be remedied. No parish is complete till it has schools adequate to the needs of its children, and the pastor and people of such a parish should feel that they have not accomplished their entire duty until the want is supplied.

But then, we must also perfect our schools. We repudiate the idea that the Catholic school need be in any respect inferior to any other school whatsoever. And if hitherto, in some places, our people have acted on the principle that it is better to have an imperfect Catholic school than to have none, let them now push their praise-worthy ambition still further, and not relax their efforts till their schools be elevated to the highest educational excellence. And we implore parents not to hasten to take their children from school, but to give them all the time and all the advantages that they have the capacity to profit by, so that, in after life, their children may "rise up and call them blessed."

Ethnicity

From Ireland and Germany, from Italy and Portugal, from Spain and all of its once great empire, Roman Catholics came to America. They were still Roman Catholics, not Irish Catholics, nor German Catholics, nor Italian Catholics — or was this really the case? If, as noted above (p. 9), Scandinavian Lutherans did not find a great deal of community with each other, how much more plausible that Catholics of widely separated geography and ethnicity might have difficulty — especially in a strange and threatening land — in seeing themselves in terms other than those of national origin. The problem was easy to understand, difficult to alleviate. Three documents follow: (1) a defense by James Cardinal Gibbons of the heavy Irish emigration to America, (2) an 1886 memorial of a Milwaukee priest, P. M. Abbelen, on behalf of Catholic Germans; and (3) a recollection from the early twentieth century of problems plaguing Catholic Italians.

[Sources: (1) James Gibbons, *A Retrospect of Fifty Years* (Baltimore: John Murphy, 1916), I, pp. 280-83. (2) Colman J. Barry, *The Catholic Church and German Americans* (Milwaukee: Bruce Publishing Co., 1953), pp. 289-90, 294-95. (3) Julian Miranda, in S. J. LaGumina, *The Immigrants Speak* (New York: Center for Migration Studies, 1979), pp. 131-32.]

1.

Perhaps someone will ask what I think of Irish immigration in general. Ought the Irish to stay at home, or ought they emigrate very largely, and especially to the United States? It is a grave problem. Ireland is a very ancient nation, with a very glorious history, and her race of men is pre-eminently adapted to the soil on which they live. Divine Providence seems to have matched the lovely fertile island with a population of brave and industrious men, and pure and beautiful women. Surely this has not been in order to tear them roughly from the farm and the hamlet, the mill and the forge, the cradle and the spinning wheel, to scatter them like the leaves of the forest or the sands of the sea. . . .

Yet this same history shows us the Irish race as possessed beyond all others with the spirit of the world-wanderer. The earliest reliable utterances of their history bear witness that they were seafaring, adventurous people; and since their conversion to Christianity there can be no doubt that this spirit has been heightened and consecrated by religious ardor for the propagation of Christianity. Willingly and unwillingly, wittingly and unwittingly, they have been a people of missionaries longer than any other race. No other people ever gave themselves *en bloc* to Christian missions as they; no other people ever suffered for their Catholic faith as they. And when, with the dawn of this century, the remarkable movements began which have today produced some 130,000,000 of English-speaking people, and been the chief element in the *renaissance* of Catholicism from its Continental tomb, it was the Irish who were the pioneers, they being then almost the only English-speaking Catholics, and devoting themselves the world over to the planting of the Catholic faith, the support of its claims and its missionaries, and the sustenance of the Papal authority. They are no longer the only English-speaking Catholics, though they are yet nearly everywhere in the majority; but we would be base and ingrate to forget that it was they who bore the brunt of the struggle for many decades of this century.

I would not, therefore, discourage Irish immigration, because there are at stake more than economic considerations. There are at stake the interests of the Catholic religion, which in this land and in this age are largely bound up with the interests of the Irish people. God's hand is upon them, going and coming; and I prefer to believe that He who harmonizes the motion of the planets and the flow of the tides, is also First Agent and Prime Mover in those no less mysterious movements by which peoples pass from one land to another. . . .

2.

1. The question concerns the relation of non-English to English parishes, and especially the relation of German to Irish parishes in the United States of North America.

2. We ask of the Sacred Congregation de Propaganda Fide that it so define this relation that German parishes shall be entirely independent of Irish parishes, or on a par with them; that rectors of Irish parishes shall not be able to exercise any parochial Jurisdiction over Germans enrolled in any German church, or who by right should be thus enrolled, whether they be newcomers from Germany or born in America of German parents. . . .

Nearly everywhere the opinion prevails that Irish rectors are truly and by right the parish priest of all those who were born in America, as if having over them an eminent domain; that German priests are, of course, necessary to take care of the souls of Germans while they speak the German language, but that it cannot fail to happen that they shall in the course of time lose their language and learn English, and that the sooner this happens the better; that the ecclesiastical status of the Germans is therefore a transitory one, and that German parishes should not be put on an equal footing with English parishes. There are also some who think that it is contrary to canon law that there should be two independent parishes in the same territory, and for this reason also that the English should be the only parish. . . .

In all this controversy, besides a difference of language, we must not by any means make light of the difference and discrepancy of Catholic customs as they are to be found among Germans and Irish. The Irish, on account of the oppression and persecution which they suffered for religion's sake in their own land, love simplicity in divine service, and in all the practice of religion, and do not care much for pomp and splendor. But the Germans, from the liberty which as a rule they have enjoyed in the exercise of their religion from the earliest times, and the traditions of their fathers, love the beauty of the church edifice and the pomp of ceremonies, belfries and bells, organs and sacred music, processions, feast days, sodalities, and the most solemn celebration of First Communion and weddings. These and other like things, although not essential to Catholic faith and life, foster piety and are so dear and sacred to the faithful that not without great danger could they be taken away from them.

Then, again, Germans differ very much from the Irish in the administration of ecclesiastical goods and affairs. For nearly everywhere the former so manage their temporal affairs that the rectors, with a body of laymen, or even laymen alone, properly elected, carry on the administration, while the Irish leave all these things in the hands of the priests. It must be confessed, it sometimes happens among the Germans that the laymen meddle too much in such affairs, but this rarely happens; nearly everywhere the temporal affairs in German parishes are administered exceptionally well.

Finally, even manners and social customs of the two nationalities differ exceedingly. Thus it happens that scarcely ever will you find Germans and Irish united in matrimony. All this is here said neither to favor the Germans nor to disparage the Irish. Rather, these things are told by way of a narrative and as matters of fact, that it may be made clear how vastly one differs from the other, these two nationalities which are the principal parts of the Church in the United States, and how necessary it is that each should have its own priests and churches co-ordinate and independent. With the lapse of time, by a certain natural formative process one will become more assimilated to the other. But, God forbid that any one should dare, and most of all, that bishops and priests should endeavor to accelerate this assimilation by suppressing the language and customs of the Germans. The German temperament and a most sad experience demonstrate that their effort is not conducive to edification, but for the destruction and ruin of souls.

3.

On the topic of the church, it must be remembered that Southern Italian men were not so church scrupulous as the women although they were Catholic. I think no one should mistake their non-church attendance for a lack of belief in the Roman Catholic faith. The seeming lack of scrupulosity in Italians should not delude anybody about their lack of commitment to Christianity and its central ideas. I think there is a great paradox, and a great ambivalence there. Basically they dislike the clergy, and if they dislike the Italian clergy they despise the American clergy. They were very cruelly treated by this group. I remember when I was a child going for my First Communion and, I was asked by one of the nuns to recite the Our Father. I had only known it in either Sicilian or Latin (dog Latin). I knew what was going to happen but I got up and recited it and of course the class guffawed and the nun made fun of me. In a rage, I left the class. It was a Sunday and my grandfather was coming to the house, saw my face and said *che succedio?* (what happened?). At first, I did not want to tell him because of the *omerta* (you did not whine) but I finally told him that I said my prayer in Sicilian and they laughed at me. Inside of thirty seconds he had me by the arm and had propelled me up to the church. There, he got hold of Fr. Fitzsimmons and the nun and verbally laid them out. Nevertheless, this affected my church attendance. The lack of concern by the church for the immigrants and the cultural difference between the Italian and Irish Catholicism was responsible for a lot of the movement of Italians out of the Church toward Protestantism. This was also, however, a way to upward mobility. Had there been Italian clergy there is no question but that it would have made a difference. First of all the mere fact of being able to converse with the priest in your own language is important, but the role of the priest has been limited until very recently. The priest was not really a social agent by and large. I do not think priests gave social assistance beyond the performance of their strictly religious functions.

Emigrants after clearing inspection on Ellis Island, 1907 (Keystone-Mast Collection, University of California, Riverside)

Liberty

While the heavy immigration of Catholics presented enormous problems of administration and education to the Church, it raised once again widespread fears on the part of many who were not members of that Church. Nativism erupted once again in the 1880s and 1890s as it had prior to the Civil War (see Documentary History, *vol. 1, pp. 459-66). (1) Congregationalist Josiah Strong (1849-1916), though progressive in matters of social reform, saw Roman Catholicism as the enemy of America's liberties and the perverter of her grand destiny. In 1885 he wrote a book entitled* Our Country *(the "our" being understood as Anglo-Saxon):* Its Possible Future and Its Present Crisis. *A*

[Sources: (1) Josiah Strong, *Our Country . . .* (New York: Baker & Taylor, rev. ed., 1891), pp. 73-75. (2) James Gibbons, *A Retrospect of Fifty Years* (Baltimore: John Murphy, 1916), I, pp. 263-64.]

major contributor to the present crisis, in Strong's view, was the peril of
"Romanism." (2) Cardinal Gibbons, archbishop of Baltimore from 1877 to
1921, found it necessary time and again to explain, to those willing to listen,
the compatibility of Catholic theology with American democracy.

1.

We have made a brief comparison of some of the fundamental principles of
Romanism with those of the Republic. And,

1. We have seen the supreme sovereignty of the Pope opposed to the sovereignty of the people.

2. We have seen that the commands of the Pope, instead of the constitution and laws of the land, demand the highest allegiance of Roman Catholics in the United States.

3. We have seen that the alien Romanist who seeks citizenship swears true obedience to the Pope instead of "renouncing forever all allegiance to any foreign prince, potentate, state or sovereignty," as required by our laws.

4. We have seen that Romanism teaches religious intolerance instead of religious liberty.

5. We have seen that Rome demands the censorship of ideas and of the press, instead of the freedom of the press and of speech.

6. We have seen that she approves the union of church and state instead of their entire separation.

7. We have seen that she is opposed to our public school system.

Manifestly there is an irreconcilable difference between papal principles and the fundamental principles of our free institutions. Popular government is self-government. A nation is capable of self-government only so far as the individuals who compose it are capable of self-government. To place one's conscience, therefore, in the keeping of another, and to disavow all personal responsibility in obeying the dictation of another, is as far as possible from *self-government*, and, therefore, wholly inconsistent with republican institutions, and, if sufficiently common, dangerous to their stability. It is the theory of absolutism in the state, that man exists for the state. It is the theory of absolutism in the church that man exists for the church. But in republican and Protestant America it is believed that church and state exist for the people and are to be administered by them. Our fundamental ideas of society, therefore, are as radically opposed to Vaticanism as to imperialism, and it is as inconsistent with our liberties for Americans to yield allegiance to the Pope as to the Czar. It is true the Third Plenary Council[3] in Baltimore denied that there is any antagonism

3. This important council had met in 1884, with fourteen archbishops and sixty American bishops in attendance.

between the laws, institutions and spirit of the Roman church and those of our country, and in so doing illustrated the French proverb that "To deny is to confess." No Protestant church makes any such denials.

History fully justifies the teaching of philosophers that civil and political society tends to take the form of religious society. Absolutism in religion cannot fail in time to have an undermining influence on political equality. Already do we see its baneful influence in our large cities. It is for the most part the voters who accept absolutism in their faith who accept the dictation of their petty political popes, and suffer themselves to be led to the polls like so many sheep.

2.

No constitution is more in harmony with Catholic principles than is the American. And no religion can be in such accord with that constitution as the Catholic. While the State is not absorbed in the Church, nor the Church in the State, and thus there is external separation, they both derive their life from the same interior principle of truth, and in their different spheres carry out the same ideas, and thus there is between them a real internal union. The Declaration of Independence acknowledges that the rights it proclaims come from God as the source of all government and all authority. This is a fundamental religious principle in which the Church and State meet.

From it follows the correlative principle that as God alone is the source of human rights, so God alone can efficaciously maintain them. This is equivalent to Washington's warning that the basis of our liberties must be morality and religion. Shall, then, the various Christian churches have influence enough with the millions of our people to keep them in morality and religion? No question can equal this in importance to our country. For success in this noble competition the Catholic Church trusts in the commission given her by her Divine Founder to teach and bless "all nations, all days, even until the end of the world." For guarantee of the spirit in which she shall strive to accomplish it, she points confidently to history's testimony of her unswerving assertion of popular rights, and to her cordial devotedness to the free institutions of America constantly manifested, in word and in work, by her Bishops, her clergy and her people.

Judaism

Education

The commitment of America's Jews to education was matched only by their commitment to keep sectarian worship or instruction out of the public schools. Bible-reading, for so long an unquestioned tradition in the Protestant-dominated public schools, was often the crux. (1) In a famous case (Minor v. Board of Education) which reached the Superior Court of Cincinnati in 1869, the Court's majority upheld the ritual reading of the Bible in the local public schools. A persuasive dissent, however, delivered by Judge Alphonso Taft (1810-91; father of the president) led to a reversal by the Ohio Supreme Court the following year. (2) In San Francisco in 1875, the Lord's Prayer, urged upon the schools by a local Protestant clergyman, became the issue; a Jewish respondent to the "Rev. Mr. Hemphill" proclaimed as the American ideal "free thought and free, unsectarian education." (3) And in 1888, Abram S. Isaacs (1851-1920) made the case before the general public that the state — and therefore the state's schools — has "nothing to do with religion."

1. Dissenting Opinion of Judge Alphonso Taft

I can not doubt, therefore, that the use of the Bible with the appropriate singing, provided for by the old rule, and as practiced under it, was and is sectarian. It is Protestant worship. And its use is a symbol of Protestant supremacy in the schools, and as such offensive to Catholics and to Jews. They have a constitutional right to object to it, as a legal preference given by the State to the Protestant sects, which is forbidden by the Constitution.

And here, I again refer to the obvious distinction between the use of the Bible by way of worship, and its use as a reading book. . . . The question, whether the Board of Education under our Constitution could make the Bible a reading book in the schools, contrary to the conscientious scruples of the people, does not, in my opinion, arise in this case. For it is, as a form of worship and religious instruction only, and not as a reading book, that it is used in our

---

[Sources: (1) *The Bible in the Public Schools* (New York: Da Capo Press, 1967 [1870]), pp. 408-9, 410-11, 414-15. (2) L. P. Gartner, ed., *Jewish Education in the United States: A Documentary History* (New York: Teachers College Press, 1969), pp. 91-93. (3) Abram S. Isaacs, "What Shall the Public Schools Teach?" *Forum*, 6 (Oct., 1888), 207-8.]

schools, and as *such*, those who object to it, have a right to regard it; and that is the ground, as I have understood these proceedings, on which this suit has been brought.

The answer states that the children of Roman Catholic parents, equal to at least half the entire number of children who attend the common schools, are kept away by reason of this rule; that a large number of Jews, who have children in the schools, object to the rule from conscientious reasons.

The counsel for the plaintiffs insist, that the Bible can, in no just sense, be regarded as sectarian, and that the conscientious scruples alleged, are not to be regarded.

The facts on which this question turns, are simple. The Roman Catholic uses a different version of the Bible and includes the Apocrypha, as part of it, which are excluded from the Protestant Bible. The Protestant Bible, is the King James' version, which the Catholics regard as not only not a correct translation, but as distorted in the interest of the Protestant, as against the Roman Catholic Church. They object, therefore, on conscientious grounds, to having their children read it or hear it read. They say and believe, that it is a source of fatal religious error.

Nor is the incorrectness of the translation the only objection they entertain to the reading of the Bible in these schools. They hold, that the Bible is entrusted to the Church, and that it is not a suitable book to be read by, or to, children without explanation by persons authorized by the Church and of sufficient learning to explain and apply it.

We are not at liberty to doubt the conscientious objections, on the part of the Catholic parents to placing their children in the schools, while the schools are opened by the reading of the Protestant Bible and singing. . . .

It is said that the Catholic clergy demand their share of the fund, to be used in carrying on schools under their control. That can not be done under the Constitution. But this affords no reason why the Board of Education should not grant to the Catholic people, what the Bill of Rights guarantees to every sect, that their rights of conscience shall not be violated, and that they shall not be compelled to attend any form of worship, or to maintain it against their consent, or be compelled to submit to religious preferences, shown by the government to other religious societies.

It is not for a court to anticipate, before judgment, that any party will not be satisfied with what the law gives him, nor are courts accustomed to withhold what is due because something else is asked.

Another numerous class of heavy tax-payers, the Jews, object to the old rule. But it is claimed on behalf of the plaintiffs, that the Jews have met with something like a conversion, and have become reconciled to the New Testament. That they held out for a while, but afterward came in, and there was no further difficulty with them, and that their case need not to have been further regarded. There is too much evidence of dissent on their part, from the old rule, to permit us to conclude that they have ever intended to waive their rights of conscience and of religious liberty. Like the majority of us, the Jews have received their faith from their ancestors, and according to that historic faith, the assertion in the New Testament that Jesus of Nazareth is God, is blasphemy against the God of Israel. If a Protestant Christian would object to have the common schools daily opened with the forms of worship peculiar to the Catholic Church, which worships the same triune God with him, how much more serious must be the objection of the Jew, to be compelled to attend, or support, the worship of a being as God, whose divinity and supernatural history he denies?

The truth in this matter undoubtedly is, that the Jews, like many others, have found out that our common schools are munificently endowed, and, in general, well conducted, so that the privilege of attending them is inestimable, and they have wisely concluded to secure for their children the secular education of the common schools, and attend to their religious nurture at home and in their own organizations. A faith which had survived so much persecution, through so many centuries, they may well have risked in the common schools of Cincinnati, though at some cost of religious feeling.

It is in vain to attempt to escape the force of the clauses of the Bill of Rights by assuming that the Protestant Christian religion was intended in the Bill of Rights, and that the sects of Protestant Christians *only* were, therefore, entitled to protection. Between all forms of religious belief the State knows no difference, provided they do not transgress its civil regulations — a mighty contrast to some times and some countries, which have boasted of their religious liberality, because the ruling sects have tolerated the dissenting minority, as a nuisance, which they have magnanimously forborne to abate. . . .

While the Court will take cognizance of the existence of the Christian religion and of the Protestant religion, it is only for the purpose of preserving civil peace and order, and the welfare of the State; and for the same purpose, it will take cognizance of the existence of every sect. The State protects every religious denomination in the quiet enjoyment of its own mode of public worship. It protects them from blasphemy, when the public peace and order require it.

It is, therefore, an entire mistake, in my opinion, to assert, that the Protestant Christian religion has been so identified with the history and government of our State or country, that it is not to be regarded as sectarian under our Constitution; or, that, when the Bill of Rights says that "religion, morality and knowledge being essential to good government," it means the Protestant Christian religion. That would be a preference, which the same section expressly disclaims, and emphatically forbids.

To hold otherwise, and that Protestant Christians are entitled to any control in the schools, to which other sects are not equally entitled, or that they are entitled to have their mode of worship and their Bible used in the common schools, against the will of the Board of Education, the proper trustees and managers of the schools, is to hold to the union of Church and State, however we may repudiate and reproach the name. Nor is it to be presumed, that the cause of genuine religion, or of the Bible, can be permanently advanced by a struggle for this kind of supremacy. The government is neutral, and, while protecting all, it prefers none, and it *disparages* none. The State, while it does not profess to be Christian, exercises a truly Christian charity toward all. Its impartial charity extends to all kinds of Protestants, Roman Catholics, Jews and Rationalists alike, and covers them with its mantle of protection and encouragement; and no one of them, however numerous, can boast of peculiar favor with the State.

2. Joseph R. Brandon's Reply to the Reverend Mr. Hemphill

Mr. Hemphill, in his cry about Godless schools, evidently represents that class of men who must see the name of God stamped upon everything; who are uneasy because it does not appear in the Constitution of the United States, and are continually agitating to get it there, as the first step to sectarianizing the Government. What doctrine is this? Cannot things speak of God to the soul of man without the letters of His name being graven upon them? Do flowers speak to us of Him? — yet we find not His name on them. Do we see the lightning assume the form of the letters of His name, or hear the thunder pronounce the sound? — yet, *they* speak to us of Him. Does the wind shriek His name to us in the tempest, or whisper it in the zephyr? — yet they speak to us of Him. Do the heavens declare His glory, and the earth His handiwork? — "There is no speech, their is no language, yet their voice is heard." And if the name of God does not appear in the Constitution of the United States, surely to him who has God in his heart His hand is seen therein, and he may exclaim with the magicians of Egypt, "The finger of God is here." . . .

The hope of all thinking men as the means to this end is education — education of the highest order — the cultivation of science, the exercise of reason, *unlimited* in its objects; but to this end it must be UNSECTARIAN. None must be shut out from that light, which is to dissipate the clouds of bigotry and prejudice, and hasten the appearance of the cloudless sky of which we have spoken, and whence the heavenly dew distils.

Education — unsectarian education is the hope and salvation of the Jew, as of all who have passed through religious persecution; for it is from the deep, dark clouds of ignorance, which bespeak its absence among men, that the direst shafts of bigotry and persecution which have fallen upon our people and others have proceeded. Well, indeed, and earnestly may we labor for its diffusion, and seek not to drive children from, but to persuade and invite them to the common schools by removing all obstacles in the way.

Let our education be of the widest kind. Let reason and religion, too long divorced, too long at enmity, be reconciled. Let all of us, with free thought and free, unsectarian education, seek to lift ourselves and our fellows above the clouds of ignorance, sectarianism and prejudice, until these clouds can be dissipated; . . .

No, reader; because sectarian prayer has not been permitted in the schools, the friend of true education and true religion need not wail with Mr. Hemphill — that a battle has been lost — that Rome has conquered. He may rather rejoice that free thought, free education, free religion has gained a victory over the churchmen of all denominations; that the great principle has at last been enunciated, that the State, which should be the common parent and protector of all its children — majority or minority — few or many — will not lend its aid to dispense the particolored light of any particular sect, but only that colorless, illuminating principle which is common to all; and let us fervently hope, and at the same time be vigilant, that sectarianism, whether in the garb of Catholic priest, or Protestant minister, rob us not of the victory.

3. Abram S. Isaacs, "What Shall the Public Schools Teach?"

I have been general in suggestions as to what the schools should teach, leaving to specialists a more detailed answer. Upon one subject, however, a more precise reply is necessary. What is the relation of the schools to religion? Shall they teach religion in any form?

The answer was very simple decades ago, when the population was smaller and more homogeneous. But to-day, with diverse religious and non-religious elements on every side, there can be but one answer: the state has nothing to do with religion, its schools are not to instill religious teachings. Such work is for the churches and the synagogues. A godless school is not necessarily an ungodly school; the omission of the name of the Deity from the book of Esther did not interfere with its place in the canon. If your school develops character, intelligence, modesty, strength, helpfulness in the pupil, it can safely leave the distinctly religious element to other teachers and influences. The absence of any positive religious teachings, however, should not be made a pretext for the inculcation of positive irreligious teachings and the deification of the sneer. But the entire subject should be omitted from the programme. It is none of the school's business, as long as the state has no established church.

The evils in the present method are many. It is true, the law is opposed to sectarian teaching in the schools, yet it favors the reading of the Bible. Usually hymns are added of a sectarian character, suitable for a Protestant Sunday School, and admirable in their way, but in this connection out of place. Then the Lord's Prayer is repeated; on the lovely and sublime character of which I make no criticism, for I recognize its rabbinical spirit in every line. But it has become a distinctly Christian prayer, and is usually followed by Christian allusions, which are excellent in the Sunday school, but not in the public school, which is supported by hosts of tax-payers who are non-Christians. In most cases, the selections from the Bible are made without tact and contain doctrinal references. Under such circumstances, the only remedy is to withdraw religion entirely from the schools. The treatment which the Bible receives, the monotonous and perfunctory readings of disconnected chapters, is enough to make it, like Milton's "Paradise Lost," with its parsing reminiscences, a closed book to the scholars for all time.

Organization

In dealing with the public school system or with a suspicious Gentile majority, America's Jews stood together in unity. In dealing with each other, however, tensions and dissensions soon appeared. In the latter years of the nineteenth century, religious divisions emerged as observant Jews adopted varying attitudes toward Jewish law (Torah) and its interpretation (Halakah). (1) Reform Judaism, led by Isaac Mayer Wise (1819-1900), moved farthest to the left, seeing much of the ancient Mosaic or Rabbinical legislation as "altogether foreign to our present mental and spiritual state" — to quote from the 1885 Declaration of Principles. (2) Conservative Judaism, with Solomon Schechter (1847-1915) as its eloquent spokesman, would remain loyal to that which was uniquely Jewish at the same time that it avoided a "moribund rationalism" and took cognizance of an American environment and a modern world. (3) And then there was Orthodox Judaism — the faith of Abraham, Isaac, and Jacob — maintained without alteration or compromise. As a Yeshiva University professor explains below, Orthodoxy would presumably be the first "to meet the challenge of the American scene. . . . In fact, it was the last to do so."

[Sources: (1) I. M. Wise, *Selected Writings* (Cincinnati: Robert Clarke Co., 1900), pp. 260-62. (2) Solomon Schechter, *Seminary Addresses and Other Papers* (Cincinnati: Ark Publishing Co., 1915), pp. 83, 84-86. (3) Emanuel Rackman, "American Orthodoxy: Retrospect and Prospect," in Theodore Friedman and Robert Gordis, eds., *Jewish Life in America* (New York: Horizon Press, 1955), pp. 23-25.]

1. Reformed Judaism (1871)

Change, universal and perpetual, is the law of laws in this universe. Still there is an element of stability, the fact of mutation itself; the law of change changes not. This law lies in the harmony of the spheres; the mystery of truth in nature's variegation; the manifestation of the wisdom of the Immutable Deity. Progress and perfectibility are the effect, and, as far as reason penetrates, the conscious aim of this cause. The geologist, as he comes away from the lowest stratum into which his researches have gone along the crust of this planet, and the historian, who returns from the study of the life of humanity from the cradle of its birth to the nineteenth century, see the chain of conscious progress in form and idea, from the lowest to the highest known to man, see the promise of perfectibility everywhere, and see permanent retrogradation nowhere. Wisdom, boundless and ineffable, and the revelations of Deity lie in this law of laws "which God hath created to do."

Therefore, Reformed Judaism, the subject of this essay, acknowledges no necessary stability of the form, but also no change of the principle. All forms change, adapting themselves to new conditions, and all changes proceed from the same principle, which is not subject to change. This is the central idea of Jewish reasoners on Judaism in the nineteenth century.

Before following this idea in its sequence, it must be understood that the term "Reformed" in connection with "Judaism," does not imply restoration to an older form; it is intended to convey the idea of putting into a new and improved form and condition. Judaism, from this standpoint admits no retrogression, and maintains that all forms which the principle has developed and crystallized, were necessarily beneficial for each respective time or locality. But the civilization of the nineteenth century, being the sum and substance of all previous phases, has produced conditions unknown in former periods of history. Therefore, the principle of Judaism also must develop new forms corresponding to the new conditions which surround its votaries who live among the civilized nations; forms, too, which were neither necessary nor desirable in former periods of history, and would not be such now to other Israelites, although adhering to the same principle, who live among semi-barbarous, or even less enlightened nations. Again, as civilization progresses, the principle of Judaism will always develop new forms in correspondence with every progressive state of the intelligence and consciousness, until the great day when one shepherd and one flock will unite the human family in truth, justice and love. As an illustration of this, it is to be remembered that the Israelite of the reformed school does not believe in the restoration of the ancient mode of worship by the sacrifice of animal victims and by a hereditary priesthood. He considers that phase was necessary and beneficial, in its time and locality, but that it would be void of all significance in our age when entirely different conceptions of divine worship prevail, and it would appear much more meaningless to coming generations. The divine institutions of the past are not obligatory on the present generation or on coming ages, since the conditions which rendered them necessary, desirable and beneficial have been radically changed. Therefore, Progressive Judaism would be a better designation than Reformed Judaism. But, on account of common usage, the latter term has been adopted as the caption of this essay, and should be understood in this spirit alone.

2. Altar Building in America (1904)

The first settlers in this country were mostly men who had left their native land for conscience' sake, despairing of the Old World as given over to the powers of darkness, despotism and unbelief. And I can quite realize how they must have gloried in the idea of being chosen instruments of Providence who were to restore the spiritual equilibrium of the world by the conquest of new spheres of religious influence and their dedication to the worship of Almighty God.

As a Jew coming from the East of Europe, where my people are trodden down, where seats of Jewish learning and Jewish piety are daily destroyed, I am greatly animated by the same feelings and am comforted to see the New World compensating us for our many losses in the Old. I rejoice, therefore, at the privilege of being with you on this solemn occasion. . . .

We are now prepared for the minuter consideration of our text.

"And thou shalt write upon the stones all the words of the Torah very plainly." The stones are erected, and at this moment have been dedicated to the service of God. But bricks and mortar, marble pillar and gilded domes do not make an altar. What constitutes an altar are the words of the Torah, which are engraved on the very stones, which influence the lives of the worshipers and convert their homes into places of worship. The verse in Exodus 20:24, also containing injunctions regarding the altar, is paraphrased by the great Hillel as if God were saying to man, "If thou wilt come unto My house, I will come into thy house." "The word of our Lord endureth forever." This is a divine promise. But if after frequent visits to places of worship, you have experienced nothing of the nearness of God in your houses, then you may safely doubt whether you have really been in a house of God. It is the home which is the final and supreme test of the altar. A synagogue, for instance, that teaches a Judaism which finds no reverberating echo in the Jewish home, awakens there no distinctive conscious Jewish life, has failed in its mission, and is sure sooner or later to disappear as a religious factor making for righteousness and holiness. It may serve as a lecture hall or a lyceum, or as a place to which people in their *ennui* repair for "an intellectual treat;" but it will never become a place of worship, a real altar for acceptable sacrifices, bestowing that element of joy in God . . . which is the secret and strength of Judaism.

This is a test applicable to all ages and to all countries; to the New World as well as the Old. There is nothing in American citizenship which is incompatible with our observing the dietary laws, our sanctifying the Sabbath, our fixing a Mezuzah on our doorposts, our refraining from unleavened bread on Passover, or our perpetuating any other law essential to the preservation of Judaism. On the other hand, it is now generally recognized by the leading thinkers that the institutions and observances of religion are part of its nature, a fact that the moribund rationalism of a half century ago failed to realize. In certain parts of Europe every step in our civil and social emancipation demanded from us a corresponding sacrifice of a portion of the glorious heritage bequeathed to us by our fathers. Jews in America, thank God, are no longer haunted by such fears. We live in a commonwealth in which by the blessing of God and the wisdom of the Fathers of the Constitution, each man abiding by its laws, has the inalienable right of living in accordance with the dictates of his own conscience. In this great, glorious and free country we Jews need not sacrifice a single iota of our Torah; and, in the enjoyment of absolute equality with our fellow citizens we can live to carry out those ideals for which our ancestors so often had to die.

3. American Orthodoxy: Retrospect and Prospect (1955)

The earliest Jewish settlers on American soil brought with them the only Judaism they knew — Orthodox Judaism. Two centuries later Reform Judaism took root and fifty years thereafter Conservative Judaism was born. Under the circumstances, one would have expected that Orthodox Judaism would be the first to meet the challenge of the American scene, both ideologically and institutionally. In fact, it was the last to do so. Paradoxically enough, it is only in the last few decades that Orthodoxy seriously came to grips with the problem of its own future.

For too long a time Orthodoxy relied upon the fact that the preponderant number of American Jews professed to be its adherents. Majorities supporting the status quo in many social situations often rely upon the force of their numbers and their inertia, while well organized and dedicated minorities make gains or change. The Orthodox Jewish community once was such a majority. It was slow to realize the extent to which it was losing its numerical advantage. Also, the ranks of American Orthodoxy were constantly replenished with thousands of immigrants from abroad. The new arrivals more than compensated for the defections to other groups. Now the loss of the European reservoir of Jews has caused American Orthodoxy to become concerned. It had to find the way to command the loyalty of American-born Jews. Finally, Orthodoxy by its very nature compromises less easily with new environments and new philoso-

Jewish market, East Side, New York City, 1900 (Library of Congress)

phies, so that it could not avail itself of that flexibility which aided the growth of the Reform and Conservative movements. The challenge of the American scene had to be met differently and the solution came later. Nonetheless, the contributions of Orthodoxy to our dual heritage as Americans and as Jews were many and significant.

It fell to the lot of Orthodoxy to establish the legal status of Jews and Judaism in American democracy. To the everlasting credit of our pioneering forbears it must be said that they were not content with second-class citizenship in the United States. George Washington confirmed this attitude in his now famous letter to the Orthodox congregation in Newport, Rhode Island. However, the false dictum that America is a "Christian state" must be challenged again and again, even in the twentieth century, and while the battle is now waged by all Jews, and especially by the defense agencies, it is usually one Orthodox Jew or another who creates the issue. The right of Sabbath observers to special consideration where "Blue Sunday" laws are in effect; their right to special treatment in the armed forces; their right to unemployment insurance benefits when they decline employment because of religious scruples — these are typical of many problems that Orthodox Jews raise in the hope that their resolution will insure maximum expansion of the American concept of equality before the law. In many instances, bearded Orthodox Jews who retain their Eastern European dress are also a challenge to the sincerity of most Americans who boast that their way of life spells respect for differences. The resistance of many of our co-religionists to the levelling character of American mores, and its inevitable discouragement of diversity, is a healthy contribution to our understanding and practice of democracy. Altogether too often American Jews require the reminder even more than American Christians.

In the same spirit it was American Orthodoxy that bore, and still bears, the burden of resistance to world-wide calendar reform. Though all Jewish groups have cooperated, it is Orthodoxy alone that regards any tampering with the inviolability of the Sabbath day fixed at Creation as a mortal blow to Judaism and in the name of the religious freedom of minorities it seeks to alert the American conscience to desist from prejudicial action.

It was, however, in the establishment and construction of thousands of synagogues throughout the country that Orthodox Jews made manifest not only their loyalty to their ancestral heritage but their appreciation of their grand opportunity in this blessed land of freedom. How truly pauperized immigrants managed, in cities large and small, to rear beautiful edifices for worship is a saga worthy of more attention than it has heretofore received. What is particularly noteworthy is that no central agency guided or financed the movement. In every case it was individual Jews who banded together and performed the feat, a remarkable tribute to the effectiveness of our tradition in inducing in individual Jews the capacity to act on their own initiative for the greater glory of God.

2. Women's Work?

Pulpit

If women wanted to enter into the pulpit, this often meant that they must create their own church (as Ann Lee and Ellen White, for example, had done; see Documentary History, *vol. 1, pp. 357-58, 365). The older, more established denominations saw the introduction of females into their ministry as radical, unbiblical, and unsuitable to the "weaker" sex. When Antoinette Brown Blackwell (1825-1921) accepted ordination in the Congregational church in 1853, she broke a barrier by becoming the first woman to be ordained by a major denomination. Yet, other barriers of resistance remained as Blackwell was obliged to defend the capacity and propriety of women entering professional life. (1) In 1875, she took issue, on physiological and psychological grounds, with a recent (1873) Boston publication by E. H. Clarke,* Sex in Education; or, A Fair Chance for the Girls. *(2) Among those not convinced by Blackwell's argumentation or example was R. L. Dabney (1820-98), a Presbyterian minister, theologian, and professor in Virginia. Writing in 1879, Dabney explained that the Bible clearly shows woman's position in the church to be subordinate to man's.*

1.

Dr. Clarke has given voice and tangibility to many of the floating suggestions of years, insisting that women are physically incapacitated for habitual study, that

---

[Sources: (1) A. B. Blackwell, *The Sexes Through Nature* (New York: G. P. Putnam's Sons, 1875), pp. 162-63, 163-67. (2) R. L. Dabney, "The Public Preaching of Women," *Southern Presbyterian Review,* 30 (Oct., 1879), 689-90, 695-96, 711-13.]

growing young girls should not be allowed to compete with boys in an identical course of education, and leading us squarely up to the inference that the strain of persistent mental work can never be successfully borne by average woman-hood: The Dr. pronounces our national, rapidly growing method of co-education in schools and colleges "a crime before God and humanity, that physiology protests against, and that experience weeps over." The entire community, therefore, has a most vital interest in this book, which maintains that co-education is more than a mistake; that it imperils the health of the girls, curtailing their hope of posterity, and threatening their few possible children with greatly unfeebled constitutions. . . .

Many of us have felt for years that the "Woman question" must be met just here, upon a comparative physiological and psychological basis. . . .

That every-day question is, does study, a few hours of regular daily application to mental work, impair or tend to impair the vigor of the feminine constitution? Are the daily lessons which are fitting and healthful for a school boy so exacting that they must draw the blood to nurture the brain of the school girl to the detriment of her appropriate womanly growth? Does moderate study, on any day and at any period of a healthy woman's life, tend to exhaust her natural strength, or to produce a reaction so violent that it must become a direct promoter either of weakness or of disease? These questions are all one; they apply to the girl of fifteen or to the woman of thirty alike. They must be answered as bearing not only on her own welfare, but also on that of the rising generation.

There are many ways of reaching the same conclusion, but the first and best method is based upon experience. It is fitting that I add personal testimony to enforce my position, that study is as healthful to women as to men, and, as society now is, that it must prove to be relatively much more so.

In the days when mothers sent their babies for early instruction, I was a little school-girl in prompt and regular attendance at three years. I remained at school, averaging from a half to two-thirds of every intervening year, until I was twenty-four; so that I have literally "come of age" under a system of joint education for the sexes, for I never attended a girls' school. During this whole period I studied as continuously as an average boy studies, was not conspicuously deficient at recitations, and for years together did more real brain work outside of all class exercises than in connection with them; yet my health was generally good, and it continued good for years after I left the Theological Seminary,[4] though I was engaged in work more health-trying than anything in my previous experience. Once, not from ordinary overwork, but in passing through an ordeal not uncommon in modern days, in which the faith of one's fathers is shaken to the foundations, and when forced to meet the added struggle of con-

---

4. Oberlin in 1850; she left without being allowed to receive a theological degree.

tinuing to teach many things which were no longer believed, or dropping out from a profession chosen conscientiously in the face of untold obstacles, my health was seriously impaired. But I speedily gained both a broader faith and a firmer health, which remain unimpaired to this day. I am the mother of six children, five of whom enjoy a vigor of constitution above the average; and one, in the midst of apparently perfect health, was swept off by one of those scourges of infancy against which Omniscience alone could always guard effectively. . . .

We may regard this as an exceptional instance of a woman's ability to endure persistent brain work unharmed in health; but I believe it to be simply one illustration of human power to thrive on habitual daily exercise of both mind and body, alternated with sufficient rest and relaxation.

2.

In this day innovations march with rapid strides. The fantastic suggestion of yesterday, entertained only by a few fanatics, and then only mentioned by the sober to be ridiculed, is to-day the audacious reform, and will be to-morrow the recognised usage. Novelties are so numerous and so wild and rash, that in even conservative minds the sensibility of wonder is exhausted and the instinct of righteous resistance fatigued. A few years ago the public preaching of women was universally condemned among all conservative denominations of Christians, and, indeed, within their bounds, was totally unknown. Now the innovation is brought face to face even with the Southern churches, and female preachers are knocking at our doors. We are told that already public opinion is so truckling before the boldness and plausibility of their claims that ministers of our own communion begin to hesitate, and men hardly know whether they have the moral courage to adhere to the right. These remarks show that a discussion of woman's proper place in Christian society is again timely.

The arguments advanced by those who profess reverence for the Bible, in favor of this unscriptural usage, must be of course chiefly rationalistic. They do indeed profess to appeal to the sacred history of the prophetesses, Miriam, Deborah, Huldah, and Anna, as proving that sex was no sufficient barrier to public work in the Church. But the fatal answer is: that these holy women were inspired. Their call was exceptional and supernatural. There can be no fair reasoning from the exception to the ordinary rule. . . .

The argument then, whether any woman may be a public preacher of the Word, should be prevalently one of Scripture. Does the Bible really prohibit it? We assert that it does. And first, the Old Testament, which contained, in germ, all the principles of the New, allowed no regular church office to any woman. When a few of that sex were employed as mouth-pieces of God, it was in an office purely extraordinary and in which they could adduce a supernatural attestation of their commission. No woman ever ministered at the altar as either priest or Levite. No female elder was ever seen in a Hebrew congregation. No woman ever sat on the throne of the theocracy except the pagan usurper and murderess, Athaliah. Now Presbyterians at least believe that the church order of the Old Testament Church was imported into the New, with less modification than any other part of the old religion. The ritual of types was greatly modified; new sacramental symbols replaced the old; the temple of sacrifice was superseded, leaving no sanctuary beneath the heavenly one, save the synagogue, the house of prayer. But the primeval presbyterial order continued unchanged. The Christianised synagogue became the Christian congregation, with its eldership, teachers, and deacons, and its women invariably keeping silence in the assembly. The probability thus raised is strong.

Secondly, if human language can make anything plain, it is that the New Testament institutions do not suffer the woman to rule or "to usurp authority over the man." See 1 Tim. ii. 12; 1 Cor. xi. 3, 7-10; Eph. v. 22, 23; 1 Peter iii. 1, 5, 6. In ecclesiastical affairs at least, the woman's position in the Church is subordinate to the man's. . . .

The woman is not designed by God, nor entitled to all the franchises in society to which the male is entitled. God has disqualified her for any such exercise of them as would benefit herself or society, by the endowments of body, mind, and heart he has given her, and the share he has assigned her in the tasks of social existence. And as she has no right to assume the masculine franchises, so she will find in the attempt to do so only ruin to her own character and to society. For instance, the very traits of emotion and character which make woman man's cherished and invaluable "helpmeet," the traits which she must have in order to fulfil the purpose of her being, would ensure her unfitness to meet the peculiar temptations of publicity and power. The attempt would debauch all these lovelier traits, while it would leave her still, as the rival of man, "the weaker vessel." She would lose all and gain nothing.

One consequence of this revolution would be so certain and so terrible that it cannot be passed over. It must result in the abolition of all permanent marriage ties. Indeed, the bolder advocates do not scruple to avow it. The destruction of marriage would follow by this cause, if no other; that the unsexed politicating woman, the importunate manikin-rival, would never inspire in men that true affection on which marriage should be founded. The mutual attraction of the two complementary halves would be forever gone. The abolition of marriage would follow again by another cause. The rival interests and desires of two equal wills are inconsistent with domestic union, government, or peace. Shall the children of this unnatural connexion be held responsible to both of two sinful but coördinate and equally supreme wills? Heaven pity the children! Again, who ever heard of a perpetual copartnership in which the parties had no power to enforce the performance of the mutual duties nor to dissolve the tie made intolerable by violation? It would be as iniquitous as impossible. Such a copartnership of equals, with coördinate wills and independent interests, must be separable at will, as all other such co-partnerships are.

This common movement for "women's rights" and women's preaching must be regarded then as simply infidel. It cannot be candidly upheld without attacking the inspiration and authority of the Scriptures. We are convinced that there is only one safe attitude for Christians, presbyters, and church courts to assume towards it. This is utterly to discountenance it, as they do any other assault of infidelity on God's truth and kingdom. The church officer who becomes an accomplice of this intrusion certainly renders himself obnoxious to discipline, just as he would by assisting to celebrate an idolatrous mass.

We close with one suggestion to such women as may be inclined to this new claim. If they read history they find that the condition of woman in Christendom, and especially in America, is most enviable as compared with her state in all other ages and nations. Let them ponder candidly how much they possess here which their sisters have enjoyed in no other age. What bestowed those peculiar privileges on the Christian women of America? The Bible. Let them beware then how they do anything to undermine the reverence of mankind for the authority of the Bible. It is undermining their own bulwark. If they understand how universally in all but Bible lands the "weaker vessel" has been made the slave of man's strength and selfishness, they will gladly "let well enough alone," lest in grasping at some impossible prize beyond, they lose the privileges they now have, and fall back to the gulf of oppression from which these doctrines of Christ and Paul have lifted them.

Society

The reform of society, many freely argued in the nineteenth century, was a man's job. But what if men were in fact a major source of the social problem? Could the leopard change his spots? (1) With regard to the overindulgence in alcohol, men indeed were the problem, and women — perhaps — the solution. Women, if organized and dedicated and vocal, could make, would make an enormous difference. This was the conviction and firm purpose of Frances E. Willard (1839-98) who led the Women's Christian Temperance Union from modest beginnings in Ohio to world-wide organization and in-

---

[Sources: (1) Frances E. Willard, *Women and Temperance* . . . (New York: Arno Press, 1972 (1883]), pp. 636-37, 638, 640. (2) Alice T. Toomy, *Catholic World*, 57 (Aug., 1893), 674-76.]

fluence. At the first convention of the W.C.T.U. in Cleveland in 1874, the fol-
lowing "Plan of Work" was adopted. (2) On the Roman Catholic side, Alice
Toomy argued for women to take a more active role in the "public sphere"
than they had traditionally done — not just in temperance concerns but in
many other social arenas as well. Toomy made her argument in the pages of
the Catholic World, *and in those same pages she was answered by Kather-*
ine E. Conway: ". . . it seems settled beyond question that woman, as woman,
can have no vocation in public life" (p. 681).

1. Plan of Work.

I. — of Organization.

Since organization is the sun-glass which brings to a focus scattered influence
and effort, we urge the formation of a Woman's Temperance Union in every
State, city, town, and village. We will furnish a Constitution for auxiliaries, with
all needed information, to any lady applying to corresponding secretary.

II. — of Making Public Sentiment.

The evolution of temperance ideas in this order: the people are informed, convinced, convicted, pledged. With these facts in view we urge:

First. — Frequent temperance mass meetings.

Second. — The careful circulation of temperance literature in the people's
homes and in saloons.

Third. — Teaching the children in Sabbath-Schools and public schools,
the ethics, chemistry, physiology, and hygiene of total abstinence.

Fourth. — Offering prizes in these schools for essays on different aspects
of the subject.

Fifth. — Placing a copy of the engraving known as "The Railroad to
Ruin," and similar pictures, on the walls of every school-room.

Sixth. — Organizing temperance glee clubs of young people to sing temperance doctrines into the peoples' hearts as well as heads.

Seventh. — Seeking permission to edit a column in the interest of temperance in every newspaper in the land, and in all possible ways enlisting the
press in this reform.

Eighth. — Endeavoring to secure for pastors everywhere frequent temperance sermons, and special services in connection with the weekly prayer-
meeting and the Sabbath-School at stated intervals, if they be only quarterly.

Ninth. — Preserving facts connected with the general subject, and with our work, in temperance scrap-books, to be placed in the hands of a special officer appointed for this purpose. . . .

IV. — of the Pledge.

If nobody would drink, then nobody would sell.

First. — We urge the circulation of the total abstinence pledge as fast and as far as facilities permit, life signatures being sought, but names being taken for any length of time, however brief.

Second. — We have a special pledge for women, involving the instruction and pledging of themselves, their children, and as far as possible their households; banishing alcohol in all its forms from the sideboard and the kitchen, enjoining quiet, persistent work for temperance in their own social circles.

Third. — We earnestly recommend ladies to get permission to place a pledge-book in every church and Sabbath-school room, where it shall be kept perpetually open in a convenient place, indicated by a motto placed above it. Also that each member of our unions keep an autograph pledge-book on her parlor table, and carry one in her pocket. . . .

VII. — of Temperance Coffee Rooms.

If we would have men forsake saloons, we must invite them to a better place, where they can find shelter, and food, and company. We would open small, neat coffee-rooms, with reading-rooms attached, which the ladies might supply with books and papers from their own homes, and by solicited friends. When practicable, there should also be Friendly Inns, connected with which there might be provided for those willing to compensate by their labor for their food and lodging, a manufacturing shop, comprising many trades. . . .

Conclusion.

Dear sisters, we have laid before you the plan of the long campaign. Will you work with us? We wage our peaceful war in loving expectation of that day "when all men's weal shall be each man's care," when "nothing shall hurt or destroy in all my holy mountain," saith the Lord; and in our day we may live to see America, beloved mother of thrice grateful daughters, set at liberty, full and complete, from foamy King Gambrinus[5] and fiery old King Alcohol.

---

5. A mythical king associated with the invention of beer.

2. There Is a Public Sphere for Catholic Women

The Catholic Women's Congress held in Chicago, May 18 [1893], gave an outline sketch of the work of Catholic women, beginning with a paper on "The Elevation of Womanhood through the Veneration of the Blessed Virgin," and closing with the life-work of Margaret Haughery,[6] of New Orleans, the only woman in America to whom the public have raised a statue.

The enthusiasm awakened by this Congress drew a large body of Catholic women together, who organized a National League for work on the lines of education, philanthropy, and "the home and its needs" — education to promote the spread of Catholic truth and reading circles, etc.; philanthropy to include temperance, the formation of day nurseries and free kindergartens, protective and employment agencies for women, and clubs and homes for working girls; the "home and its needs" to comprehend the solution of the domestic service question, as well as plans to unite the interests and tastes of the different members of the family. Each active member of the league registers under some one branch of work according to her special attraction. The underlying idea of the league is that Catholic women realize that there is a duty devolving on them to help the needy on lines which our religious cannot reach, even were they not already so sadly overworked. Tens of thousands of our ablest Catholic women are working with the W.C.T.U. and other non-Catholic philanthropies, because they find no organization in their own church as a field for their activities. Every Catholic woman who has had much association outside the church is frequently met with the question: Why don't you Catholics take care of your own poor, and not leave so much work for other churches to do for you? The truth is that ours is the church of the poor, and manifold as is the charity work of the religious and the benevolent societies, a vast amount has to go undone because there is no one to attend to it. It seems safe to compute that fully one-half our church members are among the needy, one-tenth of our members are wealthy, and the remaining forty percent are well to do. The occupations of the very wealthy seem so all-engrossing that the care of the needy seems to fall naturally on the well to do, who are happily not so far removed from the poor in condition as to be insensible to their wants. Mankind has repeated the "Our Father" for well-nigh two thousand years, and yet the great body of humanity seems only now waking up to the fact that "*our* Father" implies a common brotherhood: that "no man liveth unto himself alone": that we are our brothers' keepers. Surely then, in the face of these facts, it can only be through misapprehension of terms that the question is asked, "Is there a public sphere for Catholic

6. Margaret Gaffney Haughery (1813-82) won the affections of the New Orleans public by her self-sacrifice, abundant charity, and simple, unaffected goodwill. Her statue, unveiled in 1884, carried only this inscription: "Margaret."

women?" As well as ask, "Is there a public sphere for the religious?" since who is so public as the man or woman who gives his whole life, with all its powers, for the good of humanity? It cannot be that the estimate of the Catholic woman is so poor that it is supposed that her love of home, her sense of duty and womanly instincts will suffer by her taking counsel with a body of women for a few hours every week as to the best methods of improving the condition of her fellow-women? Catholic women enter into the gaieties and even the follies of society. Many lose more money and time for dress and fashion than would be consumed by works of philanthropy. Yet no alarm seems to be taken as to the danger to womanliness in this sphere!

Almost every subject of practical utility to humanity has been set for discussion during the Chicago congresses. Already many vital questions of morals and progress have been ably considered by experts. Many of those experts have been women, and even some of these women were Catholics. Can anyone doubt that the church and the world have gained by their success? Is not every good thought crystallized into a plan of action — a fresh guidance in well-doing?

However wise or pious a woman may be, she meets with daily problems for which no literature offers solution, but from which the light of other women's experience may clear away the difficulty. The great power of the age is organization, and nowhere is it more needed than among Catholic women, whose consciences and hearts are so keenly alive to evils that individuals find themselves powerless to overcome. The proof that the Catholic Women's League is needed is shown by the daily applications for affiliation, and for an organizer to go to other cities and establish branches.

Academy

Some women found in the Bible the sanction for their reforming efforts, the grounds for their emancipation. Others, however, saw the Bible — at least as presently translated and widely understood — as a major part of the problem. Elizabeth Cady Stanton (1815-1902), feminist of great impact, joined with the Quaker preacher Lucretia Mott in organizing the famous 1848 convention for women's rights at Seneca Falls, New York. Later working with Susan B. Anthony, Stanton took women's suffrage as her chief cause. And in

[Source: E. C. Stanton, *The Woman's Bible,* Part I (New York: European Publishing Co., 1895), pp. 7-8, 9, 10.]

*the final decade of the nineteenth century, she courted even more controversy
by taking the leading role in preparing a new edition of the Holy Scriptures,
this one to be known as* The Woman's Bible *(in two volumes, 1895, 1898).*

From the inauguration of the movement for woman's emancipation the Bible
has been used to hold her in the "divinely ordained sphere," prescribed in the
Old and New Testaments.

The canon and civil law; church and state; priests and legislators; all political parties and religious denominations have alike taught that woman was
made after man, of man, and for man, an inferior being, subject to man. Creeds,
codes, Scriptures and statutes, are all based on this idea. The fashions, forms,
ceremonies and customs of society, church ordinances and discipline all grow
out of this idea.

Of the old English common law, responsible for woman's civil and political status, Lord Brougham said, "it is a disgrace to the civilization and Christianity of the Nineteenth Century." Of the canon law, which is responsible for
woman's status in the church, Charles Kingsley said, "this will never be a good
world for women until the last remnant of the canon law is swept from the face
of the earth."

The Bible teaches that woman brought sin and death into the world, that
she precipitated the fall of the race, that she was arraigned before the judgment
seat of Heaven, tried, condemned and sentenced. Marriage for her was to be a
condition of bondage, maternity a period of suffering and anguish, and in silence and subjection, she was to play the role of a dependent on man's bounty
for all her material wants, and for all the information she might desire on the
vital questions of the hour, she was commanded to ask her husband at home.
Here is the Bible position of woman briefly summed up.

Those who have the divine insight to translate, transpose and transfigure
this mournful object of pity into an exalted, dignified personage, worthy our
worship as the mother of the race, are to be congratulated as having a share of
the occult mystic power of the eastern Mahatmas.

The plain English to the ordinary mind admits of no such liberal interpretation. The unvarnished texts speak for themselves. The canon law, church
ordinances and Scriptures, are homogeneous, and all reflect the same spirit and
sentiments.

These familiar texts are quoted by clergymen in their pulpits, by statesmen in the halls of legislation, by lawyers in the courts, and are echoed by the
press of all civilized nations, and accepted by woman herself as "The Word of
God." So perverted is the religious element in her nature, that with faith and
works she is the chief support of the church and clergy; the very powers that
make her emancipation impossible. When, in the early part of the Nineteenth
Century, women began to protest against their civil and political degradation,

they were referred to the Bible for an answer. When they protested against their unequal position in the church, they were referred to the Bible for an answer. . . .

Listening to the varied opinions of women, I have long thought it would be interesting and profitable to get them clearly stated in book form. To this end six years ago I proposed to a committee of women to issue a Woman's Bible, that we might have women's commentaries on women's position in the Old and New Testaments. It was agreed on by several leading women in England and America and the work was begun, but from various causes it has been delayed, until now the idea is received with renewed enthusiasm, and a large committee has been formed, and we hope to complete the work within a year.

Lucretia Mott (1783-1880), Quaker minister
and human rights advocate
(National Portrait Gallery, Smithsonian Institution, Washington, D.C.)

Those who have undertaken the labor are desirous to have some Hebrew and Greek scholars, versed in Biblical criticism, to gild our pages with their learning. Several distinguished women have been urged to do so, but they are afraid that their high reputation and scholarly attainments might be compromised by taking part in an enterprise that for a time may prove very unpopular. Hence we may not be able to get help from that class.

Others fear that they might compromise their evangelical faith by affiliating with those of more liberal views, who do not regard the Bible as the "Word of God," but like any other book, to be judged by its merits. If the Bible teaches the equality of Woman, why does the church refuse to ordain women to preach the gospel, to fill the offices of deacons and elders, and to administer the Sacraments, or to admit them as delegates to the Synods, General Assemblies and Conferences of the different denominations? They have never yet invited a woman to join one of their Revising Committees, nor tried to mitigate the sentence pronounced on her by changing one count in the indictment served on her in Paradise. . . .

Forty years ago it seemed as ridiculous to timid, time-serving and retrograde folk for women to demand an expurgated edition of the laws, as it now does to demand an expurgated edition of the Liturgies and the Scriptures. Come, come, my conservative friend, wipe the dew off your spectacles, and see that the world is moving. Whatever your views may be as to the importance of the proposed work, your political and social degradation are but an outgrowth of your status in the Bible. When you express your aversion, based on a blind feeling of reverence in which reason has no control, to the revision of the Scriptures, you do but echo Cowper, who, when asked to read Paine's "Rights of Man," exclaimed, "No man shall convince me that I am improperly governed while I *feel* the contrary."

3. The West

Western Indians

Pierre Jean De Smet (1801-1873) and the Sioux

As the still young American nation occupied more and more land east of the Mississippi River, Indians ceased to be a political or military presence in that half of the continent. Farther west, however, Indian tribes continued to maintain some semblance of civil independence and of cultural integrity. Inevitably, therefore, conflicts arose between the Indian minority and the expanding United States government. Especially with the Sioux, "this large and hostile tribe," many violent confrontations took place. As potential peacemaker and as one of the few whites whom they trusted, the Belgian Jesuit Pierre Jean De Smet was repeatedly called upon to intercede. His effectiveness in that role earned this tribute from David S. Stanley, Major General of the United States Army. Writing from the Dakota Territory in 1864, Stanley addressed his letter to John Baptist Purcell, Archbishop of Cincinnati.

In the month of May of the current year the commission succeeded in convoking at Fort Laramie, on the Platte river, a certain number of chiefs belonging to the most formidable and most warlike tribes. The Hunkpapas, however, still refused to enter into any arrangement with the whites, and it is unnecessary to say that no treaty with the Sioux was possible, if this large and hostile tribe was unwilling to concur in it. In this condition of affairs, the Reverend Father De Smet, who has consecrated his life to the service of the true religion and of humanity,

---

[Source: *Life, Letters, and Travels of Father De Smet* (New York: Arno Press, 1969 [1905]), IV, pp. 1584-86, 1587-88.]

offered himself, despite his great age, to endeavor to penetrate to the hostile camps and to use his influence with the chiefs to induce them to appear before the commission at Fort Rice. As the letter of the members of the [Peace] commission will inform you, there is reason to believe that his mission has been wholly successful.

I could give you only an imperfect idea of the privations and dangers of this journey, unless you were acquainted with the great plains and the Indian character, which is naturally inclined to vengeance. Father De Smet, alone of the entire white race, could penetrate to these cruel savages and return safe and sound. One of the chiefs, in speaking to him while he was in the hostile camp, told him, "if it had been any other man than you, Black-robe, this day would have been his last."

The Reverend Father had with him, as interpreter, Mr. Galpin, who is married to an Indian woman of the Hunkpapa tribe. This lady is a good Catholic and an excellent person, a striking example of what the influence of religion and civilization can accomplish for the welfare of the Indian. On leaving Fort Rice, Father De Smet had to direct his course straight west. The enemy had pitched his camp a little above the mouth of the Yellowstone river, near Powder river. The distance to be traveled, going and coming, was 700 miles. The coun-

Nez Perce Woman's Missionary Society (Presybterian) in Idaho, 1891
(Presbyterian Historical Society)

Pierre Jean De Smet, S.J. (1801-73)
(Library of Congress)

try is a barren desert. Nothing in the way of vegetation is to be seen save sage-brush, the *artemisia* of the plains. No buffalo are to be found except along the Yellowstone, where they are very numerous.

The Reverend Father is known among the Indians by the name of "Black-robe" and "Big Medicine Man." When he is among them he always wears the cas-sock and crucifix. He is the only man for whom I have ever seen Indians evince a real affection. They say, in their simple and open language, that he is the only white man who has not a forked tongue; that is, who never lies to them. The re-ception that they gave him in the hostile camp was enthusiastic and magnificent. They came twenty miles to meet him, and the principal chiefs, riding beside him, conducted him to the camp in great triumph. This camp comprised more than 500 lodges, which, at the ratio of six persons to the lodge, gave a total of 3,000 Indians. During his visit, which lasted three days, the principal chiefs, Black Moon and Sitting Bull, who had been redoubtable adversaries of the whites for the last four years of the war, watched constantly over the safety of the missionary; they slept beside him at night, lest some Indian might seek to avenge upon his person the death of some kinsman killed by the whites. During the day time, multitudes of children flocked to his lodge, and the mothers brought him their new babies that he might lay his hands on them and bless them.

In the gathering of the Indians the head chiefs promised to put an end to the war. Sitting Bull declared that he had been the most mortal enemy of the whites, and had fought them by every means in his power; but now that the Black-robe had come to utter the words of peace, he renounced warfare and would never again lift his hand against the whites. The chiefs delegated several of their principal warriors, who, in the company with Father De Smet, arrived at Fort Rice on the 30th of June. . . .

But it is time to close this long letter. Whatever may be the result of the treaty which the commission has just concluded with the Sioux, we can never forget nor shall we ever cease to admire, the disinterested devotion of the Reverend Father De Smet, who, at the age of sixty-eight years, did not hesitate, in the midst of the heat of summer, to undertake a long and perilous journey, across the burning plains, destitute of trees and even of grass; having none but corrupted and unwholesome water, constantly exposed to scalping by Indians, and this without seeking either honors or remuneration of any sort; but solely to arrest the shedding of blood and save, if it might be, some lives, and preserve some habitations to these savage children of the desert, to whose spiritual and temporal welfare he has consecrated a long life of labor and solicitude. The head chief of the Yanktonnais, Two Bears, said in his speech: "When we are settled down sowing grain, raising cattle and living in houses, we want Father De Smet to come and live with us, and to bring us other Black-robes to live among us also; we will listen to their words, and the Great Spirit will love us and bless us."

Sheldon Jackson (1834-1909), John Brady (1848-1918), and Alaska's Natives

Like Father De Smet, the Presbyterian missionary Sheldon Jackson tirelessly crossed and recrossed the Great Plains on behalf of the Indian. As though those trackless miles were not enough, however, Jackson proceeded to the even more remote vastness of Alaska. Another appointee of the Presbyterian Board of Home Missions, John Brady, also journeyed to Alaska, arriving there a few years ahead of Jackson. And like Sheldon Jackson, Brady stayed on to become a public official, serving as Alaska's governor from 1897 to 1906. Because of the labors of men such as Brady and Jackson, the Presbyterians

[Source: Sheldon Jackson, *Alaska and Missions on the North Pacific Coast* (New York: Dodd, Mead, & Co., 1880), pp. 204-5, 206-7, 208.]

*dominated all missionary efforts in Alaska in the final quarter of the nine-
teenth century. In the excerpt below, Brady writes to Jackson shortly after arriving in Sitka in 1878.*

Sitka, Alaska, May, 1878

Rev. Sheldon Jackson, D.D.

Dear Doctor: We arrived here the night of April the 11th. Our first meeting occurred on Sunday in the castle.[7] The day was charming, for the clouds
had vanished, the sun was warm, and the scenery was all that could be asked.
Far out beyond the harbor, protected by innumerable green islets, lay the vast
Pacific, in a sort of rolling calmness. At another point rose the funnel-topped
Edgecumbe, crested with snow. Back of the town, and as far down the coast as
the eye can reach, we have all the variety of grand mountain scenery. When
these days come all nature seems to be still with solemnity, and one appears to
be near the presence-chamber of the Almighty. Alaska scenery has a peculiar effect upon my emotions.

The castle has been stripped of everything, and is in a dilapidated condition. As we began to sing some of the Moody[8] and Sankey hymns, the Indians
began to steal in and squat themselves on the floor along the wall. Most of them
had their faces painted black; some were black and red, and a few had the whole
face black with the exception of the right eye, which was surrounded with a
coat of red. All but a few of the chiefs were in their bare feet, and wrapped in
blankets of various colors.

Sitka Jack is the chief who seems to have the most influence among them,
and he is their orator. He and Annahootz, the war chief, were clad in some old
suits of the naval officers who have been here. They think a great deal of the
buttons, shoulder-pieces and the like. Several wore soldiers' caps. The rest were
bareheaded.

The natives along the coast from Cape Fox to Mount St. Elias, speak the
same tongue. Mr. Cohen, a Jew who keeps a store here, kindly volunteered to
hunt up the old Russian interpreter. This man is about sixty years old. He is a
half-breed. The Russian American Fur Company took him, when a boy, and educated him for a priest to the natives; but for some reason he was never ordained
to that office. He has always been employed as interpreter. He speaks both languages well, and can read and write the Russian. Mr. George Kastrometinoff
turned my English into Russian, and the interpreter turned that into good Indian. The people listened very attentively to all that I had to say. Jack, becoming
impatient to speak, broke into a gesticulating speech, telling how bad they were

7. This "castle" was built for Russian nobles in the period when Sitka served as headquarters for the Russian empire in North America; it still dominated the town at this time.
8. See below, pp. 278-80.

heretofore, fighting and killing one another. Now they were glad that they were going to have a school and a church, and people to teach them. . . .

I explained to them why we wished them to go to school, and the advantages which they would have if they would learn English. I centred everything upon the Bible, and tried to impress upon their minds its value to all men, because it is God speaking to us when we read it. . . .

I hired some Indians, and we all worked hard to put the upper floor of the soldiers' barracks in trim for our school and church services. Mr. Whitford, who bought nearly everything which the soldiers left, sold us twenty benches, a stove, cord of wood, two brooms, and a box of chalk. The Russian priest loaned us a blackboard with half-inch cracks between the boards. These things, together with two tables, make up the list of our furniture. The school opened on Wednesday, April 17th, with fifty present, and after asking God's blessing upon this beginning of a work, which will surely prove to be one of the most interesting in the history of missions. . . .

If our churches had known the facts concerning this people, and the wonderful coast upon which they live, missionaries would have been sent out years ago. The money spent in teaching and Christianizing these people will not be thrown away. "Blessed are they which do hunger and thirst after righteousness: for they shall be filled." This promise will surely be fulfilled to these people, for they are hungering and thirsting for more light. It would be a great wrong for the Church to neglect these people longer.

I hope that before the leaves fall we shall be able to organize the Presbytery of Alaska. This will be a great thing for this Territory, which has been so wilfully misrepresented to the public. Such a body can be the source of information concerning the people and the country and its resources which will be trusted by the reading public.

"Western Orthodoxy": Russia in America

Russian Orthodoxy in Alaska

Unlike most denominations in America which moved from East to West, Russian Orthodoxy came first to the West: to Russian America, or Alaska.

[Source: *Journal of the Ministry of National Education*, 26, no. 5 (St. Petersburg: Imperatorskaia Nauk, 1840), pp. 17, 24, 41-44. I am grateful to two colleagues for their invaluable assistance: Dr. J. Arch Getty for securing a copy of the document, and Dr. Louis A. Pedrotti for providing the translation.]

> *Under the leadership of Father John Veniaminov, Russian Orthodoxy was planted with sufficient nurture to endure to the present day. Thus, native Alaskans first heard the Christian message not as dispatched from Boston or Philadelphia, but Moscow. In 1840, Father Veniaminov published in his homeland a report on "The Condition of the Orthodox Church in Russian America." "Russian America" dipped all the way down to northern California where in 1812 at Fort Ross (or Colony Ross as the Russians had called it) a trading post had been established. Veniaminov himself had visited the area in 1836 and 1838 and now reports that the settlement is to be abandoned. But of the missionary work there as well as in Alaska, the Russian priest is confident: the light of the Gospels still shines.*

Knowing how pleasant it is for a true Christian to hear about the spread of Christianity among people who are still unilluminated by the light of the Gospels, I have decided to set forth the information I collected on the dissemination and strengthening of Christ's Faith in one of the most remote territories of our Society, where through God's pleasure I had the opportunity of spending many years. . . .

Of the number of Mr. Baranov's[9] many enterprises regarding the spread of Russian possessions in America, he succeeded in founding a settlement and establishing himself in California (38 degrees north latitude). But the local settlement, called Ross, has now been ordered to give up everything, and as a result of this all Russians and Aleuts living there will be removed to Sitka. Therefore, the Orthodox Church, which has existed for about 30 years in the local region, has to be removed from there to our colonies, along with the removal of the Russians. Its existence here, however, has also not been fruitless. In the course of this time it added to its membership more than 40 persons from the natives, who also, together with the Russians, can be removed to the colonies.

On my last visit to the village of Ross (in 1838) there were 216 Russians, Creoles and Aleuts and 39 baptized Indians, and in all the Russian Church there consisted of 255 members. . . .

We know for sure that Father Macarius finally baptized all the Aleuts of the Unalaska Department, and after this there remained not a single unbaptized person. Like all our Orthodox Preachers, Father Macarius not by sword and fire proposed to them the new Faith, which forbade them their usual enjoyments, i.e., polygamy and intemperance. But in spite of this the Aleuts accepted it gladly and quickly. As proof of this may serve the fact that Macarius spent only one year in the Unalaska Department, and, while traveling around the remote islands and moving from place to place, he had with himself neither sentry nor bodyguards, other than a single Russian male-servant. The same

9. Mr. Baranov was the Russian administrator in Sitka.

Russian Orthodox cathedral, Sitka, Alaska, c. 1900
(Keystone-Mast Collection, University of California, Riverside)

Aleuts whom he had baptized or whom he was to baptize transported him, fed him and protected him, all without the slightest reward or payment. There are several examples of this kind. One might object that the Aleuts quickly accepted the Faith out of fear of the Russians and that they received the advantage of payment of tribute in furs for accepting Baptism. And actually, such reasons are sufficiently capable of inducing savages who have submitted to the authority of powerful strangers to accept the new Faith, especially since through the advantage of tribute in furs, they rid themselves of every influence of the tax-collectors, who are more terrible for the savages than the tribute in furs itself, and since their former Faith no longer satisfied the inner needs of their souls. But these means can only force them to accept the new Faith, and they cannot serve to induce them to become zealous and true fulfillers of the laws of the new Faith. And the Aleuts have remained examples of piety even to this day. If one were to examine more closely the very reasons that might have induced the Aleuts to accept Christianity, then at first glance they will seem to be sham: for the Russians, in all their (formerly) perhaps too immoderate dealings with the Aleuts, never even thought about compelling them to do this. And the payment of tribute in furs was very negligible, and they paid it when and how they wished to; moreover, the advantage of payment of tribute in furs was made to them only for three years. And so the reason for the rapid and true conversion to Christianity of the Aleuts must be sought in their character and the disposition of their souls.

Although the Aleuts willingly and quickly accepted Christianity and prayed to God as they had been taught, still it must be said in truth that up to the time of the permanent residence among them of a Priest they believed in and prayed to *an unknown God:* because Father Macarius, as much because of the shortness of time as for the lack of good interpreters, was unable to communicate to them Christian truths, except for general concepts about God, His omnipotence, His grace, etc. In the face of all this the Aleuts remained Christian, or at least right after baptism, they not only completely gave up shamanism and destroyed all the guises and masks that they had used at their festivals and shaman rites but also the songs themselves, which might somehow have reminded them of their former faith, so much so that after I arrived among them I tried (out of my personal curiosity), but I could find nothing like this. But even from among their very superstitions, to which only a man who possessed the living Evangelical faith is alien, very many were completely abandoned, and many lost their force.

But of all the good qualities of the Aleuts nothing so gladdened and delighted my heart as their zeal, or, more accurately, their thirst for hearing the word of God, so that sooner would the indefatigable Preacher himself become tired than they would weaken their heed and zeal for hearing the Word. Let us illustrate this by examples: upon my arrival in some settlement, one and all, completely abandoning all their business and occupations, no matter how important they might be for them, at my first summons would immediately gather to hear my sermons, and one and all with remarkable attentiveness would listen to them, without becoming distracted, without taking their eyes off me, and it may even be said that during this time the tenderest of mothers became as if insensitive to the crying of their children, whom they did not even bring with them, if the children could not understand.

Before there appeared among them anything written and printed in their language, I sometimes had occasion to see one of the Aleuts, not knowing at all a single word in Russian, sitting almost the whole day and reading the Slavic Psaltery of the *Chetyi-Miney* [the Reading Minaea, lives of saints]. And when they saw the books in their own language, i.e., the Catechism that I translated and printed in first edition, even the old men began to become literate in order to read on their own (and therefore there are more than a sixth among them that are able to read).

Possessing such zeal for hearing the Word of God, they are likewise zealous toward its Preacher (but their zeal does not manifest itself in material donations, because they cannot deliver furs to anyone except to the Company, which pays them a certain price). At least I can say this on my own. My visit and my arrival in the settlement would be a true holiday for the Aleuts, an Easter, because only at this time would they be able to hear the Word and partake of the Holy Sacraments. No matter where I arrived and at what time of day or night, if only the news went around that the *father* (Adak) had come, then right away one and all, whoever could manage to walk, would come out to meet me at the very dock (i.e., on the shore of the sea, where the kayaks usually pull up). One and all would greet me with real cordiality and obvious pleasure written on their faces. Often they would bring the sick to me to meet with me and receive my blessing.

Russian Orthodoxy in Western America

Shortly before the middle of the nineteenth century, the United States, by acquiring California and the Oregon Territory, stretched all the way to the Pacific Ocean. Then, in 1867, the fortunate purchase of Alaska enormously expanded the nation's western domain. In all of this new territory, from Sitka to San Francisco, the official church of Russia (a representative of Eastern or "Greek" Orthodoxy) had been the official church for employees of the Russian American Company as well as for a significant segment of the native population. (The Aleuts, mentioned below, are Eskimo natives of the Aleutian Island chain, and "Oonalashka" is more familiarly known as Unalaska, the easternmost island in that chain.) Russian Orthodoxy continued to be the major religious force in Alaska throughout the nineteenth century, including within its fold about one-sixth of the population.

In 1861 there were in the Russian American colonies seven churches and thirty-five chapels, several of them, including the cathedral, having been built at the cost of the Russian American Company, which also kept them in repair. The cost of maintenance was defrayed by voluntary contributions, and by the profits realized from the sale of candles. At about this time the total capital of the churches amounted to more than 255,000 rubles, and was kept by the treasurer of the Company, interest at five per cent being allowed upon it. The contribu-

[Source: *Overland Monthly,* 2nd ser., 26, no. 155 (Nov., 1895), 478-79.]

tions to the Church were made partly in money and partly in furs, the Company allowing the Church from seven to fourteen rubles for the skin of a sea-otter. The Company expended on behalf of the Church nearly 40,000 rubles per annum, and built a residence for the Bishop at a cost of 30,000 rubles.

At the time of the transfer of Russian America to the United States, the Greek Church maintained a considerable establishment, consisting of a Bishop, three priests, two deacons, and numerous acolytes, at Sitka. Then the Bishop made Oonalashka his headquarters, and now San Francisco is his seat, from which place as a center he administers the whole of his vast diocese, apportioning the funds at his disposal according to the needs of the various parishes. . . .

When a community is too poor to maintain a priest or reader, the Bishop, with money supplied to him from Russia, defrays the cost of maintaining a chapel there. Where there is no resident priest, the higher rites of the church, such as baptism, marriage, etc., are performed by a regularly ordained clergyman from Oonalashka, Belkovsky, Sitka, or even from San Francisco, who makes the entire round of the religious establishments in Alaska about once in two years.

Outwardly the Aleuts are intensely pious, greeting you with a prayer, and bidding you farewell with a blessing. Before a meal they always ask the blessing of God; when they enter a neighbor's house, they cross themselves, and in most

Russian Orthodox deputation from the Soviet Union
worshipping at Fort Ross, California, 1963
(National Council of Churches)

of their dwellings there is a picture of a patron saint, towards which the members of the household turn on rising in the morning and retiring at night. They will assemble for prayer whenever a priest's services can be obtained; and no matter how long the service may be, they give it their whole attention without manifesting any signs of weariness or impatience. They listen with the greatest interest to the reading of the Bible, and keep all fast-days and other religious observances strictly. In every village there is a church or chapel; the churches being erected and kept in repair, and the chapels supported, by the natives. No other religious denominations have succeeded among the Aleuts except the Greek Church, the ornate services and frequent festivals of which appeal strongly to their taste. They willingly contribute towards the maintenance of a Reader or Deacon, who performs the daily services, and teaches the young people to read, first in the Aleut dialect, and then in Russian.

The best specimen of a Greek church and one of the most interesting structures in the United States is the cathedral at Sitka, whose dome and graceful spirelet are the most striking objects of that town, the peculiar green hue of their roofs catching the tourist's eye ere the steamer has yet touched the wharf. The church is a cruciform wooden building, consisting of a nearly square hall, with a sanctuary to the east, and chapels on its north and south sides. It is well lighted by windows in and below the dome, which is supported by columns of the Byzantine order and has suspended from its center a heavy silver candelabrum. The church also contains eight fine silver candlesticks more than four feet in height. The belfry has a fine peal of bells, the original cost of which was 8,700 rubles in silver. On the altar used to rest a representation in miniature of the Holy Sepulcher wrought in silver and gold, and the communion cup was of gold set with diamonds. But many of the books and vestments which were formerly at Sitka are now in San Francisco, brought by Bishop Vladimir.

"Western" Orient: Asia in Hawaii

As Eastern Orthodoxy reached North American lands before the United States had stretched that far, so Oriental faiths reached the Hawaiian Islands well before the annexation of 1898. Confucian, Buddhist, and Shinto shrines sprang up as Chinese and Japanese emigrants settled there. The first organized missionary activity on the part of Buddhism in Hawaii came with the arrival of Japanese laborers in the late 1880s. Japanese language schools

[Source: *The Shinshu Seiten* (Honolulu: The Honpa Hongwanji Mission, 1955), pp. 109-10.]

(largely Buddhist) were soon established, temples were built, and in 1900 a Young Men's Buddhist Association was founded. The strongest Buddhist sect in Japan, Jodo-Shinshu, is also the strongest in Hawaii. Under the auspices of the Honpa Hongwanji Mission, this Shin sect established itself as a vigorous missionary religion — teaching salvation by faith, faith in the Amita Buddha. The following excerpt, dealing with this "Buddha of Infinite Life," is taken from the holy scriptures of the Shinshu (literally, "true religion") sect, a group associated with the name of its twelfth-century founder, Shinran Shonin.

In Buddhism the Ways are many, just as there are ways difficult and easy in our earthly life. To travel by land on foot is difficult, while to go by water in a ship is easy. The way of a bodhisattva[10] can also be like this. Some there are who work hard and diligent, while others attain at once the Unretrogressive State by the expediency of the easy path of faith.

Now I will tell you in detail about the Buddha of Eternal Life. There were [many other Buddhas]. . . . All these Buddhas now live in the Pure Lands[11] of the ten quarters. They thus all pronounce His name and meditate upon the vow of Amita Buddha, which says: "Should any direct his thought toward me, pronounce my name, and take refuge in me, he will at once attain the *Right Established State*, arriving at the Highest Perfect Knowledge". Therefore we should always meditate on Him. I will now praise Him in a gatha.[12]

> O Wisdom's Light, Light Infinite!
> Thou standest like a mount of gold.
> Now, bow, my body, mouth, and mind!
> I go to Him. O my hands, fold!
>
> His light is gold'n with wondrous hues.
> It shineth bright the worlds all o'er.
> With each it varieth its hues.
> I therefore kneel and Him adore.
>
> As an end cometh to this life
> And as awake we in His land,
> There virtues countless garb us all.
> Hence I trust I my self in His hand.

---

10. One who practices the Way of Buddhism and seeks to save others.
11. Worlds of highest happiness.
12. Verse.

Pure Land Japanese Buddhist Temple
in Hawaii, on the Island of Maui
(Photo by Virginia Gaustad)

As we trust fully in His power,
The power that doth no limit know,
We at once gain the *State Assured*.
So my thoughts e'er toward Him flow.

Be it life endeth in His land,
Be it pains us again enthrall,
Once born there never see we hell.
That is why I on my knees fall.

4. A New World — Abroad and at Home

Empire or Republic: Spanish-American War

For Republic

The Spanish American War, begun in April of 1898 and effectively concluded three months later, was (said John Hay) a "splendid little war." Whether war is ever splendid, this one at least had the merit of brevity. Nonetheless, about five thousand American lives were lost, largely through disease. The war, moreover, gave the United States the aura of world power as it assumed territories and responsibilities in both the Caribbean (notably, Puerto Rico) and the Pacific (notably, the Philippines). Such swift expansionism raised serious questions of national purpose, and even of national morality. Was the nation to remain a republic (think of ancient Rome) or was it to become an empire (think of decadent Rome)? Here John Lancaster Spalding (introduced below, pp. 97-98) argues vigorously in 1899 for America as republic.

Empire or Republic

The rise and fall of nations, as of individuals, are determined by moral causes. The convictions of mankind are but feebly influenced by reason. Our ethics, politics, and religion never spring from what is wholly rational. To a greater or less extent we are all victims of passion and prejudice, are swayed by interests that are selfish and motives that are unworthy. The wise and the good therefore

---

[Source: J. L. Spalding, *Opportunity and Other Essays and Addresses* (Freeport, New York: Books for Libraries, 1968 [1900]), pp. 213-15.]

subject themselves to ceaseless self-criticism; so does a noble and generous people. The habit of reflection, of considering seriously and dispassionately whatever grave situation is presented, is a mark of maturity; it is an evidence of self-
control, of the prevalence of the true self which is constituted by obedience to
what is right and good and becoming.

It is to the power of returning upon itself that a people owes its conservative strength, its ability, in the midst of whatever events, to hold steadfastly to
the principles by which its life is nourished. We are at present in the midst of a
crisis, in which lack of thought and deliberation may lead us far from the ideals
which as Americans we have most cherished, and expose us to evils of which we
scarcely dream. We stand at the parting of the ways. It is not yet too late to turn
from the way which leads, through war and conquest, to imperialism, to standing armies, to alliances with foreign powers and finally to the disruption of the
Union itself. It is not too late, because it is still possible, probable even, that the
American people will reconsider the whole question of the complications in
which our victories over Spain have involved us. . . .

. . . We will not believe that the gaining of a few naval battles over a weak
and unprepared foe has power to throw us into such enthusiasm or such madness as to turn us permanently from the principles and policies to which we
owe our national existence, our life and liberty, or that Destiny, the divinity of
fatalists and materialists, can weaken our faith in the God of justice, righteousness and love, who scorns and thrusts far away those who, having the giant's
strength, use it to oppress or destroy the weak and ignorant.

We have never looked upon ourselves as predestined to subdue the earth, to
compel other nations, with sword and shell, to accept our rule; we have always believed in human rights, in freedom and opportunity, in education and religion,
and we have invited all men to come to enjoy these blessings in this half a world
which God has given us; but we have never dreamed that they were articles to be
exported and thrust down unwilling throats at the point of the bayonet.

For Empire

On the other hand, Lyman Abbott, influential editor of the Christian Union
and later Outlook, *and the successor to Henry Ward Beecher at Brooklyn's
Plymouth Church, warmly endorsed the "New National Policy." Writing in
the* Outlook *in June of 1898, Abbott argued against the traditional policy of
isolation and for one of "fraternization": "We believe that the United States
must henceforth take its place with the other nations of the world and share*

[Source: Lyman Abbott, *Reminiscences* (Boston: Houghton Mifflin Co., 1915), pp. 436-38.]

with them the responsibility for the world's development." In his Reminiscences *written long after this brief war, Abbott makes it clear that his opinion had not changed. That war "was a duty and peace would have been a dishonor": the history of the world records no nobler conflict.*

Three years later, in 1898, another war cloud appeared upon the horizon. For over a century America had seen with increasing disquiet the sufferings of the Cuban people under an intolerable Spanish despotism. Living themselves on the threshold of the twentieth century, they saw their neighbors oppressed under a government which retained the spirit and methods of the seventeenth century. The Spanish-American War has been often attributed to the destruction of the Maine, an American man-of-war, while on a peaceful visit to Havana. In fact, that destruction took place February 15, and war was not declared until April 24, more than two months later. The real occasion of the war was the report of Senator Proctor, of Vermont, on the conditions which he found existing in the island; it aroused in the country a storm of humanitarian indignation which proved irresistible. This time I believed that war was a duty and peace would have been a dishonor. . . .

And I have never ceased from that time to this to commend the action of our Government and our people in the Spanish-American War. I repeat here what I said at one session of the Lake Mohonk Conference: —

> I believe the proudest chapter in our history is that written by the statesmanship of McKinley, the guns of Dewey, and the administration of Taft. There is nothing to repent, nothing to retract; our duty is to go on and complete the work already so well begun. I do not defend or apologize for what we have done in the Philippines. I glory in it. We must give them a government, not for our benefit, but primarily for the benefit of the Filipinos.

I do not think that the history of the world records a nobler war. We captured Cuba and gave it to the Cubans, extending over them a protectorate which guarantees them from foreign aggression and domestic anarchy. We captured Porto Rico and retained it under the protection of our flag, giving back to the Porto Ricans for expenditure in their own island all the taxes collected from them. We captured the Philippines, sent an army of teachers to follow the army of occupation, and have pledged them our word to give them self-government as fast as they are prepared for it. We asked no war indemnity from Spain; on the contrary, we paid her for all the public works which she had constructed in the conquered Philippines. We fought the American Revolution to free ourselves, the Civil War to free a people whom we had helped to enslave, the Spanish-American War to free a people to whom we owed no other duty than that of a big nation to an oppressed neighbor.

"The Philippine Question"

Quite apart from the broad question of national policy was the narrower question of what the Literary Digest *called "The Religious Problem in the Philippines" (Feb. 10, 1900). That problem, bluntly put, was that the islands were Catholic and many Americans still thought of their country as Protestant. What was to be done about a "Catholic" possession being taken over by a "Protestant" nation? Should Protestant missionaries be sent to the Philippines? And if so, which Protestants? Or is it even appropriate to send missionaries to an already Christianized people? Two opposing points of view are presented below: (1) Archbishop John Ireland of Minneapolis makes the case for a "hands off" policy by America's Protestants; (2) Arthur J. Brown, Secretary of the Presbyterian Board of Foreign Missions, argues that the overthrow of the old civil and educational regime suggests that there should similarly be a change in the old religious regime.*

1.

You ask me what I think of cooperation between Catholics and Protestants towards religious reconstruction in our new American possessions. I will speak frankly, and give expression to my convictions as a Catholic and as an American. As a Catholic, I cannot approve of any efforts of Protestants to affect the religious duties of the inhabitants of the islands. Catholics are there in complete control; they have a thorough church organization; the inhabitants are Catholics; some of them may not live up to the teachings of their faith, but they have no idea of abandoning that faith for another. It represents all they have ever known of a higher life. Protestantism will never take the place in their hearts of that faith. To take from them their faith is to throw them into absolute religious indifference. If the inhabitants of those islands were all Protestants, would Protestants ask Catholics to unite with them in the work of Protestant disintegration? Now, as an American I will no less object to efforts to implant Protestantism in those islands. Why? Because I want to see American rule made possible in those islands. Do your Protestant missionaries realize that they are doing the greatest harm to America by making her flag unpopular? Spain has already begun to say to her former subjects: "You have objected to our rule. Very well, what have you in place? You have given up to strangers not only your civil government; they are also taking away your religion." A great mistake was made, in

[Sources: (1) John Ireland interview, *Outlook,* 62, no. 17 (Aug. 26, 1899), 933-34. (2) A. J. Brown, *The New Era in the Philippines* (New York: Fleming H. Revell Co., 1903), pp. 152-54.]

Cardinal Gibbons (center) with President William McKinley (left)
and Admiral George Dewey, 1899
(Keystone-Mast Collection, University of California, Riverside)

my opinion, by one of our military officers in Porto Rico; he put himself forth
as an official leader in establishing the Protestant Church. Now, as an American
ruler he had no right, and he was not asked, to prevent the establishment there
of a Protestant church, nor was he asked to take part in Catholic worship; but
the fact that he was foremost in founding a Protestant church was enough to
make the simple Porto Ricans take the new chapel to represent the established
church of the United States. It was enough to make them think that America
was officially opposed to the Catholic religion. If I were America's enemy to-

day, I would say to American Protestants, Hurry on your missionaries to Cuba, Porto Rico, and the Philippines, and have them tell the inhabitants of those islands that their historic faith is wrong and that they ought to become Protestants. This would be the speediest and most effective way to make the inhabitants of those islands discontented and opposed to America.

2.

Archbishop Ireland and his sympathizers in the United States, the Roman Catholic bishops and priests in the Philippines, and a considerable number of Americans both at home and abroad, never tire of reminding us that the Filipinos had a form of the Christian religion before the Americans came, and that it is neither expedient nor just to attempt to change it.

I reply that the Filipinos had a form of civil government before the Americans came and also, a form of public education, forms which were as adequate to their needs as was their form of religion. Indeed, all competent testimony is to the effect that the dissatisfaction of the people with their civil governors and their schools was less than their dissatisfaction with their priests. Nevertheless, Americans have deemed it their duty to forcibly overthrow the entire governmental and educational systems, and to replace them with our own radically different ones. The wishes of the people were not considered. The Taft Commission reports: "Many witnesses were examined as to the form of government best adapted to these Islands and satisfactory to the people. All the evidence taken, no matter what the bias of the witness, showed that the masses of the people are ignorant, credulous and childlike, and that under any government the electoral franchise must be much limited, because the large majority will not for a long time be capable of intelligently exercising it."

So Americans have proceeded on the supposition that as the people did not know what was good for them, that good must be imposed by the strong arm of military power and civil law, confident that in time the Filipinos will see that it is for their welfare. Any argument that could be framed for the inadequacy of the former civil and educational systems would, *mutatis mutandis,* apply with equal force to the Roman Catholic *régime.* Indeed, if disinterested writers are to be trusted, the rottenness of the ecclesiastical administration was the source of nearly all the evils from which the Filipinos were suffering.

Protestant missionary methods are not a tenth part as drastic and revolutionary as the American civil and educational methods. Protestants ask no assistance from soldiers or policemen. They do not wish the Filipinos to be taxed to support their work, as they are taxed to maintain the public schools to which the Roman Catholic Church so strongly objects. The Protestant Churches of the United States rely wholly upon moral suasion and the intrinsic power of the truths which they inculcate. They send to the Philippines as missionaries men and women who represent the purest and highest types of American Christian character and culture. They propose to pay all costs out of voluntary contributions. Now we insist that our justification for this effort is as clear as the justification of the Department of Public Instruction, for example, in superseding the educational control of the Roman Catholics, and that our methods are far less apt to alarm and anger the Roman hierarchy and its followers.

A New Enthusiasm for Mission

Missionary Review of the World

One of the signs of a growing interest by Americans in religious work overseas was an increasing quantity of specialized publication devoted to different aspects of missions. The most important of these serial publications was the Missionary Review of the World, *which had been founded in 1878 by a retired missionary from India, Royal G. Wilder, but which in 1888 was taken over by J. M. Sherwood of New York and A. T. Pierson of Philadelphia. Pierson (1837-1911), especially, would go on to be a major figure in mediating connections between Protestant Christians in the United States and overseas. As himself a product of the Business Men's Revival of 1857, but also of a solid New England education, Pierson was as thoroughly fired by the era's characteristic American optimism as he was thoroughly committed to evangelical Protestant beliefs. Yet he also sustained for his entire adult life an open curiosity about the world that kept him from ever looking upon American religion as the only possible form of normative religion. The excerpt below outlines his purpose for the* Missionary Review.

. . . We have no less aim than to make this Review the commanding Missionary Magazine of the World, sparing neither labor nor money to make it one of the foremost agencies for the evangelization of the world and the information, organization and co-operation of disciples in the direction of world-wide missions.

That such a Review is needed, we should be ashamed to argue. There are two great, potent factors which must enter into the solution of the problem of missions — the tongue and pen. The printing-press multiplies them both a

---

[Source: "Salutatory," *Missionary Review of the World*, new ser. I:1 (Jan. 1888): 4-6.]

thousandfold. It gives volume and compass to the voice, like the trumpet of a Titan, and it scatters the products of the pen, as though it had at command the hundred-handed giants that helped the Titans. Great is the power of type and of printers' ink! Surely we should leave out a whole division in mustering our forces, if, in going forth to a world's conquest for Christ, we should neglect the printed page.

Facts are the fingers of God. There is no logic like the logic of events; no demonstration like the demonstration of the Spirit. Apathy, and even antipathy, toward the work of missions, are turned into positive and powerful sympathy, when a true disciple learns how mightily God has wrought and is working with the little missionary band. . . .

The need of such a Review of missions is pressing. The demand is immediate and imperative. With all the existing channels for conveyance of information and the exchange of views, there is yet a wide gap to be filled. The work of missions is world-wide, and we need a missionary Review of the World; the need of man is universal, and so must be our survey; the whole church is called to this grand crusade, and the Review must be unsectarian and undenominational, gathering the whole army, with all its tribal standards, closely about the Tabernacle and Ark of God; the Christian nations are all united in the work, and hence the Review will be international; and as even the best methods are liable to be defective, and custom is often, as Cyprian says, only the "Antiquity of Error," a true Review will be critical though not controversial, and will aim, not only at a wide view, but at a close, careful, candid *review.*

The time is now especially ripe for such an undenominational, international, independent missionary organ, as a means of expression and impression, communication and co-operation, education and evangelization. Missions are comparatively modern. The Church slept for more than a thousand years; then slowly awoke to the sense of a world's destitution and her own obligation. Let us remember that it yet lacks five years of a full century since in Widow Wallis' humble cottage at Kettering, that first Missionary Society was organized in England, that was the pioneer of the whole host now numbering over one hundred organizations. And already, and within the lifetime of some veterans still living, the network of missions has overspread the globe. Surely it is time that in this special department there should be abundant and adequate agencies to put and keep before the reading public the entire progress and prospects of the grand campaign which is now conducted by all Christendom against the strongholds of the Pagan, Moslem and Papal world!

Such is our word of Salutation. The primary object of this Review is not money-making, but the informing of disciples, and the quickening of our whole church-life, the promotion of an intelligent interest in the work of missions everywhere and the inspiring of an unreserved personal consecration to the work. We desire the fullest support of a large constituency of readers, in what we undertake as an unselfish labor of love for the sake of Christ and His Church. As the circulation of the Review increases and its income allows, more and more will be expended upon the periodical itself, that we may give back to the reader and subscriber the largest returns for his investment; and it is our fond hope that by the abundant blessing of God upon our labor, direct and indirect results may follow, on the largest scale, in furthering and hastening a world's evangelization. . . .

Women Missionary Mobilization

Women in American churches constituted a great, expanding source of energy, income, and recruits for missionary work. The first women missionaries noticed by audiences in Britain and the United States were the wives of pioneering men. By the 1860s and 1870s, however, there existed several agencies in the United States that recruited primarily single women and then supported them abroad through the contributions of women in the United States. Some of these groups were non-denominational while others existed within the denominations. (The latter would mostly be incorporated into the male-dominated denominational bureaucracies by the 1920s.) The Woman's Missionary Friend *of the Methodist Episcopal Church was one of the most widely-distributed magazines reporting on these far-flung efforts. The talk below was given by one of its supporters at the Baltimore Branch Annual Meeting of the Methodists' Woman's Foreign Missionary Society that sponsored this journal.*

The Place of Foreign Missions in Our Thought and Affections.

Picture to yourself great stretches of sand at the junction of two rivers, toward which a living, moving mass approaches from all directions; the roads are full, crowds throng across the fields, a most picturesque sight in their sheet-like covering of white, turbans of various colors, and bright bits of red, yellow or blue in the clothes of the women.

These are Hindus, who have come from all over India: rich rajahs and poor peasants, alike to do worship at the many holy shrines and to bathe in the sacred Ganges.

[Source: Mrs. E. T. Hill, "The Place of Foreign Missions in Our Thought and Affections," *Woman's Missionary Friend* 27 (Jan. 1896): 190-91.]

Come with me, this beautiful cloudless day in January, and let us see the miseries and degradation of idolatry. Observe, as we pass, the booths filled with brass idols of grotesque shapes, and note the crowd of anxious buyers. Here we are startled by the sight of a naked hand outstretched from the midst of the sand, where a devotee has buried himself to expiate some sin, real or fancied. At night he comes forth to eat the food that is religiously placed for him, but during the day he is in this living grave, spending his time in reflection, entirely covered up, except a small air hole. All about the hand are copper coins which the faithful have cast down in passing, thereby earning a few years' remission of sin for themselves. All the Hindu hopes is to escape transmigration into some fearful shape.

These fakirs, or holy men, are the chief feature of this religious fair. Here is a hideous creature with his face and body dusted over with ashes, which makes him look most ghastly. His hair is in long matted rolls, never combed, and his arms, horrible to behold, have been held up over his head for so many years that they have grown into that position. They are shriveled up, and his finger-nails protrude an inch through his clenched hand.

What resolution, what patient perseverance, what force of character are requisite to keep this man and his class in this rigid course of self-denial, such as, I verily believe, is scarcely possible in Christendom. If these powers were consecrated intelligently to the spread of Christianity among their fellow countrymen, what might they not accomplish for God and humanity.

The pilgrims, who are chiefly women and old men, when they reach a certain point leading to the river, fall upon their knees, bow down to, and kiss the earth, then take off their shoes before they step on the sacred spot. They have, many of them, walked hundreds of miles, and seem ready to drop from exhaustion. As we approach the water's edge we see the ground is trampled into slimy mud by the bare feet of the people who come by the ten thousands to drink and wash away their sins. They walk boldly into the water notwithstanding the bitter chill, bow to the east, west, north and south, repeating prayers, then they swallow a mouthful, which, owing to the numbers daily bathing, is now liquid mud.

The priests hold communion with the river goddess, Gunga, by standing up to the waist in the water, for hours at a time, in contemplation.

When we know so thoroughly the miseries and needs of the people of foreign lands, when we women know of the barbarous treatment our sisters in India, China, and elsewhere receive, do we dare not seek to throw some rays of blessed sunlight into their sad lives; to do nothing to help them?

It is not as if we were ignorant. In these days, with our cable, telegraph lines and newspapers, we know as well what is transpiring the other side of the globe as in a neighboring town. We are all one people made of many. Who shall say which is foreign? Can we conscientiously avoid giving, and giving liberally, when we know that the idol worshippers come and say, "We want to be Christians, we are tired of the old life, we want to get up higher." He is bold indeed who still calls into question the value of missions to Christless lands. The results are too overwhelming compared with the small efforts that have been put forth.

The prayers offered in the first half of this century were that God would open the doors. This prayer has been so fully answered that it is just here our embarrassment occurs. The doors are open on every hand, especially in North-west India, and we have insufficient funds to push forward the work.

Our missionaries in every field are overtaxed, and their appeal is for additions to their ranks. The cry comes not only from individual seekers for light, but by representatives sent from villages, whose whole population desire to be taught the Christian religion.

The great sufferers in all non-Christian lands are the women, and the work among them must be done chiefly by us. We know the words of the Master, "Go ye into all the world and preach the Gospel to every creature." There is no distinction of sex, so there is no doubt as to our duty to either go — or send.

The Duke of Wellington, when asked by a young clergyman his opinion whether, considering the moderate results in numbers, it was the duty of the Church to send out missionaries, replied, "What are your orders, sir, what are your orders?" No intelligent, candid observer can doubt the effectiveness of Christian effort in any mission field wherever it has been persistently put forth.

We must not rest until we have enlisted in the work every woman and child in our churches, so that this great cause of the age, if not the greatest in the history of this wonderful nineteenth century, shall not be hindered. If every member will go from this meeting baptized with the spirit of work such as we see manifested in a few of our leaders, what may we not accomplish? No woman is a loser by joining and becoming an active worker in the Missionary Society, but she is a great gainer, intellectually, socially and spiritually.

World's Parliament of Religions, 1893

Hinduism

The 1893 gathering in Chicago was remarkable in many ways: it demonstrated the wide currency of the English language throughout much of the world, it presented the better nature of Oriental religions to a largely Occi-

[Source: John H. Barrows, ed., *The World's Parliament of Religions* (Chicago: The Parliament Publishing Co., 1893), II, pp. 968-69, 972.]

*dental audience, it offered some hope for tolerance in an arena more often
filled with blood, and it brought together representatives of America's
churches and synagogues who otherwise had no common meeting ground. A
most impressive visitor, Swami Vivekananda, made his case for Hinduism
with enough persuasive force that this Oriental religion, in the form of the
Vedanta Society, remained a presence in America from that time forward.*

Three religions stand now in the world which have come down to us from time
pre-historic — Hinduism, Zoroastrianism, and Judaism.

They all have received tremendous shocks and all of them prove by their
survival their internal strength; but while Judaism failed to absorb Christianity,
and was driven out of its place of birth by its all-conquering daughter, and a
handful of Parsees are all that remains to tell the tale of his grand religion, sect
after sect have arisen in India and seemed to shake the religion of the Vedas to its
very foundation, but like the waters of the seashore in a tremendous earthquake,
it receded only for a while, only to return in an all-absorbing flood, a thousand
times more vigorous, and when the tumult of the rush was over, they have been
all sucked in, absorbed and assimilated in the immense body of another faith.

From the high spiritual flights of Vedantic philosophy, of which the latest
discoveries of science seem like the echoes, the agnosticism of the Buddhas, the
atheism of the Jains, and the low ideas of idolatry with the multifarious mythology, each and all have a place in the Hindu's religion.

Where then, the question arises, where is the common center to which all
these widely diverging radii converge; where is the common basis upon which
all these seemingly hopeless contradictions rest? And this is the question I shall
attempt to answer.

The Hindus have received their religion through their revelation, the
Vedas. They hold that the Vedas are without beginning and without end. It may
sound ludicrous to this audience, how a book can be without beginning or end.
But by the Vedas no books are meant. They mean the accumulated treasury of
spiritual law discovered by different persons in different times. Just as the law of
gravitation existed before its discovery, and would exist if all humanity forgot
it, so with the laws that govern the spiritual world. The moral, ethical and spiritual relation between soul and souls and between individual spirits and the Father of all spirits were there before their discovery and would remain even if we
forgot them. . . .

Thus it is that the Vedas proclaim not a dreadful combination of unfor-
giving laws, not an endless prison of cause and effect, but that at the head of all
these laws, in and through every particle of matter and force, stands one
through whose command the wind blows, the fire burns, the clouds rain, and
death stalks upon the earth. And what is his nature?

He is everywhere the pure and formless one. The Almighty and the All-merciful. "Thou art our father, thou art our mother; thou art our beloved friend; thou art the source of all strength; give us strength. Thou art he that bearest the burdens of the universe: help me bear the little burden of this life." Thus sang the Rishis of the Veda; and how to worship him — through love. "He is to be worshiped as the one beloved," "dearer than everything in this and the next life."

This is the doctrine of love preached in the Vedas, and let us see how it is fully developed and preached by Krishna, whom the Hindus believe to have been God incarnate on earth.

He taught that a man ought to live in this world like a lotus leaf, which grows in water but is never moistened by water — so a man ought to live in this world — his heart to God and his hands to work. It is good to love God for hope of reward in this or the next world, but it is better to love God for love's sake, and the prayer goes: "Lord, I do not want wealth, nor children, nor learning. If it be thy will I will go to a hundred hells, but grant me this, that I may love thee without the hope of reward — unselfishly love for love's sake." One of the disciples of Krishna, the then Emperor of India, was driven from his throne by his enemies, and had to take shelter in a forest in the Himalayas with his queen, and there one day the queen was asking him how it was that he, the most virtuous of men, should suffer so much misery; and Yuohistera answered: "Behold, my queen, the Himalayas, how beautiful they are; I love them. They do not give me anything, but my nature is to love the grand, the beautiful, therefore I love them. Similarly, I love the Lord. He is the source of all beauty, of all sublimity. He is the only object to be loved; my nature is to love him, and therefore I love. I do not pray for anything; I do not ask for anything. Let him place me wherever he likes. I must love him for love's sake. I cannot trade in love."

Buddhism

One of the world's great missionary religions, Buddhism was scarcely known in the West prior to the nineteenth century — as the excerpt below suggests. And, except for Hawaii, Buddhism was scarcely known in America until the twentieth century. Thus, H. Dharmapala, the representative to the World Parliament from Sri Lanka [Ceylon] (where the more historical or more traditional form of Buddhism prevails), felt obliged to instruct his Chicago audience in the "fundamentals" of the religion as proclaimed by Gautama Buddha in India in the sixth and fifth centuries before the birth of Christ.

[Source: John H. Barrows, ed., *The World's Parliament of Religions* (Chicago: The Parliament Publishing Co., 1893), II, pp. 863-65.]

History is repeating itself. Twenty-five centuries ago India witnessed an intellectual and religious revolution which culminated in the overthrow of monotheism, priestly selfishness, and the establishment of a synthetic religion, a system of life and thought which was appropriately called *Dhamma* — Philosophical Religion. All that was good was collected from every source and embodied therein, and all that was bad discarded. The grand personality who promulgated the Synthetic Religion is known as Buddha. For forty years he lived a life of absolute purity, and taught a system of life and thought, practical, simple, yet philosophical, which makes man — the active, intelligent, compassionate, and unselfish man — to realize the fruits of holiness in this life on this earth. The dream of the visionary, the hope of the theologian, was brought into objective reality. Speculation in the domain of false philosophy and theology ceased, and active altruism reigned supreme.

Five hundred and forty-three years before the birth of Christ, the great being was born in the Royal Lumbini Gardens in the City of Kapilavastu. His mother was Maya, the Queen of Raja Sudohodana of the Solar Race of India. The story of his conception and birth, and the details of his life up to the twenty-ninth year of his age, his great renunciation, his ascetic life, and his enlightenment under the great Bo tree at Buddha Jaya, in Middle India, are embodied in that incomparable epic, *The Light of Asia,* by Sir Edwin Arnold. I recommend that beautiful poem to all who appreciate a life of holiness and purity.

Six centuries before Jesus of Nazareth walked over the plains of Galilee preaching a life of holiness and purity, the Tathagata Buddha, the enlightened Messiah of the World, with his retinue of Arhats, or holy men, traversed the whole peninsula of India with the message of peace and holiness to the sin-burdened world. Heart-stirring were the words he spoke to the first five disciples at the Deer Park, the hermitage of Saints at Benares.

His First Message. — "Open ye your ears, O Bhikshus, deliverance from death is found. I teach you, I preach the Law. If ye walk according to my teaching, ye shall be partakers in a short time of that for which sons of noble families leave their homes, and go to homelessness — the highest end of religious effort: ye shall even in this present life apprehend the truth itself and see it face to face." And then the exalted Buddha spoke thus: "There are two extremes, O Bhikshus, which the truth-seeker ought not to follow: the one a life of sensualism, which is low, ignoble, vulgar, unworthy and unprofitable; the other the pessimistic life of extreme asceticism, which is painful, unworthy and unprofitable. There is a Middle Path, discovered by the Tathagata — the Messiah — a path which opens the eyes and bestows understanding, which leads to peace of mind, to the higher wisdom, to full enlightenment, to eternal peace. This Middle Path, which the Tathagata has discovered, is the noble Eight-fold Path, viz.: Right Knowledge — the perception of the Law of Cause and Effect, Right Thinking, Right Speech, Right Action, Right Profession, Right Exertion, Right Mindfulness, Right Contemplation. This is the Middle Path which the Tathagata has discovered, and it is the path which opens the eyes, bestows understanding, which leads to peace of mind, to the higher wisdom, to perfect enlightenment, to eternal peace."

Continuing his discourse, he said: "Birth is attended with pain, old age is painful, disease is painful, death is painful, association with the unpleasant is painful, separation from the pleasant is painful, the non-satisfaction of one's desires is painful, in short, the coming into existence is painful. This is the Noble Truth of suffering.

Zen Buddhist meditation
(Zen Center of Los Angeles)

"Verily it is that clinging to life which causes the renewal of existence, accompanied by several delights, seeking satisfaction now here, now there — that is to say, the craving for the gratification of the passions, or the craving for a continuity of individual existences, or the craving for annihilation. This is the Noble Truth of the origin of suffering. And the Noble Truth of the cessation of suffering consists in the destruction of passions, the destruction of all desires, the laying aside of, the getting rid of, the being free from, the harboring no longer of this thirst. And the Noble Truth which points the way is the Noble Eightfold Path." This is the foundation of the Kingdom of Righteousness, and from that center at Benares, this message of peace and love was sent abroad to all humanity: "Go ye, O Bhikshus and wander forth for the gain of the many, in compassion for the world for the good, for the gain, for the welfare of gods and men. Proclaim, O Bhikshus, the doctrine glorious. Preach ye a life of holiness, perfect and pure. Go then through every country, convert those not converted. Go therefore, each one traveling alone filled with compassion. Go, rescue and receive. Proclaim that a blessed Buddha has appeared in the world, and that he is preaching the Law of Holiness."

Islam

Like Buddhism and Christianity, Islam is a vigorously missionary religion. And like Buddhism and Hinduism, Islam was virtually unknown — in its own terms — to Americans at the end of the nineteenth century. Mohammed Webb, the Moslem representative to the Parliament, therefore felt it necessary to sweep away as much misinformation and prejudice as possible. Only then could he proceed to portray with any hope of success the "Spirit of Islam." His only regret, as he tells his audience, is that "the subject is so broad that I can only touch upon it."

Do you suppose that any active religionist who has studied only his own system of religion, who knows nothing about any other system, can write fairly of any other system? It is absolutely impossible. I have read every history of Mohammed and Islam published in English, and I say to you, there is not a single one of them, except the work of Ameer Ali, of Calcutta, which reflects at all in any sense the spirit of Islam. We will take the work of Washington Irving for example. Washington Irving evidently intended to be fair and honest; it is apparent in every line that he meant to tell the truth, but his information came through

[Source: John H. Barrows, ed., *The World's Parliament of Religions* (Chicago: The Parliament Publishing Co., 1893), II, 990-91, 991-92.]

channels that were muddy, and while he is appalled at what he considers the vicious character of the prophet, he is completely surprised at times to find out what a pure and holy man he was. Now, the first book I ever read in English upon Islam was *The Life of Mohammed,* by Washington Irving, and the strongest feature of that work to me was its uncertainty.

In one page he would say Mohammed was a very good, a very pure and holy man, and it was a shame that he was not a Christian, but his impious rejection of the Trinity shut him out from salvation and made him an impostor. These were not the exact words that Irving used, but they convey practically his meaning. After saying these things, he goes on to say what a sensuous, grasping, avaricious tyrant the prophet was, and he closed his work by saying that the character of the prophet is so enigmatical that he cannot fathom it. He is uncertain, finally, whether Mohammed was a good man or a bad man.

Now, to understand the character of Mohammed and his teachings, we must learn to read between the lines; we must learn to study human nature; we must carefully analyze the condition of the Arabians at the time Mohammed lived; we must carefully analyze the existing social conditions; we must understand what woman's position was in the social system; the various conditions that had possession of the whole Arabian nation. They were not, however, a nation at that time, but divided into predatory tribes, with all the vices and weaknesses that man possesses, almost as bad as men in some of the slums of Chicago and New York. Mohammed came among his people intending to purify and elevate them, to make them a better people, and he did so. The history of Mohammedanism we have in English, as I have shown, is inaccurate, untruthful, and full of prejudice. . . .

Now, let us see what the word Islam means. It is the most expressive word in existence for a religion. It means simply and literally resignation to the will of God. It means aspiration to God. The Moslem system is designed to cultivate all that is purest and noblest and grandest in the human character. Some people say Islam is impossible in a high state of civilization. Now, that is the result of ignorance. Look at Spain in the eighth century, when it was the center of all the arts and sciences, when Christian Europe went to Moslem Spain to learn all that there was worth knowing — languages, arts, all the new discoveries were to be found in Moslem Spain and in Moslem Spain alone. There was no civilization in the world as high as that of Moslem Spain.

With this spirit of resignation to the will of God is inculcated the idea of individual responsibility, that every man is responsible not to this man or that man, or the other man, but responsible to God for every thought and act of his life. He must pay for every act that he commits; he is rewarded for every thought he thinks. There is no mediator, there is no priesthood, there is no ministry.

The Moslem brotherhood stands upon a perfect equality, recognizing only the fatherhood of God and the brotherhood of man. The Emir, who leads in prayer, preaches no sermon. He goes to the mosque every day at noon and reads two chapters from the holy Koran. He descends to the floor upon a perfect level with the hundreds, or thousands, of worshipers, and the prayer goes on, he simply leading it. The whole system is calculated to inculcate that idea of perfect brotherhood.

The Uses of Diversity

Census of 1890

In 1890 the Federal Census for the first time asked questions concerning religious membership in America. (Such questions continued to be asked through 1936.) A Methodist layman and editor, H. K. Carroll (1848-1931), was appointed "special commissioner" in charge of the division of churches for the Eleventh Census. Using his data (first published in 1893, revised in 1896), one notes that the religious picture in America is one of ever-multiplying colors. Older family groups such as Lutheran and Baptist continue to divide; newer American-born groups such as Disciples of Christ and Latter-Day Saints continue to grow. While all religious statistics must be interpreted with caution, the following list of largest denominational families provides a rough sketch of the nation's religious profile near the end of the nineteenth century.

THE FOURTEEN LARGEST DENOMINATIONAL FAMILIES (1895)

	Communicants			*Communicants*
1. Catholic	8,014,911	8.	Congregationalist	600,000
2. Methodist	5,452,654	9.	Reformed	343,981
3. Baptist	4,068,539	10.	United Brethren	262,950
4. Presbyterian	1,458,999	11.	Latter-Day Saints	234,000
5. Lutheran	1,390,775	12.	Evangelical	145,904
6. Disciples of Christ	923,663	13.	Jewish	139,500
7. Episcopalian	626,290	14.	Friends	114,711

[Source: H. K. Carroll, *The Religious Forces of the United States . . .* , rev. ed. (New York: Christian Literature Co., 1896), p. 157 (with corrections).]

African-American Expansion

Only after the Civil War did denominations predominantly or exclusively black in their membership experience great growth. Three Methodist bodies, African Methodist Episcopal and African Methodist Episcopal Zion (both essentially northern in origin) along with the Colored Methodist Episcopal Church (essentially southern), made significant strides in the second half of the nineteenth century. But the greatest number of blacks by far became Baptists. An 1890 sermonic survey, excerpted below, reviews the spectacular growth since 1865 among the "colored Baptists." Taking a text from Hebrews 11:34, editor E. M. Brawley exulted in the unmistakable evidence that "out of weakness we were made strong."

Our past was that of weakness, but our present is that of strength.

Twenty-five years ago we had, except in a few instances, no churches in the South. Now (1890) we have nearly twelve thousand church organizations, and connected with nearly every one of them is a Sunday-school. Then we had practically no ordained ministers; now we have fully eight thousand. Then there were but two or three colored associations; now there are nearly four hundred. Then we numbered a few hundred thousands; now we are more than a million and a quarter. Then we had not even one institution of learning; now we have forty, ranging from high-grade normal schools to colleges and universities. Then it was not possible for our young people to get a liberal or professional education in the South; now any young man or woman can get it, whether in the arts or sciences, in theology, law, or medicine. And he can get his training under Baptist auspices; for we now have schools of theology, law, and medicine, in addition to those which are purely literary. Then there was no education among our ministry, but few being able to read, and the masses were in the same condition; now we have hundreds of educated ministers, many of them having received their training in the best institutions of the North. Some of these men have taken high rank as scholars and orators. Then we had no educators; now we have college presidents and professors, and many thousand school teachers. One-third of all the professors employed in the educational work of the American Baptist Home Mission Society are colored. Then such a thing as a colored trustee of a college was unheard of; now all our colleges and seminaries have colored members on their boards. Then there was no general officer of a national organization; now we have one district secretary. Then we did practically no literary work, and

---

[Source: E. M. Brawley, ed., *The Negro Baptist Pulpit* . . . (Philadelphia: American Baptist Publication Society, 1890), pp. 287-89.]

could produce but few books; now we have a number of authors among us, and their books are read. Then we did not have any newspapers; now there are forty, edited by colored Baptists. Then we had no professional and but few business men; now we have a large number of lawyers, physicians, and merchants. Then our forces were not organized; now they are organized, and have reached a reasonable degree of efficiency. Then we did no mission work; now we are doing mission work in every State, and even in Africa. Then we had comparatively no church property; now we have considerable, some buildings costing between fifty thousand and one hundred thousand dollars, and the total valuation being millions. Then we had no personal property, scarcely so much as "a vine and fig tree" under which to worship God; now our total wealth is estimated to be many millions. Then we were regarded as being in character and in intellect children; now we are recognized as men. Such growth is without precedent in the history of mankind. Truly we were once weak; but out of weakness we are made strong.

But we have by no means attained the strength which we will have and must have. What we have attained is but the earnest of what we should seek after in the next quarter of a century. Our large numbers will even prove to be a source of weakness to us, unless we elevate them in point of efficiency and in moral and mental character. A tremendous work is yet on our hands. May God help us to realize it!

American Dream

In 1865 Philip Schaff had sounded a note of hope for America and its religious future (see Documentary History, *vol. 1, pp. 566-68). America was not a spiritual chaos, Schaff had argued then. Now, a generation later (1893) and in the final weeks of his life, Schaff addressed the World Parliament on his — and much of the nation's — recurring dream: "the reunion of Christendom." While the religious diversity evident at the Parliament was fascinating, it was also — at another level — threatening. How could badly divided bickering churches make a meaningful impression upon a spiritually hungry world? A current religious paper,* The Independent *(45, Apr. 13, 1893), filled its front page with talk of "Christian Union" and "A Plan for Denominational Consolidation" and "How to Prevent Waste and Reduce Rivalry." And Schaff, in this his last major address, thought the time of recrimination and harsh judgment was over: "Let us forget and forgive, remembering only each other's virtues and merits."*

[Source: John H. Barrows, ed., *The World's Parliament of Religions* (Chicago: The Parliament Publishing Co., 1893), II, pp. 1199-1201.]

American Diversity: La Cienaga, New Mexico
El Rancho de Las Golondrinas (swallow) where since the 1650s a fall
harvest festival has honored San Ysidro (St. Isidore the Farmer),
whose stature is housed in the small chapel shown here.
(Photo by Peggy Gaustad)

We welcome to the reunion of Christendom all denominations which have followed the divine Master and have done his work. Let us forget and forgive their
many sins and errors, and remember only their virtues and merits. The Greek
Church is a glorious church; for in her language have come down to us the oracles of God, the Septuagint, the Gospels and Epistles; hers are the early confes-
sors and martyrs, the Christian fathers, bishops, patriarchs and emperors; hers
the immortal writings of Origen, Eusebius, Athanasius and Chrysostom; hers
the Ecumenical Councils and the Nicene Creed, which can never die.

The Latin Church is a glorious church; she was the *Alma Mater* of the barbarians of Europe; she stimulated and patronized the Renaissance, the printing press and the discovery of a new world; she still stands, like an immovable rock, bearing witness to the fundamental truths and facts of our holy religion, and to the catholicity, unity, unbroken continuity, and independence of the church; and she is as zealous as ever in missionary enterprise and self-denying works of Christian charity.

We hail the Reformation which redeemed us from the yoke of spiritual despotism, and secured us religious liberty — the most precious of all liberties — and made the Bible in every language a book for all classes and conditions of men. The Evangelical Lutheran Church, the first-born daughter of the reformation, is a glorious church: for she set the word of God above the traditions of men, and bore witness to the comforting truth of justification by faith; she struck the keynote to thousands of sweet hymns in praise of the Redeemer; she is boldly and reverently investigating the problems of faith and philosophy, and is constantly making valuable additions to theological lore. The Evangelical Reformed Church is a glorious church: for she carried the reformation from the Alps and lakes of Switzerland "to the end of the West;" she is rich in learning and good works of faith; she keeps pace with all true progress; she grapples with the problems and evils of modern society; and she sends the Gospel to the ends of the earth. The Episcopal Church of England, the most churchly of the reformed family, is a glorious church: for she gave to the English-speaking world the best version of the Holy Scriptures and the best prayer-book; she preserved the order and dignity of the ministry and public worship; she nursed the knowledge and love of antiquity, and enriched the treasury of Christian literature. The Presbyterian Church of Scotland is a glorious church: for she turned a barren country into a garden, and raised a poor and semi-barbarous people to a level with the richest and most intelligent nations; she diffused the knowledge of the Bible and a love of the kirk in the huts of the peasant as well as the palaces of the nobleman; she has always stood up for church order and discipline, for the rights of the laity, and first and last for the crown-rights of King Jesus, which are above all earthly crowns, even that of the proudest monarch in whose dominion the sun never sets. The Congregational Church is a glorious church: for she has taught the principle, and proved the capacity, of congregational independence and self-government based upon a living faith in Christ, without diminishing the effect of voluntary cooperation in the Master's service, and has laid the foundation of New England, with its literary and theological institutions and high social culture. The Baptist Church is a glorious church: for she bore, and still bears, testimony to the primitive mode of baptism, to the purity of the congregation, to the separation of church and state, and the liberty of conscience. The Methodist Church is a glorious church: for she produced the greatest religious revival since the day of Pentecost; she preaches a free and full salvation to all; she is never afraid to fight the devil, and she is hopefully and cheerfully marching on, in both hemispheres, as an army of conquest. The Society of Friends, though one of the smallest tribes in Israel, is a glorious society: for it has borne witness to the inner light which "lighteth every man that cometh into the world"; it has proved the superiority of the Spirit over all forms; it has done noble service in promoting tolerance and liberty, in prison reform, the emancipation of slaves, and other works of Christian philanthropy. The Brotherhood of the Moravians, founded by Count Zinzendorf — a true nobleman of nature and of grace — is a glorious brotherhood: for it is the pioneer of heathen missions and of Christian union among Protestant Churches; it was like an oasis in the desert of German rationalism at home, while its missionaries went forth to the lowest savages in distant lands to bring them to Christ.

Nor should we forget the services of many who are accounted heretics. The Waldenses were witnesses of a pure and simple faith in times of superstition, and have outlived many bloody persecutions to be missionaries among the descendants of their persecutors. The Anabaptists and Socinians, who were so cruelly treated in the sixteenth century by Protestants and Romanists alike, were the first to raise their voice for religious liberty and the voluntary principle in religion. Unitarianism is a serious departure from the trinitarian faith of orthodox Christendom, but it was justified as a protest against tritheism, and against a stiff, narrow and uncharitable orthodoxy. It has brought into prominence the human perfection of Christ's character and illustrated the effect of his example in the noble lives and devotional writings of such men as Channing and Martineau. Universalism may be condemned as a doctrine; but it has a right to protest against a gross materialistic theory of hell with all its Dantesque horrors, and against the once widely spread popular belief that the overwhelming majority of the human race, including countless millions of innocent infants, will forever perish. And, coming down to the latest organization of Christian work, which does not claim to be a church, but which is a help to all churches — the Salvation Army: we hail it, in spite of its strange and abnormal methods, as the most effective revival agency since the days of Wesley and Whitefield; for it descends to the lowest depths of degradation and misery, and brings the light and comfort of the Gospel to the slums of our large cities.

There is room for all these and many other churches and societies in the Kingdom of God, whose height and depth and length and breadth, variety and beauty, surpass human comprehension.

Suggested Reading (Chapter Seven)

General works treating the difficult period of readjustment after the Civil War include David W. Blight, *Race and Reunion: The Civil War in American Memory* (2001), Eric Foner, *Reconstruction: America's Unfinished Revolution, 1863-1977* (1988), and Leon F. Litwack, *Been in the Storm So Long: The Aftermath of Slavery* (1977). Allen C. Guelzo's *The Crisis of the American Republic: A History of the Civil War and Reconstruction* (1995) is good on how circumstances of the war years affected efforts to put the country back together.

Nineteenth-century immigration is so much the story of modern America that historians have given the subject considerable attention. Classic accounts include Gerald Shaughnessy, *Has the Immigrant Kept the Faith?* (1925), Oscar Handlin, *The Uprooted* (1950), and a wide-ranging work of reference edited by Stephan Thernstrom, *Harvard Encyclopedia of American Ethnic Groups* (1980). Specifically with respect to Asian immigration, see S. C. Miller, *Unwelcome Immigrant* (1969), and the engaging story in Ronald Takaki, *Strangers from a Different Shore* (1990). The Roman Catholic situation is very well analyzed by Philip Gleason in *The Conservative Reformers: German-American Catholics and the Social Order* (1968), and more generally Jay P. Dolan, *The Immigrant Church* (1975). A fine anthropological study of immigrant Catholic life in the United States has been provided by Robert A. Orsi, *The Madonna of 115th Street: Faith and Community in Italian Harlem, 1880-1950* (1985). The Harvard edition of Josiah Strong's *Our Country* (1963), edited by Jurgen Herbst, includes a valuable introduction to this influential figure.

Immigration is also the circumstance that made the latter part of the nineteenth century so important for Jewish history in America. On that particular story, see Irving Howe and Kenneth Libo, *World of Our Fathers* (1976), Daniel Soyer, *Jewish Immigration Associations and American Identity in New York, 1880-1939* (1997), and the situations evoked powerfully by Abraham Cahan's novel, *The Rise of David Levinsky* (1917). With new Jewish immigration began also the expert writing of American Jewish history. As fine examples of that scholarship on the big picture, see Naomi W. Cohen, *Jews in Christian America* (1992), Leonard Dinnerstein, *Antisemitism in America* (1994), and Jonathan D. Sarna, *A New History of American Judaism* (2004). And for treatment of the three main Jewish traditions as they developed in America, see W. Gunther Plaut, *The Growth of Reform Judaism* (1965), Moshe Davis, *The Emergence of Conservative Judaism* (1963), and Jeffrey S. Gurock, *American Jewish Orthodoxy in Historical Perspective* (1996). A stimulating collection that tells much about Jews, Catholics, non-English-speaking Protestants and other "new" religious groups in this period has been edited by Jonathan D. Sarna, *Minority Faiths and the American Protestant Mainstream* (1998).

For orientation on the history of women in American religion, see Susan Hill Lindley, *You Have Stept Out of Your Place: A History of Women and Religion in America* (1996), Ann Braude, *Women and American Religion* (2000), and the thirteen topical essays in Janet W. James, ed., *Women in American Religion* (1980). For important studies on different strands of the American religious population, see Margaret Lamberts Bendroth and Virginia Lieson Brereton, *Women and Twentieth-Century Protestantism* (2002), Pamela S. Nadell and Jonathan D. Sarna, eds., *Women and American Judaism* (2001), Karen Kennelly, ed., *American Catholic Women* (1989), and Maureen Ursenbach Beecher and Lavina Fielding Anderson, *Sisters in Spirit: Mormon Women in Historical and Cultural Perspective* (1987). An excellent collection of documents plus interpretation is found in R. S. Keller and R. R. Ruether, eds., *In Our Own Voices: Four Centuries of American Women's Religious Writings* (1995). Antoinette Brown Blackwell has received biographical treatment in Laura Kerr's *Lady in the Pulpit* (1951). Francis Willard's life has been often told, but by no one as well as Ruth Bordin, *Frances Willard: A Biography* (1986). But see also on Willard and the whole temperance movement in this period, Ruth Bordin, *Women and Temperance: The Quest for Power and Liberty, 1873-1900* (1981). Also useful on the same subject is Barbara Leslie Epstein, *The Politics of Domesticity: Women, Evangelicalism, and Temperance* (1981). Elizabeth Cady Stanton provided her own reminiscences: *Eighty Years and More* (1898). The influence of Lucretia Mott (1793-1880) upon these later women can be traced in Dana Greene, ed., *Lucretia Mott: Her Complete Speeches and Sermons* (1980). The varying roles of women in the evangelical community may be followed in Leonard I. Sweet's fine study, *The Minister's Wife: Her Role in Nineteenth-Century American Evangelicalism* (1983), and for the place of women in conservative Protestant communities at a somewhat later period, see Margaret Bendroth, *Fundamentalism and Gender* (1993). The debates surrounding the public religious activities of women are well chartered in Mark Chaves, *Ordaining Women* (1997).

For a solid general introduction to a once-neglected region, see Ferenc Morton Szasz, *Religion in the Modern American West* (2000), and for an example of a fruitful state in the region, Laurie F. Maffley-Kipp, *Religion and Society in Frontier California* (1994). For the American West, missionary work with the Indians can be followed in Henry W. Bowden, *American Indians and Christian Missions* (1981). The indigenization of Christianity in one Native American tribe is well treated by Michael D. McNally, *Ojibwe Singers: Hymns, Grief, and a Native Culture in Motion* (2000), and more generally in Clara Sue Kidwell, et al., *A Native American Theology* (2001). Francis P. Prucha, *American Indian Policy in Crisis: Christian Reformers and the Indians, 1865-1900* (1976), remains a valuable study. The Alaskan story for Orthodoxy is well told in Gregory Afonsky, *A History of the Orthodox Church in Alaska (1794-1917)* (1977) and well illustrated through an excellent collection of documents in Michael Oleska, ed., *Alaskan*

Missionary Spirituality (1987). The Spanish-American War has been set in a more general context by David Traxel, *1898: The Birth of the American Century* (1998). For the two churchmen taking opposing sides in this chapter, see Ira V. Brown, *Lyman Abbott* (1953), and D. F. Sweeney, O.F.M., *The Life of John Lancaster Spalding* (1965).

A. T. Pierson's stimulating guidance of American interest in foreign missionary service is now the subject of careful biographical study in Dana L. Robert, *Occupy Until I Come: A. A. Pierson and the Evangelization of the World* (2003). Robert's general account, *American Women in Mission* (1996), is also the best treatment of its subject.

With respect to Buddhism on the American scene, see Thomas A. Tweed, *The American Encounter with Buddhism, 1844-1912* (1992), and the valuable documents collected in Tweed and Stephen Prothero, eds., *Asian Religions in America* (1999). A general picture for the important 1893 gathering in Chicago has been supplied by Richard Hughes Seeger, *The World's Parliament of Religions: The East/West Encounter, Chicago, 1893* (1995), while for what that parliament meant for one particular world religion, see Judith Snodgrass, *Presenting Japanese Buddhism to the West: Orientalism, Occidentalism, and the Columbian Exposition* (2003).

The religious picture in America toward the end of the nineteenth century is well depicted in many studies of particular subjects, including Richard Wightman Fox, *Trials of Intimacy: Love and Loss in the [Henry Ward] Beecher-Tilden Scandal* (1999), Paul A. Carter, *The Spiritual Crisis of the Gilded Age* (1971), Ferenc Morton Szasz, *The Divided Mind of Protestant America, 1880-1930* (1982), and Robert T. Handy, *Undermined Establishment: Church-State Relations in America, 1880-1920* (1991). For fruitful use of the early religious censuses, see Kevin J. Christiano, *Religious Diversity and Social Change in American Cities, 1890-1906* (1987). For the writing of religious history with specific attention to the great early practitioner, see Henry Warner Bowden, ed., *A Century of Church History: The Legacy of Philip Schaff* (1988).

EIGHT

Religion and Society Engaged

By the end of the nineteenth century, the nation's "manifest destiny" had been fulfilled — at least in a territorial sense. Covered wagons and handbarrows had pushed their way across mountains, plains, and more mountains to a sparkling Pacific Ocean. Alaska had been purchased (1867), Hawaii annexed (1898), and the Philippines and Puerto Rico ceded to the United States at the conclusion of the Spanish-American War. By the opening of the twentieth century, the nation stood at the threshold of world power. Seventy-six million Americans could proudly survey a land mass far larger than all of Western Europe combined, could confidently flex muscles of both military and industrial might.

Love and Justice

Great growth had its measure of pain, and world power inevitably brought world responsibility. Internal problems pressed hard upon a citizenry weaned on Jefferson's dream of an agricultural republic of virtuous villages and independent farmers. Suddenly — or so it seemed — the thinly populated frontier had given birth to large cities: Chicago's population by 1900 was second only to New York's, while the top ten urban areas included such "frontier" hamlets as St. Louis, Cleveland, San Francisco, and Cincinnati. These and other cities boasted large factories that had produced sharp divisions of class that had, in turn, produced alienation, violence, and despair. It was not merely another case of the popular complaint that "things aren't what they used to be." In fact, things, almost all things, *were* different. Even in agriculture, the independent Jeffersonian farmer would no longer recognize a land now marked by chilled-iron plows and huge steam tractors, by the miles of barbed wire and railroads, by the huge domains now made available for ranching or grazing. The world was being created anew, and many were not pleased by what they saw unfolding all around them.

The city, for example, seemed less a center of culture and promise than it did a blight upon a heretofore healthy pastoral scene. "The modern city a menace," proclaimed Josiah Strong: disease, dirt, death, crime, and corruption made it so. Within the city, growth in population and corporate wealth outran growth in morality and goodwill. Huge companies acted not as faithful stewards of their economic power but as exploiters interested only in profit — and more power. "Our Christianity has not much vigor," Washington Gladden observed, "if it cannot make men ashamed of such unneighborly conduct." Men and women crowded into tenement housing no longer constituted families, and "lodging houses where people sleep and eat" no longer constituted homes. What happens to the fabric of a nation, John Lancaster Spalding anxiously asked, when family life collapses, when traditional values can no longer be passed on from one generation to the next? Not only did the city make it difficult for its denizens to cling to their own values, the city itself often flaunted prevailing morality and courted corruption on a frighteningly large scale. Churches and synagogues found themselves obliged to do more than encourage and exhort their own flock: they must shield those flocks from wholesale manipulation and abuse by new and unregulated powers. In the streets and slums and labor marts of the modern city, what was one to do? Well, what would Jesus do?, asked a Topeka, Kansas, clergyman in a novel of unprecedented popularity. He along with many others endeavored to turn abstract issues of "social gospel" and "social justice" into religiously guided options of daily life.

Rapid industrial growth posed especially difficult problems, partly because that growth threatened permanently to divide American society into warring classes called "Capital" and "Labor." Could religion prevent such deep division, could it provide some bridges between those so divided, could it at the very least press the claims of "love and justice" upon both the factory owner who had nothing to guide him but gain and upon the laborer who had nothing to sell but his sweat? These questions were not merely theoretical, for in the 1880s and 1890s tensions turned into confrontations, boycotts into general strikes, and demonstrations into bloody riots. Haymarket (1886) and Pullman (1894) stood as symbols of a society under siege. "Man has killed or maimed his fellow-man," Boston's Frederic D. Huntington sadly observed in 1886, only "for lack of knowing who the fellow-man was and what he meant." The time had come to abandon bloodshed and embrace brotherhood — a principle which "includes justice and wisdom along with charity, as in fact love is the fulfilling of the law."

Baltimore's Cardinal Gibbons, finding the prejudices against organized labor to be strong in Protestant America but perhaps even stronger in Catholic Europe, pleaded before the Vatican in 1887 for "the right of the laboring classes to protect themselves." That meant, for Gibbons as for many others besides, the right of laborers to associate and to organize (as the predominantly Catholic Knights of Labor had done in 1869 and as the predominantly non-Catholic American Federation of Labor had done in 1881). Rochester's Walter Rauschenbusch followed Gibbons's plea with a protest against the dehumanizing of the laborer, against the tendency to turn the worker into a "thing" whose only task was to "produce more things." "It is the function of religion," Rauschenbusch argued, "to teach the individual to value his soul more than his body, and his moral integrity more than his income." With similar sentiments, much of the nation's religious leadership put forth social creeds, called welfare conferences, wrote pastoral letters, and issued commission reports. In various ways, they contended that "machinery and industry exist for man and not man for them."

In the last years of the nineteenth century, and well into the twentieth, some theologians and prophets moved beyond the questions of urbanization and industrialization to probe the very character of society itself. Beyond curing the specific municipal ills and beyond ameliorating the bitterness between capital and labor, religion might hold promise for redeeming, for refashioning, the national fabric as a whole. Christianity is, in fact, a revolutionary religion, Rauschenbusch wrote. Equality was a cornerstone of the American creed, but exactly what did that imply in the economic sphere? "All men, inalienably, always, everywhere," announced New York pastor Edward McGlynn in 1887, "have a common right to all the general bounties of nature. . . ." The mission of the church, added Richard T. Ely, is to bring a "kingdom of righteousness" to the earth, "to redeem all our social relations." And whether by a new devotion to Christian socialism (George Herron) or by a new application of papal moralism (John A. Ryan), "the whole field of human action" falls under religion's sacred canopy.

War and Peace

Difficult and perplexing as these problems were, neither the nation nor the nation's churches escaped serious distraction from other quarters. The Spanish-American War (1898) had drawn the United States into hitherto unprecedented contact with far-distant parts of the world. World War I, of course, involved the country even more profoundly, evoked moral passions even more lastingly. As the nation's first full plunge into world affairs, it proved for some a heady and exhilarating experience, for others a disillusioning and sobering one. Many of the clergy who proudly "presented arms" in 1917 and 1918 pursued world peace earnestly, even frantically, in the decades that followed. A Church Peace Union was formed in 1914, a Washington Disarmament Conference called in 1921, and a Briand-Kellogg Peace Pact signed in 1928 — all this with strong and determinative support from Protestants, Catholics, and Jews. In the 1930s Frank Buchman attracted international attention by proclaiming that the only re-armament which the world needed was a "moral re-armament."

Evangelization of the World

Yet, the contest over who should rule the world was fought on other fronts, with other weapons. If from the perspective of world history, the nineteenth century was (as historian Kenneth Scott Latourette called it) the "great century" of mis-sionary advance, in America's history the twentieth century revealed the most impressive development. Despite World War I, or in some ways because of it, Protestants envisioned an evangelization that would transcend and triumph over all boundaries political and ecclesiastical. The nation's Roman Catholics, themselves regarded for so long as the passive *object* of missions, now assumed the role of active *sponsors.* "The Church in America," as Chicago's Archbishop Quigley announced in 1908, "is at the beginning of a new era in its history . . . prepared to go forth conquering . . . in the cause of Christ." And even those groups sometimes ignored or mocked in the United States ventured to Asia, Af-rica, or Europe to win victories abroad often denied them at home. Enormous amounts of energy, money, and zeal flowed into "foreign missions" in the early decades of the twentieth century. Was it worth all that effort? Questions con-cerned not only "cost effectiveness," to use a modern cliché, but more funda-mentally the appropriateness of intruding into other cultures, of enticing per-sons away from their own ancient religious heritages. In some quarters "evangelism" began to be justified as only part of a larger effort, as one noted the "social achievements of missionaries" or the humanitarian goal of improv-ing the quality of life. On what grounds, ultimately, were missions all around the world to be defended or promoted?

New Structures

Meanwhile back home, many churches and synagogues found themselves ill-equipped to minister effectively to a burgeoning population of the vagrant, poor, and despairing. Other institutions, born of the times and specific in their purposes, arose to feed the hungry, rescue the fallen, and provide temporary shelter for those who knew no home. The Salvation Army, an import from En-gland, quickly adapted to American soil, offering as an unshakeable article of faith that "the poor were to be treated with love, and not with suspicion or con-tempt." Young Men's and Young Women's Christian Associations found their initial reason for being in the great numbers of young people, uprooted from farm and family, thrust into an environment devoid of almost everything except temptation. In New York City alone, where so many of the impoverished immigrants arrived and stayed, the demands upon charity and goodwill multiplied beyond the capacity of traditional institutions to respond. In a society that had not yet heard of medicare, social security, unemployment compensation, or food stamps, it was up to private resources, and largely religious ones, to cope with urgent and expanding needs. About half of the population in New York City was Roman Catholic in 1868, and "it is notorious," a fellow Catholic wrote, that our own people "comprise a great deal more than half the pauper population. Are we doing a fair proportion of the work of taking care of our poor?" Though the answer at that time was "no," the creation of new societies and orders (for example, the Sisters of Charity and Mercy, the Society of St. Vincent de Paul) helped change that answer to "Yes."

Confronted by social needs that threatened to overwhelm them, many of the nation's religious leaders began to explore ways of working together. What needed to be done was too much for any to do alone. In 1908, some thirty denominations representing a membership of about eighteen million agreed to create a "Federal Council of the Churches of Christ in America." In the midst of World War I, some sixty-eight dioceses together with many national Catholic organizations formed the National Catholic War Council, a "temporary" structure refashioned in 1919 into the enduring National Catholic Welfare Council. This Council (later "Conference"), like the Federal Council, saw its social responsibilities in the broadest terms, as indeed did the Synagogue Council of America, formed in 1926. All three groups embraced this unity not for its own sake, but for the sake of a society whose only hope seemed to lie in a collective ministry of concern. The question in those days was not so much how religious institutions might merge as it was how churches and synagogues might effectively address themselves to common tasks. Christian unity will come, Charles Macfarland observed, "not so much by abstract process as by concrete experience. . . ."

One memorable instance of concrete experience transpired in this period: the passage of the Eighteenth Amendment in 1917 and its ratification a little over a year later. This Prohibition Amendment (repealed in 1933) represented the climax of a long history of condemnation — in the name of religion — of alcoholic beverages. Tracts had been written, sermons preached, crusades launched, and organizations developed to fight the "liquor traffic" and to rescue or assist liquor's victims. The best-known revivalist of this period, Billy Sunday, battled "booze" with every theatrical trick and oratorical flourish at his command. But as with the ecumenical entities noted above, an organized religious force was required to confront and defeat an organized enemy. That force, the Anti-Saloon League, emerged by 1895 as a national organization. Led by Methodists and heavily supported by Baptists, Presbyterians, and others (including significant leaders within Roman Catholicism), the League provided an early and effective example of "single-issue politics": one question and one question only was asked of every politician at every level — "Will you vote dry?" Enough life remained in the Evangelical Empire to launch, if not to sustain, the Noble Experiment of the 1920s.

Through urban growth, industrial strife, world war, and probes toward peace, a nation moved from adolescence to adulthood. Many of religion's resources were marshalled to attend to and assist in that time of maturation, to be engaged in the public problems of the day and not withdrawn, involved and not aloof. There were risks, of course, in being drawn into the messy world of politics and economics, of foreign policy and international relations. Those whose voices follow, however, saw even faith itself as a kind of risk.

1. Love and Justice

Redeeming the City

Josiah Strong (1847-1916)

*A native of Illinois and a graduate of Western Reserve in Ohio, Congrega-
tionalist Josiah Strong left the Midwest in 1886 to assume leadership of the
American Evangelical Alliance. He had come into national prominence the
year before with the publication of his first book,* Our Country *(see above,
p. 21). More than twenty years after that early work, Strong concentrated his
attention more narrowly upon the city and its promises and perils.*

The problems of government increase with the increase in population. As cities
become more populous, relations whose harmony must be preserved increase
in number and complexity. A mistake is further reaching; it has a longer leverage; and as efficient government grows more essential it becomes increasingly
difficult. To administer the affairs of a village of 1,000 inhabitants is a simple
matter, requiring only ordinary intelligence; the government of a city of
100,000 is much more complicated; while that of a city of 1,000,000 or of
5,000,000 demands expert knowledge, ability, and character of the very highest
order.

Our political development in the United States has been along national
and state lines rather than municipal. The principles of the state and national
governments are well settled and clearly defined, but those of municipal organization and government are confused and uncertain. We are as yet in the ex-

[Source: Josiah Strong, *The Challenge of the City* (New York: Young People's Missionary Movement of the United States and Canada, 1909 [1907]), pp. 44-46.]

perimental stage, and need the insight and genius of the highest statesmanship to solve the new and complex problems of the city, which are the problems of the new civilization. Among them are those created by the industrial revolution which has taken place during the nineteenth century — such as adjusting an aristocratic system of industry to a democratic system of government.

If upon these and other municipal problems we should bring to bear the wisdom of the fathers who framed the constitution, not a scrap of it would be wasted. It does not seem to me extravagant to say that higher intellectual qualities are required to solve these problems than to administer successfully the office of the nation's chief executive.

Does any one imagine that we are meeting these high demands? As our cities grow larger are we calling to office larger-minded men, capable of grappling with these profound problems? As a general rule, the larger our cities the worse and more incompetent is their government. We are permitting the most ignorant classes to control them. Only as far as the intelligence of a city is brought to bear upon public affairs, does it practically exist.

Washington Gladden (1836-1918)

Unlike Strong, Washington Gladden began in the East but spent the last third of his life in the Midwest: namely, Columbus, Ohio. As minister of the First Congregational Church there, Gladden established a reputation in "applied Christianity," to use the title of his first book (published in 1886, one year after Strong's first book). Before his career ended, Gladden had written some thirty-eight books and delivered countless sermons and speeches. His many efforts made him a powerful leader in what came to be called the "Social Gospel." Here, in his autobiographical reflections, he describes his own direct involvement in the municipal government of Columbus, together with the moral or theological lessons to be derived therefrom.

. . . No plan can be devised which will give us good city government, so long as the great majority of our citizens are unwilling to take any responsibility for the government of our cities. It is not the fashion, in America, for men of substance and standing to take any active part in the administration of city affairs. Many of them seem to think it bad form to interest themselves in such matters; more of them feel that they cannot afford the sacrifice of their business interests which such a service would require of them. So long as anything resembling

---

[Source: Washington Gladden, *Recollections* (Boston: Houghton Mifflin Co., 1909), pp. 336-37, 345-46, 351-52.]

this is true, we shall, of course, have bad government in our cities. We are shirking the primary obligations of our democracy, and we shall get our deserts.

Some sense of these obligations constrained me, in the spring of 1900, to take upon myself a task for which I could claim no special fitness, and which might have been far better performed by some of my neighbors. . . . Without taking counsel with any one, I announced . . . over my own signature, in all the daily papers, that if the people of the Seventh Ward desired to have me serve them the next term in the city council, I would endeavor to do so. This was all that I found it necessary to do. My neighbors took up the matter and elected me; not only did I make no canvass for the place, I scarcely mentioned the matter in conversation to any one.

In April, 1900, I took up the duties of this office, and served in it for two years. . . .

I am not at all sorry that I had a chance to serve the city . . . and that I was able to contribute toward the formation of the public opinion which resulted in the adoption, to this extent, of the principle of municipal ownership. For I am as sure as I can be of anything that the municipal ownership and control of public-service industries is the right policy, — the only policy under which there is any hope of preventing corruption and oppression. As I have already

Congregationalist Washington Gladden (1836-1918) in his study in Columbus, Ohio
(Library of Congress)

tried to show, the public-service industries are necessarily monopolies; they are monopolies which furnish us with the necessaries of life; and monopolies of that nature must belong to the people. It would be just as rational to give a private corporation the right of levying taxes, as it is to give it the exclusive control of an industry by which the welfare of all the people is affected. No such control as this over the public welfare can rationally be delegated by the people to any private agency. If this does not belong to the rudiments of democracy, it would be hard to think of anything that does.

To say that the people cannot be trusted to manage such matters is simply to say that the people cannot govern themselves. Even, therefore, if it could be shown that municipal ownership resulted, for a time, in increasing the cost of the service, that would be no reason why it should not be chosen. If the people thus, by their carelessness and neglect, bring suffering upon themselves, that is just as it should be; they will know that they have brought it upon themselves, and will know how to avoid it. Nothing is safe in a democracy but the method which brings directly home to the people themselves the consequences of their own misdoing. That is the only way in which they can be educated. . . .

I took my leave of the Columbus city council in April, 1902, with a sincere regret. I had no consciousness of having achieved great things; but I had come into close contact with the vital needs of my city, and I had had some part in solving some of its most pressing problems. I laid the burden down because it was not possible for me to bear it any longer. The work of my church was heavy and exacting, it could not be delegated, I must resign either my charge or my office. The results of my experience were a deepened sense of the seriousness of the business of municipal government and a more vivid realization of the lack of knowledge and skill on the part of those who are handling it. This is the crying evil — incompetency. There were not many occasions on which I suspected the presence of corrupting influences in the council; I do not think that money was often used; but the lack of the adequate knowledge and experience for the tasks in hand was often painfully apparent. I believe that this is true of city governments as a rule, — perhaps of state governments also. They are generally in the hands of men who have no fitness to deal with them; and this is mainly because the men who have the necessary equipment for such work almost uniformly refuse to undertake it.

John Lancaster Spalding (1840-1916)

A Kentuckian, John Lancaster Spalding served as bishop of Peoria, Illinois, for over thirty years. But his most significant service to Roman Catholicism in America came in the form of his articulate leadership in many a political or social cause. He spoke well and wrote well, defending his Church when that was necessary but more often goading his Church in directions which he thought it needed to go. The Church, he argued, could not avoid the problems of modernity, not even the problems of the modern industrial and secular state. Here his concern is for the modern family and the unhappy effects which city life seem to have upon it.

Moral degradation accompanies great physical wretchedness; and the low moral state of manufacturing populations affords inexhaustible matter for discussion and consideration. The conditions of life are not favorable to purity, and the grossest sensuality prevails. Where people have no settled home and no local traditions the loss of good name is often looked upon as a mere trifle; and the sense of shame is stifled in the young who from their earliest years have lived in an atmosphere polluted by foul language. In the city old age and childhood are thrust out of sight, and the domestic morals and simple manners, which are above all price, cease to be handed down as sacred heirlooms.

One of the greatest evils which afflicts a manufacturing population is the breaking down of the family life. What family life is possible where there is no continuity, where there are no traditions that descend from father to son? The soul of the family is respect for ancestors, and where there are no traditions this respect dies out and the family becomes an accidental collection of individual existences. A home is essential to the family, and the traditional spirit is transmitted with the home from father to son. With the possession of a fireside the family receives a life of its own, and its permanency and complete identity can be assured only by the hereditary transmission of the home. To take from it the perpetuity of its fireside is to deprive it of a great part of its strength. A house that is occupied but not owned is not a home. A true family ought to be abiding; it ought to endure while the nation exists. It reposes upon love and religion; it is nurtured by traditions of honor and virtue; and the symbol of its continuity and permanence is the home owned and transmitted from generation to generation.

Now, the poor in our great cities and manufacturing towns have no homes. They live in tenements and hired rooms; or if the more fortunate own

---

[Source: J. L. Spalding, *The Religious Mission of the Irish People and Catholic Colonization* (New York: The Catholic Publication Society, 1880), pp. 87-89.]

their cottages they can have little hope of leaving them to their children, who will go to swell the great floating population that is up for universal hire, and which, work failing, sinks lower to join the army of paupers and outcasts who form, to use the modern phrase, the dangerous classes of our great commercial and manufacturing centres. What hope can we have of men or women whose childhood has never been *consecrated* by home-life to pure thoughts and generous deeds, and who too often carry through the world the heavy burden of physical and moral disease planted in the infant heart, in which the whole human being was yet enfolded like the rose within the tender bud? Lodging-houses where people sleep and eat are not homes. Hired rooms which are changed from year to year, and often from month to month, are not homes. The operative's cottage, without yard or garden, without flowers or privacy, is not a home. The house which is empty day after day, because the mother and her little ones are chained to the great machine in the factory mill, is the grave of the family, not its home.

Samuel S. Mayerberg (1892-1964)

As the rabbi of Congregation B'nai Jehudah in Kansas City, Missouri, in the 1930s, Samuel Mayerberg did not have to search hard or far for municipal corruption. One of the nation's most notorious political machines, that of Thomas J. Pendergast, controlled every appointment to political office, every building dependent on city permits, and — according to Mayerberg — "People were actually told what physicians they might use, what lawyers might practice, what merchants might do business." Kansas City had a good charter; the only problem was that no politician paid any attention to it. Forming a Charter League and speaking to any who would listen, Rabbi Mayerberg led a risky crusade against crime, greed, and corruption. He fought many fights, but the hardest one of all, he writes, was "to convince thoroughly nice people, honorable men," that they too should join in the fight.

Pendergast is one of the most interesting personalities I have ever known. He is broken in spirit and in body now. He has suffered the tortures of the damned from his illness, while he has been incarcerated in a Federal prison. The humiliation, as his empire crumbled upon him, has been agonizing. You will not think me maudlin if I tell you sincerely that I feel a deep sympathy for this man who

---

[Source: Samuel S. Mayerberg, *Chronicle of an American Crusader* (New York: Bloch Publishing Co., 1944), pp. 107-8, 109, 110-11, 118-20, 130-31.]

could have been great. He possessed the powers of mind and heart to have served the people nobly. He chose rather to play a ruthless political gamble, and he won huge stakes for a while; but he lost ultimately, as they all must.

He was a saloonkeeper in his early years and inherited his political kingdom from his uncle. Through the years, by his indomitable will and through those tricks known only to politicians, he became the dominant boss within his party. Then a quirk in American history helped him gain complete control of Kansas City. The Prohibition amendment had given rise to "bootlegging," and illicit sale of forbidden liquor had built the racketeering system in the United States, with unscrupulous leaders like Capone in Chicago and John Lazia in Kansas City. I shall have much more to say about this gangster; it will suffice to relate here that he was a minor politician, who controlled, by fear and crime, thousands of voters in the North End. At that time 7,500 votes could swing any election in Kansas City. Lazia threw his political strength to Pendergast; the reasons will become obvious. In the next election, Pendergast, with his machine and the machine's use of fraudulent ballots, elected the Mayor and all the members of the City Council.

As a result the City Manager gleefully announced that the people had given him a mandate to conduct city affairs on a strictly partisan basis. He dismissed every city employee affiliated with the opposition party. Any person desiring city employment could obtain it only by receiving a card from his precinct captain and having it endorsed by the "big boss" at 1908 Main Street. The card was then taken personally to the City Manager, who unhesitatingly put the man to work. When the city hall was filled to overflowing, the job-seekers were listed in various departments and were assigned no work. . . .

Other political workers were abundantly enriched by contracts given to favorites. Competitive bidding was ignored or became a farce. Gasoline and oil for city purposes were bought entirely through one firm, which had been formed for that purpose. Half interest in it belonged to Pendergast. Top prices were invariably paid. Pendergast rapidly increased his growing fortune through a perfectly legitimate business. He owned the Red-D-Mix Concrete Co., which produced a good cement, mixed and ready for use. No building, public or private, could be erected unless the builder used Pendergast's product. If one dared to defy the "boss" in this respect, he was allowed to excavate the basement and lay cement foundations; then the city inspector would nonchalantly appear upon the scene, chip off a bit of the foundation and regretfully say, "This cement isn't up to specification. You will have to tear it out and use the right material." In desperation the recalcitrant builder would plead for permission to continue. When he had been sufficiently humbled, he would be told that one cement met all requirements; if he used it, no hindrance would disturb him. Thus through political control of the City Manager and his hirelings, Pendergast obtained a complete monopoly of that essential product.

It is difficult for us to imagine how extensively political control gripped our city. It ranged far beyond the limits of municipal activities. It reached out in subtle ways to affect private lives. People were actually told what physicians they might use, what lawyers might practice, what merchants might do business. Personnel men in our factories came under the domination of the machine; and for years they would refuse to employ men unless they had passes from the boss. All city insurance and all surety bonds for contractors working for the city or county had to be negotiated through one insurance broker, a very good man, a close personal friend of the boss. Respcectable business men soon found it a matter of safety to have Pendergast or [Henry J.] McElroy identified with them in their concerns; in some instances they received blocks of stock; in others they were paid for serving on executive boards. These are some of the methods by which the tyrants of the machine profited personally. Later, it was proved in Federal court that Pendergast had also been receiving hundreds of thousands of dollars over a period of years from the big and the little gamblers who, in turn, were given complete political protection. . . .

In brief, this is a sketch of the deplorable and menacing conditions which prevailed in my city on the afternoon of May 21, 1932, when I addressed the Government Study Club. I knew beyond the peradventure of a doubt that there was an alliance between our city administration of Kansas City and the underworld.

In that address I contrasted the successful administration of Cincinnati under Colonel Sherrill with that in our own city under McElroy. I showed paragraph by paragraph how the City Manager was violating the letter and spirit of the Charter. Without equivocation I called him the biggest law-breaker in the city. I properly laid the blame upon him for the disastrous conditions existing on the grounds that organized crime cannot exist without the protection of civic authorities. I charged him with manipulation and misuse of public funds. My indictment included all elements of malfeasance and misfeasance in office. I claimed that he had spoken falsely when he annually made a statement, under oath, that the city treasury contained a surplus. It was proved that this so-called surplus was, in reality, only a daily bank balance, which he maintained by juggling public funds. After an hour's exposure of the multifarious iniquities of the administration, I read the charter provisions for the legal punishment of those officials who violated the charter. I demanded that the City Council dismiss the City Manager. In its failure to do so, I challenged the County Prosecutor to exercise his authority under the state law to remove him from office.

The reception given that address amazed me. Those gentlewomen, leaders in the club life of the city, arose and shouted their approval. The same afternoon *The Kansas City Star,* one of America's great newspapers, which had from time to time attacked the machinations of the boss, carried in its home edition a two-column lead on the front page, containing a very full account. The next day editorial comment followed.

That night my telephone rang constantly. Some calls were from friends anxious about my welfare. Some were fearful that the gangsters would speedily hire retaliation upon me. Some exhorted me to drop the matter entirely; it was too dangerous. Other calls brought invitations from luncheon clubs and churches to repeat the address for them. The largest and most powerful organization in the city, the Chamber of Commerce, was silent. Its president was an intimate friend of Pendergast and McElroy. Its attorney was a member of the City Council. Of course I was pleased with the eager and enthusiastic interest displayed by the groups who wanted me to appear. It told me that the community wanted direction and stimulation in a mighty struggle, which they knew must ultimately come. During that week I delivered three or four addresses a day, and wherever I spoke the audiences overflowed the room. The boss only chuckled and McElroy insultingly denied my charges; the Council scoffed. Politicians try to laugh their opponents to shame. Being a preacher, I was an easy target for their jeering.

On May 24th I was cordially invited to lay the case before the Ministerial Alliance of Kansas City. One hundred and twenty-five ministers were present; at the conclusion of the address, after a few questions were asked, a ringing resolution endorsing my stand was passed unanimously. Aid was promised and many ministers later held meetings in their churches for me. I regret, however, that only four, Roy O. Chanel, Joseph Myers, Edmund Kulp and G. Charles Gray, remained with me to the end. . . .

Sufficient evidence had now been compiled to lend significance to the recall movement I would inaugurate through the Charter League. *The Kansas City Star* magnificently carried full length items, as we continued to expose the knavery of our city officials. Without the columns and the editorials of the *Star* our best efforts would have been futile.

It is difficult for me to describe succinctly the reactions that came from two groups, the racketeering politicians and my own congregational membership. The politicians were plainly worried and raised a great clamor over the self-righteous closing of a few dives and houses of ill fame. To this petty boasting I replied: "The elimination of a few filthy saloons and brothels will not satisfy the people of Kansas City. Those are only pimples on the body politic; only symptoms of the corruption within the body which has existed for years." As long as our charter group spent its time in harassing the gang merely by oratory at large and excited public gatherings, especially in churches, the politicians were not disturbed. They could scoff and sneer and be smug in the expressed thought, "The preachers will soon grow tired and the noise will blow over." However, as soon as plans for the Charter League progressed, the politicians saw clearly that we were translating words and ideals into action. The racketeers began to fight back in their vicious way. They tapped my telephones in my Temple study and in the Charter League offices. They ransacked the files in my study and stole the records from the League office. They threatened me and they attempted to bribe me. Pendergast, McElroy and Council members used their vast and powerful influence upon my highly-respected members to exert all pressure upon me to force me out of the fight. All through the years until the city was cleansed, one of my hardest jobs was not fighting the underworld, but in using my energy and time to convince thoroughly nice people, honorable men, that conscience and the power of religious conviction drove me unswervingly into the fray and that, as respectable citizens, they ought to be in it also.

In His Steps (1897)

A large percentage of the millions who read — and passed along — the popular novel In His Steps; or, What Would Jesus Do? *hardly realized that they too were caught up in the social gospel. In a Kansas town (Topeka), a Congregationalist pastor, Charles M. Sheldon (1857-1946), offered in fictional form the pressing dilemmas that modernity imposed. Even small-town America at the turn of the century faced questions of labor and capital, immigration and race, city and slum. In the excerpt below, the novelist presents his message in the form of a sermon by the fictional minister, Henry Maxwell, in the fictional town of Raymond. Little could Sheldon realize that, more than a century after the publication of this book, WWJD (What Would Jesus Do?) would remain a popular slogan in the nation at large.*

Sunday morning the great church was filled to its utmost. Henry Maxwell, coming into the pulpit from that all-night vigil, felt the pressure of a great curiosity on the part of the people. . . .

He had never been what would be called a great preacher. He had not the force or the quality that makes remarkable preachers. But ever since he had promised to do as Jesus would do, he had grown in a certain quality of persuasiveness that had all the essentials of true eloquence. This morning the people felt the complete sincerity and humility of a man who had gone deep into the heart of a great truth.

After telling briefly of some results in his own church in Raymond since the pledge was taken, he went on to ask the question he had been asking since the Settlement meeting. He had taken for his theme the story of the young man who came to Jesus, asking what he must do to obtain eternal life? Jesus had tested him: "Sell all that thou hast and give to the poor and thou shalt have trea-

[Source: Charles M. Sheldon, *In His Steps* (Chicago: John C. Winston Co., 1957) [1897, and countless editions thereafter]), pp. 254-57, 259.]

sure in heaven, and come, follow Me." But the young man was not willing to suffer to that extent. If following Jesus meant suffering in that way, he was not willing. He would like to follow Jesus, but not if he had to give so much.

"Is it true," continued Henry Maxwell, and his fine, thoughtful face glowed with a passion of appeal that stirred the people as they had seldom been stirred, "is it true that the church of to-day, the church that is called after Christ's own name, would refuse to follow Him at the expense of suffering, of physical loss, of temporary gain? The statement was made, at a large gathering in the Settlement last week by a leader of workingmen, that it was hopeless to look to the church for any reform or redemption of society. On what was that statement based? Plainly on the assumption that the church contained, for the most part, men and women who thought more of their own ease and luxury than of the sufferings and needs and sins of humanity. How far was that true? Are the Christians of America ready to have their discipleship tested? How about the men who possess large wealth? Are they ready to take that wealth and use it as Jesus would? How about the men and women of great talent? Are they ready to consecrate that talent to humanity as Jesus undoubtedly would do?

"Is it not true that the call has come in this age for a new exhibition of discipleship, Christian discipleship? You who live in this great, sinful city must know that better than I do. Is it possible you can go your ways careless or thoughtless of the awful condition of men and women and children who are dying, body and soul, for need of Christian help? Is it not a matter of concern to you personally that the saloon kills its thousands more surely than war? Is it not a matter of personal suffering in some form for you, that thousands of able-bodied, willing men tramp the streets of this city, and all cities, crying for work, and drifting into crime and suicide because they cannot find it? Can you say that this is none of your business? Let each man look after himself!. Would it not be true, think you, that if every Christian in America did as Jesus would do, society itself, the business world, yes, the very political system under which our commercial and governmental activity is carried on, would be so changed that human suffering would be reduced to a minimum? . . .

"What would be the result, if in this city every church member should begin to do as Jesus would do? It is not easy to go into details of the result. But we all know that certain things would be impossible that are now practiced by church members. What would Jesus do in the matter of wealth? How would He spend it? What principle would regulate His use of money? Would He be likely to live in great luxury and spend ten times as much on personal adornment and entertainment as He spent to relieve the needs of suffering humanity? How would Jesus be governed in the making of money? Would He take rentals from saloon and other disreputable property, or even from tenement property that was so constructed that the inmates had no such thing as a home and no such possibility as privacy or cleanliness?

"What would Jesus do about the great army of unemployed and desperate who tramp the streets and curse the church, or are indifferent to it, lost in the bitter struggle for the bread that tastes bitter when it is earned, on account of the desperate conflict to get it. Would Jesus care nothing for them? Would He go His way in comparative ease and comfort? Would He say it was none of His business? Would He excuse Himself from all responsibility to remove the causes of such a condition?

"What would Jesus do in the center of a civilization that hurries so fast after money that the very girls employed in great business houses are not paid enough to keep soul and body together without fearful temptations, so great that scores of them fall and are swept over the great, boiling abyss; where the demands of trade sacrifice hundreds of lads in a business that ignores all Christian duties toward them in the way of education and moral training and personal affection? Would Jesus, if He were here today, as a part of our age and commercial industry, feel nothing, do nothing, say nothing, in the face of these facts, which every business man knows? . . .

"Are we ready to make and live a new discipleship? Are we ready to reconsider our definition of a Christian? What is it to be a Christian? It is to imitate Jesus. It is to do as He would do. It is to walk in His steps."

When Henry Maxwell finished his sermon, he paused and looked at the people with a look they never forgot, and at the moment did not understand. Crowded into that fashionable church that day were hundreds of men and women who had for years lived the easy, satisfied life of a nominal Christianity. A great silence fell over the congregation. Through the silence, there came to the consciousness of all the souls there present a knowledge, stranger to them now for years, of a Divine Power. Everyone expected the preacher to call for volunteers who would do as Jesus would do. But Maxwell had been led by the Spirit to deliver his message this time and wait for results to come.

Redeeming the Factory

Frederic Dan Huntington (1819-1904)

While most of his life was spent in and around Boston, Huntington did serve for thirty-five years as the Episcopal bishop of central New York. Along with

[Source: F. D. Huntington, "Some Points in the Labor Question," *The Church Review*, 48 (July, 1886), 7-8, 14-15.]

his steady theological development, he reflected with increasing clarity upon the obligations and opportunities which the new economic order presented to the Christian. In a denominational journal in 1886, Huntington argued that Christianity must be relevant to the awful clashes between capital and labor — otherwise, it is tragically irrelevant to the most pressing problems of the day. The "labor question" is a religious question, and the church must take its place on the side of the powerless and oppressed.

What is wanted most of all in these social distractions and industrial confusions is that any two parties in opposition should take pains to look at the issue from one another's point of view. This requires some breadth of mind as well as a benevolent regard to the common good; but neither of these, in a land of general education and Christian traditions, is entirely impracticable. It is only necessary to use the faculty of thinking patiently, to quiet anger, to dismiss jealousy, to go out of the petty sphere of immediate occupations, and to examine facts. Let intelligent workmen who work for wages make a candid study of the actual methods, aims, and condition of the masters of the particular industry in which they are engaged. Let the employer, on the other hand, give an equally candid hearing to half a dozen of the best operatives in his employ, while both are in good temper and at leisure. Each party will learn a great deal, and very likely be somewhat surprised. If they could break bread together so much the better. Nothing is plainer to observers at a little distance than that the contestants in these recent struggles are fighting in the dark, striking with strokes that hit friends along with foes and are often suicidal, — a pathetic repetition of a thousand tragedies where man has killed or maimed his fellow-man for lack of knowing who the fellow-man was and what he meant. The "classes" are suffering for want of a mutual introduction and mutual interpretation, though they may live close together, serve the same establishment, and really depend upon each other's good will. . . .

More profound and far-reaching yet as a remedy for these barbarous quarrels in a half-civilised civilisation is the principle of human brotherhood. It includes Justice and wisdom along with charity, as in fact love is the fulfilling of the law. It will be difficult to find any social disruption not curable by the rule so simply laid down in the New Testament as a precept, "Let no man seek his own but every man another's wealth;" i.e., allowing for the idiom, Let no man seek exclusively his own but every man also another's welfare. Call it Utopianism, call it altruism, call it impracticable theory; it is at any rate Christianity, and it yet remains for objectors to discover a spot where it has been fairly tried without certain effects following, viz., the allaying of discord and malice; the abatement of crime; the increase of thrift, contentment, economy, and every species of virtue; the growth of public prosperity and private liberty. That it would extinguish the natural distinctions in men's gifts and powers, in gain or external fortune, any more than in sex, size, or feature, is nowhere promised. But that it would reduce excessive inequalities, and prevent the evil of violent or unrighteous contrasts, and forestall or heal social shocks, no political economy or experience is in a position to deny. One of the most deplorable results of these rash uprisings of an oppressed or injured class, therefore, is that it discourages the hopes of a true philanthropy, disappoints the best friends that labor and poverty and ignorance have, and chills our sympathies where they ought to go out with the most generous and practical activity. There can be no question on which side in the debate the voice of Christ and the Gospel and the Church is most distinctly heard. Whoever reads the sharp instructions of S. James in the fifth chapter of his Epistle, or the repeated warnings of the other Apostles, or the most tender and yet piercing commands of the Great Master Workman Himself, will be obliged to confess that it is the rich and prosperous, not the less successful and less favored, who are most severely denounced, most in danger of ruin, and most in need of a changed and watchful mind, and of a quickened conscience.

James Cardinal Gibbons (1834-1921)

Cardinal Gibbons stood as the laborer's stalwart friend in the testy confrontations between workers and owners in America. In the second half of the nineteenth century, the right of workers to organize was sharply questioned, and the dangers of allowing them to organize were repeatedly asserted. Labor unions were seen as radical, perhaps even communistic (the first volume of Marx's Das Kapital *was published in 1867); they were also seen as a threat to private property, and perhaps to Christianity as well. This was the common "wisdom" in many circles, both European and American. In Europe, the Roman Catholic Church had suffered severe reversals of fortune in revolutions that seemed simultaneously prolabor and anti-Church. Thus, it took great courage for Cardinal Gibbons in 1887 to take his case to Europe, indeed to the Vatican itself, there to defend labor's right to form unions. He did more: he defended the right of Catholic workers to form a Catholic union. And should the pope be so ill-advised as to condemn such a union, the Church in America would suffer severe and permanent damage.*

2. That there exist among us, as in all other countries of the world, grave and threatening social evils, public injustices which call for strong resistance and le-

---

[Source: James Gibbons, *A Retrospect of Fifty Years* (Baltimore: John Murphy, 1916), I, pp. 194-98.]

gal remedy, is a fact which no one dares to deny — a fact already acknowledged by the Congress and the President of the United States. Without entering into the sad details of these evils, whose full discussion is not necessary, I will only mention that monopolies, on the part of both individuals and of corporations, have everywhere called forth not only the complaints of our working classes, but also the opposition of our public men and legislators; that the efforts of monopolists, not always without success, to control legislation to their own profit, cause serious apprehensions among the disinterested friends of liberty, that the heartless avarice which, through greed of gain, pitilessly grinds not only the men, but even the women and children in various employments, make it clear to all who love humanity and justice that it is not only the right of the laboring classes to protect themselves, but the duty of the whole people to aid them in finding a remedy against the dangers with which both civilization and social order are menaced by avarice, oppression and corruption.

It would be vain to dispute either the existence of the evils, or the right of legitimate resistance, or the necessity of a remedy. At most a doubt might be raised about the legitimacy of the form of resistance, and of the remedy employed by the Knights of Labor. This, then, is the next point to be examined.

3. It can hardly be doubted that, for the attainment of any public end, association — the organization of all interested — is the most efficacious means — a means altogether natural and just. This is so evident, and besides so comfortable to the genius of our country, of our essentially popular social conditions, that it is unnecessary to insist upon it. It is almost the only means to invite public attention, to give force to the most legitimate resistance, to add weight to the most just demands.

Now, there already exists an organization which presents innumerable attractions and advantages, but with which our Catholic workingmen, filially obedient to the Holy See, refuse to unite themselves; this is the Masonic Order, which exists everywhere in our country, and which, as Mr. [Terence] Powderly has expressly pointed out to us, unites employers and employed in a brotherhood very advantageous to the latter, but which numbers in its ranks hardly a single Catholic. Nobly renouncing advantages which the Church and conscience forbid, our workingmen join associations in no way in conflict with religion, seeking nothing but mutual protection and help, and the legitimate assertion of their rights. Must they here also find themselves threatened with condemnation, hindered from their only means of self-defense?

4. Let us now consider the objections made against this sort of organization.

(a) It is objected that in such organizations, Catholics are mixed with Protestants, to the peril of their faith. Naturally, yes; they are mixed with Protestants at their work; for, in a mixed people like ours the separation of religious creeds in civil affairs is an impossibility. But to suppose that the faith of our

James Cardinal Gibbons (1834-1921), Archbishop of Baltimore, Maryland
(Library of Congress)

Catholics suffers thereby is not to know the Catholic working men of America, who are not like the working men of so many European countries — misguided children, estranged from their Mother, the Church, and regarding her with suspicion and dread — but intelligent, well-instructed and devoted Catholics, ready to give their blood, if necessary, as they continually give their hard-earned means, for her support and protection. And, in fact, it is not here a question of Catholics mixed with Protestants, but rather that Protestants are admitted to share in the advantages of an association, many of whose members and officers are Catholics; and, in a country like ours, their exclusion would be simply impossible.

(b) But it is asked, instead of such an organization, could there not be confraternities, in which the working men would be united under the direction of the clergy and the influence of religion? I answer frankly that I do not consider this either possible or necessary in our country. I sincerely admire the efforts of this sort which are made in countries where the working people are led astray by the enemies of religion, but, thanks be to God, that is not our condition. We find that in our country the presence and direct influence of the clergy would not be advisable where our citizens, without distinction of religious belief, come together in regard to their industrial interests alone. Short of that we have abundant means for making our working people faithful Catholics, and simple good sense advises us not to go to extremes.

(c) Again, it is objected that, in such organizations, Catholics are exposed to the evil influences of the most dangerous associates, even of atheists, communists and anarchists. That is true, but it is one of those trials of faith which our brave American Catholics are accustomed to meet almost daily, and which they know how to face with good sense and firmness. The press of our country tells us, and the president of the Knights has related to us, how these violent, aggressive elements have endeavored to control the association, or to inject poison into its principles, but they also inform us with what determination these machinators have been repulsed and beaten.

The presence among our citizens of those dangerous social elements, which have mostly come from certain countries of Europe, is assuredly for us an occasion of great regret and of vigilant precautions; it is a fact, however, which we have to accept, but which the close union between the Church and her children that exists in our country renders comparatively free from danger. In truth, the only thing from which we would fear serious danger would be a cooling of this relationship between the Church and her children, and I know nothing that would be more likely to occasion it than imprudent condemnations.

Walter Rauschenbusch (1861-1918)

If any Protestant deserves more credit than Washington Gladden for applying Christian principles to social problems, it is clearly Walter Rauschenbusch. Professor at Rochester Seminary in New York from 1897 until his death, this German Baptist gave the social gospel its firmest theological support (in A Theology for the Social Gospel, *1917) and its most untiring leadership. Nothing in the out-of-joint world around him escaped his attention or comment, but industry's monopolistic control and rapacious methods made that segment of modern life a first order of religion's business. To put it simply, "materialism and mammonism" must go.*

[Source: Walter Rauschenbusch, *Christianity and the Social Crisis* (New York: Harper & Row, 1964 [1907]), pp. 369-70, 370-71, 372.]

The spiritual force of Christianity should be turned against the materialism and mammonism of our industrial and social order.

If a man sacrifices his human dignity and self-respect to increase his income, or stunts his intellectual growth and his human affections to swell his bank account, he is to that extent serving mammon and denying God. Likewise if he uses up and injures the life of his fellow-men to make money for himself, he serves mammon and denies God. But our industrial order does both. It makes property the end, and man the means to produce it.

Man is treated as a *thing* to produce more things. Men are hired as hands and not as men. They are paid only enough to maintain their working capacity and not enough to develop their manhood. When their working force is exhausted, they are flung aside without consideration of their human needs. Jesus asked, "Is not a man more than a sheep?" Our industry says "No." It is careful of its live stock and machinery, and careless of its human working force. It keeps its electrical engines immaculate in burnished cleanliness and lets its human dynamos sicken in dirt. . . .

"Life is more than food and raiment." More, too, than the apparatus which makes food and raiment. What is all the machinery of our industrial organization worth if it does not make human life healthful and happy? But is it doing that? Men are first of all men, folks, members of our human family. To view them first of all as labor force is civilized barbarism. It is the attitude of the exploiter. Yet unconsciously we have all been taught to take that attitude and talk of men as if they were horse-powers or volts. Our commercialism has tainted our sense of fundamental human verities and values. We measure our national prosperity by pig-iron and steel instead of by the welfare of the people. . . .

It is the function of religion to teach the individual to value his soul more than his body, and his moral integrity more than his income. In the same way it is the function of religion to teach society to value human life more than property, and to value property only in so far as it forms the material basis for the higher development of human life. When life and property are in apparent collision, life must take precedence. This is not only Christian but prudent. When commercialism in its headlong greed deteriorates the mass of human life, it defeats its own covetousness by killing the goose that lays the golden egg. Humanity is that goose — in more senses than one. It takes faith in the moral law to believe that this penny-wise craft is really suicidal folly, and to assert that wealth which uses up the people paves the way to beggary. Religious men have been cowed by the prevailing materialism and arrogant selfishness of our business world. They should have the courage of religious faith and assert that "man liveth not by bread alone," but by doing the will of God, and that the life of a nation "consisteth not in the abundance of things" which it produces, but in the way men live justly with one another and humbly with their God.

Pastoral Letter, 1920

The pontificate of Leo XIII (1878-1903) demonstrated an awareness of modern social and economic forces not evident in his immediate predecessor, Pius IX. Leo's 1891 encyclical Rerum Novarum, *cited for decades after by all those concerned with the industrial order, encouraged many Catholics to apply Christian tenets broadly to the marketplace. In 1920, the bishops and archbishops of the United States leaned heavily on* Rerum Novarum *as they signalled that the American hierarchy was committed — if somewhat timidly — to an even-handed justice for capital, for labor, and for the entire community.*

"It is the opinion of some," says Pope Leo XIII, "and the error is already very common, that the social question is merely an economic one, whereas in point of fact, it is first of all a moral and religious matter, and for that reason its settlement is to be sought mainly in the moral law and the pronouncements of religion" (Apostolic Letter, *Graves de communi,* January 18, 1901). These words are as pertinent and their teaching as necessary today as they were nineteen years ago. Their meaning, substantially, has been reaffirmed by Pope Benedict XV in his recent statement that "without justice and charity there will be no social progress." The fact that men are striving for what they consider to be their rights, puts their dispute on a moral basis; and wherever justice may lie, whichever of the opposing claims may have the better foundation, it is Justice that all demand.

In the prosecution of their respective claims, the parties have, apparently, disregarded the fact that the people as a whole have a prior claim. The great number of unnecessary strikes which have occurred within the last few months, is evidence that justice has been widely violated as regards the rights and needs of the public. To assume that the only rights involved in an industrial dispute are those of capital and labor, is a radical error. It leads, practically, to the conclusion that at any time and for an indefinite period, even the most necessary products can be withheld from general use until the controversy is settled. In fact, while it lasts, millions of persons are compelled to suffer hardship for want of goods and services which they require for reasonable living. The first step, therefore, toward correcting the evil is to insist that the rights of the community shall prevail, and that no individual claim conflicting with those rights shall be valid. . . .

"The great mistake in regard to the matter now under consideration is to take up with the notion that class is naturally hostile to class, and that the

[Source: John A. Ryan and Joseph Husslein, eds., *The Church and Labor* (New York: Macmillan Co., 1920), pp. 243-45.]

wealthy and the workingmen are intended by nature to live in mutual conflict" *(Rerum Novarum)*. On the contrary, as Pope Leo adds, "each needs the other: Capital cannot do without Labor, nor Labor without Capital. Religion is a powerful agency in drawing the rich and the bread-winner together, by reminding each class of its duties to the other and especially of the obligation of justice. Religion teaches the laboring man and the artisan to carry out honestly and fairly all equitable agreements freely arranged, to refrain from injuring person or property, from using violence and creating disorder. It teaches the owner and employer that the laborer is not their bondsman, that in every man they must respect his dignity and worth as a man and as a Christian; that labor is not a thing to be ashamed of, if we listen to right reason and to Christian philosophy, but is an honorable calling, enabling a man to sustain his life in a way upright and creditable; and that it is shameful and inhuman to treat men like chattels, as means for making money, or as machines for grinding out work." The moral value of man and the dignity of human labor are cardinal points in this whole question. Let them be the directive principles in industry, and they will go far toward preventing disputes. By treating the laborer first of all as a man, the employer will make him a better workingman; by respecting his own moral dignity as a man, the laborer will compel the respect of his employer and of the community.

Commission on Social Justice, 1928

Jewish immigrants of the late nineteenth century, like Catholic immigrants of a generation or so earlier, often found themselves at the lower rungs of the economic ladder. In such a vulnerable position, they needed no lessons but their own lives to learn of exploitation, uneven distribution of wealth, class conflict, and an economy seemingly divorced from morality. Speaking on behalf of these and other workers, and speaking most of all on behalf of social justice, the Central Conference of American Rabbis (the organizational arm of Reform Judaism; see above, pp. 29-31) drew upon the heritage of ancient Israel to make their case for "applied Judaism."

Deriving our inspiration for social justice from the great teachings of the prophets of Israel and the other great traditions of our faith, and applying these teachings concretely to the economic and social problems of today, we, the Central Conference of American Rabbis, make this declaration of social principles: . . .

[Source: Albert Vorspan and Eugene Lipman, *Justice and Judaism: The Work of Social Action* (New York: Union of American Hebrew Congregations, fourth ed., 1959), pp. 255-57.]

II. The Distribution and Responsibilities of Wealth

We regard those tendencies to be unjust which would make the fundamental goal of industry the exploitation of the material world on the basis of unbridled competition and the unlimited and unrestricted accretion of goods in the hands of a few while millions are in want. Inequalities of wealth can find no moral justification in a society where poverty and want, due to exploitation, exist. We sympathize with measures designed to prevent private monopoly. We regard all ownership as a social trust implying the responsibility of administration for the good of all mankind. We maintain that the unrestrained and unlimited exercise of the right of private ownership without regard for social results is morally untenable.

III. Industrial Democracy

In the production and distribution of the material goods of life, the dictatorship of any class, capital or labor, employer or employee, is alike autocracy. The solution of the ills which beset our social order is to be found not in any class conscious struggle but in the triumph of sound humanitarian principles which regard mankind as ONE. No materialistic philosophy, whether it be exploitation for the many or the few, can solve these problems. It is in a finer industrial democracy that we place our hopes. The worker who invests his life's energies and stakes the welfare of his family in the industry in which he works has inviolable rights along with him who stakes his family's welfare in that industry through the investment of capital.

IV. The Sacredness of the Individual Personality

The mechanization of our present age and the building of large industries employing hundreds and thousands of workers have led to the custom of regarding labor as a mass in which the personality of the individual is lost or is not considered. We who uphold a religious philosophy of life cannot sanction this practice which tends more and more to treat labor as only an instrument. The dignity of the individual soul before God cannot be lost sight of before men. Machinery and industry exist for man and not man for them.

V. The Right of Organization

The same rights of organization which rest with employers rest also with those whom they employ. Modern life has permitted wealth to consolidate itself through organization into corporations. Workers have the same inalienable right to organize according to their own plan for their common good and to bargain collectively with their employers through such honorable means as they may choose.

VI. The Fundamental Rights of Society

Contribution to the common good and not the selfish service of a class is the touchstone of all moral endeavor. A moral order in industry must achieve the betterment of society as a whole above all else. Those who labor, those who lead labor, as well as those who employ labor or invest capital in industry must alike recognize this principle in the exercise of any and all functions, rights and privileges.

Redeeming the Land

Walter Rauschenbusch

One could reform the city or restrain the factory or, on a grander scale, one could think in terms of an entirely new social order. Broad principles, moral or religious principles, might in that event be followed wherever they led. When Rauschenbusch begins the excerpt below by announcing that "Christianity is in its nature revolutionary," it is obvious that to follow his broad principles could upset many. Indeed, the work from which this selection is taken, though written in the 1890s, was not published until 1968. For even if one were to agree that what happened two thousand years ago was a revolution, many would prefer to believe that one Christian revolution was quite enough.

Christianity is in its nature revolutionary. Its revolutionary character is apparent from the spiritual ancestry to which it traces its lineage. Jesus was the successor of the Old Testament prophets. The common people of his day discerned this kinship and whispered that he must be Elijah or Jeremiah or some other of the prophets. (Lk. 9, 19.) Although he denied his identification with them, he

---

[Source: Walter Rauschenbusch, *The Righteousness of the Kingdom* (New York: Abingdon Press, 1968), pp. 70-72.]

himself repeatedly drew the parallel between the work and lot of the prophets and his own. Like the prophets he was rejected in his own country. (Matt. 13, 57.) Like the prophets he was to suffer at the hands of the wicked husbandmen. (Lk. 20, 9-18.) Like all the prophets he must perish at Jerusalem. (Lk. 13, 34-35.) His forerunner he calls a prophet, a second Elijah (Mk. 9, 11-13; Lk. 7, 26); and to his followers he predicts that like the prophets they will be slandered and persecuted (Matt. 5, 10-12), and at last like the prophets meet their death. (Matt. 23, 29-36.)

Now what were these prophets, to whose spirit and purpose Jesus felt so close a kinship, and whose lot he expected to share?

The prophets were the revolutionists of their age. They were dreamers of Utopias. They pictured an ideal state of society in which the poor should be judged with equity and the cry of the oppressed should no longer be heard; a time in which men would beat their idle swords into ploughshares and their

Walter Rauschenbusch (1861-1918)
(Religion News Service)

spears into pruning hooks, for then the nations would learn war no more. (Isa. 2, 4.) No slight amelioration contented them, nothing but a change so radical that they dared to represent it as a repealing of the ancient and hallowed covenant and the construction of a new one. A proposal to abolish the Constitution of the United States would not seem so revolutionary to us as this proposal must have seemed to the contemporaries of the prophets. . . .

Nor were the prophets mere impractical dreamers and declaimers. They were men of action. They overthrew dynasties. They were popular agitators, tribunes of the people. They rebuked to their faces kings who had robbed the plain man of his wife or tricked him out of his ancestral holding.

These were the men whose successor Christ professed to be. This does not imply that he sanctioned all their actions or proposed to copy all their methods. But it does imply that of all the forces in the national history of Israel the prophets were the most worthy of his approval and most akin to his spirit.

The revolutionary character of Christ's work appears also from the elements in contemporary life to which he allied himself.

The Messianic hope, kindled and fanned by the prophets, was still glowing in the hearts of the people. When John the Baptist lifted up his voice by the Jordan, men were on the alert immediately, querying "whether haply he were the Messiah." (Lk. 3, 15.) The atmosphere of Palestine was surcharged with this electricity. When, in the synagogue at Nazareth, Jesus chose for his text that passage of Isaiah which tells of glad tidings to the poor, of release to the captives, of liberty to the bruised, and of the acceptable year of the Lord, "the eyes of all in the synagogue were fastened upon him." The passage was universally understood to refer to the Messianic era. They were breathlessly eager to hear what attitude he would assume. And what was his attitude? He told them the time had now come: "To-day hath this scripture been fulfilled in your ears." (Lk. 4, 16-21.)

It is plain that the people counted him as their own. They were waiting to see him raise the standard of revolt and were ready to follow him as their king. (John 6, 14-15.) And in spite of all apparent disappointments to which he subjected them, they had their eye on him still. When at the very end he entered Jerusalem with something of public state, all their hopes revived and they hailed him as the Messiah coming to claim the Kingdom of his father David. . . .

The contents of the Messianic hope of course varied. With some it was dyed in blood, with others it was irradiated by heaven. But this element was common to all who entertained it: they were weary of present conditions; they were longing for a radically different state of affairs; and they were sure that it would come and were ready to help it on. In other words, the Messianic hope was a revolutionary hope.

Edward McGlynn (1837-1900)

One way to redeem the land, it could be argued, was to ensure that all the people possessed it and derived equal benefit from it. In that way, the enormous disparity between rich and poor would even out. All land for which men compete would be taxed — rented to the highest bidder — and "a magnificent ever-increasing fund to supply the wants of increasing civilization" would in this way be created. Directly influenced by the economic reformer Henry George (1839-97), Father McGlynn of New York City campaigned so vigorously for land reform (and for Henry George) as to be censured for his socialist views. When he refused to report to Rome for a trial, he was excommunicated in 1887. Five years later, however, with some friends interceding on his behalf, he was restored to the Church and to his clerical position. Being returned to the bosom of the Church implied no change of mind or heart in McGlynn's social views. The earth was first of all the Lord's, but after that it belonged equally "to the human family, to the community, to the people, to all the children of God."

It is not for nothing that He who came to save the souls of men did so much to minister to the relief of their bodily wants. He healed their diseases; He raised their dead; He cured their distempers; He bore their sorrows; He felt compassion for the multitude, lest they should faint by the wayside. He miraculously supplemented the laws of nature and fed them with miraculous loaves and fishes in the wilderness. He did all this, because doing it He knew full well that the bodies of men as well as their souls are the creatures of God, and that their bodies and the capacities of those bodies are but signs and symbols of the spiritual things within, even as all the vast universe of God is but His garment, is but the sign and symbol and the thin veil that surrounds Him, through the rifts in which we catch on every hand glimpses of God and of heaven. . . .

This is the word of an apostle of Christ: "This is true religion — to visit the widow and the fatherless in their affliction, and to keep one's self unspotted from the world." So it is necessarily a part of true religion to insist on what is essentially the equality of man, regardless of the comparatively trifling differences in their gifts and acquirements. This is the political economy, the teaching and reducing of which to practice are the core and essence of this new crusade. All men, inalienably, always, everywhere, have a common right to all the general bounties of nature; and this is in perfect and beautiful keeping with the other law of labor that every mouth has two hands with which to feed itself, a neces-

[Source: Aaron I. Abell, ed., *American Catholic Thought on Social Questions* (New York and Indianapolis: Bobbs-Merrill Co., 1968), pp. 166-67, 168-69.]

Child laborers in Indiana Glass Works, Midnight, Indiana
(National Archives and Records Administration)

sary corollary of which is that these hands must have equal direct or indirect access to the general bounties of nature out of which to make a living. That is the whole of the doctrine of this new crusade in a nutshell, that the land as well as the sunlight, and the air, and the waters, and the fishes, and the mines in the bowels of the earth, all these things that were made by the Creator through the beautiful processes of nature, belong equally to the human family, to the community, to the people, to all the children of God. . . .

How are we going to give back to the poor man what belongs to him? How shall we have that beautiful state of things in which naught shall be ill and all shall be well? Simply by confiscating rent and allowing people nominally to own, if you choose, the whole of Manhattan Island, if it will do them any good to nominally own it; but while they have the distinguished satisfaction of seeming to own it we are going to scoop the meat out of the shell and allow them to have the shell. And how are we going to do that? By simply taxing all this land and all kindred bounties of nature to the full amount of their rental value. If there isn't any rental value then there won't be any tax. If there is any rental value then it will be precisely what that value is. If the rental value goes up, up goes the tax. If the rental value comes down, down comes the tax. If the rental value ceases, then the tax ceases. Don't you see? It is as clear as the nose on your face.

Richard T. Ely (1854-1943)

Presbyterian become Episcopalian, Ely found his career in academia as an economist first at Johns Hopkins, then at the University of Wisconsin, and finally at Northwestern. His whole career, however, was infused with a moral intensity and religious concern that would not allow the "science" of economics to be driven only by an impersonal market and a mindless laissez-faire. A righteous social order can be achieved, Ely argued; at least, it can be worked at. But to work at it, one must make decisions, and one must have a sense of direction. And Ely found in his religious understanding the motivating force as well as the purpose. "The mission of the Church is to redeem the world. . . ."

I take this as my thesis: Christianity is primarily concerned with this world, and it is the mission of Christianity to bring to pass here a kingdom of righteousness and to rescue from the evil one and redeem all our social relations.

I believe it a common impression that Christianity is concerned primarily with a future state of existence, and to this unfortunate error I trace an alliance between the Church and the powers of this world which found its exemplification in the alleged conversion of Constantine the Great. The mission of the Church is to redeem the world, and to make peace with it only on its unconditional surrender to Christ. Now, a surrender is one thing, an alliance is another. If peace and harmony prevailed between the powers of the world and the Church because the world had become thoroughly Christian, we would have reason for joy, and joy only. Men, angels, and archangels would then lift up their voices in songs of triumph, and the morning stars would join them all in a glorious chorus.

Unhappily, peace has never been made after this fashion. Whenever an agreement has been reached between the Church and the world, the terms have been a division of territory, as it were, and that on this wise: The world has transferred the domain of dogma and the future life to the Church, but has kept for itself the present life. . . .

But let it never be forgotten that Salvation means infinitely more than the proclamation of glittering generalities and the utterance of sweet sentimentalities. Salvation means righteousness, positive righteousness, in all the earth, and its establishment means hard warfare. The "Church militant" is something more than a phrase, or the Church itself is a mockery. Preaching the gospel means going to men with the words, "Thou, thou, art the man." It means a

[Source: Richard T. Ely, *Social Aspects of Christianity* (New York: Thomas Crowell and Co., 1899), pp. 53, 73-77.]

never-ceasing attack on every wrong institution, until the earth becomes a new earth, and all its cities, cities of God.

It is as truly a religious work to pass good laws, as it is to preach sermons; as holy a work to lead a crusade against filth, vice, and disease in slums of cities, and to seek the abolition of the disgraceful tenement-houses of American cities, as it is to send missionaries to the heathen. Even to hoe potatoes and plant corn ought to be regarded, and must be regarded by true Christians, as religious acts; and all legislators, magistrates, and governors are as truly ministers in God's Church as any bishop or archbishop.

I will now mention, without any attempt at scientific classification, some of the subjects which, it seems to me, ought to be taken up by the Church, — all of them religious subjects: —

1. Child labor — a growing evil — diminishing in other countries, increasing in this, removing children from home at a tender age, ruining them morally, dwarfing them physically and mentally.

2. The labor of women under conditions which imperil the family. . . .

3. Sunday labor, an increasing evil, against which workingmen throughout the length and breadth of the land are crying out bitterly. . . .

4. Playgrounds and other provision for healthful recreation in cities — an antidote to the saloon and other forms of sin.

5. Removal of children from parents who have ceased to perform the duties of parents. Homes, real homes, should be found for these.

6. Public corruption, — about which let us have something precise and definite. The moral iniquity of city councilmen, who accept street-car passes, of writers for the press, of legislators and judges, who accept railroad passes, might profitably be treated under this head.

7. Saturday half-holidays, — a great moral reform which has been accomplished in England, where men work but fifty-four hours a week. . . .

8. A juster distribution of wealth. Under this head a refutation of those ridiculous persons who would have us believe that wage-earners now receive nine-tenths of all the wealth produced — quackery and jugglery which must delight Satan.

9. A manly contest against the deadly optimism of the day which aims to retard improvement and to blind men to actual dangers. After careful thought and observation, I believe the social consequences of optimism even more disastrous than those of pessimism, though both are bad enough. Less spread-eagleism in America, more repentance for national sins, *e.g.* the most corrupt city governments to be found in the civilized world.

George D. Herron (1862-1925)

*Like Ely, Herron also labored in academia, but with less conspicuous success.
At his post in Iowa (Grinnell College), Herron even held a chair in "applied
Christianity," the very title indicating the temper of much American religion
determined to engage the social problems. Herron joined the Socialist Party
around the turn of the century and embraced Christian socialism with such
unbending vigor that he alienated many and diminished his influence as organizer and leader. As a writer, however, he effectively argued against a "competitive individualism" that lacked both rational order and moral purpose.*

There is but one deliverance from the rule of the people by property, and that is
the rule of property by the people. If much of what has been considered private
property is to be absorbed in great monopolistic ownership, as seems to be the
inevitable outcome of the competitive struggle, then the people should become
the monopolists. The whole movement of modern industrial organization has
been toward monopoly, and the movement will become more rapid, comprehensive, and powerful as present social tendencies increase. The only hope of
the people for either industrial or political freedom lies in their taking lawful
possession of the machinery, forces, and production of great industrial monopolies. Through the instrumentality of the state the people, constituted in the realized democracy of a social commonwealth, could organize their social economy in justice, that would insure work and bread for all who would work, as
well as make common to all many social benefits now exclusively enjoyed by the
privileged few; and would find some service that would give a measure of profit
and hope to even the weakest. So organized, the state as the social organ of the
people would furnish and compel work that would be redemptive to many now
given over as worthless by our unsocial order of selfish and competitive individualism. . . .

The Christian collectivist would take away no liberty from the individual
that would not be returned to him a hundred-fold in the liberty which association would give. The Christian economic state would take away the liberty to
oppress and defraud, but give the liberty to work, to have faith, and to do justice. The real property rights of the people, the preservation of the home, and
the perpetuity of the family, have their future dependence in the association of
rights under the guardianship of the state as the social organ of a Christian democracy. Such a mutual surrender and investiture of rights, instead of endan-
gering the individual and the family, would be the freedom of the individual to

[Source: George D. Herron, *The Christian State: A Political Vision of Christ* (New York:
Thomas Y. Crowell and Co., 1895), pp. 102-3, 106-7.]

develop the highest personal life, and the security of the family from the invasion of want and oppression. The collection of rights and interests in the state as the organ of the Christian economy of the people, would remove life from the sphere of chance to that of a moral social certainty, and give opportunity for that free individual development which is the true end of civilization.

John A. Ryan (1869-1945)

For herculean effort on behalf of Catholic social action, the long and busy career of Monsignor John Ryan is impossible to match. Preparing himself carefully in economic and ethical theory, Ryan published his first book in 1906: A Living Wage. *A decade later, a second book entitled* Distributive Justice *urged fundamental reforms in the national economic structure, while a third book (*Social Reconstruction, *1920) helped give leadership and voice to the wider Catholic community. When President Franklin D. Roosevelt proposed sweeping social reforms in the 1930s, Ryan — who for thirty years had been arguing along similar lines — joined in with enthusiasm. "The Right Reverend New Dealer," as one biographer called him, saw the Church as responsible for "the whole field of human action," all of which is under moral law. And "moral law is the business of the Church."*

The mission of the Church is to teach and help men to save their souls, to make men fit for the Kingdom of Heaven. They save their souls not alone by faith (the Protestant notion) but by works, by conduct. They must not only believe correctly but live righteously. Now righteous living takes in the whole field of human action. It is not confined to those of man's actions which affect merely himself and his God, nor to those which relate to his family. It concerns those actions which have an economic character, such as, theft, fraud, extortion, slothful performance of labor, oppression of the laborer, violence against property, etc., etc. In a word, all free human actions, whether without or within the field of industry, come under the control of the moral law; and the teaching and application of the moral law is the business of the Church. The notion that business actions and business relations are somehow an exempt territory, free from regulation by the moral law, neither morally good nor morally bad, is a heritage partly from the Protestant Reformation, partly from the false liberalism of the early English economists, and partly from the commercialized ethical code which came into practice owing to the failure of the state or any other

---

[Source: John A. Ryan, *Declining Liberty and Other Papers* (Freeport, New York: Books for Libraries Press, 1968 [1927]), pp. 181-83.]

Monsignor John A. Ryan (1869-1945) of the National Catholic Welfare Council
(Library of Congress)

powerful social authority to apply and enforce the principles of justice in the province of industry. It never has been and never can be the Catholic doctrine.

Having reasserted the Catholic doctrine and reasoning about the authority of the Church over industrial and business relations, let us see whether there is anything at all that can be said for the viewpoint expressed by our Catholic business man. To answer this question it will be helpful to distinguish between *principles* and *methods*.

The Pope and the Bishops have authority to lay down the moral *principles* which govern industrial relations. Under this head come Pope Leo's declarations concerning the right of labor to a living wage, the duty of labor to perform a fair day's work, the duty of employers to refrain from overburdening their employees, the right of the State to intervene in the affairs of industry whenever there exist no other means of remedying great abuses, and a host of other specific pronouncements. All these are merely applications of general moral principles to particular economic conditions.

It is conceivable that the Pope and the Bishops should go further, and pronounce judgment upon particular *methods* by which the particular moral principles may be or might be made operative. For example, Pope Leo XIII passed judgment upon and against Socialism as a method of effectuating the principles of justice in the industrial order. Incidentally, one is tempted to observe that the condemnation of Socialism, whether by Pope, Bishop, or priest, is never complained of by Catholic business men as an improper interference in matters of business. However, let that pass. The Pope might declare that a minimum wage law would or would not be a morally lawful method of making effective the doctrine of a living wage. As a matter of fact, no Pope has made any declaration on this subject, but such a declaration would be an entirely proper exercise of the Pope's authority to apply the general principles of morality to particular industrial situations.

There is a further step which may be taken by the authorities of the Church in their dealing with the moral problems of industry. It consists in not merely pronouncing certain concrete methods morally lawful, but in advocating the adoption of such methods. Pope Leo's great encyclical, "On the Condition of Labor," contains a good number of such specific recommendations; for example, concerning the multiplication of property owners by the State; the means by which the State should prevent strikes, the various kinds of associations that ought to be formed by workers and employers, etc., etc. In their "Program of Social Reconstruction" the Bishops who constituted the Administrative Committee of the National Catholic War Council, advocated many specific measures, such as the legal minimum wage, labor participation in management, and so on.

These, then, are the three principal ways in which the authorities of the Church may properly make pronouncements concerning business and industrial relations: by applying the general principles of morality to particular economic practices; by passing judgment upon the morality of particular methods or measures of reform, and by advocating and urging the adoption of certain methods and measures. All the great encyclicals and other declarations of the Popes on the social question exemplify all three of these forms of "Intervention."

2. War and Peace

Ploughshares to Swords: World War I

"To Love Is to Hate"

War divides not only the opposing armies, but also the respective civilian populations. Just as national motivations in the decision to go to war are inevitably mixed, so individuals support or oppose in varying degrees and for varying reasons their country's choice. World War I began for Europe in 1914, for America in 1917. Some religious leaders made every effort to keep the nation out of war, while others saw the nation as the world's enforcer of approved moral ends. Two spokesmen support the war effort: (1) Lyman Abbott once again in his editorial pages of Outlook, *and (2) N. D. Hillis (1858-1929), pastor of Henry Ward Beecher's famous church in Brooklyn, who goes further than Abbott in stirring up mankind's darker passions.*

1. "To Love Is to Hate"

Does not Christ command us to love our enemies? Yes. But he nowhere commands us to love God's enemies or those who treat his children with malignant cruelty.

"I hate every false way."

"I hate vain thoughts."

"I hate and abhor lying."

[Sources: (1) Lyman Abbott, *Outlook,* 19 (May 15, 1918), 99. (2) N. D. Hillis, *The Blot on the Kaiser's Scutcheon* (New York: Fleming H. Revell Co., 1918), pp. 56-57, 58-59.]

"The fear of Jehovah is to hate evil."

"Let none of you desire evil in your hearts against your neighbor; and love no false thing; for all these things do I hate."

Have these human experiences recorded in the Old Testament been abolished by the New Testament? No; Jesus Christ looked with infinite pity upon men and women who were the victims of vicious parentage, false education, or their own baser natures — who were their own enemies. But his life affords an excellent illustration of such sayings of the ancient prophets as "I, Jehovah, love justice; I hate robbery with iniquity." Literature, ancient and modern, sacred and secular, will be searched in vain to find a more awful expression of wrath against the deliberate and purposed oppression by man of his fellow-men than is furnished in the invective poured out by Jesus against the Pharisees:

> Woe unto you, scribes and Pharisees, hypocrites! for ye tithe mint and anise and cummin, and have left undone the weightier matters of the law, justice, and mercy, and faith: but these ye ought to have done, and not to have left the other undone. Ye blind guides, that strain out the gnat, and swallow the camel.
>
> Woe unto you, scribes and Pharisees, hypocrites! for ye cleanse the outside of the cup and of the platter, but within they are full from extortion and excess. Thou blind Pharisee, cleanse first the inside of the cup and of the platter, that the outside thereof may become clean also.
>
> Woe unto you, scribes and Pharisees, hypocrites! for ye are like unto whited sepulchers, which outwardly appear beautiful, but inwardly are full of dead men's bones, and of all uncleanness. Even so ye also outwardly appear righteous unto men, but inwardly ye are full of hypocrisy and iniquity.
>
> Woe unto you, scribes and Pharisees, hypocrites! for ye build the sepulchers of the prophets, and garnish the tombs of the righteous, and say, If we had been in the days of our fathers, we should not have been partakers with them in the blood of the prophets. Wherefore ye witness to yourselves, that ye are sons of them that slew the prophets. Fill ye up then the measure of your fathers. Ye serpents, ye offspring of vipers, how shall ye escape the judgment of hell?

I do not hate the Predatory Potsdam Gang because it is my enemy. I do not hate it for any evil which it has done to me. I hate it for what it has done to my defenseless neighbor across the sea. I hate it for what it is. I hate it because it is a robber, a murderer, a destroyer of homes, a pillager of churches, a violator of women. I do well to hate it. Dr. Fosdick[1] says, "We know, when we think of it, that had we been born in Germany, there is not one chance in a million that we

---

1. Dr. Harry Emerson Fosdick; see below, pp. 128, 130-31.

would be doing other than the Germans do." If I could believe this true, I should be other than I am. If I could believe that such lust and cruelty were possible in me, being what I am, I should hate myself with a bitter hatred.

2. Must German Men Be Exterminated?

A singular revulsion of sentiment as to what must be done with the German army after the war, is now sweeping over the civilized world. Men who once were pacifists, men of chivalry and kindness, men whose life has been devoted to philanthropy and reform, scholars and statesmen, whose very atmosphere is compassion and magnanimity towards the poor and weak, are now uttering sentiments that four years ago would have been astounding beyond compare. These men feel that there is no longer any room in the world for the German. Society has organized itself against the rattlesnake and the yellow fever. Shepherds have entered into a conspiracy to exterminate the wolves. The Boards of Health are planning to wipe out typhoid, cholera and the Black Plague. Not otherwise, lovers of their fellow man have finally become perfectly hopeless with reference to the German people. They have no more relations to the civilization of 1918 than an orang-outang, a gorilla, a Judas, a hyena, a thumbscrew, a scalping knife in the hands of a savage. These brutes must be cast out of society.

Some of us, hoping against hope, after the reluctant confession of the truth of the German atrocities, have appealed to education. We knew that Tacitus said, nearly two thousand years ago, that "the German treats women with cruelty, tortures his enemies, and associates kindness with weakness." But nineteen centuries of education have not changed the German one whit. The mere catalogue of the crimes committed by German officers and soldiers and set forth in more than twenty volumes of proofs destroys the last vestige of hope for their future. . . .

The sense of hopelessness as to civilizing the German and keeping him as an element in the new society grew out of the breakdown of education and science in changing the German of the time of Tacitus. Plainly the time has come to make full confession of the fact that education can change the size but not the sort. The German in the time of Tacitus was ignorant when he took the children of his enemy and dashed their brains out against the wall; the German of 1914 and 1918 still butchers children, the only difference being that the butchery is now more efficient and better calculated, through scientific cruelty, to stir horror and spread frightfulness. The leopard has not changed its spots. The rattlesnake is larger and has more poison in the sac; the German wolf has increased in size, and where once he tore the throat of two sheep, now he can rend ten lambs in half the time. In utter despair, therefore, statesmen, generals, diplomats, editors are now talking about the duty of simply exterminating the German people.

The Madness of Men

As strong counterpoint to the jingoism of Abbott and Hillis, other clerical voices condemned war, or urged great caution before plunging into war, or exposed the hideous, thoroughly de-romanticized side of war. (1) John Haynes Holmes (1879-1964), New York City Unitarian minister of wide impact, in 1915 denounced war "universally and unconditionally." (2) His good friend, Rabbi Stephen Wise (1874-1949), also of New York City, wrote to President Woodrow Wilson late in 1915 to express his dismay that the country seemed to be preparing for war. (3) Still another New York voice, that of Harry Emerson Fosdick (1878-1969), professor at Union Theological Seminary at this time, was lifted in 1917 against war; those who call it glorious are "mad." All three men, moreover, joined in various peace-making efforts and organizations.

1.
Is War Ever Justifiable?

From every point of view — from the standpoint of things spiritual as well as of things material, from the standpoint of the future as well as of the present — war is the antithesis of life. Its one end is to destroy what has been builded up through many years by the sweat and tears of men. Its one aim is to kill the lives which men have conceived in joy, women borne in agony, and both together reared in love. Its one supreme triumph is to turn a busy factory into a pile of wreckage, a fertile field into a desert, a home of joy into an ash-heap of sorrow, a living soul into a rotting carcass. Why, if war could once be carried through to its logical conclusions — if there were not a limit to all strength, and a point of exhaustion for every passion — mankind would long since have annihilated itself and this planet become as tenantless as the silent moon! And yet there are some — yea, there are many! — who are ready to assert that this foul business is sometimes and somewheres justifiable. This I deny without qualification or evasion of any kind. War is never justifiable at any time or under any circumstances. No man is wise enough, no nation is important enough, no human interest is precious enough, to justify the wholesale destruction and murder which constitute the essence of war. Human life is alone sacred. The interests of human life are alone sovereign. War, as we have now

[Sources: (1) J. H. Holmes, *A Summons Unto All Men . . .* (New York: Simon and Schuster, 1970), p. 116. (2) Carl H. Voss, ed., *Stephen Wise: Servant of the People* (Philadelphia: Jewish Publication Society of America, 1969), p. 68. (3) H. E. Fosdick, *The Challenge of the Present Crisis* (London: Student Christian Movement, [1917]), pp. 59-62.]

seen, is the enemy of life and all its interests. Therefore, in the name of life and for the sake of life, do I declare to you that war must be condemned universally and unconditionally.

2.

November 12, 1915

To The President, The White House, Washington

From time to time during the last two years, it has been my privilege to write to you in order to express my agreement with the things you have said and done. I therefore regard it as my duty to tell you how deeply I deplore the necessity under which you have found yourself of accepting and advocating a preparedness program. . . .

It is occasion for profound regret to some of us that you have seen fit at this time to urge that so-called defensive preparedness, which at other times and in other hands than your own is not unlikely to be used in the interests of aggression. You will pardon my pointing out that your program, moderate

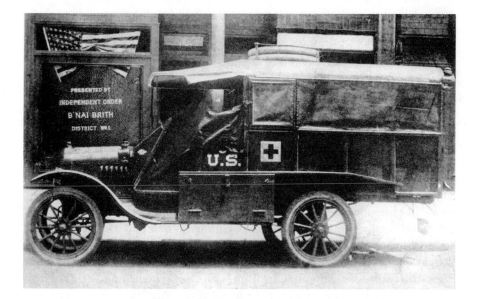

Red Cross ambulance in World War I, donated by B'nai B'rith
(B'nai B'rith, Washington, D.C.)

though you believe it to be, will not and of necessity cannot satisfy those advocates of military preparedness who will for a time purport to assent to preparedness measures.

I should not, my dear Mr. President, have written in this way nor would I burden you with my thought on this question if I did not feel in conscience bound to dissent in pulpit and on platform from your position. I regret this not only on personal grounds but because I believe that issues of deepest moment are at stake touching which you will not expect even the most revering of friends should remain silent.

3.

One who knows what really is happening on European battlefields to-day and calls war glorious is morally unsound. Says an eye-witness: "Last night, at an officers' mess there was great laughter at the story of one of our men who had spent his last cartridge in defending an attack. 'Hand me down your spade, Mike,' he said; and as six Germans came one by one round the end of a traverse, he split each man's skull open with a deadly blow." That is war. Says a Young Men's Christian Association secretary: "Many times these fingers have reached through the skulls of wounded men and felt their throbbing brains." That is war. An officer's letter from the front reads:

> An enemy mine exploded here a few days ago and buried our brigade. Many of the men were killed, but some were not much hurt; so we dug them out and used them over again.

Sons of God and brothers of Jesus Christ — "dug them out and used them over again"! That is war. Said a group of German prisoners, as they bared their gashed forearms, "We were dying with thirst, we had our choice of doing what some men do in such case — drink the blood of an enemy, or else drink our own. We are Christians: so we cut our own arms to get drink." That is war. War is not the gay colour, the rhythmic movement, the thrilling music of the military parade. War is not even killing gallantly as knights once did, matched evenly in armour and in steel and fighting by the rules of chivalry. War now is dropping bombs from aeroplanes and killing women and children in their beds; it is shooting, by telephonic orders, at an unseen place miles away and slaughtering invisible men; it is murdering innocent travellers on merchant ships with torpedoes from unknown submarines; it is launching clouds of poisoned gas and slaying men with their own breath. War means lying days and nights wounded and alone in No-Man's Land; it means men with jaws gone, eyes gone, limbs gone, minds gone; it means countless bodies of boys tossed into the incinerators that follow in the train of every battle; it means prison camps vicious with the inevitable results of enforced idleness; it means untended wounds and gangrene and the long time it takes to die; it means mothers who look for letters they will never see, and wives who wait for voices they will never hear, and children who listen for footsteps that will never come. That is war — "its heroisms are but the glancing sunlight on a sea of blood and tears" — and a man who calls it glorious is mad.

"The Lessons of War"

America's first World War formally ended on November 11, 1918. The time for evaluation then began: what did it achieve? what did it mean? what lessons are to be drawn from it? (1) The nation's Catholic bishops, in addressing themselves to "the lessons of war" in 1919, acknowledged the moral evil inherent in all war. (2) Presbyterian Robert E. Speer (1867-1947), missionary executive for over forty years, drew more positive lessons in 1919, seeing the war in essentially moral terms and its idealism as essentially unsullied.

1.

In order that our undertakings may be wisely selected and prudently carried on, we should consider seriously the lessons of the War, the nature of our present situation and the principles which must guide the adjustment of all our relations.

Our estimate of the War begins, naturally, with the obvious facts: with the number of peoples involved, the vastness and effectiveness of their armaments, the outlay in treasure and toil, the destruction of life and the consequent desolation which still lies heavy on the nations of Europe. Besides these visible aspects, we know somewhat of the spiritual suffering — of the sorrow and hopelessness which have stricken the souls of men. And deeper than these, beyond our power of estimation, is the moral evil, the wrong whose magnitude only the Searcher of hearts can determine.

For we may not forget that in all this strife of the peoples, in the loosening of passion and the seeking of hate, sin abounded. Not the rights of man alone but the law of God was openly disregarded. And if we come before Him now in thankfulness, we must come with contrite hearts, in all humility beseeching Him that He continue His mercies toward us, and enable us so to order our human re-

---

[Sources: (1) Peter Guilday, ed., *The National Pastorals of the American Hierarchy, 1792-1919* (Westminster, Md.: Newman Press, 1954), p. 297. (2) R. E. Speer, *The New Opportunity of The Church* (New York: Macmillan Co., 1919), pp. 48-49.]

lations that we may atone for our past transgressions and strengthen the bond of peace with a deeper charity for our fellowmen and purer devotion to His service.

2.

I venture to say again, accordingly, what was said at the outset of this chapter, that the war has clarified and confirmed our fundamental religious ideas and revealed the power of their appeal to the present day mind. The war also has unmistakably set in the supreme place those moral and spiritual principles which constitute the message of the Church. It has revealed the responsiveness of men to the essential ethical ideals of Christianity. Christianity proclaims that moral and spiritual values are absolute and dominant. Much of our modern teaching denied this. The war has affirmed it. It has shown that these values are supreme over personal loss and material interest. Fathers and mothers have given up their only sons to die for a cause. Soldiers have served in the war for pay so small as to be negligible. Thousands of men have served for nothing. More than that, they have made untold sacrifices. In the case of Belgium we have seen a nation give up its material interests utterly and lay the very body of its national existence upon the altar. For four years it was a national soul without a body or a home. The war itself in its essence was a moral not a material struggle and it was moral ideas which prevailed. The very materialism of the struggle was marked by the idealism of self denial. It avowed itself as nothing but the vehicle and weapon of a righteous purpose and a human hope. What is idealism but the belief in the possibility of the best, a confidence in the good faith of all who love liberty and are ready to die for it, the brotherly trust of the democratic principle? We succeeded in the war whenever and wherever this was our spirit and elsewhere and always we failed and will fail. The war says that what Christ said is forever true.

Peace and Disarmament

Church Peace Union

Once the guns of World War I were silent, a great many religious leaders in America expressed their strong reservations about war as a proper instru-

---

[Source: Charles S. Macfarland, *Pioneers for Peace Through Religion* (New York: Fleming H. Revell Co., 1946), pp. 21-23.]

ment of national policy. In the 1920s and 1930s pacifist sentiment spread far beyond the small, traditionally antiwar churches to include a far broader spectrum of American religion. Pacifism was respectable; peace-making was popular. Indeed, a thoroughly establishment figure, Andrew Carnegie (1835-1919), who made his enormous fortune in steel, dedicated a sizable segment of that fortune to the search for peace. Among his many spectacular philanthropies were the Carnegie Endowment for International Peace (1910) and the Church Peace Union (1914). The latter organization, consisting of Protestant, Catholic, and Jewish leaders, became the principal voice of institutional religion on behalf of peace-seeking and peace-making. What follows are Carnegie's welcoming words to those who came to his home in New York City on the afternoon of February 10, 1914, to join in the creation of this Union; his words reveal, among other things, his extraordinarily high hope that peace would indeed break out around the world, enabling the endowment monies then to be used for other purposes.

In greeting his guests, Mr. Carnegie said: "We meet today under wholly exceptional conditions, for never in the history of man has such a body assembled for such a purpose; no less than twelve of the chief religious bodies of the civilized world being here represented by their prominent official leaders . . . to cooperate as one body in the holy task of abolishing war." "Yours," concluded Mr. Carnegie, "is a 'divine mission.' You are making history."

After the meeting had organized itself as "The Church Peace Union (Founded by Andrew Carnegie)," Mr. Carnegie resumed:

"Gentlemen of many religious bodies all irrevocably opposed to war and devoted advocates of peace, we all feel, I believe, that the killing of man by man in battle is barbaric and negatives our claim to civilization. This crime we wish to banish from the earth; some progress has already been made in this direction, but recently men have shed more of their fellows' blood than for years previously. We need to be aroused to our duty and banish war.

"Certain that the strongest appeal that can be made is to members of the religious bodies, to you I hereby appeal, hoping that you will feel it to be not only your duty but your pleasure to undertake the administration of Two Millions of Dollars in five per cent bonds, the income to be used as in your judgment will most successfully appeal to the people in the cause of peace through arbitration of international disputes; that as man in civilized lands is compelled by law to submit personal disputes to courts of law or through other channels, this trust shall have fulfilled its mission.

"After the arbitration of international disputes is established and war abolished, as it certainly will be some day, and that sooner than expected, probably by the Teutonic nations, Germany, Britain and the United States first deciding to act in unison, other powers joining later, the trustees will divert the revenues of this fund to relieve the deserving poor and afflicted in their distress, especially those who have struggled long and earnestly against misfortune and have not themselves to blame for their poverty. Members of the various churches will naturally know such members well, and can therefore the better judge, but this does not debar them from going beyond membership when that is necessary or desirable. As a general rule, it is best to help those who help themselves, but there are unfortunates from whom this cannot be expected.

"After war is abolished by the leading nations, the trustees by a vote of two-thirds may decide that a better use for the funds than that named in the preceding paragraph has been found and are free according to their own judgment to devote the income to the best advantage for the good of their fellowmen.

"I am happy in the belief that the civilized world will not, cannot, long tolerate the killing of man by man as a means of settling its international disputes, and that civilized men will not, cannot long enter a profession which binds them to go forth and kill their fellowmen as ordered, although they will continue to defend their homes if attacked, as a duty, which also involves the duty of never attacking homes of others."

Mr. Carnegie was gracious and full of humor in the reception of his guests, but impressive in the earnestness with which he gave expression to his faith and hope.

Such was the birth of The Church Peace Union. It was the first occasion on which any substantial funds had been made available for a peace movement by an organized religious body and it was also the first peace society to unite official and representative members of the three major faiths in that capacity. From this time on The Church Peace Union became the hub about which revolved a world-wide movement.

Kirby Page and the Churches

As the sentiment for peace spread ever more widely throughout American society, minister after minister, church after church, lined up to issue a renunciation of war. War was "utterly destructive," entirely "nefarious," hopelessly "archaic," and totally "incompatible with the teaching and example of our Lord Jesus Christ." A Disciples of Christ minister, Kirby Page (1890-1957), proved a most effective and vigorous leader in rallying the churches behind the cause for peace. Peace was his passion, a passion manifest in hundreds of lectures and magazine articles (he even edited the important pacifist organ, The World Tomorrow, *from 1926 to 1934) and more than two dozen books*

[Source: Kirby Page, *Must We Go to War?* (New York: Farrar & Rinehart, 1937), pp. 182-86.]

whose impact reached far beyond the borders of the United States. In the excerpt below, we hear not only his voice but also, along with it, many voices from the nation's households of faith.

Should followers of a religion based on reverence for every person and recognition of kinship of all peoples seek justice and security by resorting to planned devastation of extensive territories and organized slaughter of men, women and children indiscriminately? Should they endeavor to starve entire populations and to burn whole cities? Should they deal in falsehood and devote themselves to the engendering of hatred and fury?

If premeditated and deliberate planning to perpetrate the countless atrocities of war is not a flagrant violation of Jesus' way of life, then no method of resisting aggression and tyranny can be contrary to that way. To say that the method of war may be consistent with his teaching and example is to say that he could consistently have joined the zealots and taken up arms against the invading Romans. But surely it is indisputable that if he had resorted to the sword against tyranny he would not now be revered as the noblest of all religious leaders. He could not have manifested active goodwill toward the Romans by plunging a dagger to their hearts. He could not have set an example of forgiveness seventy times seven by calling upon his fellow countrymen to massacre the Romans. The way of Jesus and the method of war stand in utter opposition to one another. We can choose the road of atrocity or the way of the cross, but we cannot at the same time travel both highways since they lead in opposite directions. War with its atrocities is irreconcilable with the religion of Jesus and this incontestable truth has been widely proclaimed by numerous religious bodies:

The General Conference of the Methodist Episcopal Church in 1936 said officially: "War as we now know it is utterly destructive. It is the greatest social sin of modern times; a denial of the ideals of Christ, a violation of human personality and a threat to civilization. Therefore, we declare that the Methodist Episcopal Church as an institution does not endorse, support or purpose to participate in war. . . . We therefore petition the government of the United States to grant to members of the Methodist Episcopal Church, who may be conscientious objectors to war, the same exemption from military service as has long been granted to members of the Society of Friends and similar religious organizations."

The College of Bishops of the Methodist Episcopal Church, South, in 1935 issued an official statement on war: "We shall hold in contempt this entire nefarious war business. War as a method of settling international disputes has not one single defensible argument in its behalf. We reiterate what we said a year ago to the General Conference: 'It is archaic, belongs to the jungle period of human development and should be branded as an iniquitous and inhuman procedure. . . . It is an unhallowed thing utterly contrary to the genius of Christianity.' . . . We shall teach our children and youth to despise the unclean thing and to swear eternal loyalty to the ways of peace and to the sacred honor of their brother man."

The General Convention of the Protestant Episcopal Church said: "As stated by the last Lambeth Conference: 'War, as a method of settling international disputes, is incompatible with the teaching and example of our Lord Jesus Christ. We believe that as the Christian conscience has condemned infanticide and slavery and torture, it is now called to condemn war as an outrage on the fatherhood of God and the brotherhood of all mankind.'" In a Pastoral Letter issued by the House of Bishops of the Protestant Episcopal Church the statement is made that "war is murder on a colossal scale. . . . The Christian Church cannot and will not deny loyalty and fealty to its Lord by being partner in any scheme, national or international, that contemplates the wholesale destruction of human life." The Northern Baptist Convention went on record: "War is the supreme social sin, and so long as the war system is maintained there can be no safety for our homes or for our civilization and no realization of the kingdom of heaven on earth." The Synod of the Reformed Presbyterian Church declared: "War is essentially and inherently a supreme violation of the teachings and spirit of Jesus . . . as a method for securing national ends, however just and right, [it] is antichristian."

The International Convention of the Disciples of Christ said: "We believe that war is pagan, futile, and destructive of the spiritual values for which the churches of Christ stand . . . we therefore dissociate ourselves from war and the war system, and hereby serve notice to whom it may concern that we never again expect to bless or sanction war." The Universalist Convention of California resolved: "That the Universalist principles of the Fatherhood of God and the Brotherhood of Man cannot be reconciled with the deliberate taking of life in war. That, since our country has renounced all war, we urge our people to adopt the historical position of the Friends, and take the attitude of conscientious objection to all war. That the faith of the Universalist Church should be recognized by all governmental agencies in the same way as they accept the belief of the Society of Friends."

The General Council of Congregational and Christian Churches thus went on record: "The cleavage between the way of Jesus and the system of war is clear. We of this council are convinced that we must now make this declaration, 'The church is through with war!' We of this council call upon the people of our churches to renounce war and all its works and ways and to refuse to support, sanction or bless it." The 1934 General Assembly of the Presbyterian Church in the U.S.A. "declares anew its break with the entire war system. . . . Christians cannot give their support to war as a method of carrying on international conflict." The Southern Presbyterian Church asserts that "the church should never again bless a war, or be used as an instrument in the promotion of war."

A *Manifesto Against War* was released on Armistice Day, 1934, under the auspices of the Church Peace Union. This forthright declaration was signed by more than 200 outstanding citizens of the United States, *including 60 bishops and 45 college presidents*. Here is a quotation from this pronouncement: "The time has come when organized religion must proclaim that never again shall war be waged under the sanction of the Church. . . . With the ruins of the last war piled high at its feet the Church should solemnly declare herself the implacable enemy of war . . . We have had in our generation an appalling revelation of the true nature of war. War is not what it was. When science added the airplane, the submarine and poison gas, warfare entered on a new stage. With the advent of poison gas and bacteriological germs it laid aside the last vestige of decency. War has always been bloody and brutal. It is now an atrocity. . . . War is as futile as it is barbarous. . . . There is no victor. All are defeated. . . . Modern war is suicide. The sword is so sharp that a nation can cut not only the throats of its neighbors but its own throat also. Civilization itself is in jeopardy."

The Ohio State Pastors' Conference asserted: "We are convinced that war is un-Christian, futile, and suicidal, and we renounce completely the whole war system. We will never again sanction or participate in any war. We will not use our pulpits or classrooms as recruiting stations. We set ourselves to educate and lead youth in the principles and practice of goodwill, justice, understanding, brotherhood, and peace. We will not give our financial or moral support to any war." The National Study Conference on the Churches and World Peace declared: "War denies the fatherhood of God, scorns the brotherhood of man, mocks the sacredness of human life, is merciless to helpless women and children, uses falsehood, ignores justice, releases the passions, and cultivates hate. War means everything that Jesus did not mean, and means nothing that he did mean. We therefore hold that the Churches should condemn resort to the war-system as sin and should henceforth refuse, as Institutions, to sanction it or to be used as agencies in its support." While the Commission on International Justice and Goodwill of the Federal Council of the Churches of Christ in America said bluntly: "The war system of the nations is the outstanding evil of present-day civilization. It is the most ominous antichristian phase of modern life."

Out of 20,870 clergymen who in 1934 replied to a questionnaire, 12,904 said "yes" to this question: "Are you personally prepared to state that it is your present purpose not to sanction any future war or participate as an armed combatant?" While 13,997 answered affirmatively: "Do you believe that the churches of America should now go on record as refusing to sanction or support any future war?"

Frank Buchman and Moral Re-Armament

One of the more intriguing religious developments of the 1920s and 1930s was
associated with the name of Frank Buchman (1878-1961). A Lutheran minis-
ter and sometime YMCA worker, Buchman was a revivalist — but with a
difference. Avoiding the large mass meetings and crowded tents, Buchman
preferred the intimate "house parties" where young men and women gath-
ered for prayer, Bible study, and group confession. Because of his unofficial
association with Oxford University in the early 1920s, Buchman and his fol-
lowers took the name of the "Oxford Group Movement." Gradually, however,
the energetic and visionary Buchman, growing more interested in world af-
fairs and world peace, took his message to the opinion makers and political
leaders of the nations. In 1938 he called for a worldwide spiritual mobiliza-
tion, a "Moral Re-Armament." Riding the crest of pervading pacifist desires,
the movement attracted much attention for a time, only to be drowned out
by the mighty engines of World War II. (1) The first excerpt, written by
Henry P. Van Dusen (1897-1975), long-time professor and president of Union
Theological Seminary in New York City, offers an evaluation of the Oxford
Group as of 1934. (2) In 1938 Frank Buchman issued his call for Moral Re-
Armament.

1.

It is always with the utmost hesitancy that I attempt to describe and appraise
the Oxford Group Movement. This is not at all because the facts are difficult to
ascertain and report. On the contrary, anyone passingly familiar with the history of religion who has watched this Movement's extraordinary advance over
the past ten years can readily detail its principal features and its underlying assumptions, and suggest their parallels in earlier phenomena of religion. But the
most faithful recountal of the facts must fail lamentably to convey a true impression of the Movement's extraordinary character and power to one who has
not felt its temper personally. And any estimate of its significance, however
honest, will be finally determined by the presuppositions which the appraiser
brings to his inquiry.

The protagonists of the Groups are quite right in their contention that
the inquirer may come into an adequate understanding of them in only one

[Sources: (1) H. P. Van Dusen, "The Oxford Group Movement," *Atlantic Monthly*, 154, no. 2
(Aug., 1934), 240-41. (2) Frank Buchman, *Remaking the World* (London: Blandford Press, 1961
[1947]), pp. 45-46, 47-48.]

way — by intimate acquaintance with their life from within. And they would be further justified in contending that, after such acquaintance, one's final attitude will largely reflect prior value-judgments on such basic issues as these: the inner character of true religion, the needs of the human soul, the state of religion in our day, the malaise of civilization and the possibilities for its cure — and what short-comings may be forgiven in a spiritual strategy of searching criticism and overwhelming vitality. This Movement thrusts itself upon us with a radical and drastic critique of the unchallenged assumptions of most of the readers of these words; not until its critique has been squarely faced is one entitled to give a verdict concerning the Movement.

Thus is suggested the first affirmation about the Oxford Group Movement which I should like to underscore. Any facile and categorical judgment of its importance, whether favorable or unfavorable, is to be dismissed at once as superficial and misleading. Much current comment is either extravagantly laudatory or sharply contemptuous. Neither attitude is sound. The plain truth is that there is probably no spiritual force in the world to-day which is bringing to the lives of hundreds such light and power and freedom and happiness and spiritual certainty — gifts quite beyond the measurement of any human calculus. And there is no contemporary religious movement of similar proportions which, in the judgment of many wise and consecrated persons, is so freighted with danger, self-deception, and even perversion of authentic Christian experience. Just when one has determined to dismiss it from consideration because of its excesses or its perils or its self-righteousness, one is confronted with a concrete instance of the liberation and empowerment of a defeated and despairing soul, like as not someone within one's own acquaintance. Criticism is silenced, gratitude wells spontaneously, one wonders whether even friendly questioning of so magnificent a work can be justified. Just when one is moved to lend cordial support, one meets an example of bumptious impertinence or pitiable pharisaism or tragic mishandling of a human personality so flagrant that the most tolerant sympathy cannot forgive. Doubts return, sympathy shrivels, one questions whether even qualified approval of the Movement can honestly be given. Clearly we are here face to face with something which eludes easy generalization.

In brief, the Oxford Group Movement is the most baffling religious phenomenon of our time. Nor is this a personal opinion only. Many of the foremost leaders of the Church on both sides of the Atlantic have, in personal conversation, voiced their bewilderment. Never have they encountered a movement which so defied final estimate. Never have they felt themselves so puzzled in deciding their own relationship to a vital religious work.

2.

The world's condition cannot but cause disquiet and anxiety. Hostility piles up between nation and nation, labour and capital, class and class. The cost of bitterness and fear mounts daily. Friction and frustration are undermining our homes.

Is there a remedy that will cure the individual and the nation and give the hope of a speedy and satisfactory recovery?

The remedy may lie in a return to those simple home truths that some of us learned at our mother's knee, and which many of us have forgotten and neglected — honesty, purity, unselfishness and love.

The crisis is fundamentally a moral one. The nations must re-arm morally. Moral recovery is essentially the forerunner of economic recovery. Imagine a rising tide of absolute honesty and absolute unselfishness sweeping across every country! What would be the effect, What about taxes? Debts? Savings? A wave of absolute unselfishness throughout the nations would be the end of war.

Moral recovery creates not crisis but confidence and unity in every phase of life. How can we precipitate this moral recovery throughout the nations? We need a power strong enough to change human nature and build bridges between man and man, faction and faction. This starts when everyone admits his own faults instead of spot-lighting the other fellow's.

God alone can change human nature.

The secret lies in that great forgotten truth that when man listens, God speaks; when man obeys, God acts; when men change, nations change. That power active in a minority can be the solvent of a whole country's problems. Leaders changed, a nation's thinking changed, a world at peace with itself. . . .

God has a nation-wide programme that provides inspiration and liberty for all and anticipates all political programmes.

Every employed and unemployed man employed in Moral Re-Armament; this is the greatest programme of national service — putting everybody to work remaking people, homes and businesses. A Swedish steelworker told me: 'Only a spiritual revolution goes far enough to meet the needs of men and industry.'

A Labour leader said: 'I have seen the Labour Movement triumph and felt in the midst of triumph an emptiness. The Oxford Group gave my life new content. I see in its message the only key to the future of the Labour Movement and of industry the world over.'

Only a new spirit in men can bring a new spirit in industry. Industry can be the pioneer of a new order, where national service replaces selfishness, and where industrial planning is based upon the guidance of God. When Labour, Management and Capital become partners under God's guidance, then industry takes its true place in national life.

New men, new homes, new industry, new nations, a new world.

We have not yet tapped the great creative sources in the Mind of God. God has a plan, and the combined moral and spiritual forces of the nation can find that plan.

We can, we must, and we will generate a moral and spiritual force that is powerful enough to remake the world.

3. Evangelization of the World

Protestant Empire Revived

John R. Mott (1865-1955)

If the United States were indeed becoming more empire than republic, then should not that empire be a Protestant one? It was an old idea, but previously the notion had extended only across a continent: now it embraced the whole world. John R. Mott had welcomed the twentieth century with a call in 1900 for The Evangelization of the World in This Generation. *A Methodist layman and an administrative wonder, Mott dreamed grand dreams. But his labor matched his vision, as he worked with students all over the world, creating in 1895 the World's Student Christian Federation. He also worked with churches without respect to political boundaries, becoming one of the forces behind the creation of the World Council of Churches in 1948. Here, in the excerpt below, it is his passion as missionary that is most evident.*

The closing years of the nineteenth century have witnessed in all parts of Protestant Christendom an unprecedented development of missionary life and activity among young men and young women. A remarkable manifestation of this interest in the extension of the Kingdom of Christ has been among students. The Student Volunteer Movement for Foreign Missions, taking its rise at a conference of American and Canadian students in 1886, has spread from land to land, until it has now assumed an organized form in all Protestant countries. It has been transplanted even to the colleges of mission lands, so that today the

---

[Source: J. R. Mott, *The Evangelization of the World in This Generation* (New York: Student Volunteer Movement for Foreign Missions, 1900), pp. 1-2, 4-6.]

Christian students of the Occident and the Orient, of the Northern and the Southern Hemispheres, are united in the sublime purpose of enthroning Jesus Christ as King among all nations and races of men. The reality of their consecration is proved by the fact that during the past decade over two thousand of them, after completing a thorough college or university preparation, have gone out from North America and Europe under the regular missionary societies of the Church to work in non-Christian lands. A still larger number are equipping themselves for similar service abroad.

In several countries, notably in the United States, Canada, Great Britain and Ireland, the members of this Movement have adopted as their watchword, The Evangelization of the World in This Generation. A great number of their fellow-students who, although not volunteers for foreign missions, recognize their equal burden of responsibility for the world's evangelization, have taken the same watchword as a molding influence in their life plans. The idea is taking strong hold, also, on a multitude of other men and women. Eminent leaders of the various branches of the Church of Christ, both in Christian lands and on the mission field, have endorsed the Watchword and have urged the desirability of its adoption by all Christians as expressive of an inspiring ideal as well as of a primary and urgent duty. . . .

What is it to preach the Gospel? The Greek words principally used in the New Testament mean to proclaim as heralds, or to transmit good news. Other words or expressions less frequently used are to talk or converse, to reason or discuss, to testify or bear witness, to teach and to exhort. Examples of all these forms of preaching, or of communicating a knowledge of Christ and His mission to men, are to be found in the practice of the early Church. The qualifications of the worker or speaker, and the circumstances in which he found himself placed, determined the manner of his presentation of the truth as it is in Christ.

So to-day we find the missionaries proclaiming and applying the Gospel in sermons or addresses in mission halls; expounding and discussing the truth in bazaars, inns and street chapels; conversing about Christ as they visit from house to house and as they mingle with the people socially at feasts and public gatherings; teaching the system of Christian doctrine in schools and colleges; circulating the printed Scriptures and other Christian literature; illustrating the Gospel by Christ-like ministry to the body, and by the powerful object lessons of the consistent Christian life and of the well-ordered Christian home, and ever pressing the claims of Christ upon individuals as they are met within the sphere of one's daily calling. In all these and in other ways the Christian worker by voice and by life, by pen and by printed page, in season and out of season, seeks to set forth those facts about Christ which in all lands have been found to be the power of God unto the salvation of every man that believeth.

Robert E. Speer (1867-1947)

*Having found a moral justification for World War I, Robert Speer proceeded
to offer a moral justification for "the missionary enterprise" around the
world. Speer, in his capacity as Presbyterian missionary executive, traveled
himself to most of those mission fields he supported. China, Japan, India,
Southeast Asia, the Near East, and Latin America. Like Mott, he saw denominational division as a great liability in the missionary effort and, again
like Mott, Speer labored to transcend those divisions. Speer was especially
far-sighted in his advocating that the newly created churches abroad train
their own native clergy and not continue as merely "colonial" extensions of
American denominations.*

I have named just as briefly as I could what seem to me to be five of the great
moral justifications for the war, justifications that made legitimate the sacrifices
that were poured out, and that laid the obligation of the struggle to the last effort upon every life in our land. But, when we have said this, have we said anything more than just to put into political terms, in connection with the great
struggle, the aims and ideals and purposes for which many men have been living all their lives, which have actuated the missionary enterprise, and which underlie it to-day? What does that enterprise exist for? What has it been seeking to
do, and in reality doing all the years since it began?

It has been in the world as an instrumentality of peace and international
good will. Wherever it has gone, it has erased racial prejudice and bitterness,
the great root of international conflict and struggle. It has helped men to understand one another. It has rubbed off the frictions. "Christianity continues
to spread among the Karens," said the Administration Report for British
Burmah for 1880-1881, "to the great advantage of the Commonwealth, and the
Christian Karen communities are distinctly more industrious, better educated
and more law-abiding than the Burman and Karen villages around them. The
Karen race and the British government owe a great debt to the American missionaries who have, under Providence, wrought this change among the Karens
of Burmah." . . .

It has been an agency of righteousness. As the years have gone by, it alone
has represented in many non-Christian lands the inner moral character of the
Western world. By our political agencies and activities we have forced great
wrongs upon the non-Christian peoples — commercial exploitation, the liquor
traffic, and the slave trade upon Africa and the South Sea Islands, the opium

[Source: R. E. Speer, *The New Opportunity of the Church* (New York: Macmillan Co., 1919), pp.
94-95, 97-98, 100-101.]

Graduating class of the China Bible School
(Billy Graham Center)

traffic upon China. Against these things the one element of the West that has made protest has been the missionary enterprise. Year after year in those lands it has joined with what wholesome moral sentiment existed among the people in a death struggle against the great iniquities that Western civilization had spread over the world. It has been an instrumentality of international righteousness.

It has been and is a great instrumentality of human service. It has scattered tens of thousands of men and women over many lands, teaching school in city and country, in town and village. It has built its hospitals by the thousand. It has sent its medical missionaries to deal every year with millions of sick and diseased peoples in Asia and Africa. It has been the one great, continuing, unselfish agency of unquestioning, loving, human service throughout the world, dealing not with emergency needs of famine and flood and pestilence alone, but, year in and year out, serving all human need and seeking to introduce into human society the creative and healing influences of Christ. "It is they" (the missionaries), says Sir H. H. Johnston, of British Central Africa, "who in many cases have first taught the natives carpentry, joinery, masonry, tailoring, cobbling, engineering, bookkeeping, printing, and European cookery, to say nothing of reading, writing, arithmetic, and a smattering of general knowledge. Almost invariably, it has been to missionaries that the natives of Interior Africa have owed their first acquaintance with a printing press, the turning-lathe, the mangle, the flat-iron, the sawmill, and the brick mold. Industrial teaching is coming more and more in favor, and its immediate results in British Central Africa have been most encouraging. Instead of importing painters, carpenters, store clerks, cooks, telegraphists, gardeners, natural history collectors from England or India, we are gradually becoming able to obtain them amongst the natives of the country, who are trained in the missionaries' schools, and who having been given simple, wholesome local education, have not had their heads turned, and are not above their station in life." . . .

Foreign missions have been a great agency of human unity and concord. They, at least, have believed and acted upon the belief that all men belong to one family. They have laughed at racial discords and prejudices. They have made themselves unpopular with many representatives of the Western nations who have gone into the non-Christian world, because they have not been willing to foster racial distrust, because they have insisted on bridging the divisions which separated men of different bloods and different nationalities. We are talking now about building the new world after the war. But it would be hopeless if we had not already begun it. We are talking about some form of international organization. It may need to be very simple, with few and primitive functions, but it must come. And it can come only as first, we sustain in men's hearts a faith in its possibility; as second, we devise the instrumentalities necessary to it and make them effective; as third, we build up a spirit that will support it. Across the world for a hundred years the missionary enterprise has been the proclamation that this day must come, and that some such international body of relationships as this, based on right principles, must be set up among the nations of the world.

It would not be hard to go on analyzing further what the missionary enterprise has been doing. It has been doing peacefully, constructively, unselfishly, quietly for a hundred years exactly the things that now, in a great outburst of titanic and necessarily destructive struggle, we were compelled to do by war. I say it again, that one of the most significant things of the day is to see how the great ideals and purposes of the missionary enterprise, that have been the commonplaces of some men's lives, have been gathered up as a great moral discovery and made the legitimate moral aims of the nation in the great conflict in which we have been engaged.

E. Stanley Jones (1884-1973)

A Methodist missionary who went to India in his early twenties, Jones ac-
quired fame in that capacity as well as in the role of popular lecturer and au-
thor. Elected bishop in the Methodist Episcopal Church in 1928, he soon re-
signed that office in order to return to his missionary labors. In India he
wished to reach the high caste, hoping that Christian instruction at that level
would filter down to the masses. As his widely translated Christ of the Indian Road *makes evident, however, he also thought that Christianity had*
much to learn from the rich spiritual heritage of India. In the momentous
encounter between Christianity and Hinduism, both could be transformed,
both could be enriched.

The religious genius of India is the richest in the world, the forms that it has
taken have often been the most extravagant, sometimes degrading and cruel.
These forms are falling away, or will fall away, but the spirit persists and will be
poured through other forms. As that genius pours itself through Christian
molds it will enrich the collective expression of Christianity. But in order to do
that the Indian must remain Indian. He must stand in the stream of India's culture and life and let the force of that stream go through his soul so that the expression of his Christianity will be essentially Eastern and not Western. This
does not mean that Indian Christianity will be denied what is best in Western
thought and life, for when firmly planted on its own soil it can then lift its an-
tennae to the heavens and catch the voices of the world. But it must be particular before it can be universal. Only thus will it be creative — a voice, not an
echo. . . .

The reason that the Indian Christian has not made any real contribution
to Christian theology is because he has been trying, on the whole, to think
through Western forms and here he is like a fish out of water. But now that India is awakened and self-conscious and the process of denationalization is
probably over, we may expect that genius to work. We must be willing to trust
the Indian to make his contribution.

It is no more fair to say that we cannot trust Indian genius to interpret
Christianity because of the extravagances of the past than to have said that the
Western mind could not be trusted because the Druids in England used to per-
form human sacrifices in their religion and the Scots practiced cannibalism.

Every nation has its peculiar contribution to make to the interpretation
of Christianity. The Son of man is too great to be expressed by any one portion

---

[Source: E. Stanley Jones, *Christ of the Indian Road* (New York: Abingdon Press, 1925), pp. 193-
94, 195-96.]

of humanity. Those that differ from us most will probably contribute most to our expression of Christianity. . . .

India too hopes that the world may some day be in need of a new formula. She too has her word ready. It will be spelled "Atma" — *spirit*. That word "Atma" runs like a refrain through everything in India. The followers of the Christ of the Indian Road will show us the real meaning of a *spiritual* life. They will sit lightly to earthly things and abandon themselves to the spirit.

Along with that will come the sense of the unity and harmony running through things. "Don't you think atonement would mean attunement?" said a Hindu to me one day. He felt his life was "like sweet bells jangled out of tune" by sin and evil, and to his mind, craving inward peace and harmony, atonement would bring attunement to the nature of God — music instead of a discord. No wonder peace has been the great thought and craving of India. Anything like losing one's temper is thought to be utterly incompatible with the truly religious life. "I know I haven't salvation yet," said a villager to me one day, "for while I have conquered everything else anger still remains, I haven't got it yet." The followers of the Christ of the Indian Road will be harmonized and peaceful. Meditation to them will be real. Religion will mean quiet realization. God will be the harmonizing bond of all.

Finally the followers of the Christ of the Indian Road will know the meaning of the cross, for India stands for the cost of being religious. Renunciation will be a reality, for India instinctively grasps the meaning of Jesus when he says that the way to realize life is to renounce it — to lose it is to find it. In the footprints of many of his followers as they walk along the Indian Road will be blood stains, for they will be Apostles of the Bleeding Feet. They will know the meaning of being crucified followers of a crucified Lord.

American Catholicism's New Era

Missionary Conference, 1908

Catholics in America — some fifteen million strong by 1908 — had moved from weakness to strength, from dependence to independent vigor. No longer was it necessary to send missionary priests to America: now the American Church was ready to send its own missionaries abroad. In the very year that

---

[Sources: (1) Francis C. Kelley, ed., *The First American Catholic Missionary Conference* (Chicago: J. S. Hyland and Co., 1909), pp. 43-44. (2) Ibid., pp. 362-65.]

> *the Vatican formally removed the Church in the United States from mission status, Catholics held a Missionary Conference in Chicago, November 16 to 18, 1908. (1) Chicago's Archbishop James Edward Quigley (1854-1915) opened the conference by calling attention to the "new era" into which the Church in America now entered. (2) Closing the conference, Boston's Archbishop William H. O'Connell (1859-1944) declared that "all indications point to our vocation as a great missionary nation."*

1.

The reasons and object of this Missionary Congress and its opportuneness at this time are tersely and comprehensively summed up and set forth in the following words which I quote from the call or invitation sent out by the officers of the Catholic Church Extension Society of the U.S.A., under whose auspices the Congress is held:

"To mark the change of the Church in North America from missionary conditions to its full share in the efforts of the Church Universal by striking the note of unselfishness clearly and forcibly.

"To crystallize the missionary sentiment now being awakened in the Catholic clergy and people, to the end that all may realize their common duty of preserving and extending the Church of Christ. To study missionary conditions and plan for their improvement.

"To pledge to the Holy Father America's loyal support and active cooperation in the mighty task of restoring all things in Christ."

As expressed in the first of these points, the Church in America, by Pontifical Act, is at the beginning of a new era in its history. It is practically only one hundred years old, yet it has reached its majority. The old order of things is changed and a new order established. It passes from the jurisdiction and tutelage of the great missionary organization known as the Sacred Congregation de Propaganda Fide, and takes its stand among the bright galaxy of fully organized and equipped hierarchical unities of the world-wide Church of God, that encircle and glorify the throne of the Vicar of Christ, the successor of the Prince of the Apostles, Pope Pius X. It has covered the whole land of its birth and growth with its network of provinces and dioceses and parishes; developed its own legislation and customs; taken on a character of its own; become conscious of its own mission and destiny; and full of a strength and courage born of the air and free institutions of the land whence it derives its name, is prepared to go forth conquering and to conquer in the cause of Christ.

This Congress is called at this time to give us occasion to study our duties and responsibilities as a hierarchical unity and national Church in the closer intimacy of government, association and affection, with Himself and the Church

Universal, to which we have been advanced by the Sovereign Pontiff. These duties and responsibilities are well expressed in the second and third of the reasons given for the call of this Congress — to crystallize the missionary sentiment now being awakened in the Catholic clergy and people, to the end that all may realize their common duty of preserving and extending the Church of Christ, to study missionary conditions and plan for their improvement, and to pledge to the Holy Father America's loyal support and active cooperation in the work which Pius X has made the special aim of his Pontificate, "restaurare omnia in Christo" — to restore all things in Christ.

2.

The spirit of religion, like virtue, must grow; it cannot stand still or rest in complacency upon its laurels without dealing a deadly blow to the very core of its life and progress. To rest self-satisfied with what has been accomplished is to stagnate, and stagnation is the beginning of death. So vital to the very life of religion is the fostering of the Apostolic spirit of zeal for the spread of Christ's faith that it must be nurtured at the cost of any sacrifice. The luxuries of religion we may well dispense with. Too often they have brought only harm to the Church and have been the enemies within the gates.

Magnificent buildings, splendid ceremonials, superb appurtenances are all good in their place, for the worship of Christ can never be too adequately expressed, even by all that the noblest endeavor and most brilliant genius of man may bring to its expression, but if these things are to breed a selfish content and rob the Catholics of any generation of that primitive Apostolic zeal which inflamed the breasts of their first teachers, then it is far better to dispense with these external embellishments, and in poverty and hardship cultivate the gift which made the first promulgators of the faith of Christ the conquerors of the world.

It is time, then, for the Church in America to be vigilant in preserving the unselfishness and generosity of spirit which animated the pioneer Catholic missionaries who planted on this continent the seed of faith. In no other way may the steadfastness of faith which is distinctive of our people in the United States be fully safeguarded. It is the inexorable law of self-preservation, and failure to comply with it can bring only disaster and ruin.

We may well draw a lesson from the foresight and prudence displayed by the great nations of the world. There comes a time in their history when they must reach out to find an outlet for the national life and activity. They well understand the folly of remaining quiescent and shutting the door of opportunity to the surplus talent of their people. Instinctively and inevitably led on by this feeling of self-preservation, they reach out into other lands and find new fields for the unworked energies of the nation.

They recognize that to keep doing is the law of life, and that the accumulation of unused forces is the precursor to stagnation and death. The Church in the United States must avoid this peril at all costs. It must not rest on what has been already accomplished, but even in the face of sacrifice reach out in spreading the faith of Christ where it is now either unknown or dormant, for the very necessary reason that in this way alone may it conserve intact and undimmed the brightness of the faith which has already done so much for the progress of the Church. To the isolated regions where there are scattered populations of Catholics without the ministrations of the priest the zeal of the more favored must assist actively to bring the blessings of the faith.

In the Philippines, in Porto Rico, and in all our outlying possessions, the Church must go, heralded by the missionaries of the English-speaking race who are now called upon by providential design to perform the work which has long been so nobly done by others. It is the time set by divine providence for this Apostolic undertaking. In the first ages of the Church, when imperial Rome ruled the world and Latin was the universal language, it was the missionaries of the Latin tongue who went forth from Rome, and for centuries spread the faith in the countries of Europe. In a later day, when French was the diplomatic language of the nations, France became the missionary country, and her sons and daughters have given an example of self-sacrifice and devotion in spreading the faith in foreign lands that is worthy of all emulation.

Time inevitably brings changes. Today the language of the whole Orient is English. The language of diplomatic usage has been succeeded by the language of trade, and from Port Said to the furthermost point of Japan the language which the people know best next to their own, and like best, is English. Already Japan is clamoring for English-speaking missionaries, and the field which once yielded such a fruitful harvest to the Apostolic labors of St. Francis Xavier lies ready for cultivation at the hands of English-speaking apostles.

The providential hour of opportunity has struck. We must be up and doing. All indications point to our vocation as a great missionary nation. To be recreant to such a high calling is to abdicate a blessed vantage ground and to undo gradually the good which has already been accomplished in this land by the apostolic zeal of the Church's followers. Our country has already reached out beyond her boundaries and is striving to do a work of extension of American civic ideals for other peoples. Shall it be said that the Church in this land has been outstripped in zeal and energy by the civil power under which we live?

Maryknoll, 1911

If the 1908 conference set the tone, the seminary launched in 1911 set the pace. Under the energetic leadership of two priests, Fathers Thomas F. Price and James A. Walsh, the Catholic Foreign Missionary Society of America came into being with a training center for missionaries located in New York state at Maryknoll. The formal title for this center was the "American Seminary for Foreign Missions," but "Maryknoll" became a kind of shorthand for the Roman Catholic commitment in America to missionary work around the world. By the middle of the twentieth century, that work was particularly conspicuous in Latin America.

On March 25, 1911, Cardinal Gibbons addressed a letter to the archbishops of the United States, outlining the plan of the two founders, urging the need of a foreign mission seminary, and pleading for cooperation in the new venture. His Eminence suggested that the archbishops confer with the bishops of their respective provinces and be ready to take action in the matter at their next meeting, to be held in April. Cardinal Gibbons on this occasion wrote:

"The priests of the United States number more than seventeen thousand, but I am informed there are hardly sixteen on the foreign missions. This fact recalls a warning which the late Cardinal Vaughan gave, in a kindly, brotherly letter to me twenty years ago, urging us American Catholics not to delay participation in foreign missions, LEST OUR OWN FAITH SHOULD SUFFER."

The archbishops, having conferred previously with their suffragans in accordance with the plan of Cardinal Gibbons, met in Washington, April 27, 1911, and voicing the wishes of the entire hierarchy, unanimously passed these resolutions:

"We heartily approve the establishment of an American Seminary for Foreign Missions as outlined in the letter sent by His Eminence Cardinal Gibbons to the Archbishops.

"We warmly commend to the Holy Father the two priests mentioned as organizers of this seminary, and we instruct them to proceed to Rome without delay, for the purpose of securing all necessary authorization and direction from Propaganda for the proposed work." . . .

Events followed rapidly. The two organizers left Boston for Europe on May 30, 1911, and did not return until the late summer. They took advantage of their opportunity to visit foreign mission seminaries and apostolic colleges in England and on the Continent, and made a summary study of methods and

[Source: George C. Powers, *The Maryknoll Movement* (Maryknoll: Catholic Foreign Mission Society of America, 1926), pp. 57, 59, 60-61.]

Maryknoll missionary in Molina, Chile
(Maryknoll Fathers)

rules of these institutions. They arrived in Rome on June 19, and between that date and June 29 had several interviews. . . .

On the feast of Saints Peter and Paul (June 29, 1911), with the kindly help of Doctor Schut of Mill Hill, they were able to present their formal petition for authorization and a detailed outline of their proposed operations, to the Cardinal Prefect. Cardinal Gotti at once formally authorized them to begin their

Maryknoll missionary in Kyoto, Japan
(Maryknoll Fathers)

work, to purchase property, and to appeal for students. For the present the founders were to conduct the Society jointly under the bishop in whose diocese they should begin their work; later, when they should be in a position to have a council and hold an election, they were to communicate with Propaganda; in the meantime they were to keep Propaganda informed of their progress. They then received the blessing of the Cardinal Prefect and made arrangements for an audience with the Holy Father, Pius X.

On the following day, they were graciously received by the Successor of Saint Peter and knelt before that saintly Pontiff to receive his blessing for themselves, their project, and its benefactors.

The two priests then went into consultation to decide upon the legal title of the new Society. They agreed on THE CATHOLIC FOREIGN MISSION SOCIETY OF AMERICA: *Catholic,* to distinguish it from all sectarian societies; *Foreign,* lest it be confused with home mission societies; and *of America* because it was the only society of that nature set on foot through the official sanction of the American hierarchy. Then, too, the phrase was necessary to distinguish it from all European societies of a like purpose. This title met with the instant approval of Cardinal Gibbons.

The Disinherited Abroad

Black Baptists, 1903

Missionary efforts were not the monopoly of the wealthy, nor even of the middle class. Those to whom American society had not been generous nonetheless seized the opportunity to take their messages and mission abroad. Black Baptists, growing rapidly in number after the Civil War and organizing themselves into the National Baptist Convention in 1895, saw a certain logic in selecting Africa as an area of missionary endeavor. (1) C. S. Morris, Commissioner for the Foreign Mission Board of the National Baptist Convention, in 1899 made a tour of inspection of Africa. Upon his return, he spoke of a much-abused continent: abused by slavery, by liquor, by colonialism. Victim of the world's avarice, Africa now deserved some of its charity: ". . . what a noble atonement we might make in sending missionaries." (2) In the same book that contained Morris' appeal, another denominational leader re-told the story of the conversion of the Ethiopian eunuch (Acts 8:27-39), where blacks could find all the New Testament sanction they required for both the universality of the Christian religion and the remarkable eagerness "with which the race has accepted the Gospel."

1.

If there is a continent on the face of the earth that needs the Gospel of Jesus Christ more, if possible, than any other, that continent is Africa. It has been more cruelly neglected. Sixty generations of its people have perished in rayless paganism. Africa's darkest millions have not yet begun their forward march out of centuries of midnight darkness. There are regions large as all Europe *packed with fifty million souls* without *one* single missionary. . . .

Africa has been more deeply wronged. Northern Africa gave to Christianity its first Latin Bible, produced Athanasius (who stood against the world contending for the Deity of our Lord), Tertullian, Cyprian, Augustine and Ambrose. At one time there were 500 Bishops in North Africa, but the ruthless invasion of the Vandals put thousands of Christians to the sword and scattered the remainder to the four corners of the earth. Then came the red deluge of

---

[Source: C. S. Morris, "Africa Waiting," and R. D. Baptist, sermon on Acts 8, in L. G. Jordan, ed., *Up the Ladder in Foreign Missions* (Nashville: National Baptist Publishing Board, 1903), pp. 168-69, 170-71, 173-74; 160-62.]

Mohammedanism, rolling like a bloody sea over that fair region, completing the work of annihilating the last vestiges of Christianity, and *Africa's doom was sealed.*

Then came slavery, "the heart disease of Africa." Vasco da Gama discovered West Africa about the same time that Columbus discovered America, and Africa was sacrificed for America. Europe and America inaugurated the most *gigantic crime of the Christian era* against her. Unnumbered millions of her children were slain in slave raids, other millions perished in the horrors of the "middle passage;" sometimes 700 would be stowed away on board one ship. Only sixty years ago 250,000 were being exported every year by Christian States. . . .

Then came the civilized rum traffic, *hell's masterpiece of damnation,* that has turned the whole ocean front into one long bar-room, at which *two million frenzied savages drop dead* every year of delirium tremens. Rum is deadly in the temperate regions, it is rank poison in the tropics. . . .

In the eighteenth century Europe stole the African from Africa; in the nineteenth, she is stealing Africa from the African. The unhallowed spirit of civilized greed for aggrandizement at the African's expense is not yet sated. The slave raiding of other days is to give place to the second magnificently unscrupulous conspiracy that is to partition Africa and plunder the African of the bounds of his habitation which God has determined beforehand, and thus deprive two hundred million people of their birthright; to seize upon their property and permanently drain the wealth of Africa and the African's labor into European channels, leaving her like a sucked orange, like a rifled treasure house — her keepers slain, her treasures stolen, the marauders gone.

What an awful many-sided charge the vast cloud of African witnesses will have against the civilized world on the day of judgment. A continent turned into a slave pen, a rum shop, great open running ulcers on either breast. Robbed of her children, rifled of her treasures, fettered in soul, manacled in mind, enslaved in body — *Africa lies prostrate before the rapine and avarice of the world.* . . .

The Church of Christ has been entrusted with the *great commission of the King of Kings.* She has men by the millions and money by the billions. Yet *nineteen centuries have gone over her head and there are whole continents that have not heard it.* Some say, "I don't *believe* in foreign missions;" some, "there is plenty to do at *home;*" some, "we have more *now* on hand than we can do." Jesus says, "Go ye into *all* the world, preach the gospel to *every creature,*" and in the Judgment, when the Son of Man shall sit upon the throne of His glory and behold the unreached millions for whom He died, to whom He sent a message of pardon they *never heard,* will He not turn to His recreant disciples whom He entrusted with the message and say, "I made you My stewards and you took My wealth and clothed yourselves in purple and fine linen; you fared sumptuously every day while I was hungry in India, and ye gave Me no bread; thirsty in China, and ye gave Me no drink; sick and in prison in Africa, and ye visited Me not;" "*Inasmuch as ye did it not unto the least of these my brethren, ye did it not unto Me.*" We have not done our duty to Africa, as will be seen by a comparison of what American societies spend in Asia and Africa respectively, but if, in addition to her claim on account of her numbers we should, in the spirit of the repentant Zacheus, restore unto Africa four fold that which we have taken by false accusation, what a noble atonement we might make in sending missionaries for the slaves that were taken and Bibles for the rum which America is dumping on her shores by the million gallons annually. Your money or your life is a terribly true expression of spiritual conditions. Your money is the concrete representative of your love, your gratitude, your obedience. God grant that there may come to all who read this a new vision of the whitening fields, a profounder sense of personal duty and warmer touch of the Saviour's sympathy. God grant that all may do something; that some may give grandly to this grand need, and that none may imitate those servants "who with one consent began to make excuse."

2.

The Christian religion is the exponent of the highest civilization, the highest moral and social condition of the race to-day. Where it has been accepted, and its faith and doctrines incorporated into the life and character of any people, it has in a very potential manner affected the moral, intellectual and social condition of such people. . . .

No people or race is excluded from its all-embracing provisions, nor from its divinely uplifting power when it is embraced. It should produce in the race in America, or in Africa, worthy examples of its power to save and elevate in proportion to individual or race conformity to its spirit and precepts. Its light shone early in the soul of one of the race when the Ethiopian eunuch accepted it through the preaching of Philip the evangelist, and "believed that Jesus Christ is the Son of God." He asked Baptism and was immersed by Philip, "and when they were come up out of the water the eunuch went on his way rejoicing." The large number of the [Negro] race in America who are Baptists is a living evidence of the readiness with which the race has accepted the Gospel and conformed to its doctrines and ordinances as did the eunuch of the race in the apostolic period of planting and training of Christian churches. A larger percentum of the race in America are members of evangelical Churches than of any other race in the land; and a large number of them are members of Baptist churches than of all other evangelical bodies. National Statistician for 1900 gives the number of the race members of Baptist churches in this country as 1,854,600. To this number must be added members of Baptist churches in the States not enumerated in the reports, which make a total of about 2,000,000. To this must be added the members of various other evangelical bodies in this country and we have a grand total of about 3,123,000 Negro Christians in the United States.

These should be a power as a missionary force for the evangelization of the world. They should, by their numerical strength, give to the race a distinctive character in active and effective missionary work among Christian evangelizing workers. The aggressive character of those workers who went out from the churches at Jerusalem and Antioch for the conversion of the world to Christ was marked by the strong opposition they aroused from jealous, unbelieving Jews and stolid heathen devotees, and were stigmatized as "These that have turned the world upside down." To drink in the same spirit and follow their example should produce like results of success in the same work. The world will look for results, and the great Head of the Church will hold the large number of Baptists responsible, in all work of the gospel, in proportion to their numbers, other things being considered. Some of the things to be considered are, the "talents" given, and culture, and right training in the use of the talents intrusted, including the resources vouch-safed as visible means of accomplishing the work Christ has given them to do. But in these things, as necessary accompaniments for efficiency, the responsibility of individual study is involved that they may be approved of God, workmen that need not be ashamed. This large number of Christian workers of the race owe it to Christ, who has called them into His service, to the world in which they live, the field in which Christ instructs them work, and to Africa in particular, "The rock from which they have been hewn," the original home of the race, whose benighted millions still grope in darkest heathenism, outraged and neglected, to individually measure up to the fullest possibility of resources and effort in the work of human redemption. A great work remains to be done for the race in this and other lands, and every Baptist should therefore be intensely a missionary Baptist. The command is "lift up your eyes and look on the fields, they are white already to harvest." And again, "go work to-day in my vineyard."

Mormons, 1904

No other religious body in America has made "mission" so central a part of its life, so commonplace a word in its vocabulary. Long before the Church of Jesus Christ of Latter Day Saints had settled in Utah, long before the "Gentile" persecution of Mormons had ceased, the followers of Joseph Smith and

[Source: (1) *The Latter-Day Saint Millennial Star,* 46 (Feb. 11, 1904), 81-82. (2) Ibid., 46 (Jan. 7, 1904), 1-2.]

Brigham Young had gone abroad to tell of the new revelation and to recruit members for the new church. They thereby set a pattern followed to the present wherein most able-bodied young Mormon males spend a year or two away from home on their "mission." Early in the twentieth century, two Mormon missionaries, writing for their church's paper, tell of the great work abroad: (1) Anthon L. Skanchy on Scandinavia, and (2) Francis M. Lyman on other areas of Europe and beyond.

1.

This mission, to which I have been called, is a rather extensive one — comprising Denmark, Sweden and Norway, with their numerous surrounding islands — and is known as the Scandinavian mission. Denmark is a small, level lowland, very fertile and thickly populated. It consists mainly of islands, and is located between parallels 55 and 57, north latitude, and contains 38,311 square kilometers, with a population of about 2,500,000. Copenhagen, the capital, has 500,000 inhabitants, and it was here that our venerable brother, Apostle Erastus Snow, fifty-five years ago, opened the door of the Gospel to these nations. It appears that, a couple of years before his arrival, the spirit of liberty had been poured out upon the Danish nation, upon the government and upon the royal family to such an extent that a very liberal constitution had been framed, which guaranteed religious liberty for the people in the land — a preparation for the proclamation of the Gospel. Persecutions were, nevertheless, started against our brethren when they came with the Latter-day message, and although no violent measures were taken against them by the authorities, the mob spirit sometimes ran very high. Violence went so far that blood was shed, and a young man who had embraced the Gospel fell an innocent victim to an assassin's dagger, in the city of Aalborg, in Jylland. The earthly remains of that young martyr are now resting in Aalborg cemetery, and loving hands are still keeping his grave trimmed and decorated with flowers. But here, as in other places, it was only a question of time until the Gospel should find its way to the honest among the people, and, as its principles became more and more known, many were convinced of their truth, and received the Gospel message. Charity and liberality are characteristic of the people here, and the Elders, who in those days were mostly called from among the native Saints, had but little trouble in finding shelter and subsistence. From that time until the present 46,911 noble souls have embraced the Gospel.

From the year 1850 until the end of 1903, in Denmark alone 24,039 persons have been baptized into the Church, and 16,000 of these have emigrated in charge of the Elders. These emigrants have made themselves prominent as faithful, industrious Latter-day Saints, who have taken an active part in the upbuilding of the stakes of Zion.

2.

At the close of my presidency over the European mission, it is a pleasing task to express to the ministry, the Saints and our friends, the gratitude I feel to the Lord for His abundant blessings and to them for their personal kindness and hearty support. It is also appropriate to state briefly the condition of the mission and something of the work that has been done during the past two and

Informal portrait of the First Presidency of the Church of Jesus Christ of Latter-day Saints, c. 1904: Joseph Fielding Smith, Anthon H. Lund, and John R. Winder
(Keystone-Mast Collection, University of California, Riverside)

half years. At the last October conference, the Saints will remember, Elder Heber J. Grant of the Council of Twelve Apostles was appointed to preside over this field. The business has all been turned over to him now, and he begins his administration with our love and confidence and most cordial wish that he may be prosperous and happy in his work. I hope he will find the field in a satisfactory condition.

The Elders of the European mission are, almost without exception, full of zeal and the spirit of their work. There are at the present time five hundred and ninety-seven missionaries from Zion, five of whom are sisters. They are laboring mainly in the British Isles, Scandinavia, Germany, Switzerland, and the Netherlands, but are also found in Iceland, Austria and Hungary, Palestine and South Africa. Since the time of my arrival, May 17, 1901, seven hundred and forty missionaries have registered at Liverpool; six hundred and eight have during this time departed for home. We have been called to mourn the death of three of our fellow-laborers. . . .

A cause of far greater concern and grief has been the fall of Elders from honor and virtue. During my presidency there have been seven, who disregarding their holy covenants and all that is worth living for, have yielded to the temptations of the adversary. They have been stripped of every vestige of authority and excommunicated from the Church. There was no alternative course to take with them. It is deplorable when an Elder thus turns from his high calling. The cases have been scattered, each of the large missions having had at least one. It is about one Elder in a hundred that has fallen. Let the anguish which each of them has suffered be a life's warning to the ninety and nine who thus far, by the help of the Lord, have been able to stand.

During the time it has been my privilege to labor here there have been, in the European mission, exclusive of the work done during last December, 5,193,824 tracts and 184,085 books distributed, and 4,018 baptisms performed. Greater efficiency of the Elders has been gained in the mission by doing away with what were known as conference houses. The present system of having not more than two men live together, and their lodgings to be taken with strangers, has brought the Elders into contact with more people and been followed by very satisfactory results.

The field of missionary effort is broadening. In both Austria and Hungary openings have been made and Elders are now laboring. In India Elder John H. Cooper, who has just returned after laboring alone a year and a half, raised up a thriving branch. More Elders will be sent there soon, we hope, to carry on the good work. The mission in South Africa was opened last July by President Warren H. Lyon and three companions. This is an old field which has not been worked for about forty years. The prospects are that the mission will prosper. Personally I have visited Africa, Palestine, Greece, Italy, France, Finland, Russia and Poland, and have dedicated these lands to the preaching of the

Gospel, and besought the Lord to open the way for His servants to come in and lead souls to accept His plan of salvation. Since I thus dedicated Africa, the mission has been established in the southern part, and since my visit to Russia Elder Mischa Markow has gone into that land and declared his message. These are small beginnings, but the Lord, if He wills, can make them great.

Persecuted Witnesses, 1934

In Allegheny, Pennsylvania, in 1872, "Christian persons met together . . . to consider the Scriptures relative to the coming of Christ and His Kingdom." Out of this gathering came the group ultimately to be known as "Jehovah's Witnesses." In 1916 Joseph Franklin Rutherford (1869-1942) took over leadership of the rapidly expanding fellowship, guiding it through the difficulties of World War I (the Witnesses declined to serve in the armed forces) and beyond. Noted for their vigorous missionary efforts at home, these "Watch Tower Bible Students" also pressed on with their message north to Canada, south to Latin America, east to Britain and the continent of Europe. Everywhere they met with persecution: from capitalist, communist, fascist, from devout believer, and from callous unbeliever. The excerpt below tells of their difficult days in Hitler's Germany and of their uncompromising protest against any interference in the exercise of their religion.

A convention was arranged to be held at the fair-grounds in Basel, Switzerland, from September 7 to 9, 1934. Brother Rutherford hoped to meet a number of brothers from Germany there, to hear from them firsthand about the actual situation in the country. Under most adverse conditions almost a thousand brothers from Germany were able to attend. They later reported how distressed Brother Rutherford was when he personally heard what the brothers had already been forced to suffer.

On the other hand, he was forced to recognize that even the traveling overseers present were not of one mind as regards the preaching work. He spoke to them about steps to be taken in Germany after the convention. Plans for united action were made.

October 7, 1934, will forever remain something special in the memories of all those who had the privilege of participating in the events of that day. On that day Hitler and his government were confronted by the fearless action of Jehovah's witnesses — in his eyes a ridiculous minority.

[Source: *1974 Yearbook of Jehovah's Witnesses* (Brooklyn: Watchtower Bible and Tract Society, 1974), pp. 132-33, 136-37.]

Details were spelled out in a letter from Brother Rutherford, a copy of which was to be taken by special messenger to every congregation in Germany. At the same time these messengers were instructed to make preparations for meetings to be held throughout Germany on this particular day. Brother Rutherford's letter said, in part:

"Every group of Jehovah's witnesses in Germany should gather together at a convenient place in the city where they live, on Sunday morning, October 7, 1934, at 9:00 o'clock. This letter should be read to all present. You should join together in prayer to Jehovah asking him through Christ Jesus, our Head and King, for his guidance, protection, deliverance and blessing. Immediately thereafter send a letter to German government officials which text will have been prepared beforehand and will then be available. A few minutes should be spent discussing Matthew 10:16-24, keeping in mind that by doing as this text says, you are 'standing for your lives.' (Esther 8:11) The meeting should then be closed and you should go out to your neighbors giving them a witness about Jehovah's name, about our God and his Kingdom under Christ Jesus.

"Your brothers throughout the world will be thinking of you and will direct a similar prayer to Jehovah at the same time." . . .

In harmony with the action being taken by Jehovah's witnesses throughout Germany, everyone . . . enthusiastically agreed that the following letter should be sent to the government on that day by registered mail:

"To the Officials of the Government"

"The Word of Jehovah God, as set out in the Holy Bible, is the supreme law, and to us it is our sole guide for the reason that we have devoted ourselves to God and are true and sincere followers of Christ Jesus.

"During the past year, and contrary to God's law and in violation of our rights, you have forbidden us as Jehovah's witnesses to meet together to study God's Word and worship and serve him. In his Word he commands us that we shall not forsake the assembling of ourselves together. (Hebrews 10:25) To us Jehovah commands: 'Ye are my witnesses that I am God. Go and tell the people my message.' (Isaiah 43:10, 12; Isaiah 6:9; Matthew 24:14) There is a direct conflict between your law and God's law, and, following the lead of the faithful apostles, 'we ought to obey God rather than men,' and this we will do. (Acts 5:29) Therefore this is to advise you that at any cost we will obey God's commandments, will meet together for the study of his Word, and will worship and serve him as he has commanded. If your government or officers do violence to us because we are obeying God, then our blood will be upon you and you will answer to Almighty God.

"We have no interest in political affairs, but are wholly devoted to God's kingdom under Christ his King. We will do no injury or harm to anyone. We would delight to dwell in peace and do good to all men as we have opportunity, but, since your government and its officers continue in your attempt to force us to disobey the highest law of the universe, we are compelled to now give you notice that we will, by his grace, obey Jehovah God and fully trust Him to deliver us from all oppression and oppressors."

Missions Reevaluated

W. H. P. Faunce (1859-1930)

President of Brown University for thirty years (1899-1929) and leading Baptist spokesman, Faunce in 1914 looked at the burgeoning missionary activity not in terms of the number of converts but in terms of its "social aspects." What impact have missionaries had on culture, on health and welfare, on the civilizing process itself? One should not claim too much for missions, Faunce cautioned; nor, however, should one overlook "the mainspring of human progress."

No one would claim that the Christian missionary enterprise, or even the Christian faith itself, has been the sole source of recent progress in the non-Christian world. The obligation of perfect candor, which rests on every historian, is peculiarly binding on one who deals with the facts or the narratives of religious enterprise. To view all missionary statistics through rose-colored glasses, ignoring the grim obstacles that face all noble effort, and the failures that are common to all good men at home and abroad, is to prepare for a rude awakening and reaction when the full truth is known. To suppress discouraging facts in order to secure continued support, or to ignore contributory causes in order to magnify our own effort, would be both dishonest and suicidal. The Book of Acts, the first missionary journal, is in this respect a marvel of candor. Belonging avowedly to the literature of propaganda, it nevertheless does not hesitate to record the small results of the magnificent address on Mars' Hill, the lamentable dissension of Paul and Barnabas, and the "many adversaries" to be faced at Ephesus.

There is glory enough for the foreign missionary enterprise, even when

---

[Source: W. H. P. Faunce, *The Social Aspects of Foreign Missions* (New York: Missionary Education Movement of the United States and Canada, 1914), pp. 101-3.]

all other powers have been given their full credit. Traders from Western lands, with no altruistic motive, have often carried the tools of civilization far and wide. Commercial companies are to-day sending thousands of plows into Africa, looms into India, oil into China, sewing-machines into the South Sea Islands, and are constructing railways, canals, and telephone lines throughout the Orient. It was the United States government behind Commodore Perry that compelled the opening of Japan in 1853. It is the British government that by the building of the great dam across the Nile at Assuan, and the introduction of better methods of tilling the soil, is now lifting the Egyptian peasant out of poverty six thousand years old. Applied science, as we have already seen, is reshaping vast regions of the world, both East and West. It is changing ancient modes of life, creating new wants, putting Sheffield cutlery and Lancashire cottons into Bombay and Calcutta, German rifles into Turkey, and American automobiles into Java and Borneo.

But when all this has been admitted, it remains true that the mainspring of human progress has been for nineteen hundred years, and is to-day, the Christian faith. The moral dynamic that transformed our wild forefathers, the Saxons, Celts, and Scandinavians, into civilized nations was not science — then unborn — not politics, literature, or art, it was Christianity.

William E. Hocking (1873-1966)

Professor of Philosophy at Harvard (1914-43) and Congregational churchman, Hocking led a "Layman's Inquiry" into a century of missionary activity. This probing evaluation inquired into the design and purpose of missions, their scope and effectiveness, their merit and ultimate validity. In the document below, Hocking sees this enterprise as having matured from its earlier evangelical phase to its present humanitarian one — though the two aspects are not to be thought of as mutually exclusive. And while he defends the importance of "a true and well-qualified evangelism," Hocking also urges that the "spirit of Christian service" be distinguished from "the work of conscious and direct evangelization."

When the modern missionary movement came to birth at the end of the eighteenth century its objectives were clear and definite. It was an outflow of the widespread religious awakening which came to Europe and America near the middle of that century. This movement, commonly called the "Evangelical

[Source: W. E. Hocking, *Re-thinking Missions: A Layman's Inquiry after One Hundred Years* (New York: Harper & Brothers, 1932), pp. 60-62, 63-64, 69-70.]

Awakening," put its chief emphasis on individual salvation. Under its stimulus men felt impelled to go to the ends of the earth to save souls and build them into the church. The great personalities who led this movement were primarily evangelists.

But they were more than evangelists. Their enterprise would not so profoundly have altered the course of events in the regions where they worked if they had not quickly perceived how much more than preaching was involved in their undertaking. In order to proclaim their own message they were obliged to master languages, translate the Scriptures, and produce literature in those languages. Almost from the beginning of their work in the Orient, there were missionaries who saw that a scheme of education was a necessity, if enlightened leaders and pastors were to be developed. The missionary as a man has always been sensitive to the suffering of others, and as a Christian has accepted a peculiar responsibility for relieving it. Hospitals and other medical service were natural developments. Thus there has been no time in the history of modern missions when the philanthropic objective has not had a place.

But in the course of a hundred years, this place has become a very large one, as thoughtful and forward-looking missionaries have gradually realized what is involved in their enterprise. Starting with the purpose of saving individual souls, they have been drawn on by necessity into efforts to build up the minds, and the bodies, and to improve the social life in which these souls are engaged. The educational and other associated interests have grown until in volume and variety they now outrank the parent activity. There is a visible tendency to regard them as having a value of their own, and as being legitimate functions of Christian missions apart from any explicit evangelization. It is as if "salvation" had begun to take on a new meaning: men are to be saved, not for the next world alone, and not out of human life, but within human life. A thoroughgoing acceptance of this view would mean a new epoch in the conception of the task of mission. . . .

There is a danger that diversifying the scope of effort horizontally may be at the expense of depth. Uplifters and social betterment experts easily fall into the vain supposition that by simply improving the economic basis of life or by cleverly re-shuffling human relationships they can produce the happy world of their hopes. All proposals for cure through philanthropy alone, miss the point of central importance, namely, that there must be *first of all a new kind of person as the unit of society if there is to be a new social order.* Social efforts which ignore this principle have at times brought disillusionment: impressive and stable results are difficult and rare. What count most in the progress of society are simple day by day events, such as may take place in the mind of a youth here and there or in the formation of a new friendship. These tiny rootlet processes in the long run remake civilization. The main contribution of the mission has been not in devising new social programs, but in forming the men who do the devising. Nothing therefore can displace or minimize the importance of a true and well-qualified evangelism. . . .

But there is a special reason for regarding the ministry of deeds as a fit vehicle for a Christian message. For Christianity, in contrast to religions of illusion or of pessimism, regards the condition of the human being in human society as an express object of God's concern. Human history becomes a field in which the divine life and the divine solicitude are manifested. "Inasmuch as ye have done it unto one of the least of these my brethren ye have done it unto me." To regard social service as something more than a humanitarian act of relief, namely, as an act of union with God's will, is thus in a special sense an expression of the kernel of the Christian faith.

We believe, then, that the time has come to set the educational and other philanthropic aspects of mission work free from organized responsibility to the work of conscious and direct evangelization. We must be willing to give largely without any preaching; to cooperate with non-Christian agencies for social improvement; and to foster the initiative of the Orient in defining the ways in which we shall be invited to help.

This means that we must work with *greater faith* in invisible successes. We must count it a gain when without addition to our institutional strength the societies of the East are slowly permeated with the spirit of Christian service. This attitude will be in accord with the *greater patience* implied in the permanent mission program: the universal church is to arrive, but by its own mode of building, and in God's own time.

4. New Structures

Comforting the Afflicted

Salvation Army

Organized in England in 1865, the Salvation Army spread to the United States soon thereafter. This "new structure" seemed peculiarly adapted to the human needs which urbanization and industrialization accentuated or aggravated. (1) In a 1900 description of the Army's work in America, Frederick Booth-Tucker (1853-1929; son-in-law of William Booth, the founder) tells of the organization's evolution from personal evangelism to "social salvation." (2) And in an account written one year earlier, Booth-Tucker acknowledges the central role of women in every level of ministry within the Salvation Army.

1. Social Salvation

As its name signifies, the Salvation army was originally started with the sole aim of reaching the non-church-going masses with the Gospel. Here was the appalling statement made by those who had given the matter years of patient study, that 90% of the working classes in the older civilizations of Europe habitually neglected public worship and had practically cut themselves loose from even the outward profession of religion. It was to remedy this condition of affairs that William and Catherine Booth set to work.

[Sources: Frederick Booth-Tucker, *The Social Relief Work of the Salvation Army in the United States* (1900), pp. 6-7, 9-10; and (2), by the same author, *The Salvation Army in the United States* (1899), n. p. — both found in *The Salvation Army in America* (New York: Arno Press, 1972).]

As evangelists they could crowd the largest buildings with the vast crowds who flocked to their meetings. Their converts were numbered by thousands. Yet they could not fail to notice and mourn over the fact that those who came were mostly church-goers and professors of religion. The godless multitudes drifted past their doors. To reach them, other methods must be pursued. Their habits must be studied and they must be followed to their haunts and hiding-places.

When, however, this had been done, it became daily more and more evident that the evils to be combatted were of a temporal as well as of a spiritual character. Churchlessness was with these classes the natural outcome of homelessness, worklessness and worthlessness. To combat the evil, its causes must be radically dealt with. The task was truly a gigantic one. But General Booth was not the man to shrink from it. Cautiously and experimentally at first, and finally with the confidence that was the natural outcome of repeated success, he grappled with the problem.

In traversing and transforming these melancholy wastes of woe, root principles were discovered and laid down for the guidance of the legion of well-trained workers who had been rapidly enrolled.

The poor were to be treated with love, and not with suspicion or contempt.

They were to be classified, not as the worthy and unworthy, but as those who were willing to work out their own regeneration, and the unwilling.

They were to be encouraged in every possible way to become their own deliverers.

Each institution was to aim at self-support by the labor or payments of its inmates.

Social reform to be complete must include the soul as well as the body. In other words the man himself must be changed and not merely his circumstances.

To save a man for this world should be but a stepping-stone toward saving him for the next. . . .

From the above facts it may be regarded as certain that the "submerged" classes in America, including the criminal, the vicious and the purely pauper elements, number not less than 3,000,000 under favorable sociological circumstances, while the number is liable to increase alarmingly during seasons of commercial depression.

For dealing with this mass of poverty and suffering the Salvation army in the United States has organized the various institutions and agencies described in the following pages. These include:

Shelters for homeless men; shelters for homeless women; homes for clerks and artisans; homes for girls working in stores and offices; homes for children; rescue homes for fallen women; slum posts for slum visitation and meetings; slum day nurseries for infants, cheap food depots and cent-meals; cheap clothing and second-hand stores; salvage brigades for collection of

Salvation Army coal distribution depot, 1902
(New York Public Library)

household and office waste; woodyards; employment bureaus; Knights of hope
for prison visitation and ex-criminals; winter relief; medical relief, including
free hospital and dispensaries; summer outings for the poor; penny ice wagons;
Christmas and Thanksgiving dinners; missing friends and inquiry department;
farm colonies for the poor.

The complex character of the remedies above indicated has been necessitated by the complex nature of the evil to be dealt with. To the uninitiated eye
poverty appears to be one seething cauldron of dirt, rags, hunger, hypocrisy
and misery. To the skilled eye of our officers, who devote their lives to the practical task of combatting the evil, the poor may be divided into classes which are
as sharply defined and unmixable as the castes of the Hindoos, or the stratas of
geology. To deal successfully with the monster of poverty, each of its hydra

heads must be separately handled, with methods peculiar to itself and with a staff of workers who are trained to become experts in their own particular department, whilst the sunshine of love and the tender showers of Gospel grace are made to permeate the mass.

2. A Sphere for Woman's Work

In no religious or secular organization is there so free a hand allowed to women as in The Salvation Army, and to this fact is undoubtedly due a large measure of its success. The Hallelujah Lass has from the earliest days of the movement proved herself its Joan of Arc. Into the heart of slumdom she has carried the banner of salvation, and if her bonnet has become an equally familiar sight in the offices of our merchant princes, it is only that she may plead the claims of the poor and champion their cause.

Problems that statesmanship and philanthropy have failed to solve have yielded to the gentle magic of these heroines of slumdom. "If there is a fight we make straight for the centre of it," said one of these girl warriors, who had been born and bred in the lap of luxury and had forsaken a comfortable home and brilliant social prospects in order to minister to the semi-savages of our city jungles. "Even if they are inflamed with drink or are using knives or revolvers, they never touch us. The people would almost tear them to pieces if they did."

"There are only two saloons in Chicago where we are not allowed to visit," said another of these officers, "and we go to them regularly every week. When the proprietor reminds us that he has already forbidden us to come, we answer, 'Yes, sir; but we have come to see whether you have changed your mind yet!'"

Thousands of those who never cross the threshold of a church are to be found night after night in our meetings. Even when they do not profess to be converted, a marked change comes frequently over their lives. The meetings possess for these men a strange fascination, drawing them away from the glittering allurements of the saloons and dives and low music halls.

The personal magnetism of these women, their fearless face-to-face dealing with the wicked and their patient toil in behalf of the suffering poor are not the only secrets of their success. Prayer and faith equip the most timid of them for the platform duties from which they would naturally shrink. "It is so much easier," they say, "to act than to talk." And yet the burning words which fall from their lips, powerful in their simplicity, go straight to the hearts of their hearers and result in wonderful reformations.

As organizers and administrators many of our women officers have proven themselves to be in no sense inferior to the men, and the fact that they are equally eligible for our most responsible offices has helped to draw forth gifts which have only been latent for want of exercise.

The "Y" Movement

The nation's churches and synagogues demonstrated particular concern for the young people removed from familiar and supportive surroundings, deprived of family and friends. Again, England led the way, with a London Young Men's Christian Association (YMCA) being started in 1844. Only after the Civil War, however, did the "Y" movement become a significant force in America. By the time of the nation's next great war in 1917-18, the YMCA was in a position to play a major role in providing off-duty recreation and refreshment to servicemen at home and abroad. Also by that time, all major religious groups in America were sponsoring distinct associations for their young people. The YMCA, oldest of these several groups, started out in close affiliation with evangelical religion and Protestant revivalism. Like the Salvation Army, however, the "Y" moved gradually from an emphasis on personal Bible-reading and prayer to a concern with social problems and community welfare. The 1936 statement of "Objectives and Characteristics," excerpted below, also indicates the developing inter-racial and interdenominational emphasis.

Distinctive Objectives and Characteristics

The Young Men's Christian Association we regard as being in its essential genius a world-wide fellowship of men and boys, united by a common loyalty to Jesus, for the purpose of developing Christian personality and building a Christian society.

I. Developing Christian Personality

The first Young Men's Christian Association was formed by a group of young men, who worked and lived together, for mutual helpfulness in maintaining Christian standards and growing in Christian experience in the face of their working and living conditions. What characterized the first Association group has been distinctive of the Y.M.C.A. throughout its development. It provides a medium for mutual helpfulness in Christian living to boys, young and older men, where they live, attend school, work, or spend their leisure time. It seeks to enlist boys and men in the Christian life and to lead them to avail themselves of the opportunities it offers for the development of Christian experience.

[Source: C. Howard Hopkins, *History of the Y.M.C.A. in North America* (New York: Association Press, 1951), pp. 524-25.]

To these ends Association work at its best provides:

1. *Groups* around school, vocational, neighborhood, friendship, leisuretime, and other social relations which furnish a medium for mutual helpfulness to boys and men in their everyday lives.
2. *A group program, leadership* and *methodology* through which boys and men

   - may find opportunity for a group fellowship through which they can help one another in personal problems and can reinforce one another's ideals and purposes, and in which they may share and discuss experience in meeting their life situations.
   - may live coöperatively rather than competitively amid the consequences of the competitive struggle so common in our modern world.
   - may be challenged through the study of the Bible and of the writings of others in the nineteen centuries of Christian experience to explore the meaning of the Christian religion and its applicability to one's own life, and through prayer and worship use its resources in facing personal problems.
   - may have opportunity to enrich their lives in areas of need or interest.
   - may obtain counsel from a leader or other competent individuals on their intimate personal problems, thus becoming happier and more skillful in their work, recreation, social and religious life.

3. *Service buildings* providing wholesome living, eating and recreational conditions for young and older men away from home or in the community. These centers are located near neighborhood, work, or school relationships, at railroad junction and lay-over points, important shore-leave ports for the Navy, near Army posts, industrial plants, and in student communities.
4. *Service to individuals* where there is need or strain in their living, school, work, or leisure-time relations. Counsel is made available to boys and men on personal difficulties, putting them in touch with experts where needed, helping them to make satisfactory church, social and other connections in strange communities, aiding them in vocational choice and placement and helping them to find the resources of the Christian religion. Healthful physical exercise is provided. Courses of study are offered, suited in content and method to individual needs, so that younger and older men may improve their vocational status through proper training, and that individuals may enrich their lives in fields which they have not had previous opportunity to explore.

II. Building a Christian Society

Although the Association started as an agency for personal helpfulness, more recently it has come to recognize the close inter-relation of personal and social problems. Personal problems can be successfully solved only in a society that respects personal values. Further, the Christian gospel implies both the sacredness of individual personality and the necessity of a society based on sacredness of individual personality wherein people live together coöperatively in the spirit of good-will. Consequently the Association work seeks to enlist its functional groups in such group and intergroup programs as to:

1. Stimulate competent, constructive, independent thinking and action both on personal problems and on economic, political, inter-racial, and other issues.
2. Challenge men to explore the meaning of Christian principles and of the gospel and bring them to feel and understand the tension between life as it is and as it would be if the Christian ideals operated more fully in our economic, political, business, inter-racial and national affairs.
3. Encourage groups to re-make on the Christian pattern the life of which they are a part.
4. Encourage coöperation by dissenting groups or minorities within groups with those of like mind in the community to put into effect their varying Christian convictions.
5. Bring about through such activities a fellowship characterized by understanding and friendship, in which boys and men shall work together positively and constructively to transform the contemporary life of which they are a part.

Society of St. Vincent de Paul

Like the YMCA, the Society of St. Vincent de Paul had its origins abroad (France, 1845), but also like the "Y," it had its major impact in the United States after the Civil War. By the end of the century, the society had taken the lead in cooperating with other agencies and charities in order to accomplish as much as possible. So overwhelming were the needs and so ever-multiplying the numbers that denominations must work together, must trust each other. That was the argument of Thomas M. Mulry (1855-1916), businessman and guiding hand of the Society in the city of New York.

[Source: Aaron I. Abell, *American Catholic Thought on Social Questions* (New York and Indianapolis: Bobbs-Merrill Co., 1968), pp. 179-80.]

In 1882, or thereabouts, the charity organization society was started in New York city. The objects of the society were to prevent the indiscriminate giving of relief, to evolve a system that would be acceptable to all, and to bring the various charities closer together.

The organization gave no relief, but acted as a sort of charities exchange, where all information could be obtained, and where people applying for assistance would be investigated and referred to proper relief societies. There was something repugnant to the catholic idea of charity in this new scheme. It seemed like dragging the worthy poor before the public, and there was nothing to appeal to our people in an organization which expended *all* its receipts in salaries and expenses, none going to the poor.

We refused to co-operate with them, but after a few years a better understanding developed itself. It was seen that there was a good side to the work.

After the organization had been in existence a few years, the attention of some of the members of the society of St. Vincent de Paul was called to the large number of catholic children attending the various Protestant missions and Sunday schools. Immediately the charity organization society was looked upon as the cause.

It happened that the work of investigating the matter was assigned to me. I called upon the committee of the charity organization society. What did I find? A body of ladies and gentlemen earnestly endeavoring to do something to help God's poor, and most anxious for our moral support and co-operation.

There had been some catholic gentlemen's names used, but they had taken no active part. I found letters had been sent to clergymen, to conferences of the society of St. Vincent de Paul, to the various charitable organizations; but in most cases the letter had been thrown into the waste basket, the requests to assist ignored; and yet the people needed care and looking after.

Despairing of obtaining assistance from catholic sources, other people took on themselves the care of helping the families, with the result that, in many cases, the children were weaned from the Church.

We saw at once the field this work opened for us. We saw also the danger of neglecting this great means of doing good. Therefore, several catholic gentlemen became actively connected with the association. We soon made our people familiar with its purposes; we also received a warm welcome from the charity organization society. Our assistance was valued very highly and our advice appreciated.

From this beginning has spread a better feeling, a closer relation between the various charities than we had ever hoped for. It will certainly contribute more than anything else to that Christian unity which our beloved, august, and respected Pontiff so earnestly recommends. Perhaps the grand spectacle of a body of laymen devoting their leisure time, the world over, to visiting and relieving the poor has excited the admiration of our non-catholic friends more than anything else; — no paid agents, no class distinction, no petty social differences, all working gratuitously for God's poor, following the same rule, and practicing the same methods.

I have dwelt somewhat at length on the relations of the society of St. Vincent de Paul with the charity organization society because that society has been the great means of accomplishing this co-operation and of extending all the other charities.

Jewish Welfare Board

The Jewish Welfare Board, an American creation, arose in direct response to the requirements of the nation during World War I. For one thing, the selection of Jewish chaplains for the armed services required a Jewish voice. But, as noted below, "no single agency could be selected as representative of the Jewry in America." Thus the new board met the external need even as it satisfied internal requirements for greater unity in action. In this respect, it resembled the "Y" movement (and there were also Young Men's and Young Women's Hebrew Associations) as well as the Knights of Columbus, also referred to in the following document. (The major Roman Catholic fraternal order, the Knights of Columbus started out as a heavily Irish mutual aid society in New Haven, Connecticut, in 1882. In World War I it served as the chief channel of assistance and support for Roman Catholic servicemen.)

The Jewish Welfare Board

By Chester Jacob Teller
Executive Director, Jewish Welfare Board

Primarily the purpose of the Jewish Welfare Board is to help America win the war. Despite the basic American principle of a separate Church and State, or, to be more exact, because of it, the American Government in the first days of the war perceived the necessity of calling upon certain religious welfare agencies to co-operate with it. It sought this co-operation because it recognized the value of morale in warfare, and knew how close was the relationship between morale and modern community ways of life. With a breadth of view and a degree of foresight, perhaps never before equalled by a war administration of any other

[Source: *American Jewish Yearbook*, XX (Philadelphia: Jewish Publication Society of America, 1918), pp. 88-89.]

country, the United States Government set itself to thinking out the war problems not only in terms of ships, guns, munitions, and supplies, but also in health, decency, personal improvement of the men, contentment, esprit. In short, all those elements that go to make up the concept of morale in its broadest implications received the closest study and the most thorough-going application.

A special Commission on Training Camp Activities was created, as a branch of the War Department, charged with the specific duties of making life in the new American camps and in the communities adjoining the camps as normal as conditions of actual war and the problems of an unprecedented national emergency would permit. This commission sought to utilize the potential social resources of the country, and it early brought to bear on the problem the whole strength of the Young Men's Christian Association, with its nation-wide organization, so thoroughly alive to the needs of young men, and so excellently adapted to the nation's new work.

In the same spirit and for the same purposes the War Department . . . invited the large Catholic group in America to participate in the national welfare program, with the result that the Knights of Columbus was nominated by the Catholic Church and accepted by the American Government as the authoritative Catholic agency for war purposes.

The selection of the third agency to represent what might be considered the third largest religious group in America, namely, the Jewish group, was fraught with difficulties. It is a commentary upon Jewish life in America, and particularly upon its work of national organization and management, that with 260 years of history behind it, and with literally thousands of organizations, no single agency could be selected as representative of the Jewry of America. True, one or two of them seemed to have some special claim to such recognition, but by reason of their limited constitution or platform, or for some other reason, they failed to secure the endorsement of the Jews as a whole. The result was a meeting of representatives of some ten or more national Jewish organizations, at which it was decided that each organization present should delegate certain powers to a new agency. This was the beginning of the organization which has since become known as the Jewish Welfare Board, and which has obtained the official recognition of the Government and, indeed, its mandate to contribute on behalf of the Jews of America to the national work of welfare among the nation's uniformed men.

•

Gathering the Divided

Federal Council and Christian Cooperation

The first quarter of the twentieth century saw a great increase in cooperation across denominational lines, even across religious lines. World War I, as we have seen, provided much of the impetus, but certainly not all. The Federal Council of Churches, for example, had been formed well before the war when, in 1908, thirty denominations joined together "to bring the Christian bodies of America into united service for Christ and the world." Writing more than a decade later, Charles S. Macfarland (General Secretary of the Federal Council from 1911 to 1930) explained that in the "new and complex social order" everything was getting federated and organized except religion. That condition required changing, for "we spoke with voices, but not with a voice."

Our various denominations and sects arose largely from the demand for freedom, and through much suffering we found our freedom. We are now recognizing as denominations, however, that the highest freedom we possess may be the freedom to give up some of our freedom for the sake of the common good. This was the kind of freedom to which Paul referred in his discussion of those denominational differences which had already begun in the Apostolic Church. We are ready to acknowledge, without forgetting perhaps that in our intellectual expression of truth we have been of Apollos or Cephas, that we are all of Christ, and that in allegiance to Him we must maintain or regain unity even in the midst of our diversity. We are following still farther our denominational search for freedom, and are seeking this highest freedom in our modern movements towards Christian unity. . . .

Meanwhile one of the most startling of modern discoveries is that we have been so sadly and thoughtlessly wasteful. We have wasted our mineral wealth, squandered our forests, and allowed the mighty forces of our streams to run out into an unneeding sea.

Worse still, in the development of industry, and by social neglect, we have wretchedly wasted our human power and, as our new legislation witnesses, we have been criminally prodigal with human life itself. We have poisoned, neglected, maimed, and mangled by our inefficient speeding up, by our twelve-hour days and seven-day weeks. . . .

But these are not an intimation of the worst of our dissipations, and in-

---

[Source: C. S. Macfarland, *The Progress of Church Federation* (New York: Fleming H. Revell Co., 1921), pp. 10-11, 11-12, 14-16.]

deed these wastes have been largely because of a deeper and more serious prod-igality. We have let the very light within us become darkness, and the saddest of all has been the waste of our moral powers, our finer emotions, and our religious enthusiasms, through sectarian divisions, denominational rivalries, and unrestrained caprice often deluding itself as a religious loyalty. . . .

Meanwhile the development of a new and complex social order about us was getting ready for the call of a persuasive and effective gospel. New foes were arising on every hand. They were all united, and we found ourselves facing federated vice, the federated saloon, federated corruption in political life, federated human exploitation, and then all these together multiplied in one strong federation, the federation of commercialized iniquity. All of these were bound together in a solemn league and covenant, and the reason they so confidently faced a derided Church was because they faced a divided one.

On the one hand were the federations of labor and on the other hand federations of capital, girding themselves for their conflict, waiting the voice which should speak with power and influence, that should quell their human hatreds.

Problems of social justice were looking to us with beseeching voice, and we found ourselves obliged to face them, or, worse still, to shun them, with shame upon our faces and with a bewildered consciousness, because we had no common articulation of a code of spiritual principles or moral laws. Our spiritual authority was not equal to our human sympathy, because it was divided.

On all these things we had a multitude of voices trying to express the same consciousness, but the great world of men did not know it. Why should they know it when we had not found it out ourselves, We spoke with voices, but not with a voice.

Very nearly up to our own day the Church has faced united iniquity while there has been scarcely a city in which it could be said, in any real or serious sense, that its churches moved as one great force. And in many a town and rural village we yet have churches wearying themselves to death in a vain struggle for competitive existence, or suffering from that worst of diseases, to be "sick with their brothers' health."

What wonder that we have lost our civic virtue! Why should we not lose, not only our Sabbath as a day of worship, but also our Sunday as a day of rest? Why are we surprised that we have lost not only temperance laws but also our temperate ways? Why should we be astonished that with the loss of these we have also lost our sons and filled our houses of refuge with our daughters? Why should we wonder that the rich have left us for their unrestrained, unholy pleasure and the poor because we had no united sense of power of social justice to restrain an industry that devoured widows' houses and that bound heavy burdens grievous to be borne, especially when this was sometimes done by those who for a pretense made long prayers? What wonder that, with disintegrated religions which gave no adequate sense of religion, the home should lose its sacredness and the family become the easy prey of easy divorce and of unholy marriage? Still we went on singing: "Like a mighty army moves the Church of God." And when we came to resolve it to its final analysis the only trouble was that we did not sing together.

National Catholicism

World War I did provide the direct stimulus for a more unified social engagement on the part of America's Roman Catholics. In 1917 a general convention in Washington, D.C., led to the creation of a National Catholic War Council to supervise the recruitment and training of military chaplains as well as to oversee other war-related activities. But when the war ended, the new-found unity was not allowed to lapse. A National Catholic Welfare Council (and later Conference) kept the same initials in 1919 but widened its scope to include a broad array of social concerns. The entire American hierarchy, gathered at the Catholic University of America, addressed many issues in their long Pastoral Letter of 1919, but among them were the scope and structure of this revised organization.

In view of the results obtained through the merging of our activities for the time and purpose of war, we determined to maintain, for the ends of peace, the spirit of union and the coordination of our forces. We have accordingly grouped together, under the National Catholic Welfare Council, the various agencies by which the cause of religion is furthered. Each of these, continuing its own special work in its chosen field, will now derive additional support through general cooperation. And all will be brought into closer contact with the Hierarchy, which bears the burden alike of authority and of responsibility for the interests of the Catholic Church.

Under the direction of the Council and, immediately, of the Administrative Committee, several Departments have been established, each with a specific function, as follows:

The Department of Education, to study the problems and conditions which affect the work and development of our Catholic schools;
The Department of Social Welfare, to coordinate those activities which aim at improving social conditions in accordance with the spirit of the Church;

[Source: Peter Guilday, ed., *The National Pastorals of the American Hierarchy, 1792-1919* (Westminster, Md.: Newman Press, 1954), pp. 296-97.]

The Department of Press and Literature, to systematize the work of publication;

The Department of Societies and Lay Activities, to secure a more thoroughly unified action among our Catholic organizations.

For the development and guidance of missionary activity, provision has
been made through The American Board of Catholic Missions, which will have
in charge both the Home and the Foreign Missions.

The organization of these Departments is now in progress. To complete
it, time and earnest cooperation will be required. The task assigned to each is so
laborious and yet so promising of results, that we may surely expect, with the
Divine assistance and the loyal support of our clergy and people, to promote
more effectually the glory of God, the interests of His Church, and the welfare
of our country.

Cooperative Judaism

*By the end of the first quarter of the twentieth century, the divisions in Juda-
ism described above (see pp. 29-34) were familiar across much of the American landscape. Many voices spoke for Judaism in America. Was it possible for
Judaism on certain subjects and under certain circumstances to speak with
one voice? That hope led to the formation of the Synagogue Council of America on November 9, 1926, in the city of New York. Never as integrative as some
of its founders hoped, the Council did nonetheless become the cooperative
arm of Judaism in dealing with the Federal Council of Churches as well as the
National Catholic Welfare Council. It also played a major role in the National Conference of Christians and Jews, an interfaith agency formed in
1928. A portion of the 1926 Constitution of the Synagogue Council is excerpted below, along with part of a 1931 statement of its progress to that point.*

Constitution and By-Laws of the Synagogue Council of America

Preamble

Whereas, The synagogue is the basic and essential unit of our Jewish life, and
whereas it is desirable that the representatives of the synagogues in America

---

[Source: *The Synagogue Council of America: Its Origin and Activities* (New York: n. p., 1931), pp.
2-3, 6.]

meet from time to time in order to take counsel together for the sacred purpose of preserving and fostering Judaism,

Be it resolved, That a Council composed of representatives of national congregational and rabbinical organizations of America be formed, for the purpose of speaking and acting unitedly in furthering such religious interests as the constituent organizations in the council have in common; it being clearly provided that the council interfere in no way with the religious and administrative autonomy of any of the constituent organizations.

Name

The name of the organization shall be "The Synagogue Council of America."

Membership

The organizations constituting this council shall be

> Central Conference of American Rabbis
> Rabbinical Assembly of the United Synagogue of America
> Rabbinical Council of the Union of Orthodox Jewish Congregations of
>   America
> Union of American Hebrew Congregations
> Union of Orthodox Jewish Congregations of America
> United Synagogue of America

and such other similar national organizations as may be admitted from time to time. Each constituent organization shall be entitled to three members in the Synagogue Council as well as to three alternates. The alternates shall have the privilege of attending all meetings of the Council and participating in discussion. In case of the absence or disability of a delegate, an alternate shall be entitled to vote in his stead. . . .

The Spirit of the Council

Whatever doubts existed as to the practical need of the Synagogue Council, or that representatives of different shades of religious doctrine in American Israel could meet in candor and good will for mutual action were soon dissipated. In four years of earnest and thoughtful conference the Synagogue Council of America has vindicated the high expectations of its advocates. More than good will between Jews and Christians is good will between Jews and Jews and an appreciation of their differing viewpoints is necessary and desirable.

Devotion and candor dominate the delegates. The sacred cause of advancing Judaism guides its representatives. The Council is not given over to a compilation of statistics. It is not carried away by the cry of the majority nor by passion for publicity. Essentially a deliberative body, its conclusions are arrived at only through careful and thoughtful study.

The combined membership of the three rabbinical associations in the Council represents 800 rabbis, or sixty-five percent of all the Jewish ministers in the United States. The Union of Orthodox Congregations, the United Synagogue of America, and the Union of American Hebrew Congregations have a joint membership of 800 congregations. Conservatively estimated, this means that the Synagogue Council of America speaks for at least one million Jewish men and women in our country, and is therefore representative of the religious affiliation of the majority of American Jews. If so, religious Israel has found a voice. The Synagogue Council of America must interpret that voice. Why then should it not develop a statesmanship of policy, authority, and direction?

Drying Out the Republic

Billy Sunday (1862-1935)

Serving as the prototype for Sinclair Lewis's Elmer Gantry, *Billy Sunday dominated the revivalist scene in the early years of the twentieth century. Lacking the professionalism of C. G. Finney (see* Documentary History, *vol. 1, pp. 321-24) and the quiet assurance of D. L. Moody (see below, pp. 278-81), Sunday compensated with sensationalism and high drama. A former professional baseball player, this preacher sought to be nothing more than "one of the boys": unsophisticated, sometimes coarse, given to oversimplification, and sharing the limits of the culture that spawned him. What follows is a portion of his vigorous attack on "the hell-soaked liquor business"; the excerpt also illustrates something of Billy Sunday's sermon style.*

Listen! Here is an extract from the *Saturday Evening Post* of November 9, 1907, taken from a paper read by a brewer. You will say that a man didn't say it: "It ap-

---

[Source: William T. Ellis, *"Billy" Sunday: The Man and His Message* (Philadelphia: L. T. Myers, 1914), pp. 113, 114-15.]

pears from these facts that the success of our business lies in the creation of appetite among the boys. Men who have formed the habit scarcely ever reform, but they, like others, will die, and unless there are recruits made to take their places, our coffers will be empty, and I recommend to you that money spent in the creation of appetite will return in dollars to your tills after the habit is formed."

What is your raw materials, saloons? American boys. Say, I would not give one boy for all the distilleries and saloons this side of hell. And they have to have 2,000,000 boys every generation. And then you tell me you are a man when you will vote for an institution like that. What do you want to do, pay taxes in money or in boys?

I feel like an old fellow in Tennessee who made his living by catching rattlesnakes. He caught one with fourteen rattles and put it in a box with a glass top. One day when he was sawing wood his little five-year-old boy, Jim, took the lid off and the rattler wriggled out and struck him in the cheek. He ran to his father and said, "The rattler has bit me." The father ran and chopped the rattler to pieces, and with his jack-knife he cut a chunk from the boy's cheek and then sucked and sucked at the wound to draw out the poison. He looked at little Jim, watched the pupils of his eyes dilate and watched him swell to three times his normal size, watched his lips become parched and cracked, and eyes roll, and little Jim gasped and died.

The father took him in his arms, carried him over by the side of the rattler, got on his knees and said, "O God, I would not give little Jim for all the rattlers that ever crawled over the Blue Ridge mountains."

And I would not give one boy for every dirty dollar you get from the hell-soaked liquor business or from every brewery and distillery this side of hell....

You men have a chance to show your manhood. Then in the name of your pure mother, in the name of your manhood, in the name of your wife and the poor innocent children that climb up on your lap and put their arms around your neck, in the name of all that is good and noble, fight the curse. Shall you men, who hold in your hands the ballot, and in that ballot hold the destiny of womanhood and childhood and manhood, shall you, the sovereign power, refuse to rally in the name of the defenseless men and women and native land? No.

I want every man to say, "God, you can count on me to protect my wife, my home, my mother and my children and the manhood of America."

By the mercy of God, which has given to you the unshaken and unshakable confidence of her you love, I beseech you, make a fight for the women who wait until the saloons spew out their husbands and their sons, and send them home maudlin, brutish, devilish, stinking, blear-eyed, bloated-faced drunkards.

You say you can't prohibit men from drinking. Why, if Jesus Christ were here today some of you would keep on in sin just the same. But the law can be enforced against whisky just the same as it can be enforced against anything else, if you have honest officials to enforce it. Of course it doesn't prohibit. There isn't a law on the books of the state that prohibits. We have laws against murder. Do they prohibit? We have laws against burglary. Do they prohibit? We have laws against arson, rape, but they do not prohibit. Would you introduce a bill to repeal all the laws that do not prohibit? Any law will prohibit to a certain extent if honest officials enforce it. But no law will absolutely prohibit. We can make a law against liquor prohibit as much as any law prohibits.

Anti-Saloon League

Once again effective social action demanded organization. To make the Eighteenth Amendment (1919) a reality, more was required than the passionate denunciations of a Billy Sunday. Political action was called for: organized, deliberate, and as patient and single-minded as the circumstances demanded. The Anti-Saloon League, formed in 1895, worked slowly but steadily toward its goal of a national prohibition against the manufacture and sale of alcoholic beverages. In an article written in 1908, one sees this calm, unwavering purpose. The author, Superintendent of the Oakland District (California) for the League, also explains that the churches were the "natural starting point" and most fertile soil for cultivating members, monies, and energies. Individual reform can go only so far; then, social organization and political action are required.

There are but two methods of accomplishing reforms where the action of others is necessary for success. Either the will of these others must be influenced by persuading them that the change is right, or they must be forced to take certain action because it is best for their own welfare. When a moral reform is started, its method is always that of persuasion, but the time always comes when persuasion has accomplished its purpose, and the cause of reform is abated; or it is seen that the method is useless because it is too slow; or enough people have been convinced by this method to make a use of force hopeful.

As in other reforms, the agitation and effort to curb the vice of drunkenness began by persuasion and with the individual. A hundred years ago, men began signing pledges in order to bolster up a weak will, and then set about organizing societies and persuading others to join and sign pledges. Many confirmed drunkards were reformed, and with a true missionary spirit they began

[Source: W. M. Burke, "The Anti-Saloon League as a Political Force," in *Annals of the American Academy of Political and Social Science*, 33 (Nov., 1908), 27-28, 29-30.]

to induce others to follow their example. In the United States, seventy years ago, so great was the work done by these reformed drunkards — mainly by platform lectures — that thousands of men and women were persuaded.

Thirty years later, another great wave of persuasion was started, slightly different because it aimed, not at the drinker himself, but at the man who sold the drink. Moreover, it was the women, for the most part, who never drank at all, who were most active. Their method of persuasion was to appeal to the saloon keeper in a public way, through his religious instincts and his family affection, by praying and singing hymns in his place of business or on the sidewalk before it, and by personal solicitation for the sake of his mother's memory or his wife and children, or because of the injury to his customers and their families. This method was successful, in many cases, in persuading the saloon keeper to give up the business, but its greatest success lay in the fact that out of it grew an organization whose sole purpose it was to combat drunkenness through persuasion. The Woman's Christian Temperance Union has never seriously attempted anything but to persuade children to shun intoxicants, drinkers to give it up, men in the business to get out of it, or legislators to legislate against it. In the hands of this organization, the moral suasion method has been remarkably successful, and the present attitude of the public is largely due to its incessant propaganda.

The first attempt to substitute compelling force for moral suasion is to be found in the formation of a political party with a single plank in its platform, viz., the prohibition of the manufacture and sale of intoxicating liquors. Its avowed object was to put its own candidates in office, pass the necessary laws and enforce them. Many of the leaders in this movement believed it to be hopeless, but expected to gain adherents enough to hold the balance of power. In some cases, this was accomplished, and the old parties were forced to take account of the prohibition vote. The best recognition they could force from either of the old parties was the statement in the platform of the Republican party, in one national campaign, that "That first concern of all good government is the virtue and sobriety of the people and the purity of the home. The Republican party cordially sympathizes with all wise and well-directed efforts for the promotion of temperance and morality." The work of the Prohibition party has been very largely the same as that of other temperance organizations, viz., the changing of the attitude of the people toward drunkenness and the licensing of the liquor traffic.

As a result of all this agitation, and the public sentiment adverse to the saloon, the trade began to protect itself, entrenching itself behind state laws, and for this purpose made a very effective political organization. There was no organized political opposition, and as a result they held the balance of power between the parties. . . .

The Anti-Saloon League was organized to combat the political organiza-

Suffragette picketing the White House, 1918
(National Archives and Records Administration)

tion of the liquor traffic. It was believed, and the event has largely proven it true, that in most communities there were more anti-saloon than there were pro-saloon votes, and if the great mass of anti-saloon votes could be organized, the power of the saloon in politics would be broken.

The natural starting point was the church, for here was already an organization, which, by ideal and aim, by tradition and leadership, was in direct and absolute opposition to everything the saloon was doing. It was already recognized that if the church was right, the saloon was wrong, and that the church must overcome the saloon or eventually be overcome by it. The great obstacle had been that the saloon did not go to the church, and it was contrary to church tradition and policy for the church to go where the saloon was, viz., into politics. Church forces finally found the answer to the problem thus presented in an agency more or less organically combined with the church, and in its organization rather indirectly responsible to the church which could go into politics and could in time organize and concentrate the votes of the church men and the independent anti-saloon vote against pro-saloon candidates. The organization of the church was effected by having delegates from the different denominations meet in convention and elect a board of trustees. This board of trustees outline the entire policy for the league. They elect an executive committee which is, in reality, a board of strategy, and also a superintendent who is the leader or general of the forces in the field. He appoints his subordinates or district leaders throughout the state. This is the state organization which does the actual work. The board of trustees meet once a year or oftener, while the executive committee meets at least once a month, and in the heat of a campaign will be found meeting very much oftener.

Suggested Reading (Chapter Eight)

A helpful orientation to many strands of public religion in America from the late nineteenth century forward has been offered by Martin E. Marty in his multi-volume series *Modern American Religion,* including for the period up to the Second World War, vol. 1: *The Irony of It All, 1893-1919* (1986), and vol. 2: *The Noise of Conflict, 1919-1941* (1991).

What is variously known as social justice, social action, or social gospel has received considerable attention in American religious history. Two older treatments still merit careful study: C. H. Hopkins, *The Rise of the Social Gospel in American Protestantism, 1865-1915* (1940), and Henry F. May, *Protestant Churches and Industrial America* (1949). A generous sample of the writings of three major figures (Washington Gladden, Richard Ely, and Walter Rauschenbusch) is provided in Robert T. Handy, *The Social Gospel in America, 1870-1920* (1966). For most recent treatments, consult Ralph Luker, *The Social Gospel in Black and White: American Racial Reform, 1885-1912* (1991), and Susan Curtis, *A Consuming Faith: The Social Gospel and Modern American Culture* (1991).

On the Roman Catholic side, Aaron I. Abell has provided *American Catholicism and Social Action: A Search for Social Justice, 1865-1900* (1963), and edited *American Catholic Thought on Social Questions* (1968). Equally useful is David O'Brien, *American Catholics and Social Reform: The New Deal Years* (1968). For a contemporary perspective on one of the most active Catholic social movements, see John Fitzsimmons and Paul McGuire, eds., *Restoring All Things: A Guide to Catholic Action* (1938). A solid biography of John A. Ryan has been done by F. L. Broderick, *Right Reverend New Dealer* (1963), and Robert E. Weir offers a broader context for much religious-economic history in *Beyond Labor's Veil: The Culture of the Knights of Labor* (1996). For Jewish responses to the challenges posed by city and factory, see Elias Tcherikover and Aaron Antonovsky, eds., *The Early Jewish Labor Movement in the United States* (1961), and Beth S. Wenger, *New York Jews and the Great Depression* (1996). On municipal reform — or its absence — the anthology by Robert D. Cross, *The Church and the City, 1865-1910* (1967), is most instructive. And while the Bible was appealed to by both those proposing and those resisting reform, its wide use in this and other periods of American history is considered in Ernest R. Sandeen, ed., *The Bible and Social Reform* (1982).

How religion meets the challenges of war is never a simple question of resistance or support. Generally one finds some of both, often in the same denomination, sometimes even in the same individual. In World War I, the support (often uncritical) of the clergy for the war is fully revealed in R. H. Abrams, *Preachers Present Arms* (1933). Voices for peace in this war, as well as other recent wars, are well presented in James C. Juhnke and Carol M. Hunter, *The Missing Peace: The Search for Nonviolent Alternatives in United States History* (2001). Providing balance between the bellicose and the pacifist is John F. Piper, Jr., *The American Churches in World War I* (1985). On Kirby Page specifically, see Charles Chatfield, *Kirby Page and the Social Gospel: Pacifist and Social Aspects* (1974). There is full-scale treatment of the Oxford Group Movement in Garth Lean, *On the Tail of a Comet: The Life of Frank Buchman* (1986).

For Americans learning about and taking some responsibility for the world, the early twentieth century represented a time of rapid advance in missionary effort. Understanding Christian missions in the modern period still needs the Olympian perspective provided by Kenneth Scott Latourette in his five-volume *Christianity in a Revolutionary Age* (1958-62). Efforts from the mainline Protestant churches are authoritatively treated in William R. Hutchison, *Errand to the World: American Protestant Thought and Foreign Mission* (1987), while the same is done for more evangelical groups in Joel A. Carpenter and Wilbert R. Shenk, eds., *Earthen Vessels: American Evangelicals and Foreign Missions, 1880-1980* (1990). For American involvement in China, the era's largest mission field, see Patricia R. Hill, *The World Their Household: The American Woman's Foreign Mission Movement and Cultural Transformation, 1870-1920* (1985), and on the relationship of missionaries to indigenous developments there, Daniel H. Bays, ed., *Christianity in China* (1996). The work of important individuals may be followed in C. H. Hopkins's exhaustive biography, *John R. Mott, 1865-1955* (1979), Stephen A. Graham, *The Totalitarian Kingdom of God: The Political Theology of E. Stanley Jones* (1998), and W. R. Wheeler's life of Robert Speer, *A Man Sent from God* (1956). An innovative general study of how foreign missionary service exerted an influence back on to American society has been provided by Daniel H. Bays and Grant Wacker, eds., *The Foreign Missionary Enterprise at Home* (2003), a collection that contains Wacker's perceptive essay on the tangled career of Pearl S. Buck. For Roman Catholic missions see *The Mission Apostolate: A Study of the Mission Activity of the Roman Catholic Church* (1942), issued under the auspices of the Society for the Propagation of the Faith, U.S. More recent studies include Sister Marcelline, *Sisters Carry the Gospel* (1956), Penny Lernoux, et al., *Hearts on Fire: The Story of the Maryknoll Sisters* (1993), and Jean-Paul Wiest, *Maryknoll in China . . . 1918-1955* (new ed., 1997). Contemporary responses to the criticisms of missionary activity excerpted above are included in C. H. Patton, *Foreign Missions Under Fire* (1928), C. A. Selden, *Are Missions a Failure?* (1927), and Robert E. Speer, *Are Missions Done For?* (1928). On the large participation by African American churches in foreign missionary effort, see Sylvia M. Jacobs, *Black Americans and the Missionary Movement in Africa* (1982), and especially James T. Campbell, *Songs of Zion: The African Methodist Episcopal Church in the United States and South Africa* (1998).

On the new organizations brought into existence in order to meet the new needs of industrial society, there are now many fine studies. The best recent accounts of the Salvation Army are Edward H. McKinley, *Marching to Glory: The History of the Salvation Army in the United States, 1880-1992* (new ed., 1995), and Diane Winston, *Red-Hot and Righteous: The Urban Religion of the Salvation Army* (1999). On the Society of St. Vincent de Paul, see D. T. McColgan, *A Century of Charity*, 2 vols. (1951). There are, in addition, many accounts of various Sisters of Charity and Sisters of Mercy at work in a single diocese or a single state. Christopher Kauffman's *Faith and Fraternalism: The History of the Kings of Columbus, 1882-1982* (1982) is a careful examination of this important Catholic men's organization. For general studies outlining the transatlantic forces at work in the era of increased social concern, see James T. Kloppenberg, *Uncertain Victory: Social Democracy in European and American Thought, 1870-1920* (1986), and Daniel T. Rodgers, *Atlantic Crossings: Social Politics in a Progressive Age* (1998).

The first quarter of the twentieth century witnessed intensified ecumeni-cal activity, not all of it related to World War I. The creation of the Federal Council of Churches and the fortunes of its early years may be discerned in E. B. Sanford, *Origin and History of the Federal Council* (1916) and Samuel E. Cavert, *The American Churches in the Ecumenical Movement, 1900-1968* (1968). Good recent biographies of Billy Sunday include Lyle W. Dorsett, *Billy Sunday and the Redemption of Urban America* (1991), and Robert Francis Martin, *Hero of the Heartland: Billy Sunday and the Transformation of American Society, 1862-1935* (2002). On the prohibitionist cause more generally, fine studies have been done by Norman H. Clark, *Deliver Us from Evil: An Interpretation of American Prohibition* (1976), and Thomas R. Pegram, *Battling Demon Rum: The Struggle for a Dry America, 1880-1933* (1998).

NINE

Worlds Within and Beyond

Much of American religion remains hidden from public view, operating in quiet privacy or within a subculture to which the wider world is largely oblivious. Still other religious elements do not so much engage the surrounding culture as they stand aloof from or in opposition to that "mainstream." Yet to ignore all of these manifestations of religion in America would be to ignore a very great deal; indeed, it might be to ignore the principal points at which religion bears upon the daily lives of most men and women in the nation.

Private Religion

In a sweeping oversimplification, Alfred North Whitehead once defined religion as what a man does with his solitariness, a definition that nevertheless contains a certain kernel of truth. It is in those lonely emergencies of life, to cite William James, another Harvard philosopher and colleague of Whitehead, that one's creed is tested. Not all such lonely emergencies lend themselves to documentation, of course, but one can observe those places where people turn for inspiration or solace, for guidance in how to live and in how to find meaning in whatever life has offered to them.

For a hundred years or more, one of those places to which vast segments of the American public have turned is the novel and its various fictionalized lives of Jesus. Though the novel is a modern art form (and therefore under some suspicion earlier in many religious circles), it had by the end of the nineteenth century won a place among many of the religiously minded. The novel, it was discovered, could offer instruction in virtue, could demonstrate the calamities awaiting the wicked, and could even convey insight into religious history and doctrine. For the American reading public, that last service was most conspicuously rendered in those imaginative reconstructions of the life of Jesus which, beginning with *Ben-Hur* in 1880, held millions enthralled. Through such novels, one walked the dusty roads of Judea, observed the political-military fortunes of Imperial Rome, marveled at the origins and progress of Christianity. But most of all, one found personal assurance and sustaining inspiration.

However popular such books proved to be, they of course only complemented, never challenged, that perennial best-seller, the Bible. In whatever translation or edition or abridgment, the Bible sold and the Bible was read. In red letter format (the red being used for the words of Jesus), in slim single-book paperbacks (the Gospel of John being the most popular), in pocket-size, India-paper editions (often, the New Testament plus the Book of Psalms), in mammoth pulpit size, in print enlarged for failing eyes, in braille, on records, with study outlines, commentaries, concordances, and an entire industry of "aids" and "helps," the Bible reached every hamlet and into nearly every home. Daily Bible reading, widely encouraged, was often regarded as the mark of the serious and committed believer as opposed to the mere church-attending dilettante.

Along with Bible reading (although by no means limited solely to that context), the most private moments of prayer and meditation took place. To commune with the Divine and perchance to enter into the presence of the Divine may be to approach the very heart of the religious life. Something of the nature of these activities, then, however intimate or however solitary, must be understood. For "the joy of communion with God," as Rufus Jones noted, "is the central function of prayer and it is one of the most impressive facts of life."

In the rhythms of the religious life, some celebrations coincide with such central events as birth, puberty, marriage, death. Other events superimpose an ecclesiastical calendar upon the seasonal rotations of sun, moon, and earth. Thus, for example, we observe a springtime Easter, a harvesttime Rosh Hashana, a winter solstice Christmas. But the most obvious rhythm in America's religious life is the special setting aside of one day in seven: Remember the sabbath day, to keep it holy. How that day should be remembered, and even when, has been severely contested throughout the nation's history. That contest has not been limited to the churches and synagogues, but has time and again crowded the dockets of municipal, state, and federal courts. For millions of Americans, controversy notwithstanding, being religious has had direct implications for what one did, where one went, how one's thoughts were guided on that single special day of the week.

Pulpits served as one obvious and often powerful instrument for the guidance of sabbath thoughts, the voices from some of those pulpits reverberating far beyond the walls of a local sanctuary. While not exclusively a Protestant art form, preaching was more the centerpiece, more the "main event" of Protestant services than of most others. Protestant clergy were commonly addressed as "Preacher" for such was their most obvious — and often their most influential — role. In 1924 the nondenominational *Christian Century* conducted a poll to determine the most effective practitioners of the pulpiteering art: "men of prophetic vision, of pulpit power, whose message seems most vitally to interpret the mind of Christ." From over twenty thousand responses, twenty-five ministers were selected as the country's "pulpit leaders." Four of these are presented individually later in the chapter, but here a few general comments may be in order. The denominations most generously represented among the winners were Presbyterian, Congregational, Methodist, and Baptist. While it is perhaps not surprising that in the 1920s one finds neither blacks nor women in the top twenty-five, it is surprising that such large and national groups as Lutheran and Episcopalian are wholly absent. Whatever the merits and the criteria of choice, it is evident that American pulpits, long before the electronic age, commanded large audiences and influenced many lives.

New Thought and New Thoughts

In the second half of the nineteenth century a mixture of ideas, visions, and techniques joined in varying ways to win zealous followings and fashion new institutions. Some of the mixture was foreign born. Sweden's Emmanuel Swedenborg (1688-1771), for example, left a legacy of visionary writings that migrated to America (though he did not), where they influenced a small number profoundly and a large number superficially. Swedenborg's emphasis on health and healing appealed to some, his "spiritualizing" of biblical history and law to others, his optimistic certainties to still others. He emphasized "the eternal lustre of the gospel," wrote Henry James, Sr. (one of those influenced profoundly), "by disclosing its interior or spiritual and philosophical contents. . . ." Another European, Friedrich Mesmer (c. 1734-1815), Austrian physician and astrologer, stressed the power of the mind to heal and to communicate with the beyond, thereby contributing "mesmerism" (or hypnotism; also, animal magnetism) to the American vocabulary. From the orient, religious and philosophical concepts, severed from their ancient cultural roots, made their way to the West where they competed with the traditional orthodoxies of Judaism and Christianity. All reality is one, and all reality (including humankind) is divine; evil has no independent existence, and sin leaves no enduring stain. East and West met in America, mixing and mutating in ways that brought further variety onto the national scene.

An International New Thought Alliance, organized in 1915, resolved "to teach the infinitude of the Supreme One, the Divinity of Man and his Infinite possibilities through the creative power of constructive thinking. . . ." The Alliance also dedicated itself to maintaining some semblance of unity among its many proponents and advocates, but that goal proved ever elusive. New Thought had too much rich complexity, too much wide ambiguity, too much ready opportunity for it to be able to keep everything together. And even those specific institutions discussed in the chapter — Christian Science, Unity, Religious Science — struggled within their own subcategories to keep the household of the faithful under a single roof. Those struggles never wholly succeeded.

Private proclaimers, freshly inspired healers, charismatic leaders — all cultivated their own followings. In some instances, however, as with Russell H. Conwell and Norman Vincent Peale (see below), the following was purely personal so that no new church or denomination emerged. What did emerge was the application of a transcendental optimism to the tasks or travails of this world: you *can* find health, happiness, and prosperity; you *can* win!

But connections between the spiritual and the material worlds, between mind and body, were not the preoccupations alone of the New Thought practitioners. The late nineteenth century also saw the development of psychology, psychiatry, and psychoanalysis as the names of other Europeans — Freud (1856-1939), Adler (1870-1937), Jung (1876-1961) — became familiar in more and more households. "Spiritual healing" in this context came to be discussed by the clinically trained physician along with the theologically informed clergyman. And in most of these discussions, the emphasis was not on faith versus medicine, or on the spiritual versus the physical, but on an openness to whatever therapy seemed most appropriate to the case at hand. As Seward Hiltner wrote: "In some situations the surgeon's knife must cut out the offending tissue in order to release the forces of healing; in other cases the personality analysis is the central need; and in still other cases the conscious recognition of the power of these healing influences is most needed." The point is to know the virtues and the limits of each type of therapy, then to discover how the three methods, "applied intelligently, benefit the whole person more than any single one without the others."

Society Out of Joint

Those who saw maladjustments in largely personal terms found comfort or care in many options newly available in the twentieth century. Those who saw ills more in the body social than in the body personal also proposed novel options and assorted remedies. Some argued that the time had come to put some limits on democracy in America, at least on that kind of democracy represented by an open, prodigal invitation to all the world's tired, poor, hungry, and what-have-you. For example, should America's Protestants (or was it "Protestant America") continue to be deluged by the flood of Roman Catholic immigration? New England, once the bastion of Puritanism and the Protestant work ethic, was being totally transformed. Writing for the *Forum* in 1889, a Massachusetts headmaster decried that great change from "a homogenous people of common faith and common speech and common love for the common wealth" to "populations diverse in creed and in tongue, untrained to liberty and a republican form of government, and with no respect for the ashes of the dead from which has sprung our fatherland." And so in 1894 an Immigration Restriction League was formed in New England, even as in Iowa an American Protective Association, anti-Catholic in purpose, had been organized seven years earlier. These voices helped prepare the soil for a revived Ku Klux Klan which in the 1920s became even more explicit about what constituted the true American: namely, native, white, Protestant. It was a good time for shutting down open immigration (accomplished in 1924), a bad time for Catholic Alfred Smith to run for President (defeated in 1928).

On the economic front, questions raised timidly about capitalism in the 1920s boomed boldly in the 1930s as the grim grip of the Great Depression refused to let go. The American economic system was desperately ill: none would deny that. But was it fundamentally incurable? At bottom, could one reconcile the ethics of Jesus with the mindless pursuit of profit? or the motive of love with the drive of greed? or the absolute ideals of faith with the arbitrary operations of the marketplace? These questions, not easy ones at any time, pressed cruelly when all seemed so wrong in the Western economic world, when much seemed so promising in a rising Marxist world. And to these queries that sounded more like anguished cries, what did religion in America have to say? Not much, a young Reinhold Niebuhr feared: "If religion is to contribute anything to the solution of the industrial problem, a more heroic type of religion than flourishes in the average church must be set to the task."

World Out of Time

Whatever the ills of the time, other religious voices were raised to remind Americans of a God above and beyond time, to remind them, in other words, of eternity. Revivalists of this period were the prime reminders: eternity, and how one spends it, is life's central question and most crucial choice. Nothing very complicated about the plan of salvation, Billy Sunday explained. It has only two parts: believe with your heart, and confess with your mouth. The crowds that pressed in to hear Dwight Moody in Brooklyn, Sam Jones in Atlanta, and Sunday in Chicago demonstrated that thousands shared the view that the issue of eternal life transcended all other issues. Earthly troubles, personal woes, social sicknesses — all those must be placed in the perspective of eternity. One can seek health, happiness, and prosperity, but none of these — nor anything else — can a man or woman exchange for his or her soul.

While some messengers stressed the rescue of the soul from a sinful world, others promised the rescue of that sinful world itself: a rescue in the form of the Second Coming of Jesus, the establishment of a New Jerusalem on earth. Millennialism, a familiar theme in American history (see *Documentary History*, vol. 1, pp. 357-62), in the twentieth century proved its persisting popularity yet again. Jehovah's Witnesses spoke of 1914 as the fateful year, while Aimee Semple McPherson preferred to assert with finality but with less temporal precision: "JESUS IS COMING SOON — GET READY TO MEET HIM." An especially pervasive form of millennialism, that known as dispensationalism, spread through many denominations and dominated the theology of such popular preachers as G. Campbell Morgan and Dwight L. Moody, both treated herein, and of many more besides. A single volume, the *Scofield Reference Bible*, found such wide acceptance as to insure that expectations concerning the imminent end of the world reached from pulpit into pew, from school desk to family hearth.

But if God delayed in descending from heaven to purify and redeem the earth, perhaps individual Christians could, through the aid of the Holy Spirit, reach a heavenly purification and perfection on their own. Methodism's John Wesley had written a "plain account" of Christian perfection in 1739 (revised often through 1777, and reprinted countless times thereafter) which encouraged many to move beyond "the elementary doctrines of Christ" to the maturity of entire sanctification. The holiness movement began in America before the Civil War, but flourished and proliferated abundantly after that conflict. A "National Camp Meeting for the Promotion of Christian Holiness," formed in 1867, gave promotional direction and impetus to the movement. Sired by Methodism, a whole progeny of independent holiness denominations grew up in the late nineteenth and early twentieth centuries. So also the closely related pentecostal movement, which stressed an even more charismatic, spirit-filled service of worship, the most distinctive feature of which was glossolalia, or speaking in tongues. For many, this powerful experience proved beyond doubt the presence of the Holy Spirit and the gift of God's "second blessing," the first having been salvation itself. For others, an even more dramatic evidence of the Spirit's presence and power came in the act of healing. "Once I was blind, but now I see" had proved a powerful testimony many centuries ago; it continued to draw the unbelievers, even as for the believers it sealed and confirmed their faith.

1. Private Religion

Inspirational Reading: Lives of Jesus

The Greatest Story Ever Told

Fulton Oursler (1893-1952), long associated with Reader's Digest, *became a Roman Catholic in the course of the eleven years that he spent writing* The Greatest Story Ever Told *(1949). One generalization about the novels discussed here should be offered: they were all enormously successful in sales. This was certainly true of Oursler's book, which was in no degree limited to or directed toward a specifically Catholic audience. Soon after its publication in 1949,* The Greatest Story *topped the best-seller list, was syndicated in over two hundred newspapers, and was translated into several languages. The episode below tells of Jesus' birth, though, as with all fictionalized versions of such events, it moves far beyond the meagre details offered in the Gospels of Matthew and Luke.*

Now they entered the streets of Bethlehem, and the press of pilgrims was so great that the pair could scarcely move forward; no one would even listen to Joseph when he asked the way to a hotel; one urchin laughed in his face at such a question. Five hostelries they tried but all were filled up. Joseph kept on doggedly, he forced his way through the door of the last tavern and demanded to talk to the host.

"My wife is ill," pleaded Joseph. "Her baby is about to be born."

The innkeeper was a stout and grumpy man with an enormous stomach.

[Source: Fulton Oursler, *The Greatest Story Ever Told* (Garden City: Doubleday & Co., 1951 [1949]), pp. 49-51.]

He had rolls of fat under his chin, and little dumplings hanging under his eyes, and oily gray curls.

With red hands clasped in front of him, he gaped at these four Nazarenes, and it seemed to Joseph as if all mercy fled from his little eyes. For a moment he said nothing; then he curled fat fingers around his mouth and bawled hoarsely:

"Sarah!"

His wife, just as stout as he was — she might have been himself in women's clothes — came shuffling from the back of the house.

"What you want?" she demanded, hoarse voice a replica of his own.

"Look at this woman."

"Which?"

"The young one, not the old one."

"I see her, yes."

"Is she having her baby now or is this a scheme to get lodgings?"

The greasy wife leaned forward, hardening the creases in her neck.

"This one," she announced, voice even hoarser with fright, "is having the baby now. I know. I have had ten."

"Please," implored Joseph, "for the love of God —— "

"Don't you realize," growled Sarah, "the place is full? All Bethlehem is full. There's not a bed in the town tonight. But she can't have a baby here on the floor. We've got to do something. Gabriel!"

"Hah?" answered the innkeeper obediently.

"There is one warm and comfortable place where we haven't put anybody yet."

"Is there now? Where? Just where?" demanded Gabriel.

"In the stable!"

"The stable!" echoed Joseph miserably, and Anna put her arms around Mary. But the young wife looked gratefully at the innkeeper's wife.

"You are very kind to think of it," she said. "A stable is warm. And it will be like home, because often I slept downstairs with the sheep and the goats." She turned to Joseph. "These people would surely take good care of their animals. And we will be alone there."

She turned quickly back to the old woman.

"You will not rent it to anyone else besides us?" she pleaded.

"No," smiled Sarah slowly, with a reluctant chuckle. "And I will help you. God knows we women have got to help each other."

The stable was in a roomy cave that extended under the whole building of the inn. Joseph held Mary's hand as he led her down twisting stone steps to an earthen floor; in his free hand he held a lantern that threw against the rough walls the magnified shadows of Anna and Joachim and Mary and himself.

"Where are we going to put her down?" cried Anna distractedly.

Heaving and puffing, the stout Sarah came clumping down the stairs behind them, and after her Gabriel, puffing even louder than his wife, both clasping fresh bundles of straw. They laid a bed against the inner wall, which was warmer and not so damp, and they brought linen and a coverlet and a pillow for Mary's head.

Then Gabriel and Sarah had to leave them, for business was brisk upstairs, but both of them paused to give a hoarse: "God be with you tonight!" As their footsteps died away the four at last felt relieved, if only to be alone. Anna helped Mary to undress, and then she went upstairs in search of jars of heated water, while Joseph stood near brooding.

"Why do we have no sign now?" he was asking himself. "Where is the angel? Why doesn't Anna hurry back?"

Anna soon came back with the water. She briskly exiled Joseph and Joachim through a rear door in the stable, bidding them to stay out until they were sent for. It was dark outside, the night air moist and cold.

Meanwhile Anna, with the wisdom of old wives, urged Mary not to lie on the straw but to get up and walk. Mary obeyed. Back and forth in the stable she walked, amid the braying of donkeys and bleating of sheep, her nostrils filled with the sweet, pungent odors of barley and oats and hay. To and fro she walked.

And Joseph was trudging up and down in the dark area behind the stable. Again and again he tightened and then loosened the frayed girdle around his travel-stained robe. He fingered the pouch that held his store of coins and wondered whether he had enough money to see them through. The hours dragged on. Joachim had sat down on his haunches and soon fell asleep. But Joseph walked on like a man in a nightmare, waiting, praying until at last and suddenly he heard the sound — a child's first cry.

In the dimmish light he knelt beside the bed of staw where Mary lay, pale and weak but wide-eyed and with a small, brave smile for him.

"See!" she murmured.

Joseph was on his knees. Mary held out firm hands, lifting up her son, wrapped in Grandmother Anna's swaddling clothes — lifting him up adoringly, the fate of the world reposing in the chalice of her hands.

Even in the first instant of seeing the child Joseph was aware of something extraordinarily different about him. Somehow he knew that this newborn baby, whose face was not red and crinkled but smooth and white, and whose expression was of such potent innocence and affection, had come into the world to get nothing and to give everything.

The Nazarene

A decade earlier Sholem Asch (1880-1957), a Polish-born Jew, published his life of Jesus, The Nazarene *(1939). With a thorough Hebrew education in rabbinical schools in Poland, Asch emigrated to the United States in 1914 and became a naturalized citizen six years later. Offering a much more informed commentary on Jewish life and times in the first century of the present era, Asch lifted the genre to a higher level. Though Asch hoped that his life of Jesus (Yeshua, or simply "Rabbi" in the novel) would have significant impact on the Jewish community, its great and enduring popularity was among the Gentiles. In the excerpt below, the narrator (one of the twelve disciples) relates an episode that, while it resonates with New Testament language, is the imaginative creation of the author.*

And we were then twelve disciples who had left our own, wife and child, house and field; we had forsaken all that was ours and we had followed after him. For he persuaded us and we hearkened unto him, and we became his possession, the souls which he had made. And we were in his hand as the clay in the hand of the potter, and he could do with us as he willed, for we believed in his words.

And it came to pass on a certain day that we were on the way with our Rabbi and it was the oncoming of night, and we reached a certain inn and we entered there. And we encountered therein a company of scorners, and the chief among them was a dissolute old man; and they drank beer mixed with honey and they laughed and mocked and spoke much folly. And the slave that served them was a scholar and a man of learning who had been sold into slavery for debt. And it came to pass that when the company of scorners grew merry, they threw what was left of their drinks in the face of him that served them, and they broke the vessels on his head, and the slave stood and endured the shame that they did unto him and answered not a word. And the dissolute old man laughed loudly so that his cheeks became red and the white locks of his beard shook, and he said:

"Tell me thy text, thou son of an ass."

And the learned man that was the slave answered and said: "The days of man are like the grass, he is like the blossom of the field." And when the old man heard these words he smote the slave with his fist and said:

"I have come out with my friends to rejoice and be merry, and thou comest and disturbest our joy. A bad servant art thou."

And when we saw this thing, then Jochanan, of the brothers Zebedee, spoke unto our Rabbi:

[Source: Sholem Asch, *The Nazarene* (New York: G. P. Putnam's Sons, 1939), pp. 212-14.]

"Rabbi, why sufferest thou him to have dominion? Shall I make him silent?"

And our Rabbi answered: "I am not come to destroy a soul, but to build up." And he drew near the old man and said unto him:

"I will give thee such joy as none shall ever disturb, and none shall ever take it from thee."

And the old man answered:

"Thou speakest assuredly of wine. For it is written: 'Wine rejoiceth the heart of man.'"

And the Rabbi answered him and said:

"A joy whereof the end is sadness is not a joy. Come, I will give thee a joy which is like unto a well, which groweth ever stronger and it hath no end."

And the old man asked:

"What is that joy which hath no end?"

And the Rabbi answered him:

"It is the joy which a man hath of his father, the creator of the world. This is the joy that hath no end, and the joy of the kingdom of heaven none shall take from thee, for it is not outside of thee but within thee."

And the old man said:

"That joy is hidden from me, for the path to my father in heaven is cut off by many sins which I have committed in my life."

And the Rabbi said:

"Thou makest thyself great in that thou makest thyself little. The gates are ever open for those that would return."

And the old man said:

"Is there still hope for me? I in no wise knew it."

And he drew near to the slave and fell at his feet and begged forgiveness of him; and our Rabbi said unto us:

"Come and behold: with one word canst thou fling thy brother into the nethermost pit and with one word canst thou bring him under the wings of the glory. Therefore be not deceived by that which your eyes see, but see what is in the heart of a man." And to the servant he said: "When thy brother sinneth against thee, punish him, and when he repenteth, forgive him." And he made peace between them. And he said to the old man:

"Arise, thou art comforted."

And he sat down with them, and drank wine with them, and he changed the company of the scornful into a company of brothers, as it is written: Brothers dwelling together.

The Robe

*The crucifixion scene, and specifically the untold, unknown fate of Jesus'
robe, provided the plot line for Lloyd C. Douglas (1877-1951), Lutheran clergyman turned full-time novelist. In The Robe, Douglas consciously followed
in the tradition set by Lew Wallace (1827-1905) in the much reprinted, often
dramatized, Ben-Hur: A Tale of the Christ (1880). Strictly speaking, The
Robe is not a life of Jesus, but a novelistic reflection on Christ's influence via
the garment which he wore at his death. But the whole context of the Near
East is so amply provided as to give the reader a sense of immediacy with Jesus and the first followers. In the episode below, the Roman soldier
Marcellus, hero of the story, has fortified himself with alcohol for the unpleasant task of standing guard during Jesus' hours on the cross.*

There was not as large a crowd as he had expected to see. There was no disorder,
probably because the legionaries were scattered about among the people. It was
apparent, from the negligence of the soldiers' posture, as they stood leaning on
their lances, that no rioting had occurred or was anticipated.

Demetrius moved closer in and joined the outer rim of spectators. Not
many of the well-to-do, who had been conspicuous at the Insula, were present.
Most of the civilians were poorly dressed. Many of them were weeping. There
were several women, heavily veiled and huddled in little groups, in attitudes of
silent, hopeless grief. A large circle had been left unoccupied below the crosses.

Edging his way slowly forward, occasionally rising on tiptoe to search for
his master, Demetrius paused beside one of the legionaries who, recognizing
him with a brief nod, replied to his low-voiced inquiry. The Commander and
several other officers were on the other side of the knoll, at the rear of the
crosses, he said.

'I brought him some water,' explained Demetrius, holding up the jug. The
soldier showed how many of his teeth were missing.

'That's good,' he said. 'He can wash his hands. They're not drinking water
today. The Procurator sent out a wineskin.'

'Is the man dead?' asked Demetrius.

'No — he said something awhile ago.'

'What did he say? Could you hear?'

'Said he was thirsty.'

'Did they give him water?'

'No — they filled a sponge with vinegar that had some sort of balm in it,
and raised it to his mouth; but he wouldn't have it. I don't rightly understand

[Source: Lloyd C. Douglas, *The Robe* (Boston: Houghton Mifflin Co., 1942), pp. 134-37.]

what he is up there for — but he's no coward.' The legionary shifted his position, pointed to the darkening sky, remarked that there was going to be a storm, and moved on through the crowd.

Demetrius did not look at the lonely man again. He edged out into the open and made a wide détour around to the other side of the knoll. Marcellus, Paulus, and four or five others were lounging in a small circle on the ground. A leather dice-cup was being shaken negligently, and passed from hand to hand. At first sight of it, Demetrius was hotly indignant. It wasn't like Marcellus to be so brutally unfeeling. A decent man would have to be very drunk indeed to exhibit such callous unconcern in this circumstance.

Now that he was here, Demetrius thought he should inquire whether there was anything he could do for his master. He slowly approached the group of preoccupied officers. After a while, Marcellus glanced up dully and beckoned to him. The others gave him a brief glance and resumed their play.

'Anything you want to tell me?' asked Marcellus, thickly.

'I brought you some water, sir.'

'Very good. Put it down there. I'll have a drink presently.' It was his turn to play. He shook the cup languidly and tossed out the dice.

'Your lucky day!' growled Paulus. 'That finishes me.' He stretched his long arms and laced his fingers behind his head. 'Demetrius,' he said, nodding toward a rumpled brown mantle that lay near the foot of the central cross, 'hand me that coat. I want to look at it.'

Demetrius picked up the garment and gave it to him. Paulus examined it with idle interest.

'Not a bad robe,' he remarked, holding it up at arm's length. 'Woven in the country; dyed with walnut juice. He'll not be needing it any more. I think I'll say it's mine. How about it, Tribune?'

'Why should it be yours?' asked Marcellus, indifferently. 'If it's worth anything, let us toss for it.' He handed Paulus the dice-cup. 'High number wins. It's your turn.'

There was a low mutter of thunder in the north and a savage tongue of flame leaped through the black cloud. Paulus tossed a pair of threes, and stared apprehensively at the sky.

'Not hard to beat,' said Vinitius, who sat next him. He took the cup and poured out a five and a four. The cup made the circle without bettering this cast until it arrived at Marcellus.

'Double six!' he called. 'Demetrius, you take care of the robe.' Paulus handed up the garment.

'Shall I wait here for you, sir,' asked Demetrius.

'No — nothing you can do. Go back to the Insula. Begin packing up. We want to be off to an early start in the morning.' Marcellus looked up at the sky. 'Paulus, go around and see how they are doing. There's going to be a hard storm.' He rose heavily to his feet, and stood swaying. Demetrius wanted to take his arm and steady him, but felt that any solicitude would be resented. His indignation had cooled now. It was evident that Marcellus had been drinking because he couldn't bear to do this shameful work in his right mind. There was a deafening, stunning thunderclap that fairly shook the ground on which they stood. Marcellus put out a hand and steadied himself against the central cross. There was blood on his hand when he regained his balance. He wiped it off on his toga.

A fat man, expensively dressed in a black robe, waddled out of the crowd and confronted Marcellus with surly arrogance.

'Rebuke these people!' he shouted, angrily. 'They are saying that the storm is a judgment on us!'

There was another gigantic crash of thunder.

'Maybe it is!' yelled Marcellus, recklessly.

The fat man waved a menacing fist.

'It is your duty to keep order here!' he shrieked.

'Do you want me to stop the storm?' demanded Marcellus.

'Stop the blasphemy! These people are crying out that this Galilean is the Son of God!'

'Maybe he *is*!' shouted Marcellus. '*You* wouldn't know!' He was fumbling with the hilt of his sword. The fat man backed away, howling that the Procurator should hear of this.

Circling the knoll, Demetrius paused for a final look at the lonely man on the central cross. He had raised his face and was gazing up into the black sky. Suddenly he burst forth with a resonant call, as if crying to a distant friend for aid.

Bible Reading and Daily Meditation

Advice to Catholic Girls

Books that change history are seldom the same books that change or profoundly influence the lives of "ordinary" men and women. In many American homes where few books are to be found, traditionally one of those has been the Bible. In addition, one may find a service book, a missal, a guide to

---

[Source: George Deshon, *Guide for Catholic Young Women*, 31st ed., rev. (New York: Arno Press, 1978 [1897]), pp. 77-80, 80-82.]

daily devotions. Or, in the case of those who have no books or perhaps do not read, meditations may center upon an icon, an amulet, a rosary, a crucifix. In the popular guide represented here (over thirty editions between 1868 and 1897), Paulist priest George Deshon (1823-1903) stressed the importance of good thoughts, good books, and the Good Book.

Books are, next to sermons, next to the living voice of the preacher, the most powerful means to excite us to virtue. Get, then, at least a few books, and read them when you get a chance.

"Oh!" says a good girl, "I wish I could! I have never been taught to read, and am now too old to learn; besides, I have no opportunity for learning; there is no one to teach me, and I haven't the time."

Now, do not be cast down on that account. There is one beautiful book, at least, we can read; and that is the Crucifix. What fountains of knowledge and true wisdom it contains! You can look at it, and think over what it means, from one year's end to another, yet you will never reach the bottom of it.

St. Bonaventure, who wrote so many beautiful things, was asked where he got them all? What books he had learned them out of, "There is my book," said he, pointing to the Crucifix; "all my knowledge, all my thoughts come from that."

Another lovely book you have that you can read, though you never learned a letter of the alphabet, and that is the Rosary. Millions who could not read a word have read that book every day. Get some one to teach you the meaning of the mysteries, and you will never fail to have the best of books always at hand. There is no need, then, to be cast down because you cannot read; only keep your heart simply directed to God, and he will make up abundantly for all that is lacking. Many of the saints have not been able to read, but they could pray, and think of Christ's sufferings and love for them, wonderfully well.

"But why say a word about those who cannot read, since they cannot read what you say?" That is true; but somebody else may read it to them, or tell them, and then my object will be accomplished, which is to give every one such instruction and consolation as is necessary for them.

If you can read, then it is the Lord's will that you should make use of this gift; for He required us to make good use of all our talents and opportunities. "To whom much is given, of him much will be required" (St. Luke xii.48). . . .

You need not, however, have a great many books; a few good ones are all-sufficient to furnish food for your souls. Such books can be read over and over without getting tired of them. They will always renew some good impression, and excite in you a strong desire to regulate your life so as to please God better. There is one book far above all others that have ever been written or ever will be — that is, the Holy Bible. This book is different from all other books, because we can put the most entire confidence in all that is written in it. Why? It is God Himself, the Holy Ghost, that has caused it to be written for our benefit. This is

Sharecropper in Butler County, Missouri, 1939
(Library of Congress)

what the Scripture itself says: "All Scripture, divinely inspired, is profitable to teach, to reprove, to correct, to instruct in justice, that the man of God may be perfect, furnished unto every good work" (2 Tim. iii.16).

Especially is this the case with the New Testament, which is better fitted to our times and circumstances, which is for the most part plainer and easier to be understood, and which tells us all that has been done for us by our Saviour and His apostles. . . .

Every part of it is full of holy instruction, and I am not at all afraid that any harm will come to a well-intentioned, pure-minded person, from reading it; on the contrary, such persons will not fail to derive much good from it.

But does not St. Peter say, speaking of the epistles of St. Paul and the other Scriptures, that in them "are many things hard to be understood which the unlearned and the unstable wrest to their own perdition?" (2 Peter iii.16). Undoubtedly he does, and nothing can be more true. There are even things which seem perfectly plain and easy to understand, that would certainly mislead any but a scholar unless they were explained. Such things were understood well enough at the time they were written, because all the people were accustomed to use words in the sense in which the writers meant to use them. But now that language and manners have changed, these words have lost the meaning they had at that time, and convey a very different one to us. They must be explained or we shall be misled.

Other things are very deep and difficult in themselves, even to scholars, and it is a real folly to set up one's opinion about them without an explanation.

It is the Church's office to guard and preserve the true sense of the Scripture, as you remember the Scripture itself calls her "the pillar and ground of the truth." The Church, where the meaning of a passage is obscure, or has become changed in the translation from one language to another, has placed notes and explanations to preserve the original meaning. There can be no objection to reading a Catholic Bible, and I find it strongly recommended to the faithful as the best of all books to read.

A Protestant "Book of Hours"

In the Middle Ages, richly illustrated and painstakingly copied manuals of private devotion were called Books of Hours. The most popular Protestant devotional guide of the twentieth century, The Upper Room, *was the inspiration of a southern Methodist minister, Grover C. Emmons. Launched in 1935 (at five cents per copy), this quarterly of "daily devotions for family and individual use" grew in circulation from one hundred thousand to more than three million within a single generation. During that same period of growth,* The Upper Room *had also spread far beyond the borders of the United States. Translated into at least thirty languages, this guide called upon its faithful users to make this covenant: "1) To seek an enrichment of my own spiritual life by observing a period for devotions each day; and, 2) To share Christ with my fellows and endeavor to enlist them in His service." What follows is from the first issue of April, 1935; the pattern of Bible reading, meditation, and prayer was to continue unchanged.*

[Source: *The Upper Room* (Nashville, Tenn.: Methodist Episcopal Church, South, 1935), n.p.]

APRIL 2

"Jesus . . . departed into a desert place apart." Matt. 14:13.

A one-roomed house is fatal to refinement. Where there are no privacies the sweet and holy sentiments of life are inevitably lost. This is true also of spiritual attainments. Religion is born and fostered in the secret place. Much of the drabness and listlessness of present-day Christianity is our neglect of private meditation and prayer. Is this the reason for your uncertainty, and for the lack of joy in your religious experience? Religion without a closet loses its gentle refinements, its glow, its power.

We must not fail to observe how the life of the Lord Jesus moved constantly from great thoughts to great works, from solitude to society, from the closet of prayer to the field of action. The secret place was for Him central and essential. "What was indispensable to the Redeemer must always be indispensable to the redeemed." Therefore, He says to us, "Come ye yourselves apart." "Enter into thy closet, and when thou hast shut the door, pray."

Read Matt. 14

Synagogue service during World War II (June, 1944), New York City
(Library of Congress)

Prayer

> "My God, is any hour so sweet,
> From blush of morn to evening star,
> As that which calls me to Thy feet,
> The hour of prayer," Amen.

— Charlotte Elliott

Thought for the Day

The root of the spiritual life is a continuing sense of the presence of God.

Costen J. Harrell.

The Inner Life

Prayer

While some prayers are published and some (the Lord's Prayer, for example) even set to music, prayer is for the most part a private and therefore not readily visible affair. To ignore it, however, would be as inappropriate as it is misleading, for to many prayer is the essence of the religious life. The Quaker historian and Haverford College professor of philosophy, Rufus Jones (1863-1948), makes clear in the segment below that prayer is not primarily petition or asking of God, but it is communion with God. It is "practicing the presence of God," to use the title of a medieval classic. As such, prayer is not one of religion's props or extras or frills: it is the root of the matter.

Religion is primarily and at heart the personal meeting of the soul with God and conscious communion with Him. To give up the cultivation of prayer would mean in the long run the loss of the central thing in religion; it would involve the surrender of the priceless jewel of the soul. We might try in its stead to perfect the other aspects of religion. We might make our form of divine service

---

[Source: Rufus Jones, *Pathways to the Reality of God* (New York: Macmillan Co., 1931), pp. 241-42, 243.]

very artistic or very popular; we might speak with the tongues of men and sing with the tongues almost of angels, but if we lose the power to discover and appreciate the real presence of God and if we miss the supreme joy of feeling ourselves environed by the Spirit of the living and present God, we have made a bad exchange and have dropped from a higher to a lower type of religion.

Prayer, no doubt, is a great deal more than this inner act of discovery and appreciation of God, but the joy of communion and intercourse with God is the central feature of prayer and it is one of the most impressive facts of life.

The early Franciscans remained on their knees rapt in ardent contemplation praying with their hearts rather than with their lips. It was a prayer of quiet rather than a specific request. Francis thought of prayer as a time of storing up grace and power through union with God. He called it, in his happy phrase, sharing the life of the angels — a needed preparation for the life of action and service which were to follow it. . . .

One of these deep constructive energies of life is prayer. It is a way of life that is as old as the human race is, and it is as difficult to "explain" as is our joy over love and beauty. It came into power in man's early life and it has persisted through all the stages of it because it has proved to be essential to spiritual health and growth and life-advance. Like all other great springs of life, it has sometimes been turned to cheap ends and brought down to low levels, but on the whole it has been a pretty steady uplifting power in the long story of human progress. The only way we could completely understand it would be to understand the eternal nature of God and man. Then we should no doubt comprehend why He and we seek one another and why we are unsatisfied until we mutually find one another.

Mysticism

In the whole repertoire of religious experience, no term is more badly used than "mysticism." Often treated as a synonym for the strange, occult, mysterious, and irrational, the word loses all significant content. Relying on Rufus Jones once more, we learn that the mystic is disciplined and determined in his or her strenuous search for "that more than ourselves whom we call God." Himself a mystic, Jones was fully aware of the criticism frequently levied against the mystical experience — as against all strictly private experience insofar as it seeks to be a source of knowledge. But the quest is worthy, Jones argues, and the truth possibilities are real.

[Source: Rufus Jones, *New Studies in Mystical Experience* (New York: Macmillan Co., 1928), pp. 15-16, 18-20, 22-24.]

The mystic, as I hope to show, is not a peculiarly favored mortal who by a lucky chance has received into his life a windfall from some heavenly Bread-fruit tree, while he lay dreaming of iridescent rainbows. He is, rather, a person who has cultivated, with more strenuous care and discipline than others have done, the native homing passion of the soul for the Beyond, and has creatively developed the outreach of his nature in the God-direction. The result is that he has occasions when the larger Life with which he feels himself kin seems to surround him and answer back to his soul's quest, as a sensitized magnetic needle, if it were conscious, might feel itself enveloped by the currents that sweep back upon it from the electrical storehouse of the sun. . . .

When we raise the question of the objectivity of these experiences there is no easy answer. The proof of objectivity in any field, even in that of sense perception, has been the intellectual task of all the centuries, and after all the coöperative labor it is difficult to produce an argument that is bound to convince the doubter who questions whether the external world is the way it appears. Fortunately our common sense solves the problem for most of us. That and our practical nature carry us forward without waiting for the slow proofs.

In the world of values the case is somewhat different. There is present here a private, personal aspect which does not attach, to anything like the same degree, to objects of sense perception. My appreciation of music or of poetry has a subjective color all its own. No one else would feel quite at home in my inner aesthetic world. Nor can we without much adaptation pass on to others our judgments of right and wrong or our consciousness of duty. And yet the noblest minds have always refused to admit that beauty or obligation are out and out, through and through, subjective. These experiences in some sense have their ground in the eternal nature of things, and they conform, in inner law and substance, to some overarching reality beyond us but not alien to our finite minds. It seems evident that moral practice slowly builds up a richer, deeper inner life within us and reveals a cumulative power of moral advance which indicates that something in the deepest nature of the universe *backs* a person who is making his life an organ of ethical goodness.

There is the same kind of objective evidence in the highest forms of mystical experience. There is, to begin with, a majestic *conviction of objectivity.* The mystic is sure that he has found what he has been seeking — as sure as the climber is that he has reached his peak. The sight itself is convincing. It has all the certainty that objects of sense have to the normal man. But it must be admitted that the usual verifications of our sense facts are wanting. The mystic cannot describe his object in the categories of common speech, nor can he get the corroborative testimony of other spectators. He has seen what he has seen, and in its first-hand quality of acquaintance it forever remains just his incommunicable experience. That seems, no doubt, a damaging admission and, for some, ends the debate. . . .

Important as the mystical element is, it would be a grave mistake to *re-duce* religion to the bare basis of uninterpreted experience. We cannot have knowledge in any field without a body of observed facts, but knowledge does not consist of mere observations or experiments or empirical occurrences. It consists rather of systematic interpretation of observations and experiments and facts of experience. They are lifted up and seen in the light of the laws and principles which they exhibit.

So, too, religion in its full meaning is vastly more than flashes of insight, intuitions of a Beyond, invasions of an environing Life, convictions of a Light that never was on sea or land. Religion builds on these deep-lying intimations of the soul and would be poor without them, but there is immensely more to say before the whole truth is uttered. Religion draws upon the whole nature and all the resources of man's complete life. It is essentially bound up with all the processes of the intellect and with all the deeper issues of the will as well as with these first-hand intimations of the soul's vision. The present-day revolt from doctrine is in many ways superficial. There can be no great religion without the interpretation of life, of the universe, of experience, of mind, of God. What we ought to revolt from is traditional dogma. We ought to challenge the elaborate logical constructions of bygone metaphysics, and base our interpretations on the sure ground of *vital religious experience* and on the unescapable implications of our minds as they coöperate with a universe which reveals rationality from outermost husk to innermost core. In insisting on *experience* I am not unmindful of the more yet that must go with experience. It is no lazy mysticism that we want, no vain hope that God will give all the treasures of the Spirit "to His beloved in sleep." I have no word of encouragement to offer those persons who expect the palaces of the soul to be built and furnished by magically rubbing an Aladdin's lamp, or by saying over some "blessed word" like Mesopotamia, or some phrase from "the *patois* of Canaan." The religious life is of all things strenuous business. It calls for heroic adventure. But one of the essential aspects of religion now and always is the experiment, made in the soul's inner laboratory, of the personal discovery of that more than ourselves whom we call God.

Contemplation

For some pursuers of the holy grail, contemplation is not a few moments of quiet reflection but an entire way of life. Among the many orders of the Roman Catholic Church, for example, some are described as "contemplative" to distinguish them from orders whose primary mission is teaching or nurs-

---

[Source: Thomas Merton, *Sign of Jonas* (New York: Harcourt, Brace and Co., 1953), pp. 28-30.]

ing or missions or some other specialized activity. No twentieth-century American monastic attracted more attention than Thomas Merton (1915-68), a member of the Reformed Cistercians of the Strict Observance, or Trappists. Merton's popular autobiography, Seven Storey Mountain *(1948), told of his decision to enter the monastic order that required (in addition to the traditional vows of poverty, chastity, and obedience) the vow of silence. In a later book, Merton tells of his call to contemplation and of the necessity to remember that contemplation is never the end in itself: God and his glory is the end.*

March 10 [1947]

Yesterday I read a couple of chapters of the *Cloud of Unknowing*. Every time I pick up a book in that tradition, especially Saint John of the Cross, I feel like the three wise men when they came out of Jerusalem and out of the hands of Herod, and once more saw their star. They rejoiced with great joy. They were once more delivered from questions and uncertainties, and could see their road straight ahead. In this case it is not even a question of seeing a road. It is simpler than that. For as soon as you stop traveling you have arrived.

I can remember other passages of other books that have hit me with the same impact. They bear witness to moments when I knew, right down to the

Thomas Merton with the Dalai Lama in Tibet, 1968
(Trustees of the Merton Legacy Trust)

very depths of my being, that I had found the thing that God wanted for me. I remember, for instance, Saint Teresa's chapter on the real unimportance of involuntary distractions in the prayer of quiet, in *The Way of Perfection.* Then, four years ago, in the novitiate, I discovered all that section of *The Living Flame of Love,* in the third Stanza, where Saint John of the Cross talks about the "deep caverns" and about prayer. More recently there was a chapter in *Le Paradis Blanc,* about the interior life. The chapter is called *"Un Chartreux Parle."* But it applies just as well to us. In a different mode, I have been deeply impressed by Duns Scotus's distinction on beatitude, the 49th, in the IVth book of the *Oxoniense,* and by all Saint Bonaventure has to say about desire, especially in the *Itinerarium.* These things have gone deep into me and have shaped my life and my prayer. They have not only arrested my attention, they have transformed my soul. And yet I think that they have only been the last step in processes that grace was working secretly before. They have made me realize what had been going on inside me without my having been quite aware of it. For I read much the same things before I came to Gethsemani,[1] and they did not transform me at all. In fact I was barely able to grasp what they were all about. . . .

March 11

My intention is to give myself entirely and without compromise to whatever work God wants to perform in me and through me. But this gift is not something absolutely blind and without definition. It is already defined by the fact that God has given me a *contemplative* vocation. By so doing He has signified a certain path, a certain goal to be mine. That is what I am to keep in view, because that is His will. It means renouncing the business, ambitions, honors and pleasures and other activities of the world. It means only a minimum of concern with temporal things. Nevertheless, I have promised to do whatever a Superior may legitimately ask of me. That may, under certain circumstances, involve the sacrifice of contemplation. But it seems to me this sacrifice can only be a temporary thing. It can not mean the sacrifice of the whole contemplative vocation as such.

However, the important thing is not to live for contemplation but to live for God. That is obvious, because, after all, that is the contemplative vocation. That is why it is best to take religious obedience quite literally. As soon as obedience is tempered with conditions, the mind becomes unfit for contemplation. It falls into division because it has to choose between its own solicitudes and the will of the Superior. It has reserved to itself a whole useless field of interior activity (that of judging all the commands that come to it) and this will inevitably interfere with contemplation. If activity becomes too intense — there is no reason why you should not ask your Superiors to have a little pity on you.

1. Our Lady of Gethsemani Abbey, near Bardstown, Kentucky.

March 12 Feast of Saint Gregory the Great

What I wrote yesterday is ambiguous because it assumes that the Rule of Saint Benedict is ordered to a life of pure contemplation. As a matter of fact, it is not. The Fathers would perhaps have said that the Benedictine life was active, in so far as it involved labor, asceticism, active glorification of God in the office, and even a certain amount of teaching and preaching, at least within the monastic community.

Nevertheless, work in the fields helps contemplation. Yesterday we were out in the middle bottom, spreading manure all over the gray mud of the cornfields. I was so happy I almost laughed out loud. It was such a relief to get away from a typewriter.

One Day in Seven

"Remember the Sabbath Day"

Those standing in the Judeo-Christian tradition (where in fact the vast majority of religious Americans do stand) give special attention to the rituals of religion on one day of every week. For Orthodox Jews (and Seventh-Day Baptists, Seventh-Day Adventists, Worldwide Church of God, and others), that day is the sabbath, the seventh day of the week, honored in accordance with ancient command. Hannah G. Solomon (1858-1942), Chicagoan and founder of the National Council of Jewish Women in 1893, had the difficult task of relating her organization to a Jewish constituency of varying opinions and convictions. That variety was evident in the way that the sabbath was being kept — or not being kept. "Bring the Sabbath back into our homes," she urged, for the home is "the true center of lofty inspiration and hallowing customs."

[Council of Jewish Women]

If we followed the advice of all, we would be at one and the same time orthodox, conservative, radical. We refrain altogether from attempting to settle questions of theology. The most serious step we took was to pass resolutions. The effects of these we will learn at our next convention. The one that probably interests you the most was the one relative to the observance of a rest day,

---

[Source: Hannah G. Solomon, *A Sheaf of Leaves* (Chicago: privately printed, 1911), pp. 79-81.]

championed as was the day we observe by a member of this congregation. The opinions upon the question were various. We must acknowledge that Jews have no one rest day. Some worship on Friday evening, some on Saturday, some on Sunday. The sentiments connected with those days also vary. To the large majority at the convention, the Sabbath of the early home, with hallowed memories of childhood, was too sacred to be uprooted. They were teraphim of the fathers. Sentiment and feeling are never out of date, and we must hesitate to put down that resolution as an outbreak of hysteria. Hysterical women are out of fashion, anyway. Anyone interested in that specimen must go to the antiquity shops. He will find her lolling on a sofa of a hundred years ago. We are too healthy now for that. The new rest day fails to bring to many the message of the old. We know that the hour passed in this house has been a prop to modern Judaism. It is capable of supplying the spiritual need of any human being. But if the hour is passed with longing thoughts for the hours to follow, it is no improvement upon the Saturday morning when the men who come to say Kadish cannot wait for the benediction in order to get their mail.

If we look at it squarely, we have grown satisfied with half a Sabbath. Saturday afternoon is now a legal holiday, and we may see the services transferred to the afternoon. We must admit that we, like the rest, are satisfied with half a day. Our Sunday afternoons are not passed in accordance with the spirit of the old Sabbath. I am too strong a believer in clubs to say one word against them. I consider the social club one of the finest institutions of our day, one of the most potent agencies for fostering fellowship and good feeling. But a community which is able, as is this one, to give a practical lesson to the world upon the Sunday sabbath, should do something better in those beautiful places than turn them into gambling houses upon that day. I shall not say one word against gambling. I used to do that when I was young — I mean, very young. The only way to counteract vice is to make it powerless. This lies first in proper education, in giving other resources to boys. Every good actor and artist who comes to this city, which so liberally patronizes art, should devote some of his time to the amusement of the poorer class. We know it is not the poor alone who gamble and visit cheap amusements; but they are the only ones who can have nothing better. Our social clubs could do much toward introducing other methods of enjoyment on the rest day.

The Sunday service is one of the twentieth century reforms. Its associations are but forming. As yet we should have too much conscience to offer, to anyone who has the true sentiment for the old Sabbath and the religious spirit that comes with the day, such a half-day as a substitute. We must above all keep the heart warm. We cannot force, we must allow and encourage growth. . . .

We must bring the Sabbath back into our homes — the true center of lofty inspiration and hallowing customs. We must instruct our children in religion, however little we may seem to impress them at the time. In spite of the

"Now will you be good?" *New York Herald,* March 15, 1908
(Library of Congress)

natural cynicism of youth, time comes in the life of everyone when religion affords a prop and a consolation. Without hope and faith were the world bleak indeed at times. We may not comprehend Deity, yet religion brings trust and a consciousness of the Divine that we cannot well afford to lose.

"And on the First Day of the Week . . ."

The early Christian church gradually shifted its day of worship from the seventh day to the first, the shift being in part a memorial to the Resurrection. Such a shift was not without controversy, and controversies regarding Sunday — Sunday sports, Sunday mails, Sunday shopping, and the like —

[Source: Charles H. Huestis, *Sunday in the Making* (New York: Abingdon Press, 1929), pp. 245-47.]

have continued to the present. Even among earnest Christians, many dis-
agreements arose concerning the proper observance of the "Lord's Day." In
the 1920s a Canadian Methodist, Charles H. Huestis (1863-1953), wrote a
book on the development of Sunday as opposed to the sabbath, combining
both history and homily in his presentation. Like Hannah G. Solomon,
Huestis argued that Sunday was "pre-eminently a day for the Home."

The church has a duty to perform in guiding the minds and conduct of its people in the proper observance of Sunday. The time has come for the church to
work out some definite program of Sunday observance in this modern world,
so that the minds of the people may be clear upon the question. In making the
following suggestions for such a program, I shall follow, as I have throughout
the latter part of this study, the great word of Jesus. If the Sabbath was made for
man — and Sunday also — then it was made for his threefold nature — body,
mind, spirit.

Body. Sunday should be a day of recreation. The thought of freedom and
joy is associated with the Sabbath idea from earliest times, and any attempts to
make it a day of gloom, however well intentioned, have not been a success.
Hence recreation must have its place in Sunday observance, especially for children whose natural expression is in play. It need not be said that Sunday recreation should be in harmony with the character of the day as one of rest and
spiritual uplift, so that one may go back to his work on Monday not only with
renewed corporeal vigor, but also with a deeper sense of the presence of God in
the world and in his own life.

Mind. Sunday should be a day of thought and meditation. No man can
"live on twenty-four hours a day" — really live, not simply exist — who does
not give some attention to the serious side of life and the cultivation of his
mind. Sunday affords additional leisure for this occupation, and the man who
does not devote a part of the day to reading and thinking about matters outside
his daily life and occupation, becomes a mere slave to routine, and the ability to
think quickly declines.

Spirit. Sunday is a day of worship. No man is spending Sunday well, or
doing his duty to himself, his family or his community, who does not go to
church on Sunday. "I go to church on Sunday," said Mr. Gladstone, "because I
love religion, and I go to church on Sunday because I love England." I need not
add that Sunday is pre-eminently a day for the *Home,* and family life, a day
when we have leisure to follow the beautiful injunction of Froebel: "Come, let
us live with our children."

Popular Preaching

G. Campbell Morgan (1863-1945)

When Theodore Roosevelt described the White House as a "bully pulpit," he was speaking in the days before radio and television when a good many of the nation's pulpits were, in fact, "bully": that is, excellent or splendid. Pulpit and press were twin instruments of communication and persuasion, with congregations often finding their opinions sharpened or shaped by what they heard on Sunday mornings. G. Campbell Morgan, an Englishman and Congregationalist, traveled widely in this country lecturing on Bible subjects. He also for a time held pastoral responsibilities in New York City and Philadelphia. In the brief excerpt below, Morgan reviews biblical history "from Creation to Christ" in order to draw some "evident lessons."

The evident lessons of our study are two — first, *human failure;* second, *Divine progress.* Look where you will in human history, you find failure. The Fall and the Flood, Corruption and the Cross. Every time humanity is put upon a new footing it fails. Has God failed? Not once; everything has been preparatory and progressive. Let us retrace our steps. The Cross and all that it means was prepared for throughout Judaic history. This one nation of Israel learned, through battle and smoke, murmuring and forgiveness, captivity and deliverance, the great truth that there is but one God. Monotheism is the lesson which humanity has learned through Israelitish history. From the time when Israel came back out of Babylon, she never again set up idols. When that truth was enshrined for the world in the chosen nation, then the one God became flesh. God was preparing through the wonderful history of their times for the Incarnation. What of the failure that preceded the Flood? Sin worked itself out to the utmost head of corruption. God allowed it to have its own free working, and then He swept it away, and started man upon the next stage of history, having behind him that terrific example of what sin is when it is left to its own course. I am bold to say that human corruption, so far as its actual effects upon men's lives are concerned, has never reached the awful depths of degradation which prevailed before the flood, when the sons of men were holding intercourse with evil spirits.

Thus we have sin manifested and the one God seen; while the Incarnate Word takes that sin upon Himself, that the world may ever know, from that

---

[Source: G. C. Morgan, *God's Methods with Man* (New York: Fleming H. Revell Co., 1898), pp. 26-27.]

point onward, the meaning of sin as well as the meaning of God and His Divine government.

George W. Truett (1867-1944)

An intense and effective speaker, George W. Truett was long identified with all things Baptist in the state of Texas. For nearly half a century he occupied the pulpit of the First Baptist Church in Dallas, exercising wide influence throughout the South and, in his capacity as president of the Baptist World Alliance from 1934 to 1939, throughout much of the world. "Soul winning" was what he preached, and what he practiced. In this sample of his sermon style, one sees an explicit and unapologetic evangelism which indeed characterized the Southern Baptist Convention of which Truett was a vital part.

A Quest for Souls.

Text: "And he brought him to Jesus." — John 1:42.

The bringing of a soul to Jesus is the highest achievement possible to a human life. Some one asked Lyman Beecher,[2] probably the greatest of all the Beechers, this question: "Mr. Beecher, you know a great many things. What do you count the greatest thing that a human being can be or do?" And without any hesitation the famous pulpiteer replied: "The greatest thing is, not that one shall be a scientist, important as that is; nor that one shall be a statesman, vastly important as that is; nor even that one shall be a theologian, immeasurably important as that is; but the greatest thing of all," he said, "is for one human being to bring another to Christ Jesus the Savior."

Surely, he spoke wisely and well. The supreme ambition for every church and for every individual Christian should be to bring somebody to Christ. The supreme method for bringing people to Christ is indicated here in the story of Andrew, who brought his brother Simon to Jesus. The supreme method for winning the world to Christ is the personal method, the bringing of people to Christ one by one. That is Christ's plan. When you turn to the Holy Scriptures, they are as clear as light, that God expects every friend He has to go out and see if he cannot win other friends to the same great side and service of Jesus.

"Ye shall be witnesses unto me," said Jesus, "both in Jerusalem, and in all

---

[Source: George W. Truett, *A Quest for Souls* (Dallas: Texas Baptist Book Store, 1917), pp. 57-58.]
  2. See *Documentary History*, vol. 1, pp. 304-10.

Judea, and in Samaria, and unto the uttermost parts of the earth." The early church went out and in one short generation shook the Roman empire to its very foundation. It was a pagan, selfish, sodden, rotten empire, and yet in one short generation, that early church had shaken that Roman empire from center to circumference, and kindled a gospel light in every part of the vast domain. And they did it by the personal method. The men and the women and the children who loved Christ, went out everywhere, and talked for Christ, in the hearing of those who knew Him not, and the hearers became interested, and followed on, and found out for themselves the saving truth that there is in Christ's gospel. Every Christian, no matter how humble, can win somebody else to Christ. You would not challenge that, would you? Let me say it again. Every Christian, however humble, can win somebody to Christ.

Francis J. McConnell (1871-1953)

Bishop of the Methodist Episcopal Church and from 1909 to 1912 president of De Pauw University, Francis McConnell was a prolific author as well as an effective spokesman from the pulpit. He was in particular demand by college audiences, and the following "chapel address" is an example of his art as well as a hint as to his theology. A social activist, McConnell nonetheless saw the responsible individual as the only foundation for any program of social improvement.

Zebedee

"And they left their father Zebedee in the boat with the hired servants." — Mark 1.20

The passage tells us that at the call of Jesus James and John left their father Zebedee, a fisherman, with his hired servants and followed the new Master. Because Zebedee remained in his boat he has suffered some rather severe treatment from homiletic interpretation. He has been painted as the stay-at-home who did not heed the call of Jesus. A brilliant preacher of the last generation had a notable sermon from the text which tells us that the mother of Zebedee's sons came with her sons upon one occasion to honor Jesus. The preacher entitled his sermon "Where was Zebedee?" And Zebedee was duly cudgeled for his lack of interest in religion.

[Source: Francis J. McConnell, *The Just Weight and Other Chapel Addresses* (New York: Abingdon Press, 1925), pp. 151-54, 155-56.]

On the occasion to which the brilliant pulpiteer referred it seems to me rather to the credit of Zebedee that he was not present. The motive that brought the mother of Zebedee's sons, with her sons, to Jesus was not wholly to honor Jesus but to seek the chief places in the Kingdom for James and John. It will be recalled that Jesus had to use some harsh words on that occasion. Probably the mother and the sons were in the after-years heartily ashamed of their request.

Another famous preacher has made it appear that this call to the men in the boat was a call to repentance and salvation and that Zebedee missed his chance. This explanation is hardly convincing. Jesus was not just then on an evangelistic tour. He was seeking men for membership in that group of disciples which was to be with him and learn of his teaching and his ways. It does not seem from the narrative that Jesus called Zebedee to discipleship. These preachers just mentioned are typical of the point of view from which many have approached Zebedee. I have known of revival appeals in which the deadness of Zebedee's heart has been dwelt upon with various expositions as to what had hardened his heart. He was too old, and had let too many appeals pass ever to be stirred again, an explanation which is, of course, sheer imagination. Or he was too much interested in fish. I once heard a young preacher shrewdly suspect that Zebedee was a capitalist, and had the capitalistic lack of interest in spiritual adventure.

Why not take the narrative just as it stands? Jesus called James and John, and they left Zebedee and followed Jesus. There is no hint that Zebedee was not a well-meaning man of good will, a hard-working fisherman, attending to his own business and taking things almost as they came, after the manner of fishermen. It was rather remarkable that he did not utter any word of remonstrance when his sons so summarily left him. There is this much of point in the hint that he was a capitalist — he had a boat and some nets. Those were tools. He hired and fired servants. That made him an employer of labor. All of which gives us a clue to his industry and sensible management, but none of which conveys a hint of any sort of dishonesty and exploitation.

Zebedee seems to me to stand out as the type of man who is an honorable stay-at-home, the man who keeps the ordinary work of the world going while the selected and called younger men fit themselves for special forms of service to God and man and move forth to make the world better. There is not much place for Zebedee personally in the field of such service itself. He is a little too old. It is no reflection on him that he does not at first glance recognize the Christ in this or that new movement. The trained disciples in the day of Jesus were themselves slow in recognizing the Christ in Jesus, or at least in recognizing the implications of Messiahship. Zebedee's age, however, prevents his making the readjustments necessary for active carrying out into apostleship the truth which he recognizes. It is best for him to stay where he is. . . .

An interesting and fruitful question concerning any forward social movement is, "Who pays?" War has had to meet the question, "Who pays?" and the question is deadly for the militarist. So with the constructive movements. All of these cost something, and somebody has to pay. Now, it may seem farfetched to ask of the school of the disciples, "Who paid?" but the question is pertinent. Zebedee paid. He paid in the fact that his sons left him and he allowed them to go, apparently without demur. He had to work harder because James and John were away with Jesus, or he had to hire more servants. The cost fell on Zebedee. He was not likely to be called on to suffer martyrdom, but he had to pay nevertheless. That he pays ungrudgingly is a mighty item to be put down to his credit. We see and hear James and John. We are charmed by their eloquence and zeal. Let us not forget Zebedee, who gave them their chance. He never writes any Gospels or Epistles but his signature is eloquent at the bottom of a check. The bright, ardent, young apostle starts out from the college amid the plaudits of those who expect him to turn the world upside down. If he ever does thus revolutionize the world, it will be because Zebedee, back among the boats and the nets and the fish, supplied him the leverage.

Does this seem fanciful? James and John, it appears, had some of this world's goods. They were not directly earning anything. Where did the contribution they made toward the upkeep of the little group come from? Where, but from Zebedee's nets? Zebedee knew that James and John were with Jesus. He did not understand what Jesus was trying to do. All he knew was that his sons believed in Jesus, that Jesus seemed to him to be in the right path, and that good for Israel might come out of it all. So he kept at his nets and helped feed the villages while the Master got his chance, occasionally sending fish and money to James and John. Let us not forget Zebedee who helped pay to teach the disciples.

Henry S. Coffin (1877-1954)

The youngest of the four ministers presented here, Henry Sloane Coffin had the advantage of an excellent education at Yale, in Edinburgh, and then in Marburg, Germany. Such heavy academic training made it highly probable that Coffin would have a career as seminary professor or even president — both of which he became at Union Theological Seminary in New York City. But Coffin was also a Presbyterian preacher (Madison Avenue Presbyterian Church) of major influence, and it is in that capacity that we read his explication of the "new life" in Christ.

[Source: H. S. Coffin, *Some Christian Convictions* (New Haven: Yale University Press, 1915), pp. 160-61.]

The New Life — Individual and Social

The health department of a modern city is charged with a double duty: it has to care for cases of disease, and it has to suggest and enforce laws to keep the city sanitary. The former task — the treament of sickness — is much more widely recognized as the proper function of the medical profession; the latter — the prevention of the causes of illness — is a newer, but a more far-reaching, undertaking. When Pasteur was carrying on his investigations into the origins of certain diseases, most of the leading physicians and surgeons made light of his work: "How should this chemist, who cannot treat the simplest case of sickness nor perform the most trifling operation, have anything to contribute to medical science?" But Pasteur's discovery of the part played by bacilli not only altered profoundly the work of physicians and surgeons, but opened up the larger task of preventive medicine.

The Gospel of Christ, in its endeavor to make and keep men whole, faces a similarly double labor. It has its ministry of rescue and healing for sinning men and women; it has its plan of spiritual health for society. It comes to every man with its offer of rebirth into newness of life: "If any man be in Christ, he is a new creature." It comes to society with its offer of a regenesis, a paradise of love on earth. The life of God enters our world by two paths — personally, through individuals whom it recreates, and by whom it remakes society; socially, through a new communal order which reshapes the men and women who live under it. The New Testament speaks of both entrances of the Spirit of God into human life: it pictures "*one* born from above," and "the holy *city* coming down from God out of heaven." The two processes supplement each other. Consecrated man and wife make their home Christian; a Christian home renders the conversion of its children unnecessary; they know themselves children of God as soon as they know themselves anything at all. Saved souls save society, and a saved society saves souls.

2. New Thought and New Thoughts

Theosophy and New Thought

H. P. Blavatsky (1831-91)

A native of Russia, Madame Blavatsky came to America in 1873, though "settled" in America would not be the proper expression. For a restlessness of mind, body, and spirit characterized all of her adult life. As Robert Ellwood wrote, ". . . always a wanderer, [she was] a colorful misfit in whatever society she found herself." Together with Henry S. Olcott (1832-1907), she founded the Theosophical Society in 1875. This organizational structure permitted expression of her deep interest in psychic phenomena, in the ancient wisdom of India, in the comparative study of the world's religions, and in universal brotherhood. She wrote voluminously, notably Isis Unveiled *(in two volumes, 1877) and* The Secret Doctrine *(in three volumes, 1888-97). In a dialogue between the "Enquirer" and the "Theosophist," the document below tells of the Society's broad purpose.*

ENQ. What are the objects of the Theosophical Society?

THEO. They are three, and have been so from the beginning. (1) To form the nucleus of a Universal Brotherhood of Humanity without distinction of race, colour, or creed. (2) To promote the study of the world's religion and sciences, and to vindicate the importance of old Asiatic literature, namely, of the Brahmanical, Buddhist, and Zoroastrian philosophies. (3) To investigate the hidden mysteries of Nature under every aspect possible, and the

[Source: H. P. Blavatsky, *The Key to Theosophy: An Abridgement* (ed. by Joy Mills) (Wheaton, Ill.: Theosophical Publishing House, 1972 [1889]), pp. 24-27.]

psychic and spiritual powers latent in man especially. These are, broadly
stated, the three chief objects of the Theosophical Society.

ENQ. Can you give me some more detailed information upon these?

THEO. We may divide each of the three objects into as many explanatory clauses
as may be found necessary.

ENQ. Then let us begin with the first. What means would you resort to, in order
to promote such a feeling of brotherhood among races that are known to
be of the most diversified religions, customs, beliefs, and modes of
thought?

THEO. Allow me to add that which you seem unwilling to express. Of course we
know that every nation is divided, not merely against all other nations,
but even against itself. Hence your wonder, and the reason why our first
object appears to you a Utopia. Is it not so?

ENQ. Well, yes; but what have you to say against it?

THEO. Nothing against the fact; but much about the necessity of removing the
causes which make Universal Brotherhood a Utopia at present.

ENQ. What are, in your view, these causes?

THEO. First and foremost, the natural selfishness of human nature. All the unselfishness of the altruistic teachings of Jesus has become merely a theoretical subject for pulpit oratory; while the precepts of practical selfishness, against which Christ so vainly preached, have become ingrained
into the innermost life of the Western nations. "An eye for an eye and a
tooth for a tooth" has come to be the first maxim of your law. Now, I state
openly and fearlessly that the perversity of this doctrine and of so many
others *Theosophy alone* can eradicate.

ENQ. How?

THEO. Simply by demonstrating on logical, philosophical, metaphysical, and
even scientific grounds that: *(a)* All men have spiritually and physically
the same origin, which is the fundamental teaching of Theosophy. *(b)* As
mankind is essentially of one and the same essence, and that essence is
one — infinite, uncreate, and eternal, whether we call it God or Nature —
nothing, therefore, can affect one nation or one man without affecting all
other nations and all other men.

ENQ. But this is not the teaching of Christ, but rather a pantheistic notion.

THEO. That is where your mistake lies. It is purely *Christian.*

ENQ. Where are your proofs for such a statement?

THEO. They are ready at hand. Christ is alleged to have said: "Love each other"
and "Love your enemies"; for "if ye love them (only) which love you,
what reward (or merit) have ye? Do not even the *publicans* the same? And
if you salute your brethren only, what do ye more than others? Do not
even publicans so?" These are Christ's words. But *Genesis,* ix, 25, says
"Cursed be Canaan; a servant of servants shall he be upon his brethren."

And, therefore, Biblical people prefer the law of Moses to Christ's law of love. They base upon the Old Testament, which panders to all their passions, their laws of conquest, annexation, and tyranny over races which they call *inferior*. What crimes have been committed on the strength of this infernal (if taken in its dead letter) passage in Genesis, history alone gives us an idea, however inadequate.

ENQ. I have heard you say that the identity of our physical origin is proved by science, that of our spiritual origin by Wisdom-Religion. Yet we do not find Darwinists exhibiting great fraternal affection.

THEO. This is what shows the deficiency of the materialistic systems, and proves that we Theosophists are in the right. The identity of our physical origin makes no appeal to our higher and deeper feelings. Matter, deprived of its soul and spirit, or its divine essence, cannot speak to the human heart. But the identity of the soul and spirit, of real, immortal man, as Theosophy teaches us, once proven and deep-rooted in our hearts, would lead us far on the road of real charity and brotherly goodwill.

ENQ. But how does Theosophy explain the common origin of man?

THEO. By teaching that the *root* of all nature, objective and subjective, and everything else in the universe, visible and invisible, *is, was,* and *ever will be* one absolute essence, from which all starts, and into which everything returns.

ENQ. What do the statutes of your Society advise its members to do besides this? On the physical plane, I mean?

THEO. In order to awaken brotherly feeling among nations we have to assist in the international exchange of useful arts and products, by advice, information, and cooperation with all worthy individuals and associations. What is also needed is to impress men with the idea that, if the root of mankind is *one*, then there must also be one truth which finds expression in all the various religions.

ENQ. This refers to the common origin of religions, and you may be right there. But how does it apply to practical brotherhood on the physical plane?

THEO. First, because that which is true on the metaphysical plane must be also true on the physical. Secondly, because there is no more fertile source of hatred and strife than religious differences. When one party or another thinks himself the sole possessor of absolute truth, it becomes only natural that he should think his neighbour absolutely in the clutches of Error or the Devil. But once get a man to see that none of them has the *whole* truth, but that they are mutually complementary, that the complete truth can be found only in the combined views of all, after that which is false in each of them has been sifted out — then true brotherhood in religion will be established.

Warren Felt Evans (1817-89)

Starting out as a Methodist minister, Evans grew increasingly interested in the power of the mind over the body and in the intimate connection between the physical and the spiritual worlds. Cured himself through the ministrations of Phineas P. Quimby (1802-66), that fascinating clockmaker, hypnotist, and mental healer of antebellum America, and influenced as well by the writings of Emmanuel Swedenborg (see above, p. 195), Evans became one of the founders of New Thought. Though a specific organization did not emerge until the 1890s, Evans's books in the 1870s and 1880s enunciated many of New Thought's characteristic themes: the overriding significance of spiritual reality, the unity of all religions, the harmony between science and religion, and the ability of the individual to harness the Divine Nature in order to effect all manner of change — including the change from sickness to health. All of these themes are evident in the excerpt below.

Christ and Disease; or, The Power of the Spiritual Life over the Body.

The highest form of existence is that of a true religious life, which, in its essence, is a harmonious union of goodness and truth, love and wisdom, benevolence and faith, in the character and activity of the individual. Where intellect and love are harmoniously united and blended, and act in perfect concordance, the resulting product is spiritual power. The omnipotence of God is the union of infinite wisdom and infinite love, or the knowing how to do what His goodness inclines Him to do. He who is, in this respect, an image of God, partakes of His spiritual almightiness. When a true philosophy is taken into the mount of transfiguration, and transformed into a divinely human religion, its face shines from the radiance of a higher sun, and possesses a power over ourselves and others that it could not otherwise have. When philosophy and religion are combined into a harmonious unity, each adds power and influence to the other. All religion should be made scientific, and all science religious. There is no inharmony between them when both are properly understood. The attempt to demonstrate the perfect agreement and concordance of the two, which is being made by many at the present time, is a laudable one, and promotive of the best interests of the race, though to accomplish this the current religious creeds must part company with some of their irrational dogmas, and science give up

---

[Source: W. F. Evans, *The Divine Law of Cure* (Boston: H. H. Carter & Co., 1886), pp. 119-20, 120-23.]

many of its unproved assumptions. But this will be no loss to either, as it is only eliminating an element of weakness from each. . . .

The founders of the great religions of the world were men in whom the intellect and the religious nature were blended more or less harmoniously. This is what gives their systems of doctrine such an almost unyielding grasp upon the minds of men, and such influence over so great masses of the world's population. Such men were Confucius, Buddha, Zoroaster, and we may add Mohammed. In all these examples which we have given of spiritual power there is some common principle. Can we discover what it is? It is that they were men of strong intellect, and were profoundly religious men. They were religious, not superficially, not in momentary and transient moods, but all through their being. Their religious fervor transported them into the third heavens, but also carried the intellect with it into a Divine realm of life and thought. Hence their thoughts, when given to others in their writings, have a Divine warmth and spiritual vitality in them, and are not mere cold and logical intellectual conceptions, like moonbeams reflected from polar ice. The religious nature exalted the intellect to a Divine realm of thought, where they became inspired, and recipient of the living Word, the indwelling Logos, of which they became in a true sense the incarnations. In all such men, in a mitigated sense, the Word is made flesh and dwells among us. It is impossible to be spiritual in our intellectual conceptions without being religious. To reach the higher degrees of inspiration, or quickened intuition, without a fervor of religious feeling is as impossible as to fly without wings.

The highest example in human history of the perfect union of the intellect with the religious nature, and the resultant spiritual power, is seen in Jesus the Christ. In him there was the most intimate blending of the purely human and the truly Divine, so that in his personality where the human nature ended and the Divinity commenced no one can perceive. The boundary line between the Godhead and manhood is not clearly drawn. There is in him a deification of humanity and a humanization of God, and somehow in him God comes very near to the souls of men. In him we witness the spectacle of a human nature and soul filled with God, — with all the fullness of God. But he expected, and expressed the wish, that all his disciples in every age should be, in this respect, a copy of the Master, — that they should be one with God as he and the Father were one. (John xvii: 20-23.) As the highest representation of God in human history, there is in his life, as unfolded in the Gospels, a revelation of the thoughts and feelings of God. No man can be actuated by a Divine influence and afflatus without in some way, and to some extent, manifesting the feelings of the Deity. But Paul affirms that God gave the Spirit to the Christ without measure, and the Divine love was the motive power of all his activity. He spent a large fraction of his public life in the cure of "all manner of sickness and disease" among the people. His activity seemed naturally to take that beneficent direction. So far as the Christ-principle is in us, we shall have power to do the same. The drift and current of our inner life will exhibit itself as a spontaneous impulse to do good to the souls and bodies of men. Jesus seemed to have a divinely clear conception of the spiritual origin of disease, and of the efficacy of spiritual remedies in its cure. He did not look upon sickness of the flesh as the real disease, but as the effect of an *a priori* spiritual malady; and when this antecedent cause ceases to operate, the morbid effect comes to an end. As Jesus the Christ was perpetually moved by a Divine influence and impulse in his career as the great Physician, it shows that in God there is a perpetual *conatus,* an irrepressible endeavor, an unchangeable willingness to heal our diseases of mind and body. In all our struggles against every morbid condition, within and without, we can, with unerring certainty, count upon God and his omnipotent love as our unfailing ally in the battle with evil and suffering. If God be for us, what can prevail against us? Here is the standing-ground of an assured and unyielding faith in Him for the cure of our own sicknesses and those of others through us. If I have any understanding of the system of the Christ in the cure of disease, he found the cause of it in some prior disturbance of the spiritual principle in man, and he applied his healing power to the mental root of the malady. All his *mighty works* had a redemptive aim, that is, they were designed primarily to deliver men from spiritual evil. Matter was viewed by him as an unsubstantial *appearance,* and mind was the only reality. Through the restored and redeemed soul he healed the body of its diseases, both functional and organic. To illustrate his Divine method of cure, and to make it an available, practical system, will be the aim of all I have to say in the subsequent chapters of this volume.

Ralph Waldo Trine (1866-1958)

If Evans planted the seeds of New Thought, R. W. Trine harvested that crop and broadcast more seeds. Trine's conviction that all that men and women needed was to get "in tune with the Infinite" struck responsive chords from coast to coast. He knew What All the World's A-Seeking, *to use the title of his first book (1896) — or so it seemed, as the products of his pen sold in the millions of copies. Not only health was in one's grasp, but success, power, and prosperity as well. "Hold to this thought, never allow it to weaken. . . ."*

Recognize, working in and through you, the same Infinite Power that creates and governs all things in the universe, the same Infinite Power that governs the

[Source: R. W. Trine, *In Tune with the Infinite* (Indianapolis: Bobbs-Merrill, 1970 [1908]), pp. 137, 138-39.]

endless systems of worlds in space. Send out your thought — thought is a force, and it has occult power of unknown proportions when rightly used and wisely directed — send out your thought that the right situation or the right work will come to you at the right time, in the right way, and that you will recognize it when it comes. Hold to this thought, never allow it to weaken, hold to it, and continually water it with firm expectation. You in this way put your advertisement into a psychical, a spiritual newspaper, a paper that has not a limited circulation, will make its way not only to the utmost bounds of the earth, but of the very universe itself. It is an advertisement, moreover, which, if rightly placed on your part, will be far more effective than any advertisement you could possibly put into any printed sheet, no matter what claims are made in regard to its being "the great advertising medium." In the degree that you come into this realization and live in harmony with the higher laws and forces, in that degree will you be able to do this effectively. . . .

This is the law of prosperity: When apparent adversity comes, be not cast down by it, but make the best of it, and always look forward for better things, for conditions more prosperous. To hold yourself in this attitude of mind is to set into operation subtle, silent and irresistible forces that sooner or later will actualize in material form that which is today merely an idea. But ideas have occult power, and ideas, when rightly planted and rightly tended, are the seeds that actualize material conditions.

Never give a moment to complaint, but utilize the time that would otherwise be spent in this way in looking forward and actualizing the conditions you desire. Suggest prosperity to your self. See yourself in a prosperous condition. Affirm that you will before long be in a prosperous condition. Affirm it calmly and quietly but strongly and confidently. Believe it, believe it absolutely. Expect it — keep it continually watered with expectation. You thus make yourself a magnet to attract the things that you desire. Don't be afraid to suggest, to affirm these things, for by so doing you put forth an ideal which will begin to clothe itself in material form. In this way you are utilizing agents among the most subtle and powerful in the universe. If you are particularly desirous for anything that you feel it is good and right for you to have, something that will broaden your life or that will increase your usefulness to others, simply hold the thought that at the right time, in the right way and through the right instrumentality there will come to you or there will open up for you the way whereby you can attain what you desire.

Institutions of New Thought

Christian Science

The very name suggesting the harmony between religion and science of which W. F. Evans wrote, this highly visible, highly successful institution gained its first charter from the state of Massachusetts in 1879. The founder, Mary Baker Eddy (1821-1910), had like Evans come into contact with Phineas Quimby and had — again like Evans — herself experienced a mental or spiritual care of physical infirmity. In 1875, Mrs. Eddy published the basic text, the sacred text, of her theology: Science and Health with Key to the Scriptures. *The book and the church (Boston's "Mother Church") had won an impressive following by the time of Mrs. Eddy's death in 1910. What follows is a portion of her address to adherents gathered in Chicago in 1888.*

Science and the Senses.

Substance of my address at the National Convention in Chicago, June 13, 1888.

The National Christian Scientist Association has brought us together to minister and to be ministered unto; to mutually aid one another in finding ways and means for helping the whole human family; to quicken and extend the interest already felt in a higher mode of medicine; to watch with eager joy the individual growth of Christian Scientists, and the progress of our common cause in Chicago, — the miracle of the Occident. We come to strengthen and perpetuate our organizations and institutions; and to find strength in union, — strength to build up, through God's right hand, that pure and undefiled religion whose Science demonstrates God and the perfectibility of man. This purpose is immense, and it must begin with individual growth, a "consummation devoutly to be wished." The lives of all reformers attest the authenticity of their mission, and call the world to acknowledge its divine Principle. Truly is it written: —

> "Thou must be true thyself, if thou the Truth would'st teach;
> Thy heart must overflow, if thou another's heart would'st reach."

[Source: Mary B. G. Eddy, *Miscellaneous Writings, 1883-1896*, 3rd ed. (Boston: Joseph Armstrong, 1897), pp. 98-99, 100-2.]

Science is absolute and final. It is revolutionary in its very nature; for it upsets all that is not upright. It annuls false evidence, and saith to the five material senses, "Having eyes ye see not, and ears ye hear not; neither can you understand." To weave one thread of Science through the looms of time, is a miracle in itself. The risk is stupendous. It cost Galileo, what? This awful price: the temporary loss of his self-respect. His fear overcame his loyalty; the courage of his convictions fell before it. Fear is the weapon in the hands of tyrants.

Men and women of the nineteenth century, are you called to voice a higher order of Science? Then obey this call. Go, if you must, to the dungeon or the scaffold, but take not back the words of Truth. How many are there ready to suffer for a righteous cause, to stand a long siege, take the front rank, face the foe, and be in the battle every day? . . .

Past, present, future, will show the word and Spirit of Truth — healing the sick and reclaiming the sinner — so long as there remains a claim of error for Truth to deny or to destroy. Love's labors are not lost. The five personal senses, that grasp neither the meaning nor the magnitude of self-abnegation, may lose sight thereof; but Science voices unselfish love, unfolds infinite Good, leads on irresistible forces, and will finally show the fruits of Love. Human reason is inaccurate; and the scope of the senses is inadequate to grasp the word of Truth, and teach the eternal.

Science speaks when the senses are silent, and then the evermore of Truth is triumphant. The spiritual monitor understood is coincidence of the divine with the human, the acme of Christian Science. Pure humanity, friendship, home, the interchange of love, bring to earth a foretaste of Heaven. They unite terrestrial and celestial joys, and crown them with blessings infinite.

The Christian Scientist loves man more because he loves God most. He understands this Principle, — Love. Who is sufficient for these things? Who remembers that patience, forgiveness, abiding faith, and affection, are the symptoms by which our Father indicates the different stages of man's recovery from sin and his entrance into Science? Who knows how the feeble lips are made eloquent, how hearts are inspired, how healing becomes spontaneous, and how the divine Mind is understood and demonstrated? He alone knows these wonders who is departing from the thraldom of the senses and accepting spiritual Truth, — that which blesses its adoption by the refinement of joy and the dismissal of sorrow.

Christian Science and the senses are at war. It is a revolutionary struggle. We already have had two in this nation; and they began and ended in a contest for the true idea, for human liberty and rights. Now cometh a third struggle; for the freedom of health, holiness, and the attainment of Heaven.

The scientific sense of Being which establishes harmony, enters into no compromise with finiteness and feebleness. It undermines the foundations of mortality, of physical law, breaks their chains, and sets the captive free, opening the doors for them that are bound.

He who turns to the body for evidence, bases his conclusions on mortality, on imperfection; but Science saith to man, "God hath all power."

The Science of Omnipotence demonstrates but one power, and this power is good, not evil, not matter, — but Mind. This virtually destroys matter and evil, including sin and disease.

If God is all, and God is good, it follows that all must be good; and no other power, law, or intelligence can exist. On this proof rest premise and conclusion in Science, and the facts that disprove the evidence of the senses.

God is individual Mind. This one Mind and His individuality comprise the elements of all forms and individualities, and prophesy the nature and stature of Christ, the ideal man.

Christian Science sanitarium in San Francisco, c. 1935
(Keystone-Mast Collection, University of California, Riverside)

A corporeal God, as often defined by lexicographers and scholastic theologians, is only an infinite finite being, an unlimited man, — a theory to me inconceivable. If the unlimited and immortal Mind could originate in a limited body, and eventually return to those limits, it would be forever limited.

In this limited and lower sense God is not personal. His infinity precludes the possibility of corporeal personality. His being is individual, but not physical.

God is like Himself, and like nothing else. He is universal and primitive. His character admits of no degrees of comparison. God is not part, but the whole. In His individuality I recognize the loving, divine Father, Mother God. Infinite personality must be incorporeal.

God's ways are not ours. His pity is expressed in modes above the human. His chastisements are the manifestations of Love. The sympathy of His eternal Mind is fully expressed in Divine Science, which blots out all our iniquities and heals all our diseases. Human pity often brings pain.

Science supports harmony, denies suffering, and destroys it with the sympathy of Truth. Whatever seems material, seems thus only to the material senses, and is but the subjective state of mortal and material thought.

Science has inaugurated the irrepressible conflict between sense and Soul. Mortal thought wars with this sense as one that beateth the air, but Science outmasters it, and ends the warfare. This proves daily that "one with God is a majority."

Unity School of Christianity

While Christian Science managed to build and maintain a substantial organization, it did not escape factionalism and schism. Some persons (for example, Emma C. Hopkins and Ursula Gestefeld) were dismissed from the parent church for expressing divergent views and attracting personal followings. The Fillmores, Charles (1854-1948) and Myrtle (1845-1931), came under the influence of these excommunicants, even as they too had already been influenced by Phineas Quimby and W. F. Evans. Beginning a publishing program in 1889, the Fillmores (husband and wife) in 1903 applied for incorporation of the "Unity School of Practical Christianity." With headquarters in Kansas City, Missouri, the Unity School at first saw its mission as working within the established churches. Gradually, however, Unity developed its own professional ministry, its widely scattered centers, and its standards of orthodoxy. Another New Thought movement had become a church. In the excerpt

[Source: Charles Fillmore, *Unity*, June, 1947, pp. 3-6.]

*below, Charles Fillmore informs his readers that they can be either an Adam
or a Christ: "The choice lies with you."*

Let us repeat that the body of man is the visible record of his thoughts. It is the
identification of the individual's interpretation of man, and each individual
shows in his body just what his views of man are. The body is the corporeal record of the mind of its owner, and there is no limit to its infinite differentiation.
The individual may become any type of being that he elects to be. Man selects
the mental model and the body images it. So the body is the image and likeness
of the individual's idea of man. We may embody any conception of life or being
that we can conceive. The body is the exact reproduction of the thoughts of its
occupant. As a man thinks in his mind, so is his body.

   You can be an Adam if you choose, or you may be a Christ, or any other
type of being that you see fit to idealize. The choice lies with you. The body
merely executes the mandates of the mind. The mind dictates the model according to which the body shall manifest. Therefore, "as he thinketh within
himself [in his vital nature], so is he." Each is just what he believes he is.

   It is safe to say that nine hundred and ninety-nine people out of every
thousand believe that the resurrection of the body has something specifically
to do with the getting of a new body after death; so we find more than ninety-
nine percent of the world waiting for death to get something new in the way
of a body. This belief is not based on the principles of Truth, for there is no
ready-made-body factory in the universe, and none will get the body that
thus he expects. Waiting for death in order to get a new body is the folly of ignorance. The thing to do is to improve the body that we now have; it can be
done, and it must be done by those who would follow Jesus in the regeneration.

   The "resurrection" of the body has nothing whatever to do with death,
except that we may resurrect ourselves from every dead condition into which
sense ignorance has plunged us. To be resurrected means *to get out of the place
that you are in* and to get into another place. Resurrection is a rising into new
vigor, new prosperity; a restoration to some higher state. It is absurd to suppose
that it applies only to the resuscitation of a dead body.

   Paul hints at a time when the body will be changed, and he says that it is
when "Death is swallowed up in victory." Here are Paul's words: "When this
corruptible shall put on incorruption, and this mortal shall have put on immortality . . . Death is swallowed up in victory."

   This transformation is worked out by the individual himself, and is not
the result of physical death, but rather of the death or annihilation of the erroneous ideas that ignorance has stored in the cells of the body. It is first a mental
resurrection, followed by a body demonstration.

   It is the privilege of the individual to express any type of body that he sees fit to idealize. Man may become a Christ in mind and in body by incorporating into his every thought the ideas given to the world by Jesus.

"But we all, with unveiled face beholding as in a mirror the glory of the Lord, are transformed into the same image from glory to glory, even as from the Lord the Spirit."

Creative Mind has imaged in the soul of every one a picture of the perfect-man body. The imaging process of creative Mind may well be illustrated by the picture that light makes on the photographic plate, which must be "developed" before it becomes visible. Or man's invisible body may be compared to the blue prints of a building that the architect delivers to the builder. Man is a builder of flesh and blood. Jesus was a carpenter. Also He was indeed the Master Mason. He restored "the temple of Jehovah," the Lord's body, in Jerusalem, in His mind and heart.

When we call ourselves fleshly, mortal, finite, we manifest bodily upon a fleshly, mortal and finite plane. We sow to the flesh, and of the flesh reap corruption. The time has arrived for the whole human family to repudiate the estimate of man as corrupt and instead to think of him as he was designed by creative Mind. "This corruptible must put on incorruption, and this mortal must put on immortality," says Paul.

We must stop calling our bodies flesh and blood, but see them as they are in Spirit-Mind — pure and incorruptible. This realization of man's perfect body will arrest decay, disintegration, and death.

We must rise above material thoughts into spiritual realization, and live, move, and have our being in a divine reality. When our views of man are elevated to spiritual understanding, we shall begin the expression of bodily perfection. Our thoughts must first be perfect before we can expect to manifest perfection in body. The issues of life are within man; the body is merely the record of the state of mind of the individual.

Church of Religious Science

Christian Science began in New England, Unity in the Midwest, and the Church of Religious Science in the Far West. New Thought had spread across the nation. Ernest S. Holmes (1887-1960), though born in Maine, settled in Los Angeles where he organized a New Thought group and in 1927 launched a popular New Thought magazine, Science of Mind. *His book of the same title, published the previous year (and much revised and reprinted thereaf-*

[Source: E. S. Holmes, *The Science of Mind* (New York: Dodd, Mead & Co., 1959 [1926]), pp. 202-5.]

ter), stood as the charter document of this twentieth-century church. Like
those before him, Holmes saw the secret of life as lying in a right relationship
with Divine Being. Rightly related, the believer possessed the key that could
unlock all of the inexhaustible powers of the universe.

How to Heal

In our work, we treat man, not as a physical body, neither do we treat the disease as belonging to him, *the reason being that if we do, we cannot subsequently*
free him from it. We do not think of the disease as being connected with him or
a part of him. The practitioner seeks to realize man as *perfect,* not needing to be
healed of anything. This is nothing less than the realization of the Presence and
the Power of God, or Spirit, as Man's Life, as the only life there is, as complete
and perfect in him right now.

First recognize your own perfection, then build up the same recognition
for your patient. You are then ready to directly attack the *thought* that binds
him, *recognizing that your word destroys it, and stating that it does.* You may then
take into account and specifically mention everything that needs to be changed,
every so-called broken law or false thought. Then finish your treatment with a
realization of peace, remaining for a few moments in silent recognition *that*
your work is done, complete and perfect.

The work must not be thought of as hard. When we know that there is
but One Mind, we shall realize that this work could not be difficult or laborious. *Mental treatment is a direct statement of belief into Mind, coupled with a re-*
alization that the work is already an accomplished fact. The spiritual man needs
no healing, health is an omnipresent reality, and when the obstructions that
hinder healing are removed, *it will be found that health was there all the time.* So
in your work, do not feel that you must heal anyone. Your only responsibility is
to uncover the Truth.

Never say: "Here is a patient whom I must heal," for if you think of him
from this viewpoint, how are you going to heal him? If you mentally see a sick
man, he will remain mentally sick. *We cannot heal successfully while we recognize*
sickness as a reality to the Spirit. In spiritual healing by this method, no one believes in disease, it has no action nor reaction, it has neither cause nor effect, it
has no law to support it and no one through whom it can operate. There is no
one to talk with about it, and no one to believe in it. While we maintain that
disease is primarily a thing of thought, we do not deny the actuality of its experience nor the suffering it causes, instead we seek to heal it, and we co-operate
with all, no matter what method they are using to relieve distress.

You have nothing to do with the patient's thought as a personality, for as
your own thought clears, he will be helped. First eliminate doubt and fear from

your own thought; realize that your patient is a Divine Being, and that your word is the law unto the thing unto which it is spoken. This is what gave Jesus His power: "For He taught them as one having authority, and not as the scribes."

Healing is Clear Thinking

Scientific mental healing is the result of clear thinking and logical reasoning, which presents itself to consciousness and is acted upon by Mind. It is a systematic process of reasoning, which unearths the mental cause or idea underlying disease, and presents the Truth about man's being.

For instance, say to yourself: "God is all there is. There is only One Life." When you are treating, if there is any slight point which is not clear, do not continue with the treatment. Stop at once, go back to your analysis of Ultimate Reality, and build your whole argument upon It, in order to get a clear consciousness.

Repeat: "God is All. There is but One Power, Intelligence and Consciousness in the Universe, but One Presence. This One Presence cannot change. There is nothing for It to change into but Itself. It is Changeless, *and It is my life now, It is in me now.*" Claim that no form of race-suggestion, belief in limitation, subjective idea of limitation, thought of karma, fatalism, theology or hell, horoscope, or any other false belief, has power. Accept none of them. If you have ever believed in them, if you have ever believed that the stars govern you, or that your environment governs you, or that your opportunities govern you, recognize this as an hypnotic condition into which you have fallen, and deny every one of them until there is no longer anything in you that believes in them.

This is a good way to clear your consciousness. We can readily see what it does: it induces a clear concept of Reality, which must reproduce Itself. This process of clear thinking, if carried out every day, will heal.

When you are giving a treatment, you are *thinking.* You are meeting, opposing, neutralizing, erasing and obliterating suppression, fear, doubt, failure, morbid emotion and sense of loss — whatever the trouble may be. Every time your thought hits fairly and squarely, it erases just as definitely as one would erase a chalk line. Such is the mystery of the appearance and the disappearance of thought.

Right thought, constantly poured into consciousness, will eventually purify it. Discord might be likened to a bottle of impure water; healing might be likened to the process of dropping pure water into the bottle, a drop at a time, until the whole is clean and pure. Someone might ask why the bottle could not be turned upside down and at once drain out all the impurities. Sometimes this happens but not often. Meanwhile, a drop at a time will finally eliminate the impurities and produce a healing.

In treating, go beyond the disease and supply a spiritual consciousness. A treatment is not complete without a great realization of Life and Love, of God and Perfection, of Truth and Wisdom, of Power and Reality. Sense the Divine Presence in and through the patient at all times.

Peace and Prosperity

Acres of Diamonds (1890)

While much of New Thought concentrated on the healing of disease, all understood that the power of the universe could be applied to any good purpose. (The Fillmores thought of Unity as merely applied or practical Christianity.) Russell H. Conwell (1843-1925), not a member of any New Thought organization but a Baptist minister in Philadelphia, nonetheless shared the view that life's problems were largely internal, life's potential essentially unlimited. His most famous sermon by far, Acres of Diamonds, *delivered over and over again, printed over and over again, made the point that so many wanted to hear — over and over again: you ought to be rich, you can be rich, it is your duty to be rich.*

Now then, I say again that the opportunity to get rich, to attain unto great wealth, is here in Philadelphia now, within the reach of almost every man and woman who hears me speak tonight, and I mean just what I say. I have not come to this platform even under these circumstances to recite something to you. I have come to tell you what in God's sight I believe to be the truth, and if the years of life have been of any value to me in the attainment of common sense, I know I am right; that the men and women sitting here, who found it difficult perhaps to buy a ticket to this lecture or gathering to-night, have within their reach "acres of diamonds," opportunities to get largely wealthy. There never was a place on earth more adapted than the city of Philadelphia to-day, and never in the history of the world did a poor man without capital have such an opportunity to get rich quickly and honestly as he has now in our city. I say it is the truth, and I want you to accept it as such; for if you think I have come to simply recite something, then I would better not be here. I have no time to waste in any such talk, but to say the things I believe, and unless some of you get richer for what I am saying to-night my time is wasted.

[Source: R. H. Conwell, *Acres of Diamonds* (New York: Harper & Brothers, 1915 [1890]), pp. 17-18, 20.]

I say that you ought to get rich, and it is your duty to get rich. How many of my pious brethren say to me, "Do you, a Christian minister, spend your time going up and down the country advising young people to get rich, to get money?" "Yes, of course I do." They say, "Isn't that awful! Why don't you preach the gospel instead of preaching about man's making money?" "Because to make money honestly is to preach the gospel." That is the reason. The men who get rich may be the most honest men you find in the community. . . .

For a man to have money, even in large sums, is not an inconsistent thing. We preach against covetousness, and you know we do, in the pulpit, and often-times preach against it so long and use the terms about "filthy lucre" so ex-tremely that Christians get the idea that when we stand in the pulpit we believe it is wicked for any man to have money — until the collection-basket goes around, and then we almost swear at the people because they don't give more money. Oh, the inconsistency of such doctrines as that!

Money is power, and you ought to be reasonably ambitious to have it. You ought because you can do more good with it than you could without it. Money printed your Bible, money builds your churches, money sends your missionar-ies, and money pays your preachers, and you would not have many of them, ei-ther, if you did not pay them. I am always willing that my church should raise my salary, because the church that pays the largest salary always raises it the eas-iest. You never knew an exception to it in your life. The man who gets the larg-est salary can do the most good with the power that is furnished to him. Of course he can if his spirit be right to use it for what it is given to him.

I say, then, you ought to have money. If you can honestly attain unto riches in Philadelphia, it is your Christian and godly duty to do so.

You Can Win (1938)

Far more famous for his later book on The Power of Positive Thinking *(1952), Norman Vincent Peale (1898-1993) announced those themes in the 1930s that many longed to hear. Religion is not so much obligation as it is op-portunity; life is not so much frustration as it is conquest, the universe is not so much beyond as it is within. Like Conwell, Peale was not a member of New Thought; he was in fact a Methodist minister who became a Dutch Re-formed pastor in New York City. And again like Conwell, Peale proved to be enormously popular. In the case of both men, their spectacular success brought professional and financial reward enabling both to underwrite edu-cational and religious enterprises.*

[Source: N. V. Peale, *You Can Win* (New York: Abingdon Cokesbury Press, 1938), pp. 21-23.]

Thus your religion, which may now consist largely of the framework of belief, tradition and ceremonial, and from which you derive not a little comfort and help, can be — and this is the greatest truth you will ever encounter — a force and power to completely revolutionize your life. From it you can draw a power beyond anything you have ever experienced, a power sufficient to overcome any weakness, carry any burden, conquer any sin. Through a surrendered faith in Christ and a daily intimate living in spirit with him you can win over adversaries which formerly seemed too great for the human spirit to bear.

Call the roll of all those things which can defeat a man — suffering and pain, sorrow, disappointment, hardship, frustration, sin. There they stand, challenging, menacing, all but invincible. Who can hope to overcome them? But if one is armed with a strange and wonderful secret, these giants are at his mercy. This secret is not some cure-all, nicely wrapped in cellophane, which you can purchase in a store. It is not an achievement for which you may valiantly struggle. It cannot be purchased, nor can it be won by effort. It is a gift freely offered to you. All you need do is to take it by an act of faith and begin to live on it. Why go on being a victim of fear, anxiety, trouble, and weakness, with vigor of mind and spirit and body being steadily drained off? Great new power and strength can be yours.

Turn to the Bible. In the Bible you read a statement by a man who long ago discovered the truth. He said, "I can do all things through Christ who giveth me the strength." You can learn to say the same thing. That secret can be yours if you want it. You can win. I mean that because I know it is true. It is immaterial what your difficulty is. If it is the worst difficulty in the world, it does not invalidate the fact that you can win if you will adopt this plan of living. There is nothing magical about the Bible, but the secret I am talking about is to be found within its pages. Why sit there defeated when you have at your very elbow a book that can make a new person of you? When you open it, the most human people come walking out of its pages and sit down with you or me and say: "Listen, I have a secret and I want to share it with you. If you take Christ into your life and put your life in his hands, you too can win over anything." "I can do all things through Christ," says the Bible.

I realize that many people do not understand religion in this vital way. They think of religion as something that has to do with what they regard as stale and musty churches and dull services of worship. But that isn't religion at all. Religion deals with an electric power or force which is all about us, just as sound waves are in the air. When you come into your living room, for instance, your radio is silent and lifeless. You turn a dial. You tune your radio to the sound waves that are filling the air and immediately these sounds are brought into your room and you take into your consciousness that with which the air is filled but which the moment before were meaningless to you because you had not tuned in. All about us in the universe is this value called the power of God, but we are impervious to it. It means nothing to us. We are closed to it. We go on day by day living in our own feeble human strength, which is drawn from inside ourselves and which soon runs dry. Accordingly, we are worried; we are nervous; we are defeated time and time again; we have no sense of conquest at all. Religion means that you get tired of living like that. You become aware of a power in the world that you do not possess. What, then, do you do? You tune in. You bring your spirit into harmony with the Spirit of God. That's very simply done too. You say with the faith of a little child, "Lord, I bring my human spirit to you and I ask you to fill me with your power." Then the miracle happens. As the strains of an orchestra fill the room when a radio is tuned in, so the marvelous melody of God comes into your life.

Psychology and Religion

Emmanuel Movement

Apart from the congeries of ideas gathered under the heading of New Thought, the new science of psychology, even more of psychoanalysis and psychiatry, made its impact upon religion in America. Elwood Worcester (1862-1940), Episcopal clergyman in Boston and among the earliest to relate psychology to the pastoral ministry, launched the Emmanuel Movement in 1906. The aim of the movement, as an early associate wrote, was "to unite in friendly alliance a simple New Testament Christianity as modern Biblical scholarship corroborates it and the proved conclusions of modern medicine, and more especially of modern psychological medicine, in the interests of suffering humanity" (Samuel McComb, Independent, May 21, 1908, p. 1122). In the words of Elwood Worcester below, one also sees an openness to multiple approaches in the curing of human hurts.

As we are attempting to establish no new dogma, and as our motives are entirely disinterested, our single desire is to give each patient the best opportunity of life and health which our means allow. We believe in the power of the mind over the body, and we believe also in medicine, in good habits, and in a wholesome, well-regulated life. In the treatment of functional nervous disorders we make free use of moral and psychical agencies, but we do not believe in overtaxing these valuable aids by expecting the mind to attain results which can be effected more easily

---

[Source: Elwood Worcester et al., *Religion and Medicine: The Moral Control of Nervous Disorders* (New York: Moffat Yard and Co., 1908), pp. 2-5.]

through physical instrumentalities. Accordingly we have gladly availed ourselves of the services of the skilled medical and surgical specialists who have offered to co-operate with us, and we believe that our freedom in this respect and the combination of good psychical and physical methods have had much to do with our success. If a bad headache is caused by eye-strain, or a generally enfeebled condition is obviously the result of a digestive disturbance, a pair of glasses or a belt is frequently far more effective than suggestion. Most religious workers in this field have made the mistake of supposing that God can cure in only one way and that the employment of physical means indicates a lack of faith. This is absurd. God cures by many means. He uses the sunlight, healing and nourishing substances, water and air. The knitting of a broken bone, or the furrowing out of new blood courses in a diseased limb, is just as truly His work as the restoration of a wounded spirit. There is no peculiar piety involved in the use of suggestion. We have seen the consumptive nursed back to life, by rest, fresh air, abundant food and kindness, and we have seen more spectacular recovery from other diseases through confident expectation and the spoken word, but we have never felt that the one was necessarily more the act of God than the other. The fact remains that consumption can be cured in no other way, and that those who take a different view of the subject do not cure consumptives, they kill them by robbing them of their last chance of life; the same is true of other diseases.

For this reason we have confined our practice to that large group of maladies which are known to-day as functional nervous disorders. Although a sound psychical and moral method is a valuable adjunct in every branch of medicine, yet viewed as an independent remedial agent the legitimate sphere of psychotherapy is strictly limited. It is in the field of the functional neuroses that all its real victories have been won. Here again our conception of our mission differs decidedly from that of our predecessors. In answer to their taunt: "If you believe in God's power to cure disease, how dare you place any limit to that power?" we are content to reply: "We believe God has power to cure all disease, but we do not believe God cures all disease by the same means." At all events an authentic instance of recovery from organic disease through psychical means is what we are waiting for. While we do not believe that any man knows all that is to be known on this subject, or that we are in a position to affirm dogmatically what the mind can or cannot accomplish, yet we are surely safe in accepting as to this the overwhelming weight of scientific opinion, and in confining our practice to a field in which it is known to be efficacious. By so doing we avoid the one valid objection which has ever been urged against psychotherapeutics, namely, its employment in diseases which obviously require physical interference, with the result that many patients have died through sheer neglect.

Apart from this, it is in the domain of functional nervous disorders that such service as we are able to render is most needed, not merely because this branch of medicine is least developed in America and adequate treatment is difficult to obtain, especially by the poor, but because disorders of this nature are peculiarly associated with the moral life. An attack of typhoid fever may spring from no moral cause and it may have no perceptible influence upon character, but neurasthenia, hysteria, psychasthenia, hypochondria, alcoholism, etc., are afflictions of the personality. They spring from moral causes and they produce moral effects. In this domain the beneficent action of drugs and medicines is extremely limited, and the personality of the physician is everything. Other agencies such as electricity, baths, etc., probably owe much of their value to their suggestional effect, and so long as the training of our physicians is strictly material, such patients will continue to be their despair, for the reason that moral maladies require moral treatment.

Physicians of the Soul

In colonial America, it was not uncommon for the local minister to serve also as the town doctor (the "angelic conjunction," as Cotton Mather called it). The nineteenth century's dedication to professionalism changed all that. In the important work of Anton T. Boisen (1876-1965), however, steps were taken to close the gap between physician and clergyman. Boisen, the founder of clinical pastoral education, helped establish a whole new field with its own extensive literature and collection of learned journals (for example, Journal of Religion and Health, Journal of Pastoral Counseling, Journal of Pastoral Care, *and* Pastoral Psychology*). In 1936, Boisen called for doctors and ministers to understand each other better, approach each other more closely. In writing of "spiritual healing," Boisen had much to say about what a later generation would call "holistic medicine."*

In venturing to use the term "spiritual healing" I am probably laying myself open to criticism. Only a few weeks ago I was taken severely to task for using the term "cure of souls." A professor of religious education thought it most unfortunate that I should cling to such an outworn and misleading word as "soul," while a psychiatrist friend suggested that it would be much wiser if I should avoid the use of words like "cure," to which the medical profession laid an exclusive claim. I am afraid the present title will be open to the same objections.

Now I have no desire to become involved in any controversy over the use of words and I should be happy to substitute another phrase if I could find it. I am concerned only to follow out the logical consequences of our findings as re-

[Source: A. T. Boisen, *The Exploration of the Inner World: A Study of Mental Disorder and Religious Experience* (New York: Harper & Brothers, 1936), pp. 238-39, 242-43, 247-48.]

gards the distinctive task of the clergyman and the conditions essential to its ac-
complishment. We have found that mental illness of the functional type has to
do with the philosophy of life and usually with the sense of personal failure. We
have arrived at the conclusion that acute upheavals are really attempts at reorganization which are closely related to those eruptive solutions of inner conflicts so familiar to the religious worker under the name of "conversion experiences." We have furthermore concluded that in mental illness there are
operative those profound and delicate laws of the spiritual life with which theology deals. If our findings are correct it follows that the religious worker, as his
major problem, is dealing with precisely those same inner adjustments and
conflicts which come within the province of the psychiatrist. It is of course true
that he is dealing with these difficulties in their incipient rather than in their
terminal stages. But that only makes his task the more important. If only he
have understanding, there is no one who has it in his power to do more effective
preventive work than the minister who in his professional capacity goes in and
out among his people, visiting them in their homes, talking with them individually about their personal problems, and preaching from his pulpit on that
which has to do with the end and meaning of life. For the same reason, if he
have not understanding, he may be worse than ineffective. He may do actual
harm. But the fact remains that so long as the church is in existence and so long
as it retains any influence whatsoever, the minister will be engaged in the same
general task as the psychiatrist. Regardless of the name we use, for better or for
worse, he will be doing psychotherapeutic work. It would seem advisable that
this fact should be recognized and that he should be enabled to do his rightful
part toward the achievement of mental health among those whom he serves.

I count it, therefore, as not the least important of my obligations as a student of the advanced disorders of the personality that I should do my part toward acquainting ministers generally with the insights derived from dealing
with serious mental illness. In endeavoring to perform this task before groups
of ministers I have not infrequently encountered among them a certain impatience. They want to be told at once what to do. They want rules of procedure
which they can apply and they are apt to be restive under the attempt to discover the meaning of the different forms of mental illness. . . .

Probably there is no more important lesson for the average minister or
teacher than this art of listening, for not uncommonly he likes to do the talking
himself. From the good psychiatrist he should learn the need of beginning with
the other fellow, of listening without condemning, of trying to understand his
language, particularly that symbolic language which is intended to be understood only by those who have eyes to see and ears to hear. And seeing back of
symptom and symbol to the real needs and the unspoken longings, the man of
understanding will be little concerned about creed or formula but will concern
himself with the task of leading the sufferer in terms of his own formulations to

discover for himself that solution of his problem which is socially acceptable and constructive.

While it is necessary to bear in mind the primary importance of the imponderable and elusive personal factors, we should not fail to recognize that there are different psychotherapeutic techniques, each with its particular point of view and its particular uses.

The methods which in the past have generally been employed by the church belong in the "faith healing" group. This form of psychotherapy is characterized by the fact that it relies chiefly upon suggestion. It takes the patient as he is, making little or no attempt to discover the roots of his difficulty, and directs his attention to comforting and constructive thoughts through prayer, friendly advice and devotional books. It would do the church serious injustice not to recognize that considerable good sense has been brought to bear by individual workers and that rather generally a great deal of stress has been placed on facing the facts and squaring accounts and correcting misunderstandings. But there has never been any systematic attempt at treatment on the basis of diagnosis, while in such forms as Christian Science suggestion is even carried to the point of denying the reality of evil and pain and asserting the absolute omnipotence of Mind and Love and Truth.

A somewhat different form of faith healing is that which some years ago received much publicity through M. Coué and his little formula about "getting better and better." Still another is that which makes use of hypnosis. With the patient in the hypnotic condition the practitioner makes constructive suggestions. Of recent years the use of deep hypnosis has been limited. The tendency among those who use hypnosis at all is merely to give suggestions to the patient while the latter is in relaxed condition or under light hypnosis. It is also used for exploratory purposes in order to discover hidden causes of trouble. The disfavor with which hypnosis is now regarded is due to the view that results secured with its help, while often striking, are not permanent. They are suggestions imposed from without and may even tend to weaken the patient's will.

The results secured at religious revivals in the years gone by have undoubtedly been due largely to the influence of suggestion; so also the cures effected at such shrines as Lourdes and Ste. Anne de Beaupré. . . .

. . . We find a striking contrast between the training of the medical man and that of the clergyman. The medical man is trained to deal at first hand with living human nature. He knows particularly the dangers and diseases to which flesh is heir, and if he be a psychiatrist, he knows the vagaries of the human spirit. He has not, however, as an essential part of his training, been introduced to human nature at its best. In the case of the clergyman the primary stress is laid upon character and purpose and he is introduced in his training to the noblest experiences of the race and to its most important insights. As yet however it is not an essential part of his training that he should be introduced under guidance to the raw material of life or that he should learn to recognize and understand experiences that are morbid or pathological.

Now I have no brief for either profession. I have had almost as much difficulty with the one as with the other. I can only say that from the standpoint of the mentally ill, in whose behalf I speak, I scarcely know which is worse, to have to depend upon a clergyman who has never come to close grips with the realities of human nature, or to be at the mercy of a physician who has no understanding of the spiritual needs and aspirations and of the nobler potentialities of mankind. I am merely convinced that our present system of training experts in the maladies of the personality is in need of improvement.

What Spiritual Healing Is

The integration between what medicine had to offer and what religion had to offer grew closer in the 1930s and 1940s, especially where levels of education and competence were on a par. Seward Hiltner (b. 1909), graduate of the University of Chicago Divinity School, worked with the Federal Council of Churches, taught at Chicago, and concluded an active career at Princeton Theological Seminary. In his many journal articles and books, Hiltner won broad acceptance for the potentially productive interaction among surgeon, psychiatrist, and minister.

What Spiritual Healing Is. One theological assumption has been suggested in previous sections but it remains to be stated directly. It would seem so obviously true as to require no proof. This is that any distinction made between "religious healing" or "spiritual healing" and other healing is only a practical difference so far as method is concerned. That is, healing influences which are permitted to operate through the method of prayer, for example, are not necessarily more "religious" or more "spiritual" than those set in motion by the surgeon's knife or the psychiatrist's analysis. For all healing comes from the *vis medicatrix naturae*, or the *vis medicatrix Dei*, the healing power of nature or of God, depending upon whether we are making an empirical or a religious statement. It is legitimate to make a practical distinction between the surgeon's knife, on the one hand, and prayer, on the other, and even to call the beneficent influence of one "spiritual healing," so long as it is recognized that one is not basically more "spiritual" or "religious" than the other. For both may be looked on in the broader sense as channels of the *vis medicatrix Dei*, which is another way of saying that the healing influences are ready to operate if the conditions

---

[Source: Seward Hiltner, *Religion and Health* (New York: Macmillan Co., 1943), pp. 100-102.]

are set up to permit them to work. In some situations the surgeon's knife must cut out offending tissue in order to release the forces of healing; in other cases the personality analysis is the central need; and in still other cases the conscious recognition of the power of these healing influences is most needed. In the majority of cases, something of all three may be helpful. We know more about when the surgeon's knife (or drug, or a new diet) is needed than we know about the others. We know more about when personality analysis is needed than we do about when prayer is needed; but we are learning new things about both. And we find increasingly that the three, applied intelligently, benefit the whole person more than any single one without the others.

Perhaps the central matter in what we distinguish practically as "spiritual healing" relates to consciousness in a special sense, to the degree of awareness of the beneficent influences which are ready to operate in a healing direction if they can be released — that is, it relates to affirmation of things which can really be affirmed on the basis of all sound religious experience and which do not conflict with the findings of science. It involves something which has not usually been recognized by those interested in "spiritual healing," a special relation between conscious awareness and the unconscious driving forces of human life. Real spiritual healing is not symptomatic. It does not deal with making affirmations about how wonderful God is to look after us as he does . . . when at the same time these affirmations are used as a cloak shrouding recognition of basic problems (and sins) within us which remain unexamined. Real spiritual healing brings forgiveness for guilt about things concerning which one ought to feel guilty, after the real guiltiness has been recognized. It brings personality reorganization after the powerful elements of disorganization have been investigated. It brings peace after the causes of "internal warfare" have been subjected to scrutiny and have been accepted as "emotional facts." It brings love after one's capacities for hostility have been seen and diagnosed. It brings security after one's anxieties have been understood and faced.

This does not mean that the process is mainly an intellectual one; for it is not. The kind of analysis which we might give of the situation, with some verbal precision required on account of the need to communicate what we mean, is not the basic factor in the situation. It makes comparatively little difference whether the person is capable of carrying out conscious and deliberate analysis of the type we have been doing; but it makes a great difference whether the "conscious" acceptance of one's "unconscious self" is basically honest emotionally, or whether it is merely an intellectual smoke-screen. Generally, intellectual knowledge of what happens in such processes should help, provided it is sound knowledge. But possession of the knowledge does not necessarily bring the forces into operation. The psychiatrists make a similar point in their reference to the difference between "intellectual" and "emotional" insight. All of these phrases are inadequate to explain the reality, but they do offer suggestions.

3. Society Out of Joint

Unsafe for Democracy

American Protective Association and Immigration

When nativism erupted again in the 1880s and 1890s, its focus tended to be on the largely unrestricted immigration into America. Up until the Civil War, immigration was generally thought of as a "good thing" — new blood, fresh hands, eager settlers. At this period, however, many were having second thoughts, those thoughts prompted not so much by the size of this later immigration as by its character. So many of the "new" immigrants tended, for example, not to be Protestants. In 1887 at Clinton, Iowa, Henry Francis Bowers (1837-1911) founded the American Protective Association (APA), the leading anti-Catholic organization of the closing years of the nineteenth century. Son of a German Lutheran father and an Anglo Methodist mother, Bowers pledged his followers to a "true Americanism," those code words being further explained as demanding that citizenship be denied to all who are subject to "any ecclesiastical power not created and controlled by American citizens. . . ." (1) Disciples of Christ minister, lecturer, and author John L. Brandt (1860-1946) in 1895 published a vigorously anti-Catholic work which carried the "imprimatur" of the APA's second president, W. J. H. Traynor. (2) An Immigration Restriction League was formed in 1894, and in 1924 a National Origins Act was passed that attempted to turn the clock back to the earlier pattern of immigration.

[Sources: (1) John L. Brandt, *America or Rome, Christ or the Pope* (Toledo, Ohio: The Loyal Pub. Co., 1895), pp. 4, 5-8. (2) R. L. Garis, *Immigration Restriction* (New York: Macmillan Co., 1927), pp. 203-4, 212-13.]

1.

The United States is Rome's favorite missionary field. The extent of our territory, the fertility of our soil, and the freedom of our institutions, offer such
strong inducements that our country has been flooded with hordes of foreigners, many of whom are uneducated Roman Catholics, and who, from infancy,
have yielded implicit obedience to the Pope. The Jesuits have been expelled
from nearly every country in Europe, and they are now turning their eyes to the
western hemisphere, and are exerting might and main to take possession of the
United States, as the following bold declarations will testify.

At the Centenary Celebration of the Catholic Church in the United States,
Archbishop Ireland declared: "The great work, which in God's providence the
Catholics in the United States are called to do within the coming century, is, to
make America Catholic, and to solve for the Church Universal the all-absorbing
problem with which the age confronts her."

At the Baltimore Catholic Congress, Henry F. Brownson, LL.D., said:
"The American system is also anti-Protestant, and must either reject Protestantism, or be overthrown by it." . . .

Says Pope Leo XIII., in his encyclical of January 29, 1895: "The church
would bring forth more abundant fruits, if, in addition to liberty, she enjoyed
the favor of the laws and the patronage of public authority."

In these bold declarations and avowed intentions, Rome is either right or
wrong. As Cardinal Manning has put it: "The Catholic Church is either the
masterpiece of Satan, or the kingdom of the Son of God." Or to use the words of
Cardinal Newman: "Either the Church of Rome is the house of God, or the
house of Satan; there is no middle ground between them." If the Church of
Rome is the Church of God, we ought to know it. If the Pope is infallible, we
ought to know it. If Rome's presence in our country and the objects she has determined to accomplish are for the highest good, the sooner we are convinced
of this, the better. On the other hand, if the Church of Rome is the house of Satan, if the Pope is the Antichrist, if her doctrines are the commandments of
men, if she is the enemy of our liberties, then our people ought to know it. It is
the purpose of this book to assist in settling these questions, and to furnish
knowledge that will awaken sympathy and prepare for wise action. I have
quoted, at great length, from Rome's highest authorities on the various subjects
discussed; for out of her own mouth she must stand condemned or acquitted,
and from her own history she must stand approved or disapproved.

There are those who may not see the need of another book upon this subject; I would ask such to reserve their judgment until they have carefully studied
the question; until they have read the encyclicals, decrees, catechisms, theologies, and authoritative utterances of this hierarchy; until they have read an account of some of Rome's dogmas, practices and intrigues as depicted by those

who have made the subject a lifelong study. Our country is a paradise for Rome. She has, without being disputed, introduced into our beautiful and fair land, many dogmas, founded upon pretended visions and fabulous tales, more fit for pagan darkness than for evangelical light; she has burdened millions of our people with masses, auricular confessions, priestly celibacy, and fears of purgatory; she has attacked our public schools; she has denounced our Bible; she has favored the union of church and state; she has thrust her hand into our treasury; she has monopolized the funds donated to the religious bodies for Indian education; she controls our telegraphic system; she censures and subsidizes the public press; she manipulates many of our political conventions; she rules many of our large cities; she has put eighty men, out of every hundred, at work in the public department at Washington; she has put officers in charge of our army and navy; she has put judges upon the bench; she has muzzled the mouths of many of our ablest statesmen, editors and ministers; she has plotted to destroy our Government; she has made her subjects swear allegiance to a foreign power, and Archbishop Ireland says: "She has the power to speak; she has an organization by which her laws may be enforced. . . . She is the sole living and enduring Christian authority."

These things being true, is it not time to watch this cunning enemy? Is it not time to arouse sleepy Protestants? Is it not time to call a halt? Have we not had enough bloodshed, Tammany rings, anarchism and Jesuitism? The preservation of American liberties is no small consideration, for without these liberties, an American is without a home.

At the very outset I desire to state that there are many good Catholic men and women identified with the Roman Catholic Church, but there is a broad line of distinction between the unsuspecting confidence of the laity and the deliberate scheming of the Roman Catholic priesthood. There is, also, credit due to Rome for the preservation of some learning during the dark ages of the world's history; but the claim that she has done some good, does not prevent us from seeing the evils that have followed in her footsteps.

In this discussion, we have no denunciation to hurl against any individual. We shall discuss Romanism as it is. We shall discuss it as a system. We shall discuss its doctrines, principles, spirit and practices.

2.

At the present time European immigration to the United States may be divided into two groups, the "old" and the "new." The "old" immigration has extended from the beginning of our colonial and national history to the present time and has been and still is derived chiefly from Great Britain and Ireland, Germany, Holland, and the Scandinavian countries. Since practically all the immigrants to 1890 belonged to this "old" immigration, they were predominantly Anglo-Saxon-Germanic in blood and Protestant in religion — of the same stock as that which originally settled the United States, wrote our Constitution and established our democratic institutions. The English, Dutch, Swedes, Germans, and even the Scotch-Irish, who constituted practically the entire immigration prior to 1890, were less than two thousand years ago one Germanic race in the forests surrounding the North Sea. Thus, being similar in blood and in political ideals, social training and economic background, this "old" immigration has merged with the native stock fairly easily and rapidly. Assimilation has always been only a matter of time and this has been aided by the economic, social and political conditions of the country. Even though those already here objected at times to others coming in, yet once in they have soon become Americans, so assimilated as to be indistinguishable from the natives; for this old immigration has consisted almost wholly of families who have come to this country with the full intention of making it their home and of becoming American citizens. It was this immigration that aided so much in the development of agriculture in the great Central West and in the construction of our incomparable transportation system. Furthermore, in comparison with the recent "new" immigration, it has always been small in volume, while the abundance of free land in the past, our need of pioneers and the willingness of these "old" type immigrants to go into the West and settle on the land, prevented the rise of many serious problems.

In the period centering about the year 1880, and in particular in the decade 1880-1890, there was a distinct shift in the immigration movement. Whereas before 1890 most of our immigrants were Anglo-Saxons and Teutons from Northern Europe, since 1890 and prior to the quota legislation in 1924 the great majority were members of the Mediterranean and Slavic races from Southern, Eastern and Southeastern Europe. The great bulk of this "new" immigration has its sources in Russia, Poland, Austria, Hungary, Greece, Turkey, Italy, and the Balkan countries. It is this "new" immigration which constitutes *the* immigration problem of *today.* . . .

Prior to the World War [I] the race map of this [Austro-Hungarian] Empire showed the most complicated social mosaic of all modern nations and as far as present day immigration is concerned the same situation exists despite the break up of the empire. Prior to the war there existed a juxtaposition of hostile races and a fixity of language held together only by the outside pressure of the powerful neighboring nations. This conflict of races aggravated the conditions which caused millions to emigrate. Not only were there five grand divisions of the human family — the German, the Slav, the Magyar, the Latin, and the Jew — within what was formerly Austria-Hungary, but these had to be subdivided to really understand the situation. In the northern mountainous and hilly sections were the Slavic peoples, the Czechs, or Bohemians, with their closely related Moravians, and the Slavic Slovaks, Poles, and Ruthenians (Russniaks); while in the southern hills and along the Adriatic were other Slavs, the Croatians, Servians, Dalmatians, and Slovenians. Between these divisions were the two dominant races, the Magyars and the Germans. To the southwest was the Italian element and in the east were the Latinized Slavs, the Rumanians. In general the Slavs were the conquered peoples, being dominated by the Germans and Magyars. The northern Slavs were subject to Austria and Hungary. The Ruthenians suffered a double subjection, being serfs of their fellow Slavs, the Poles, whom they hate. The Southern Slavs and Rumanians were subject to Hungary. In general it may be said that the Slavic immigrant furnishes a most difficult problem in assimilation due to the fact that his past, his customs and his inherited traditions make change slow.

"With all of this confusing medley of races, with its diversity of Greek and Roman Catholicism and Judaism, with its history of race oppression and hatred, with its almost universal serfdom and low standards of living, it is not surprising that in America the different races should group and settle together and often break out into factions and feuds wherever thrown together among us."

For, from such a conglomeration of races it is impossible that political and social entanglements and difficulties should not arise. Coming in millions it has been impossible to even begin to assimilate and Americanize them. Practically the entire immigration has been that of peasants. As in other countries of low standards, the number of births in this section of Europe is large in proportion to the inhabitants. Thus poverty, ignorance, inequality and helplessness all play their part in producing a very high birthrate. The result has been the emigration to America of many whose low standards of living, whose ignorance and racial hatreds have made it impossible for us under present conditions to assimilate and have marked them, in the minds of those who favor immigration restriction, along with the Italians and Russians, as undesirable immigrants.

The Klan's Americanism

While the APA worried chiefly about Roman Catholics, the Ku Klux Klan (KKK) worried about Catholics, Jews, blacks, and anyone else who did not measure up to the Klan's definition of American: native, white, Protestant. And like the APA, the Klan took its stance on behalf of an Americanism which "can only be achieved if the pioneer stock is kept pure." The prominence of Klan activity in the 1920s is evident by the space which the presti-

---

[Sources: (1) *North American Review*, 223 (March, April, May, 1926), 52-53, 53-55. (2) Ibid. (June, July, August, 1926), 286-88.]

gious North American Review *gave to it. (1) The first selection by Hiram Wesley Evans, "Imperial Wizard and Emperor, Knights of the Ku Klux Klan," sets forth that organization's firm convictions. (2) A succeeding issue of the* Review *carried responses from Catholic, Jew, and black. The Jewish rejoinder by Rabbi Joseph Silverman of Temple Emanu-El of New York City is excerpted below.*

1.

The fundamentals of our thought are convictions, not mere opinions. We are pleased that modern research is finding scientific backing for these convictions. We do not need them ourselves; we know that we are right in the same sense that a good Christian knows that he has been saved and that Christ lives — a thing which the intellectual can never understand. These convictions are no more to be argued about than is our love for our children; we are merely willing to state them for the enlightenment and conversion of others.

There are three of these great racial instincts, vital elements in both the historic and the present attempts to build an America which shall fulfill the aspirations and justify the heroism of the men who made the nation. These are the instincts of loyalty to the white race, to the traditions of America, and to the spirit of Protestantism, which has been an essential part of Americanism ever since the days of Roanoke and Plymouth Rock. They are condensed into the Klan slogan: "Native, white, Protestant supremacy."

First in the Klansman's mind is patriotism — America for Americans. He believes religiously that a betrayal of Americanism or the American race is treason to the most sacred of trusts, a trust from his fathers and a trust from God. He believes, too, that Americanism can only be achieved if the pioneer stock is kept pure. There is more than race pride in this. Mongrelization has been proven bad. It is only between closely related stocks of the same race that interbreeding has improved men; the kind of interbreeding that went on in the early days of America between English, Dutch, German, Huguenot, Irish and Scotch.

Racial integrity is a very definite thing to the Klansman. It means even more than good citizenship, for a man may be in all ways a good citizen and yet a poor American, unless he has racial understanding of Americanism, and instinctive loyalty to it. It is in no way a reflection on any man to say that he is un-American; it is merely a statement that he is not one of us. It is often not even wise to try to make an American of the best of aliens. What he is may be spoiled without his becoming American. The races and stocks of men are as distinct as breeds of animals, and every boy knows that if one tries to train a bulldog to herd sheep, he has in the end neither a good bulldog nor a good collie. . . .

The second word in the Klansman's trilogy is "white". The white race

must be supreme, not only in America but in the world. This is equally unde-
batable, except on the ground that the races might live together, each with full
regard for the rights and interests of others, and that those rights and interests
would never conflict. Such an idea, of course, is absurd. The colored races today, such as Japan, are clamoring not for equality but for their supremacy. The

Ku Klux Klan parade in St. Petersburg, Florida, c. 1926
(Keystone-Mast Collection, University of California, Riverside)

whole history of the world, on its broader lines, has been one of race conflicts, wars, subjugation or extinction. This is not pretty, and certainly disagrees with the maudlin theories of cosmopolitanism, but it is truth. The world has been so made that each race must fight for its life, must conquer, accept slavery or die. The Klansman believes that the whites will not become slaves, and he does not intend to die before his time.

Moreover, the future of progress and civilization depends on the continued supremacy of the white race. The forward movement of the world for centuries has come entirely from it. Other races each had its chance and either faded or stuck fast, while white civilization shows no sign of having reached its limit. Until the whites falter, or some colored civilization has a miracle of awakening, there is not a single colored stock that can claim even equality with the white; much less supremacy.

The third of the Klan principles is that Protestantism must be supreme; that Rome shall not rule America. The Klansman believes this not merely because he is a Protestant, nor even because the Colonies that are now our nation were settled for the purpose of wresting America from the control of Rome and establishing a land of free conscience. He believes it also because Protestantism is an essential part of Americanism; without it America could never have been created and without it she cannot go forward. Roman rule would kill it.

Protestantism contains more than religion. It is the expression in religion of the same spirit of independence, self-reliance and freedom which are the highest achievements of the Nordic race. It sprang into being automatically at the time of the great "upsurgence" of strength in the Nordic peoples that opened the spurt of civilization in the fifteenth century. It has been a distinctly Nordic religion, and it has been through this religion that the Nordics have found strength to take leadership of all whites and the supremacy of the earth. Its destruction is the deepest purpose of all other peoples, as that would mean the end of Nordic rule.

It is the only religion that permits the unhampered individual development and the unhampered conscience and action which were necessary in the settling of America. Our pioneers were all Protestants, except for an occasional Irishman — Protestants by nature if not by religion — for though French and Spanish dared and explored and showed great heroism, they made little of the land their own. America was Protestant from birth.

She must remain Protestant, if the Nordic stock is to finish its destiny. We of the old stock Americans could not work — and the work is mostly ours to do, if the record of the past proves anything — if we became priest-ridden, if we had to submit our consciences and limit our activities and suppress our thoughts at the command of any man, much less of a man sitting upon Seven Hills thousands of miles away. This we will not permit. Rome shall not rule us. Protestantism must be supreme.

2.

The head and front of the offending on the part of this underground conspiracy are directed, not only against Negroes, but also against Catholics, Jews and aliens, the fixed policy of the organization being based on the "Know Nothing" principle of "America for Americans only", with the modification that America shall be restricted to a citizenry of white Protestants. The Klan also maintains that all other people in America shall only be tolerated, shall be deprived of the right of suffrage and of holding office, and that all further immigration shall be entirely cut off.

On the Klan's efforts for further restricting immigration, or cutting it off altogether, I shall here offer no extended criticism. Immigration comes under the political and economical policies of a country, and its regulation is subject to fluctuating internal conditions. Restriction of immigration, even when justified, may sometimes work injustice to certain classes of foreigners who seek entrance into our shores. The immigration phase of the Klan's policy is, however, to be censured because it is not coupled with a national political or economic policy, but is part of the Klan's general scheme for placing this country under the control of white Protestants. We resent the reasons and the motives for the Klan's restrictive measures because they are not associated with the best interests of the Nation.

It is not difficult to infer that the programme of the Ku Klux Klan includes religious propaganda for the purpose of repressing and oppressing members of the Catholic and Jewish faiths. Indications have already been given in no uncertain terms by local sections that the plan is to Christianize America, to Christianize the public schools, to elect only white Protestants to office — that is, to enforce everywhere the teachings and the practices of the Protestant Church and to place the Government under the control of that branch of Christianity.

This is, in truth, an ambitious programme, and it is well that the country is aware thereof, for to be forewarned, in this respect, is certainly to be forearmed. The Klan had deserved condemnation and punishment for its political and other secret machinations against the Negro, for instigating racial prejudice; and now that it has entered upon a religious crusade against Jews and Catholics, and against the Constitution of the Nation, it has invited additional execration and progressive punishment even up to its total extinction.

It passeth all understanding how American citizens, and especially such as profess to be followers of Christianity, can undertake to carry out any programme that savors of the Spanish Inquisition and the Massacre of the Innocents. We are constantly inveighing against the terrible crimes committed in the name of religion in the Dark Ages, and we speak deprecatingly of those times as the "Dark Ages." But what shall we say of the Klan's ways, that we see are dark, in this so-called enlightened age, and in this noble and free America, that we love and cherish!

What justification is there for this twentieth century religious persecution on American soil? Is the Klan afraid that America may become Romanized? There is more danger (if it is a danger) that America may become Evangelized. Or is the Klan perhaps afraid that America may become Judaized? I have no such fears, or even hopes. Or is the Klan fearful that Catholics, Jews, Negroes, free thinkers and nondescript naturalized citizens may combine to control elections and perhaps place a Catholic, a Jew, a Negro or a free thinker in the Presidential chair? Why does the Klan harrow up such hallucinations? Is it not better to trust the good sense of the American people to do, under any given circumstances, what is best for the country? And let the Klansmen remember that after all, Catholic, Jewish, Negro and atheistic or non-religious citizens are also true Americans — as genuine Americans as the Klansmen claim to be. The American Constitution does not discriminate against the religious or non-religious citizen. It is opposed to a religious test for public office; it is based on the principle of separation of State from Church. The Government, to be sure, is courteous to religion and grants to all sects equal protection — and it behooves religion to be courteous to the Government and it is the duty of all sects to obey and preserve intact the principles and articles of the federal law. The Klan, by injecting into the political life of these States a religious issue, convicts itself thereby of being un-American in principle and act. *The Ku Kluxers violate Americanism in order to enforce their stamp of Americanism.*

Moreover, by what warrant does the Klan assume that white Protestants would make the best Americans? Is Protestantism a better religion than Catholicism? Are they not, both, part of Christianity? Do they not both believe in the same Messiah and in the same Bible? And is not a Protestant or Catholic of the Negro race, if he is sincere, equally as acceptable to God as a Protestant or Catholic of the white race? Or does the Klan wish us to believe that God also draws the color line, and is also prejudiced either against one sect or another of the Christian Church? For my part, I believe that the Klansmen have involved themselves in a hypocritical attitude and dilemma from which it will be impossible to extricate themselves, unless they destroy their unworthy Order.

I am tempted also to defend the Jew against the discrimination to which he is subjected by the Klan on the score of his religion, but I refrain, when I remember that Christianity paid Judaism the greatest compliment that was ever paid to any race or religion when it claimed that God had selected a Son of Israel to be the Messiah to the heathen world two thousand years ago in order to convert it to a better faith, a higher culture and a nobler civilization. We Jews still have the same religion that Jesus originally professed, and it seems to us nothing short of folly for any devotees of Jesus to declare that only self-elected white Protestant Christians are fit to be Americans, and that Jews, from whom

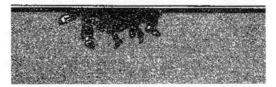

A 1924 KKK anti-immigration pamphlet,
"The Menace of Modern Immigration:
An Address Outlining Fully the Policies of the Knights
of the Ku Klux Klan," by H. W. Evans
(Michigan State University Library, Special Collections Division)

Jesus sprang, should be barred from American life. *Verily, the Ku Kluxers violate religion in order to enforce their own type of religion.*

Rum and Rome

In 1928 nativism had a specific target: a Roman Catholic had for the first time in American history won the nomination of a major political party and was now running for the presidency of the United States. That he was no special friend of the Prohibition Amendment (see above, p. 91) only aggravated Protestant anxieties and steeled their resolve to keep this Catholic out of the White House. (1) In September of 1928 the Methodists of Ohio, meeting in their newly formed conference, heard Mabel Walker Willebrandt plead for the defeat of Alfred E. Smith and for the election of Herbert C. Hoover. (2) In that same fall, candidate Smith, on the campaign trail in Oklahoma City, responded to the Klan, to Mrs. Willebrandt, and to all who would divide American voters along religious lines.

1. Special to *The New York Times*

SPRINGFIELD, Ohio, Sept. 7 [1928]

The newly formed Ohio conference of the Methodist Episcopal Church today unanimously adopted a resolution endorsing the candidacy of Herbert Hoover, Republican nominee for the Presidency. The conference went on record as being unalterably opposed to the election of Governor Smith. The conferring ministers insisted that the action was taken solely on the prohibition issue.

The action of the conference this afternoon divided interest with an address in the evening by Mrs. Mabel Walker Willebrandt, Assistant Attorney General of the United States. Mrs. Willebrandt described Governor Smith's candidacy as a result of an alliance between Tammany Hall and wealthy anti-prohibitionists.

She charged that since the repeal of the New York State Mullan-Gage act, in Governor Smith's second term, dry enforcement had completely broken down in the State. New York City, she said, was one of the worst wet spots in the country. She alleged that liquor was pouring over the Canadian border into New York, and called on the Methodists to support Mr. Hoover. . . .

[Sources: (1) *New York Times,* Sept. 8, 1928, pp. 1, 3. (2) Alfred E. Smith, *Campaign Addresses . . .* (Washington, D.C.: Democratic National Committee, 1929), pp. 52- 53, 56-58.]

Following a reference to the fact that all but two States ratified the 18th Amendment, Mrs. Willebrandt said that there remained in the nation many "willful sections" in which the local sentiment was largely against prohibition.

"The worst of these spots," she continued, "was in New York City. The Empire State as a whole achieved the 'will to unselfishness' which ratification of the 18th Amendment typifies. But Manhattan is ruled by Tammany, an organization that for underworld connections and political efficiency is matched no place else in America.

Anti-Prohibitionists Scored.

"Scattered over the United States were members of the intelligentsia who organized the Association Against the Prohibition Amendment. They worked along more or less futilely through 1921, 1922 and 1923. In 1924, at the Democratic convention in Madison Square Garden, Tammany tried to capture the Democratic Party.

"Tammany didn't then realize that it could not sweep that party off its feet by typical Tammany methods. Screaming whistles and brass bands failed to win Southern leaders. Tammany's candidate was the man who had just abandoned the policy of cooperation between State and National Government, provided for in the concurrent clause of the Eighteenth Amendment.

"He was the one Governor in all the American States who, notwithstanding his oath to support the Constitution of the United States, pulled down one of the forty-six pillars the people had erected for its support. New York had ratified the amendment. That ratification was a pledge to concurrent effort. But the audacious Governor was unconvinced by such reasoning. Tammany wanted the least possible prohibition. Tammany had reared him; gave him his power. Tammany's desires were his convictions.

"Triple Alliance" Is Alleged.

"Certain leaders in the Association Against the Prohibition Amendment saw the importance of securing as spokesman of their cause so powerful a leader as the Governor of New York.

"Thus the wealthy groups of anti-prohibitionists and Tammany, symbol of predatory politics, and Governor Smith were found in early alliance.

"They have prepared well for this critical hour. Newspapers in rural and Southern communities were bought by New York money and have switched from a long-settled dry policy to preaching the doctrine of 'It can't be enforced.' At the same time there have been insinuated into strategic positions in dry enforcement men who were members of the Association Against the Prohibition Amendment. They have left office proclaiming from the lecture platform and through the press one general chorus that 'prohibition can never be enforced.' . . .

Defense of Amendment Urged.

"Anti-prohibitionists have never won against united drys. It is clever strategy, therefore, to divide their forces. That is what is attempted in making prohibition a party issue. . . . You did not make it a political issue. Your adroit Tammany foe has done so. You can do nothing else but follow wherever defense of the Eighteenth Amendment leads.

"It is not abandoning your non-partisan policy of not discussing politics or letting your organization be torn by political dissensions to take a stand against the Democratic nominee and for the Republican national ticket this year. In fact, there is no choice. The Republican Party platform and both its candidates are, by declaration and record, committed to the principle and the enforcement of prohibition. . . .

"It is reasonable to assume that the Governor's oath promising to 'support the Constitution of the United States' binds him to assist in the letter and spirit of enforcement of the Federal Constitution, but New York since, through Governor Smith's leadership, the enforcement act of the State was repealed, has become the centre, not only of lawlessness and disregard for the Constitution of the United States and Free and open distribution of liquor, but it has also become the centre of the dissemination of the false doctrine that the law can't be enforced.

"That statement could be received with more conviction if it emanated from a State where Federal Government and State had joined hands and worked valiantly to do the job. In New York State there are between 2,000 and 3,000 State police; there are more than 16,000 city police; there are 113 Supreme Court State judges and sixty-two County Prosecutors.

Says Bootlegging Has Risen.

"All of these agencies might be enlisted to reduce the crime and lawlessness that is alleged to flow from disregard of the prohibition law, but they are now and have been inactive as to prohibition since New York repealed its enforcement act.

"As a consequence bootlegging has vastly increased; liquor running over the Canadian border has multiplied, blind-pigs that used to operate secretly and with some degree of shame operate openly with bars and brass rails; hun-

dreds of night clubs in Manhattan are just a new form of the old-fashioned saloons that Tammany used to protect. These night clubs have open bars, and yet
they can exist only so long as they get licenses from the City Administration.

"Of course the law is not being enforced in New York; it is being evaded
and nullified; a few hundred Federal agents and thirteen Federal judges with
four United States Attorneys cannot alone cope successfully with so much lawlessness.

"There are 2,000 pastors here. You have in your churches more than
600,000 members of the Methodist Church in Ohio alone. That is enough to
swing the election. The 600,000 have friends in other States. Write to them. Every day and every ounce of your energy are needed to rouse the friends of prohibition to register and vote.

"The Eighteenth Amendment is new in politics. You did not put it there.
The Republican Party did not put it there.

"Neither did the rank and file of the loyal constitutional Democrats. Neither did the National Democratic Convention put it there. It was put there by
its enemies; and Governor Smith by a formal act as ruthless as was ever recorded in American politics became their leader. You have a chance to prove by
electing Herbert Hoover that obedience to law can be secured and that America
does not retreat before organized crime."

2.

I can think of no greater disaster to this country than to have the voters of it divide upon religious lines. It is contrary to the spirit, not only of the Declaration
of Independence, but of the Constitution itself. During all of our national life
we have prided ourselves throughout the world on the declaration of the fundamental American truth that all men are created equal.

Our forefathers, in their wisdom, seeing the danger to the country of a division on religious issues, wrote into the Constitution of the United States in no
uncertain words the declaration that no religious test shall ever be applied for
public office, and it is a sad thing in 1928, in view of the countless billions of
dollars that we have poured into the cause of public education, to see some
American citizens proclaiming themselves 100 per cent. American, and in the
document that makes that proclamation suggesting that I be defeated for the
presidency because of my religious belief.

The Grand Dragon of the Realm of Arkansas, writing to a citizen of that
State, urges my defeat because I am a Catholic, and in the letter suggests to the
man, who happened to be a delegate to the Democratic convention, that by voting against me he was upholding American ideals and institutions as established by our forefathers.

The Grand Dragon that thus advised a delegate to the national convention to vote against me because of my religion is a member of an order known as the Ku Klux Klan, who have the effrontery to refer to themselves as 100 per cent. Americans.

Yet totally ignorant of the history and tradition of this country and its institutions and, in the name of Americanism, they breathe into the hearts and souls of their members hatred of millions of their fellow countrymen because of their religious belief.

Nothing could be so out of line with the spirit of America. Nothing could be so foreign to the teachings of Jefferson. Nothing could be so contradictory of our whole history. Nothing could be so false to the teachings of our Divine Lord Himself. The world knows no greater mockery than the use of the blazing cross, the cross upon which Christ died, as a symbol to install into the hearts of men a hatred of their brethren, while Christ preached and died for the love and brotherhood of man. . . .

Giving them [the Republicans] the benefit of all reasonable doubt, they at least remain silent on the exhibition that Mrs. Willebrandt made of herself before the Ohio Conference of the Methodist Episcopal Church when she said:

"There are two thousand pastors here. You have in your church more than 600,000 members of the Methodist Church in Ohio alone. That is enough to swing the election. The 600,000 have friends in other states. Write to them."

This is an extract from a speech made by her in favor of a resolution offered to the effect that the conference go on record as being unalterably opposed to the election of Governor Smith and to endorse the candidacy of Herbert Hoover, the Republican candidate.

Mrs. Willebrandt holds a place of prominence in the Republican administration in Washington; she is an Assistant Attorney-General of the United States. By silence, after such a speech, the only inference one can draw is that the administration approves such political tactics. Mrs. Willebrandt is not an irresponsible person. She was Chairman of the Committee on Credentials in the Republican National Convention at Kansas City.

What would the effect be upon these same people if a prominent official of the government of the State of New York under me suggested to a gathering of the pastors of my church that they do for me what Mrs. Willebrandt suggests be done for Hoover?

It needs no words of mine to impress that upon your minds. It is dishonest campaigning. It is un-American. It is out of line with the whole tradition and history of this government. And, to my way of thinking, is in itself sufficient to hold us up to the scorn of the thinking people of other nations.

One of the things, if not the meanest thing, in the campaign is a circular pretending to place someone of my faith in the position of seeking votes for me because of my Catholicism. Like everything of its kind, of course, it is unsigned, and it would be impossible to trace its authorship. It reached me through a member of the Masonic order who, in turn, received it in the mail. It is false in its every line. It was designed on its very face to injure me with members of churches other than my own.

I here emphatically declare that I do not wish any member of my faith in any part of the United States to vote for me on any religious grounds. I want them to vote for me only when in their hearts and consciences they become convinced that my election will promote the best interests of our country.

By the same token, I cannot refrain from saying that any person who votes against me simply because of my religion is not, to my way of thinking, a good citizen.

Let me remind the Democrats of this country that we belong to the party of that Thomas Jefferson whose proudest boast was that he was the author of the Virginia statute for religious freedom. Let me remind the citizens of every political faith that that statute of religious freedom has become a part of the sacred heritage of our land.

The constitutional guaranty that there should be no religious test for public office is not a mere form of words. It represents the most vital principle that ever was given any people.

I attack those who seek to undermine it, not only because I am a good Christian, but because I am a good American and a product of America and of American institutions. Everything I am, and everything I hope to be, I owe to those institutions.

Unsure of Capitalism

Economic Disaster

The stockmarket crash of 1929, followed by the Great Depression of the 1930s, stamped both the nation and its citizenry with such disaster as to leave the national psyche permanently marked. In those years, the nation was on trial, capitalism was on trial, traditional religion was on trial. (1) Writing even before the awful truth was known, Harry F. Ward (1873-1966), Methodist minister and seminary professor turned social radical, saw an irrecon-

---

[Sources: (1) H. F. Ward, *Our Economic Morality and the Ethic of Jesus* (New York: Macmillan Co., 1929), pp. 318-20, 321, 322-23. (2) C. E. Coughlin, *A Series of Lectures on Social Justice, 1935-1936* (Royal Oak, Mich.: Radio League of the Little Flower, 1936), pp. 7, 9-11.]

cilable conflict between the ethic of Jesus and the economic system of America. (2) In the depth of the depression, Charles E. Coughlin (1891-1979), Roman Catholic priest and radio preacher turned Populist (and later turned anti-Semite), formed a National Union for Social Justice. Coughlin's Union would radically alter the economic structure of the nation, "nationalizing those public necessities which by their very nature are too important to be held in the control of private individuals."

1.

It is the vision of ends that Western life lacks. It has no sense of direction. It is all motion — at unequaled speed — but what is its goal? It is atomic, chaotic — not yet corporate. Why do its millions work and fight and breed and die? Do even their leaders know? For what shall man live? For all, says Communism. For each, says Individualism. For both, says the ethic of Jesus. Having in the course of its development rescued the individual from both the early communal society of the East and the aristocratic society of the West that he may find himself in a voluntary brotherhood, this religious morality is not to be deceived by the suicidal separatism of individualistic democracy nor the equally fatal subordination which dogmatic Communism imposes upon personality. If there is one thing that the ethic of Jesus can help an inevitably collectivist world to remember, it is the creative function of the individual. If there is anything it can help those who have been nurtured in the individualistic tradition to appreciate, it is that personality is social in its origin and nature, needing the Great Society for its fulfillment.

The obligation involved in this relationship has been expressed in the motto, "Each for all and all for each." To choose to live for all in the search for justice and fellowship with the consciousness that they are the eternal values, to achieve solidarity by self-surrender in activity toward the common good and so to find the self — this is the realization of life according to the word of the Nazarene. Whatever theology may make of this view of life — and the Communists have certainly made it into a powerful enough God — it is the necessity of life if human society is to continue. To make the future, man must have some idea of what he would make. To be the creator he must have the creator's vision. What task is more divine than to make and remake human nature, and whatever our ultimate relation to the cosmos, whatever the extent to which we draw on the Eternal Spirit, this is our responsibility. . . .

The final clash between our current economic morality and the ethic of Jesus is over the nature of man. The capitalist economy rests on the hypothesis that man is a creature who prefers material comforts to moral values, who would rather have an increase in goods than in the quality of existence. The only future it can offer man is one in which he will get more conveniences but less freedom, justice, and fellowship, believing that thus he will be content. The ethic of Jesus rejects this estimate of human nature; insists moreover that the very making of it is the negation of personality, whose essence lies in the making of choices and whose development consists in preferring moral satisfactions to material, the ultimate to the immediate, the eternal to the temporal. . . .

Because the central issue in the conflict between our current economic morality and the ethic of Jesus is this difference of judgment concerning the capacities of man, the struggle between them is a matter of life and death for both religion and civilization. "Ye cannot serve God and Mammon!" Either religion proves itself able to bring to the acquisitive society redemption from the making and selling of things, and release from the struggle of greed for power, or it blindly leads this blind age into the twilight that has fallen upon all other civilizations. Therefore if the salvation which an ethical religion has to offer industrial society is to be available in time, the present duty of those to whom the development of this type of religion has been committed is to help this generation to see clearly the nature of the choice which a money-making economy puts before modern man.

2.

. . . Let us turn our attention to the specific program of the National Union for Social Justice. It has been called to my attention that loose-lipped whisperers of various breeds, together with certain mad-cap newspaper columnists, have written the obituary notice of our organization.

Much to the chagrin of these literary crystal-gazers, the National Union will prove to be a most dynamic corpse. There will be no let down. Principles, not men; justice, not partisanship; courage, not cowardice — these motivating forces will not be surrendered, nor shall I stoop either to compromise or betray the members of the National Union. . . .

The two major political parties which already exist, and to which the vast bulk of American citizens already belong, long since have been seized by powerful groups of manipulators. The American Liberty League, the United States Chamber of Commerce, the American Bankers Association, the Manufacturers Association, the oil industries and many other groups so jockeyed your Representative into position that, oftentimes, he became nothing more than the Washington secretary of plutocratic overlords.

Oftentimes there was as little distinction between a Democratic and a Republican member of Congress as there was between two worms gnawing on the one apple. Exploitation of the inarticulate people continued until wealth was concentrated in the hands of a few. The Constitution of the United States was degraded while Congress after Congress supported the private coinage and fixation of money. Consistently they permitted profits to pile up prodigiously for the owners of industry in a machine age when the laborer was being paid less and when his toil was wanted less. Consistently they forced the farmers of the nation, at least since 1920, to operate at a loss. Instead of supplying the country with honest American credit, Congress has flooded it with bankers' credit. Instead of regulating our national credit based on our national wealth, Congress has cooperated with the privately owned Federal Reserve bankers, permitting them to create credit out of nothing while the same Congress expects us and future generations to repay these bankers with currency money that does not exist.

Beyond all doubt, the old economic system of ragged, rugged individualism was nurtured at the twin breasts of successive Republican and Democratic Administrations — the right breast exuding the sour milk of plutocracy and the left breast the skimmed milk of socialistic remedies. The anemic body of our citizenry, nurtured upon such a fatal diet, witnessed the whitening of the bones of justice, experienced the weakening of the flesh of morality, while the tuberculosis of want spread in the midst of plenty. This individualism was clothed by the unclean, ragged garments of putrid politics, among whose folds there were bred the germs of radicalism.

Want in the midst of plenty! Millions of acres of fertile fields beckoning to the millions of idle to come and drink at their breasts! Thousands of factories with cunning machines anxious to produce clothing and conveniences for the mass of our citizens! Stately pine and hemlock and sturdy oak, willing to surrender their timbers for fuel and shelter! Yet, because of some fiat, because of some strange enchantment, because of some diabolical greed in the minds and hearts of a small group of unchristian men, there was echoed down the centuries the sacrilegious philosophy of Cain, denying that men are their brothers' keepers!

Our scientists knew how to harness a Niagara! Dare they intimate to us, in this year of grace, that they do not know how to harness an unnecessary poverty? Our Congressmen knew how to marshal the forces of our nation to fight a commercial war which they called "making the world safe for democracy." Dare you tell me that they know not how to marshal the wealth and the intelligence of the nation to fight our domestic enemies of greed and exploitation?

The National Union is hopeful enough to conquer these domestic enemies. . . .

Christian Love

Of all the solutions proposed for curing America's terrible economic ills, none seemed more improbable than Christian love and none more unlikely a warrior in that struggle than Dorothy Day (1897-1980). Converted to Roman Catholicism in 1927, this pacifist, impoverished social radical had no trump cards to play, occupied no important position, held no impressive title. Yet, she inspired thousands through her writing, her simplicity, her single-minded dedication to Christian love. In 1933 she founded the Catholic Worker, *a monthly periodical designed to be the Christian answer to the Marxist* Daily Worker. *Both papers described a society scandalously out of joint, but the solutions proffered were worlds apart. In her autobiography,* The Long Loneliness, *Day wrote (1) of publication and poverty; then (2) of community and love.*

1.

We started publishing *The Catholic Worker* at 436 East Fifteenth Street (now at 39 Spring Street) in May, 1933, with a first issue of 2,500 copies. Within three or four months the circulation bounded to 25,000, and it was cheaper to bring it out as an eight-page tabloid on newsprint rather than the smaller-sized edition on better paper we had started with. By the end of the year we had a circulation of 100,000 and by 1936 it was 150,000. It was certainly a mushroom growth. It was not only that some parishes subscribed for the paper all over the country in bundles of 500 or more. Zealous young people took the paper out in the streets and sold it, and when they could not sell it even at one cent a copy, they gave free copies and left them in streetcar, bus, barber shop and dentist's and doctor's office. We got letters from all parts of the country from people who said they had picked up the paper on trains, in rooming houses. . . .

One of the reasons for the rapid growth was that many young men were coming out of college to face the prospect of no job. If they had started to read *The Catholic Worker* in college, they were ready to spend time as volunteers when they came out. Others were interested in writing, and houses in Buffalo, Chicago, Baltimore, Seattle, St. Louis and Philadelphia, to name but a few cities, published their own papers and sold them with the New York *Catholic Worker*. A *Catholic Worker* was started in Australia and one in England. . . .

Voluntary poverty means a good deal of discomfort in these houses of

---

[Sources: (1) Dorothy Day, *The Long Loneliness* (New York: Harper & Brothers, 1952), pp. 207, 212-13. (2) Ibid., pp. 317-18.]

ours. Many of the houses throughout the country are without central heating and have to be warmed by stoves in winter. There are back-yard toilets for some even now. The first Philadelphia house had to use water drawn from one spigot at the end of an alley, which served half a dozen other houses. It was lit with oil lamps. It was cold and damp and so unbelievably poverty-stricken that little

Fritz Eichenberg woodcut of a Catholic Worker Movement House of Hospitality
(from Peter Maurin, *The Green Revolution*)

children coming to see who were the young people meeting there exclaimed that this could not be a *Catholic* place; it was too poor. We must be Communists. They were well acquainted with the Communist point of view since they were Puerto Rican and Spanish and Mexican and this was at the beginning of the Spanish Civil War.

How hard a thing it is to hear such criticisms made. Voluntary poverty was only found among the Communists; the Negro and white man on the masthead of our paper suggested communism; the very word "worker" made people distrust us at first. We were not taking the position of the great mass of Catholics, who were quite content with the present in this world. They were quite willing to give to the poor, but they did not feel called upon to work for the things of this life for others which they themselves esteemed so lightly. Our insistence on worker-ownership, on the right of private property, on the need to de-proletarize the worker, all points which had been emphasized by the popes in their social encyclicals, made many Catholics think we were Communists in disguise, wolves in sheep's clothing.

2.

The most significant thing about *The Catholic Worker* is poverty, some say. The most significant thing is community, others say. We are not alone any more.

But the final word is love. At times it has been, in the words of Father Zossima,[3] a harsh and dreadful thing, and our very faith in love has been tried through fire.

We cannot love God unless we love each other, and to love we must know each other. We know Him in the breaking of bread, and we know each other in the breaking of bread, and we are not alone any more. Heaven is a banquet and life is a banquet, too, even with a crust, where there is companionship.

We have all known the long loneliness and we have learned that the only solution is love and that love comes with community.

It all happened while we sat there talking, and it is still going on.

3. In Dostoyevsky's *Brothers Karamazov*.

Political Realism

The most widely read American theologian of the 1930s was Reinhold Niebuhr (1892-1971), member of the Evangelical and Reformed church (which later merged into a new United Church of Christ). After graduating from Yale Divinity School in 1914, Niebuhr assumed a pastorate in the nation's industrial center, Detroit, Michigan. There the young minister found his sentimental liberalism inadequate to cope with or speak to brutal economic realities all around him. Attracted to Marxism, he became a severe critic of capitalism. Then disillusioned with Marxism, he came to criticize its easy dogmatisms as well. Rejecting what he saw as naiveté on the part of communists, capitalists, and sentimental moralists, Reinhold Niebuhr advanced to a position of Christian and political realism. (1) In his autobiographical work, Leaves from the Notebook of a Tamed Cynic, *one can follow some of this painful progression in 1925 and 1926. (2) In 1934, Niebuhr set forth the "political realism of Christian orthodoxy."*

1.

But why not be specific? Why doesn't the church offer specific suggestions for the application of a Christian ethic to the difficulties of our day? If that suggestion is made, the answer is that such a policy would breed contention. It certainly would. No moral project can be presented and no adventure made without resistance from the traditionalist and debate among experimentalists. But besides being more effective, such a course would be more interesting than this constant bathing in sentimentalities. If the church could only achieve schisms on ethical issues! They would represent life and reality. Its present schisms are not immoral as such. They are immoral only in the sense that they perpetuate issues which have no relevancy in our day.

When I sit through a church conference I begin to see a little more clearly why religion is on the whole so impotent ethically, why the achievements of the church are so meager compared to its moral pretensions. Sermon after sermon, speech after speech is based upon the assumption that the people of the church are committed to the ethical ideals of Jesus and that they are the sole or at least chief agents of redemptive energy in society.

It is very difficult to persuade people who are committed to a general

[Sources: (1) Reinhold Niebuhr, *Leaves from the Notebook of a Tamed Cynic* (Chicago: Willett, Clark, and Colby, 1929), pp. 74-75, 79, 112-13. (2) Reinhold Niebuhr, *Reflections on the End of an Era* (New York: Charles Scribner's Sons, 1934), pp. 215-17.]

ideal to consider the meaning of that ideal in specific situations. It is even more difficult to prompt them to consider specific ends of social and individual conduct and to evaluate them in the light of experience.

The church conference begins and ends by attempting to arouse an emotion of the ideal, usually in terms of personal loyalty to the person of Jesus, but very little is done to attach the emotion to specific tasks and projects. Is the industrial life of our day unethical? Are nations imperialistic? Is the family disintegrating? Are young people losing their sense of values? If so, we are told over and over again that nothing will help but "a new baptism of the spirit," a "new revival of religion," a "great awakening of the religious consciousness." . . .

The morality of the church is anachronistic. Will it ever develop a moral insight and courage sufficient to cope with the real problems of modern society? If it does it will require generations of effort and not a few martyrdoms. We ministers maintain our pride and self-respect and our sense of importance only through a vast and inclusive ignorance. If we knew the world in which we live a little better we would perish in shame or be overcome by a sense of futility. . . .

The churches of America are on the whole thoroughly committed to the interests and prejudices of the middle classes. I think it is a bit of unwarranted optimism to expect them to make any serious contribution to the reorganization of society. I still have hopes that they will become sufficiently intelligent and heroic to develop some qualifying considerations in the great industrial struggle, but I can no longer envisage them as really determining factors in the struggle. Neither am I able for this reason to regard them as totally useless, as some of the critics do.

The ethical reconstruction of modern industrial society is, to be sure, a very important problem, but it is not the only concern of mankind. The spiritual amenities and moral decencies which the churches help to develop and preserve in the private lives of individuals are worth something for their own sake. Yet it must be obvious that if anyone is chosen by talent and destiny to put his life into the industrial struggle, the church is hardly his best vehicle.

The church is like the Red Cross service in war time. It keeps life from degenerating into a consistent inhumanity, but it does not materially alter the fact of the struggle itself. The Red Cross neither wins the war nor abolishes it. Since the struggle between those who have and those who have not is a never-ending one, society will always be, in a sense, a battleground. It is therefore of some importance that human loveliness be preserved outside of the battle lines. But those who are engaged in this task ought to realize that the brutalities of the conflict may easily negate the most painstaking humanizing efforts behind the lines, and that these efforts may become a method for evading the dangers and risks of the battlefield.

If religion is to contribute anything to the solution of the industrial problem, a more heroic type of religion than flourishes in the average church must be set to the task. I don't believe that the men who are driven by that kind of religion need to dissociate themselves from the churches, but they must bind themselves together in more effective association than they now possess.

2.

According to the absolute ideal, man was intended to live in perfect love and complete equality with his fellowmen. But his fall into sin made this impossible and created a situation in which the evil lusts of men needed to be checked by the coercion of governments, the restrictions of property and even the inequalities of slavery. The problems of economics and politics were to be regulated by the requirements of "natural law" rather than the absolute ideal of love, a conception which Christianity borrowed from Stoicism. The requirements of the natural law were, broadly speaking, the demands of *justice* (though never equalitarian justice) and they were assumed to have been written into all human hearts by God. In as far as they were not voluntarily obeyed (and the prevalence of sin would make infractions inevitable) they were to be enforced by governments. Government had, in fact, been expressly instituted by God for this purpose. Here the orthodox church from the earliest day to the present has leaned heavily on the words of Paul. "There is no power but of God; the powers that be are ordained of God."

If one were to reconstruct this general philosophy of politics in nonmythological terms it might be put in the following words: The highest moral ideal for human life, the ideal of love can neither be renounced nor completely realized. Its imperative and convincing reality proves that human life has its source and its goal above and beyond the frustrations and hindrances of the world of nature in which man lives. In this world the inordinate egoism of individuals and groups constantly threatens life with self-destruction through anarchy. Since obedience to the absolute demands of love is impossible to natural man he must be restrained by an ideal less rigorous but nevertheless effective in preventing the strong from devouring the weak and from living in the anarchy of constant conflict. The law of justice is such an ideal. It is the moral ideal in a more negative form than the ideal of love. It demands not that the interests of the neighbor be affirmed but that interests of the self be restricted so that they will not infringe upon those of the neighbor. Furthermore it sanctions the coercive force of governments to restrain those who will not voluntarily abide by the rule of rational justice.

4. World Out of Time

Revivalism

Dwight L. Moody (1837-99)

"As early as 7 o'clock the streets of Brooklyn presented the unwonted spectacle of long streams of well-dressed men and women hurriedly moving in the direction of the Rink. All the cars from the New-York ferries, as well as from East and South Brooklyn and other outlying points, were crowded to their utmost capacity. The building was filled to its utmost capacity both morning and afternoon. . . ." So the New York Times *(Oct. 25, 1875) began its front-page story of the electric revival in which the polar attractions were Dwight L. Moody, preacher, and Ira D. Sankey (1840-1908), song leader. And this meeting was typical of the excitement generated wherever Moody and Sankey went. Fresh from a successful two-year revival in Great Britain, the team returned to an America ready to give them every bit as much extravagant praise as the British had. What follows is the account by a New York journalist (William H. Coleman) of the super-charged atmosphere of a Moody meeting.*

Imagine yourself on the platform of the Madison Avenue Hall at 7.15 P.M., five minutes before the opening of the doors. Platform and near gallery are already well filled by the choir, Christian workers and their escorts, and special-ticket holders; the floor of the house is unoccupied, save by knots of ushers with their wands, no one being allowed to sit there until the doors are opened. In the railed inclosure, just back of the speaker's place, is a telegraph operator, usually

---

[Source: William R. Moody, *The Life of Dwight L. Moody* (New York: Fleming H. Revell Co., 1900), pp. 278-80, 280-81.]

a lady. Near by sits the chief superintendent, with aids at hand to transmit orders. At the other end of the hall sit another superintendent and operator. These control the lighting and heating and the seating of the audience.

"Ting! ting! ting!" goes a distant bell ten times — attention! "Ting! ting!" again, and the outer and inner doors slip back at three points, and three streams of people pour into the hall. The foremost enters at a run that would become disorder did not the usher check it, divide the stream, direct it into the front and middle seats, and when a section is filled bar the way with his wand. In ten minutes five thousand persons are seated. The galleries fill more slowly, and when all parts are full the doors are closed, and no one is allowed to stand in the aisles or along the gallery front save a few blue-coated policemen, whose services seem rarely called for.

The half-hour before meeting time passes quickly. One studies the vast throng before him with unceasing interest. The bright light of the many reflectors falls full upon the faces of all sorts and conditions of men — to say nothing of women and children. A more mixed multitude it would be hard to find. At the four o'clock meetings women are the leading element, next to old people, some of them so feeble as almost to be carried to their seats. But at night all classes and ages are present. There is a quiet stir everywhere, but no noise or levity. At 7.45 Mr. Thatcher leads the choir in singing, and shows great skill in managing both choir and congregation in combined and separate parts and in producing tender and powerful effects. One reason is, he has capital music to do it with. The 'Moody and Sankey Hymn-book' is the best for congregational use ever printed. Its words are full of the Gospel, its tunes express the thoughts they are allied to, and are so simple and yet positive in character that any one can sing them after once hearing them. When this vast congregation sings, "Safe in the arms of Jesus" or "I hear Thy welcome voice," one gets a new idea of the power of sacred song.

Eight o'clock, and Mr. Moody is at his post. It is a pleasant night, and though every seat is filled there is a large crowd outside. . . .

How he preaches has already been described. The evening sermon is usually of a bolder offhand character than that of the afternoon, which is intended more specially for Christians. He makes a marked distinction between preaching the Gospel and teaching Christians. His afternoon sermon on the Holy Spirit seemed meant for himself as well as for others, and at the close his voice trembled with emotion as he said: "I want more of this power. Pray for me, that I may be so filled with the Holy Spirit when coming on this platform that men may feel I come with a message from God." The quiet of the audience during Moody's preaching and Sankey's singing is remarkable. Even the rough young fellows who crowd the gallery passages make no sound. At the close Mr. Moody announces a men's meeting in the other hall, a boys' meeting in one of the smaller rooms, and the usual work in the inquiry meeting. Those attending these meetings are requested to go to them while the last hymn is being sung.

Moody and Sankey revival meeting in Brooklyn
(Billy Graham Center)

The Hippodrome work is a vast business enterprise, organized and conducted by business men, who have put money into it on business principles, for the purpose of saving men. But through all the machinery vibrates the power without which it would be useless — the power of the Holy Ghost. Of course it is successful. Men are being saved day and night, and a moral influence is felt round about the building itself. Two Sundays ago the police returns of that precinct showed no arrests — a thing before unknown — and a recent statement says that in spite of increased destitution among the poor this winter there has been no increase of crime.

Christians have been warmed, "limbered up," and taught to work as they have never worked before; taught how to study their Bibles and how to use them for the good of others; how to reach men simply, naturally, and successfully, how to live consistently and whole-heartedly themselves. The easy-going church life of multitudes has been sharply rebuked by these laborious evangelists. Worshipping in the rude-walled Hippodrome, sitting on wooden chairs, led in song by a man with a melodeon, and preached to by a man without a pulpit, they have learned that costly churches, stained windows, soft cushions, great organs, and quartette choirs are not necessary to the worship of God, and tend to drive away the poor, leaving the rich to enjoy their luxuries alone.

Sam Jones (1847-1906)

For Moody, for Jones, and for revivalists generally, every message was a single message: "Believe on the Lord Jesus Christ and thou shalt be saved." In whatever form, drawn from whatever text, the single concern was salvation. Sometimes called the "Moody of the South," Sam Jones started out as a lawyer in Georgia (1868-72), then became a Methodist circuit rider (1872-80), and spent the last several years of his life as an urban evangelist throughout the South — and well beyond that region. For an understanding of the excerpt below, no sophisticated theological education is required, no program of preparation is demanded. He that has ears to hear, let him hear. Even more crucial, let him choose life and not death.

How To Be Saved.

What must I do to be saved? And they said, Believe on the Lord Jesus Christ and thou shalt be saved and thy house."
                                                    — Acts XVI, 30, 31.

This is the language of the Philippian jailer to St. Paul, and Paul's answer. As a minister of the Gospel of Jesus Christ, I have no right to advise a man to do any thing that he may not die doing and die saved. I might advise a man to join the Church — I know that is helpful and good advice, and I wish every man was a member of the Church of Jesus Christ, and was living up to the precepts of his blessed religion; and yet I see how a man may join the Church, and live in the Church and die in the Church, and yet be lost at last. And that's the saddest reflection of a human soul — gone from the heights of profession down to the depths of damnation. I might advise a man to read good books, and I wish there were no bad books in the universe. I am sorry that a bad book was ever published. I am sorry that any bad book ever had an entrance into your home, brother. I am sorry that one of your children, or one of you, ever sat down and worse than threw away your time reading bad books. I wish there were only good books, and that men would read them, and when I advise a man to read good books I am giving him good advice; but I see how men may go from the best libraries of earth down to hell at last. I might advise a man to be baptized in the name of the Trinity, and, brethren, this is a rite commanded of God; yet a man who has been baptized may go down to hell, unsaved at last.

[Source: *Sam Jones' Own Book: A Series of Sermons* (Cincinnati: Cranston & Stowe, 1886), pp. 131-33.]

I might advise a man to take the sacrament of the Lord's-supper. This is one of the sacraments of the Church of God, and I am sorry for any man who lies down to die with the consciousness, "These hands have never handled the cup of my Lord, and have never tasted of the bread which is emblematic of the broken body of the Son of God." Yet I see how a man may take communion regularly, may partake of the sacrament once a month, and die and be lost at last.

I might advise a man to keep good company, and I wish all men were good, so that there would be no bad company, for nothing can be more injurious than bad company, and nothing more helpful than good company; and yet I see how it is possible for a man to keep good company all his life and die unsaved. These things are all good. I would not, I say, underestimate a single one of these efficient means to take us to God; but there is only one sufficiency, and that is faith in the Lord Jesus Christ. And he who has this faith with works of love, and purifies his heart and overcomes the world shall be among that blood-washed number that shall shout and shine forever in heaven.

"What must I do to be saved?" The question is given, the question is answered, and I have often thought how good God is to us. He asks us questions and there on the pages of that book six thousand years old, some of them four thousand, some two thousand years, are the answers. But now here's a trembling, ruined man who cries out, "What must I do to be saved?" And the answer in the twinkling of an eye comes ringing down through his soul: "Believe on the Lord Jesus Christ and thou shalt be saved." Thank God for an answer as quick as heaven can give it to all who ask in sincerity and truth what they must do to be saved.

We might stop profitably to-night on the question itself, "What must I do to be saved?" Now, this term, "saved," "salvation," is not a song; it is not a sentiment; it is not a tear; it is not a shout; it is not feeling happy; but in its broadest, highest sense it means simply this — deliverance from sin; deliverance from all that God despises.

Billy Sunday (1862-1935)

Sunday, already introduced above (see pp. 183-85) in connection with prohibition, spent far more of his time on that same fundamental concern of the revivalist: salvation, and how to achieve it. The flamboyant, acrobatic Billy Sunday received much criticism from clergy and press, but he gave as good as he got. "If God could convert the preachers," he said, "the world would be

[Source: William T. Ellis, *"Billy" Sunday: The Man and the Message* (Philadelphia: L. T. Meyers, 1914), pp. 148-49. Quotations above are taken from pp. 200-201.]

*saved. Most of them are a lot of evolutionary hot-air merchants." Semi-
naries, in Sunday's opinion, were a kind of cold storage facility where young
ministers were kept "until they get cold enough to practice preaching." And
with real insight, he described himself as the "half-way house between the
brown-stone church and the Salvation Army."*

What does converted mean? It means completely changed. Converted is not
synonymous with reformed. Reforms are from without — conversion from
within. Conversion is a complete surrender to Jesus. It's a willingness to do
what he wants you to do. Unless you have made a complete surrender and are
doing his will it will avail you nothing if you've reformed a thousand times and
have your name on fifty church records.

Believe on the Lord Jesus Christ, in your heart and confess him with your
mouth and you will be saved. God is good. The plan of salvation is presented to
you in two parts. Believe in your heart and confess with your mouth. Many of
you here probably do believe. Why don't you confess? Now own up. The truth is
that you have a yellow streak. Own up, business men, and business women, and
all of you others. Isn't it so? Haven't you got a little saffron? Brave old Elijah ran
like a scared deer when he heard old Jezebel had said she would have his head,
and he beat it. And he ran to Beersheba and lay down under a juniper tree and
cried to the Lord to let him die. The Lord answered his prayer, but not in the
way he expected. If he had let him die he would have died with nothing but the
wind moaning through the trees as his funeral dirge. But the Lord had something better for Elijah. He had a chariot of fire and it swooped down and carried him into glory without his ever seeing death.

So he says he has something better for you — salvation if he can get you
to see it. You've kept your church membership locked up. You've smiled at a
smutty story. When God and the Church were scoffed at you never peeped, and
when asked to stand up here you've sneaked out the back way and beat it. You're
afraid and God despises a coward — a mutt. You cannot be converted by thinking so and sitting still.

Maybe you're a drunkard, an adulterer, a prostitute, a liar; won't admit
you are lost; are proud. Maybe you're even proud you're not proud, and Jesus
has a time of it.

Jesus said: "Come to me," not to the Church; to me, not to a creed; to me,
not to a preacher; to me, not to an evangelist; to me, not to a priest; to me, not
to a pope; "Come to me and I will give you rest." Faith in Jesus Christ saves you,
not faith in the Church.

You can join church, pay your share of the preacher's salary, attend the
services, teach Sunday school, return thanks and do everything that would apparently stamp you as a Christian — even pray — but you won't ever be a
Christian until you do what God tells you to do.

That's the road, and that's the only one mapped out for you and for me. God treats all alike. He doesn't furnish one plan for the banker and another for the janitor who sweeps out the bank. He has the same plan for one that he has for another. It's the law — you may not approve of it, but that doesn't make any difference.

Millennialism

Jehovah's Witnesses

The Pennsylvania sect founded by Charles Taze Russell in 1872 began as a Bible study group, that study having a special focus: the coming of Christ and his kingdom. Like other groups in America eagerly awaiting the "restitution of all things," the temptation to name a specific date grew irresistible. The time? For the early Witnesses, the year 1914 was "the farthest limit of the rule of imperfect men." At that time God would rule, and the "Kingdom of Jehovah's Anointed" would begin. Thus, the slogan was repeatedly proclaimed in the early years of the twentieth century: "Millions now living shall never die." From Witness literature, the "Bible evidence" for that proclamation is presented below.

In this chapter we present the Bible evidence proving that the full end of the times of the Gentiles, i.e., the full end of their lease of dominion, will be reached in A.D. 1914; and that that date will be the farthest limit of the rule of imperfect men. And be it observed, that if this is shown to be a fact firmly established by the Scriptures, it will prove: —

Firstly, That at that date the Kingdom of God, for which our Lord taught us to pray, saying, "Thy Kingdom come," will obtain full, universal control, and that it will then be "set up," or firmly established, in the earth, on the ruins of present institutions.

Secondly, It will prove that he whose right it is thus to take the dominion will then be present as earth's new Ruler; and not only so, but it will also prove that he will be present for a considerable period before that date; because the overthrow of these Gentile governments is directly caused by his dashing them to pieces as a potter's vessel (Psa. 2:9; Rev. 2:27), and establishing in their stead his own righteous government.

[Source: *Studies in Scripture*, series II, "The Time is at Hand" (Brooklyn: Watch Tower, Bible and Tract Society, 1910 [1889]), pp. 76-79.]

Thirdly, It will prove that some time before the end of A.D. 1914 the last member of the divinely recognized Church of Christ, the "royal priesthood," "the body of Christ," will be glorified with the Head; because every member is to reign with Christ, being a joint-heir with him of the Kingdom, and it cannot be fully "set up" without every member.

Fourthly, It will prove that from that time forward Jerusalem shall no longer be trodden down of the Gentiles, but shall arise from the dust of divine disfavor, to honor; because the "Times of the Gentiles" will be fulfilled or completed.

Fifthly, It will prove that by that date, or sooner, Israel's blindness will begin to be turned away; because their "blindness in part" was to continue only "*until* the fulness of the Gentiles be come in" (Rom. 11:25), or, in other words, until the full number from among the Gentiles, who are to be members of the body or bride of Christ, would be fully selected.

Sixthly, It will prove that the great "time of trouble such as never was since there was a nation," will reach its culmination in a world-wide reign of anarchy; and then men will learn to be still, and to know that Jehovah is God and that he will be exalted in the earth. (Psa. 46:10) . . .

Seventhly, It will prove that *before that date* God's Kingdom, organized in power, will be in the earth and then smite and crush the Gentile image (Dan. 2:34) — and fully consume the power of these kings. Its own power and dominion will be established as fast as by its varied influences and agencies it crushes and scatters the "powers that be" — civil and ecclesiastical — iron and clay. . . .

The beginning of these Gentile Times is clearly located by the Scriptures. Hence, if they furnish us the length *also* of the fixed period, or lease of Gentile dominion, we can know positively just when it will terminate. The Bible does furnish this fixed period, which must be fulfilled; but it was furnished in such a way that it could not be understood when written, nor until the lapse of time and the events of history had shed their light upon it; and even then, only by those who were watching and who were not over-charged by the cares of the world.

The Bible evidence is clear and strong that the "Time of the Gentiles" is a period of 2520 years, from the year B.C. 606 to and including A.D. 1914. This lease of universal dominion to Gentile governments, as we have already seen, began with Nebuchadnezzar — not when his reign began, but when the typical kingdom of the Lord passed away, and the dominion of the whole world was left in the hands of the Gentiles. The date for the beginning of the Gentile Times is, therefore, definitely marked as at the time of the removal of the crown of God's typical kingdom, from Zedekiah, their last king.

Foursquare Gospel

Aimee Semple McPherson (1890-1944) reached the height of her fame as minister-revivalist in Los Angeles (Angelus Temple) during the final twenty years of her turbulent life. Jesus' ministry, she taught, is a fourfold one: as savior, baptizer, healer, and returning king of kings. A gospel which is faithful to all of these roles is a foursquare gospel. With her own denomination (officially, the International Church of the Foursquare Gospel), her own building, and her own keen sense for the dramatic and newsworthy, McPherson was a religious phenomenon. In the excerpt below, it is that fourth aspect of Jesus' work — a returning king of kings who would rule over a New Jerusalem — that attention is being called to. Mrs. McPherson presents her millennialism not in terms of dates and times, but in a very personalized "vision and prophecy."

There came a great voice from Heaven as of a trumpet, crying: JESUS IS COMING SOON — GET READY TO MEET HIM.

My soul longed to see His face. My heart had been cleansed by His blood, and the Spirit had entered the tabernacle. I cried out:

"Yea, Lord," and ran to meet Him.

"Get ready! Get ready!" cried the great voice, again and again. "Get ready! Get ready!!" yet echoed over the hills and through the valleys. "*Get* ready!"

"O! Lord, Lord!" I cried, "Wherefore sayest thou unto me, 'Get ready?' Have I not left all for thee? Didst Thou not wash me in Thy blood? Wherein shall I get ready?"

He held an open Bible before my face and it shone as a mirror. Then showed He me myself, dark and tanned, and uncomely.

"O Lord," I wept, "have thy way. Get Thou me ready, I pray."

Then I lifted up my eyes and beheld a man, tall of stature, clothed in raiment of light, that shone as the sun. A sharp sword gleamed in His hand. I beheld His brightness, and saw His armour gleaming upon Him. He advanced and drew near me. He towered above me. His beauty was of such brightness my eyes could not gaze upon Him. Then I saw my own imperfections, my blemishes, my failures. I withered under His gaze, and was ashamed in His presence. I wept for my foolish blindness, that had boasted of readiness.

Who can dwell in His brightness without showing a blemish?

"O, Lord," I cried, "I am a failure. I am all blackness. I am undone." Then He spake: "Wilt thou let me have My way? Wilt thou let Me make thee ready, no matter what the cost?"

[Source: Aimee Semple McPherson, *This Is That: Personal Experiences, Sermons, and Writings* (Los Angeles: Bridal Call Publishing House, 1919), pp. 653-54, 655.]

"O Lord," I cried, "I am utterly unworthy, but have your way." . . .

Then I looked and behold! a New creation, as of a beautiful woman. I beheld her coming from the West, and walking towards the East. She approached. I beheld her white raiment, dazzling as the snow in the sunshine. Her movements were gracious and tender. Her voice was mellow and full of sweet fragrance. I smelled the fragrance of her garments, as sweet lilies grown in the valleys, and as the rose of Sharon. Her eyes beheld no guile, but they were tender as

Aimee Semple McPherson (1890-1944) built a powerful
revivalist ministry headquartered in Los Angeles and attained
national fame during the last two decades of her turbulent life.
(The International Church of the Foursquare Gospel)

a dove's eyes. Her lips were pure, and dropped as the honey-comb. No foolish-ness, no criticism marred their sweetness. No fleshly words, her ears were kept for His alone, her Lover, her Bridegroom, her King.

As she drew nigh, I gazed with amazement into her face, and saw that it was myself. I heard the voice of the Master speaking unto me, saying: "This is My beloved. How far you have fallen short of the standard of my perfections!"

Dispensationalism

In America that view of the world's history and destiny known as "dispensa-tionalism" was most effectively promoted by Cyrus I. Scofield (1843-1921). Converted to Christianity when he was in his late thirties, Scofield turned from a career in law to one in biblical study and instruction. He lectured widely, trained teachers, offered popular correspondence courses in Bible study, and more. Most of all, he prepared what became known as the Scofield Reference Bible, *a work of enormous and enduring impact. First appearing in 1909, this Bible enjoyed a second edition in 1917, and in 1967 Oxford University Press published the* New Scofield Reference Bible. *Notes and outlines in all these Bibles highlight that particular view of the past, present, and future which divides all time into seven periods or "dispensa-tions." The mysteries of biblical prophecy are unlocked, and the exact nature of the events during the "last times" is unfolded. Here, in compact form from one of his popular lecture series, are Scofield's views on "The Seven Dispen-sations."*

The Scriptures divide time, by which is meant the entire period from the cre-ation of Adam to the "new heaven and a new earth" of Rev. 21:1, into seven un-equal periods, called, usually, "dispensations" (Eph. 3:2), although these periods are also called "ages" (Eph. 2:7) and "days" — as, "day of the Lord," etc.

These periods are marked off in Scripture by some change in God's method of dealing with mankind, or a portion of mankind, in respect of the two questions of sin and of man's responsibility. Each of the Dispensations may be regarded as a new test of the natural man, and each ends in judgment — marking his utter failure.

Five of these Dispensations, or periods of time, have been fulfilled; we are living in the sixth, probably toward its close, and have before us the seventh, and last — the millennium.

[Source: C. I. Scofield, *Rightly Dividing the Word of Truth (2 Timothy 2:15),* 2nd ed. (Philadel-phia: Philadelphia School of the Bible, 1923), pp. 20-25.]

1. MAN INNOCENT. — This dispensation extends from the creation of Adam, Gen. 2:7, to the Expulsion. Adam, created innocent, and ignorant of good and evil, was placed in the garden of Eden with his wife, Eve, and put under responsibility to abstain from the fruit of the tree of the knowledge of good and evil. The Dispensation of Innocence resulted in the first and, in its far-reaching effects, the most disastrous of the failures of the natural man, and was closed by judgment — "So He drove out the man." See Gen. 1:26; Gen. 2:16, 17; Gen. 3:6; Gen. 3:22-24.

2. MAN UNDER CONSCIENCE. — By the Fall Adam and Eve acquired, and transmitted to the race, the knowledge of good and evil. This gave conscience a basis for right moral judgment, and hence the race came under this measure of responsibility — to do good and eschew evil. The result of the Dispensation of Conscience was that "all flesh had corrupted his way on the earth;" that "the wickedness of man was great in the earth, and that every imagination of the thoughts of his heart was only evil continually;" and God closed the second testing of the natural man with Judgment — the Flood. See Gen. 3:7, 22; Gen. 6:5, 11, 12; Gen. 7:11, 12, 23.

3. MAN IN AUTHORITY OVER THE EARTH. — Out of the fearful judgment of the Flood God saved eight persons to whom, after the waters were assuaged, He gave the purified earth with ample power to govern it. This, Noah and his descendants were responsible to do. The Dispensation of Human Government resulted, upon the plain of Shinar, in the impious attempt to become independent of God and closed in judgment — the Confusion of Tongues. See Gen. 9:1, 2; Gen. 11:1-4; Gen. 11:5-8.

4. MAN UNDER PROMISE. — Out of the dispersed descendants of the builders of Babel God now calls one man, Abram, with whom He enters into covenant. Some of the promises to Abram and his descendants were purely gracious and unconditional. These either have been, or will yet be, literally fulfilled. Other promises were conditional upon the faithfulness and obedience of the Israelites. Every one of these conditions was violated, and the Dispensation of Promise resulted in the utter failure of Israel, and closed in the judgment of the Egyptian Bondage.

The book of Genesis, which opens with the sublime words, "In the beginning God created," closes with, "in a coffin in Egypt." [See] Gen. 12:1-3; Gen. 13:14-17; Gen. 15:5; 26:3; 28:12, 13; Ex. 1:13, 14.

5. MAN UNDER LAW. — Again the grace of God came to the help of helpless man and redeemed the chosen people out of the hand of the oppressor. In the Wilderness of Sinai He proposed to them the Covenant of Law. Instead of humbly

pleading for a continued relation of grace, they presumptuously answered: "All that the Lord hath spoken we will do." The history of Israel in the Wilderness and in the Land is one long record of flagrant, persistent violation of the Law, and at last, after multiplied warnings, God closed the testing of man by law in judgment, and first Israel, and then Judah, were driven out of the Land into a dispersion which still continues. A feeble remnant returned under Ezra and Nehemiah, of which, in due time, Christ came: "Born of a woman — made under the law." Him both Jews and Gentiles conspired to crucify. See Exodus 19:1-8; 2 Kings 17:1-18; Romans 10:5; 2 Kings 25:1-11; Gal. 3:10; Acts 2:22, 23; Romans 3:19, 20; Acts 7:51, 52.

6. MAN UNDER GRACE. — The sacrificial death of the Lord Jesus Christ introduced the dispensation of pure grace — which means undeserved favor, or God GIVING righteousness, instead of God REQUIRING righteousness, as under Law.

Salvation, perfect and eternal, is now freely offered to Jew and Gentile upon the one condition of faith.

Jesus answered and said unto them, This is the work of God, that ye BELIEVE on him whom he hath sent. John 6:29.

Verily, verily, I say unto you, He that BELIEVETH on me HATH everlasting life. John 6:47.

Verily, verily, I say unto you, He that heareth my word, and BELIEVETH him that sent me, HATH eternal life, *and cometh not into judgment,* but hath passed out of death into life. John 5:24. R. V. [Revised Version]

My sheep hear my voice, and I know them, and they follow me: and I give unto them eternal life; and *they shall never perish.* John 10:27, 28.

For by grace have ye been saved through faith; and that not of yourselves: *it is* the gift of God: not of works, that no man should glory. Eph. 2:8, 9. R. V.

The predicted result of this testing of man under grace is, judgment upon an unbelieving world and an apostate Church. [See] Rev. 3:15, 16; Luke 17:26-30; Luke 18:8; 2 Thess. 2:7-12.

The first event in the closing of this dispensation will be the descent of the Lord from Heaven, when sleeping saints will be raised and, together with believers then living, caught up "to meet the Lord in the air: and so shall we ever be with the Lord." 1 Thess. 4:16, 17.

Then follows the brief period called "the great tribulation." [See] Matt. 24:21, 22; Dan. 12:1; Zeph. 1:15-18; Jer. 30:5-7.

After this occurs the personal return of the Lord to the earth in power and great glory, and the judgments which introduce the seventh, and last dispensation. [See] Matt. 24:29, 30; Matt. 25:31-46.

7. MAN UNDER THE PERSONAL REIGN OF CHRIST. — After the purifying judgments which attended the personal return of Christ to the Earth, He will reign

over restored Israel and over the earth for one thousand years. This is the period commonly called the Millennium. The seat of His power will be Jerusalem, and the saints, including the saved of the Dispensation of Grace, viz., the Church, will be associated with Him in His glory. See Acts 15:14-17; Rev. 19:11-21; Isa. 2:1-4; Rev. 20:1-6; Isa. 11: entire.

But when Satan is "loosed a little season" he finds the natural heart as prone to evil as ever, and easily gathers the nations to battle against the Lord and His saints, and this last dispensation closes, like all the others, in judgment. The "great white throne" is set, the wicked dead are raised and finally judged, and then come the "new heaven and a new earth" — eternity begun. [See] Rev. 20:3, 7-15; Rev. 21 and 22.

Holiness and Pentecostalism

Doctrine

The father of Methodism, John Wesley (1703-91), stimulated profound interest in "Christian perfection" among his followers both in Britain and in America. Some so stimulated went on to create new denominations and associations, greatly adding to this nation's religious variety. The "holiness" movement stressed the process that goes on after salvation. As noted above, the revivalist theme was often salvation and nothing more; for the believer in Christian perfection, however, there was more, much more. Beyond justification lay sanctification, and beyond the new birth lay a life-long process of maturing, of growing in God's grace. But when did one become holy — and how? The notion of perfection was easy to ridicule, difficult to define how it might apply to obviously imperfect human beings. In 1898, Methodist De Witt Clinton Huntington (1830-1912), native of Vermont, pastor and presiding elder and professor, undertook to state clearly what sin was and was not, what holiness was and was not. What follows cannot be described as the holiness position, for there were several, but only as one sustained effort to be both helpful and precise.

We shall now attempt to show that Christian holiness, on the human side, belongs to the voluntary states of the mind, that it consists in an abiding state of

---

[Source: D. W. C. Huntington, *Sin and Holiness, Or What It Is to Be Holy* (Cincinnati: Curts & Jennings, 1898), pp. 152-54, 156-58.]

the will. In submitting a definition, we will say that Christian holiness is *a state of unreserved consecration of the being to God, secured through the constant revelation of Christ to the soul of the believer by the Holy Spirit.* It is distinguished from an *act of consecration* by the feature of *continuousness.* It includes *living* consecration, uninterrupted faith in Christ as a present and sufficient Savior from sin, and a continuous presence and incoming of the Holy Spirit in the soul of the Christian. It is abiding in Christ. It is such a Divinely-strengthened state of the soul, that the will stands in a "supreme preference for God." It is that state in which the will constantly chooses the will of God as the law of its entire activity. In a word, it is voluntary and continuous obedience to all the known will of God, a state in which the believer *does not commit sin.*

On the Divine side it is not so much what the Holy Spirit does in the believer at any given moment, as what he does and what he is at each and every moment. It is his pervading presence, revealing Christ to the soul as all-sufficient for its utmost exigency, and thus strengthening us to abide in unbroken acceptance of the will of God. It is Christ conquering *in* us as he conquered *for* us. It is that state in which, by the power of God through faith, the Christian believer is *kept from committing sin.* In support of this view of Christian holiness we offer the following remarks:

Holiness is the exact opposite of sin. We have endeavored to show that sin is all and always voluntary transgression of law. If this be so, it follows that holiness is voluntary and entire obedience to the known will of God. If, on the other hand, there are two kinds of sin, there must be two kinds of holiness. But if sin is disobedience to the known will of God, then holiness is entire obedience to the apprehended will of God. "All sin has its seat in the will. The appetites and passions and intellectual aspirations are not sins. They belong to the original furnishings of the soul. Sin is volitional indulgence in contravention of law." Holiness, then, is salvation from indulgence in contravention of law, and, by consequence, obedience to known law. . . .

This view of Christian holiness recognizes and necessarily implies the very distinctions in Christian experience and character which are taught in the Bible. The fact has already been noticed that the twofold classification of believers into somewhat distinct bodies, distinguished by the specific fact of the existence or non-existence in them of "inbred sin," does not appear in the Scriptures. But the Bible does recognize the fact that some Christian believers are weak and wavering, that they have need to be "confirmed," to be "established, strengthened, settled." They are exhorted to "grow up into him [Christ] in all things," to "go on unto perfection," to be "made perfect," to be "holy." They are encouraged to expect a realization of a state of entire sanctification, in which they may be preserved blameless; that is, in which they will commit no known sin. The converts of the New Testament stand before us essentially like those of our own day, ardent and sincere, but not in a state of constant, unbroken obedi-

Storefront Holiness church on Virginia's eastern shore (Exmore)
(Photo by Edwin S. Gaustad)

ence to God. They committed more or less sin. The differences in Christian experience recognized in such passages are the differences between a weak and wavering state, in which sin is sometimes committed, and a state in which the high Christian privilege is realized of being saved and kept from all sin.

It is true that believers are exhorted to "holiness," to "sanctification," and are encouraged to expect that they shall be "sanctified wholly;" but this in no way proves that the holiness and sanctification here enjoined and promised consist in the destruction or removal of an "inbeing of sin." There is nothing in the passages alluded to in reference to a "second blessing" of "inbred sin" destruction in distinction from a previous or partial one of "inbred sin" subjugation. It would seem impossible so to construe their meaning by any whose minds were not preoccupied by the thought.

Experience

Pentecostalism, taking its name from that first Pentecost described in the Book of Acts (2:1-5), arose in close association with the holiness movement. Once more, dozens of new denominations emerged on the American scene. One may think of Pentecostalism as the more radical sting of the holiness movement: more extravagant and uninhibited services of worship, more adventurism in theology (for example, the "Jesus only" faction, a kind of right-wing unitarianism), far more emphasis upon healing. Indeed, so radical did Pentecostalism seem in the eyes of some holiness churches that the latter took steps to separate themselves or at least distinguish themselves from the former. Pentecostals found the validity of their theology in their experience, especially the experiences of healing and of speaking in tongues. For some, glossolalia or speaking in tongues was not merely a sign of God's "second blessing" — it was the sign. The largest black Pentecostal group, the Church of God in Christ (founded in 1895 by C. H. Mason [1866-1961]), includes in its official history this explanation of and justification for speaking in tongues.

And these signs shall follow those that believe: In my name shall they cast out devils; they shall speak with new tongues. Our Lord Jesus did not say that some of those that believe should speak with new tongues, but those that believe shall speak with new tongues. This promise is to those that believe; it is not to the unbeliever. When did this great work begin? On the day of Pentecost (Acts 2:1-5). And when the day of Pentecost was fully come, they were all with one accord in one place. Suddenly there came a sound from heaven, as of rushing, mighty wind, and it filled all the house where they were sitting and there appeared unto them cloven tongues like as of fire, and it sat upon each of them; and they were all filled with the Holy Ghost and began to speak with new tongues as the spirit gave them utterance.

This promise is to all that believe. Acts 2:38-39. They spake with tongues at Caesarea, when the Holy Ghost fell upon them which heard the word. Acts 10:44-45.

Believers that went with Peter knew that these Gentiles had received the Holy Ghost when they heard them speak with tongues and magnify God. Acts 10:45-46. The Church at Ephesus spake with tongues when they received the Holy Ghost. Acts 19:6. When we are baptized with the Holy Ghost the glory of the son will be revealed to us as never before. He will glorify Christ. He will show us the things of Christ. John 16:14.

[Source: *History and Formative Years of the Church of God in Christ* (Memphis: Church of God in Christ Publishing House, 1969), pp. 37-39.]

Did God intend the speaking in tongues to be in the Church? And God hath set some in the Church, First Apostles; secondly, prophets; thirdly, teachers. After that, miracles; then gifts of healing — and helps, governments, diversities of tongues. 1 Cor. 12:28. For he that speaketh in an unknown tongue, speaketh not to men, but unto God, for no man understandeth him; howbeit in the spirit he speaketh mysteries. 1 Cor. 14:2. No man understands him, but the spirit is speaking the mysteries of God, through us. Is it wrong for one to pray in tongues? No, for if I prayed in an unknown tongue, my spirit prayeth but my understanding is unfruitful. 1 Cor. 14:14. Should we let the spirit pray in us if we do not know what he is saying? Yes, what is it then, I will pray with the spirit and with the understanding also. 1 Cor. 14:15. We do not understand what to pray for as we ought to. Rom. 8:26. Likewise the spirit also helpeth our infirmities, for we know not what we should pray for as we ought; but the spirit itself maketh intercession for us with groanings which can't be uttered. How many ways can the spirit speaking in tongues in us edify the Church? We see four ways. 1 Cor. 14:6. First way, by revelations; second, by knowledge; third, by

Speaking in tongues
(St. Columba Roman Catholic Church in Hopewell, New Jersey, 1973)
(Religion News Service)

prophesying; fourth, by doctrinal teaching. What more can we say, wherefore tongues are a sign not to them that believe, but to them that believe not; but prophesying serveth not for them that believe not, but for them which believe. 1 Cor. 14:22. Should we forbid to speak with tongues? No. Wherefore, brethren, covet to prophesy and forbid not to speak with tongues. 1 Cor. 14:39.

Are we helped in any way to speak in tongues? Yes. He that speaketh in an unknown tongue edifieth himself. 1 Cor. 14:4. Would the Holy Ghost have all to speak with tongues? Yes. I would that ye all speak with tongues, but rather that ye prophesy; for greater is he which prophesieth than he that speaketh with tongues except he interpret, that the church may receive edifying, and when he that speaketh with tongues cannot interpret. But if he can interpret he is great or greater, for he may speak in the mysteries of God (1 Cor. 14:2), and he can speak unto men to edification and exhortation and comfort (verse 3). You can see in verse 6 that we may prophesy in tongues and he may speak a revelation with tongues and he may speak the word of knowledge with tongues, teach doctrines with tongues. May the Lord open the eyes of all His people to this great mystery. Paul was one of the greatest of the apostles, and he spoke with tongues more than all. 1 Cor. 14:18. Oh, how the Holy Ghost doth reveal Christ to us when we are baptized with Him, and we do speak with tongues as He gives utterance; He will make us know that we are in Christ and Christ in us; and in the Father and the Father in Christ. John 14:20.

What a sweet unity. Christ is all. What a sweet rest. Christ is all. God speaks Himself in tongues in us. Isa. 28:11; for with stammering lips and other tongue will He speak to His people, to rest. This is the refreshing, yet they would not hear. Rest and refreshing from the Lord when He, the Holy Ghost, is speaking in us with tongues; still the people will not hear. Speaking in tongues is the wonderful work of God. All that did not have this work in them on that day were amazed and in doubt about the wonderful work of God, and so it is today with all that have not this blessed work going on in them — they cannot understand it; they will say everything about it. Sinners, converted ones and sanctified ones and all wonder and will wonder when they hear or see this movement of the Holy Ghost going on in the saints of God. If the Holy Ghost does not speak in them, they can't understand His speaking the wonderful works of God in other tongues. Oh, dear ones, the word of every promise of God must enter into us before we can understand the wonderful works of the promise in others. The word giveth light and understanding that all may be baptized with this one baptism of the Holy Ghost. He will show us then Christ is coming soon again to the earth. Prepare to meet your God in His glory.

ELDER C. H. MASON.

Cure of Souls

As noted above, the Pentecostal service featured not only speaking in tongues but often even more dramatically the cure of physical and spiritual ills. Healing in these instances comes not through the steady application of a religious science, nor through the careful interaction of psychiatry and theology, but through the sudden and powerful manifestation of the presence of the Holy Spirit in the moment of cure. The most nationally visible healer of the twentieth century, Oral Roberts, was born in Pontococ County, Oklahoma, in 1918. Originally a member of the Pentecostal Holiness Church, Roberts in 1968 moved into that Methodism out of which so many of the newer churches had come. But his nationally televised healing services continued, even as his nationally prominent university in Tulsa continued to evolve from a "University of Evangelism" into a general liberal arts institution. In the selection below, Roberts describes himself both as healer and as one healed.

Jesus is not here today with the seamless robe, nor Paul with his blessed cloths, nor Peter with his shadow that brought healing, nor the elders of the church with their anointing oil, but God has not left Himself without human instrumentalities to deliver this generation. I have heard His voice: first that I was to be healed, next, that I was to bring healing to the sick and demon-possessed, and that His healing power would be felt in my right hand for all who would believe. It is happening just as the Lord said. I seldom feel anything in my left hand, but through my right hand I feel the healing virtue of the Son of God. Thousands have witnessed this power as it surged through every fiber of their being. God uses this human agency as a point of contact. The time is set when I lay my right hand upon the captive and adjure the afflictions to come out of him in the name of the Master, Jesus Christ of Nazareth. I feel the pressure of the disease rising to meet my right hand, but then as God's healing virtue surges into the person, this pressure is relieved and deliverance is wrought: The deaf ears are opened, the cancers wither and die and pass from the body, demons come out and humanity is set free through faith in God. This gift in my humble life is for the deliverance of my generation and not for my personal gratification. Any gift from God is to be used only for the deliverance of others.

But a gift of healing is not the only means of healing or point of contact for your faith. There is the anointing oil which God's minister anoints you with in Jesus' Name for the purpose of praying the prayer of faith for your healing,

---

[Source: Oral Roberts, *If You Need HEALING Do These Things*, rev. ed. (Tulsa: Healing Waters, Inc., 1954), pp. 35-38.]

using the anointing oil as a point of contact. The moment it is applied turn your faith loose. This was my point of contact when I was healed in 1935 in a big healing revival in Ada, Oklahoma where Rev. George W. Muncie prayed the prayer of faith for my deliverance. As I was being brought to the meeting on a mattress in the back seat of a car, after being bed-fast five months with tuberculosis in both lungs, I was led to use the anointing oil and laying on of hands as a point of contact. Down deep in my heart I was believing in God for deliverance and I told the Lord that when Brother Muncie anointed me and laid his hands on my head that then, and then alone, would I believe the work was done. The healing line was long. Midnight came and I was still waiting. I was suffering but I did not become discouraged nor angry with having to be the last one prayed for. Trembling with anticipation, I was waiting for him to anoint and touch me with his hands, through which God was performing miracles. At last my time had come.

They helped me to my feet. I watched every move they made; above all, I was watching for his hands to be laid on my head. Then the anointing oil touched my forehead. His hands were upon me and at that instant I turned my faith loose; the deepest desires and emotions of my hungry spirit pushed outward toward God. I believed God! I found myself thanking Him for deliverance. Every ache and pain disappeared. The glory rushed into my soul. I was tingling from head to toe with new life. And, then, for several minutes I was lost in the sheer ecstacy of divine deliverance. I opened my eyes to the surroundings a little later, astonished to realize that I was leaping and shouting and running on the long platform. I was healed! Faith had wrought it!

Oh, suffering friend, turn your faith loose. Hang it on some Bible means of deliverance and let go of it. Hold nothing back. Pour all your pent-up faith-emotions into the act of believing God for your deliverance.

Suggested Reading (Chapter Nine)

One avenue which opens into that often dimly lit world of private religion, the inspirational "best seller," can be readily followed through the many reprintings of these works. Scholarly studies are harder to come by, though one solid effort is Allene S. Phy, ed., *The Bible and Popular Culture in America* (1983), especially the editor's own chapter, "Retelling the Greatest Story Ever Told: Jesus in Popular Fiction." In addition to the lives of Jesus excerpted in this chapter itself, other immensely popular works were the businessman's biography by Bruce Barton, *The Man Nobody Knows* (1925), and the journalist's you-were-there biographies, Jim Bishop, *The Day Christ Died* (1957) and *The Day Christ Was Born*

(1960). The literature of private devotion and Bible reading is largely "in house," with most of the guides, manuals, and "aids to devotion" coming from denominational presses. An exceptionally useful study that includes treatment of such literature in one denomination is *The Confessional Mosaic: Presbyterians and Twentieth-Century Theology* (1990), one part of a major seven-volume series edited by Milton J. Coalter, John M. Mulder, and Louis B. Weeks. Academic works that take such literature and other popular expressions seriously include Ann Taves, *The Household of Faith: Roman Catholic Devotions in Mid-Nineteenth-Century America* (1986), Colleen McDannell, *The Christian Home in Victorian America, 1840-1900* (1986), and David Morgan, *Visual Piety: A History and Theory of Popular Religious Images* (1998).

On mysticism and prayer, the literature is large but not necessarily attuned to historical questions. Abraham Heschel, himself a Jewish mystic, provided an excellent discussion, "The Mystical Element in Judaism," in Louis Finkelstein, ed., *The Jews: Their Religion and Culture* (1971). The sometimes forbidding subject of mysticism is made less so in Evelyn Underhill's charming essay, *Practical Mysticism: A Little Book for Normal People* (1914). Hal Bridges in his *American Mysticism from William James to Zen* (1970) includes Heschel along with Rufus Jones and Thomas Merton in this important monograph. For a full volume of Jones's insights, see Kerry S. Walters, ed., *Rufus Jones: Essential Writings* (2001). Merton's own *Contemplative Prayer* (1969) should be read alongside Lawrence Cunningham, *Thomas Merton and the Monastic Vision* (1999). Louis Jacobs' *Hasidic Prayer* (1973) reveals much that is similar, but also dissimilar, from other main religious traditions in America. The centrality of worship, and therefore of the day of the week specifically set aside for worship, is the subject of Horton Davies, *Christian Worship and Meaning* (1957), and Louis Finkelstein (in the volume cited above), "The Jewish Religion: Its Beliefs and Practices." Sabbath keeping is only one of the subjects explored insightfully in Dorothy C. Bass, *Practicing Our Faith* (1997). Not enough has been done to study the modern sermon, but the Library of America's anthology, *American Sermons* (1999), offers useful context. From Marsha G. Witten, *All Is Forgiven: The Secular Meaning of American Protestantism* (1993), comes probably the most searching study of sermonizing in modern America.

To wend one's way through the intricate labyrinth of New Thought, one is grateful for expert guides, like Catherine L. Albanese, *Nature Religion in America: From the Algonkian Indians to the New Age* (1991), Albanese, *Reconsidering Nature Religion* (2002), Amanda Porterfield, *The Transformation of American Religion* (2001), and Stephen J. Stein, *Alternative American Religions* (1999). While Robert S. Ellwood's *Alternative Altars: Unconventional and Eastern Spirituality in America* (1979) is not limited to New Thought, it does place the movement very skillfully in the context of other "unconventional" religion in America.

For, respectively, narrower and broader aspects of Mary Baker Eddy's work in founding Christian Science, see Ronald L. Numbers, *Prophetess of Health: Ellen G. White and the Origins of Seventh-day Adventist Health Reform* (new ed., 1992), and Rennie B. Schoepflin, *Christian Science on Trial: Religious Healing in America* (2003). On Unity's founder, see Hugh D'Andrade, *Charles Fillmore, Herald of the New Age* (1974). A valuable scholarly treatment of the tradition out of which Russell Conwell and Norman Vincent Peale speak is Donald B. Meyer, *The Positive Thinkers: A Study of the American Quest for Health, Wealth, and Personal Power from Mary Baker Eddy to Norman Vincent Peale* (1965). The literature on psychology and religion has become voluminous beyond measure, but some purchase on it can be gained by perusing periodicals like the *Journal of Religion and Health, Journal of Psychology and Christianity,* or *Journal of Psychology and Theology.*

The fear of new immigrants and resulting organized resistance are effectively presented in an older work that has worn well, John Higham, *Strangers in the Land: Patterns of American Nativism, 1860-1925* (1955). For more specific studies, see Les Wallace, *The Rhetoric of Anti-Catholicism: The American Protective Association, 1887-1911* (1990), and Nancy MacLean, *Behind the Mask of Chivalry: The Making of the Second Ku Klux Klan* (1994). E. A. Moore, *A Catholic Runs for President* (1956), captures well Alfred Smith's campaign of 1928. The economic ills of the 1930s, together with the passionate remedies offered by some, can be followed in Alan Brinkley's *Voices of Protest: Huey Long, Father Coughlin, and the Great Depression* (1982), and the extremist opinions they promoted are covered in Leo P. Ribuffo, *The Old Christian Right* (1983). For Dorothy Day, there have been a series of outstanding works, including Mel Piehl, *Breaking Bread: The Catholic Worker and the Origin of Catholic Radicalism in America* (1982), William D. Miller, *Dorothy Day: A Biography* (1982), Robert Coles, *Dorothy Day: A Radical Devotion* (1987), and Paul Elle, *The Life You Save May Be Your Own: An American Pilgrimage* (2003).

The broader religious and theological context in which Reinhold Niebuhr made his social criticism has been nicely outlined by Heather A. Warren, *Theologian of a New World Order: Reinhold Niebuhr and the Christian Realists, 1920-1948* (1997). Richard Fox's *Reinhold Niebuhr* (1985) is an excellent biography, Robert McAfee Brown has edited a useful set of documents in *The Essential Reinhold Niebuhr* (1986), and there are helpful interpretations in Robin W. Lovin, *Reinhold Niebuhr and Christian Realism* (1995) and Langdon Gilkey, *On Niebuhr* (2001).

A full account of twentieth-century revivalism, giving full attention to all three revivalists excerpted in this chapter (Moody, Jones, and Sunday) is William G. McLoughlin, *Modern Revivalism: Charles Grandison Finney to Billy Graham* (1959). D. L. Moody has been the beneficiary of noteworthy biographical studies from several angles, including James F. Findlay, Jr., *Dwight L. Moody:*

American Evangelist, 1837-1890 (1969), Lyle W. Dorsett, *A Passion for Souls: The Life of D. L. Moody* (1997), and Bruce J. Evensen, *God's Man for the Gilded Age* (2003). For Billy Sunday, see the books suggested at the end of chapter eight.

The Jehovah's Witnesses are one of the groups helpfully illuminated by Paul Conkin, *American Originals: Homemade Varieties of Christianity* (1997). Aimee Semple McPherson, founder of the International Church of the Foursquare Gospel, has been blessed with two outstanding recent studies, Daniel Mark Epstein, *Sister Aimee* (1993), and Edith Blumhofer, *Aimee Semple McPherson: Everybody's Sister* (1993). Timothy P. Weber is a sure guide to modern dispensationalism in *Living in the Shadow of the Second Coming: American Premillennialism, 1875-1982* (3rd ed., 1987).

The Holiness and Pentecostal Movements are now receiving the attention they so long deserved. Surveys that range widely include books by the dean of Pentecostal historians, Vinson Synan, *The Century of the Holy Spirit* (2001), and by a talented team of experts, Edith L. Blumhofer, et al., eds., *Pentecostal Currents in American Protestantism* (1999). Grant Wacker breaks new ground with fresh interpretive perspective in *Heaven Below: Early Pentecostalism and American Culture* (2001). The books of David Edwin Harrell, Jr. were pioneering efforts that remain essential, including *All Things Are Possible: The Healing and Charismatic Revivals in Modern America* (1975), and *Oral Roberts: An American Life* (1985). For reference, the indispensable volume is now Stanley M. Burgess and Ed Van der Maas, eds., *The New International Dictionary of Pentecostal and Charismatic Movements* (2002). Finally, the connections between religion, health, and pastoral care have been well treated by E. Brooks Holifield, *A History of Pastoral Care in America: From Salvation to Self-Realization* (1983), and then more generally in Martin E. Marty and Kenneth L. Vaux, eds., *Health/ Medicine in the Faith Traditions* (1982).

TEN

Religion and the Life of the Mind

or new categories.

In the realm of ideas, the Western World bubbled and boiled over in the late nineteenth and early twentieth centuries. Whole new disciplines were born: anthropology, sociology, psychology, and more. History turned scientific, and biology interpreted history. Literary critics crossed the line separating the secular from the sacred, while philosophy — so long religion's partner and ally — began to chart its separate course. Modernity had arrived, and the bumptious new guest faced a mixed welcome.

Philosophy and Religion

The Enlightenment had struck a hard blow against abstract speculation, metaphysical musing, and pompous system-building. In early-nineteenth-century America, Scottish Realism or Common Sense (both names sounding reassuringly unmetaphysical) continued to exercise its influence through eastern colleges and prevailing textbooks. A few Hegelian idealists in St. Louis argued that at least one great system remained as an option. But these philosophical possibilities were clearly derivative, imported from afar, not a product of the native soil.

Not until the pragmatic school arose did America begin to make its own contribution to the field, even though pragmatism, as one critic observed, was not so much a philosophy as it was a method of doing without one. But it was a method, and a method of considerable import for religion. Abstract theological system-building tended to give way to creeds clearly based upon experience, upon observable consequences — here and now — of religious belief. Metaphysics yielded to ethics, as the question "Does God exist?" was replaced by the query, "What do you believe about God?"

Yet pragmatism did not drive away all idealism. Josiah Royce, for example, represented that "genteel tradition" effectively as he pursued his life-long interest in religion. The "process philosophy" of Alfred North Whitehead had religious implications as Whitehead himself noted, but in the generation following his death in 1947 a whole school of process theologians emerged. George Santayana, though he created no school, sharply rebuked those acculturated liberals, those mystical modernists, who consciously or otherwise abandoned the historic faith. "The modernist wishes to reconcile the church and the world," Santayana noted. "Therein he forgets what Christianity came into the world to announce and why its message was believed."

Science and Religion

From the Middle Ages well into the nineteenth century, most scientists sustained some connection to churches, and theology remained in theory the queen of the sciences. By the middle of the nineteenth century, that state of affairs was passing away. Polemic spokespeople, claiming to speak for scientists in general or theologians in general, increasingly pictured their different enterprises as offering competing avenues to the truth. Dialogue, listening, and a good bit of cooperation continued, but deliberate caricature, sharp ridicule, and some false hope that "the enemy" would soon fade away came more and more to dominate public perception.

While strident polemicists talked boldly about "warfare" between science and religion, quite a few scientists with religious convictions and theologians with scientific interests went on as they had for centuries past with their poorly coordinated, often confusing, but mutually beneficial dialogue. In light of the great practical successes of modern industry and the burgeoning of new discoveries from scientists in the expanding universities, traditional theology was by the nature of the case giving up much of its former assurance. But when polemicists on behalf of science went so far as to assert their own omniscience, critics were quick to respond.

In the nineteenth century and beyond, academic questions concerning religion and science rarely remained isolated from broader public issues. This reality was conspicuously true in the case of evolution, the doctrine that has received the most public attention. Evolution was not some abstract and far-away theory about the cosmic pull of gravity or the strange orbits of planetary motion: it was about life — everyone's life. Evolution said things, or at least could be made to imply things, about design and purpose, value and meaning, ancestry and destiny. It could not be ignored, and it was not ignored. For a brief period in the summer of 1925, the "greatest show on earth" was not a circus tent run by Barnum & Bailey but a county courthouse in Dayton, Tennessee, where the subject was — evolution. At the trial held there, it was no surprise that those who wanted to see evolution taught in the Tennessee public schools evoked the general "pursuit of knowledge in the world," while William Jennings Bryan, who opposed the teaching of evolution, was mostly concerned about the ways in which unfettered science had been used to create the horrors of World War I.

Studying and Reading the Bible

The metaphor of battle is least metaphorical in the many clashes concerning the Bible. In those instances, metaphor became reality as the bitterest passions were aroused, institutions torn apart, and careers ruined. Words like "inspiration," "infallibility," "plenary," and "inerrancy" competed against other words like "heresy," "atheism," "modernism," and "betrayal." Modern biblical scholarship or, to use a common and more commonly offensive term, "higher criticism" was in one sense only a special category of the science-versus-religion confrontation, but at the same time it was a category all unto itself. For now the "scientific" study of the Bible — empirical, verifiable, wholly without presuppositions or devotional predispositions — threatened to weaken and undermine, perhaps even to destroy, that foundation on which most of Western religion rested.

This challenge hit Protestantism hardest. For out of the Reformation had come a Protestant rejection of tradition in favor of an elevation of scripture. It was then commonly assumed, first, that the two could be completely separated, and, second, that scripture constituted a source, an authority of unshakable integrity. In the nineteenth century, both assumptions came under repeated attack. It was tradition that, by the fourth century of the Christian era, had determined the bounds of scripture. And it was scripture that within its own canon mirrored that development called tradition. Nothing in this world sprang forth full blown, fixed, unchanged and unchanging; all evolved, all developed. Even inspiration, even dogma, had a history. While Protestantism suffered most in seeking or resisting accommodation to this bitterly barbed edge of modernity, neither Catholicism nor Judaism escaped the persisting, nagging force of a "criticism" directed against that which had heretofore been immune to all criticism.

The results of this sharply focused fight are incalculable, for the battle goes on. But quite early one witnessed bruising confrontation and sweeping condemnation. One also witnessed, however, a rebirth of biblical investigation, translation, and interpretation. New societies were born, new commentaries provided, new archaeological expeditions undertaken, and a new intensity in searching the scriptures displayed on both sides. For liberals and conservatives alike, the question of what one did with and said about the Bible was insistent, adamant, and impossible to shake. Even more basic, of course, was the fact that the Bible continued to be read — and as the years rolled on, to be translated into a stunning variety of new versions.

Modernism/Fundamentalism

Critique of Liberalism

Partaking of all the elements noted above (and of more, besides), the struggle between modernists and fundamentalists early in the twentieth century cannot be understood as a simple, single issue. At any one moment, the debate may have centered on one proposition or a specific article of faith, but behind each verbal dispute lay a universe of attitudes, approaches, methods, motives, sentiments, and predilections. Opponents rarely understood each other, hardly heard each other.

Roman Catholicism faced the problems first in Europe, where so much that came to be tagged "modernism" first arose. Indeed, a good deal of what the Church officially condemned in 1907 could be located much more readily in Europe than in the United States. An earlier encyclical censuring "Americanism" was, despite the terminology, also aimed at ominous tendencies to be resisted in Europe no less than in America. Yet, parties or factions or wings clearly did exist within the Roman Catholic community in this country. The liberalizing influences, evident for example in the group agitating for a Catholic University of America (realized in 1888), found no support in the papal strictures about biblical investigation, public education, private religious feeling, error and its rights, and modern civilization in general. Indeed, the papal condemnation of 1907 was so sweeping, its administrative enforcement so efficient, that Catholic scholarship was stunted in its development for an entire generation or more.

In Protestantism, authority was decentralized, if not invisible. Consequently, all who wished spoke freely, published profusely, and contended against the opposing side unceasingly. Between the extremes of modernism and fundamentalism, a preponderant majority of Protestants hoped that the middle ground they thought they stood on really existed. This majority did not wish to turn its back upon modern philosophy, nor upon the evident blessings of modern science, nor upon the colleges which they had attended or their forefathers had founded. At the same time, however, they had no intention of turning their backs upon the "faith once delivered to the saints," nor upon those scriptures whose very words were woven into the fabric of their daily lives. So all they could do was live with tension and uncertainty, remembering that "all things work together for good to them that love God, to them who are called according to his purpose" (Romans 8:28).

Judaism, in its "denominational" separation into Reform, Conservative, and Orthodox, responded with at least that much variety to the several messages of modernity. Only in Reform, for example, did biblical criticism early find a home. At Hebrew Union College (Cincinnati, Ohio), Jewish scholars joined with Gentiles in exploring the merits of both textual and "higher" criticism. Conservative Judaism urged caution in any hasty abandonment of Mosaic laws, criticizing those too eager to prove themselves cosmopolitan citizens of a sophisticated and scientific world. Orthodoxy, which to some seemed only a vestige of medieval Judaism and therefore destined soon to wither away, preserved a fully observant community of believers, maintaining a strong "fence" around the Law (Torah), rejoicing in being God's covenanted and chosen people. For this status, as for one's own soul, one would not exchange a trendy and tawdry world.

Theological Aftermath

An old hymn concludes with the refrain, "And when the battle's over, we shall wear a crown, in the New Jerusalem." Whether or not the battle between modernism and fundamentalism was over in the 1940s and 1950s, none wore unchallenged crowns and none knew exactly where the New Jerusalem was to be found. Both sides were busy adjusting and regrouping, and both sides had been much distracted by depression and war. In the midst of great uncertainty and intellectual confusion, with the future cloudy and a bit scary, the path of wisdom turned toward the past.

The time of "neo's" had arrived: neo-Orthodox, neo-Thomist, neo-Fundamentalist. Whether attention fastened upon the sixteenth century, the thirteenth, or the first, the past appeared to hold more theological gold suitable for mining than did any vague claims staked in the future. Of course, a "neo" is never a precise replication of a "paleo." Such duplication is, to be sure, impossible; it is, moreover, undesirable — even to those whose theme song is "Give Me That Old-Time Religion." The contemporary world poses problems and demands solutions for which no previous age provides the precise pattern. So whether the backward glance was toward the theology of the reformers, or the "high" scholasticism of Thomas Aquinas, or the charismatic assurance of the apostles, the theology that resulted belonged to the twentieth century — and to no other.

1. Philosophy and Religion

William James (1842-1910)

Around the turn of the century, no one did more to make philosophy palatable (if not actually tasty) to the average American than William James. Nor in his frequent attention to religion has anyone proved more durable, this being true of many essays as well as the major monograph, The Varieties of Religious Experience, *first published in 1902. James, along with his less lionized contemporary, Charles S. Peirce (1839-1914), helped bring into being that characteristically American school of philosophy known as pragmatism. According to this view, the truth of a proposition lies in its predictability, its effect upon future possible experience. And in the view of William James, this gave great significance to religious attitudes and beliefs. For, as James explained in an essay first published in 1897, faith is full of meaning for it is full of productivity and predictive quality. Faith shapes destinies; it has momentous consequences. And if this be true, it is ridiculous — "trebly asinine" — for philosophers to ignore it or dismiss it.*

Now, there is one element of our active nature which the Christian religion has emphatically recognized, but which philosophers as a rule have with great insincerity tried to huddle out of sight in their pretension to found systems of absolute certainty. I mean the element of faith. Faith means belief in something concerning which doubt is still theoretically possible; and as the test of belief is willingness to act, one may say that faith is the readiness to act in a cause the prosperous issue of which is not certified to us in advance. It is in

---

[Source: William James, *Essays on Faith and Morals* (New York: Longmans, Green and Co., 1949 [this essay, 1897]), pp. 90-92, 93-97.]

fact the same moral quality which we call courage in practical affairs; and there will be a very widespread tendency in men of vigorous nature to enjoy a certain amount of uncertainty in their philosophic creed, just as risk lends a zest to worldly activity. Absolutely certified philosophies seeking the *inconcussum*[1] are fruits of mental natures in which the passion for identity (which we saw to be but one factor of the rational appetite) plays an abnormally exclusive part. In the average man, on the contrary, the power to trust, to risk a little beyond the literal evidence, is an essential function. Any mode of conceiving the universe which makes an appeal to this generous power, and makes the man seem as if he were individually helping to create the actuality of the truth whose metaphysical reality he is willing to assume, will be sure to be responded to by large numbers.

The necessity of faith as an ingredient in our mental attitude is strongly insisted on by the scientific philosophers of the present day; but by a singularly arbitrary caprice they say that it is only legitimate when used in the interests of one particular proposition, — the proposition, namely, that the course of nature is uniform. That nature will follow to-morrow the same laws that she follows to-day is, they all admit, a truth which no man can *know;* but in the interests of cognition as well as of action we must postulate or assume it. . . .

With regard to all other possible truths, however, a number of our most influential contemporaries think that an attitude of faith is not only illogical but shameful. Faith in a religious dogma for which there is no outward proof, but which we are tempted to postulate for our emotional interests, just as we postulate the uniformity of nature for our intellectual interests, is branded by Professor [Thomas] Huxley as "the lowest depth of immorality." Citations of this kind from leaders of the modern *Aufklärung* might be multiplied almost indefinitely. Take Professor [W. K.] Clifford's article on the 'Ethics of Belief.' He calls it 'guilt' and 'sin' to believe even the truth without 'scientific evidence.' But what is the use of being a genius, unless *with the same scientific evidence* as other men, one can reach more truth than they? . . .

The coil is about us, struggle as we may. The only escape from faith is mental nullity. What we enjoy most in a Huxley or a Clifford is not the professor with his learning, but the human personality ready to go in for what it feels to be right, in spite of all appearances. The concrete man has but one interest — to be right. That for him is the art of all arts, and all means are fair which help him to it. Naked he is flung into the world, and between him and nature there are no rules of civilized warfare. The rules of the scientific game, burdens of proof, presumptions, *experimenta crucis,* complete inductions, and the like, are only binding on those who enter that game. As a matter of fact we all more or less do enter it, because it helps us to our end. But if the means presume to frus-

---

1. Constant, unshakable.

trate the end and call us cheats for being right in advance of their slow aid, by guesswork or by hook or crook, what shall we say of them? Were all of Clifford's works, except the *Ethics of Belief,* forgotten, he might well figure in future treatises on psychology in place of the somewhat threadbare instance of the miser who has been led by the association of ideas to prefer his gold to all the goods he might buy therewith.

In short, if I am born with such a superior general reaction to evidence that I can guess right and act accordingly, and gain all that comes of right action, while my less gifted neighbor (paralyzed by his scruples and waiting for more evidence which he dares not anticipate, much as he longs to) still stands shivering on the brink, by what law shall I be forbidden to reap the advantages of my superior native sensitiveness? Of course I yield to my belief in such a case as this or distrust it, alike at my peril, just as I do in any of the great practical decisions of life. If my inborn faculties are good, I am a prophet; if poor, I am a failure: nature spews me out of her mouth, and there is an end to me. In the total game of life we stake our persons all the while; and if in its theoretic part our persons will help us to a conclusion, surely we should also stake them here, however inarticulate they may be.

But in being myself so very articulate in proving what to all readers with a sense for reality will seem of platitude, am I not wasting words? We cannot live or think at all without some degree of faith. Faith is synonymous with working hypothesis. The only difference is that while some hypotheses can be refuted in five minutes, others may defy ages. A chemist who conjectures that a certain wall-paper contains arsenic, and has faith enough to lead him to take the trouble to put some of it into a hydrogen bottle, finds out by the results of his action whether he was right or wrong. But theories like that of Darwin, or that of the kinetic constitution of matter, may exhaust the labors of generations in their corroboration, each tester of their truth proceeding in this simple way, — that he acts as if it were true, and expects the result to disappoint him if his assumption is false. The longer disappointment is delayed, the stronger grows his faith in his theory.

Now, in such questions as God, immortality, absolute morality, and freewill, no non-papal believer at the present day pretends his faith to be of an essentially different complexion; he can always doubt his creed. But his intimate persuasion is that the odds in its favor are strong enough to warrant him in acting all along on the assumption of its truth. His corroboration or repudiation by the nature of things may be deferred until the day of judgment, The uttermost he now means is something like this: "I *expect* then to triumph with tenfold glory; but if it should turn out, as indeed it may, that I have spent my days in a fool's paradise, why, better have been the dupe of *such* a dreamland than the cunning reader of a world like that which then beyond all doubt unmasks itself to view." . . .

Now, I wish to show what to my knowledge has never been clearly pointed out, that belief (as measured by action) not only does and must continually outstrip scientific evidence, but that there is a certain class of truths of whose reality belief is a factor as well as a confessor; and that as regards this class of truths faith is not only licit and pertinent, but essential and indispensable. The truths cannot become true till our faith has made them so.

Suppose, for example, that I am climbing in the Alps, and have had the ill-luck to work myself into a position from which the only escape is by a terrible leap. Being without similar experience, I have no evidence of my ability to perform it successfully; but hope and confidence in myself make me sure I shall not miss my aim, and nerve my feet to execute what without those subjective emotions would perhaps have been impossible. But suppose that, on the contrary, the emotions of fear and mistrust preponderate; or suppose that, having just read the Ethics of Belief, I feel it would be sinful to act upon an assumption unverified by previous experience, — why, then I shall hesitate so long that at last, exhausted and trembling, and launching myself in a moment of despair, I miss my foothold and roll into the abyss. In this case (and it is one of an immense class) the part of wisdom clearly is to believe what one desires; for the belief is one of the indispensable preliminary conditions of the realization of its object. *There are then cases where faith creates its own verification.* Believe, and you shall be right, for you shall save yourself; doubt, and you shall again be right, for you shall perish. The only difference is that to believe is greatly to your advantage.

The future movements of the stars or the facts of past history are determined now once for all, whether I like them or not. They are given irrespective of my wishes, and in all that concerns truths like these subjective preference should have no part; it can only obscure the judgment. But in every fact into which there enters an element of personal contribution on my part, as soon as this personal contribution demands a certain degree of subjective energy which, in its turn, calls for a certain amount of faith in the result, — so that, after all, the future fact is conditioned by my present faith in it, — how trebly asinine would it be for me to deny myself the use of the subjective method, the method of belief based on desire!

Josiah Royce (1855-1916)

A native of California but, like James, associated principally with Harvard University in his mature years, Royce was a philosophical idealist, the last great representative of a disappearing breed. Royce was also the last major philosopher of his era to mix philosophy with theology so easily, so unself-consciously. He could take a biblical text (in this instance Romans 7), give exegesis like a preacher and explication like a philosopher. His first major work, The Religious Aspect of Philosophy *(1885), augured a life-long interest in religion, for it was religion (he later noted) that drove him to philosophy. Almost thirty years later, he concentrated on "The Problem of Christianity," developing the three "essential ideas" of that religion: The Beloved Community, the individual's moral responsibility, and atonement. The excerpt below concerns the second of these ideas, that moral burden which, as George Santayana said, "spoiled the pantheistic serenity" of Royce's system. But it was that moral burden which also gave human life its unique dignity and its special purpose.*

"All things excellent," says Spinoza, "are as difficult as they are rare;" and Spinoza's word here repeats a lesson that nearly all of the world's religious and moral teachers agree in emphasizing. Whether such a guide speaks simply of "excellence," or uses the distinctively religious phraseology and tells us about the way to "salvation," he is sure, if he is wise, to recognize, and on occasion to say, that whoever is to win the highest goal must first learn to bear a heavy burden. It also belongs to the common lore of the sages to teach that this burden is much more due to the defects of our human nature than to the hostility of fortune. "We ourselves make our time short for our task": such comments are as trite as they are well founded in the facts of life.

But among the essential ideas of Christianity, there is one which goes beyond this common doctrine of the serious-minded guides of humanity. For this idea defines the moral burden, to which the individual who seeks salvation is subject, in so grave a fashion that many lovers of mankind, and, in particular, many modern minds, have been led to declare that so much of Christian doctrine, at least in the forms in which it is usually stated, is an unreasonable and untrue feature of the faith. This idea I stated at the close of our first lecture, side by side with the two other ideas of Christianity which I propose, in these lectures, to discuss. The idea of the Church, — of the universal community, — which was our topic in the second lecture, is expressed by the assertion that

[Source: Josiah Royce, *The Problem of Christianity* (with a new introduction by John E. Smith) (Chicago: University of Chicago Press, 1968 [1913]), pp. 99-100, 102-4.]

there is a real and divinely significant spiritual community to which all must belong who are to win the true goal of life. The idea of the moral burden of the individual is expressed by maintaining that (as I ventured to state this idea in my own words): "The individual human being is by nature subject to some overwhelming moral burden from which, if unaided, he cannot escape. Both because of what has technically been called original sin, and because of the sins that he himself has committed, the individual is doomed to a spiritual ruin from which only a divine intervention can save him."

This doctrine constitutes the second of the three Christian ideas that I propose to discuss. I must take it up in the present lecture. . . . Let us turn, then, to our new topic. The moralists, as we have already pointed out, are generally agreed that whoever is to win the highest things must indeed learn to bear a heavy moral burden. But the Christian idea now in question adds to the common lore of the moralists the sad word: "*The individual cannot bear this burden.* His tainted nature forbids; his guilt weighs him down. If by salvation one means a winning of the true goal of life, the individual, unaided, cannot be saved. And the help that he needs for bearing his burden must come from some source entirely above his own level, — from a source which is, in some genuine sense, divine."

The most familiar brief statement of the present idea is that of Paul in the passage in the seventh chapter of the epistle to the Romans, which culminates in this cry: "O wretched man that I am!" What the Apostle, in the context of this passage, expounds as his interpretation both of his own religious experience and of human nature in general, has been much more fully stated in the form of well-known doctrines, and has formed the subject-matter for ages of Christian controversy.

In working out his own theory of the facts which he reports, Paul was led to certain often cited statements about the significance and the effect of Adam's legendary transgression. And, as a consequence of these words and of a few other Pauline passages, technical problems regarding original sin, predestination, and related topics have come to occupy so large a place in the history of theology, that, to many minds, Paul's own report of personal experience, and his statements about plain facts of human nature, have been lost to sight (so far as concerns the idea of the moral burden of the individual) in a maze of controversial complications. To numerous modern minds the whole idea of the moral burden of the individual seems, therefore, to be an invention of theologians, and to possess little or no religious importance.

Yet I believe that such a view is profoundly mistaken. The idea of the moral burden of the individual is, as we shall see, not without its inherent complications, and not without its relation to very difficult problems, both ethical and metaphysical. Yet, of the three essential ideas of Christianity which constitute our list, it is, relatively speaking, the simplest, and the one which can be most easily interpreted to the enlightened common sense of the modern man.

Its most familiar difficulties are due rather to the accidents of controversy than to the nature of the subject.

The fate which has beset those who have dealt with the technical efforts to express this idea is partly explicable by the general history of religion; but is also partly due to varying personal factors, such as those which determined Paul's own training. This fate may be summed up by saying that, regarding just this matter of the moral burden of the individual, those who, by virtue of their genius or of their experience, have most known what they meant, have least succeeded in making clear to others what they know.

Paul, for instance, grasped the essential meaning of the moral burden of the individual with a perfectly straightforward veracity of understanding. What he saw, as to this matter, he saw with tragic clearness, and upon the basis of a type of experience that, in our own day, we can verify, as we shall soon see, much more widely than was possible for him. But when he put his doctrine into words, both his Rabbinical lore, and his habits of interpreting tradition, troubled his speech; and the passages which embody his theory of the sinfulness of man remain as difficult and as remote from his facts, as his report of these facts of life themselves is eloquent and true.

Similar has been the fortune of nearly all subsequent theology regarding the technical treatment of this topic. Yet growing human experience, through all the Christian ages, has kept the topic near to life; and today it is in closer touch with life than ever. The idea of the moral burden of the individual seems, to many cheerful minds, austere; but, if it is grave and stern, it is grave with the gravity of life, and stern only as the call of life, to any awakened mind, ought to be stern. If the traditional technicalities have obscured it, they have not been able to affect its deeper meaning or its practical significance. Rightly interpreted, it forms, I think, not only an essential feature of Christianity, but an indispensable part of every religious and moral view of life which considers man's business justly, and does so with a reasonable regard for the larger connections of our obligations and of our powers.

Alfred North Whitehead (1861-1947)

Also at Harvard (from 1924 to 1936), Whitehead brought to the problems of philosophy and religion a background strikingly different from that of James

[Source: Alfred North Whitehead, *Process and Reality: An Essay in Cosmology* (New York: Harper & Brothers, 1957 [1929]), pp. 519-21.]

or Royce. A native of England and son of a Church of England clergyman, Whitehead began his academic contributions in the field of mathematics, his first major work being A Treatise on Universal Algebra *(1898). Between 1910 and 1913 Whitehead joined with Bertrand Russell in writing the epoch-making* Principia Mathematica, *thereby establishing his reputation as one of the world's front-rank thinkers. Soon thereafter he turned his attention to persisting problems of metaphysics and cosmology. While at Harvard, he published his major work in this area,* Process and Reality, *the final chapter of which is entitled (with grand simplicity) "God and the World." God is Process rather than static Being; God is Love rather than established Ruler; God moves by persuasion rather than by coercion, which is why — White-head explained — the mills of the gods grind so slowly. Great ideas, includ-ing great religious ideas, need time to work their way — say a thousand or two thousand years — "nerving the race in its slow ascent"* (Adventures of Ideas, *chap. 2, section V).*

So long as the temporal world is conceived as a self-sufficient completion of the creative act, explicable by its derivation from an ultimate principle which is at once eminently real and the unmoved mover, from this conclusion there is no escape: the best that we can say of the turmoil is, 'For so he giveth his beloved — sleep.' This is the message of religions of the Buddhistic type, and in some sense it is true. In this final discussion we have to ask, whether metaphysical principles impose the belief that it is the whole truth. The complexity of the world must be reflected in the answer. It is childish to enter upon thought with the simple-minded question, What is the world made of? The task of reason is to fathom the deeper depths of the many-sidedness of things. We must not ex-pect simple answers to far-reaching questions. However far our gaze penetrates, there are always heights beyond which block our vision.

The notion of God as the 'unmoved mover' is derived from Aristotle, at least so far as Western thought is concerned. The notion of God as 'eminently real' is a favourite doctrine of Christian theology. The combination of the two into the doctrine of an aboriginal, eminently real, transcendent creator, at whose fiat the world came into being, and whose imposed will it obeys, is the fallacy which has infused tragedy into the histories of Christianity and of Mahometanism.

When the Western world accepted Christianity, Caesar conquered; and the received text of Western theology was edited by his lawyers. The code of Justin-ian and the theology of Justinian are two volumes expressing one movement of the human spirit. The brief Galilean vision of humility flickered throughout the ages, uncertainly. In the official formulation of the religion it has assumed the trivial form of the mere attribution to the Jews that they cherished a misconcep-tion about their Messiah. But the deeper idolatry, of the fashioning of God in the image of the Egyptian, Persian, and Roman imperial rulers, was retained. The Church gave unto God the attributes which belonged exclusively to Caesar.

In the great formative period of theistic philosophy, which ended with the rise of Mahometanism, after a continuance coeval with civilization, three strains of thought emerge which, amid many variations in detail, respectively fashion God in the image of an imperial ruler, God in the image of a personification of moral energy, God in the image of an ultimate philosophical principle. Hume's *Dialogues* criticize unanswerably these modes of explaining the system of the world.

The three schools of thought can be associated respectively with the divine Caesars, the Hebrew prophets, and Aristotle. But Aristotle was antedated by Indian, and Buddhistic, thought; the Hebrew prophets can be paralleled in traces of earlier thought; Mahometanism and the divine Caesars merely represent the most natural, obvious, theistic idolatrous symbolism, at all epochs and places.

The history of theistic philosophy exhibits various stages of combination of these three diverse ways of entertaining the problem. There is, however, in the Galilean origin of Christianity yet another suggestion which does not fit very well with any of the three main strands of thought. It does not emphasize the ruling Caesar, or the ruthless moralist, or the unmoved mover. It dwells upon the tender elements in the world, which slowly and in quietness operate by love, and it finds purpose in the present immediacy of a kingdom not of this world. Love neither rules, nor is it unmoved; also it is a little oblivious as to morals. It does not look to the future; for it finds its own reward in the immediate present.

Apart from any reference to existing religions as they are, or as they ought to be, we must investigate dispassionately what the metaphysical principles, here developed, require on these points, as to the nature of God. There is nothing here in the nature of proof. There is merely the confrontation of the theoretic system with a certain rendering of the facts. But the unsystematized report upon the facts is itself highly controversial, and the system is confessedly inadequate. The deductions from it in this particular sphere of thought cannot be looked upon as more than suggestions as to how the problem is transformed in the light of that system. What follows is merely an attempt to add another speaker to that masterpiece, Hume's *Dialogues Concerning Natural Religion*. Any cogency of argument entirely depends upon elucidation of somewhat exceptional elements in our conscious experience — those elements which may roughly be classed together as religious and moral intuitions.

John Dewey (1859-1952)

✱ Dewey & Reconstruction

Like each of the philosophers already treated, Dewey believed that philosophy must relate directly to life, must deal with the problems of men and women, not of philosophers alone. "While saints are engaged in introspection, burly sinners run the world." Dewey was determined to end that deplorable state of affairs by offering a Reconstruction in Philosophy *(1920) that would produce a reconstruction in society. He came closer than most. Unlike the three philosophers above, however, Dewey's interest in religion was more peripheral than central. Art, logic, politics, science, education — these all gripped him far more. In 1934, however, as the nation's best-known and most influential philosopher, John Dewey (professor at Columbia University) was invited to Yale to deliver the Terry lectures which, according to their founder, should treat of "a broadened and purified religion." The resulting book,* A Common Faith, *demonstrated little confidence in historic religions and none in revelation. One may have faith, but faith in and a dedication to the "one method for ascertaining fact and truth — that conveyed by the word 'scientific' in its most general and generous sense. . . ."*

The obvious and simple facts of the case are that some views about the origin and constitution of the world and man, some views about the course of human history and personages and incidents in that history, have become so interwoven with religion as to be identified with it. On the other hand, the growth of knowledge and of its methods and tests has been such as to make acceptance of these beliefs increasingly onerous and even impossible for large numbers of cultivated men and women. With such persons, the result is that the more these ideas are used as the basis and justification of a religion, the more dubious that religion becomes.

Protestant denominations have largely abandoned the idea that particular ecclesiastic sources can authoritatively determine cosmic, historic and theological beliefs. The more liberal among them have at least mitigated the older belief that individual hardness and corruption of heart are the causes of intellectual rejection of the intellectual apparatus of the Christian religion. But these denominations have also, with exceptions numerically insignificant, retained a certain indispensable minimum of intellectual content. They ascribe peculiar religious force to certain literary documents and certain historic personages. Even when they have greatly reduced the bulk of intellectual content to be accepted, they have insisted at least upon theism and the immortality of the individual.

[Source: John Dewey, *A Common Faith* (New Haven: Yale University Press, 1934), pp. 30-33.]

It is no part of my intention to rehearse in any detail the weighty facts that collectively go by the name of the conflict of science and religion — a conflict that is not done away with by calling it a conflict of science with theology, as long as even a minimum of intellectual assent is prescribed as essential. The impact of astronomy not merely upon the older cosmogony of religion but upon elements of creeds dealing with historic events — witness the idea of ascent into heaven — is familiar. Geological discoveries have displaced creation myths which once bulked large. Biology has revolutionized conceptions of soul and mind which once occupied a central place in religious beliefs and ideas, and this science has made a profound impression upon ideas of sin, redemption, and immortality. Anthropology, history and literary criticism have furnished a radically different version of the historic events and personages upon which Christian religions have built. Psychology is already opening to us natural explanations of phenomena so extraordinary that once their supernatural origin was, so to say, the natural explanation.

The significant bearing for my purpose of all this is that new methods of inquiry and reflection have become for the educated man today the final arbiter of all questions of fact, existence, and intellectual assent. Nothing less than a revolution in the "seat of intellectual authority" has taken place. This revolution, rather than any particular aspect of its impact upon this and that religious belief, is the central thing. In this revolution, every defeat is a stimulus to renewed inquiry; every victory won is the open door to more discoveries, and every discovery is a new seed planted in the soil of intelligence, from which grow fresh plants with new fruits. The mind of man is being habituated to a new method and ideal: There is but one sure road of access to truth — the road of patient, cooperative inquiry operating by means of observation, experiment, record and controlled reflection.

The scope of the change is well illustrated by the fact that whenever a particular outpost is surrendered it is usually met by the remark from a liberal theologian that the particular doctrine or supposed historic or literary tenet surrendered was never, after all, an intrinsic part of religious belief, and that without it the true nature of religion stands out more clearly than before. Equally significant is the growing gulf between fundamentalists and liberals in the churches. What is not realized — although perhaps it is more definitely seen by fundamentalists than by liberals — is that the issue does not concern this and that piecemeal *item* of belief, but centers in the question of the method by which any and every item of intellectual belief is to be arrived at and justified.

The positive lesson is that religious qualities and values if they are real at all are not bound up with any single item of intellectual assent, not even that of the existence of the God of theism; and that, under existing conditions, the religious function in experience can be emancipated only through surrender of the whole notion of special truths that are religious by their own nature, together with the idea of peculiar avenues of access to such truths. For were we to admit that there is but one method for ascertaining fact and truth — that conveyed by the word "scientific" in its most general and generous sense — no discovery in any branch of knowledge and inquiry could then disturb the faith that is religious. I should describe this faith as the unification of the self through allegiance to inclusive ideal ends, which imagination presents to us and to which the human will responds as worthy of controlling our desires and choices.

George Santayana (1863-1952)

> *Santayana has already been quoted above (p. 304); indeed, it is difficult to resist quoting Santayana. He wrote widely and well: poetry, fiction, reminiscence, philosophy. Born in Spain, growing up in Boston, lecturing at Oxford, the Sorbonne, and Harvard, and dying in a convent hospital in Rome, Santayana was the true cosomopolitan. In his twenty years or more at Harvard (mostly from 1889 to 1912), Santayana shrewdly observed and later pointedly wrote about Character and Opinion in the United States (1920). In "A Brief History of My Opinions," written in 1930, he noted: ". . . I have always set myself down officially as a Catholic; but this is a matter of sympathy and allegiance, not of philosophy." The sympathy which was real tended to grow stronger as Santayana grew older. But even in earlier years, he defended Catholicism against the modern tendency to subject it either to a cold impersonal rationalism or to a purely private mysticism. Here he anticipates some of the discussion to be found later in this chapter.*

Modernism is the infiltration into minds that begin by being Catholic and wish to remain so of two contemporary influences: one the rationalistic study of the Bible and of church history, the other modern philosophy, especially in its mystical and idealistic forms. The sensitiveness of the modernists to these two influences is creditable to them as men, however perturbing it may be to them as Catholics; for what makes them adopt the views of rationalistic historians is simply the fact that those views seem, in substance, convincingly true; and what makes them wander into transcendental speculations is the warmth of their souls, needing to express their faith anew, and to follow their inmost inspiration, wherever it may lead them. A scrupulous honesty in admitting the probable facts of history, and a fresh

[Source: George Santayana, *Winds of Doctrine* (London: J. M. Dent & Sons, 1913), pp. 40-43, 56-57.]

up-welling of mystical experience, these are the motives, creditable to any spiritual man, that have made modernists of so many. But these excellent things appear in the modernists under rather unfortunate circumstances. For the modernists to begin with are Catholics, and usually priests; they are pledged to a fixed creed, touching matters both of history and of philosophy; and it would be a marvel if rationalistic criticism of the Bible and rationalistic church history confirmed that creed on its historical side, or if irresponsible personal speculations, in the manner of Ritschl[2] or of M. Bergson,[3] confirmed its metaphysics.

I am far from wishing to suggest that an orthodox Christian cannot be scrupulously honest in admitting the probable facts, or cannot have a fresh spiritual experience, or frame an original philosophy. But what we think probable hangs on our standard of probability and of evidence; the spiritual experiences that come to us are according to our disposition and affections; and any new philosophy we frame will be an answer to the particular problems that beset us, and an expression of the solutions we hope for. Now this standard of probability, this disposition, and these problems and hopes may be those of a Christian or they may not. The true Christian, for instance, will begin by regarding miracles as probable; he will either believe he has experienced them in his own person, or hope for them earnestly; nothing will seem to him more natural, more in consonance with the actual texture of life, than that they should have occurred abundantly and continuously in the past. When he finds the record of one he will not inquire, like the rationalist, how that false record could have been concocted; but rather he will ask how the rationalist, in spite of so many witnesses to the contrary, has acquired his fixed assurance of the universality of the commonplace. An answer perhaps could be offered of which the rationalist need not be ashamed. We might say that faith in the universality of the commonplace (in its origin, no doubt, simply an imaginative presumption) is justified by our systematic mastery of matter in the arts. The rejection of miracles *a priori* expresses a conviction that the laws by which we can always control or predict the movement of matter govern that movement universally; and evidently, if the material course of history is fixed mechanically, the mental and moral course of it is thereby fixed on the same plan; for a mind not expressed somehow in matter cannot be revealed to the historian. This may be good philosophy, but we could not think so if we were good Christians. We should then expect to move matter by prayer. Rationalistic history and criticism are therefore based, as Pius X. most accurately observed in his Encyclical on modernism, on rationalistic philosophy; and we might add that rationalistic philosophy is

2. Albrecht Ritschl (1822-89), German Protestant theologian who emphasized the inner life of Christ as the basis for theology.

3. Henri Bergson (1859-1941), French philosopher who also stressed the inner life and the direct insights of conscience.

based on practical art, and that practical art, by which we help ourselves, like Prometheus, and make instruments of what religion worships, when this art is carried beyond the narrowest bounds, is the essence of pride and irreligion. Miners, machinists, and artisans are irreligious by trade. Religion is the love of life in the consciousness of impotence.

Similarly, the spontaneous insight of Christians and their new philosophies will express a Christian disposition. The chief problems in them will be sin and redemption; the conclusion will be some fresh intuition of divine love and heavenly beatitude. It would be no sign of originality in a Christian to begin discoursing on love like Ovid or on heaven like Mohammed, or stop discoursing on them at all; it would be a sign of apostasy.

Now the modernists' criterion of probability in history or of worthiness in philosophy is not the Christian criterion. It is that of their contemporaries outside the church, who are rationalists in history and egotists or voluntarists in philosophy. The biblical criticism and mystical speculations of the modernists call for no special remark; they are such as any studious or spiritual person, with no inherited religion, might compose in our day. But what is remarkable and well-nigh incredible is that even for a moment they should have supposed this non-Christian criterion in history and this non-Christian direction in metaphysics compatible with adherence to the Catholic church. That seems to presuppose, in men who in fact are particularly thoughtful and learned, an inexplicable ignorance of history, of theology, and of the world. . . .

Now religious experience, as I have said, may take other forms than the Christian, and within Christianity it may take other forms than the Catholic; but the Catholic form is as good as any intrinsically for the devotee himself, and it has immense advantages over its probable rivals in charm, in comprehensiveness, in maturity, in internal rationality, in external adaptability; so much so that a strong anti-clerical government, like the French, cannot safely leave the church to be overwhelmed by the forces of science, good sense, ridicule, frivolity, and avarice (all strong forces in France), but must use violence as well to do it. In the English church, too, it is not those who accept the deluge, the resurrection, and the sacraments only as symbols that are the vital party, but those who accept them literally; for only these have anything to say to the poor, or to the rich, that can refresh them. In a frank supernaturalism, in a tight clericalism, not in a pleasant secularisation, lies the sole hope of the church. Its sole dignity also lies there. It will not convert the world; it never did and it never could. It will remain a voice crying in the wilderness; but it will believe what it cries, and there will be some to listen to it in the future, as there have been many in the past. As to modernism, it is suicide. It is the last of those concessions to the spirit of the world which half-believers and double-minded prophets have always been found making; but it is a mortal concession. It concedes everything; for it concedes that everything in Christianity, as Christians hold it, is an illusion.

2. Science and Religion

Confrontation

John W. Draper (1811-82)

The "conflict" or "warfare" between science and religion should not be thought of as a battle by only one side: theologians fighting and sniping away while scientists, hidden away in their monastic laboratories, kept a steady course in their pursuit of Truth. Scientists fought battles too. In the late nineteenth and well into the twentieth century, many scientists were convinced that religion was on its way out and that it ought to be on its way out. Like magic and superstition, religion was a stage of civilization now outmoded, now outgrown. John W. Draper, son of a Methodist minister, received his medical degree from the University of Pennsylvania in 1836, soon thereafter joining the science faculty at New York University where he made notable contributions in chemistry, photography, telegraphy, and physiology. But he is represented here as scientist turned historian, a historian who is delighted to report that the "ecclesiastical spirit no longer inspires the policy of the world."

Whoever has had an opportunity of becoming acquainted with the mental condition of the intelligent classes in Europe and America, must have perceived that there is a great and rapidly-increasing departure from the public religious faith, and that, while among the more frank this divergence is not concealed, there is a far more extensive and far more dangerous secession, private and unacknowledged.

[Source: John W. Draper, *History of the Conflict of Religion and Science* (New York: D. Appleton & Co., 1889), pp. v-viii.]

So wide-spread and so powerful is this secession, that it can neither be treated with contempt nor with punishment. It cannot be extinguished by derision, by vituperation, or by force. The time is rapidly approaching when it will give rise to serious political results.

Ecclesiastical spirit no longer inspires the policy of the world. Military fervor in behalf of faith has disappeared. Its only souvenirs are the marble effigies of crusading knights, reposing in the silent crypts of churches on their tombs.

That a crisis is impending is shown by the attitude of the great powers toward the papacy. The papacy represents the ideas and aspirations of two-thirds of the population of Europe. It insists on a political supremacy in accordance with its claims to a divine origin and mission, and a restoration of the medieval order of things, loudly declaring that it will accept no reconciliation with modern civilization.

The antagonism we thus witness between Religion and Science is the continuation of a struggle that commenced when Christianity began to attain political power. A divine revelation must necessarily be intolerant of contradiction; it must repudiate all improvement in itself, and view with disdain that arising from the progressive intellectual development of man. But our opinions on every subject are continually liable to modification, from the irresistible advance of human knowledge.

Can we exaggerate the importance of a contention in which every thoughtful person must take part whether he will or not? In a matter so solemn as that of religion, all men, whose temporal interests are not involved in existing institutions, earnestly desire to find the truth. They seek information as to the subjects in dispute, and as to the conduct of the disputants.

The history of Science is not a mere record of isolated discoveries; it is a narrative of the conflict of two contending powers, the expansive force of the human intellect on one side, and the compression arising from traditionary faith and human interests on the other.

No one has hitherto treated the subject from this point of view. Yet from this point it presents itself to us as a living issue — in fact, as the most important of all living issues.

A few years ago, it was the politic and therefore the proper course to abstain from all allusion to this controversy, and to keep it as far as possible in the background. The tranquillity of society depends so much on the stability of its religious convictions, that no one can be justified in wantonly disturbing them. But faith is in its nature unchangeable, stationary; Science is in its nature progressive; and eventually a divergence between them, impossible to conceal, must take place. It then becomes the duty of those whose lives have made them familiar with both modes of thought, to present modestly, but firmly, their views; to compare the antagonistic pretensions calmly, impartially, philosophically. History shows that, if this be not done, social misfortunes, disastrous and enduring, will ensue. When the old mythological religion of Europe broke down under the weight of its own inconsistencies, neither the Roman emperors nor the philosophers of those times did any thing adequate for the guidance of public opinion. They left religious affairs to take their chance, and accordingly those affairs fell into the hands of ignorant and infuriated ecclesiastics, parasites, eunuchs, and slaves.

The intellectual night which settled on Europe, in consequence of that great neglect of duty, is passing away; we live in the daybreak of better things. Society is anxiously expecting light, to see in what direction it is drifting. It plainly discerns that the track along which the voyage of civilization has thus far been made, has been left; and that a new departure, on an unknown sea, has been taken.

John Wesley Powell (1834-1902)

Powell, a geologist, is best known for his explorations of the Colorado River. In those and other western travels, he studied the American Indian, defended the natural environment, and reflected on the course of human development — especially as this development related to science and religion. Like Draper, Powell saw the old domination of men's minds by religion as an earlier phase of civilization now happily passing away. We have moved from savagery through barbarism to what Powell calls "monarchacy." From there, with the aid of science, we can enter into a new age of democratic enlightenment. And in the bright future, it will be science, not religion, that gives hope; science, not religion, that offers the "pure water of truth" in place of the "hashish of mystery." In this excerpt, he describes that evolution from barbarism to "monarchacy."

The [physical theism] of barbarism is transformed into [psychological theism], and the deities have psychic attributes, though to a large extent the names of the deities remain the same. Thus there is a god of war and a god of love, a god of agriculture and a god of commerce, a god of hunting and a god of fishing, and in like manner the chief psychic attributes of mankind and the vocation which they follow are all represented by deities in the pantheon. At first the gods constitute a tribe, then they inhabit a city which is above on some mountain like Olympus or in the sky. As time goes on the constitution of the tribe of deities is changed, and the supreme deity is exalted more and more until a qualified monotheism is established.

[Source: John Wesley Powell, *The Monist*, 8 (1898), 199-200, 203-4.]

Worship changes and terpsichorean ceremonies are gradually abandoned, sacrifices are continued, but modified and ameliorated, becoming symbolic. Ceremony is refined and becomes a vast system of symbolism, so that worship becomes highly poetical. Gradually a new element is added to religion, and at last becomes its chief characteristic. Gods who were supposed to be pleased with dancing and then pleased with oblations are now supposed to be best pleased with opinions, and to be worshipped in spirit and in truth through creeds that work their effects in the hearts of men impelling them to righteous conduct. Religion is fiducial, and men are held to be pious who acknowledge God in all their ways. Another change comes, for men pray less for present blessings and more for blessings in the future world.

The crime of crimes in savagery is witchcraft, in which it is supposed that the gods are induced to do evil to men. This crime lasts on through barbarism and is punished with still greater rigor; it still continues in the third stage and those who practice it are condemned to death. In barbarism the crime of blasphemy is developed, consisting in the omission of rites or in acts of disrespect. This also appears in the third stage. In monarchacy yet a new crime is developed, for creed now becomes essential and the heretic receives more horrible punishment than the witch or the blasphemer.

During the stage of monarchacy six great religions were developed: Judaism, Confucianism, Hindooism, Buddhism, Islamism, and Christianity. In all these religions the priests are propagandists and desire to make their doctrines universal. The great majority of the peoples of the globe are worshippers in one or another of these systems, but there are a few followers of Zoroaster and of Lau-tsze, a few barbarians, and a few savages. Idolatry has never been a religion, but in all the three stages idols are found as insignia of shrines. . . .

The schools were devoted to philosophy and disputation. But little by little the disciplines of science, when they could no longer be ignored, were introduced into the seats of learning. The leaven worked a transformation, so that the schools became agencies of research and instruction in science as well as in philosophy. Gradually philosophy itself came to be known as metaphysics by the accident of a word. At last schools, individuals, and finally governments were enlisted in the work of research, and metaphysics has been relegated to a discipline for one of the years or even one of the scholastic terms in the life of the student. The public schools, colleges, and universities are now engaged mainly in the teaching of science. At last a fourth factor or potent mental agency in civilization has been developed, so that now industry, militancy, religion, and science are the four supreme agencies of change, and the new agency subordinates them all.

It is important to note here the metamorphosis wrought on religion by science, which comes to purify but not to slay. Not as the ages go by, not as the centuries lapse, but as decades fly, a change is wrought in the human conception of the attributes of deity. The pleasure of worship is becoming the contemplation of perfection, the form of worship the agency of instruction, the cause of worship the love of humanity, the purpose of worship the purification of conduct. This is the ideal state to which religion is tending, and it must be understood in order properly to appreciate the characteristics of the existing religions. In the primitive world religions were many, because tribes were many and languages many, names many, and totems many; but they were all on one plan, to secure one purpose, namely, that of pleasure, and to give pleasure to the gods. They were still many in barbarism, though not so many, but all designed to obtain welfare and to give welfare to ancestors. Then religions became few and sought to yield tribute of praise and allegiance to gods, and to gain bliss hereafter with incidental prosperity now. Much of ceremonial worship remains yet in this the first period of the new stage in the evolution of religion. Much of theoretic and practical sacrifice remains; much of creed remains, but more of scientific truth. As this last agency approaches perfection religion advances, for science has no conflict with it but only with metaphysics.

From time to time during the stage of monarchacy prophets arose who became great teachers. Seeing that true ceremony is only impressive symbolism, that true sacrifice is only immolation of unwise desire, and that true creed is only expression of opinion, and being profoundly convinced that true religion is righteous deed, they sought to convert men to better ways and taught a religion of ethics. Some of these great teachers for a time were successful, but by reason of ignorance and sin disciples continually relapsed into ceremony, sacrifice, and creed as true religion and forgot religion itself. But when Moses and Confucius and Buddha and Mahomet and Jesus could teach the world through the magical speech of books, great teachers multiplied and ethical religions gained ground. In democracy one of the great historic religions prevails, and has attained to Catholicity in that stage; though it has many subdivisions, the teaching of Jesus ever more and more in the spirit of the Sermon on the Mount is becoming the religion of the people. Though this religion is represented by diverse ceremonies and by differing theories of sacrifice, it is unified in practical ethics, but not in theoretical ethics. As the years pass, insistence on ceremony, insistence on sacrifice, and insistence on creed grows less and less, while instruction in ethics grows more and more. Ethical religion, though now often vaguely taught, will triumph in Catholicity.

T. DeWitt Talmage (1832-1902)

An almost exact contemporary of Powell's, the popular Calvinist preacher
saw science more as menace than as salvation. A graduate of the University
of the City of New York and of New Brunswick Seminary in New Jersey,
Talmage achieved his great fame in Brooklyn's Free Tabernacle, "free" in the
sense that no pew rents were charged, but also free in the sense that Talmage
stood above denominational discipline. This pulpit orator inspired thou-
sands with his "Talmagic," and his collected sermons fill twenty volumes.
The notion of evolution, if that was the best science could do, did not speak
well for science. It was a notion "atheistic and absurd," a "stenchful and
damnable doctrine." Any true Christian would be foolish to trade that de-
grading dogma for the ennobling teaching found in the Bible.

Evolution is one great mystery. It hatches out fifty mysteries, and the fifty hatch
out a thousand, and the thousand hatch out a million. Why, my brother, not admit the one great mystery of God, and have that settle all the other mysteries? I
can more easily appreciate the fact that God, by one stroke of His omnipotence
could make man, than I could realize how, out of five millions of ages, He could
have evolved one, putting on a little here and a little there. It would have been
just as great a miracle for God to have turned an orang-outang into a man as to
make a man out and out — the one job just as big as the other.

It seems to me we had better let God have a little place in our world somewhere. It seems to me if we cannot have Him make all creatures, we had better
have Him make two or three. There ought to be some place where He could stay
without interfering with the evolutionists. "No," says Darwin, and so for years
he is trying to raise fan-tailed pigeons, and to turn these fantail pigeons into
some other kind of pigeon, or to have them go into something that is not a pigeon — turning them into quail, or barnyard fowl, or brown thresher. But pigeon it is. And others have tried with the ox and the dog and the horse, but they
stayed in their species. If they attempt to cross over it is a hybrid, and a hybrid is
always sterile and goes into extinction. There has been only one successful attempt to pass over from speechless animal to the articulation of man, and that
was the attempt which Balaam witnessed in the beast that he rode; but an angel
of the Lord, with drawn sword, soon stopped that long-eared evolutionist.

But, says some one, "If we can not have God make a man let us have Him
make a horse." "Oh, no!" says Huxley, in his great lectures in New York several
years ago. No, he does not want any God around the premises. God did not

---

[Source: T. DeWitt Talmage, "The Missing Link," in *Live Coals* (New York: Wilbur B. Ketcham,
1885), pp. 271-75.]

make the horse. The horse came of the pliohippus, and the pliohippus came from the protohippus, and the protohippus came from the mio-hippus, and the mio-hippus came from the meshohippus, and the meshohippus came from the orohippus, and so away back, all the living creatures, we trace it in a line, until we get to the moneron, and no evidence of divine intermeddling with the creation until you get to the moneron, and that, Huxley says, is of so low a form of life that the probability is it just made itself, or was the result of spontaneous generation. What a narrow escape from the necessity of having a God.

As near as I can tell, these evolutionists seem to think that God at the start had not made up His mind as to exactly what He would make, and having made up his mind partially, He has been changing it all through the ages. I believe

ANOTHER PIED PIPER

E. J. Pace cartoon, 1920s
(Billy Graham Center)

God made the world as He wanted to have it, and that the happiness of all the species will depend upon their staying in the species where they were created.

But, my friends, evolution is not only infidel and atheistic and absurd; it is *brutalizing in its tendencies.* If there is anything in the world that will make a man bestial in his habits it is the idea that he was descended from the beast. Why, according to the idea of these evolutionists, we are only a superior kind of cattle, a sort of Alderney among other herds. To be sure, we browse on better pasture, and we have better stall and better accommodations, but then we are only Southdowns among the great flocks of sheep. Born of a beast, to die like a beast; for the evolutionists have no idea of a future world. They say the mind is only a superior part of the body. They say our thoughts are only molecular formation. They say when the body dies, the whole nature dies. The slab of the sepulchre is not a milestone on a journey upward, but a wall shutting us into eternal nothingness. We all die alike — the cow, the horse, the sheep, the man, the reptile. Annihilation is the heaven of the evolutionist.

From such a stenchful and damnable doctrine turn away. Compare that idea of your origin — an idea filled with the chatter of apes, and the hiss of serpents, and the croak of frogs — to an idea in one or two stanzas which I shall read to you from an old book of more than Demosthenic, or Homeric, or Dantesque power: "What is man, that thou art mindful of him? and the son of man, that thou visitest him? Thou hast made him a little lower than the angels, and hast crowned him with glory and honor. Thou madest him to have dominion over the works of thy hand; thou hast put all things under his feet. All sheep and oxen, yea, and the beasts of the field; the fowl of the air, and the fish of the sea, and whatsoever passeth through the paths of the seas. Oh, Lord, our Lord, how excellent is Thy name in all the earth."

How do you like that origin? The lion the monarch of the field, the eagle the monarch of the air, behemoth the monarch of the deep, but man monarch of all. Ah! my friends, I have to say to you that I am not so anxious to know what was my origin as to know what will be my destiny. I do not care so much where I came from as where I am going to. I am not so interested in who was my ancestry ten million years ago as I am to know where I will be ten million years from now. I am not so much interested in the preface to my cradle as I am interested in the appendix to my grave. I do not care so much about protoplasm as I do about eternasm. The "was" is overwhelmed with the "to be." And here comes in the evolution I believe in: not natural evolution, but gracious and divine and heavenly evolution — evolution out of sin into holiness, out of grief into gladness, out of mortality into immortality, out of earth into heaven! That is the evolution I believe in.

James Cardinal Gibbons (1834-1921)

*Introduced above (see p. 106), Baltimore's Cardinal Gibbons took a some-
what higher ground in his assessment of the "conflict" between science and
religion. There is no conflict, he argued, nor can there be, for God is the Author of all Truth. Sometimes the teachings of the Church are improperly understood, and sometimes the claims of science are irresponsible and false.
But Thomas Huxley and John Draper are both wrong, Gibbons declared,
and the tendency of their writings is pernicious. Science must be humble and
not profane. It remains the responsibility of the Catholic Church, furthermore, to rebuke and reprove when science advocates "some crude theory" or
"some hypothesis" at variance with "the Divine Oracle of which she is the
custodian." Then the Church must cry out, "Thus far . . . and no farther!"*

It cannot be denied that there dwells in many sincere minds a lurking suspicion,
amounting in some persons almost to a painful conviction, that antagonism
exists between certain dogmas of revelation and the results of scientific investigation. Mr. Huxley, Dr. Draper, and other acknowledged leaders of modern
thought, have done their utmost to confirm these sinister impressions and to
widen the breach between the teachers of religion and those of physical science.
They will tell you that the study of nature leads us away from God and ultimately results in the denial of His existence. They maintain that there is and
must be an irrepressible conflict between these two great branches of knowledge; that they cannot coexist; and that, in the long run, theology must surrender to her younger and more progressive rival.

They affect to believe that the champions of Christianity, conscious of the
unequal conflict, view with alarm the rapid strides of the natural sciences, and
do all in their power to discourage the study of them altogether. You will be
told, dear reader, by this modern school of thought, that the more you are attached to the teachings of Christian faith, the more will your judgment be
warped — your intellect stunted, and the more you will be retarded in the investigation of scientific truth. They will try to persuade you that, in exploring
the regions of science, you will be in constant danger of falling foul of some ecclesiastical ukase warning you away from the poisoned tree of knowledge, just
as our primitive parents were forbidden to eat the fruit of a certain tree in Paradise. They will tell you that your path is likely to be intercepted by some Pope's
bull, which may metaphorically gore you to death. They will, in a word, contend that, to enjoy full freedom in searching the secrets of the physical world,

---

[Source: James Cardinal Gibbons, *Our Christian Heritage* (Baltimore: John Murphy & Co.,
1889), pp. 301-4, 309-10, 319-20.]

you must emancipate yourself from the intellectual restraints imposed on you by the Christian religion.

Such are the statements deliberately made in our times against Christian revelation. But though they are uttered by bearded men, we call them childish declamations. We call them also ungrateful assertions, since they are spoken by men who are indebted to Christianity for the very discoveries they have made. Many a Christian Moses has wandered for years through the wilderness of investigation, and died almost in sight of the promised land of scientific discovery. And his successors, guided by the path that he had opened, and who might otherwise have died unknown after vain wanderings, entered the coveted territory and enjoyed its fruits. . . .

The truth is, that how much soever scientists and theologians may quarrel among themselves, there will never be any collision, but the most perfect harmony wilt ever exist between science and religion, as we shall endeavor to demonstrate in the following pages.

There are, indeed, and there ever will remain, truths of religion difficult to be reconciled with facts of science. If the ideas of time and space and the relation of soul to body are beyond our comprehension, we cannot be expected with our unaided reason to explain away the apparent incongruities that we find between the unseen and the visible kingdom of the universe. But difficulties do not necessarily involve doubts, still less denials. If we hold the two ends of a chain, we know that the connection is complete, though some of the links may be concealed from us.

Science and Religion, like Martha and Mary, are sisters, because they are daughters of the same Father. They are both ministering to the same Lord, though in a different way. Science, like Martha, is busy about material things; Religion, like Mary, is kneeling at the feet of her Lord.

The Christian religion teaches nothing but what has been revealed by Almighty God, or what is necessarily derived from revelation. God is truth. All truth comes from Him. He is the Author of all scientific truth, as He is the Author of all revealed truth. "The God who dictated the Bible," as Archbishop Ryan has happily said, "is the God who wrote the illuminated manuscript of the skies." You might as well expect that one ray of the sun would dim the light of another, as that any truth of revelation can be opposed to any truth of science. No truth of natural science can ever be opposed to any truth of revelation; nor can any truth of the natural order be at variance with any truth of the supernatural order. Truth differs from truth only as star differs from star, — each gives out the same pure light that reaches our vision across the expanse of the firmament. . . .

Now, since reason and revelation aid each other in leading us to God, the Author of both, it is manifest that the Catholic Church, so far from being opposed to the cultivation of reason, encourages and fosters science of every kind.

The more secrets science will elicit from nature's bosom, the more the Church will rejoice; because she knows that no new revelation of nature will ever utter the words: "There is no God!" Rather will they whisper to the eager investigator, "He made us, and not we ourselves."

Each new discovery of science is a trophy with which religion loves to adorn her altars. She hails every fresh invention as another voice adding its harmonious notes to that grand choir which is ever singing the praises of the God of nature.

At no period of the Church's history did she wield greater authority than from the twelfth to the sixteenth century. She exercised not only spiritual, but also temporal power; and she had great influence with the princes of Christendom. Now, this is the very period of the rise and development of the universities in Europe. During these four centuries, nineteen universities were opened in France, thirteen in Italy, six in Great Britain and Ireland, two in Spain and one in Belgium. At no time did the human intellect revel in greater freedom. No question of speculative science escaped the inquisitive search of men of thought. Successful explorations were made in every field of science and art. The weapons of heathendom were employed in fighting the battles of truth....

The position of the Catholic Church in reference to modern scientists may be thus briefly summarized: The Church fosters and encourages every department of science. But just because she is the friend of true science she is opposed to all false pretensions of science. There is as much difference between true and false science as there is between authority and despotism, liberty and license. When she hears a man advancing some crude theory at variance with the received doctrines of revelation, — with the existence of God, for example, or His superintending providence or His wisdom or His sanctity; when she hears him advocating some hypothesis opposed to the unity of the human species, to the spirituality and the immortality of the soul, to the future destiny of man, and to those other great doctrines that involve at once the dignity and moral responsibility of the human race, she knows that his assumptions must be false, because she knows that God's revelation must be true. She stands between such a man and the Divine Oracle of which she is the custodian; and when she sees him raise his profane hands and attempt to touch the temple of faith, she cries out, "Thus far shalt thou go and no farther!"

Mediation

Joseph Le Conte (1823-1901)

From a Georgia family of Huguenot heritage, Joseph Le Conte moved from the University of South Carolina to the University of California at Berkeley as professor of geology. In both states, it had been Le Conte's custom to offer lectures to a "Bible-class of young men," assuring them that modern science — of which he was a practitioner — constituted no threat to Christianity — in which he was a devout believer. To be sure, science and religion have occasionally collided, and the apparent discrepancies between the two are numerous. But Christianity returns from each battle stronger or purer than before. The true scientist, moreover, must see that faith is neither unsettled nor destroyed, but built upon foundations "more solid, enduring, and rational."

My Christian Friends: In all my lectures thus far I have tried to show a general accordance between the teachings of Scripture and the teachings of Nature. I have tried to show that the truths revealed in the one are also revealed in the other. But some one will say, perhaps many have already said: "Is there not a radical discordance between these two books in many passages? Does not skepticism draw its weapons principally from the armory of Nature? If some departments of science and some departments of Nature seem to be in general accordance with Scripture, are there not other departments, especially geology, in which there seems to be a fatal discordance?" It is indeed true, I frankly confess it, that, according to traditional interpretation of Scripture, there are many particular passages which seem to be in discordance with the teachings of Nature. But let me ask you, shall not the general spirit of the two books outweigh what seems to be the literal interpretation of some passages? Shall not the accordance of the two books, in those grand spiritual truths which form the basis of religion, overbalance apparent minor discrepancies in matters which are of little spiritual significance? Nevertheless, lest some persons should be distressed in mind by these apparent discrepancies in particular passages, I have determined, in this lecture and the next, to take up this subject. It seemed to me appropriate that, in connection with, and introductory to, the subject of man, which will occupy the remainder of these lectures — man the crown of Nature, and the culminating point of the whole *history of creation* — I should say something concerning the supposed *discrepancies in this history,* as recorded in the two books.

[Source: Joseph Le Conte, *Religion and Science: A Series of Sunday Lectures* . . . (New York: D. Appleton & Co., 1874), pp. 227-30, 231-33.]

Throughout the whole history of Christianity, from the earliest times until now, there have been from time to time collisions between religious faith and
the prevailing systems of philosophy. We find it first in St. Paul preaching the
unknown God to the scoffing philosophers of ancient Athens; we find it again
in the metaphysical discussions of the schoolmen of the middle ages; we find it
again, and more severe, in the conflict between faith and the acute metaphysical
philosophy of Hume; and last of all, and most serious of all, in the conflict now
going on with the material philosophy of the present day. The enemy has inces-
santly shifted the field of conflict from one ground to another. First it is in the
field of metaphysics, then in the field of science. In the field of science, again, it
is first in the department of astronomy, then in the department of geology and
natural history. Wherever the intellectual activity is greatest, there we find the
field of contest.

The general result of these collisions has ever been the same. In every case
Christianity has risen from the contest stronger and purer, and in this day, I believe, stronger and purer than ever before. How different, in this respect, is it
from all other forms of faith! These simply succumb unresistingly before advancing knowledge — like shadows, or spectres, they simply disappear before
the light of science. Christianity, on the contrary, loves the light, seeks the light,
lives in the light; it loves the truth, seeks the truth, lives in the truth; its Divine
founder was both light and truth. Is this the nature of spectres and shadows, Is
it not rather the nature of a permanent living reality? The last conflict has been
longest and most deadly. It is still going on. But those who have studied the history of such conflicts cannot doubt the final result.

What, then, are the subjects of conflict? What are the points of discrepancy between the two books? We will very briefly mention the most important.

The Scriptures, according to traditional interpretation, seem to teach —
1. That the age of this earth, and of the whole cosmos, is about six thousand
years or earth-revolutions. 2. That creation took place by successive instantaneous acts in the course of six natural days or earth-rotations. (Let me here
draw your attention parenthetically to the enormous improbability, not to say
absurdity, that the steps of evolution of the infinite cosmos should be determined by the rotations of this our little earth!) 3. By traditional interpretation,
it seems to teach that death reigned from Adam until now.

On the other hand, Nature seems very plainly to teach the inconceivable
antiquity of the earth and of the cosmos. Again, it seems to teach that creation took place, not by instantaneous acts occupying in all six natural days,
but was a gradual process of becoming — each successive condition of the
universe having come out of the previous condition by a gradual process of
evolution according to law. In the third place, it seems to teach that death has
reigned from the beginning of organic creation until now; that death and life
are correlative; life cannot exist without its counterpart death, and therefore

they are coextensive, and that during an inconceivable lapse of time. You see the discrepancy. . . .

My object, therefore, is rather to adjust, if possible, the *general relations of science and theology.* I wish to show that these two have the same general end and object, viz., the seeking of Divine truth. I wish to change, if possible, their angry conflict into generous emulation.

The science of astronomy is so old, its truths so long and well established, and the changes of interpretation of Scripture necessitated by the discovery of these truths have been now so long accepted, that any attempt to adjust the claims of astronomy with those of theology would be considered unnecessary. We even look back with wonder at the disturbance of religious faith produced by these truths when first established. But with geology the case is quite different. Geology is born of the present century. The generation is not yet gone which saw, and perhaps despised, its helpless infancy. It has advanced with such prodigious strides, it has opened such immense and unexpected fields of intellectual vision, its truths are of so startling a character, and have followed each other in such quick succession, that the popular mind is wholly unprepared to adjust their relations with faith; religious faith has not yet been able to incorporate these truths and to assimilate them to itself, as it eventually must and will do. Thus every step in the advance of the science of geology has tended to sap, and finally to overthrow, our faith in certain dogmas concerning the antiquity of the earth and the introduction of death, dogmas which we have learned at our mothers' knee, and taken in with our mothers' milk; dogmas which, therefore, have been loved and reverenced as Divine truth. These objects of our love and reverence, these our household gods, these images of Divine truth (for have they not been proved to be images made by ourselves?), these images of Deity have been rudely torn from the sanctuary of our hearts, and by some inconsiderate iconoclasts in science have been even trampled upon and defaced. In an agony we are ready to cry out, in the words of Micah to the plundering Danites, "Ye have taken away our gods: what have we more?"

Now, my Christian friends, I do believe that we cannot do a man a greater and a more irreparable injury than to unsettle in any way his religious faith. Faith is the very fountain of all noble activity. Without faith of some kind nothing worthy was ever accomplished, either for this life or the life to come. The faith may be lower or higher. It may be only faith in *self,* it may be faith in our *destiny,* it may be faith in *humanity,* it may be faith in a loving heavenly Father; but without faith of some kind there never was and never will be a noble or successful life. Life is noble in proportion to the nobleness of faith; it is successful in proportion to the fixedness of faith. There is no form of religious faith, however gross, no, not even idolatry or superstition, but is better than no faith at all. Superstition may be spiritual deformity, but unbelief is spiritual death. The light of science is indeed a glorious light — a light absolutely necessary for the perfect growth of the human spirit and its development into forms of perfect beauty and strength, a light absolutely necessary to the tree of humanity, in order that it should bear flower and fruit worthy of its divine origin; but, unless this light be assisted by the dews and showers of heaven received only through faith, it only scorches and withers and blasts; where we look for luxuriant verdure and abundant harvest, we find only blackened trunks and naked, outstretched limbs — noble trunks, it may be, "majestic even in ruin," but yet only dead.

I believe, therefore, it is the duty of every scientific man, who is also a lover of his fellow-men, to attempt to restore again the faith which he himself, perhaps, has helped to destroy; to wrest again, if possible, from the hands of infidelity, the weapons which perhaps he himself has furnished; to build again the foundations of faith upon a more solid, enduring, and rational basis.

James McCosh (1811-94)

A native of Scotland and a Presbyterian clergyman, McCosh came to America in 1868 to assume the presidency of Princeton. A philosopher of considerable reputation even before beginning his career in this country, McCosh put that reputation on the line by becoming the first prominent clergyman in the United States strongly to support the theory of evolution. Much of the controversy had bubbled over in the 1870s, and McCosh quickly entered the fray. Later, when things had quieted down somewhat, he published The Religious Aspect of Evolution *in 1888. In the preface to the "enlarged and improved edition" issued two years later, he wrote: "I am pleased to discover that intelligent Christians are coming round gradually to the views which I have had the courage to publish."*

In my first published work, "The Method of Divine Government," I sought to unfold the plan by which God governs the world, and I found it to be in an orderly manner — that is, by law. As having pursued this line of research, I was prepared to believe that there might be the like method in the organic kingdoms, and to listen to Darwin when he showed that there was a regular instrumentality in the descent of plants and animals. I noticed that he and others, such as Lewes, Huxley, and Spencer, who took the same view, were not swayed by any religious considerations, and that religious people generally were strongly prepossessed against the new doctrine. But I saw, at the same time, that

[Source: James McCosh, *The Religious Aspect of Evolution* (New York: Charles Scribner's Sons, 1890), pp. vii-x.]

Darwin was a most careful observer, that he published many important facts, that there was great truth in the theory, and that there was nothing atheistic in it if properly understood — that is, in the acknowledged tenet of the government of organic nature by means and according to law.

I felt it to be my only course not to reject the truth because it was proclaimed by some who turned it to an irreligious use, but to accept it wherever it might lead, and to turn it to a better use. I let it be known that while I thought there was truth, I believed there was error in the common expositions of evolution, and that the work of the coming age must be to separate the truth from the error, when it would be found, I was sure, that this, like every other part of God's work, would illustrate his existence and his wisdom.

When I was called from the Old World to the office which I now hold as president of an important college, I had to consider — I remember seriously pondering the question in the vessel which brought me to this country — whether I should at once avow my convictions or keep them in abeyance because of the prejudices of religious men, and lest I might unsettle the faith of the students committed to my care. I decided to pursue the open and honest course, as being sure that it would be the best in the end. I was not a week in Princeton till I let it be known to the upper classes of the college that I was in favor of evolution properly limited and explained; and I have proclaimed my views in lectures and papers in a number of cities and before various associations, literary and religious. I have been gratified to find that none of the churches has assailed me, and this has convinced me that their doubts about evolution have proceeded mainly from the bad use to which the doctrine has been turned. I am pleased to discover that intelligent Christians are coming round gradually to the views which I have had the courage to publish.

I have all along had a sensitive apprehension that the undiscriminating denunciation of evolution from so many pulpits, periodicals, and seminaries might drive some of our thoughtful young men to infidelity, as they clearly saw development everywhere in nature, and were at the same time told by their advisers that they could not believe in evolution and yet be Christians. I am gratified beyond measure to find that I am thanked by my pupils, some of whom have reached the highest position as naturalists, because in showing them evolution in the works of God, I showed them that this was not inconsistent with religion, and thus enabled them to follow science and yet retain their faith in the Bible.

B. B. Warfield (1851-1921)

One of James McCosh's students as an undergraduate at the College of New
Jersey later went on to a distinguished career as a theologian at Princeton
Theological Seminary. Benjamin Breckinridge Warfield testified as an old
man that McCosh's advocacy for evolution had electrified him as an under-
graduate, that he had then given up McCosh's view, only then to construct
his own version of how traditional Christianity might accommodate mod-
ern evolutionary theories. From the mid-1890s to his death, Warfield wrote
steadily about how that accommodation might take place, even as he was
also busy upholding thoroughly conservative positions in other debates then
swirling within his Presbyterian church. In 1915 Warfield published a histor-
ical article on how he felt John Calvin, the early leader of Reformation Prot-
estantism, would have responded to modern science if he had lived to see it
develop. The approval he thought he could find for evolution in Calvin's
works doubtless spoke for his own convictions as well.

It should be observed that in this and similar discussions founded on the progressive completion of the world, Calvin does not intend to attribute what we
may speak strictly of as progressive creation to God. With Calvin, while the per-
fecting of the world — as its subsequent government — is a process, creation,
strictly conceived, tended to be thought of as an act. "In the beginning God created the heavens and the earth": after that it was not "creation" strictly so called
but "formation," gradual modelling into form, which took place. Not, of course,
as if Calvin conceived creation deistically; as if he thought of God as having created the world-stuff and then left it to itself to work out its own destiny under
the laws impressed on it in its creation. A "momentary Creator, who has once
for all done His work," was inconceivable to him: and he therefore taught that it
is only when we contemplate God in providence that we can form any true conception of Him as Creator. But he was inclined to draw a sharp distinction in
kind between the primal act of creation of the heavens and the earth out of
nothing, and the subsequent acts of moulding this created material into the
forms it was destined to take; and to confine the term "creation," strictly conceived, to the former. . . .

It is important further that we should not suppose that Calvin removed
the production of the human soul out of the category of immediate creation, in
the strictest sense of that term. When he insists that the works of the days subsequent to the first, when "in the beginning God created the heavens and the

---

[Source: B. B. Warfield, "Calvin's Doctrine of Creation," *Princeton Theological Review* 13 (Apr.
1915): 202-03, 207-09.]

earth," were not strictly speaking "creations," because they were not productions *ex nihilo*, he is thinking only of the lower creation, inclusive, no doubt, of
the human body; all this is made out of that primal "indigested mass" which
sprang into being at the initial command of God. The soul is a different matter;
and not only in the first instance, but in every succeeding instance, throughout
the whole course of human propagation, is an immediate creation *ex nihilo*.
Moses, he tells us, perfectly understood that the soul was created from nothing;
and he announces with emphasis, that it is certain that the souls of men are "no
less created than the angels," adding the decisive definition: "now, creation is
the origination of essence *ex nihilo*." It is thus with the lower creation alone in
his mind that Calvin insists that all that can justly be called by the high name of
"creation" was wrought by God on the first day, in that one act by which He created, that is, called into Being out of nothing, the heavens and the earth.

It should scarcely be passed without remark that Calvin's doctrine of creation is, if we have understood it aright, for all except the souls of men, an evolutionary one. The "indigested mass," including the "promise and potency" of
all that was yet to be, was called into being by the simple *fiat* of God. But all that
has come into being since — except the souls of men alone — has arisen as a
modification of this original world-stuff by means of the interaction of its intrinsic forces. Not these forces apart from God, of course: Calvin is a high theist,
that is, supernaturalist, in his ontology of the universe and in his conception of
the whole movement of the universe. To him God is the *prima causa omnium*
[first cause of all] and that not merely in the sense that all things ultimately —
in the world-stuff — owe their existence to God; but in the sense that all the
modifications of the world-stuff have taken place under the directly upholding
and governing hand of God, and find their account ultimately in His will. But
they find their account proximately in "second causes"; and this is not only
evolutionism but pure evolutionism. What account we give of these second
causes is a matter of ontology; how we account for their existence, their persis-
tence, their action, — the relation we conceive them to stand in to God, the up-
holder and director as well as creator of them. Calvin's ontology of second
causes, was, briefly stated, a very pure and complete doctrine of *concursus*, by
virtue of which he ascribed all that comes to pass to God's purpose and directive government. But that does not concern us here. What concerns us here is
that he ascribed the entire series of modifications by which the primal "indigested mass," called "heaven and earth," has passed into the form of the ordered
world which we see, including the origination of all forms of life, vegetable and
animal alike, inclusive doubtless of the bodily form of man, to second causes as
their proximate account. And this, we say, is a very pure evolutionary scheme.
He does not discuss, of course, the factors of the evolutionary process, nor does
he attempt to trace the course of the evolutionary advance, nor even expound
the nature of the secondary causes by which it was wrought. It is enough for

Lyman Abbott (1835-1922) in 1905, author of *The Theology of an Evolutionist*
(Keystone-Mast Collection, University of California, Riverside)

him to say that God said, "Let the waters bring forth, . . . Let the earth bring forth", and they brought forth. Of the interaction of forces by which the actual production of forms was accomplished, he had doubtless no conception: he certainly ventures no assertions in this field. How he pictured the process in his imagination (if he pictured it in his imagination) we do not know. But these are subordinate matters. Calvin doubtless had no theory whatever of evolution; but he teaches a doctrine of evolution. He has no object in so teaching except to preserve to the creative act, properly so called, its purity as an immediate production out of nothing. All that is not immediately produced out of nothing is therefore not created — but evolved.

John Augustine Zahm (1851-1921)

In 1896 a Holy Cross priest and professor of physics at Notre Dame offered his reconciliation of Darwinian investigation and Roman Catholic instruction. Like McCosh, Zahm did not see evolution as a threat to the Christian faith nor an attack upon the Bible. We must remember that much being said about evolution is still hypothetical, he noted, but even supposing it all were to be established as incontrovertible fact, still "Catholic Dogma would remain absolutely intact and unchanged." Evolution for the agnostic or atheist means one thing, but for the "theistic evolutionist" everything "is a part of a grand unity betokening an omnipotent Creator." Within two years of its publication, Zahm's work was placed on the Index of Prohibited Books and withdrawn from further circulation.

Suppose, then, that a demonstrative proof of the theory of Evolution should eventually be given, a proof such as would satisfy the most exacting and the most skeptical, it is evident, from what has already been stated, that Catholic Dogma would remain absolutely intact and unchanged. Individual theorists would be obliged to accommodate their views to the facts of nature, but the doctrines of the Church would not be affected in the slightest. The hypothesis of St. Augustine and St. Thomas Aquinas would then become a thesis, and all reasonable and consistent men would yield ready, unconditional and unequivocal assent.

And suppose, further, that in the course of time science shall demonstrate — a most highly improbable event — the animal origin of man as to his body. There need, even then, be no anxiety so far as the truths of faith are concerned. Proving that the body of the common ancestor of humanity is descended from some higher form of ape, or from some extinct anthropopithecus, would not necessarily contravene either the declarations of Genesis, or the principles regarding derivative creation which found acceptance with the greatest of the Church's Fathers and Doctors.

Mr. Gladstone, in the work just quoted from,[4] expresses the same idea with characteristic force and lucidity. "If," he says, "while Genesis asserts a separate creation of man, science should eventually prove that man sprang, by a countless multitude of indefinitely small variations, from a lower, and even from the lowest ancestry, the statement of the great chapter would still remain

---

4. William E. Gladstone, introduction to G. C. Lorimer, ed., *The People's Bible History . . .* (1895).

[Source: J. A. Zahm, *Evolution and Dogma* (Chicago: D. H. McBride & Co., 1896), pp. 428-30, 435-38.]

undisturbed. For every one of those variations, however minute, is absolutely separate, in the points wherein it varies, from what followed and also from what preceded it; is in fact and in effect a distinct or separate creation. And the fact that the variation is so small that, taken singly, our use may not be to reckon it, is nothing whatever to the purpose. For it is the finiteness of our faculties which shuts us off by a barrier downward, beyond a certain limit, from the small, as it shuts us off by a barrier upward from the great; whereas for Him whose faculties are infinite, the small and the great are, like the light and the darkness, 'both alike,' and if man came up by innumerable stages from a low origin to the image of God, it is God only who can say, as He has said in other cases, which of those stages may be worthy to be noted with the distinctive name of creation, and at what point of the ascent man could first be justly said to exhibit the image of God."

But the derivation of man from the ape, we are told, degrades man. Not at all. It would be truer to say that such derivation ennobles the ape. Sentiment aside, it is quite unimportant to the Christian "whether he is to trace back his pedigree directly or indirectly to the dust." St. Francis of Assisi, as we learn from his life, "called the birds his brothers." Whether he was correct, either theologically or zoölogically, he was plainly free from that fear of being mistaken for an ape which haunts so many in these modern times. Perfectly sure that he, himself, was a spiritual being, he thought it at least possible that birds might be spiritual beings, likewise incarnate like himself in mortal flesh; and saw no degradation to the dignity of human nature in claiming kindred lovingly with creatures so beautiful, so wonderful, who, as he fancied, "praised God in the forest, even as angels did in heaven." . . .

And as Evolution ennobles our conceptions of God and of man, so also does it permit us to detect new beauties, and discover new lessons, in a world that, according to the agnostic and monistic views, is so dark and hopeless. To the one who says there is no God, "the immeasurable universe," in the language of Jean Paul, "has become but a cold mass of iron, which hides an eternity without form and void."

To the theistic evolutionist, however, all is instinct with invitations to a higher life and a happier existence in the future; all is vocal with hymns of praise and benediction. Everything is a part of a grand unity betokening an omnipotent Creator. All is foresight, purpose, wisdom. We have the entire history of the world and of all systems of worlds, "gathered, as it were, into one original, creative act, from which the infinite variety of the universe has come, and more is coming yet." And God's hand is seen in the least as in the greatest. His power and goodness are disclosed in the beauteous crystalline form of the snow-flake, in the delicate texture, fragrance and color of the rose, in the marvelous pencilings of the butterfly's wing, in the gladsome and melodious notes of the lark and the thrush, in the tiniest morning dew-drop with all its gorgeous prismatic hues and wondrous hidden mysteries. All are pregnant with truths of the highest order, and calculated to inspire courage, and to strengthen our hope in faith's promise of a blissful immortality. . . .

Science and Evolution tell us of the transcendence and immanence of the First Cause, of the Cause of causes, the Author of all the order and beauty in the world, but it is revelation which furnishes us with the strongest evidence of the relations between the natural and supernatural orders, and brings out in the boldest relief the absolute dependence of the creature on its Maker. It is faith which teaches us how God "binds all together into Himself;" how He quickens and sustains "each thing separately, and all as collected in one."

I can, indeed, no better express the ideas which Evolution so beautifully shadows forth, nor can I more happily conclude this long discussion than by appropriating the words used long ago by that noble champion of the faith, St. Athanasius. "As the musician," says the great Alexandrine Doctor, in his "Oratio Contra Gentiles," "having tuned his lyre, and harmonized together the high with the low notes, and the middle notes with the extremes, makes the resulting music one; so the Wisdom of God, grasping the universe like a lyre, blending the things of air with those of earth, and the things of heaven with those of air, binding together the whole and the parts, and ordering all by His counsel and His will, makes the world itself and its appointed order one in fair and harmonious perfection; yet He, Himself, moving all things, remains unmoved with the Father."

Litigation: The Scopes Trial

The most famous, if not necessarily the most significant, controversy between science and religion did not come until 1925. By then most minds in the scholarly community had already been made up, the courses of most universities and seminaries already charted. But "Scopes" was the main event in the public arena. A young biology teacher in Dayton, Tennessee, John Thomas Scopes (1900-70), taught evolution in opposition to a state law. Or at least he was so charged, for the precise thrust of the state law was one of the points at issue (as is evident below). One reason for the trial's fame was the reputation of the major figures involved: Clarence S. Darrow (1857-1938), outstanding Chicago trial lawyer for the defense; Kirtley F. Mather

[Source: Leslie Allen, ed., *Bryan and Darrow at Dayton* (New York: A. Lee & Co., 1925), (1) pp. 16-19; (2) pp. 64-66; (3) pp. 112-14; (4) pp. 195-96.]

(1888-1978), Harvard geologist and expert witness for the defence (also the author a few years later of Science in Search of God, *1928); but above all others, William Jennings Bryan (1860-1925), thrice presidential candidate and the prosecution's tireless voice. Bryan's final summation was never delivered because both sides had agreed to conclude the sweltering proceedings on July 21, 1925. Five days later Bryan died, and two days after that his widow released the remarks that he would have given if the trial had reached its final drama. Without further introduction, four documents follow: (1) Darrow early in the trial; (2) Bryan in response; (3) Mather as Bible student and scientist; and (4) Bryan's never-delivered summation. All of this comes from a reporter's transcription of the events of which a nation waited eagerly to hear.*

1.

Clarence Darrow

"There is not a single line of any constitution that can withstand bigotry and ignorance when it seeks to destroy the rights of the individual; and bigotry and ignorance are ever active. Here we find today as brazen and as bold an attempt to destroy learning as was ever made in the Middle Ages, and the only difference is we have not provided that they shall be burned at the stake. But there is time for that, your Honor. We have to approach these things gradually.

"Now let us see what we claim with reference to this law. If this proceeding, both in form and substance, can prevail in this court, then, your Honor, any law, no matter how foolish, wicked, ambiguous, or ancient, can come back to Tennessee. All the guarantees go for nothing. All of the past has gone to waste, been forgotten, if this can succeed.

"I am going to begin with some of the simpler reasons why it is absolutely absurd to think that this statute, indictment, or any part of the proceedings in this case are legal; and I think the sooner we get rid of it in Tennessee the better for the people of Tennessee, and the better for the pursuit of knowledge in the world; so let me begin at the beginning.

"The first point we made in this suit is that it is unconstitutional on account of divergence and the difference between the statute and the caption and because it contains more than one subject.

"Every Constitution with which I am familiar has substantially this same proposition, that the caption and the law must correspond.

"Lots of things are put through the Legislature in the night time. Everybody does not read all of the statutes, even members of the Legislature — I have been a member of the Legislature myself, and I know how it is. They may vote for them without reading them, but the substance of the act is put in the caption, so it may be seen and read, and nothing may be in the act that is not contained in the caption. There is not any question about it, and only one subject shall be legislated on at once. Of course, the caption may be broader than the act. They may make a caption and the act may fall far short of it, but the substance of the act must be in the caption, and there can be no variance.

"Now let us see what they have done. There is not much dispute about the English language, I take it. Here is the caption:

> "'Public Act, Chapter 37, 1925, an act prohibiting the teaching of the evolution theory in all the universities, normals, and all the public schools of Tennessee which are supported in whole or in part by the public school funds of the State, and to prescribe penalties for the violation thereof.'

"Now what is it — an act to prohibit the teaching of the evolution theory in Tennessee? Is this the act? Is this statute to prevent the teaching of the evolution theory? There is not a word said in the statute about evolution. There is not a word said in the statute about preventing the teaching of the theory of evolution — not a word.

"This caption says what follows is an act forbidding the teaching of evolution, and the Catholic could have gone home without any thought that his faith was about to be attacked. The Protestant could have gone home without any thought that his religion could be attacked. The intelligent, scholarly Christians, who by the millions in the United States find no inconsistency between evolution and religion, could have gone home without any fear that a narrow, ignorant, bigoted shrew of religion could have destroyed their religious freedom and their right to think and act and speak; and the nation and the State could have laid down peacefully to sleep that night without the slightest fear that religious hatred and bigotry were to be turned loose in a great State.

"Any question about that? Anything in this caption whatever about religion, or anything about measuring science and knowledge and learning by the Book of Genesis, written when everybody thought the world was flat? Nothing.

"They went to bed in peace, probably, and they woke up to find this, which has not the slightest reference to it; which does not refer to evolution in any way; which is, as claimed, a religious statute.

"That is what they found and here is what it is:

"'Be it enacted by the General Assembly of the State of Tennessee, that it shall be unlawful for any teacher in any of the universities, normals, and all other public schools in the State, which are supported in whole or in part by the public school funds of the State, to teach' — what, teach evolution? Oh, no. — 'To teach the theory that denies the story of the divine creation of man as taught in the Bible, and to teach instead that man has descended from a lower order of animals.'

"That is what was foisted on the people of this State, under a caption which never meant it, and could give no hint of it; that it should be a crime in the State of Tennessee to teach any theory, — not evolution, but any theory of the origin of man, except that contained in the divine account as recorded in the Bible.

"But the State of Tennessee, under an honest and fair interpretation of the Constitution, has no more right to teach the Bible as the Divine Book than that the Koran is one, or the Book of Mormon, or the Book of Confucius, or the Buddha, or the Essays of Emerson, or any one of the 10,000 books to which human souls have gone for consolation and aid in their troubles."

2.
William Jennings Bryan

"Our Position is that the statute is sufficient. The statute defines exactly what the people of Tennessee decided and intended and did declare unlawful, and it needs no interpretation.

"The caption speaks of the evolutionary theory, and the statute specifically states that teachers are forbidden to teach in the schools supported by taxation in this State any theory of creation of man that denies the Divine record of man's creation as found in the Bible, and that there might be no difference of opinion — there might be no ambiguity — that there might be no such confusion of thought as our learned friends attempt to inject into it. The Legislature was careful to define what is meant by the first of the statute.

"It says 'to teach that man is a descendant of any lower form of life.' If that had not been there, if the first sentence had been the only sentence in the statute, then these gentlemen might come and ask to define what that meant or to explain whether the thing that was taught was contrary to the language of the statute in the first sentence. But the second sentence removes all doubt, as has been stated by my colleague.

"The second sentence points out specifically what is meant, and that is the teaching that man is the descendant of any lower form of life; and if the defendant taught that, as we have proved by the textbook that he used and as we have proved by the students that went to hear him, if he taught that man is a descendant of any lower form of life, he violated the statute, and more than that, we have his own confession that he knew he was violating the statute."

After summarizing the evidence, Mr. Bryan continued:

"We do not need any expert to tell us what the law means. An expert cannot be permitted to come in here and try to defeat the enforcement of a law by testifying that it isn't a bad law, and it isn't — I mean a bad doctrine — no matter how these people phrase that doctrine, no matter how they eulogize it. This is not the place to try to prove that the law ought never to have been passed. The place to prove that was at the Legislature.

"If these people were so anxious to keep the State of Tennessee from disgracing itself, if they were so afraid that by this action taken by the Legislature, the State would put itself before the people of the nation as ignorant people and bigoted people — if they had half the affection for Tennessee that you would think they had as they come here to testify — they would have come at a time when their testimony would have been valuable, and not at this time to ask you to refuse to enforce a law because they did not think the law ought to have been passed.

"And if the people of Tennessee were to go into a state, into New York, the one from which this impulse comes to resist this law, or go into any state . . . and try to convince the people that a law they had passed ought not to be enforced (just because the people who went there didn't think it ought to have been passed), don't you think it would be resented as an impertinence? . . .

"The people of this State passed this law. The people of this State knew what they were doing when they passed the law, and they knew the dangers of the doctrine that they did not want it taught to their children. And, my friends, it isn't proper to bring experts in here to try to defeat the purpose of the people of this State by trying to show that this thing that they denounce and outlaw is a beautiful thing that everybody ought to believe in. . . .

"These people want to come here with experts to make your Honor believe that the law should never have been passed, and because in their opinion it ought not to have been passed, it ought not to be enforced. It isn't a place for expert testimony. We have sufficient proof in the book. Doesn't the book state the very thing that is objected to and outlawed in this State? Who has a copy of that book?"

JUDGE RAULSTON — Do you mean the Bible?

MR. BRYAN — No, sir, the biology. [Laughter]

A VOICE — Here it is, Hunter's Biology.

MR. BRYAN — "No, not the Bible. You see, in this State they cannot teach the Bible. They can only teach things that declare it to be a lie, according to the learned counsel. These people in the State, Christian people, have tied their hands by their Constitution. They say we all believe in the Bible, for it is the overwhelming belief in the State, but we will not teach that Bible, which we believe — even to our children, through teachers that we pay with our money.

"No, no, it isn't the teaching of the Bible, and we are not asking it.

"The question is, Can a minority in this State come in and compel a teacher to teach that the Bible is not true and make the parents of these children pay the expenses of the teacher to tell their children what these people believe is false and dangerous?

"Has it come to a time when the minority can take charge of a state like Tennessee and compel the majority to pay their teachers while they take religion out of the heart of the children of the parents who pay the teachers?"

3.
Kirtley F. Mather

Dr. Mather's statement was introduced as coming from a student of the Bible, lecturer to Bible students at the Boston University School of Religious Education, member of the Baptist Church at Newton Center, Mass., and teacher of the Mather Class in its Bible school. Professor Mather said that evolution was "not a power, not a force," but "a process, a method." God was "a power, a force"; He necessarily uses processes and methods in displaying His Power and exerting force.

Not one of the facts of evolution "contradicts any teaching of Jesus Christ known to me," his statement read. "None could, for His teachings deal with moral law and spiritual realities. Natural science deals with physical laws and material results. When men are offered their choice between science, with its confident and unanimous acceptance of the evolutionary principle on the one hand, and religion, with its necessary appeal to things unseen and unproven on the other, they are more likely to abandon religion than to abandon science. If such a choice is forced upon us the churches will lose many of their best educated young people, the very ones upon whom they must depend for leadership in the coming years.

"Fortunately such a choice is absolutely unnecessary. To say that one must choose between evolution and Christianity is exactly like telling the child as he starts for school that he must choose between spelling and arithmetic. Thorough knowledge of each is essential to success — both individual and racial — in life.

"Good religion is founded on facts, even as the evolutionary principle. A true religion faces the facts fearlessly, regardless of where or how the facts may be found. The theories of evolution commonly accepted in the scientific world do not deny any reasonable interpretations of the story of Divine creation as recorded in the Bible. Rather they affirm that story and give it larger and more profound meaning.

"This, of course, depends upon what the meaning and interpretation of the stories are to each individual. I have been a Bible student all of my life, and ever since my college days I have been intensely interested in the relations between science and the Bible.

"It is obvious to any careful and intelligent reader of the Book of Genesis that some interpretation of its account must be made by each individual. Very evidently, it is not intended to be a scientific statement of the order and method of creation.

"In the first chapter of Genesis we are told that man was made after the plants and the other animals had been formed, and that man and woman were both created on the same day.

"In the second chapter of Genesis we read that man was formed from the dust of the ground before plants and other animals were made; that trees grew until fruit was upon them; that all the animals passed in review before man to be named, and then, after these events, woman was made.

"There is obvious lack of harmony between these two Biblical accounts of creation so far as details of process and order of events are concerned. They are, however, in perfect accord in presenting the spiritual truth that God is the author and the administrator of the universe, and that is the sort of truth we find in the Bible.

"It is a textbook of religion, not a textbook of biology or astronomy or geology. Moreover, it is just exactly the Biblical spiritual truth concerning God which rings clearly and unmistakably through every theory of theistic evolution. With it, modern science is in perfect accord.

"There are a number of reasons why sincere and honest Christians have recently come to distrust evolution. . . . Too many people who loudly proclaim their allegiance to the Book, know very little about what it really contains.

"The Bible does not state that the world was made about 6,000 years ago. The date 4004 B.C., set opposite Genesis 1:1 in many versions of the Bible, was placed there by Archbishop Ussher only a few centuries ago. It is a man's interpretation of the Bible; it is in the footnotes added recently; it is not a part of the book itself.

"Concerning the length of earth history and of human history, the Bible is absolutely silent. Science may conclude that the earth is 100,000,000 or 100,000,000,000 years old; the conclusion does not affect the Bible in the slightest degree. Or, if one is worried over the progressive appearance of land, plants, animals, and man on the successive six days of a 'Creation Week,' there is a well-known Biblical support for the scientists' contention that eons rather than hours elapsed while these things were taking place.

"'A day in the sight of the Lord is as a thousand years, and a thousand years as a day.'

"Taking the Bible itself as an authority dissipates many of the difficulties which threaten to make a gulf between religion and science."

4.
Bryan

"Let us, then, hear the conclusion of the whole matter. Science is a magnificent material force, but it is not a teacher of morals. It can perfect machinery, but it adds no moral restraints to protect society from the misuse of the machine. It can also build gigantic intellectual ships, but it constructs no moral rudders for the control of storm-tossed human vessels. It not only fails to supply the spiritual element needed, but some of its unproven hypotheses rob the ship of its compass and thus endanger its cargo.

"In war, science has proven itself an evil genius; it has made war more terrible than it ever was before. Man used to be content to slaughter his fellowmen on a single plane — the earth's surface. Science has taught him to go down into the water and shoot up from below, and to go up into the clouds and shoot down from above, thus making the battlefield three times as bloody as it was before; but science does not teach brotherly love.

"Science has made war so hellish that civilization was about to commit suicide; and now we are told that newly discovered instruments of destruction will make the cruelties of the late war seem trivial in comparison with the cruelties of wars that may come in the future.

"If civilization is to be saved from the wreckage threatened by intelligence not consecrated by love, it must be saved by the moral code of the meek and lowly Nazarene. His teachings, and His teachings alone can solve the problems that vex the heart and perplex the world.

"The world needs a saviour more than it ever did before, and there is only one name under heaven given among men whereby we must be saved. It is this name that evolution degrades, for, carried to its logical conclusion, it robs Christ of the glory of a Virgin birth, of the majesty of His deity and mission, and of the triumph of His resurrection. It also disputes the doctrine of the atonement.

"This case is no longer local; the defendant ceases to play an important part. The case has assumed the proportions of a battle royal between unbelief that attempts to speak through so-called science and the defenders of the Christian faith, speaking through the legislators of Tennessee.

"It is again a choice between God and Baal, it is also a renewal of the issue in Pilate's court.

"In that historic trial — the greatest in history — force, impersonated by Pilate, occupied the throne. Behind it was the Roman Government, mistress of the world, and behind the Roman Government were the legions of Rome. Before Pilate stood Christ, the Apostle of love. Force triumphed; they nailed him to the tree and those who stood around mocked and jeered and said, 'He is dead.' But from that day the power of Caesar waned and the power of Christ in-

Mr. and Mrs. William Jennings Bryan, two decades before the Scopes trial
(Keystone-Mast Collection, University of California, Riverside)

creased. In a few centuries the Roman Government was gone and its legions forgotten; while the crucified and risen Lord has become the greatest fact in history and the growing figure of all time.

"Again force and love meet face to face, and the question, 'What shall I do with Jesus,' must be answered. A bloody, brutal doctrine — evolution — demands, as the rabble did 1900 years ago, that He be crucified. That cannot be the answer of this jury, representing a Christian State and sworn to uphold the laws of Tennessee.

"Your answer will be heard throughout the world; it is eagerly awaited by a praying multitude. If the law is nullified, there will be rejoicing wherever God is repudiated, the Saviour scoffed at, and the Bible ridiculed. Every unbeliever of every kind and degree will be happy.

"If, on the other hand, the law is upheld[5] and the religion of the school children protected, millions of Christians will call you blessed and, with hearts full of gratitude to God, will sing again that grand old song of triumph:

> *Faith of our Fathers, living still,*
>   *In spite of dungeon, fire and sword;*
> *O, how our hearts beat high with joy,*
>   *Whene'er we hear that glorious word!*
> *Faith of our fathers — holy faith;*
> *We will be true to thee till death!*

---

5. Scopes was found guilty and fined $100; the conviction, however, was overturned on a technicality by the Tennessee Supreme Court.

3. Studying and Reading the Bible

Text and Context

"Bibles within the Bible"

In the sixteenth-century Reformation, Protestants had discounted tradition in order to magnify scripture. Scripture was the only foundation of faith and practice; scripture was sufficient in and of itself — sola scriptura. But in the nineteenth century that single and firm foundation began to weaken, or at least came to be looked at in a different way. Private universities such as Harvard and Yale, not under strict denominational control by this time, took the lead in both textual and "higher" criticism. Harvard's Ezra Abbot (1819-94), for example, in his capacity as professor of New Testament criticism forged ahead in textual analysis, with the American Revised Version of the Bible (1901) standing as his monument. Yale's Benjamin W. Bacon (1860-1932) moved a generation later from efforts to arrive at the best text to those "higher" questions of authorship, editing, revision, and layers of development and understanding within any given text. In the document below, Bacon explores the several sources that lie behind or within the book of Genesis, thereby — as his title page says — "illustrating the presence of Bibles within the Bible."

The attention of the reading public of America has been called frequently of late to the claims of the science of Higher Criticism, a study all-important to a correct understanding of the Scriptures; and in particular to that theory of the

---

[Source: B. W. Bacon, *The Genesis of Genesis* (Hartford: Student Publishing Co., 1893), pp. vii-viii, ix-x, xii-xiii.]

science which maintains the origin of the Pentateuch from a compilation of older documents. They have been assured of the practically unanimous acceptance of this theory abroad, and have been themselves witnesses of the divided opinions of scholars at home. Considering the importance of the subject, the enormous mass of accumulated evidence pro and con, the conflicting claims of scholars as to the resulting benefit or injury to accrue to Christian faith from the acceptance of the theory, it should be apparent to all, as a primary axiom, that the reading public are entitled to judge for themselves.

As to the method of presenting the facts to the public, two propositions are easily established.

I. The public require, not controversial argument, but explanation.

The method of the controversialist, which ever side be championed, rarely gains more than a partisan applause guaranteed in advance, and the converts to be made among those "convinced against their will." It assumes that the public has already made up its mind, or else to judge for the public. The assumption is either false or impertinent. A public accustomed to exercise the right of private judgment demands, in the case of so important and widely supported a theory, a plain statement of the case, an explanation of the general principles involved, of the nature, rather than the details, of the argument, and as simple a presentation of methods and results as possible. It wants "the documents in the case."

II. It is not necessary that the presentation of the case should be made from a standpoint of hostility to the new theory, nor even from one of indifference.

The public wishes to do justice to the new theory. Until it has had opportunity to obtain a general conspectus thereof it occupies the standpoint of traditional opinion. It has not time to give to the minutiae of controversial discussion, but desires to be informed in general outline of the method pursued by the critics and the results propounded. Such an explanation can only be given by one familiar with the critical argument and at least in some degree in sympathy with the theory. The position of such an expositor differs however from that of the advocate and special pleader, in that he undertakes to explain and not to argue. He does not pretend to have no opinion, but refrains from obtruding his opinion upon the reader, preferring to state the most general facts and grounds of critical procedure in an unbiassed way, and leave the reader to draw his own conclusions.

In accordance with the general proposition first laid down, the present work is addressed not merely to scholars and technical investigators, but to the general public. The author believes that critics and biblical scholars will find contributions of value to the science of documentary analysis within its pages; but argument in support of these original investigations has been relegated to technical reviews, and even notes which require the use of Hebrew text have been inserted in a special appendix. . . .

In recent years, thanks largely to the efforts of Profs. W. R. Harper of Chicago and C. A. Briggs of Union Seminary, the claims of Semitic literature to a position in the curriculum of study for every person of liberal education are coming to be felt. The literary and scientific study of the development of the Hebrew and Hellenistic religious consciousness as exhibited in their literature — the Bible — is beginning to be recognized as something not to be left merely to the pulpit orator and the Sunday-school teacher, but to be eagerly welcomed into the domain of school, college and university training. With the recognition has come a perception of the transcendent interest of these studies and a growing demand from beyond the academic walls for admission to at least a gleaner's share in these new fields of scientific investigation.

The author desires to meet this demand, and to present to all classes of Bible students, in churches, Sunday-schools, academies and other institutions of learning, as well as to the general public, that which might be expected to be gained from a course of lectures on the Documentary Theory of the Pentateuch, if delivered on one of the recently endowed university foundations for instruction in Biblical Literature. . . . To the reader who may approach these pages in the endeavor to find a deeper, clearer meaning in the ancient book than hitherto, he would express the sincere and sanguine hope that new light upon the unknown history of this long revered and cherished literature may prove it ever more and more clearly a "word of God," fragments providentially preserved of religious thought from that people whose history is the history of the development of the religious consciousness. If "given unto the fathers in the prophets by divers portions and in divers manners," it was no less "given of God," because the gift extended over many centuries, "line upon line and precept upon precept." It is no less divine if the fruit of generations of consecrated human hearts and consciences, rather than the utterance of a single individual.

What is true of the individual investigator is in a still higher degree true of any science, the science of criticism included. "We can do nothing against the truth, but for the truth." If reassurance is needed in regard to the effect of presenting to the public these claims of the higher criticism, I prefer to give it in the words of others rather than my own. Says Prof. Briggs of Union Seminary: "The higher criticism has rent the crust with which rabbinical tradition and Christian scholasticism have encased the Old Testament, overlaying the poetic and prophetic elements with the legal and the ritual. Younger biblical scholars have caught glimpses of the beauty and glory of biblical literature. The Old Testament is studied as never before in the Christian Church. It is beginning to exert its charming influence upon ministers and people. Christian theology and Christian life will be ere long enriched by it. God's blessing is in it to those who have the Christian wisdom to recognize, and the grace to receive and employ it."

In the firm confidence that a general acquaintance with the discoveries claimed to have been made by the higher criticism in the Pentateuch can only conduce to the lasting benefit of His cause, who said, "Thy word is Truth," this volume is respectfully submitted to the Christian public.

Benjamin Wisner Bacon.

Parsonage, Oswego, N. Y., October, 1891.

Origins of the New Testament

Not only did scholars raise questions about the specific books in the Bible, they also asked why these books and not others were designated as "sacred." What was the process by which the New Testament, for example, came to consist of twenty-seven particular writings from the first century or so of Christian history? Did other Christian writings exist at that time? Who made the decision about this collection, and when, and by what criteria? Edward C. Moore (1857-1943), Harvard professor of theology, wrote in 1904 of this "evolution of a simple literature into an authoritative Canon." And like Bacon, Moore hoped to communicate his views to a wider public. We simply carry on the spirit of the Reformation, Moore explained, being true to its passion for truth and understanding as we trace the gradual development evident in all things.

We have spoken thus far in these lectures of the origin and growth of that collection of the literature of early Christianity which we know under the name of the New Testament. We need now to stand apart a little from this movement, to set it in what appears to be its true light. The remarkable development which we have endeavored to trace, the evolution of a simple literature into an authoritative Canon, is then first really understood when it is seen in the light of parallel developments which took place in the same age. It has been said that all the great intellectual and spiritual phenomena of a given era may safely be assumed to be but the manifestations of a common impulse, which pervades and possesses the minds of the men of that era. But there are two main comparisons which in this and in the following lecture we shall need to institute. We shall discern that that movement with which we have thus far been dealing is only a part of a far greater movement. Not less illuminating than the discovery that the New Testament has a history such as that which we have tried to sketch, is the recognition that even that history is but the evidence of tendencies and the product of causes which had at least two other issues that are hardly less won-

---

[Source: E. C. Moore, *The New Testament in the Christian Church* (New York: Macmillan Co., 1904), pp. 213-14, 215-18.]

derful than the one which we have named. Nothing in the life of the race is isolated, just as nothing in our own personal experience stands apart and out of relation to all other things. . . .

We cannot heartily adhere to the historic evolution of Scripture, without holding to the evolution of church government, and of doctrine and ritual as well. Or, rather, inasmuch as we, in common with most men since the Reformation, do hold to the evolution of church government, from the simplest and most natural beginnings in the time of the Apostles to the great structure and colossal organization which in the Middle Ages overshadowed all the world; and since, if we ever thought of it, we do hold to the growth of the great historic forms of worship, we cannot therefore consistently do otherwise than hold to the historic development of Scripture and of dogma as well. We do but bring to bear to-day upon the Scripture the same criticism which the Reformers employed so justly and effectively upon the tradition of the church four hundred years ago. We do but vindicate ourselves the children of their spirit. And surely a far nobler and more vital conception of the church has come through the criticism which in the Reformation was applied to the traditional theory of the church.

This is true as to dogma. The confessions, whatever be their names, to which men give their assent, have tended to become to the Protestant church exactly what the tradition is to the Roman church. It has been made in the Protestant polemic a standing reproach to the Roman Catholic church that it rests upon the Scripture and upon the tradition. It has been deemed the fame of the Protestant churches that they rest upon the Scripture alone. But this contention can scarcely be maintained. In the name of creeds and confessions, from the Apostles' Creed down to the confessions of our own time, the attempt has been made to fix an authoritative interpretation of Scripture, and to praise or to blame men as they accord or disagree with that interpretation. But assuredly this is only traditionalism over again. Indeed, one may say that the Roman tradition has this advantage, that it receives its utterance, in the concrete case, from living men. Confessionalism tends to confer the power of the authoritative interpretation of Scripture only upon men who are dead. We have passed through a period of abuse of doctrine, and of the assumption upon the part of some that we can get on without doctrine. But this is merely reaction against an unhistoric notion of the nature of doctrine. Doctrine is nothing but the adjustment of men's thoughts concerning religion to their thoughts concerning all other things. That adjustment is a perennially necessary task. The attempt to hold our thoughts concerning religion out of all relation to our other thoughts is the sure road by which men, according to temperament, arrive at one of two conditions. They end either in having thoughts without any religion or else in having religion without thoughts. Either condition is deplorable. These are signs that we are on the eve of a noble reconstruction of Christian doctrine.

That reconstruction is made possible by the clear historic sense which we have gained as to what doctrine is.

So is it also as to Scripture. It was not unnatural that the men of four hundred years ago should set up against the authority of an infallible church an authority of Scripture which they soon came to apprehend in an almost equally external way. Those men could not have done differently. Their theory of Scripture had a certain historic inevitableness and a great historic right. But they did not perceive that the light of history, and that right reasoning upon history which they so successfully applied to the prevailing theory of the authority of the church, would one day have its way with the idea of an external authority of Scripture as well. It ought to be repeated, to the honor of the first generation of the Reformers, that they began thus to reason upon the problem. There is something pathetic in the defection of the later generations of Protestants from this true example of the Reformers. The authority of Scripture, when thought of as something external and not subject to rational review, has come near to being as great a tyranny and source of darkness as was ever the authority of the church. But, as we have seen, the most vital and potent conception of Scripture has been regained for us, the most reverent and worshipful acknowledgment of the authority of Scripture has been again made possible for us, exactly through the historic sense of what the Christian Scripture really is.

"A Jewish Interpretation"

Within Judaism, and especially within the Reform branch, scholars also wrestled with the implications of both the lower (textual) and higher (contextual) criticism. At Hebrew Union College in Cincinnati, the intellectual stronghold of Reform, Julian Morgenstern (1881-1976), professor of Bible and Semitic languages — and later the college's president, presented "a Jewish interpretation" of the Book of Genesis. The scholarship for Hebrew scriptures as well as for the New Testament had been largely if not exclusively a Gentile enterprise. Morgenstern argued that the Pentateuch, the first Five Books of Moses, could "be correctly understood only when interpreted from a positive Jewish standpoint." This perspective Morgenstern endeavored to provide as early as 1919 in his own commentary on the Book of Genesis. The excerpt below is taken from the preface to the second edition of this book "designed primarily for use by Jewish religious school teachers."

[Source: Julian Morgenstern, *The Book of Genesis: A Jewish Interpretation*, rev. ed. (New York: Schocken Books, 1965 [1919]), pp. 7-9.]

The book aims to be precisely what its title indicates, a Jewish interpretation of Genesis. We have had countless books on Genesis by Jewish authors. But, with rare exceptions, they have sought only to recount the stories of Genesis literally, without penetrating adequately to the fundamental Jewish spiritual truth beneath, and without consideration of the many significant discoveries and teachings of modern Biblical science with regard to Genesis. They have confounded Biblical myths, legends and traditions with what they have mistakenly called Biblical history. Thereby they have, on the one hand, only too frequently worked mischievous confusion and misunderstanding in the minds of those whom they sought to instruct, and, on the other hand, they have missed almost entirely the golden opportunity to impart the really basic truths of Judaism to the most receptive minds.

We have also had numerous scientific interpretations of Genesis, almost all by non-Jewish scholars. Their work has been almost entirely analytic in character. They have picked Genesis, and the entire Old Testament in fact, to pieces. They have resolved it into its component sources, and have determined with quite reliable accuracy when and under what conditions these were written. They have also determined when, how and by whom these originally independent sources were gradually combined, until at last our present Old Testament came into being.

But singularly enough, they have failed in considerable measure to determine the ends for which these sources were combined and the thoughts and aims which animated the editors. They have, apparently, tacitly assumed that this was an inevitable and largely incidental and purposeless process. Therefore they have failed to realize and to stress that the Old Testament, and particularly the Torah, the Five Books of Moses, is entirely a Jewish work, written by Jewish authors and edited by Jewish thinkers, the product of Jewish religious genius and a unit of Jewish religious thought and doctrine, and that it must be animated throughout by some deeply Jewish purpose, and can, in the final analysis, be correctly understood only when interpreted from a positive Jewish standpoint. Consequently, while science has taught us much about the Old Testament, new, unsuspected, and significant truths, it has failed almost entirely to catch its real Jewish purpose, spirit and flavor. For this reason the usual scientific, analytic interpretation of the Old Testament is inadequate and fails to achieve its ultimate and positive potentials.

The present work aims to be a popular scientific interpretation of Genesis, but an interpretation which is not merely analytic, and therefore largely negative and destructive, but which is also, and more pronouncedly, synthetic, constructive and Jewish. It accepts the established and irrefutable teachings of science with regard to Genesis, and seeks constantly to determine what is the fundamental Jewish thought and teaching of the various stories and groups of stories, for the sake of which their Jewish authors and editors cast them into their present form. It operates on the principle that the Old Testament is a Jewish work throughout, and that it can be understood correctly and authoritatively only when interpreted from the standpoint of its Jewish teachings. It proceeds with deep love and reverence for Judaism and its teachings and practices and for Jewish tradition and history. But it is animated by equal love and reverence for the future of Judaism and for the evolution and expansion which its beliefs and teachings must inevitably undergo in the constant and steady progress of human thought and knowledge and in the irresistible compulsion to adapt and apply these teachings and principles to the needs and standards of modern existence, in order that Judaism may continue to be, what it has always been, a true religion of life, by which men may not only die resignedly but, even more, may live nobly, bravely and usefully.

In this spirit and for this purpose and with this eager hope this book is offered once again, in this second edition, to the public, to a new, a larger and, religiously, a broader and more composite public. May this hope be richly fulfilled.

"The New Approach"

Introduced above (p. 128), Harry Emerson Fosdick — unlike Bacon, Moore, or Morgenstern — was not primarily a biblical scholar or student of the early church. He was a pastor and preacher caught up in the turmoil of modern philosophy, science, and biblical criticism. But Fosdick did resemble the three men named above in his desire to communicate the results of modern speculations and investigations to a broader public, to let Americans at large know what was going on and to assist them in their accommodation to or assimilation of all this new knowledge. And in this role, Fosdick was enormously successful, his Modern Use of the Bible *(1924) being often reprinted and widely read.*

The results of the modern study of Scripture can be grouped under two heads, and to one of these we now turn our attention. For the first time in the history of the church, we of this generation are able to arrange the writings of the Bible in approximately chronological order. That statement, like other summaries of human knowledge such as that the earth is round, can be swiftly and simply made, but its involved meanings reach far and deep. The total consequence of all the work of the Higher Criticism is that at last we are able to see the Bible a

---

[Source: H. E. Fosdick, *The Modern Use of the Bible* (New York: Association Press, 1926), pp. 6-8, 11-12, 28-31.]

good deal as a geologist sees the strata of the earth; we can tell when and in what order the deposits were laid down whose accumulated results constitute our Scriptures. Was there ever such an unfortunate label put upon an entirely legitimate procedure as the name "Higher Criticism"? Were one to search the dictionary for two words suggestive of superciliousness, condescension, and destructiveness, one could hardly find any to surpass these. Yet the Higher Criticism simply asks about the books of the Bible: who wrote them, when and why they were written, and to whom. Every efficient Sunday School teacher, according to his own ability, has always been a Higher Critic. This process, however, armed with our modern instruments of literary, historical, and archeological research, pushed with unremitting zeal and tireless labor, after following many false trails and landing in many cul-de-sacs, has gotten a result, at least in its outlines, well assured. . . .

From the purely scientific point of view this is an absorbingly interesting matter, but even more from the standpoint of practical results its importance is difficult to exaggerate. It means that we can trace the great ideas of Scripture in their development from their simple and elementary forms, when they first appear in the earliest writings, until they come to their full maturity in the latest books. Indeed, the general soundness of the critical results is tested by this fact that as one moves up from the earlier writings toward the later he can observe the development of any idea he chooses to select, such as God, man, duty, sin, worship. Plainly we are dealing with ideas that enlarge their scope, deepen their meaning, are played upon by changing circumstance and maturing thought, so that from its lowliest beginning in the earliest writings of the Hebrews any religious or ethical idea of the Bible can now be traced, traveling an often uneven but ascending roadway to its climax in the teaching of Jesus.

That this involves a new approach to the Bible is plain. To be sure, our fathers were not blind to the fact that the New Testament overtops, fulfils, and in part supersedes the Old. They had the Sermon on the Mount and the opening verses of the Epistle to the Hebrews to assure them of that. But our fathers never possessed such concrete and detailed illustration of that idea as we have now. . . .

Fortunately for us, spiritual efficiency in the use of the Bible is not entirely dependent upon correctness of exegesis. These older interpreters who used the Book in ways now impossible for us did not on that account fail to find there the sustenance and inspiration which we may miss if we trust too much to our keener instruments and too little to spiritual insight. Just as men raised life-sustaining crops from the earth's soil long before they analyzed the earth's strata, so they got from Scripture the bread of life even if the chronological arrangement of the documents was yet undreamed. Nevertheless, it is of obvious importance that a new approach to the Bible has been forced upon us. No longer can we think of the Book as on a level, no longer read its maturer messages back into its earlier sources. We know now that every idea in the Bible started from primitive and childlike origins and, with however many setbacks and delays, grew in scope and height toward the culmination in Christ's Gospel. We know now that the Bible is the record of an amazing spiritual development. . . .

This leads us to our final statement about the consequences of the new approach to the Bible. It restores to us the whole Book. It gives to us a comprehensive, inclusive view of the Scriptures and enables us to see them, not piece-

E. J. Pace cartoon, 1920s
(Billy Graham Center)

meal, but as a whole. Those of us who accept the modern knowledge of the Bible as assured and endeavor to put it to good use are continually being accused of tearing the Book to pieces, of cutting out this or that, and of leaving a mere tattered patchwork of what was once a glorious unity. The fact is precisely the opposite. The new approach to the Bible once more integrates the Scriptures, saves us from our piecemeal treatment of them, and restores to us the whole book seen as a unified development from early and simple beginnings to a great conclusion.

One who has mastered the new approach is at home in any part of the Bible and can use all of it. He opens its pages at any point and knows where he is. He knows the road by which the thought that he finds there has traveled. He knows the contribution that there is being made to the enlarging revelation. He knows where next the road will turn and climb, and he knows where it all comes out in the Gospel. Once more, in a new way, he has regained what once our fathers had and what recently the church has lost: ability to see the Bible in its entirety and to use it as a whole.

For no part of it is without its usefulness. People to-day are living in all the stages of development which its records represent. Its earliest, crudest sins and shames, views of God, and ideals of man are all among us. As one travels through the Book there is no place on the road where one does not meet some problems which modern folk are facing, some points of view which they ought to get or ought to outgrow, some faiths which they ought to achieve or ought to improve upon. So long as a man knows the whole road and judges every step of it by the spirit of Christ, who is its climax, he can use it all.

This is the finest consequence of the new approach to the Bible: it gives us the whole Book back again.

If some one protests that it spoils the idea of inspiration, I ask why. We used to think that God created the world by fiat on the instant, and then, learning that the world evolves, many were tempted to cry out that God did not create it at all. We now know that changing one's idea of a process does not in itself alter one's philosophy of origins. So we used to think of inspiration as a procedure which produced a book guaranteed in all its parts against error, and containing from beginning to end a unanimous system of truth. No well-instructed mind, I think, can hold that now. Our idea of the nature of the process has changed. What has actually happened is the production of a Book which from lowly beginnings to great conclusions records the development of truth about God and his will, beyond all comparison the richest in spiritual issue that the world has known. Personally, I think that the Spirit of God was behind that process and in it. I do not believe that man ever found God when God was not seeking to be found. The under side of the process is man's discovery; the upper side is God's revelation. Our ideas of the method of inspiration have changed; verbal dictation, inerrant manuscripts, uniformity of doctrine between 1000 B.C. and 70 A.D. — all such ideas have become incredible in the face of the facts. But one who earnestly believes in the divine Spirit will be led by the new approach to the Bible to repeat with freshened meaning and deepened content the opening words of the Epistle to the Hebrews:

> "God, having of old time spoken unto the fathers in the prophets by divers portions and in divers manners, hath at the end of these days spoken unto us in his Son."

Reactions and Results

Protestant Trials

So much to adjust to, and it came so fast. Denominational officers and institutions confronted controversy that would not go away and could not be quietly contained. (1) An early trial of the spirit — not a formal proceeding — involved Crawford Howell Toy (1836-1919) when he was on the faculty of Southern Baptist Seminary, recently moved to Louisville, Kentucky. Having studied abroad in Berlin, Toy had absorbed the latest techniques and conclusions of biblical scholarship. When he returned to the seminary in 1869, his introduction of some of this into the classroom (though "some things I have not thought expedient to state in my classes") led to growing uneasiness in a financially insecure institution. After much uneasiness on both sides, Toy wrote the letter below much more in sorrow than in anger. He taught thereafter at Harvard for nearly thirty years. (2) A trial in the fullest sense was the lot of Charles A. Briggs (1841-1912; mentioned by B. W. Bacon above). Associated with Union Theological Seminary in New York City for virtually all of his adult life, this leading Old Testament scholar was tried before the Presbyterians' judicial body in New York. He was charged with many deviations from orthodoxy, among them his questioning of the "inerrancy of Holy Scripture." A portion of Briggs's defense on this point is given below. Adjudged guilty, Briggs was suspended from the Presbyterian ministry, casting his lot in 1899 with the Episcopalians. His association with Union, however, continued uninterrupted until the end of his life.

[Sources: (1) George Shriver, ed., *American Religious Heretics* (Nashville: Abingdon Press, 1966), pp. 79-81, 82-84. (2) C. A. Briggs, *The Defence of Professor Briggs before the Presbytery of New York* (New York: Charles Scribner's Sons, 1893), pp. 84-85, 88-90.]

1.

To the Board of Trustees of the Southern Baptist Theological Seminary.

Dear Brethren: — It having lately become apparent to me that my views of Inspiration differ considerably from those of the body of my brethren, I ask leave to lay my opinions on that subject before you, and submit them to your judgment.

At the outset I may say that I fully accept the first article of the Fundamental Principles of the Seminary, "the Scriptures of the Old and New Testament were given by inspiration of God, and are the only sufficient, certain and authoritative rule of all saving knowledge and obedience," and that I have always taught and do now teach in accordance with, and not contrary to it.

It is in the details of the subject that my divergence from the prevailing views in the denomination occurs. This divergence has gradually increased in connection with my studies, from year to year, till it has become perceptible to myself and others.

In looking for light on Inspiration, my resort has been, and is, to the Scriptures themselves alone, and I rest myself wholly on their testimony. It seems to me that while they declare the fact of Divine Inspiration, they say nothing of the manner of its action. We are told that men spake from God, borne along by the Holy Ghost, and that all Scripture is given by Inspiration of God, and is profitable for doctrine, for reproof, for correction, for instruction in righteousness, that the man of God may be complete, thoroughly furnished for every good work. The object of the Scriptures is here said to be an ethical, spiritual one. They were given man for his guidance and edification in religion, as our Lord also says: "Sanctify them in the truth; Thy word is truth."

As nothing is said of the mode of operation of the Divine Spirit, of the manner in which the divine saving truth is impressed on the mind, of the relation of the divine influence to the ordinary workings of the human intellect, we must, as to these points, consult the books of the Bible themselves and examine the facts. Against facts, no theory can stand, and I prefer, therefore, to have no theory, but submit myself to the guidance of the actual words of Holy Scripture.

As the result of my examination, I believe that the Bible is wholly divine and wholly human; the Scripture is the truth of God communicated by Him to the human soul, appropriated by it and then given out with free, human energy, as the sincere, real conviction of the soul. To undertake to say what must be the outward forms of God's revelation of himself to man, seems to me presumptuous. If rationalism be the decision of religious questions by human reason, then it appears to me to be rationalistic to say that a Divine revelation must conform to certain outward conditions; to insist, for example, that it must be written in a certain style, or that it *must* teach certain things in geography, or astronomy, or similar matters.

I hold all *a priori* reasoning here to be out of place, and all theories based on it to be worthless. Such procedure seems to me to be out of keeping with the simple, reverent spirit appropriate to him who comes to search into the truth of God. For this reason I am forced to discard the theories of some pious men as Fichte and Wordsworth, who have proceeded in this *a priori* way, and to keep myself to the facts given in the Bible itself.

These facts make on me the impression that the Scripture writers are men who have received messages from God and utter them under purely free, human conditions. The inspired man speaks his own language, not another man's, and writes under the conditions of his own age, not under those of some other age. His personality, his individuality, has the freest play, all under the control of the guiding Divine Spirit. . . .

In one word, I regard the Old Testament as the record of the whole circle of the experiences of Israel, the people whom God chose to be the depository of His truth, all whose life He so guided as to bring out of it lessons of instruction which He then caused to be written down for preservation. The nation lived out its life in a free, human way, yet under divine guidance, and its Prophets, Priests and Psalmist recorded the spiritual, religious history under the condition of their times. The divine truth is presented in a framework of relatively unessential things, as Christ in his Parables introduced accessories merely for the purpose of bringing out a principle, so that the Parable of the Ten Virgins, for example, may properly be said to be the framework or vehicle of religious truth. As a whole the Parable may in a sense be called a religious teaching, but speaking more precisely we should say that a part of it is such teaching, or that the teaching is contained in it.

What I have said of the outward form of the Old Testament applies, as I think, to the outward form of the New Testament. I will not lightly see a historical or other inaccuracy in the Gospels or the Acts, but if I find such, they do not for me affect the divine teachings of these books. The centre of the New Testament is Christ himself, salvation is in Him, and a historical error cannot affect the fact of His existence and His teachings. The Apostles wrote out of their personal convictions of the reality of the truth of Christ. If Paul makes a slip of memory, . . . that cannot affect his spiritual relation to Christ and to the Father, nor detract from his power as an inspired man. If his numerical statements do not always agree with those of the Old Testament, (as in Gal. iii. 17, compared with Exodus xii. 40), that seems to me a matter of no consequence.

If the New Testament writers sometimes quote the Old Testament in the Greek Version, which does not correctly render the Hebrew, (as in Heb. x:5, quoted from Psa. xl:6.) that does not affect the main thought or the religious teaching. And it may be that in some cases my principles of exegesis lead me to a different interpretation of an Old Testament passage from that which I find given by some New Testament writer, as in Psa. xl:6, above mentioned; this again I look on as an incidental thing, of which the true religious teaching is independent. I should add that in the majority of cases I hold that the New Testament quotations correctly represent the sense of the Old Testament, and there is always a true spiritual feeling controlling them. I think that Peter's discourse, in Acts ii, gives the true spiritual sense of the passage in Joel, and so, many references of Old Testament passages to Christ throughout the New Testament. It ought also to be noticed that the ancient ideas of quotations were different from ours: ancient writers cite in a general way from memory for illustration, and permit themselves without remark such alterations as a modern writer would think it necessary to call attention to. This is to be regarded as a difference of habit arising from a difference of the times. The freeness of quotation in the Scripture writers does not, for example, affect their general honesty and truthfulness, nor their spiritual train of thought, nor their spiritual authority. It is only a human condition of the divine truth they utter. In these men the Spirit of God dwelt, and out of their writings comes a divine power. Recognizing in them a divine element, I cannot reject it because of what seems to me outward or non-spiritual limitation. I do not condition divine action, but accept it in the form in which I find it.

As to criticism (question of date and authorship) and exegesis, these stand by themselves, and have nothing to do with Inspiration. The prophecy in Isa. xl-lxvi. is not less inspired if it be assigned to the period of the Babylonian Exile, and the "Servant of Jehovah" be regarded as referring primarily to Israel. These are questions of interpretation and historical research, in which, as it seems to me, the largest liberty must be allowed. If some of the Psalms should be put in the Maccabean period (B.C. 160), this is no reason for doubting their inspiration; God could as easily act on men in the year B.C. 160 as B.C. 400 or B.C. 700.

It is proper to add that the above statement of my views of Inspiration is the fullest that I have ever expressed. Some things I have not thought it expedient to state to my classes in the Seminary. At the same time I regard these views as helpful for Bible study. If at first they seem strange, I am convinced that they will appear more natural with further strict study of the text.

I beg leave to repeat that I am guided wholly by what seems to me the correct interpretation of the Scriptures themselves. If an error in my interpretation is pointed out, I shall straightway give it up. I cannot accept *a priori* reasoning, but I stake everything on the words of the Bible, and this course I believe to be for the furtherance of the truth of God.

And now, in conclusion, I wish to say distinctly and strongly that I consider the view above given to be not only lawful for me to teach as Professor in the Seminary, but one that will bring aid and firm standing-ground to many a perplexed mind and establish the truth of God on a firm foundation.

But that I may relieve the Board of all embarrassment in the matter, I tender my resignation as Professor in the Southern Baptist Theological Seminary.

Respectfully submitted,
C. H. Toy

May, 1879

2.

"The Presbyterian Church in the United States of America charges the Rev. Charles A. Briggs, D.D., being a Minister of the said Church and a member of the Presbytery of New York, with teaching that errors may have existed in the original text of the Holy Scripture, as it came from its authors, which is contrary to the essential doctrine taught in the Holy Scriptures and in the Standards of the said Church, that the Holy Scripture is the Word of God written, immediately inspired, and the rule of faith and practice." . . .

(1) The Charge alleges three offences. It alleges that the doctrine taught by me is contrary to these three essential doctrines — *(a)* that Holy Scripture is the Word of God written; *(b)* that Holy Scripture is immediately inspired; and *(c)* that Holy Scripture is the rule of faith and practice.

(2) It is alleged that I teach "that errors may have existed in the original text of the Holy Scripture, as it came from its authors." This statement of my doctrine I can admit as fairly accurate. But when we look at the specification, notice that it consists of a long extract from the Inaugural Address. You should bear in mind that the only proper use of this extract is to prove the doctrine attributed to me in the Charge, which doctrine I admit. You have no right to use it to impute to me any other objectionable doctrine. You have no right to vote me guilty on the ground of any other objection to my words than that stated in the Charge. This is all the more important in view of the irrelevant passages of Scripture cited to sustain the Charge, which may be interpreted by you in a sense different from the true sense. You have no right to vote me guilty on the basis of these passages. You can consider nothing but my doctrine as stated in the Charge and determine whether that is contrary or not contrary to the essential doctrines named in the Charge.

(3) The only question which need concern us, therefore, is whether my doctrine is contrary to any one, or any two, or all three of the essential doctrines of the Confession stated in the Charge. Doubtless the prosecution think that there is contradiction here; and it may be that a majority of this Presbytery think so. . . .

I agree to the doctrines (1) that "Holy Scripture is the Word of God written;" (2) "immediately inspired;" and (3) "the rule of faith and practice."

Do these statements necessarily involve the doctrine that there are no errors in Holy Scripture? *(a)* The doctrine that "the Holy Scriptures are the rule of faith and practice" clearly does not involve that "the Holy Scriptures are the rule in matters other than faith and practice." If I find fallibility in Holy Scripture in matters of faith and practice, I am inconsistent with the Confession. But in the Inaugural, I expressly disclaimed such fallibility. . . .

The only errors I have found or ever recognized in Holy Scripture have been beyond the range of faith and practice, and therefore they do not impair the infallibility of Holy Scripture as a rule of faith and practice.

But it is claimed that if I recognize errors in matters beyond the range of faith and practice, I excite suspicion as to the infallibility of Holy Scripture within the range of faith and practice. You are entitled to that opinion for yourselves, but you have no right to force your opinion upon me. The Confession does not say "rule of all things," but "the rule of faith and practice." You must judge by the Confession, not by your fears, or your impressions, or by the conclusions you have made. But is it true that fallibility in the Bible in matters beyond the scope of the divine revelation impairs the infallibility in matters within the scope of divine revelation? We claim that it does not. The sacred writings were not composed in heaven by the Holy Spirit, they were not sent down from heaven by angel hands, they were not committed to the care of perfect men, they were not kept by a succession of perfect priests from that moment until the present time. If these had been the facts in the case, we might have had a Bible infallible in every particular. But none of these things are true. God gave His Holy Word to men in an entirely different way. He used the human reason and all the faculties of imperfect human nature. He used the voice and hands of imperfect men. He allowed the sacred writings to be edited and re-edited, arranged and re-arranged and rearranged again by imperfect scribes. It is improbable that such imperfect instrumentalities should attain perfect results. It was improbable that fallible men should produce a series of writings infallible in every respect. It was sufficient that divine inspiration and the guidance of the Holy Spirit should make their writings an infallible rule of faith and practice, and that the divine energy should push the human and the fallible into the external forms, into the unessential and unnecessary matters, into the human setting of the divine ideals. As the river of life flowing forth from the throne of God, according to Ezekiel's Vision, entering into the Dead Sea quickens its waters and fills them with new life, so that "everything shall live whithersoever the river cometh" "But the miry places thereof and the marshes thereof shall not be healed" (Ez. xlvii. 9-11); so may it be with that divine influence which we call inspiration, when it flows into a man. It quickens and enriches his whole nature, his experience, his utterance, his expressions, with truth and life divine, and yet leaves some human infirmities unhealed in order that the revelation may be essentially divine and infallible and yet bear traces of the human and fallible into the midst of which it came.

Catholic Concerns

Catholic biblical scholarship had not advanced far enough in America by the end of the nineteenth century to alarm the Vatican. But in Europe, Alfred F. Loisy (1857-1940) had aroused much anxiety and calls for caution. In 1893 Pope Leo XIII issued Providentissimus Deus, *a statement designed to discourage the newer critical methods being applied to biblical study. "There has arisen, to the great detriment of religion," the pope wrote, "an inept method, dignified by the name of 'higher criticism,' which pretends to judge the origin, integrity, and authority of each book from internal indications alone." The authority of the Church, mother and teacher, was being by-passed in the name of science. Six years later in an encyclical dealing with "Americanism," the papacy rejected the notion that "the Church ought to adapt herself somewhat to our advanced civilization, and, relaxing her ancient vigor, show some indulgence to modern popular theories and methods." Then in 1907 Pope Pius X in a long letter* (Pascendi Dominici Gregis) *condemned the Modernists without equivocation, the Church having already earlier that year listed some sixty-five "Errors of the Modernists." Many of those "errors," as is evident below, pertained to the proper approach to and understanding of "the Sacred Books." (Loisy was excommunicated in 1908.)*

With truly lamentable results, our age, casting aside all restraint in its search for the ultimate causes of things, frequently pursues novelties so ardently that it rejects; the legacy of the human race. Thus it falls into very serious errors, which are even more serious when they concern sacred authority, the interpretation of Sacred Scripture, and the principal mysteries of Faith. The fact that many Catholic writers also go beyond the limits determined by the Fathers and the Church herself is extremely regrettable. In the name of higher knowledge and historical research (they say), they are looking for that progress of dogmas which is, in reality, nothing but the corruption of dogmas.

These errors are being daily spread among the faithful. Lest they captivate the faithful's minds and corrupt the purity of their faith, His Holiness, Pius X, by Divine Providence, Pope, has decided that the chief errors should be noted and condemned by the Office of this Holy Roman and Universal Inquisition.

Therefore, after a very diligent investigation and consultation with the Reverend Consultors, the Most Eminent and Reverend Lord Cardinals, the General Inquisitors in matters of faith and morals have judged the following

---

[Source: *Lamentabili Sane,* July 3, 1907 (Washington: National Catholic Welfare Conference, 1963), pp. 45-47.]

propositions to be condemned and proscribed. In fact, by this general decree, they are condemned and proscribed.

* * *

1. The ecclesiastical law which prescribes that books concerning the Divine Scriptures are subject to previous examination does not apply to critical scholars and students of scientific exegesis of the Old and New Testament.

2. The Church's interpretation of the Sacred Books is by no means to be rejected; nevertheless, it is subject to the more accurate judgment and correction of the exegetes.

3. From the ecclesiastical judgments and censures passed against free and more scientific exegesis, one can conclude that the Faith the Church proposes contradicts history and that Catholic teaching cannot really be reconciled with the true origins of the Christian religion.

4. Even by dogmatic definitions the Church's magisterium cannot determine the genuine sense of the Sacred Scriptures.

5. Since the deposit of Faith contains only revealed truths, the Church has no right to pass judgment on the assertions of the human sciences.

6. The "Church learning" and the "Church teaching" collaborate in such a way in defining truths that it only remains for the "Church teaching" to sanction the opinions of the "Church learning."

7. In proscribing errors, the Church cannot demand any internal assent from the faithful by which the judgments she issues are to be embraced.

8. They are free from all blame who treat lightly the condemnations passed by the Sacred Congregation of the Index or by the Roman Congregations.

9. They display excessive simplicity or ignorance who believe that God is really the author of the Sacred Scriptures.

10. The inspiration of the books of the Old Testament consists in this: The Israelite writers handed down religious doctrines under a peculiar aspect which was either little or not at all known to the Gentiles.

11. Divine inspiration does not extend to all of Sacred Scriptures so that it renders its parts, each and every one, free from every error.

12. If he wishes to apply himself usefully to Biblical studies, the exegete must first put aside all preconceived opinions about the supernatural origin of Sacred Scripture and interpret it the same as any other merely human document.

13. The Evangelists themselves, as well as the Christians of the second and third generation, artificially arranged the evangelical parables. In such a way they explained the scanty fruit of the preaching of Christ among the Jews.

14. In many narrations the Evangelists recorded, not so much things that

are true, as things which, even though false, they judged to be more profitable for their readers.

15. Until the time the canon was defined and constituted, the Gospels were increased by additions and corrections. Therefore there remained in them only a faint and uncertain trace of the doctrine of Christ.

16. The narrations of John are not properly history, but a mystical contemplation of the Gospel. The discourses contained in his Gospel are theological meditations, lacking historical truth concerning the mystery of salvation.

17. The fourth Gospel exaggerated miracles not only in order that the extraordinary might stand out but also in order that it might become more suitable for showing forth the work and glory of the Word Incarnate.

18. John claims for himself the quality of witness concerning Christ. In reality, however, he is only a distinguished witness of the Christian life, or of the life of Christ in the Church at the close of the first century.

19. Heterodox exegetes have expressed the true sense of the Scriptures more faithfully than Catholic exegetes.

Biblical Societies and Studies

In 1880 in the home of Philip Schaff (see Vol. I, pp. 566-68) in New York City, the Society of Biblical Literature came into being, with its own journal appearing two years later. A dozen years after the Society's founding, its president (J. H. Thayer) recommended the establishment of "an American School of Oriental Studies in Palestine," now the American School for Oriental Research. The great energies expended in the new biblical scholarship around this time may be suggested by noting a few titles: Strong, Exhaustive Concordance of the Bible (1894); Smith, Historical Geography of the Holy Land (1894); Cheyne and Black, Encyclopedia Biblica (1899) in four volumes; and Hastings, Dictionary of the Bible (1908) in five volumes. And the list is by no means exhaustive. (1) An ambitious biblical commentary, the International Critical Commentary, also began publication in this period, its earliest volumes appearing in 1895. This work, an Anglo-American effort, was under the general editorship of S. R. Driver of Oxford, Alfred Plummer of Durham, and the aforementioned Charles A. Briggs of Union. The excerpt below is from the preface to Driver's own commentary on the Book of Deuteronomy. (2) The "Catholic concerns" noted above delayed the full par-

---

[Sources: (1) S. R. Driver, *A Critical and Exegetical Commentary on Deuteronomy* (Edinburgh: T. & T. Clark, 1895), pp. xi-xiii. (2) *Divino Afflante Spiritu*, 1943 (Washington: National Catholic Welfare Conference, n. d.), pp. 14-15, 17, 18-19, 22.]

*ticipation of America's Roman Catholic scholars in this renaissance of bibli-
cal study. In 1938, however, the Catholic Biblical Association was founded,
with the* Catholic Biblical Quarterly *emerging the following year. When in
1943 Pope Plus XII issued an encyclical giving his encouragement and blessing to such scholarly undertakings, biblical study in the Catholic community
was placed on solid footing. A portion of that 1943 statement is given below.*

1.

The aim of the present volume (in accordance with the plan of the series, of
which it forms part) is to supply the English reader with a Commentary which,
so far as the writer's powers permit it, may be abreast of the best scholarship and
knowledge of the day. Deuteronomy is one of the most attractive, as it is also one
of the most important, books of the Old Testament; and a Commentary which
may render even approximate justice to its many-sided contents has for long
been a desideratum in English theological literature. Certainly the Hebrew text
(except in parts of c. 32. 33) is not, as a rule, difficult; nevertheless, even this has
frequently afforded me the opportunity of illustrating delicacies of Hebrew usage, which might escape the attention of some readers. On the other hand, the
contents of Deuteronomy call for much explanation and discussion: they raise
many difficult and controverted questions —, and they afford frequent scope for
interesting and sometimes far-reaching inquiry. Deuteronomy stands out conspicuously in the literature of the Old Testament: it has important relations, literary, theological, and historical, with other parts of the Old Testament; it possesses itself a profound moral and spiritual significance; it is an epoch-making
expression of the life and feeling of the prophetic nation. I have done my best to
give due prominence to these and similar characteristic features; and by pointing
out both the spiritual and other factors which Deuteronomy presupposes, and
the spiritual and other influences which either originated with it, or received
from it a fresh impulse, to define the position which it occupies in the national
and religious history of Israel. Deuteronomy, moreover, by many of the observances which it enjoins, bears witness to the fact that Israel's civilization, though
permeated by a different spirit from that of other ancient nations, was nevertheless reared upon the same material basis; and much light may often be thrown,
both upon the institutions and customs to which it alludes, and upon the manner in which they are treated by the Hebrew legislator, from the archaeological
researches of recent years. Nor is this all. The study of Deuteronomy carries the
reader into the very heart of the critical problems which arise in connexion with
the Old Testament. At almost every step, especially in the central, legislative part
(c. 12-26), the question of the relation of Deuteronomy to other parts of the Pentateuch forces itself upon the student's attention. In dealing with the passages

where this is the case, I have stated the facts as clearly and completely as was possible within the limits of space at my disposal, adding, where necessary, references to authorities who treat them at greater length. As a work of the Mosaic age, Deuteronomy, I must own, though intelligible, *if it stood perfectly alone,* — *i.e.* if the history of Israel had been other than it was, — does not seem to me to be intelligible, when viewed in the light shed upon it by other parts of the Old Testament: a study of it in that light reveals too many features which are inconsistent with such a supposition. The entire secret of its composition, and the full nature of the sources of which its author availed himself, we cannot hope to discover; but enough is clear to show that, however regretfully we may abandon it, the traditional view of its origin and authorship cannot be maintained. The adoption of this verdict of criticism implies no detraction either from the inspired authority of Deuteronomy, or from its ethical and religious value. Deuteronomy marks a stage in the Divine education of the chosen people: but the methods of God's spiritual providence are analogous to those of His natural providence: the revelation of Himself to man was accomplished not once for all, but through many diverse channels (Heb. I), and by a gradual historical process; and the stage in that process to which Deuteronomy belongs is not the age of Moses, but a later age. Deuteronomy gathers up the spiritual lessons and experiences not of a single lifetime, but of many generations of God-inspired men. It is a nobly-conceived endeavour to stir the conscience of the individual Israelite, and to infuse Israel's whole national life with new spiritual and moral energy. And in virtue of the wonderful combination of the national with the universal, which characterizes the higher teaching of the Old Testament, it fulfils a yet wider mission: it speaks in accents which all can still understand; it appeals to motives and principles, which can never lose their validity and truth, so long as human nature remains what it is: it is the bearer of a message to all time.

2.

23. Being thoroughly prepared by the knowledge of the ancient languages and by the aids afforded by the art of criticism, let the Catholic exegete undertake the task, of all those imposed on him the greatest, that namely of discovering and expounding the genuine meaning of the Sacred Books. In the performance of this task let the interpreters bear in mind that their foremost and greatest endeavor should be to discern and define clearly that sense of the biblical words which is called literal. Aided by the context and by comparison with similar passages, let them therefore by means of their knowledge of languages search out with all diligence the literal meaning of the words; all these helps indeed are wont to be pressed into service in the explanation also of profane writers, so that the mind of the author may be made abundantly clear.

24. The commentators of the Sacred Letters, mindful of the fact that where there is question of a divinely inspired text, the care and interpretation of which have been confided to the Church by God Himself, should no less diligently take into account the explanations and declarations of the teaching authority of the Church, as likewise the interpretation given by the Holy Fathers, and even "the analogy of faith" as Leo XIII most wisely observed in the Encyclical Letter *Providentissimus Deus*. With special zeal should they apply themselves, not only to expounding exclusively these matters which belong to the historical, archeological, philological and other auxiliary sciences — as, to Our regret, is done in certain commentaries, — but, having duly referred to these, in so far as they may aid the exegesis, they should set forth in particular the theological doctrine in faith and morals of the individual books or texts so that their exposition may not only aid the professors of theology in their explanations and proofs of the dogmas of faith, but may also be of assistance to priests in their presentation of Christian doctrine to the people, and in fine may help all the faithful to lead a life that is holy and worthy of a Christian. . . .

31. Moreover we may rightly and deservedly hope that our times also can contribute something towards the deeper and more accurate interpretation of Sacred Scripture. For not a few things, especially in matters pertaining to history, were scarcely at all or not fully explained by the commentators of past ages, since they lacked almost all the information, which was needed for their clearer exposition. How difficult for the Fathers themselves, and indeed well nigh unintelligible, were certain passages is shown, among other things, by the oft-repeated efforts of many of them to explain the first chapters of Genesis; likewise by the reiterated attempts of St. Jerome so to translate the Psalms that the literal sense, that, namely, which is expressed by the words themselves, might be clearly revealed.

32. There are, in fine, other books or texts, which contain difficulties brought to light only in quite recent times, since a more profound knowledge of antiquity has given rise to new questions, on the basis of which the point at issue may be more appropriately examined. Quite wrongly therefore do some pretend, not rightly understanding the conditions of biblical study, that nothing remains to be added by the Catholic exegete of our time to what Christian antiquity has produced; since, on the contrary, these our times have brought to light so many things, which call for a fresh investigation and a new examination, and which stimulate not a little the practical zeal of the present-day interpreter.

35. What is the literal sense of a passage is not always as obvious in the speeches and writings of the ancient authors of the East, as it is in the works of the writers of our own time. For what they wished to express is not to be determined by the rules of grammar and philology alone, nor solely by the context; the interpreter must, as it were, go back wholly in spirit to those remote centu-

ries of the East and with the aid of history, archaeology, ethnology and other sciences, accurately determine what modes of writing, so to speak, the authors of that ancient period would be likely to use, and in fact did use.

36. For the ancient peoples of the East, in order to express their ideas, did not always employ those forms or kinds of speech, which we use today; but rather those used by the men of their times and countries. What those exactly were the commentator cannot determine as it were in advance, but only after a careful examination of the ancient literature of the East. The investigation, carried out, on this point, during the past forty or fifty years with greater care and diligence than ever before, has more clearly shown what forms of expression were used in those far off times, whether in poetic description or in the formulation of laws and rules of life or in recording the facts and events of history. The same inquiry has also clearly shown the special preeminence of the people of Israel among all the other ancient nations of the East in their mode of compiling history, both by reason of its antiquity and by reason of the faithful record of the events; qualities which may well be attributed to the gift of divine inspiration and to the peculiar religious purpose of biblical history.

37. Nevertheless no one, who has a correct idea of biblical inspiration, will be surprised to find, even in the Sacred Writers, as in other ancient authors, certain fixed ways of expounding and narrating, certain definite idioms, especially of a kind peculiar to the Semitic tongues, so-called approximations, and certain hyperbolical modes of expression, nay, at times, even paradoxical, which help to impress the ideas more deeply on the mind. For of the modes of expression which, among ancient peoples, and especially those of the East, human language used to express its thought, none is excluded from the Sacred Books, provided the way of speaking adopted in no wise contradicts the holiness and truth of God. . . .

46. But this state of things is no reason why the Catholic commentator, inspired by an active and ardent love of his subject and sincerely devoted to Holy Mother Church, should in any way be deterred from grappling again and again with these difficult problems, hitherto unsolved, not only that he may refute the objections of the adversaries, but also may attempt to find a satisfactory solution, which will be in full accord with the doctrine of the Church, in particular with the traditional teaching regarding the inerrancy of Sacred Scripture, and which will at the same time satisfy the indubitable conclusions of profane sciences.

47. Let all the other sons of the Church bear in mind that the efforts of these resolute laborers in the vineyard of the Lord should be judged not only with equity and justice, but also with the greatest charity; all moreover should abhor that intemperate zeal which imagines that whatever is new should for that very reason be opposed or suspected. Let them bear in mind above all that in the rules and laws, promulgated by the Church there is question of doctrine

regarding faith and morals; and that in the immense matter contained in the Sacred Books — legislative, historical, sapiential and prophetical — there are but few texts whose sense has been defined by the authority of the Church, nor are those more numerous about which the teaching of the Holy Fathers is unanimous. There remain therefore many things, and of the greatest importance, in the discussion and exposition of which the skill and genius of Catholic commentators may and ought to be freely exercised, so that each may contribute his part to the advantage of all, to the continued progress of the sacred doctrine and to the defense and honor of the Church.

New Bible Translations

Bible Translations Explained

The King James Version (KJV) of the English Bible, first published in 1611, occupies a unique niche in all of English literature. By common agreement and long usage, it has become the English Bible: "the noblest monument of English prose." By the latter decades of the nineteenth century, however, with the discovery of many ancient manuscripts unknown in 1611 and with a new surge in biblical scholarship, the need for new translations was widely recognized. In 1870, the Church of England authorized such an effort, the result eleven years later being the English Revised Version. An American counterpart, with many different readings, followed in 1901: the American Standard Version (ASV). These newer versions represented scholarly advances over the KJV but did not gain widespread public acceptance. And so the search for reliable, yet readable, translations went on. From the 1920s more and more translations appeared. (1) Edgar J. Goodspeed (1871-1962) of the University of Chicago offers below a good-humored account of what happened when he brought out his own New Testament: An American Translation, *in 1923. But despite increasing interest in such new efforts, it was not until 1952, with the publication of the long-awaited Revised Standard Version (RSV), that a new trans-*

[Sources: (1) E. J. Goodspeed, *As I Remember* (New York: Harper & Brothers, 1953), pp. 155-56, 166-69. (2) W. A. Irwin, in *An Introduction to the Revised Standard Version of the Old Testament* (New York: Thomas Nelson & Sons, 1952), pp. 12-14. (3) "Preface," *Tanakh: A New Translation of the Holy Scriptures According to the Traditional Hebrew Text* (Philadelphia: Jewish Publication Society, 5746/1985), pp. xv, xvii, xviii, xix-xxi. (4) "Preface," *The Holy Bible: New International Version, Inclusive Language Edition* (London: Hodder & Stoughton, 1996), pp. vii-viii.]

lation was accepted by large sections of the American reading public. To be sure, there was also considerable opposition, but some of that opposition was itself eventually poured into the production of still other translations. (2) In the excerpt below, written to help introduce the RSV to a potentially skeptical audience, William A. Irwin (1884-1967), also of the University of Chicago, explained something of the methods of the translators working to produce a Bible for modern readers. After the RSV, the floodgates of new translations were opened wide. One of the most important contributors to that flood was a new version of the Hebrew Scriptures prepared under the auspices of the Jewish Publication Society. (3) At its appearance in 1985, it was again important to point out in a Preface what the new effort was about. In recent years, questions of Bible translation have naturally shared in broader debates about how the English language is now used, especially with respect to gender. Since the early 1990s, many attempts have been made to translate faithfully and yet also to meet what many regard as fundamental alterations in the language. (4) As one example, the last document explains how the translation team of the New International Version (NIV), now the most widely-used modern translation in the English-speaking world, tried to deal with questions of gender. The excerpt comes from the introduction to a version of the NIV that was released in Britain but then withheld in the U.S. because of objections to the treatment of gender outlined here.

1.

Many other men have translated the New Testament into English and published it, but I don't believe any of them has found the experience such an exciting and bewildering romance as I did. And yet I found my way to the task and performed it without the slightest expectation of any such result.

It may seem ungracious to revive a controversy thirty years old, when the international verdict has gone so sweepingly in one's favor, and yet it has such instructive and amusing aspects that one cannot pass it over. For it was in the year 1923 that I performed the horrendous deed of publishing an American translation of the New Testament. This simple act, obscurely done, in my own field of specialization, on the basis of many years of close study, with no expectation of any publicity at all, and quietly published at the University of Chicago Press, called forth from the public press a nationwide, indeed world-wide and vehement protest, though now [1953], when Jews, Catholics, and Protestants, yes and the Jehovah's Witnesses also are engaged upon modern speech translations or revisions of the Old Testament, or the New Testament, or the Old and New Testament and the Apocrypha, hardly an editor dares lift up his voice against these dreadful undertakings. . . .

Stamp celebrating the five hundredth anniversary of the
Gutenberg Bible, coinciding with the publication of
the Revised Standard Version of the Bible in 1952
(Religion News Service)

The *Examiner* had sent out a reporter, Bruce Grant, for an interview and I gave him a long one, talking steadily for nearly two hours. He did not take a note but seemed to be listening closely. I read his interview the next morning with grave apprehensions but it was admirable. He got my points and presented them clearly and fairly in what I believe is called a six-column spread. This was about the way the papers handled the matter, the news columns generally fairly and informedly. The excitement was provided by the editorials. On Thursday I parted with the last section of the final proof, and in the afternoon I was interviewed for an hour by Duncan Clark, for *Success* magazine.

Friday the 24th began early, for at 7:45 the United Press was on the wire. Somehow or other it had become possessed of a galley proof of the eleventh chapter of Luke, with its somewhat abbreviated form of the Lord's Prayer, and the U.P. man, one H. E. Caylor, mistakenly supposing that that was where the Lord's Prayer came from, leaped to the conclusion that I had shortened the Lord's Prayer. Now if there is one thing the English-speaking world will not tolerate, it is shortening the Lord's Prayer, and the U.P. proceeded to make the most of it.

In Philadelphia the *Bulletin* recorded the unanimous disapproval of the clergy. In Boston it so aroused the old Boston *Transcript* that it devoted two editorials to excoriating me for abbreviating the Lord's Prayer, and the long shadow of this altogether groundless accusation reached even to Capetown, South Africa, where further editorial disapproval was evinced. Of course, it is actually from the Sermon on the Mount in Matthew that all churches derive the Lord's Prayer, as well as the Beatitudes and the Golden Rule, of all of which

Luke has variant forms. Certainly the charge made against me can be made just as truly against every serious New Testament translation or revision from Alexander Campbell in 1826 down to the Catholic revision of 1941, the *Revised Standard Version* of 1946, and the Jehovah's Witnesses New Testament of 1951. Not one has transferred Matthew's Lord's Prayer to Luke; that is, as the U.P. puts it, they have all shortened the Lord's Prayer!

The fact was, nothing could have been more mistaken than to say I had tampered with the text. I had taught textual criticism for twenty years, and had the utmost confidence in its results. No translator had been more rigorously faithful to them, to the very last, minutest detail. I had deciphered, collated and published half a dozen Greek manuscripts of the gospels. The United Press was attacking the book on the point on which it was strongest, in fact unassailable, by any truthful means.

That Friday afternoon Underwood sent its photographer around to take my picture, and at 10:30 Friday night the *Tribune* telephoned for my translation of the Beatitudes to print side by side with those of King James next morning. . . .

Monday morning I was awakened from a troubled sleep by a friend calling, "Have you seen the *Tribune*?" It was Ernest Wilkins, afterward President of Oberlin College, who thus introduced me to the *Tribune*'s tribute, entitled "Monkeying with the Bible." The *Tribune* spoke up strongly for the King James version. "Tampering with it," it declared, "is chipping a cathedral." It regarded the King James version as a seamless coat, a perfect version. I was reminded that the King James version, the first issue of the first edition of which I have before me, underwent a lamentable amount of chipping after the appearance of Samuel Johnson's dictionary in 1755, to which of course it had to be conformed. The current forms of it, as we all know, go back without exception to Professor Benjamin Blayney's revision of 1769. These alterations have so far as I know never been counted, but it is safe to say they are not less than eighty thousand, and they may reach a hundred thousand. But as I hastened to inform the *Tribune*, this was all done a hundred years before my birth so that it is unreasonable to hold me responsible for any part of it. Worse, yet, the Apocrypha, the whole transept of the *Tribune*'s noble cathedral, has long since disappeared from the King James version, and the *Tribune* has never missed it!

2.

The present work . . . is primarily a revision. Its official title declares this: it is the Revised Standard Version, that is, a revision of the American Standard Version of 1901, which had its ultimate inception in the official action of the Church of England in 1870 that authorized a revision of the King James Version. Through its entire activity the committee for the Revised Standard Version has been conscious of its role as reviser. The American Standard Version was its basic English text, and from it deviations were permitted only by majority vote, subject to final ratification by a two-thirds vote.

A task of revision entails all the problems and difficulties of translation, and in addition, one that is peculiarly its own: what degree of change from the basic text is permissible? It is a question of peculiar urgency when the revision concerns the Bible, for its very words quickly endear themselves to the devout student, so that any alteration, however slight, can well appear almost a desecration.

But further, any process of translation is in a sense an effort at the impossible. Languages differ; they are projections of the personalities of those for whom the speech learned in childhood is as intimate and personal as their native air. From these, the translators are separated by insuperable psychological barriers. The best that can be hoped is an approximation to the thought of the original, but its finer points, its overtones, its allusions, the feeling and atmosphere of its words lie beyond any process of translation. This is especially true

Catholic University of America professor, Monsignor Patrick Skehan,
studies notes for the New American Bible, 1970
(Baptist Joint Committee on Public Affairs)

when the task is that of rendering classics of an ancient language, such as the Old Testament includes, into a modern tongue of far remote genius and relationships. All speech develops its peculiar expressions that vary from mere slang across a diverse terrain to proverbial sayings at the other end. Colloquialisms soon pass, either into standard speech, or into desuetude as derelicts of a once pulsing reality; then life moves on and forgets their occasion and significance. One who works long and seriously with the Hebrew Old Testament grows steadily more conscious that much of its allusive and delicate meaning has been for ever lost; the words are known — generally — but their significance in particular combinations allures, but evades, the student.

However this may be, the responsibility of the translator is clear. Representing the best extant understanding of the language with which he deals, he is charged to tell as accurately as he can in his own language precisely what the original says. This is of an importance to bear some emphasis. The Bible translator assumes a strict responsibility to say in English just what the Biblical writers said in Hebrew, or in Aramaic, or in Greek, as the case may have been. In response to early publicity about the launching of the Revised Standard project, letters came in to one or another of the committee pointing out their opportunity to deal a blow to certain anti-social views which unfortunately base themselves on this or that Bible passage — the committee should change the offending passage! The only answer that could be given was that the committee did not intend, nor had it any authority, to change the Bible. The purpose was to give a more accurate rendering of what it said, even in these passages. Correction of wrong uses of the Bible, important as this may be, lay entirely outside its responsibility.

Yet this is not all. The danger here is of a subtle sort. A recent speaker has told of a project to issue "a theologically conservative translation of the Bible." Doubtless this is an appealing undertaking in the eyes of many. But the fact must be stressed that there is no place for theology in Bible translation, whether conservative or radical or whatever else. A "theological translation" is not a translation at all, but merely a dogmatic perversion of the Bible. Linguistic science knows no theology; those of most contradictory views can meet on common ground devoid of polemic, agreed that Hebrew words mean such and such, and their inflection and syntactical relations imply this or that. These facts establish an agreed translation. Then, and then only, may the exegete and dogmatist busy himself with theological deductions from the thoughts of the Biblical writers. The Bible translator is not an expositor; however pronounced his views about Biblical doctrines, he has no right whatever to intrude his opinions into the translation, or to permit his dogmatic convictions to qualify or shape its wording. His one responsibility, and it is absolute, is to render the Biblical meaning as accurately and effectively as is possible into appropriate English.

3.

This translation of *Tanakh,* the Holy Scriptures, produced by the Jewish Publication Society, was made directly from the traditional Hebrew text into the idiom of modern English. It represents the collaboration of academic scholars with rabbis from the three largest branches of organized Jewish religious life in America. Begun in 1955, the ongoing translation was published in three main stages: *The Torah* in 1962, *The Prophets (Nevi'im)* in 1978, and *The Writings (Kethuvim)* in 1982. These three volumes, with revisions, are now brought together in a complete English *Tanakh (Torah-Nevi'im-Kethuvim),* the latest link in the chain of Jewish Bible translations. . . .

After World War II, when the Jewish Publication Society began to consider a new edition of the Bible, the idea of a modest revision of the 1917 translation met with resistance, and the concept of a completely new translation gradually took hold. The proposed translation would reproduce the Hebrew idiomatically and reflect contemporary scholarship, thus laying emphasis upon intelligibility and correctness. It would make critical use of the early rabbinic and medieval Jewish commentators, grammarians, and philologians and would rely on the traditional Hebrew text, avoiding emendations. The need for this new translation was the focus of the Jewish Publication Society's annual meeting in 1953. Later that year the Society announced its intention to proceed with the project, and in 1955 the committee of translators began their task. . . .

The committee profited much from the work of previous translators; the present rendering, however, is essentially a new translation. A few of its characteristics may be noted. The committee undertook to follow faithfully the traditional Hebrew text, but there were certain points at which footnotes appeared necessary: (1) where the committee had to admit that it did not understand a word or passage; (2) where an alternative rendering was possible; (3) where an old rendering, no longer retained, was so well known that it would very likely be missed, in which case the traditional translation was given in the name of "Others" (usually referring to the Society's version of 1917); (4) where the understanding of a passage could be facilitated by reference to another passage elsewhere in the Bible; and (5) where important textual variants are to be found in some of the ancient manuscripts or versions of the Bible.

The translators avoided obsolete words and phrases and, whenever possible, rendered Hebrew idioms by means of their normal English equivalents. For the second person singular, the modern "you" was used instead of the archaic "thou," even when referring to the Deity ("You"). A further obvious difference between this translation and most of the older ones is in the rendering of the Hebrew particle *waw,* which is usually translated "and." Biblical Hebrew demanded the frequent use of the *waw,* but in that style it had the force not only of "and" but also of "however," "but," "yet," "when," and any number of other such words and particles, or none at all that can be translated into English. Always to render it as "and" is to misrepresent the Hebrew rather than be faithful to it. Consequently, the committee translated the particle as the sense required, or left it untranslated.

In preparing the translation of *The Prophets,* the translators faced a recurring problem that deserves special mention. The prophetic books contain many passages whose meaning is uncertain. Thus, in order to provide an intelligible rendering, modern scholars have resorted to emending the Hebrew text. Some of these emendations derive from the ancient translators, especially of the Septuagint and the Targums, who had before them a Hebrew text that sometimes differed from today's traditional text. Where these ancient versions provide no help, some scholars have made conjectural emendations of their own. Many modern English versions contain translations of emended texts, sometimes without citing any departure from the traditional Hebrew text.

Like the translation of *The Torah,* the present translation of the prophetic books adheres strictly to the traditional Hebrew text; but where the text remains obscure and an alteration provides marked clarification, a footnote is offered with a rendering of the suggested emendation. If the emendation is based on one or two ancient versions, they are mentioned by name; if more than two versions agree, they are summed up as "ancient versions." Conjectural emendations are introduced by "Emendation yields." Sometimes, however, it was deemed sufficient to offer only a change of vowels, and such modifications are indicated by "Change of vocalization yields." In all cases, the emendation is given in a footnote, which may be readily disregarded by those who reject it on either scholarly or religious grounds. The only exceptions involve such changes in grammatical form as those, say, from second person to third or from singular to plural. In such rare instances, the change is incorporated in the text, and the traditional Hebrew is translated in a footnote. . . .

The Jewish Publication Society joins the members of the committees of translators in the hope that the results of our labors will find favor with God and man.

4.

Soon after its first appearance in 1978, the New International Version established its place among the leading translations of the Bible. It received wide acceptance in the English-speaking world as a Bible suitable for both church and private use.

No living language ever stands still, however, and the English language in particular is continuously subject to influences and developments worldwide.

Even though only a comparatively short time has elapsed since the New International Version was first produced, it is already clear that it needs to be brought up to date in certain areas. The Committee on Bible Translation have therefore given themselves to the task of continuing to keep this translation available in contemporary English while remaining faithful to its established text.

A major challenge facing the Committee is how to respond to the significant changes that are taking place within the English language in regard to gender issues. The word 'man', for example, is now widely understood to refer only to males, even though that is often not the intention of the corresponding Greek or Hebrew words. Instances of potential confusion abound, as in instructions about preparing for the Lord's Supper ('A man ought to examine himself', 1 Corinthians 11:28), or in pronouncements of beatitude such as in Psalm 1:1 ('Blessed is the man . . .'). In these and many other passages, it has become increasingly necessary to have a translation that makes it clear that women and men are both included.

Recognising this need, the Committee on Bible Translation made a decision in 1992 that the New International Version should be made available in an inclusive language edition. Many of the issues are of a sensitive nature. So to guide its inclusive language revision, the Committee adopted a set of principles.

The first principle was to retain the gender used in the original languages when referring to God, angels and demons. At the same time, it was recognised that it was often appropriate to mute the patriarchalism of the culture of the biblical writers through gender-inclusive language when this could be done without compromising the message of the Spirit. This involved distinguishing between those passages in which an activity was normally carried out by either males or females, and other cases where the gender of the people concerned was less precisely identified. While in cases of the former the text could be left unaltered, in cases of the latter words like 'workmen' could be changed to 'worker' or 'craftsman' to 'skilled worker'.

A further problem presented itself in handling pronouns. In order to avoid gender-specific language in statements of a general kind, it was agreed that the plural might be substituted for the singular and the second person for the third person. On the other hand, inclusive singular subjects such as 'everyone' or 'whoever' would only occasionally be followed by plural pronouns such as 'they' or 'their'.

Female words such as 'maid' or 'girl', which in recent years have developed a more pejorative connotation, would usually be replaced. Awkward generic terms like 'human' used as a noun or 'humankind' would be used as sparingly as possible. Some expressions, however, would be left unchanged, as in specific references to either males or females or in wisdom literature where young men on the threshold of adult life were being addressed. The feminine gender of cities and states or nations would also be retained.

It was further determined that the revisions must be sensitive to the varying demands of context. Gender-specific features in literary genres such as parables or exemplary stories were not to be altered without good reason, nor were specific features of metaphorical language.

A common feature in the language of both Old and New Testaments is the use of 'brothers' to refer to members of social units broader than the nuclear family. In cases where reference is to communities that are inclusive of women, 'brothers' should be replaced with some more gender-inclusive expression. Where the noun is vocative (and in a few other passages), the rendering should be expanded to 'brothers and sisters', without the addition of a footnote.

The Committee on Bible Translation have sought to keep faith with the original principles of the New International Version, and at the same time ensure that the recognised text of the New International Version reflects the contemporary use of English around the world. We believe that the changes introduced will remove the obstacles to understanding experienced by some readers, and so enable a new generation to read the Word of God in language they can understand. We pray that God will bless this modern revision as richly as he has done the earlier editions of the New International Version.

Bible Translations Illustrated

In the end, new translations of the Bible rise and fall on whether they can make an ancient text sound convincingly natural in modern idiom. Although far fewer Americans today know the vocabulary, cadences, and eccentricities of the KJV than was the case as late as the 1960s, it still remains the norm. Whether other translations succeed is, thus, almost always a question of how they compare with that standard. The examples below allow for a test. First are versions of the 23rd Psalm from the Hebrew Scriptures or Old Testament, taken from (1) the KVJ; (2) the 1978 version of the New International Version, which was sponsored by an ad hoc group of conservative Protestants and has become the most widely distributed English-language Bible in the world, after the KVJ; and (3) the Tanakh, which was brought out

[Sources: (2) *Holy Bible: New International Version* (Grand Rapids: Zondervan, 1978), pp. 511-12; (3) *Tanakh: A New Translation of the Holy Scriptures According to the Traditional Hebrew Text* (Philadelphia: Jewish Publication Society, 5746/1985), pp. 1131-32. (5) *The Holy Bible: Revised Standard Version* (New York: Thomas Nelson & Sons, 1952), pp. 4-5. (6) *The Living Bible: Paraphrased* (Wheaton, IL: Tyndale House, 1971), p. 748.]

in a revised form in 1985 at the completion of the Jewish Publication Society's long effort to secure its own English version for America. The next three selections present different versions of the Beatitudes (Matthew 5:1-16) from the New Testament: (4) the KJV; (5) the Revised Standard Version of 1952; and (6) the Living Bible, *a popular and self-described paraphrase (and so deliberately less literal in its translation) prepared by Kenneth Taylor and published as part of the complete New Testament in 1971.*

1.

The LORD *is* my shepherd; I shall not want.

2 He maketh me to lie down in green pastures, he leadeth me beside the still waters.

3 He restoreth my soul: he leadeth me in the paths of righteousness for his name's sake.

4 Yea, though I walk through the valley of the shadow of death, I will fear no evil; for thou *art* with me; thy rod and thy staff they comfort me.

5 Thou preparest a table before me in the presence of mine enemies; thou anointest my head with oil; my cup runneth over.

6 Surely goodness and mercy shall follow me all the days of my life: and I will dwell in the house of the LORD for ever.

2.

1   The LORD is my shepherd, I shall lack nothing.
2   He makes me lie down in green pastures,
      he leads me beside quiet waters,
3   he restores my soul.
      He guides me in paths of righteousness
           for his name's sake.
4   Even though I walk
           through the valley of the shadow of death,
      I will fear no evil,
           for you are with me;
      your rod and your staff,
           they comfort me.

5   You prepare a table before me
           in the presence of my enemies.
      You anoint my head with oil;

    my cup overflows.
6 Surely goodness and love will follow me
      all the days of my life,
    and I will dwell in the house of the LORD
      forever.

3.

    The LORD is my shepherd;
      I lack nothing.
2 He makes me lie down in green pastures;
      He leads me to water in places of repose;
3   He renews my life;
      He guides me in right paths
      as befits His name.
4 Though I walk through a valley of deepest darkness,
      I fear no harm, for You are with me;
      Your rod and Your staff — they comfort me.

5 You spread a table for me in full view of my enemies;
      You anoint my head with oil;
      my drink is abundant.
6 Only goodness and steadfast love shall pursue me
      all the days of my life,
    and I shall dwell in the house of the LORD
      for many long years.

4.

    And seeing the multitudes, he went up into a mountain: and when he was
set, his disciples came unto him:
2 And he opened his mouth, and taught them, saying,
3 Blessed *are* the poor in spirit: for theirs is the kingdom of heaven.
4 Blessed *are* they that mourn: for they shall be comforted.
5 Blessed *are* the meek: for they shall inherit the earth.
6 Blessed *are* they which do hunger and thirst after righteousness: for they
shall be filled.
7 Blessed *are* the merciful: for they shall obtain mercy.
8 Blessed *are* the pure in heart: for they shall see God.
9 Blessed *are* the peacemakers: for they shall be called the children of God.

10 Blessed *are* they which are persecuted for righteousness' sake: for theirs is the kingdom of heaven.

11 Blessed are ye, when *men* shall revile you, and persecute *you*, and shall say all manner of evil against you falsely, for my sake.

12 Rejoice, and be exceeding glad: for great *is* your reward in heaven: for so persecuted they the prophets which were before you.

13 Ye are the salt of the earth: but if the salt have lost his savour, wherewith shall it be salted? it is thenceforth good for nothing, but to be cast out, and to be trodden under foot of men.

14 Ye are the light of the world. A city that is set on an hill cannot be hid.

15 Neither do men light a candle, and put it under a bushel, but on a candlestick; and it giveth light unto all that are in the house.

16 Let your light so shine before men, that they may see your good works, and glorify your Father which is in heaven.

5.

Seeing the crowds, he went up on the mountain, and when he sat down his disciples came to him. ²And he opened his mouth and taught them, saying:

³"Blessed are the poor in spirit, for theirs is the kingdom of heaven.

⁴"Blessed are those who mourn, for they shall be comforted.

⁵"Blessed are the meek, for they shall inherit the earth.

⁶"Blessed are those who hunger and thirst for righteousness, for they shall be satisfied.

⁷"Blessed are the merciful, for they shall obtain mercy.

⁸"Blessed are the pure in heart, for they shall see God.

⁹"Blessed are the peacemakers, for they shall be called sons of God.

¹⁰"Blessed are those who are persecuted for righteousness' sake, for theirs is the kingdom of heaven.

¹¹"Blessed are you when men revile you and persecute you and utter all kinds of evil against you falsely on my account. ¹²Rejoice and be glad, for your reward is great in heaven, for so men persecuted the prophets who were before you.

¹³"You are the salt of the earth; but if salt has lost its taste, how shall its saltness be restored? It is no longer good for anything except to be thrown out and trodden under foot by men.

¹⁴"You are the light of the world. A city set on a hill cannot be hid. ¹⁵Nor do men light a lamp and put it under a bushel, but on a stand, and it gives light to all in the house. ¹⁶Let your light so shine before men, that they may see your good works and give glory to your Father who is in heaven."

6.

One day as the crowds were gathering, he went up the hillside with his disciples and sat down and taught them there.

³"Humble men are very fortunate!" he told them, "for the Kingdom of Heaven is given to them. ⁴Those who mourn are fortunate! for they shall be comforted. ⁵The meek and lowly are fortunate! for the whole wide world belongs to them.

⁶"Happy are those who long to be just and good, for they shall be completely satisfied. ⁷Happy are the kind and merciful, for they shall be shown mercy. ⁸Happy are those whose hearts are pure, for they shall see God. ⁹Happy are those who strive for peace — they shall be called the sons of God. ¹⁰Happy are those who are persecuted because they are good, for the Kingdom of Heaven is theirs.

¹¹"When you are reviled and persecuted and lied about because you are my followers — wonderful! ¹²Be *happy* about it! Be *very glad!* for a *tremendous reward* awaits you up in heaven. And remember, the ancient prophets were persecuted too.

¹³"You are the world's seasoning, to make it tolerable. If you lose your flavor, what will happen to the world? And you yourselves will be thrown out and trampled underfoot as worthless. ¹⁴You are the world's light — a city on a hill, glowing in the night for all to see. ¹⁵,¹⁶Don't hide your light! Let it shine for all; let your good deeds glow for all to see, so that they will praise your heavenly Father."

4. Modernism/Fundamentalism

Roman Catholicism

Battle of the Bishops

On the American scene the tensions within Catholicism are dramatically revealed in the antagonism between John Ireland (1838-1918), Archbishop of St. Paul, Minnesota, from 1888 to 1918, and Bernard J. McQuaid (1823-1909), Bishop of Rochester, New York, from 1869 to 1909. Ireland and McQuaid, temperamentally different and philosophically opposed, contested for the mind of America's Catholics and for the ear of the Vatican. Ireland was politically progressive, interested in urban reform, in "Americanizing" the Catholic church, in democratic reform and public education, in better relations with all races and religions. McQuaid, politically conservative and a strict disciplinarian, opposed the liberalizing tendencies within his Church, resisted the founding of Catholic University of America, and vigorously supported the parochial school system as the only means of assuring a faithful constituency for generations to come. (1) Ireland's sentiments are revealed in a preface that he wrote in 1891 for a biography of Isaac Hecker (see Documentary History, *vol. 1, pp. 445-51). (2) In angry remarks delivered in the Rochester Cathedral in 1894, McQuaid denounces Ireland publicly not only for being wrong on nearly everything but also for being wrong in McQuaid's own territory.*

[Sources: (1) John Ireland in Walter Elliott, *The Life of Father Hecker* (New York: Columbus Press, 1891), pp. ix-xiii. (2) F. J. Zwierlein, *The Life and Letters of Bishop McQuaid* (Rome & Louvain, no pub., 1927), III, pp. 207-8, 210.]

1.

Father Hecker was the typical American priest; his were the gifts of mind and heart that go to do great work for God and for souls in America at the present time. Those qualities, assuredly, were not lacking in him which are the necessary elements of character of the good priest and the great man in any time and place. Those are the subsoil of priestly culture, and with the absence of them no one will succeed in America any more than elsewhere. But suffice they do not. There must be added, over and above, the practical intelligence and the pliability of will to understand one's surroundings, the ground upon which he is to deploy his forces, and to adapt himself to circumstances and opportunities as Providence appoints. I do not expect that my words, as I am here writing, will receive universal approval, and I am not at all sure that their expression would have been countenanced by the priest whose memory brings them to my lips. I write as I think, and the responsibility must be all my own. It is as clear to me as noon-day light that countries and peoples have each their peculiar needs and aspirations as they have their peculiar environments, and that, if we would enter into souls and control them, we must deal with them according to their conditions. The ideal line of conduct for the priest in Assyria will be out of all measure in Mexico or Minnesota, and I doubt not that one doing fairly well in Minnesota would by similar methods set things sadly astray in Leinster or Bavaria. The Saviour prescribed timeliness in pastoral caring. The master of a house, He said, "bringeth forth out of his treasury new things and old," as there is demand for one kind or the other. The apostles of nations, from Paul before the Areopagus to Patrick upon the summit of Tara, followed no different principle.

The circumstances of Catholics have been peculiar in the United States, and we have unavoidably suffered on this account. Catholics in largest numbers were Europeans, and so were their priests, many of whom — by no means all — remained in heart and mind and mode of action as alien to America as if they had never been removed from the Shannon, the Loire, or the Rhine. No one need remind me that immigration has brought us inestimable blessings, or that without it the Church in America would be of small stature. The remembrance of a precious fact is not put aside, if I recall an accidental evil attaching to it. Priests foreign in disposition and work were not fitted to make favorable impressions upon the non-Catholic American population, and the American-born children of Catholic immigrants were likely to escape their action. And, lest I be misunderstood, I assert all this is as true of priests coming from Ireland as from any other foreign country. Even priests of American ancestry, ministering to immigrants, not unfrequently fell into the lines of those around them, and did but little to make the Church in America throb with American life. Not so Isaac Thomas Hecker. Whether consciously or unconsciously I do not know, and it matters not, he looked on America as the fairest conquest for divine truth, and he girded himself with arms shaped and tempered to the American pattern. I think that it may be said that the American current, so plain for the last quarter of a century in the flow of Catholic affairs, is, largely at least, to be traced back to Father Hecker and his early co-workers. It used to be said of them in reproach that they were the "Yankee" Catholic Church; the reproach was their praise.

Father Hecker understood and loved the country and its institutions. He saw nothing in them to be deprecated or changed; he had no longing for the fleshpots and bread-stuffs of empires and monarchies. His favorite topic in book and lecture was, that the Constitution of the United States requires, as its necessary basis, the truths of Catholic teaching regarding man's natural state, as opposed to the errors of Luther and Calvin. The republic, he taught, presupposes the Church's doctrine, and the Church ought to love a polity which is the offspring of her own spirit. . . .

He laid stress on the natural and social virtues. The American people hold these in highest esteem. They are the virtues that are most apparent, and are seemingly the most needed for the building up and the preservation of an earthly commonwealth. Truthfulness, honesty in business dealings, loyalty to law and social order, temperance, respect for the rights of others, and the like

Archbishop John Ireland (1839-1918) of St. Paul, Minnesota
(Library of Congress)

virtues are prescribed by reason before the voice of revelation is heard, and the absence of specifically supernatural virtues has led the non-Catholic to place paramount importance upon them. It will be a difficult task to persuade the American that a church which will not enforce those primary virtues can enforce others which she herself declares to be higher and more arduous, and as he has implicit confidence in the destiny of his country to produce a high order of social existence, his first test of a religion will be its powers in this direction. This is according to Catholic teaching. Christ came not to destroy, but to perfect what was in man, and the graces and truths of revelation lead most securely to the elevation of the life that is, no less than to the gaining of the life to come. It is a fact, however, that in other times and other countries the Church has been impeded in her social work, and certain things or customs of those times and countries, transplanted upon American soil and allowed to grow here under a Catholic name, will do her no honor among Americans. The human mind, among the best of us, inclines to narrow limitations, and certain Catholics, aware of the comparatively greater importance of the supernatural, partially overlook the natural. . . .

On a line with his principles, as I have so far delineated them, Father Hecker believed that if he would succeed in his work for souls, he should use in it all the natural energy that God had given him, and he acted up to his belief. I once heard a good old priest, who said his beads well and made a desert around his pulpit by miserable preaching, criticise Father Hecker, who, he imagined, put too much reliance in man, and not enough in God. Father Hecker's piety, his assiduity in prayer, his personal habits of self-denial, repel the aspersion that he failed in reliance upon God. But my old priest — and he has in the church to-day, both in America and Europe, tens of thousands of counterparts — was more than half willing to see in all outputtings of human energy a lack of confidence in God. We sometimes rely far more upon God than God desires us to do, and there are occasions when a novena is the refuge of laziness or cowardice. God has endowed us with natural talents, and not one of them shall be, with His permission, enshrouded in a napkin. He will not work a miracle, or supply grace, to make up for our deficiencies. We must work as if all depended on us, and pray as if all depended on God.

2.

You are well aware that, since I came to Rochester as bishop, I have most sedulously refrained from taking sides in politics, because I did not wish to throw the weight of my official position into the scales of either party, or to drag my episcopal robes in the mire of political partisanship. In my forty-seven years of priesthood, I have never put myself under obligation to any party, or to any official of national, state, or municipal government. No applicant for office has ever been helped by my personal solicitation, or by the signing of an application for office to the party in power. In other words, the sacredness of my office has never been a matter of barter in the mart of the political office-seeker. In this city of Rochester, I have been more frequently classed as a Republican than as a Democrat. No one has ever had warrant to put me in either class, and for twenty-seven years I have never cast a vote, out of anxiety not to put it in any man's power to say that I had voted for one party or the other. While it may have been a duty to exercise the privilege of a citizen and vote, I have felt that a more sacred duty devolved on me of preserving unsullied the high and holy office of bishop by keeping clear of entanglements with any political party. It has been traditional in the Church of the United States for Bishops to hold aloof from politics. This tradition has been handed down to us by Bishops, whose greatness was real, and not mere newspaper greatness, pandering to the sensational popularity of the day. Although often accused, by our enemies, of actively participating in political plottings and partisanship, we have been able, until of late, to deny and repel the false accusation.

Having said this much by way of preface, I will now advert to the late scandal, which caused these remarks. Every Catholic, having respect for his bishops and priests and the honor and good name of his Church, must have been pained and mortified when he learned, during the late political campaign, that one of our bishops, the Archbishop of St. Paul [John Ireland], cast to one side the traditions of the past and entered the political arena like any layman. The newspapers were careful to keep the public daily informed of his arrival in New York weeks before the election, of his appearance on the platform of ratification meetings, surrounded by the leaders of the Republican party, of his views of political questions, strongly expressed through interviews carefully prepared for the press, and of his mingling in a crowd of excited politicians and partisans on the night of election.

I contend that this coming to New York of the Archbishop of St. Paul, to take part in a political contest, was undignified, disgraceful to his episcopal office, and a scandal in the eyes of all right-minded Catholics of both parties. It was, furthermore, a piece of meddlesome interference on his part, to come from his State to another to break down all discipline among our priests and to justify the charge of those inimical to us, that priests are partisans and use their office and opportunities for political work. If Archbishop Ireland had made himself as conspicuous in favor of the Democratic party, he would be just as blameworthy in my estimation. If his conduct in the last political campaign were not censured and condemned, it would not be possible for me to restrain the priests of this diocese from imitating his example and descending from the pulpit to the political platform and marshalling their parishioners up to the polls on the day of election. Not one of them but has an equal right, with his

Grace of St. Paul, to turn electioneering agent for one party or another and absent himself from his parish, as the Archbishop absented himself from his diocese. It is no excuse to say that the Archbishop was working in the interest of good government. Every other clerical aspirant to political distinction would say the same. New York is abundantly able to take care of itself, without extraneous help, as the last election showed. And if the newspapers report correctly, the legislature of Minnesota is itself sadly in need of purification, and his Grace might have found full scope for his political scheming and skill right at home, if politician he would be. . . .

These remarks will suffice for the present. If no other remedy can be found, then recourse to Rome will teach prelates that they would do well to stay at home and give their undivided attention to the field assigned them. I have made these remarks, because I want it understood that it is the policy of the Catholic Church in this country that her bishops and priests should take no active part in political campaigns and contests; that what bishops can do in political matters with impunity priests also can do; that neither have any right to become tools or agents of any party; that, when they do so, they descend from their high dignity, lay themselves open to censure and bitter remarks from those whom they oppose, remarks which recoil upon the sacred office they hold, and expose themselves and office to the vituperation so common in electioneering times.

I also wish it to be understood that this meddling in the political affairs of another state by Archbishop Ireland is altogether exceptional, — as he is the only bishop who thus interfered with others, that this scandal deserved rebuke as public as the offense committed. I sincerely hope that the Church will be spared its repetition.

Rome Speaks — and Is Spoken To

(1) The encyclical condemning modernism noted above, Pascendi Dominici Gregis, *was issued by Pope Pius X in September of 1907.˙While modernism was never a "school" nor quite so systematic as the encyclical suggests, the pope made clear what was objectionable in the new philosophy, history, psychology, science, and biblical study. Only a small portion of the text is excerpted below. (2) The major representatives of modernism were more often European than American (though Bishop Ireland had some fear that the en-*

[Sources: (1) *Pascendi Dominici Gregis* (Washington: National Catholic Welfare Conference, 1963), pp. 3, 8-9, 18-19, 20-21. (2) *Letters to His Holiness Pope Pius X*, by a Modernist (Chicago: Open Court Publishing Co., 1910), pp. 186-88.]

cyclical was aimed at him too), but in 1910 a strong American reply to the pope appeared. Published anonymously but written by W. L. Sullivan (1872-1935), priest and Paulist father until leaving the Church in 1909, the reply took the form of a series of "letters to his Holiness." Sullivan spoke without gentleness or restraint — or effect.

1.
The Modernist Personality.

5. To proceed in an orderly manner in this somewhat abstruse subject, it must first of all be noted that the Modernist sustains and includes within himself a manifold personality; he is a philosopher, a believer, a theologian, an historian, a critic, an apologist, a reformer. These roles must be clearly distinguished one from another by all who would accurately understand their system and thoroughly grasp the principles and the outcome of their doctrines.

Agnosticism.

6. We begin, then, with the philosopher. Modernists place the foundation of religious philosophy in that doctrine which is commonly called *Agnosticism.* According to this teaching human reason is confined entirely within the field of *phenomena,* that is to say, to things that appear, and in the manner in which they appear: it has neither the right nor the power to overstep these limits. Hence it is incapable of lifting itself up to God, and of recognizing His existence, even by means of visible things. From this it is inferred that God can never be the direct object of science, and that, as regards history, He must not be considered as an historical subject. Given these premises, everyone will at once perceive what becomes of *Natural Theology,* of the *motives of credibility,* of *external revelation.* The Modernists simply sweep them entirely aside; they include them in *Intellectualism,* which they denounce as a system which is ridiculous and long since defunct. . . .

Evolution of dogma.

13. Dogma is not only able, but ought to evolve and to be changed. This is strongly affirmed by the Modernists, and clearly flows from their principles. For among the chief points of their teaching is the following, which they deduce from the principle of *vital immanence,* namely, that *religious formulas,* if they are to be really *religious* and not merely intellectual speculations, ought to

be living and to live the life of the *religious sense*. This is not to be understood to mean that these formulas, especially if merely imaginative, were to be invented for the religious sense. Their origin matters nothing, any more than their number or quality. What is necessary is that the *religious sense* — with some modification when needful — should vitally assimilate them. In other words, it is necessary that the *primitive formula* be accepted and sanctioned by the heart; and similarly the subsequent work from which are brought forth the *secondary formulas* must proceed under the guidance of the heart. Hence it comes that these formulas, in order to be living, should be, and should remain, adapted to the faith and to him who believes. Wherefore, if for any reason this adaptation should cease to exist, they lose their first meaning and accordingly need to be changed. In view of the fact that the character and lot of dogmatic formulas are so unstable, it is no wonder that Modernists should regard them so lightly and in such open disrespect, and have no consideration or praise for anything but the religious sense and for the religious life. In this way, with consummate audacity, they criticise the Church, as having strayed from the true path by failing to distinguish between the religious and moral sense of formulas and their surface meaning, and by clinging vainly and tenaciously to meaningless formulas, while religion itself is allowed to go to ruin. "Blind" they are, and "leaders of the blind" puffed up with the proud name of science, they have reached that pitch of folly at which they pervert the eternal concept of truth and the true meaning of religion. . . .

The Modernist as believer.

14. Thus far, Venerable Brethren, We have considered the Modernist as a philosopher. Now if We proceed to consider him as a believer, and seek to know how the believer, according to Modernism, is marked off from the philosopher, it must be observed that, although the philosopher recognises the *reality of the divine* as the object of faith, still this *reality* is not to be found by him but in the heart of the believer, as an object of feeling and affirmation, and therefore confined within the sphere of phenomena; but the question as to whether in itself it exists outside that feeling and affirmation is one which the philosopher passes over and neglects. For the Modernist believer, on the contrary, it is an established and certain fact that the reality of the divine does really exist in itself and quite independently of the person who believes in it. If you ask on what foundation this assertion of the believer rests, he answers: In the personal *experience* of the individual. On this head the Modernists differ from the Rationalists only to fall into the views of the Protestants and pseudo-mystics. . . .

The evolution of doctrine.

26. To conclude this whole question of faith and its various branches, we have still to consider, Venerable Brethren, what the Modernists have to say about the development of the one and the other. First of all they lay down the general principle that in a living religion everything is subject to change, and must in fact be changed. In this way they pass to what is practically their principal doctrine, namely, *evolution.* To the laws of evolution everything is subject under penalty of death — dogma, Church, worship, the Books we revere as sacred, even faith itself. The enunciation of this principle will not be a matter of surprise to anyone who bears in mind what the Modernists have had to say about each of these subjects. Having laid down this law of evolution, the Modernists themselves teach us how it operates. And first, with regard to faith. The primitive form of faith, they tell us, was rudimentary and common to all men alike, for it had its origin in human nature and human life. Vital evolution brought with it progress, not by the accretion of new and purely adventitious forms from without, but by an increasing perfusion of the religious sense into the conscience. The progress was of two kinds: *negative,* by the elimination of all extraneous elements, such, for example, as those derived from the family or nationality; and *positive,* by that intellectual and moral refining of man, by means of which the idea of the divine became fuller and clearer, while the religious sense became more acute. . . .

The Modernist complex.

With all this in mind, one understands how it is that the Modernists express astonishment when they are reprimanded or punished. What is imputed to them as a fault they regard as a sacred duty. They understand the needs of consciences better than anyone else, since they come into closer touch with them than does the ecclesiastical authority. Nay, they embody them, so to speak, in themselves. Hence, for them to speak and to write publicly is a bounden duty. Let authority rebuke them if it pleases — they have their own conscience on their side and an intimate experience which tells them with certainty that what they deserve is not blame but praise. Then they reflect that, after all, there is no progress without a battle and no battle without its victims; and victims they are willing to be like the prophets and Christ Himself. They have no bitterness in their hearts against the authority which uses them roughly, for after all they readily admit that it is only doing its duty as authority. Their sole grief is that it remains deaf to their warnings, for in this way it impedes the progress of souls, but the hour will most surely come when further delay will be impossible, for if the laws of evolution may be checked for a while they cannot be finally evaded.

And thus they go their way, reprimands and condemnations notwithstanding, masking an incredible audacity under a mock semblance of humility. While they make a pretence of bowing their heads, their minds and hands are more boldly intent than ever on carrying out their purposes. And this policy they follow willingly and wittingly, both because it is part of their system that authority is to be stimulated but not dethroned, and because it is necessary for them to remain within the ranks of the Church in order that they may gradually transform the collective conscience. And in saying this, they fail to perceive that they are avowing that the collective conscience is not with them, and that they have no right to claim to be its interpreters.

2.

Your Holiness:

I have now finished the first and greater part of my task, which is to set forth frankly the reasons for that antipathy to Rome which has been for three centuries so striking a feature in the religious life of the most progressive and enlightened nations of the world. I have tried to show, what I think must be obvious to every man of sound sense, that this antipathy does not rest on blind bigotry or unreasonable malice, but is based upon the notorious past history and the perfectly evident present policy of the Roman See. The Papal and Italian autocracy is considered by the world to be in theoretical and practical hostility to the main principles of modern civilization — to freedom of conscience, democracy, respect for individual personality, and liberty of intellect. How it is that peoples who were once in union with Rome have arrived at so momentous a change of conviction, the foregoing letters, I think, will help toward explaining.

Holy Father, if you have any desire to emerge out of the darkness of inexcusable sophistication which surrounds you, and look honestly at reality, these letters, or any other similar expression of candid criticism, may help you in no small degree. If you wish to make Catholicism respectable, and avert from it the ruin and death which now appear inevitable, is it possible for you not to see that no other means will avail to this end than the spiritualizing, and let us not shrink from the word, the modernizing of the Church? If the Catholic religion is to continue holding to persecution in principle, to the present doctrine of church and state, to Italian absolutism, to the prevailing attitude toward indulgences and other superstitions, and to its war of extermination upon critical scholars, then may we as well begin to write its epitaph; then may those honest students who, in the teeth of despair have been faintly hoping for some spiritualizing change, as well go forth into exile, and seek peace in a strange land, since peace and even honor are becoming impossible in what they loved as home.

That the changes which spirituality and scholarship demand from Roman Catholicism are profound and even perilous, there can be no denying. The perplexity indeed is awful. To remain as of old means certain death; to obey the summons of Reform may mean distress and scandal to many, and great injury to some. But surely we cannot lessen the gravity of the situation by not thinking of it. Think of it we must in prudence; provide for it we must in conscience. The adaptations called for need not after all, be the work of a day. Only let the Roman Church begin to show even common courtesy to our civilization, and in this, small as it is, we shall recognize the beginning of a better day, a sign of life in the midst of death. Let Catholics be allowed to hold that freedom of conscience is an inalienable right of man. Let some Pope speak out a brave word of execration upon the Inquisition. Let there be liberty for Catholic professors to teach that union of Church and State is not demanded by the Christian religion as an ideal. Let indulgences and all other heathenism be abolished. Let a representative government, autonomous local synods, and home-rule generally, supersede the present Italian and Papal despotism. Let scholars hold the modernist views as to the nature of dogma and the function of authority. Above all — and this is the one condition which will prevent these concessions from resulting in any great measure of harm — let the whole endeavor of the Church and hierarchy be to promote the Christ-ideal on earth.

Protestantism

Christianity and Liberalism

It is easy to caricature fundamentalism as the religion of the illiterate and untrained. J. Gresham Machen (1881-1937) effectively refutes that stereotype. Graduate of Johns Hopkins University and Princeton Seminary, further educated in Germany, and for over twenty years engaged as professor of New Testament at Princeton, Machen ultimately broke with his own Presbyterian church over the growing divergence between their respective theological positions. While Machen did not flaunt the label of "fundamentalism," he wrote that if it were necessary for him to choose between only two alternatives, namely, liberalism and fundamentalism, he would without hesitation choose the latter. Fundamentalism had to do with Christianity, while liberalism — in Machen's view — was something quite separate and distinct.

[Source: J. G. Machen, *Christianity and Liberalism* (New York: Macmillan Co., 1923), pp. 6-8, 15-16.]

What is the relation between Christianity and modern culture; may Christianity be maintained in a scientific age?

It is this problem which modern liberalism attempts to solve. Admitting that scientific objections may arise against the particularities of the Christian religion — against the Christian doctrines of the person of Christ, and of redemption through His death and resurrection — the liberal theologian seeks to rescue certain of the general principles of religion, of which these particularities are thought to be mere temporary symbols, and these general principles he regards as constituting "the essence of Christianity."

It may well be questioned, however, whether this method of defence will really prove to be efficacious; for after the apologist has abandoned his outer defences to the enemy and withdrawn into some inner citadel, he will probably discover that the enemy pursues him even there. Modern materialism, especially in the realm of psychology, is not content with occupying the lower quarters of the Christian city, but pushes its way into all the higher reaches of life; it is just as much opposed to the philosophical idealism of the liberal preacher as to the Biblical doctrines that the liberal preacher has abandoned in the interests of peace. Mere concessiveness, therefore, will never succeed in avoiding the intellectual conflict. In the intellectual battle of the present day there can be no "peace without victory"; one side or the other must win.

As a matter of fact, however, it may appear that the figure which has just been used is altogether misleading; it may appear that what the liberal theologian has retained after abandoning to the enemy one Christian doctrine after another is not Christianity at all, but a religion which is so entirely different from Christianity as to belong in a distinct category. It may appear further that the fears of the modern man as to Christianity were entirely ungrounded, and that in abandoning the embattled walls of the city of God he has fled in needless panic into the open plains of a vague natural religion only to fall an easy victim to the enemy who ever lies in ambush there.

Two lines of criticism, then, are possible with respect to the liberal attempt at reconciling science and Christianity. Modern liberalism may be criticized (1) on the ground that it is un-Christian and (2) on the ground that it is unscientific. We shall concern ourselves here chiefly with the former line of criticism; we shall be interested in showing that despite the liberal use of traditional phraseology modern liberalism not only is a different religion from Christianity but belongs in a totally different class of religions. But in showing that the liberal attempt at rescuing Christianity is false we are not showing that there is no way of rescuing Christianity at all; on the contrary, it may appear incidentally, even in the present little book, that it is not the Christianity of the New Testament which is in conflict with science, but the supposed Christianity of the modern liberal Church, and that the real city of God, and that city alone, has defences which are capable of warding off the assaults of modern unbelief.

However, our immediate concern is with the other side of the problem; our principal concern just now is to show that the liberal attempt at reconciling Christianity with modern science has really relinquished everything distinctive of Christianity, so that what remains is in essentials only that same indefinite type of religious aspiration which was in the world before Christianity came upon the scene. In trying to remove from Christianity everything that could possibly be objected to in the name of science, in trying to bribe off the enemy by those concessions which the enemy most desires, the apologist has really abandoned what he started out to defend. Here as in many other departments of life it appears that the things that are sometimes thought to be hardest to defend are also the things that are most worth defending.

In maintaining that liberalism in the modern Church represents a return to an un-Christian and sub-Christian form of the religious life, we are particularly anxious not to be misunderstood. "Un-Christian" in such a connection is sometimes taken as a term of opprobrium. We do not mean it at all as such. Socrates was not a Christian, neither was Goethe, yet we share to the full the respect with which their names are regarded. They tower immeasurably above the common run of men; if he that is least in the Kingdom of Heaven is greater than they, he is certainly greater not by any inherent superiority, but by virtue of an undeserved privilege which ought to make him humble rather than contemptuous.

Such considerations, however, should not be allowed to obscure the vital importance of the question at issue. If a condition could be conceived in which all the preaching of the Church should be controlled by the liberalism which in many quarters has already become preponderant, then, we believe, Christianity would at last have perished from the earth and the gospel would have sounded forth for the last time. If so, it follows that the inquiry with which we are now concerned is immeasurably the most important of all those with which the Church has to deal. Vastly more important than all questions with regard to methods of preaching is the root question as to what it is that shall be preached. . . .

. . . The condition of mankind is such that one may well ask what it is that made the men of past generations so great and the men of the present generation so small. In the midst of all the material achievements of modern life, one may well ask the question whether in gaining the whole world we have not lost our own soul. Are we forever condemned to live the sordid life of utilitarianism? Or is there some lost secret which if rediscovered will restore to mankind something of the glories of the past?

Such a secret the writer of this little book would discover in the Christian religion. But the Christian religion which is meant is certainly not the religion of the modern liberal Church, but a message of divine grace, almost forgotten now, as it was in the middle ages, but destined to burst forth once more in

God's good time, in a new Reformation, and bring light and freedom to mankind. What that message is can be made clear, as is the case with all definition, only by way of exclusion, by way of contrast. In setting forth the current liberalism, now almost dominant in the Church, over against Christianity, we are animated, therefore, by no merely negative or polemic purpose; on the contrary, by showing what Christianity is not we hope to be able to show what Christianity is, in order that men may be led to turn from the weak and beggarly elements and have recourse again to the grace of God.

The Faith of Modernism

Shailer Mathews (1863-1941), professor of Historical and Comparative Theology at Chicago and dean of the Divinity School from 1908 to 1933, did not shy away from the term "modernism" — an epithet even more frightening than "liberalism." Believing that one must accept development in all things, even religious doctrines, and further affirming that the scientific method was the best avenue to truth, Mathews saw modernism not as negative and destructive, but as a positive religious force. A lifelong Baptist, the Chicago professor remained committed to the churches and to their important role in modern life.

What then is Modernism? A heresy? An infidelity? A denial of truth? A new religion? So its ecclesiastical opponents have called it. But it is none of these. To describe it is like describing that science which has made our modern intellectual world so creative. It is not a denomination or a theology. *It is the use of the methods of modern science to find, state and use the permanent and central values of inherited orthodoxy in meeting the needs of a modern world.* The needs themselves point the way to formulas. Modernists endeavor to reach beliefs and their application in the same way that chemists or historians reach and apply their conclusions. They do not vote in convention and do not enforce beliefs by discipline. Modernism has no Confession. Its theological affirmations are the formulation of results of investigation both of human needs and the Christian religion. The Dogmatist starts with doctrines, the Modernist with the religion that gave rise to doctrines. The Dogmatist relies on conformity through group authority; the Modernist, upon inductive method and action in accord with group loyalty. . . .

While by its very nature the Modernist movement will never have a creed

---

[Source: Shailer Mathews, *The Faith of Modernism* (New York: Macmillan Co., 1924), pp. 22-23, 179-82.]

or authoritative confession, it does have its beliefs. And these beliefs are those attitudes and convictions which gave rise to the Christian religion and have determined the development of the century long Christian movement. No formula can altogether express the depths of a man's religious faith or hope to express the general beliefs of a movement in which individuals share. Every man will shape his own credo. But since he is loyal to the on-going Christian community with its dominant convictions, a Modernist in his own words and with his own patterns can make affirmations which will not be unlike the following:

> I believe in God, immanent in the forces and processes of nature, revealed in Jesus Christ and human history as Love.
> I believe in Jesus Christ, who by his teaching, life, death and resurrection, revealed God as Savior.
> I believe in the Holy Spirit, the God of love experienced in human life.
> I believe in the Bible, when interpreted historically, as the product and the trustworthy record of the progressive revelation of God through a developing religious experience.
> I believe that humanity without God is incapable of full moral life and liable to suffering because of its sin and weakness.
> I believe in prayer as a means of gaining help from God in every need and in every intelligent effort to establish and give justice in human relations.
> I believe in freely forgiving those who trespass against me, and in good will rather than acquisitiveness, coercion, and war as the divinely established law of human relations.
> I believe in the need and the reality of God's forgiveness of sins, that is, the transformation of human lives by fellowship with God from subjection to outgrown goods to the practice of the love exemplified in Jesus Christ.
> I believe in the practicability of the teaching of Jesus in social life.
> I believe in the continuance of individual personality beyond death; and that the future life will be one of growth and joy in proportion to its fellowship with God and its moral likeness to Jesus Christ.
> I believe in the church as the community of those who in different conditions and ages loyally further the religion of Jesus Christ.
> I believe that all things work together for good to those who love God and in their lives express the sacrificial good will of Jesus Christ.
> I believe in the ultimate triumph of love and justice because I believe in the God revealed in Jesus Christ.

Such affirmations are more than the acceptance of biblical records, ancient facts or the successive doctrinal patterns of the Christian church. They are the substance of a faith that will move mountains. Under their control no man can deliberately seek to injure his neighbor or distrust his God. They are moral motive and direction for social action.

To trust God who is good will is to find a cure for the cynical doubt born of war and its aftermath.

To be loyal to the sinless Son of Man is to gain new confidence in the possibility of transforming human nature and society from selfishness to brotherliness.

To discover in the death of Jesus that God himself shares in sacrifice for the good of others is to gain confidence in the struggle for the rights of others.

To know that the God of law and love has made good will the only source of permanent happiness is to possess a standard of moral judgment.

To follow Jesus in international affairs is to end war.

To find God in natural law and evolution is an assurance that love is as final as any other cosmic expression of the divine will.

To embody the spirit of Jesus Christ in all action is to enjoy the peace which can come only to those who are at one with the cosmic God.

To experience the regenerating power of God is to have new hope for the ultimate completion of the human personality through death as well as life.

The final test of such generic Christianity is the ability of the Christian movement to meet human needs. And of this we have no doubt. Whoever does the will of God will know that the gospel of and about Jesus Christ is not the dream of a noble though impracticable victim of circumstance, but the revelation of the good will of the God of nature, the Father of our spirits, the Savior of His world. And through that knowledge he will gain the fruit of the Spirit — love, joy, peace, long-suffering, kindness, goodness, faithfulness, meekness, self-control.

Judaism

Reform Platforms

(1) In 1885 Reform Jews gathered in Pittsburgh and adopted a set of principles which has come to be known as the "Pittsburgh Platform." A "Declara-

---

[Sources: (1) Central Conference of American Rabbis *Yearbook,* vol. 45 (New York: CCAR, 1935), pp. 198-200. (2) W. Gunther Plaut, *The Growth of Reform Judaism* (New York: World Union for Progressive Judaism, 1965), pp. 96-99.]

tion of Independence," Rabbi Isaac Mayer Wise had called it, and indeed it did set Reform on a path apart from traditional or Orthodox Judaism. This 1885 platform accepted biblical criticism, spoke of "the Bible reflecting the primitive ideas of its own age," and stated regarding the laws of Moses: we "reject all such as are not adapted to the views and habits of modern civilization." Modernity was whole-heartedly embraced. (One should also note the anti-Zionist stance at this time; the large question of Zionism will be taken up in Chapter 11.) (2) About a half-century later, in Columbus, Ohio, Reform Jews adopted another set of principles which placed a somewhat higher value on tradition and heritage. While still holding to the developmental view of the Bible, the framers of the 1937 statement emphasized that the Mosaic Law or Torah "remains the dynamic source of the life of Israel." And "such customs, symbols and ceremonies as possess inspirational value" are to be cherished, not forsaken.

1.

(1885)

In view of the wide divergence of opinion and of the conflicting ideas prevailing in Judaism today, we, as representatives of Reform Judaism in America, in continuation of the work begun at Philadelphia in 1869, unite upon the following principles:

First — We recognize in every religion an attempt to grasp the Infinite One, and in every mode, source or book of revelation held sacred in any religious system the consciousness of the indwelling of God in man. We hold that Judaism presents the highest conception of the God-idea as taught in our holy Scriptures and developed and spiritualized by the Jewish teachers in accordance with the moral and philosophical progress of their respective ages. We maintain that Judaism preserved and defended amid continual struggles and trials and under enforced isolation this God-idea as the central religious truth for the human race.

Second — We recognize in the Bible the record of the consecration of the Jewish people to its mission as priest of the One God, and value it as the most potent instrument of religious and moral instruction. We hold that the modern discoveries of scientific researches in the domains of nature and history are not antagonistic to the doctrines of Judaism, the Bible reflecting the primitive ideas of its own age and at times clothing its conception of divine providence and justice dealing with man in miraculous narratives.

Third — We recognize in the Mosaic legislation a system of training the Jewish people for its mission during its national life in Palestine, and today we accept as binding only the moral laws and maintain only such ceremonies as elevate and sanctify our lives, but reject all such as are not adapted to the views and habits of modern civilization.

Fourth — We hold that all such Mosaic and Rabbinical laws as regulate diet, priestly purity and dress originated in ages and under the influence of ideas altogether foreign to our present mental and spiritual state. They fail to impress the modern Jew with a spirit of priestly holiness; their observance in our day is apt rather to obstruct than to further modern spiritual elevation.

Fifth — We recognize in the modern era of universal culture of heart and intellect the approach of the realization of Israel's great Messianic hope for the establishment of the Kingdom of truth, justice and peace among all men. We consider ourselves no longer a nation but a religious community, and therefore expect neither a return to Palestine, nor a sacrificial worship under the administration of the sons of Aaron, nor the restoration of any of the laws concerning the Jewish state.

Sixth — We recognize in Judaism a progressive religion, ever striving to be in accord with the postulates of reason. We are convinced of the utmost necessity of preserving the historical identity with our great past. Christianity and Islam, being daughter religions of Judaism, we appreciate their mission to aid in the spreading of monotheistic and moral truth. We acknowledge that the spirit of broad humanity of our age is our ally in the fulfilment of our mission, and therefore we extend the hand of fellowship to all who co-operate with us in the establishment of the reign of truth and righteousness among men.

Seventh — We reassert the doctrine of Judaism, that the soul of man is immortal, grounding this belief on the divine nature of the human spirit, which forever finds bliss in righteousness and misery in wickedness. We reject as ideas not rooted in Judaism the belief both in bodily resurrection and in Gehenna and Eden (hell and paradise), as abodes for everlasting punishment or reward.

Eighth — In full accordance with the spirit of Mosaic legislation which strives to regulate the relation between rich and poor, we deem it our duty to participate in the great task of modern times, to solve on the basis of justice and righteousness the problems presented by the contrasts and evils of the present organization of society.

2.

Guiding Principles of Reform Judaism (1937)

In view of the changes that have taken place in the modern world and the consequent need of stating anew the teachings of Reform Judaism, the Central

Conference of American Rabbis makes the following declaration of principles. It presents them not as a fixed creed but as a guide for the progressive elements of Jewry.

A. Judaism and Its Foundations

1. *Nature of Judaism.* Judaism is the historical religious experience of the Jewish people. Though growing out of Jewish life, its message is universal, aiming at the union and perfection of mankind under the sovereignty of God. Reform Judaism recognizes the principle of progressive development in religion and consciously applies this principle to spiritual as well as to cultural and social life.

Judaism welcomes all truth, whether written in the pages of scripture or deciphered from the records of nature. The new discoveries of science, while replacing the older scientific views underlying our sacred literature, do not conflict with the essential spirit of religion as manifested in the consecration of man's will, heart and mind to the service of God and of humanity.

2. *God.* The heart of Judaism and its chief contribution to religion is the doctrine of the One, living God, who rules the world through law and love. In Him all existence has its creative source and mankind its ideal of conduct. Through transcending time and space, He is the indwelling Presence of the world. We worship Him as the Lord of the universe and as our merciful Father.

3. *Man.* Judaism affirms that man is created in the Divine image. His spirit is immortal. He is an active co-worker with God. As a child of God, he is endowed with moral freedom and is charged with the responsibility of overcoming evil and striving after ideal ends.

4. *Torah.* God reveals Himself not only in the majesty, beauty and orderliness of nature, but also in the vision and moral striving of the human spirit. Revelation is a continuous process, confined to no one group and to no one age. Yet the people of Israel, through its prophets and sages, achieved unique insight in the realm of religious truth. The Torah, both written and oral, enshrines Israel's ever-growing consciousness of God and of the moral law. It preserves the historical precedents, sanctions and norms of Jewish life, and seeks to mould it in the patterns of goodness and of holiness. Being products of historical processes, certain of its laws have lost their binding force with the passing of the conditions that called them forth. But as a depository of permanent spiritual ideals, the Torah remains the dynamic source of the life of Israel. Each age has the obligation to adapt the teachings of the Torah to its basic needs in consonance with the genius of Judaism.

5. *Israel.* Judaism is the soul of which Israel is the body. Living in all parts of the world, Israel has been held together by the ties of a common history, and above all, by the heritage of faith. Though we recognize in the group loyalty of Jews who have become estranged from our religious tradition, a bond which still unites them with us, we maintain that it is by its religion and for its religion that the Jewish people has lived. The non-Jew who accepts our faith is welcomed as a full member of the Jewish community.

In all lands where our people live, they assume and seek to share loyally the full duties and responsibilities of citizenship and to create seats of Jewish knowledge and religion. In the rehabilitation of Palestine, the land hallowed by memories and hopes, we behold the promise of renewed life for many of our brethren. We affirm the obligation of all Jewry to aid in its upbuilding as a Jewish homeland by endeavoring to make it not only a haven of refuge for the oppressed but also a center of Jewish culture and spiritual life.

Throughout the ages it has been Israel's mission to witness to the Divine in the face of every form of paganism and materialism. We regard it as our historic task to cooperate with all men in the establishment of the kingdom of God, of universal brotherhood, justice, truth and peace on earth. This is our Messianic goal.

B. Ethics

6. *Ethics and Religion.* In Judaism religion and morality blend into an indissoluble unity. Seeking God means to strive after holiness, righteousness and goodness. The love of God is incomplete without the love of one's fellowmen. Judaism emphasizes the kinship of the human race, the sanctity and worth of human life and personality and the right of the individual to freedom and to the pursuit of his chosen vocation. Justice to all, irrespective of race, sect or class is the inalienable right and the inescapable obligation of all. The state and organized government exist in order to further these ends.

7. *Social Justice.* Judaism seeks the attainment of a just society by the application of its teachings to the economic order, to industry and commerce, and to national and international affairs. It aims at the elimination of man-made misery and suffering, of poverty and degradation, of tyranny and slavery, of social inequality and prejudice, of ill-will and strife. It advocates the promotion of harmonious relations between warring classes on the basis of equity and justice, and the creation of conditions under which human personality may flourish. It pleads for the safeguarding of childhood against exploitation. It champions the cause of all who work and of their right to an adequate standard of living, as prior to the rights of property. Judaism emphasizes the duty of charity, and

strives for a social order which will protect men against the material disabilities of old age, sickness and unemployment.

8. *Peace.* Judaism, from the days of the prophets, has proclaimed to mankind the ideal of universal peace. The spiritual and physical disarmament of all nations has been one of its essential teachings. It abhors all violence and relies upon moral education, love and sympathy to secure human progress. It regards justice as the foundation of the well-being of nations and the condition of enduring peace. It urges organized international action for disarmament, collective security and world peace.

C. Religious Practice

9. *The Religious Life.* Jewish life is marked by consecration to these ideals of Judaism. It calls for faithful participation in the life of the Jewish community as it finds expression in home, synagog and school and in all other agencies that enrich Jewish life and promote its welfare.

The Home has been and must continue to be a stronghold of Jewish life, hallowed by the spirit of love and reverence, by moral discipline and religious observance and worship.

The Synagog is the oldest and most democratic institution in Jewish life. It is the prime communal agency by which Judaism is fostered and preserved. It links the Jews of each community and unites them with all Israel.

The perpetuation of Judaism as a living force depends upon religious knowledge and upon the Education of each new generation in our rich cultural and spiritual heritage.

Prayer is the voice of religion, the language of faith and aspiration. It directs man's heart and mind Godward, voices the needs and hopes of the community, and reaches out after goals which invest life with supreme value. To deepen the spiritual life of our people, we must cultivate the traditional habit of communion with God through prayer in both home and synagog.

Judaism as a way of life requires in addition to its moral and spiritual demands, the preservation of the Sabbath, festivals and Holy Days, the retention and development of such customs, symbols and ceremonies as possess inspirational value, the cultivation of distinctive forms of religious art and music and the use of Hebrew, together with the vernacular, in our worship and instruction.

These timeless aims and ideals of our faith we present anew to a confused and troubled world. We call upon our fellow Jews to rededicate themselves to them, and, in harmony with all men, hopefully and courageously to continue Israel's eternal quest after God and His kingdom.

Conservative Approaches

The major rabbinical training center for Conservative Judaism, the Jewish Theological Seminary of America (New York City), was presided over from 1901 to 1915 by the able scholar, Solomon Schechter (1850-1915). (1) Schechter found "higher criticism" to be ill-informed, damaging in its effect, and possibly anti-Semitic in its intent. "Our great claim to the gratitude of mankind," Schechter declared, "is that we gave to the world the word of God, the Bible." And it is just this great gift "which the Higher anti-Semitism is seeking to destroy, denying all our claims for the past, and leaving us without hope for the future." (2) A half century later, the Jewish Theological Seminary undertook the publication of a series of volumes on "The Heritage of Biblical Israel." Now, higher criticism is accepted and the fundamentalists and literalists are being set aside. Nahum Sarna (b. 1923), long a professor of biblical studies at Brandeis University, but formerly on the faculty of the Jewish Theological Seminary, wrote Understanding Genesis. *This book, Sarna noted, is "based on the belief that the study of the Book of Books must constitute a mature intellectual challenge, an exposure to the expanding universe of scientific biblical scholarship." Those who continue to reject or ignore that "expanding universe" (and Orthodox Judaism manifests no great interest therein), taking refuge in "tradition," really rely on medieval authority that is now superseded by the "modern sciences of literary and textual criticism."*

1.

Now, the first thing that we have to recover is the Bible. There is a story of a Catholic saint who was beheaded by his pagan persecutors, but, like a good saint, he took his head under his arm and walked off. You smile, and think it perhaps too much of a miracle, but a Judaism without a Bible is even a greater miracle. It would mean a headless Judaism, for, gentlemen, Judaism is not merely an ethical society placed under the auspices of Abraham, Isaac, Jacob, Moses and Aaron. . . .

Judaism is a revealed religion, with sacred writings revealing the history of the past, making positive demands on the present and holding out solemn promises for the future. And these sacred writings are the Bible, and they ought to be the possession of every Jew, interpreted and commented on in the

---

[Sources: (1) Solomon Schechter, *Seminary Addresses and Other Papers* (Cincinnati: Ark Publishing Co., 1915), pp. 3-5, 6-7, 37-38. (2) Nahum Sarna, *Understanding Genesis* (New York: Jewish Theological Seminary of America, 1966), pp. xx-xxiii.]

Jewish spirit. I am in no way antagonistic to all that is modern. I confess that my sympathies for Wellhausen are not very strong and that I have a tolerable antipathy against "painted Bibles" and mutilated Scriptures.[6] But I know that the demands of science are inexorable. . . . But the question may be asked whether it is really all science that is claimed as such. My studies within the past years, which centered largely around the Bible, have convinced me that there is much in the higher criticism, which is at best theology of a kind, not philology and history.

But apart from this question there is another consideration. An old friend of mine once said to me, "Even if you are able to translate a Psalm, you understand only the Psalm but not the Psalmist." Now I put it to you, whether in a school where a man like Duhm, one of the oracles of higher criticism, can declare that the Psalms are all mere rancorous party pamphlets, the Psalmist is understood or not.

Another instance is the attempt by a majority of higher critics to eliminate the personal element from the Psalms — I mean the *ich* question. You will agree with me, I think, that our grandmothers and grandfathers, who did read the Psalms and had a good cry over them, understood them better than all the professors. I am not pleading here for an orthodox commentary to the Bible, but there is a Jewish liberalism and a Christian liberalism and even from the point of view of liberalism let a commentary be written in the spirit of a Jewish and not a Christian liberalism. Remember that the Bible was not discovered by Cheyne[7] and Wellhausen. We worked over it thousands of years before the Occidentals could read a Hebrew sentence correctly. . . .

Perhaps you will allow me to conclude with a passage from the Zohar[8] which I have often used before, and possibly many others before me, but it bears repetition. The story runs that a certain Rabbi once sailed in a ship. When the ship came upon the high seas, a storm arose and wrecked the vessel. Down it went, but the Rabbi was a saint, and, of course, a miracle happened. The vessel came out at the other side of the globe, and he found men engaged in prayer; but he did not understand them. It is supposed by the commentaries, which are still to be written, that the cause of his inability to understand them was that they did not pray in Hebrew. But even worse would it be if the religious literature of the Jews should not be accessible to all the Jews. And here in New York, where the West and the East meet in such close proximity, it is especially neces-

6. Julius Wellhausen (1844-1918) was an early biblical critic out of German Protestantism. The reference to painted and mutilated Bibles is to the printing of early Old Testament materials in such a way as to indicate the several sources or "documents" that lay behind the final product.

7. T. K. Cheyne (1841-1915), contemporary of Wellhausen, introduced much of German scholarship into England.

8. The central book of the medieval cabala (or kabbala) literature of Judaism.

Main building of Orthodox Judaism's Yeshiva University, founded in 1928
(Yeshiva University)

sary if we are all to remain brothers on earth, as we hope to be in heaven, that our religious literature should be based on and developed from that Sacred Book and Sacred Language which have always been the means of communion between Israel and Israel, and between Israel and his God.

Some time ago I saw in one of the numerous sheets of this country a reference to the Hammurabi Code, concluding with the words, "this means a blow to Orthodoxy." I hold no brief for Orthodoxy in this country or elsewhere. But, may I ask: Is there any wing in Judaism which is prepared to confirm the reproach of Carlyle, who, in one of his anti-Semitic fits, exclaimed, "The Jews are always dealing in old clothes; spiritual or material." We are here between ourselves, so we may frankly make the confession that we did not invent the art of printing; we did not discover America, in spite of Kayserling; we did not inaugurate the French Revolution, in spite of some one else; we were not the first to utilize the power of steam or electricity, in spite of any future Kayserling. Our great claim to the gratitude of mankind is that we gave to the world the word of

God, the Bible. We have stormed heaven to snatch down this heavenly gift. . . , we threw ourselves into the breach and covered it with our bodies against every attack; we allowed ourselves to be slain by hundreds and thousands rather than become unfaithful to it; and we bore witness to its truth and watched over its purity in the face of a hostile world. The Bible is our sole *raison d'être,* and it is just this which the Higher anti-Semitism is seeking to destroy, denying all our claims for the past, and leaving us without hope for the future.

Can any section among us afford to concede to this professorial and im-perial anti-Semitism and confess "for a truth we and our ancestors have sinned;" we have lived on false pretenses and were the worst shams in the world? Forget not that we live in an historical age in which everybody must show his credentials from the past. The Bible is our patent of nobility granted to us by the Almighty God, and if we disown the Bible, leaving it to the tender mercies of a Wellhausen, Stade and Duhm, and other beautiful souls working away at diminishing the "nimbus of the Chosen People," the world will disown us. There is no room in it for spiritual parvenus. But this intellectual persecu-tion can only be fought by intellectual weapons and unless we make an effort to recover our Bible and to think out our theology for ourselves, we are irrevoca-bly lost from both worlds. A mere protest in the pulpit or a vigorous editorial in a paper, or an amateur essay in a monthly, or even a special monograph will not help us. We have to create a really living, great literature, and do the same for the subjects of theology and the Bible that Europe has done for Jewish history and philology.

2.

. . . The crux of the matter is that in the eyes of modern, secularized man, the Bible has very largely lost its sanctity and relevance.

It would not be profitable to trace here in any detail the rather complex pattern of events that has produced this unprecedented situation. It was proba-bly an inevitable outgrowth of various intellectual movements which had long been gathering momentum and which converged in the nineteenth century. Al-ready in 1670, Benedict Spinoza, in his *Theologico-Political Treatise,* had con-ceived of biblical studies as a science, and had formulated a methodology in-volving the use of rationalism and historical criticism. For this alone, and for his revolutionary conclusions, he must be regarded as the true founder of the modern scientific approach to the Bible. But he was not the primary inspiration for further studies in this direction. The new cosmology that had been gaining ground for three centuries and the later evolutionary theories were bound to lead to a questioning of the Genesis narrative. Moreover, the scope of the evolu-tionary thesis was sure to be broadened beyond the realms of geology and biology, so that it is not surprising that attempts were made to explain thereby the religious, cultural and social history of Israel. The revolt against intellectual and ecclesiastical authority that marked the rise of humanism, and the new concept of history that underplayed the supernatural and made the decisions of men predominant, could not but affect the approach to the theocentricity of the biblical narrative. But above all, biblical scholarship was touched decisively by the development and application of critical, historical and analytical methods used in the identification and isolation of literary sources and the determination of their dating. No longer could the Pentateuch be regarded as a unitary work, divinely dictated, word for word, to Moses. It became one of the finalities of scholarship that the narrative portions of the Pentateuch were thoroughly unreliable for any attempted reconstruction of the times about which they purported to relate. The devastating effect of all this upon faith, when faith was exclusively identified with a literalist approach to Scripture, is abundantly obvious. No wonder that the Bible became desanctified in the eyes of so many educated men.

Interior of traditionalist synagogue in Colchester, Connecticut, 1940
(Library of Congress)

Unfortunately, the response of the fundamentalists to the challenge of scientism served only to exacerbate the situation. They mistakenly regarded all critical biblical studies as a challenge to faith. There remained no room for the play of individual conscience; the validity of genuine intellectual doubt was refused recognition. By insisting dogmatically upon interpretations and doctrines that flagrantly contradicted the facts, the fundamentalist did not realize the self-exposure of an obvious insecurity that was more a reflection upon his own religious position than a judgment upon biblical scholarship. For it declared, in effect, that spiritual relevance can be maintained only at the expense of the intellect and the stifling of conscience.

The deadly effects of this approach can be easily measured by discussing the Bible with university students. It becomes immediately apparent that the literature of ancient Israel is not treated with the same seriousness and respect as that of ancient Greece. The childish image of the Scriptures, imparted at an early age, is well-nigh ineradicable. For this reason, the teaching of the Bible in the religious schools has, more often than not, become a self-defeating exercise in futility. Any intelligent child who studies mathematical logic in school, and most children now do, cannot but note the contrast in intellectual challenge between this and his biblical studies. He must, willy-nilly, conclude that the latter is inferior, an attitude hardly calculated to instil or encourage a feeling for the sanctity and relevance of Scripture. Why the elementary pedagogical absurdity of present-day Bible teaching in the religious schools is not obvious to those in control of curriculum and teacher training, is an utter mystery.

Of course, the fundamentalists frequently take refuge from modern scholarship by appealing to "tradition," by which they mean medieval authority. The illegitimacy of this position as an argument of faith is, however, easily demonstrable. The medieval scholars made the most of all the limited tools at their disposal. But they did not have access, naturally, to the modern sciences of literary and textual criticism and to the disciplines of sociology, anthropology, linguistics and comparative religion. We simply do not know how they would have reacted had all this material been available to them. To assume a blind disregard of evidence on their part is as unwarranted as it is unfair. Be this as it may, it is clear, at any rate, that "pietism," no less than its "scientific" opposition, bears a goodly measure of responsibility for the alienation of modern man from the sacred Scriptures.

This book, the first of a projected series, is designed to make the Bible of Israel intelligible, relevant and, hopefully, inspiring to a sophisticated generation, possessed of intellectual curiosity and ethical sensitivity. It recognizes the fact that the twentieth century has transformed our categories of thought and has provided us with new criteria for critical judgment. It is based on the belief that the study of the Book of Books must constitute a mature intellectual challenge, an exposure to the expanding universe of scientific biblical scholarship. It is predicated upon the profound conviction, born of personal experience, that the findings of modern biblical studies, in all their scholarly ramifications, provide the means to a keener understanding of the Hebrew Scriptures and may prove to be the key to a deeper appreciation of their religious message. Far from presenting a threat to faith, a challenge to the intellect may reinforce faith and purify it.

5. Theological Aftermath

Neo-Orthodoxy

H. Richard Niebuhr (1894-1962)

The problem, Walter Rauschenbusch had written in 1917, was to see that men and women no longer had "to believe with all their hearts what they could not possibly understand with all their heads." A generation later, however, the problem was whether anything remained to be believed with all one's heart. The time for theological reconstruction or return had come. And in once more turning toward the transcendent, moving beyond the "modern" and the natural to the timeless and the supernatural, none rendered more valiant service than Richard Niebuhr and his brother, Reinhold (introduced above, pp. 275-77). A native of Missouri and reared in the German Evangelical tradition, Richard Niebuhr spent his professional life chiefly at Yale University. In the course of his own theological maturing, he discovered new value in old ideas, notably in those of Jonathan Edwards (see Documentary History, *vol. 1, pp. 183-90), even as he assisted his students and a wide reading public to appreciate and apprehend anew the insights of basic Christian doctrines. His* Kingdom of God in America *(1937) recognized liberalism's deficiencies, orthodoxy's resilient and enduring strengths. In 1941, he addressed the subject of revelation, but not in the stale terms of battles over this text or that, this emendation or that. We must see revelation, Niebuhr argued, not as a part of apologetics, not as a record of things past, but as an encounter in the present with the ever-living, ever-revealing God.*

[Source: H. Richard Niebuhr, *The Meaning of Revelation* (New York: Macmillan Co., 1941), pp. 1-4, 38-42.]

What is the meaning of revelation? The question has been raised many times in the history of the Christian church. But its reappearance in contemporary theological discussion puzzles many men who are accustomed to associate the word revelation with ancient quarrels and their fruitless issue. They remember particularly the turgid debate about miracles, prophecy, revelation and reason in which Deists and Supernaturalists engaged at the beginning of the eighteenth century. The defense of revelation at that time seemed to mean social and intellectual conservatism; what was at stake in the quarrel was the right of the church, clergy, and traditional authority in general to exercise their ancient guardianship over society; the appeal to revelation seemed simply a defensive device. The cause of reason on the other hand was espoused by the rebellious and fresh powers of democratic, mercantile civilization which used it for the attainment of other victories than those of reason. And whatever the fortunes of the contending parties in that conflict were, reason and revelation were sadly damaged. At its close, as at the end of every war, victor and victim were almost indistinguishable. Scepticism, clothed in the episcopal vestments Butler gave it, or in the more worldly armor Hume supplied, was left in possession of the intellectual field. . . .

With Wesley, Whitefield, Edwards and their associates, Christianity abandoned the defense of revelation as well as the attack on reason; it turned rather to its proper work of preaching the gospel, of exorcising the demons which inhabit human hearts and of guiding souls to fellowship with a holy spirit. Problems of relationship between reason and faith, theology and philosophy, natural and religious experience arose occasionally, of course, but for a while it seemed that a Platonic justice had been established in which each part of the Christian soul and each institution in Christian society minded its own business and made its contribution to the whole without lapsing again into imperialistic adventures. As for "revelation," the word was used sparingly, however much Scriptures and Christian history were employed in the preaching of the gospel.

When we recall that quarrel and its consequences we are tempted to turn away with some distaste from a revival of the revelation idea. Does not the reestablishment of a theology of revelation mean the renewal of a fruitless warfare between faith and reason? Is it not the sign of a retreat to old entrenchments in which only those veterans of a lost cause, the fundamentalists, are interested? To speak of revelation now seems to imply a reversal of the enlightenment in religious thought which began when Schleiermacher asked and answered his rhetorical question to the cultured despisers of faith: "Do you say that you cannot away with miracles, revelation, inspiration? You are right; the time for fairy tales is past." Such a reversal appears to be as impossible as it is undesirable. The work of a hundred and fifty years in theology cannot be ignored; the methods and the fruits of Biblical and historical criticism as well as of natural and social science cannot be so eliminated from men's minds as to allow them to recover the same attitude toward Scriptures which their seventeenth-century forbears had. We may admire the simplicity and directness with which these answered the question about the meaning of revelation by pointing to the Scriptures and may be ready to concede that there was a wisdom in this simplicity which is lacking in our complicated and analytical scholarship. Nevertheless it is evident that we cannot achieve their innocence of vision by wishing for it. . . .

The justification of the Christian, or of the church, or of religion, or of the gospel, or of revelation seems forever necessary in the face of the attacks which are made upon these from the outside and in view of the doubts that arise within. Fear of defeat and loss turn men away from single-minded devotion to their ends in order that they may defend themselves and their means of attaining their ends. We not only employ methods for the discovery of truths but somehow feel it necessary to show, otherwise than by the fruits of our work, that these methods are the best. We not only desire to live in Christian faith but we endeavor to recommend ourselves by means of it and to justify it as superior to all other faiths. Such defense may be innocuous when it is strictly subordinated to the main task of living toward our ends, but put into the first place it becomes more destructive of religion, Christianity and the soul than any foe's attack can possibly be.

A theology of revelation which begins with the historic faith of the Christian community is no less tempted to self-justification and so to abandonment of its starting point than any other theology. It may seek to make a virtue out of its necessity and to recommend itself as not only inescapable but as superior in results to all other methods. It may direct attention away from the God visible to the community of faith and seek to defend that community, its faith and its theology. The idea of revelation itself may be employed, not for the greater glory of God, but as a weapon for the defense and aggrandizement of the church or even of the individual theologian. A recent book on the subject of revelation states that "the question of revelation is at the very root of the claim of the Christian religion to universal empire over the souls of men." Such an apologetic statement contains an evident inherent self-contradiction; for revelation and the "claim of the Christian religion to universal empire over the souls of men" are absolute incompatibles. The faith of Christian revelation is directed toward a God who reveals himself as the only universal sovereign and as the one who judges all men — but particularly those directed to him in faith — to be sinners wholly unworthy of sovereignty. To substitute the sovereignty of Christian religion for the sovereignty of the God of Christian faith, though it be done by means of the revelation idea, is to fall into a new type of idolatry, to abandon the standpoint of Christian faith and revelation which are directed toward the God of Jesus Christ and to take the standpoint of a faith directed toward religion or revelation. A revelation that can be used to undergird the claim of Christian faith to universal empire over the souls of men must be something else than the revelation of the God of that Jesus Christ who in faith emptied himself, made himself of no reputation and refused to claim the kingly crown.

The inherent self-contradiction in all such self-defensive uses of the revelation idea indicates that every effort to deal with the subject must be resolutely confessional. As we begin with revelation only because we are forced to do so by our limited standpoint in history and faith so we can proceed only by stating in simple, confessional form what has happened to us in our community, how we came to believe, how we reason about things and what we see from our point of view.

Other considerations also warn against the apologetic use of revelation and make necessary the adoption of a confessional method. Whenever the revelation idea is used to justify the church's claims to superior knowledge or some other excellence, revelation is necessarily identified with something that the church can possess. Such possessed revelation must be a static thing and under the human control of the Christian community — a book, a creed, or a set of doctrines. It cannot be revelation in act whereby the church itself is convicted of its poverty, its sin and misery before God. Furthermore, it cannot be the revelation of a living God; for the God of a revelation that can be possessed must be a God of the past, a God of the dead who communicated his truths to men in another time but who to all effects and purposes has now retired from the world, leaving the administration of his interests to some custodian of revelation — a church, a priesthood, or a school of theology.

Paul Tillich (1886-1965)

Neither the Niebuhrs nor Tillich fits neatly under narrow labels nor sits politely behind the desks of some particular "school." But Tillich, like the Niebuhrs, turned squarely toward the supernatural and engaged heroically with the ancient doctrines of the Christian religion. Refugee from Hitler's Germany, Tillich — through the good offices of Reinhold Niebuhr — came to America in 1933 to start a new career at Union Theological Seminary in New York City. Tillich made theology respectable again, one measure of his impact being the cover story in Time *magazine (March 16, 1959) on Tillich and his theology for a new age. His influences moved well beyond the confines of Protestantism as artists, philosophers, historians, psychotherapists,*

[Source: Paul Tillich, *Systematic Theology,* Vol. I (Chicago: University of Chicago Press, 1951), pp. 3-4, 11-12, 15-16.]

and others not confessionally identified as Protestants found themselves
speaking "god talk." In mid-twentieth-century America, this was a surpris-
ing thing to be doing. Even more surprising was the attempt at such a time
and in such a fragmented world to do "systematic theology." But in 1951
Tillich undertook just such a task, bringing that labor to completion (in
three volumes) a dozen years later. The excerpt below, taken from the intro-
duction to the first volume, describes the task of theology in the current "sit-
uation."

Theology, as a function of the Christian church, must serve the needs of the
church. A theological system is supposed to satisfy two basic needs: the statement of the truth of the Christian message and the interpretation of this truth
for every new generation. Theology moves back and forth between two poles,
the eternal truth of its foundation and the temporal situation in which the eternal truth must be received. Not many theological systems have been able to balance these two demands perfectly. Most of them either sacrifice elements of the
truth or are not able to speak to the situation. Some of them combine both
shortcomings. Afraid of missing the eternal truth, they identify it with some
previous theological work, with traditional concepts and solutions, and try to
impose these on a new, different situation. They confuse eternal truth with a
temporal expression of this truth. This is evident in European theological orthodoxy, which in America is known as fundamentalism. When fundamentalism is combined with an antitheological bias, as it is, for instance, in its
biblicistic-evangelical form, the theological truth of yesterday is defended as an
unchangeable message against the theological truth of today and tomorrow.
Fundamentalism fails to make contact with the present situation, not because it
speaks from beyond every situation, but because it speaks from a situation of
the past. It elevates something finite and transitory to infinite and eternal validity. In this respect fundamentalism has demonic traits. It destroys the humble
honesty of the search for truth, it splits the conscience of its thoughtful adherents, and it makes them fanatical because they are forced to suppress elements
of truth of which they are dimly aware.

Fundamentalists in America and orthodox theologians in Europe can
point to the fact that their theology is eagerly received and held by many people
just because of the historical or biographical situation in which men find themselves today. The fact is obvious, but the interpretation is wrong. "Situation," as
one pole of all theological work, does not refer to the psychological or sociological state in which individuals or groups live. It refers to the scientific and artistic, the economic, political, and ethical forms in which they express their interpretation of existence. The "situation" to which theology must speak relevantly
is not the situation of the individual as individual and not the situation of the
group as group. Theology is neither preaching nor counseling; therefore, the

Paul Tillich (1886-1965)
(Religion News Service)

success of a theology when it is applied to preaching or to the care of souls is not necessarily a criterion of its truth. The fact that fundamentalist ideas are eagerly grasped in a period of personal or communal disintegration does not prove their theological validity, just as the success of a liberal theology in periods of personal or communal integration is no certification of its truth. The "situation" theology must consider is the creative interpretation of existence, an interpretation which is carried on in every period of history under all kinds of psychological and sociological conditions. . . .

We have used the term "ultimate concern" without explanation. Ultimate concern is the abstract translation of the great commandment: "The Lord, our God, the Lord is one; and you shall love the Lord your God with all your heart, and with all your soul and with all your mind, and with all your strength." The religious concern is ultimate; it excludes all other concerns from ultimate significance; it makes them preliminary. The ultimate concern is unconditional, independent of any conditions of character, desire, or circumstance. The unconditional concern is total: no part of ourselves or of our world is excluded from it; there is no "place" to flee from it. The total concern is infinite: no moment of relaxation and rest is possible in the face of a religious concern which is ultimate, unconditional, total, and infinite.

The word "concern" points to the "existential" character of religious experience. We cannot speak adequately of the "object of religion" without simultaneously removing its character as an object. That which is ultimate gives itself only to the attitude of ultimate concern. It is the correlate of an unconditional concern but not a "highest thing" called "the absolute" or "the unconditioned," about which we could argue in detached objectivity. It is the object of total surrender, demanding also the surrender of our subjectivity while we look at it. It is a matter of infinite passion and interest (Kierkegaard), making us its object whenever we try to make it our object. For this reason we have avoided terms like "*the* ultimate," "*the* unconditioned," "*the* universal," "*the* infinite," and have spoken of ultimate, unconditional, total, infinite concern. Of course, in every concern there is *something* about which one is concerned; but this something should not appear as a separated object which could be known and handled without concern. This, then, is the first formal criterion of theology: *The object of theology is what concerns us ultimately. Only those propositions are theological which deal with their object in so far as it can become a matter of ultimate concern for us.*

The negative meaning of this proposition is obvious. Theology should never leave the situation of ultimate concern and try to play a role within the arena of preliminary concerns. Theology cannot and should not give judgments about the aesthetic value of an artistic creation, about the scientific value of a physical theory or a historical conjecture, about the best methods of medical healing or social reconstruction, about the solution of political or international conflicts. The theologian *as* theologian is no expert in any matters of preliminary concern. And, conversely, those who are experts in these matters should not *as such* claim to be experts in theology. The first formal principle of theology, guarding the boundary line between ultimate concern and preliminary concerns, protects theology as well as the cultural realms on the other side of the line. . . .

If taken in the broadest sense of the word, theology, the *logos* or the reasoning about *theos* (God and divine things), is as old as religion. Thinking pervades all the spiritual activities of man. Man would not be spiritual without words, thoughts, concepts. This is especially true in religion, the all-embracing function of man's spiritual life. It was a misunderstanding of Schleiermacher's definition of religion ("the feeling of absolute dependence") and a symptom of religious weakness when successors of Schleiermacher located religion in the realm of feeling as one psychological function among others. The banishment of religion into the nonrational corner of subjective emotions in order to have the realms of thought and action free from religious interference was an easy way of escaping the conflicts between religious tradition and modern thought.

But this was a death sentence against religion, and religion did not and could not accept it.

Every myth contains a theological thought which can be, and often has been, made explicit. Priestly harmonizations of different myths sometimes disclose profound theological insights. Mystical speculations, as in Vedanta Hinduism, unite meditative elevation with theological penetration. Metaphysical speculations, as in classical Greek philosophy, unite rational analysis with theological vision. Ethical, legal, and ritual interpretations of the divine law create another form of theology on the soil of prophetic monotheism. All this is "theo-logy," *logos* of *theos,* a rational interpretation of the religious substance of rites, symbols, and myths.

Christian theology is no exception. It does the same thing, but it does it in a way which implies the claim that it is *the* theology. The basis of this claim is the Christian doctrine that the Logos became flesh, that the principle of the divine self-revelation has become manifest in the event "Jesus as the Christ." If this message is true, Christian theology has received a foundation which transcends the foundation of any other theology and which itself cannot be transcended. Christian theology has received something which is absolutely concrete and absolutely universal at the same time. No myth, no mystical vision, no metaphysical principle, no sacred law, has the concreteness of a personal life. In comparison with a personal life everything else is relatively abstract. And none of these relatively abstract foundations of theology has the universality of the Logos, which itself is the principle of universality. In comparison with the Logos everything else is relatively particular. Christian theology is the theology in so far as it is based on the tension between the absolutely concrete and the absolutely universal.

Neo-Thomism

The French Philosophers

The herculean theological achievement of Thomas Aquinas (c. 1225-74; "Saint" Thomas by 1323) represents the high point of medieval scholasticism, even as it constitutes the masterful synthesizing of Hebrew and Greek, of

---

[Sources: (1) Jacques Maritain in *Religion and the Modern World* (Philadelphia: University of Pennsylvania Press, 1941), pp. 10, 11-13. (2) Etienne Gilson, *The Philosopher and Theology* (New York: Random House, 1962), pp. 201-4.]

Christian doctrine and "worldly" thought. By the twentieth century, however, given all of the new knowledge and new methods which had come to the fore, "Thomism" — it could be argued — was thoroughly obsolete and archaic, hopelessly "unmodern." Yet, like traditional orthodoxy among Protestants, the thought of Thomas Aquinas enjoyed a great revival of interest in a very modern world. The two principal popularizers (in the best sense) of Thomism in America were not Americans but "imports": Jacques Maritain (1882-1973) and Etienne Gilson (1884-1978). Both were French and both were laymen, not clergymen. (1) Maritain in 1941 described the scope and significance of "the Thomist renaissance." (2) Gilson, in an autobiographical work published in 1962, discussed what it meant to be a Thomist.

1.

The historical importance of the Thomist renaissance comes from the fact that it constitutes a vast movement of thought affecting the life itself of the Church and the efforts of lay Christian workers, and from the fact that it consists of something rare in intellectual work, namely, a durable and progressive collaboration founded upon common principles and a living tradition. . . .

The tendencies that the Thomist revival represent are at once philosophical and theological. Accordingly, as Dom Chapman remarked with penetration, if one wishes to compare Thomism with modern thought, which has assumed all the divine and human problems of our destiny, one must compare modern philosophy not merely with Thomist philosophy, which is strictly limited to problems accessible to reason, but with the ensemble of Thomist philosophy and Thomist theology.

Thomism states as an absolute principle the unconditional affirmation of faith in the divine order, and it also affirms in the human order the unshakable intrinsic value of nature and reason, for every creature of God is good, as St. Paul said. Thomist thought appears from the very first as an effort to distinguish and to unite or rather to distinguish in order to unite.

Thomism can be characterized as an integralist and progressive Christian position. If we seek our conceptual weapons in the arsenal of Aristotle and Thomas Aquinas, it is not in order to return to ancient Greece or to the Middle Ages. We think that it is a sort of blasphemy against the Providence of God in history to want to go back to a past age, and we hold that there is an organic increase both in the Church and in the world. Hence the task of the Christian is, we believe, to save those "truths gone mad," as Chesterton said, which four centuries of Anthropocentric Humanism have disfigured, and to reconcile them with the truths of higher origin misunderstood by this Humanism, and to return them to Him who is Truth and to whose voice faith listens.

The Humanism of Thomas Aquinas is an Integral Humanism; I mean a Humanism which neglects nothing present in man. Such Humanism knows that man is made of nothing and that everything that comes from nothing tends of itself towards nothing; and it also knows that man is the image of God and that within man there is more than man; it knows that man is inhabited by a God who not only gives him life and activity but who gives him His Very Self and wishes him to have as final fruition the three Divine Persons.

It is a Humanism of the redemptive Incarnation — a Gospel-minded Humanism. I think that St. Thomas Aquinas is the apostle of modern times because these times have loved intelligence and have abused it and can be truly cured by it alone; and because Thomas Aquinas is the saint of the intellect; he reduces all things to the light of the Word, that Light which is at once — and this Karl Barth does not see — the Light that illuminates the reason of all men coming into this world and the Light that illuminates supernaturally all men reborn by faith. All the philosophy and all the theology of St. Thomas are constructed in the illumination of the word received by Moses: "I am Who Am."

The philosophy of St. Thomas is a philosophy not of essences but of existence; it lives from the natural intuitions of sensory experience and of the intelligence. His theology lives from faith; it is a theology of the incomprehensible Pure Act *to be* which subsists by itself and does not exist in the same Way as anything exists, and whose inmost life we cannot know except by its own Word. Accordingly, it can be said that Thomist thought is above all an existential one, although it is existential in a different manner from that of the various philosophies which have adopted this term. And it must be also said that it is a personalist thought, according as the philosophic realism of St. Thomas implies at every moment the act of the entire human person, body and soul, confronted with being to penetrate; and according as the theological Transcendentalism of St. Thomas is a perpetual dialogue between Christ speaking through the Church and Scripture, and reason listening and seeking.

The synthetic character of Thomistic thought has been often emphasized, and rightly so. It tends to make for unity in man and to prepare him for that peace which surpasses all understanding, in joining or reconciling in him grace and nature, faith and reason, theology and philosophy, the supernatural virtues and the natural virtues, the spiritual order and the temporal order, the speculative order and the practical one, mystical contemplation and knowledge merely human, fidelity to eternal data and understanding of time. But this view would be incomplete if we did not add that such a reconciliation has nothing to do with the more or less easy arrangements of bookish reason; it demands repeatedly surmounting conflicts repeatedly arising; it demands of man a tension and an extension which are possible only in the agony of the Cross. For the words of St. Paul are valid also in the order of things of the spirit: "Without shedding of blood there is no redemption." The reconciliation we spoke of is a false reconciliation if it is not a redemption; and it cannot be accomplished without mysterious suffering, the focus of which is the spirit itself.

2.

How does one become a Thomist? At what moment? This is not easy to say. For some reason or other a philosopher begins to read Saint Thomas. If he happens to be allergic to that way of thinking, he drops the book and never picks it up again. But if there exists between him and Saint Thomas some spiritual affinity, he will read and reread it. He will then talk about Thomism, write about it, with no other intention than to help others to dispel their ignorance as he slowly dispels his, but many will want something else. They will want to know, not what Saint Thomas Aquinas thinks, but whether you are a Thomist. The only honest answer to give is that, before proclaiming yourself a Thomist, you ought first to try to find out what the Saint actually thought. To do so is a long undertaking and it is an insult to the Saint's memory to proclaim oneself his disciple without knowing exactly what he said. Such scruples are foreign to the noisiest among his followers. What they want you to do is to say that you are a Thomist. They want you to join the Thomist party. Knowing what some of them call Thomism, and that they do not even suspect there is a problem in knowing what it is, the proposition *I am a Thomist* hardly makes sense. Unfortunately, the contrary proposition has a very definite sense. It would seem that many accept being called Thomists because of their deep reluctance to say that they are not.

He who enters upon this road must be ready for some surprises. The first one is that from this moment on he will be treated by the "Thomists" according to their customary ways, which are not always gentle. Should he be French, he can expect to become the object of particular attentions on the part of integrists whose theological fanaticism is matched by the intolerance so common among Frenchmen. The only Thomist in contemporary France whose thought was lofty, bold, and creative, capable of meeting the most urgent problems and, so to speak, to stand ever ready before all emergencies, was rewarded for his zeal by the incessant, active, and venomous hostility of unhappy creatures who have little else to put in the service of God than their hatred of their neighbors.[9] True enough, greatness as such is unbearable in their eyes. The disciple is not above the master. Every victim of their injustice will remember that Saint Thomas himself suffered from it.

Another possible surprise for the man who "turns Thomist" is that for the rationalist, that is for the "true philosopher," he will have ceased to exist. This is

---

9. The allusion here is to Maritain who, encountering much hostility in his native France, left for North America.

easily understood. Confronted with the prodigious inflation of books, philosophical journals and conventions prevalent in all civilized countries, it becomes necessary for readers to choose. Now the Thomist is a man who makes it
a point to think in philosophy what another man already thought in the thirteenth century. What an excellent pretext to get rid of him! From then on he
will find himself honorably classified as belonging among the modern survivors of the "Thomistic school." More simply still, he will find himself labeled a
"Neoscholastic," a man neither to be read nor discussed. . . .

The professed Thomist, then, should not be surprised at the solitude that
will surround him. If his own country does not want him, Christendom is vast
enough and some countries are generous enough to offer him the public he
cannot find at home. Such things have happened. If the synagogue of the
"laicists" excludes him, he still will have the opportunity, no doubt without enthusiasm, to turn to the Gentiles. The main thing is that, in a great mind that is
also a great heart, such isolation never breeds bitterness. Let his generosity be
an example to us. A man may have to live in isolation from his own country and
his own time, but he should not let his country and time become foreign to
him. On the contrary, the only legitimate reason to call oneself a Thomist is
that one feels happy to be one and is anxious to share this happiness with those
who are receptive to it.

A man becomes aware of being a Thomist on the day he realizes that from
then on he will no longer be able to live without the company of Saint Thomas
Aquinas. He feels in the *Summa Theologiae* as a fish in the sea; away from it he
feels out of his element, and cannot wait to go back to it. More deeply, this is
what gives the Thomist the joyous feeling that he is free. Essentially a Thomist is
a free mind. His freedom does not consist in having neither master nor God but
rather in having no master other than God. And indeed God is for man the only
bulwark against the tyrannies of other men. God alone delivers from fears and
timidities a mind that otherwise would die of starvation in the midst of plenty.
Left to itself, it will be unable to choose and will therefore die either from starvation or from indigestion. The happiness of the Thomist is the joy he experiences in feeling free to welcome all truth from whichever side it may come. The
perfect expression of this liberty of the Christian man is that of Saint Augustine: *Dilige et quod vis fac: Love and do what you will.* In exactly the same spirit
and the same deep sense, but in no other, the disciple of Saint Thomas can likewise say: *Believe, and think what you will.* Like charity, faith is a liberator. Incidentally, this is a reason why the Christian should willingly accept being considered as a rather unusual specimen by non-Christian thinkers.

An American Perspective

The remarkable popularity of Gilson and Maritain in the American Catholic community is helpfully commented on below. America itself really had no "central" Catholic theologian to put forward, though some were on the horizon. Thus, these two Europeans filled a void even as they gave "American Catholics the assurance of continuity with the past that they need. . . ." Walter J. Ong (b. 1912), long-time member of the faculty of English of St. Louis University and also a member of the Society of Jesus, explains that the French philosophers met "some deep-felt emotional need."

The first half of the twentieth century will doubtless go down in history as the age when American Catholics were specializing in symbols of frontier or borderline operations. Their idols (the word is hardly too strong) include not only figures such as Chesterton, Waugh, Greene, Mrs. Clare Boothe Luce, and numbers of converted Communists and other converts who have appeared in England and the United States to testify to the religio-intellectual charge at the borderline between the Church and her surroundings, as well as similar figures in France . . . but most especially two Europeans who have been first borrowed and more recently simply annexed by the English-speaking Catholics of North America, MM. Gilson and Maritain.

There can be little doubt that Professor Gilson has been sponsored by American Catholics not only out of admiration for his superb scholarship, but also out of some deep-felt emotional need. American Catholics commonly think of M. Gilson simply as a Thomist, but the author of *Thomism* himself has credited much of his interest in philosophy and inspiration to Bergson; and Bergson's sense of history, of a present which is and has always been the frontier where the past moves into the future, is undoubtedly one of the things which gave M. Gilson his appeal to the contemporary American Catholic mind. For this mind, Gilson helps symbolically to endow even the reputed static qualities of the Middle Ages, and with them the similar qualities imputed (mistakenly) by Americans to Europe in general, with the sense of movement in history so congenial to the American sensibility.

As a symbol, M. Gilson affects the American Catholic mind apparently well below the threshold of consciousness, for he himself appears much more explicitly aware of the necessity of establishing a dialogue between the Faith and America and more inclined explicitly to view his own work as contributing to this dialogue than are his own American backers. So far as I have observed,

[Source: Walter J. Ong, S. J., *Frontiers in American Catholicism* (New York: Macmillan Co., 1957), pp. 113-14.]

American Catholics seem quite unaware that the title of M. Gilson's Harvard lectures in honor of their fellow American William James which they so widely read, *The Unity of Philosophical Experience,* is a take-off and commentary on the title of an earlier series of Gifford Lectures by William James himself, *The Varieties of Religious Experience.* It is fascinating to note that in this exchange of views — at a distance of some years — it is James whose sense of history was not very compelling and who studies the various manifestations of drives common to all, or many individuals, focusing on an anhistorical diversity, whereas Gilson focuses on the unity evinced within movement or history, and thus gives comfort to the American Catholic unconscious in its own orientation toward movement.

The other favorite symbol of borderline activity, Professor Maritain, has been sponsored even more than Professor Gilson in the United States, where he is now more eminent than in his own country. Emerging from the same European-medieval context as Gilson, and thus giving American Catholics the assurance of continuity with the past that they need, Maritain puts the American Catholic ethos in contact less with the movement of history than with something else in its surroundings: the post-Newtonian scientific developments of a generation or two ago. It may fairly be said that he predigested these developments for American Catholic consumption. On the whole, his work in this field has been more widely attended to in America than his own more valuable work on Church-state relationships, which has had to compete with the parallel work of an American Jesuit, Father John Courtney Murray.[10]

Neo-Fundamentalism: Evangelical Responsibility

"The recovery of interest in special divine revelation is," wrote Carl F. H. Henry (b. 1912) in 1957, "one of the gracious providences of our century." So saying in Christianity Today, *a conservative journal of which Henry became the first editor, he called for a return to biblical theology and a rejection of that natural theology so dear to modernism. But the new fundamentalism, or "evangelical theology" to use Henry's term, is not a mere replication of the older fundamentalism. In the earlier time, genuine Christian living was so often interpreted as "personal abstinence from dubious social externals." Now, one moves toward "comprehending the whole of the moral law in fuller*

---

10. On Murray, see below, p. 543.

[Source: Carl F. H. Henry, in *Christianity Today,* July 8, 1957, p. 18; July 22, 1957, pp. 23-24.]

exposition of love for God and neighbor. . . ." The time for negativism and narrow legalism is over; the time for "positive preaching" and the "social application of Christian theology" is at hand.

The way theology defines the relation of revelation and reason will color its comprehension of Christianity and culture, Christianity and science, Christianity and philosophy, no less than the exposition of Christian doctrine and apologetics. If divine revelation stands in essential contrast to human reason, or if it impinges only dialectically upon the human mind, so that divine revelation cannot be grasped in concepts and words, then a Christian philosophy is a vain hope. It is part of the glory of evangelical theology that it rises above the modern contrast between God-truth and world-truth which divides human reason and precludes the intellectual integration of experience.

The recovery of interest in special divine revelation is one of the gracious providences of our century. It comes significantly at a time when the world must contend with the tactical initiatives of Communism and of irreligion. Protestant modernism deflected Western Christianity's theological interest from biblical revelation to natural theology.

This retrograde idealistic philosophy only briefly resisted a further decline to humanism. Evangelicals once reveled in the divine oracles; the modernists now asked whether God exists. Modernism's surrender of biblical revelation finally enmeshed American Christianity in the loss of the self-revealed God; in the noncommunist world, as well as the communist, naturalism surged to ascendancy. Now that special revelation is once again recognized as integral to Hebrew-Christian redemptive religion, it becomes a duty of evangelical theology to conserve this gain, and to shield it from speculative misunderstanding.

A higher spirit to quicken and to fulfill the theological fortunes of this century will require more than the displacement of modernism, more than the revision of neo-orthodoxy, more than the revival of fundamentalism. Recovery of apostolic perspective and dedication of the evangelical movement to biblical realities are foundational to this hope.

Exalt Biblical Theology

Evangelical theology has nothing to fear, and much to gain, from aligning itself earnestly with the current plea for a return to biblical theology. To measure this moving front of creative theology sympathetically, to understand its concern and courage and to name its weaknesses without depreciating its strength will best preserve relevant theological interaction with the contemporary debate.

The evangelical movement must make its very own the passionate concern for the reality of special divine revelation, for a theology of the Word of

God, for attentive hearing of the witness of the Bible, for a return to biblical theology.

Positive Preaching

Rededication to positive and triumphant preaching is the evangelical pulpit's great need. The note of Christ's lordship over this dark century, of the victory of Christianity, has been obscured. If it be evangelical, preaching must enforce the living communication of the changeless realities of divine redemption. The minister whose pulpit does not become the life-giving center of his community fails in his major mission. Perspective on Christianity's current gains and final triumph will avoid a myopic and melancholy discipleship. The Christian pulpit must present the invisible and exalted Head of the body of Christ; linked to him this earthly colony of heaven moves to inevitable vindication and glory. The perplexing problems of our perverse social orders find their hopeful solution only in this regenerative union. Out of its spiritual power must spring the incentives to creative cultural contributions.

Enlarge Christian Living

The evangelical fellowship needs a fresh and pervading conception of the Christian life. Too long fundamentalists have swiftly referred the question, "What distinguishes Christian living?" to personal abstinence from dubious social externals. The Christian conscience, of course, will always need to justify outward behavior, in home, in vocation and in leisure. But Christian ethics probes deeper. It bares the invisible zone of personality where lurk pride, covetousness and hatred.

Unfortunately, fundamentalism minimized the exemplary Jesus in the sphere of personal ethics. The theme of Christ's oneness with God was developed so exclusively in terms of his deity that the import of his dependence upon God for all human nature was lost. . . .

Another way in which evangelicals need to move beyond the fundamentalist ethic is in comprehending the whole of the moral law in fuller exposition of love for God and neighbor, and in the larger experience of the Holy Spirit in New Testament terms of ethical virtue. Often quite legalistically, and with an absoluteness beyond New Testament authority, fundamentalism's doctrine of surrender, of rededication, has merely proscribed worldly practices, from which the believer was discouraged. Unemphasized, however, are the fruit of the Spirit and those many virtues which differentiate dedicated living in terms of biblical Christianity.

Social Concern

We need a new concern for the individual in the entirety of his Christian experience. He is a member of all life's communities, of faith, of the family, of labor, of the state, of culture. Christianity is by no means the social gospel of modernism, but is nonetheless vibrant with social implications as a religion of redemptive transformation. To express and continue the vitality of the gospel message, marriage and the home, labor and economics, politics and the state, culture and the arts, in fact, every sphere of life, must evidence the lordship of Christ. . . .

Approach to Science

Evangelical confidence in the ontological significance of reason makes possible a positive, courageous approach to science. For more than a century and a half modern philosophy has regrettably minimized the role of reason. Kant disjoined it from the spiritual world. Darwin naturalized and constricted it within the physical world. Dewey allowed it only a pragmatic or an instrumental role. These speculations took a heavy toll in Christian circles. A segment of evangelical Christianity nonetheless maintained its insistence upon the Logos as integral to the Godhead, the universe as a rational-purposive order, and man's finite reason as related to the image of God.

Yet for more than a generation the evangelical attitude in scientific matters has been largely defensive. Evolutionary thought is met only obliquely. American fundamentalism often neglected scrutinizing its own position in the light of recent historical and scientific research. It even failed to buttress its convictions with rigorous theological supports.

Yet modernism, despite its eager pursuit of such revision, achieved no true correlation of Christianity and science. While modernism adjusted Christianity swiftly to the prevailing climate of technical conviction, its scientific respect was gained by a costly neglect of Christianity's import to science.

Today a new mood pervades the scientific sphere. That mood may not fully validate the evangelical view of nature, but it does at least deflate the presuppositions on which the older liberalism built its bias against the miraculous. The evangelical movement is now given a strategic opportunity to transcend its hesitant attitude toward scientific endeavor, and to stress the realities of a rational, purposive universe that coheres in the Logos as the agent in creation, preservation, redemption, sanctification and judgment.

Suggested Reading (Chapter Ten)

On the many connections between religion and the major philosophers excerpted in this chapter (James, Royce, Dewey, and Whitehead), outstanding historical accounts have been provided by Bruce Kuklick, *Churchmen and Philosophers from Jonathan Edwards to John Dewey* (1985), Ann Taves, *Fits, Trances, and Visions: Experiencing Religion and Explaining Experience from Wesley to James* (1999), Louis Menand, *The Metaphysical Club: A Story of Ideas in America* (2001), and Kuklick, *A History of Philosophy in America* (2002). For an engaged modern encounter with John Dewey and other pioneers of modern American philosophy, see Cornel West, *The American Evasion of Philosophy: A Genealogy of Pragmatism* (1989). Expert editing of William James's key work, *The Varieties of Religious Experience*, was provided by Martin E. Marty in a 1985 edition.

The encounters between science and religion, which have been generating much heat along with considerable light for more than a century and a half, have also generated a huge literature. Outstanding orientation, including matters far beyond America's shores, is provided by Gary B. Ferngren, ed., *Science and Religion* (2002), John Hedley Brooke, *Science and Religion: Some Historical Perspectives* (1991), David C. Lindberg and Ronald L. Numbers, eds., *God and Nature* (1986), John C. Greene, *Science, Ideology, and World View: Essays in the History of Evolutionary Ideas* (1981), and David N. Livingstone, et al., eds., *Evangelicals and Science in Historical Perspective* (1999). For the complex and often very political struggles over evolution, there is now a lineup of exceptional books that convey much less confusion in their history than is promoted by polemicists on the many sides of this issue. See especially James R. Moore, *The Post-Darwinian Controversies* (1979), Ronald L. Numbers, *The Creationists* (1992), Ronald L. Numbers, *Darwin Comes to America* (1998), Jon H. Roberts, *Darwinism and the Divine in America: Protestant Intellectuals and Organic Evolution, 1859-1900* (new ed., 2001), Edward J. Larson, *Trial and Error: The American Controversy over Creation and Evolution* (new ed., 2003), and Karl W. Giberson and Donald A. Yerxa, *Species of Origins: America's Search for a Creation Story* (2003). A work attuned to the history rather than the mythology of the 1925 Scopes Trial in Dayton, Tennessee, is Edward J. Larson, *Summer for the Gods: The Scopes Trial and America's Continuing Debate Over Science and Religion* (1997). On some of the individuals whose comments are excerpted in this chapter, see Donald Worster, *A River Running West: The Life of John Wesley Powell* (2000), Lester Stephen, *Joseph LeConte: Gentle Prophet of Evolution* (1982), J. David Hoeveler, Jr., *James McCosh and the Scottish Intellectual Tradition from Glasgow to Princeton* (1981), Mark A. Noll and David N. Livingstone, eds., *B. B. Warfield on Evolution, Science, and Scripture* (2000), and Ralph E. Weber, *Notre Dame's John Zahm* (1961). Cardinal Gibbons talked about evolution because he addressed almost all important issues of his era. For a still-useful biography, see John Tracy Ellis, *The Life of James Cardinal Gibbons* (1963).

A good approach to early American contributions to the "scientific" study of the Bible is through the history of divinity schools and seminaries associated with major universities, for example, George H. Williams, ed., *The Harvard Divinity School* (1954), and Roland A. Bainton, *Yale and the Ministry* (1957). For its 100th anniversary, the Society for Biblical Literature commissioned a number of volumes examining the pervasive and multi-faceted American engagement with Scripture. Several attempted broad surveys of how Scripture has been appropriated in various faith traditions, including Gerald P. Fogarty, *American Catholic Biblical Scholarship . . . from the Early Republic to Vatican II* (1989), David S. Sperling, Baruch A. Levine, and Barry B. Levy, *Students of the Covenant: A History of Jewish Biblical Scholarship in North America* (1992), and Mark A. Noll, *Between Faith and Criticism: Evangelicals, Scholarship, and the Bible in America* (1991). Particularly insightful on related themes was an essay that appeared in another one of the commissioned volumes, Jonathan D. Sarna and Nahum M. Sarna, "Jewish Biblical Scholarship and Translation in the United States," in E. S. Frerichs, ed., *The Bible and Bibles in America* (1988). For an account of many of these commissioned volumes, see Mark A. Noll, "Review Essay: The Bible in America," *Journal of Biblical Literature* 106 (1987): 493-509. The two best books ever done on, respectively, the physical production and the translation of the Bible in American history appeared nearly simultaneously at the end of the century, Paul P. Gutjahr, *An American Bible: A History of the Good Book in the United States, 1777-1880* (1999), and Peter J. Thuesen, *In Discordance with the Scriptures: American Protestant Battles over Translating the Bible* (1999). Mark S. Massa clarified the position of one important early moderate on Bible criticism, *Charles Augustus Briggs and the Crisis of Historical Criticism* (1990). For a set of essays considering broader matters of Scripture and culture, see Nathan O. Hatch and Mark A. Noll, eds., *The Bible in America* (1982).

For background on the rise of modernism within American Catholicism, see David J. O'Brien, *Isaac Hecker: An American Catholic* (1992), and for its development over a short career, R. Scott Appleby, *"Church and Age Unite": The Modernist Impulse in American Catholicism* (1992). The finest studies of the contending forces that battled for the soul of American Protestant life early in the twentieth century remain William R. Hutchison, *The Modernist Impulse in American Protestantism* (1976), and George M. Marsden, *Fundamentalism and American Culture . . . 1870-1925* (1980). Insightful studies of key figures are provided by D. G. Hart, *Defending the Faith: J. Gresham Machen and the Crisis of Conservative Protestantism in Modern America* (1994), and Robert Moats Miller, *Harry Emerson Fosdick: Preacher, Pastor, Prophet* (1985). Judaism's varying responses to modernity may be followed in Mel Scult, *Judaism Faces the Twentieth*

Century: A Biography of Mordecai M. Kaplan (1993), Samuel Belkin, *Essays in Traditional Jewish Thought* (1956), Solomon Poll, *The Hasidic Community of Williamsburg* (1962), Michael A. Meyer, *Response to Modernity: A History of the Reform Movement in Judaism* (1988), and Pamela Susan Nadess, *Conservative Judaism in America* (1988).

On the development of one strand of modern Protestant theology, a major interpretation entitled *The Making of American Liberal Theology* is being presented in three volumes by Gary J. Dorrien, including vol. 1: *Imagining Progressive Religion, 1805-1900* (2001), and vol. 2: *Idealism, Realism, and Modernity, 1900-1950* (2003). The useful anthologies edited by Mark G. Toulouse and James O. Duke contain a great deal of material on their subject for the twentieth century: *Makers of Christian Theology in America* (1997), and *Sources of Christian Theology in America* (1999). Works on Reinhold Niebuhr were suggested at the end of chapter nine. For other important Protestant voices, see Ronald F. Thiemann, ed., *The Legacy of H. Richard Niebuhr* (1991), and F. Forester Church, ed., *The Essential Tillich* (1987). For Neo-Thomism, besides the many writings of Maritain and Gilson themselves, there is an engaging contemporary account by the influential Chicago educator, Mortimer J. Adler, who provided his positive appraisal in *Saint Thomas and the Gentiles* (1938). The modern viability of philosophical Thomism is suggested by Alasdair C. MacIntyre in *Three Rival Versions of Moral Enquiry* (1990). For the way in which Neo-Thomism provided the grounding for Catholic higher education (and also for Catholic higher education floundered when Neo-Thomism gave way), see the splendid study by Philip Gleason, *Contending with Modernity: Catholic Higher Education in the Twentieth Century* (1995). For the new evangelical movements in which Carl Henry took the lead, see especially Joel A. Carpenter, *Revive Us Again: The Reawakening of American Fundamentalism* (1997). For Henry's own account, the autobiographical *Confessions of a Theologian* (1986) is quite useful. Richard F. Lovelace provided the most attractive historical and theological account of the movement in *Dynamics of Spiritual Life: An Evangelical Theology of Renewal* (1979).

ELEVEN

Consensus and Conflict

In the period since World War II, the relationship between American religions and American culture has been as robust as it has been uneasy. That uneasiness was evident in the years immediately following the war, which are the focus for most of the documents presented in this chapter. And it has continued to the present, as is suggested by the excerpts below that follow postwar situations closer to the present. On the one hand, a postwar "revival" of religion suggested a scene that was upbeat and positive. On the other hand, theology grew less assured and less constructive while a statistical profile of mainline denominations suggested that, by the end of the 1960s, all was not well. So too, from one perspective, the postwar years brought a flood of ecumenical activity, enough so that one might even characterize this period as the "era of good will." Yet, from another perspective, the country and its churches were deeply divided over civil rights, over communist and anticommunist crusades, over moral obligations to the culturally and economically deprived, and over moral integrity — or the conspicuous absence thereof — in the nation's highest offices. The signals were mixed, as religion now and then functioned as the agent of consensus, now and then as the occasion of conflict.

The World and Its Wars

As in all of the nation's other wars before and since, World War II had its religious dissenters — those who for cause of conscience could not bear arms or agree to slay the enemy. Yet, unlike many of America's other wars, this one created no widespread dissent, resulted in no sharp social division. No "loyalists" to purge or force into exile as in the American Revolution, no antiimperialists to suppress or denounce as in the Mexican or in the later Spanish-American War, and of course no horrible clash between brother and brother as in the Civil War. Aside from the disgraceful treatment of the Japanese Americans,

World War II was a national effort: reviving the economy, unifying the nation internally, and elevating the United States to the highest peak of world influence and power. Nevertheless, for all its glory and unconditional victories over Germany, Italy, and Japan, this World War left two haunting legacies. Hiroshima revealed the enormity of mankind's new power to destroy; the Holocaust revealed the enormity of mankind's old power to hate. Both legacies were of such a scale as to defy comparisons, and both demanded new efforts to "justify the ways of God to man."

One of the by-products of World War II and the Allied victory was the creation of the state of Israel in 1948. Sentiment for such a Jewish homeland did not originate, of course, in the 1940s. For generations before, those favoring such a state *somewhere* (and at times, anywhere) — the Zionists — had appealed to Jews around the world and to consciences in all the world for help in bringing such a homeland into being. The Zionist movement, European in origin, found wide though not universal support in America. After the founding of Israel, however, and even more after the 1967 Six Day War, anti-Zionism in America was reduced to a whisper. Vindication had at last come for the Hungarian Theodor Herzl, Zionism's passionate and persuasive nineteenth-century voice.

If Israel's brief war in 1967 was a conspicuous success, America's long war of the 1960s and 1970s was a tragic failure: tragic on the battlefield, and tragic at home. Never since the Civil War had the nation found itself so bitterly divided, so much at cross purposes with its own vision of what "America" as symbol had meant since 1776. One of the reasons for swelling criticism was simply the Vietnam War's interminable course. It turned out to be the country's longest war, from 1964 to 1975, and surely its least satisfying one. What were the vital interests of the United States in far-off Indochina? What were our purposes: politically, economically, militarily, morally? The whole encounter, moreover, had a kind of David and Goliath aspect, with this nation seen as the heavy-handed, bullying giant. "The picture of the world's greatest superpower killing or seriously injuring 1,000 noncombatants a week, while trying to pound a tiny backward nation into submission," wrote Secretary of Defense Robert S. McNamara to President Lyndon B. Johnson on May 19, 1967, "is not a pretty one." And the picture turned even uglier as the costs mounted in both dollars and lives, as the cries and acts of dissent grew more desperate. By war's end, 57,000 Americans had died and untold thousands of Vietnamese. The living were left shaken, sobered, morally confused. The course of the long cold war with the Union of Soviet Socialist Republics eventually turned out differently. Whether the U.S. "won" the cold war or the U.S.S.R. "lost" it remains a matter for ongoing debate. What cannot be debated is the large and looming presence that, early and late, the cold war exerted on the American consciousness, including religious consciousness.

Society and Its Conflicts

The 1950s and 1960s were difficult times for synagogue and church, for politician and president. The World War II alliance with the Soviet Union, an alliance of convenience for some and a pact with the devil for others, did not long survive the postwar negotiating and global positioning by England, France, the Soviet Union, and the United States. As the Cold War cast its pall, the whole world seemed divided between communist (despotic and atheistic) and noncommunist (free and godly) halves. In the 1950s the Americans' pledge of allegiance to the flag was amended to include the phrase "under God," as if to emphasize that the Cold War was also, to some degree, a Holy War. The passions aroused on all sides were equal to such a crusade. In the days of Senator Joseph McCarthy's greatest power, from around 1948 to around 1954 (he died in 1957), mainline churches, and especially Protestant churches, found themselves thrown on the defensive, shielding themselves from being attacked as dupes, cowards, or traitors. For the historic Protestant churches of America, it was a position of striking anomaly: surprising in its novelty and unnerving in its severity. Like measles or whooping cough, this epidemic also passed, but it left a religious establishment weakened and unwell.

Remarkably, however, near the close of the "McCarthy era," the United States Supreme Court (under the leadership of Chief Justice Earl Warren) unanimously decided that separate education (for blacks and for whites) did not constitute equal education. Then, under the even more remarkable leadership of Martin Luther King, Jr., the late 1950s and the 1960s saw Protestant, Catholic, Jew — and Orthodox — caught up in and effectively contributing to the civil rights movement. The rhetoric was moving, the dedication widespread, the resistance (including, of course, religious resistance) deep-seated and often bloody. It would be a mistake, to be sure, to regard that struggle as now over, or to delude oneself into thinking that some permanent peace had been agreed upon. But advances were made (notably in the presidential years of Lyndon B. Johnson, 1963-69), as the nation inched closer to the ideal proclaimed long ago of all men's equal creation.

In 1960, the Democratic party put forward its nomination for the presidency of the United States: John F. Kennedy, then a U. S. senator, formerly a U. S. representative, a veteran of World War II, a graduate of Harvard, and a native of the colonial state of Massachusetts. To some segments of the voting public, however, the only fact about him that really mattered was that he was a Roman Catholic. In 1928, the Democrats had nominated Alfred E. Smith (see above, pp. 263, 266-68), and while his Catholicism was not the only issue, it was a highly inflammatory one. Would 1960 be a repeat of 1928? It was not, as everyone knows, but "the religious issue" occupied a disproportionate amount of time and space in press, pulpit, and presidential coverage. A kind of maturing, it could be argued, had taken place between 1928 and 1960, a maturing also evident in the effort that followed Kennedy's assassination in 1963 to extend the benefits of an affluent society to all its citizens. The argument for maturity became harder to make in the early 1970s, however, as a vice president resigned for the first time in American history amid charges of bribery and corruption; and then, as a president resigned for the first time in American history amid charges of lying, covering up a crime, and attempting to create an imperial presidency. The Great Society had so soon become the Betrayed Society.

The Nation and Its Churches

On the domestic religious front, the second half of the twentieth century began with the reorganizing of the old (1908) Federal Council of Churches into a strengthened and more visible National Council of Churches (1950). The World Council of Churches, founded two years earlier in Amsterdam, selected the United States for its second great gathering: at Evanston, Illinois, in 1954. In 1956, the fortnightly magazine, *Christianity Today,* began publication, giving a more cohesive and unifying voice to large segments of conservative Christianity in America. Billy Graham was a prime mover behind the founding of this journal, and he would also play a leading role in calling together the Lausanne Congress on World Evangelization of 1974. This meeting and its subsequent committees have represented for Protestant evangelicals and many emerging Pentecostal groups worldwide what the World Council of Churches has meant for mainline Protestants. In 1960 Presbyterian Eugene Carson Blake and Episcopalian James Albert Pike stimulated the formation of the Consultation on Church Union, a wide-ranging "Proposal Toward the Reunion of Christ's Church." In the decade that followed, Episcopalians and Presbyterians, Congregationalists and Methodists (both black and white denominations), Disciples of Christ, and others probed into the nature of the church and its ministry, the sacraments and liturgy, the creeds and theology in search of that firm foundation on which all could build together. By the end of the century the Consultation had been transformed into a new organization, Churches Uniting in Christ, which exists to further shared worship and activity among the ten denominations that made up the Consultation.

Of course, not all church activity moved in the direction of ecumenical good will. The Lutherans, who had sailed rather majestically through the troubled waters of modernism and fundamentalism earlier in the century, found themselves thrown against the rocks in the 1970s. At that time the Lutheran Church–Missouri Synod fired faculty, expelled students, and drove away churches — all on grounds repeatedly marched over in America's religious history. Only the timing was occasion for surprise. In the 1980s, the Southern Baptist Convention followed the path taken by the Missouri Synod in fighting its own tardy battle over biblical inerrancy and ministerial authority. On the other hand, northern and southern Presbyterians merged in 1983, while major branches of American Lutheranism (Missouri Synod aside) came together in 1987 — creating an Evangelical Lutheran Church of over five million members.

By any accounting, the top religious story, worldwide, of the early sixties concerned the convening of the most important church council since the sixteenth century. Vatican II (1962-65) met not in secret but in open daylight, as an entranced world listened on radio, watched on television, and read the countless pamphlets, articles, columns of newsprint, and books which poured forth like an avalanche. Pope John's "revolution," as it has been called without exaggeration, was the heroic if tardy struggle of the Roman Catholic Church to come to terms with the modern world, such a "settlement" having been emphatically rejected by Pope Pius IX (*Syllabus of Errors,* 1864), by Vatican I (Dogma of Papal Infallibility, 1870), and by Pius X (*Pascendi Dominici Gregis,* 1907). Decades after the fourth and final session of Vatican II (concluded ceremonially with a mass in St. Peter's Square in Rome, December 8, 1965), Roman Catholics in America — and elsewhere around the world — still busily worked at the far-reaching implications of this Council.

In 1955 Jewish sociologist-theologian Will Herberg published a popular treatment of religion in America; he called it *Protestant, Catholic, Jew* and spoke of these affiliations as America's three ways of being religious. But there was then, and is now, a fourth way of major significance: Eastern Orthodoxy. The Orthodox in America, chiefly gathered into Greek and Russian communions, had an affiliated membership of nearly four million in 2000, roughly equivalent to the number of religiously observant Jews at that time. Yet, these Americans have been scarcely visible, except for an occasional "fourth" prayer at presidential inaugurations (who is that bearded man?). The reason for this near invisibility has nothing to do with that church's numbers, nothing to do with its long history, and certainly nothing to do with the nature of its worship and pageantry. Anyone who has attended an Eastern Orthodox service where every one of his or her senses was stimulated if not overwhelmed would have real difficulty imagining how such a church could escape wide public notice. The answer to the mystery lies in ethnicity and unbending tradition. Ethnic enclaves are nothing new to American religion: the colonial period is full of such small groups huddled together for survival, while in the nineteenth century Lutheranism provides the best example of those who found their togetherness more in terms of language, ethnicity, and national origin than in terms of theological tradition or creedal loyalty. For the twentieth century, Eastern Orthodoxy affords the best example. Language, ethnicity, and national ties are clung to, while steps toward Americanization or acculturation are taken only tentatively. Joined with this ethnic environment is the firm dedication to tradition, to — if you will — "Orthodoxy." The Eastern Orthodox churches have undergone no Reformation, no Enlightenment, no direct challenge by the familiar forces of modernism and fundamentalism, no Vatican II (though observers did attend that Council and have participated in various ways in the National and World Council of Churches). As a result of all this, it becomes deplorably easy, unjustifiably easy, to write of "religion in America" with little or no attention to this ancient, colorful, sometime powerful force in world Christendom.

Revivalism and Retreat

In three hundred or so years of American history, it would be difficult to find a more "American" phenomenon or one more potent with possibility than the religious revival. Over and over, revivalism has been dismissed as only a feeble survivor of an earlier and simpler time: weak, wobbly, and barely able to thump some crude pulpit in some obscure church. Over and over, this caricature has proved to be utterly false. The person most responsible for revivalism's enduring vitality in the decades after World War II is Billy Graham. Since 1949 at least, Graham has captured national and international headlines; he has been interviewed, acclaimed, excoriated, and written off as a mere flash in the pan. The flash has been a long time fading. Being in the limelight for so long almost guarantees a kind of arrested development, a refusal to do anything but echo the sure formulas of success. Graham has defied this pattern, however, as he has over many years become more socially sensitive, more politically wary, and more theologically self-critical. So with Graham, and quite apart from Graham, religion revived in the 1950s, some of the larger churches beginning to falter by the end of the 1960s.

Theology also faltered, as the most popular religious books could hardly be distinguished from the best-selling self-help books. New Thought (see above, pp. 227-51) proved highly marketable thought, but now emerging from the bosoms of the older ecclesiastical traditions. Then for a time in the 1960s it became fashionable to speak of the "death of God" or to argue for a "religious humanism" that could preserve all the old values with few of the old verities. No wonder, then, that religious statistics that had arched ever upward took a surprising, discomforting downward turn. In many of the mainline denominations, if there was any growth at all, it did not even match the modest increase in national population. In other instances, the decline was absolute. So, a line portraying a centuries-old trend of enlarging membership — from, say, less than 20 percent in the colonial period to over 60 percent in the 1960s — leveled out or slid slightly toward the bottom of the graph. In 1970, according to the Gallup Poll, only 14 percent of the sampled population were prepared to agree that religion in this country was "increasing its influence." Tables, graphs, charts, and polls did not reveal a bullish market in religion; nor did the older schools of theology, monasteries, convents, and the ranks of young recruits for ministry and mission. Things would change in the 1960s and 1990s, but only because the forces of both religious renewal and religion-ignoring secularism became more assertive.

1. The World and Its Wars

Legacy of World War II

Hiroshima

The world was introduced into the atomic age neither gradually nor gently. That abrupt introduction came on August 6, 1945. Nearly one hundred thousand people were killed almost instantly, another hundred thousand fatally injured, a whole city left in rubble, and a whole world left in anxious dread and moral confusion. "America's Atomic Atrocity," a leading Protestant journal editorialized (Christian Century, *August 29, 1945), this after a second bomb had been dropped on Nagasaki, obliterating that urban center as well. The task of reconciliation, the editor noted, falls to the churches who must restore "the spiritual basis of community between the Christian church and the Japanese people." In the document below, Richard M. Fagley (b. 1910), a member of the Federal Council of Churches' Commission on a Just and Durable Peace, also insisted that "we cannot escape this crisis by secularist means."*

If there was any doubt that beneath the crisis of the Second World War lay a more profound crisis of man, the explosions in New Mexico, Hiroshima and Nagasaki should have shattered the illusion. The fact that the illusion widely persists reveals the depth of our present, and possibly final, crisis.

Through the sacrifices of young men and scientific discovery, our secularized society survived the crisis of Hitler's pagan conspiracy. The faith of

[Source: R. M. Fagley, "The Atomic Bomb and the Crisis of Man," *Christianity and Crisis,* Oct. 1, 1945, p. 5.]

Refugees at Ibinokuchi, near Nagasaki, Japan, on August 10, 1945
(© by Hiroshima City and Nagasaki City)

modern man in his own self-sufficiency unfortunately also survived, weakened perhaps but not broken. Consequently, the end of one crisis becomes, with the discovery of atomic power, the beginning of a far greater crisis. From this crisis there is no escape by the ways familiar to secularism or worldliness. The inexorable "either-or" of the atomic bomb, upon which hangs the fate of life on this planet, leaves the pride of man no means by which to save itself. The only alternative to Armageddon is repentance and regeneration.

One tragic reflection of the present crisis is the picture, conjured up by some of our writers, of vast power and plenty made possible by atomic energy. The Promised Land of freedom from want lies just ahead. Man has made the power of the sun his servant, and freed himself for luxury and leisure. How distorted is our vision to see so easily the vista of mechanical progress in this Atomic Age, and to fail to see clearly the greed, pride and fear in ourselves which have now brought us to the doorstep of doom! Of course, atomic energy can lift the burden of poverty from the backs of countless millions and give all mankind the material basis for creative living. What should be equally obvious is that only if man has a new spirit within him can he pass over into this Promised Land. The Atomic Age is otherwise almost certain to be extremely short and extremely brutish!

Equally revealing is the naive faith of many in the ability of science to control the threat of atomic bombs by creating effective counter-weapons. The end of a scientific race between the development of anti-bombs and the development of bigger, faster bombs is not hard to see. It is the end of man on this earth. Not machines but man with God's help can control the power God has permitted man to discover.

Again, there is the common illusion that fear can protect mankind from atomic war. Fear, it is true, may help — if it leads men to seek, with a contrite heart, the protection and guidance of God. But fear by itself offers a shortcut to catastrophe. The fear of destruction from atomic bombs in the present world of competing states would insure and hasten sudden, ruthless attacks with atomic bombs. Total aggression would become the strategy for survival. As Norman Cousins writes: "If history teaches us anything, it is that the possibility of war increases in direct proportion to the effectiveness of the instruments of war."

Of a piece with the above patterns of thought is the notion that the present crisis might be exorcised, if only the inventors would destroy their infernal machine, or if they would discontinue the manufacture of bombs, while the nations signed a pledge not to use them. For better or worse, however, the clock of history does not run backwards. Nor can its cosmic hands be stayed by Kellogg-Briand pacts. Atomic power is here to stay for the remainder of human history. And unless man can control himself as well as atomic power according to the moral law, both will no doubt terminate within a comparatively few years.

The argument for world government as a way to control the perils and potentialities of atomic energy is logical in detail. But its fundamental premise, that changes in political institutions by themselves would assure human survival, is false like the rest of the secularist arguments. No form of government is foolproof. No system of international control can provide a final answer. Political institutions can be corrupted. Controls can break down.

This does not mean that the form of institution or the differences among types of political controls are unimportant. Far from it. Yet twist and turn as we may, we cannot escape from this crisis by secularist means. We are driven inexorably from one false solution to another, unless and until we seek a more profound, religious solution. A deeper faith in God and therefore in man as a child of God and a more sacrificial effort to make brotherhood a guiding principle of society, alone offer real hope that atomic rockets can be kept under control, and the new energy be put to the service of human needs. Unless men everywhere are moved to confess their own inadequacy, and seek to follow God's will rather than their own, no other strategy can save mankind.

The fate of the world, therefore, in a literal sense, depends upon the ability of the moral and religious forces, and above all, of the Christian churches, to call men effectively to repentance, worship, and service. The conversion of man, who, as Cousins puts it, "has exalted change in everything but himself," has suddenly become a life-and-death issue, not merely for individuals, but for the race. Beyond all other groups, our churches are confronted with the ultimatum of the atomic bomb, for they alone can provide a significant answer.

Holocaust   *Laura Hildebrand's book Unbroken*

> *If the enormity of Hiroshima was almost instantaneously evident, the horror of the Holocaust came only by degrees. Even that way, it proved impossible to absorb: millions of Jews, along with hundreds of thousands of others, systematically imprisoned, degraded, experimented with, tortured, gassed, buried. The camp at Auschwitz came to symbolize the depravity of this event, an event unique in "the whole history of human depravity." And Auschwitz became for many a kind of moral and theological line of demarcation. After Auschwitz, one could never reflect in quite the same way concerning the nature of God or man, and concerning the meaning of human history. Emil L. Fackenheim (b. 1916), rabbi and professor of philosophy at the University of Toronto, writes below of "The Commanding Voice of Auschwitz."*

My mind and spirit are still numbed. I have, however, acquired one religious certainty as great as any in this religiously uncertain age. Søren Kierkegaard once perceived his "knight of faith" as forever obliged to retrace Abraham's road to Mount Moriah, the place where he was to sacrifice Isaac. The Jewish believer and theological thinker today — as well as a century or a millennium hence — is obliged to retrace, again and again, the *via dolorosa* that led one-third of his people to the human sacrifice in the Nazi gas chambers. He is forbidden the cheap and often sacrilegious evasions that tempt him on every side:

[Source: E. L. Fackenheim, *The Jewish Return into History* (New York: Schocken Books, 1978), pp. 44-47.]

the "progressive" ideology that asserts that memory is unnecessary, that Auschwitz was an accidental "relapse into tribalism" (an insult to any tribe ever in existence); the "psychiatric" ideology that holds that memory is masochism even as Auschwitz itself was sadism, thus safely belittling both; the "liberal-universalist" ideology that asserts that memory is actually immoral, that because Jews must care about Vietnam, the Black ghetto, and Arab refugees, they are obliged to forget the greatest catastrophe suffered by their own people.

That last-named ideology is especially insidious, for good Jews are tempted by it. When I first called Auschwitz unique my assertion was at once taken to mean that a dead Jewish child at Auschwitz is a greater tragedy than a dead German child at Dresden. That was a misunderstanding possible only because of an antisemitism (conscious or unconscious) that distinguishes "universalistic" Jews concerned with others to the point of consenting to group suicide, and "particularistic" Jews who deserve this nasty epithet if they show any concern whatever for the fate of their own people. This ideology, I say, tempts many: witness the countless Jews today who risk much in behalf of Vietnam or the Black ghetto but will not utter a word against Polish or Soviet antisemitism. Hatred of Jews on the part of others has always produced self-hating Jews — never more so than when disguised as a moral ideology.

I call Auschwitz unique because it *is* unique. As my wife, Rose, put it in a letter to a minister, Auschwitz was

> overwhelming in its scope, shattering in its fury, inexplicable in its demonism. Unlike Hiroshima, it was no miscalculation of a government at war. It was minutely planned and executed over a twelve-year period, with the compliance of thousands of citizens, to the deafening silence of the world. Unlike slaughtered Russian villages, these were no chance victims of the fury of war. They were carefully chosen, named, listed, tabulated, and stamped. The Nazis went to incredible lengths to find even a single missing Jew. It did not help but hindered the war effort. For while antisemitism was in the beginning politically advantageous to the Nazis the actual crime of genocide had often to be carefully hidden from their own people. Troop trains were diverted from the Russian front in order to transport Jews to Auschwitz. Unique in all human history, the Holocaust was evil for evil's sake.

The woman who wrote those words is a Christian. I doubt whether I or any other Jew could have been so relentless as she was in her evaluation.

No wonder the mind seeks refuge in comparisons — some shallow, some obscene, all false — between Auschwitz and Hiroshima, or Vietnam, or the Black ghetto, or even the American campus. Indeed, the very words "Holocaust" and "six million" are evasive abstractions, empty universal substitutes for the countless particulars each of which is an inexhaustible mystery of sin and suffering. . . .

Let me take just one of those particulars. In issuing "work permits" that were designed to separate "useless" Jews to be murdered at once from "useful" ones to be kept useful by diabolically contrived false hopes and murdered later, the Nazis customarily issued two such permits to an able-bodied Jewish man. One was untransferable, to be kept for himself; the other was to be given at his own discretion to his able-bodied mother, father, wife, or one child. The Nazis would not make the choice, even though to do so would have produced a more efficient labor force. Jewish sons, husbands, or fathers themselves were forced to decide who among their loved ones was — for the time being — to live, who to die at once.

I search the whole history of human depravity for comparisons. In vain. I would reject the comparisons cited above even if they compared the comparable: let each human evil be understood in its own terms. What makes the comparisons utterly odious is that in effect if not intention they abuse Auschwitz, deny that it ever happened, rob its victims even of memory. There is a qualita-

Desecrated synagogue in Munich, Germany
(Archives, City of Munich)

tive distinction between evils — even gigantic ones — perpetuated for such "rational" ends as gain, victory, real or imagined self-interest, and evils perpetrated for evil's sake.

Moreover, there can be a difference even among evils for evil's sake. Theologians call these "the demonic," and I myself once found escape in this theological abstraction. I find it no more. In the history of demonic evil (which, incidentally, in this age of uncritical theological celebrations, someone should write) conceivably there are examples comparable to the Nazi custom of issuing the two work permits. But until such examples are found my religious life and theological thought must lack the comfort of comparisons as I retrace the *via dolorosa* that leads to Auschwitz, trying at the desperate utmost to match the solitude, the despair, the utter abandonment of every one of my brethren who walked that road. And I shall always fail.

Zionism and the State of Israel

"Let Sovereignty Be Granted"

The history of Zionism in the modern world as well as its place in power politics must begin with Theodor Herzl (1860-1904), native of Budapest, student of law, of German language and culture, and a journalist. The infamous 1894 trial of Alfred Dreyfus, a French army officer, proved the persisting force of anti-Semitism and turned Herzl into a passionate Zionist. He wrote The Jewish State *(excerpted below) in 1896, launched the Zionist newspaper,* Die Welt, *in 1897, and gathered Jews together in World Congresses to educate them concerning the absolute necessity for Jews to be granted sovereignty "over a portion of the globe adequate to meet our rightful national requirements." Then, Herzl added, "we will attend to the rest."*

No one can deny the gravity of the Jewish situation. Wherever they live in appreciable number, Jews are persecuted in greater or lesser measure. Their equality before the law, granted by statute, has become practically a dead letter. They are debarred from filling even moderately high offices in the army, or in any public or private institutions. And attempts are being made to thrust them out of business also: "Don't buy from Jews!"

[Source: Arthur Hertzberg, ed., *The Zionist Idea* (Westport, Conn.: Greenwood Press, 1959 [this document 1896]), pp. 215-16, 220-21.]

Attacks in parliaments, in assemblies, in the press, in the pulpit, in the street, on journeys — for example, their exclusion from certain hotels — even in places of recreation are increasing from day to day. The forms of persecutions vary according to country and social circle. In Russia, special taxes are levied on Jewish villages; in Romania, a few persons are put to death; in Germany, they get a good beating occasionally; in Austria, anti-Semites exercise their terrorism over all public life; in Algeria, there are traveling agitators; in Paris, the Jews are shut out of the so-called best social circles and excluded from clubs. The varieties of anti-Jewish expression are innumerable. But this is not the occasion to attempt the sorry catalogue of Jewish hardships. We shall not dwell on particular cases, however painful.

I do not aim to arouse sympathy on our behalf. All that is nonsense, as futile as it is dishonorable. I shall content myself with putting the following questions to the Jews: Is it not true that, in countries where we live in appreciable numbers, the position of Jewish lawyers, doctors, technicians, teachers, and employees of every description becomes daily more intolerable? Is it not true that the Jewish middle classes are seriously threatened? Is it not true that the passions of the mob are incited against our wealthy? Is it not true that our poor endure greater suffering than any other proletariat? I think that this pressure is everywhere present. In our upper economic classes it causes discomfort, in our middle classes utter despair.

The fact of the matter is, everything tends to one and the same conclusion, which is expressed in the classic Berlin cry: *"Juden 'raus!"* ("Out with the Jews!").

I shall now put the question in the briefest possible form: Shouldn't we "get out" at once, and if so, whither?

Or, may we remain, and if so, how long?

Let us first settle the point of remaining. Can we hope for better days, can we possess our souls in patience, can we wait in pious resignation till the princes and peoples of this earth are more mercifully disposed toward us? I say that we cannot hope for the current to shift. And why not? Even if we were as near to the hearts of princes as are their other subjects, they could not protect us. They would only incur popular hatred by showing us too much favor. And this "too much" implies less than is claimed as a right by any ordinary citizen or ethnic group. The nations in whose midst Jews live are all covertly or openly anti-Semitic.

The common people have not, and indeed cannot have, any comprehension of history. They do not know that the sins of the Middle Ages are now being visited on the nations of Europe. We are what the ghetto made us. We have without a doubt attained pre-eminence in finance because medieval conditions drove us to it. The same process is now being repeated. We are again being forced into money-lending — now named stock exchange — by being kept out of other occupations. But once on the stock exchange, we are again objects of contempt. At the same time we continue to produce an abundance of mediocre intellectuals who find no outlet, and this endangers our social position as much as does our increasing wealth. Educated Jews without means are now rapidly becoming socialists. Hence we are certain to suffer acutely in the struggle between the classes, because we stand in the most exposed position in both the capitalist and the socialist camps. . . .

The Plan

The whole plan is essentially quite simple, as it must necessarily be if it is to be comprehensible to all.

Let sovereignty be granted us over a portion of the globe adequate to meet our rightful national requirements; we will attend to the rest.

"Zionism in America"

For more than half a century, the spiritual descendants of Herzl agitated, cajoled, bargained, and prayed until at last in 1948 the state of Israel came into being. It was an occasion of incalculable significance for Jews throughout the whole world, of course, but Jews in America had a special role: "to marshal political and financial support" that would not only help bring such a state into being but also would insure its stability and safety in the years ahead. Writing in the year of America's own bicentennial in 1976 (with Israel not yet a full generation old), Rabbi Arthur Hertzberg (b. 1921), author, lecturer, and member of the World Zionist Organization, wrote of the way in which "America is different." In that Diaspora (that is, in that land far away from the Holy Land), the "overarching religion of American Jews" is a "pride and glory in American Jewry's sharing in Israel. . . ."

Zionism is supposed to make Jews realize how uncomfortable they are in the Diaspora and how such living has too little dignity. In the United States, Zionism has acted to the contrary — to make Jews more comfortable in the Diaspora and a greater force within the society at large. Rhetoric obscures this truth, for do not American Zionists and even non-Zionists march through the streets of Jerusalem proclaiming their assent to the "centrality of Israel," which is the

[Source: Arthur Hertzberg, *Being Jewish in America: The Modern Experience* (New York: Schocken Books, 1979), pp. 220-24.]

very core of Zionism's Jerusalem platform? The truth is that those from Kansas, California, and even New York who assert this mean not that they condemn their *galut* [exile] but that the involvement in Israel gives content and verve to lives they intend to continue to live in the American Diaspora.

It is therefore relatively easy to conceive of a celebration by Israelis of the bicentenary year of the United States of America. This is not more difficult than the Canadian celebration of that event. America's neighbor to the north has a complex relationship to the powerful giant to the south, on which it is overdependent but from which it nonetheless maintains substantial distance. Comparably, as I sometimes imagine, the true emotional border of Israel is not on the Mediterranean but immediately off the coast of the United States.

To define an attitude toward the American bicentennial is, however, much more difficult when "Jewish issues" are involved. Can one praise the United States as the home of a unique freedom and influence for Jews, whose power there is a critical factor in the very building of Israel, without raising the troubling question: Is this American Diaspora therefore unthinkable as an abode for Jews?

From its very beginnings American Zionism has answered this question by insisting that "America is different." Here the Zionist task was to marshal political and financial support. A small elite continued to emigrate to Zion, but the great Zionist crisis in America was not a quarrel between Zionists and others over the question: Is America a fit habitation for Jews? That ideological quarrel was fought in Russia, in Poland, and even in Germany, but never in the United States. Here the Zionists fought within the Jewish community for half a century before they succeeded in making support of the Jewish homeland the almost universally shared central purpose of American Jewish life. More crucial and more difficult still was the concurrent struggle to establish in America the right of Zionists to battle for their political aims.

Politically, the most damaging charge ever hurled against any group in America was that of being a hyphenated American, or, as it was later put, of being guilty of "dual loyalty." This charge silenced the German-Americans in World War I and it acted to keep all other ethnic groups, including the Irish, from having a particular foreign policy of their own for any significant length of time.

The only group in America which withstood the charge, both within its own community and in the politics of the larger society, was the Zionists. American Zionists were crucial to making an end of the "melting pot" image of America in the name of a minority commitment of their own. . . . Only Zionism has translated itself into a second and third generation. The one commitment that is universally shared in American Jewry is to make sure that the foreign policy of the United States does not turn against Israel. At this bicentenary moment all other major special-interest groups are defined in America by their domestic programs: labor, blacks, ethnics in the big cities, and even big business, except, in part, for big oil. The only special-interest group which is defined by its foreign policy is the Jews.

The great success of Zionism is to have made this acceptable on the American scene. This has represented a profound change in America's conception of itself, and it has consequences in other realms. The insistence of blacks in America for "affirmative action," that is, for acts of special reparation in this generation for three centuries of injustice done to them by slavery, fell on ears which had been hearing for decades the Zionist claim that the Jewish people was entitled to an act in this century of unique reparation for twenty centuries of exile by having its homeland returned to it. All other kinds of dissent from the American consensus, such as the movement against the Vietnam War, became possible in a society which no longer equated, as it had at the beginning of the twentieth century, patriotism with conformity. To reverse the argument, in the America of 1976 a Jewish community deeply devoted to Israel is no longer outrageously unique. This represents a fundamental change in American life from the self-definition of this society at the beginning of the twentieth century.

Within American Jewry, Zionism has also successfully conquered the community's inner life so that the labors that it commands have become American Jewry's "religion."

It is simply not true that excommunication no longer exists in modern Judaism. On the contrary, it has reappeared in new forms. One can, indeed, no longer be excommunicated in modern America for not believing in God, for living totally outside the tradition, or even for marrying out. Indeed, none of these formerly excommunicable offenses debar one today from occupying high offices in positions of Jewish leadership — but that does not mean that all is permitted. On the contrary, the case of the American Council for Judaism, the well-known anti-Zionist body, is instructive. It has been effectively debarred from any participation in Jewish life on any issue, even, for example, a matter as uncontroversial and as universally acceptable as the American Jewish struggle for the rights of Soviet Jews. . . .

The overarching religion of American Jews is therefore not Orthodox, Conservative, or Reform; it is not Hebrew or the national culture. It is pride and glory in American Jewry's sharing in Israel — and it is therefore disappointed in rebbes who do not perform miracles on order, who are sometimes fallible on Yom Kippur when a war breaks out, even as mortal men, and whose courts are not as perfect as dreams would have them.

Most important of all, I think, is a cliché which is even more deeply true than it seems to be. Zionism and Israel have, indeed, provided American Jews with great dignity in the eyes of the American majority. Even in today's less glorious times than those which followed June 1967, Israel remains in America the symbol of achievement against odds and of the kind of pioneering creativity that Americans respect.

"Fighting for Israel"

The Six Day War of 1967 galvanized the opinion of American Jewry behind the state of Israel as no single event has done, before or since. Israel, whose very survival was threatened, had defended itself successfully, dramatically, even gloriously. From that point on, to be a Jew meant to be committed to Israel. This, at least, is the argument of Nathan Glazer (b. 1923), sociologist, professor, and author of the popular survey American Judaism *(1957; revised, 1972, mainly to take into account the 1967 war and its impact on American Jews). Like Hertzberg, Glazer also suggests that "Israel has become* the *Jewish religion for American Jews," but — unlike Hertzberg — he is less sanguine about the future in that regard.*

Israel has become the pre-eminent issue in American Jewish life, to a degree that could not have been envisaged in 1948, or 1957, or 1966. Newspapers, the mass media generally, political candidates (especially presidential candidates) are aware of how important Israel is to American Jews. What is not often realized is how relatively new is the absolute predominance of Israel in American Jewish concerns.

In the early postwar period, the Jewish community of Israel amounted to only six percent of the Jewish people. Within individual Jewish communities, including that of the United States, Zionism had been a minority movement. Jewish organizations fought over how much of the money raised for Jewish causes should go to Israel and how much to other claimants. Jews in other countries who were in distress (particularly those who emerged from the concentration camps of Europe and the Jews of Arab lands) had a strong claim to Jewish charitable funds. Domestic needs — synagogues, temples, schools, hospitals, social service agencies — also rated high among Jewish priorities.

The exclusive and overwhelming concern of American Jews with Israel dates from the Six Day War of 1967, when it appeared at first that Israel might be defeated and its Jewish inhabitants massacred. American Jews discovered then that Israel meant much more to them than they realized. Everything possible was done to save Israel. Political pressure was mobilized, large sums of money were raised in a surprisingly short time, and thousands of U.S. volunteers left to fight. If in the past it was possible for some Jews to separate their commitment to Judaism from their commitment to Israel, after 1967 this was no longer possible.

Israel has become *the* Jewish religion for American Jews. To those who

---

[Source: Nathan Glazer, "Jewish Loyalties," *Wilson Quarterly*, 5 (1981), 137-38.]

think in terms of Christianity — and perhaps to some Jews, too — that may sound blasphemous or heretical. How can anything of this world be absolutized to the point where it becomes the central theme of religion, while "other-worldly" themes are put aside? That, I would argue, is a rather non-Jewish way of looking at religion.

The Jewish religion has always been linked to a single people. Among the great religions, it is perhaps unique in this respect. Judaism is inconceivable without Jews, the actual and living people. Christianity is quite conceivable without the adherence of any particular ethnic group, as is Islam. After the Holocaust, this apparently archaic feature of the Jewish religion became very modern again. The most creative Jewish theologian on the North American continent, Emil Fackenheim, emphasizes in his theology the centrality of the *physical* survival of the Jewish people — particularly in the aftermath of a diabolical effort, which enjoyed considerable success, to destroy them.

One can thus make an argument out of Jewish theology and history that the Jewish commitment to Israel has something of a religious character. The problem is that Israel is a state, as well as the Zion whose restoration God promised to the Jews. And therein hangs a potential difficulty that Jews have only recently become aware of — one that can only become more serious with time, it appears to me. The difficulty is the potential conflict between loyalty to the United States and loyalty to Israel.

"After Zionism"

Hillel Halkin is an American-born Jew who in 1970 emigrated to Israel. In 1977 he published a book urging Jews in the Diaspora to come to Israel as he had done (Letters to an American Jewish Friend: A Zionist's Polemic). *In the article excerpted below from 1997, he now looks back over two decades filled with climactic events and substantial changes for Jews in both Israel and America. While there was much to ponder in thinking about those decades, including Halkin's prediction that assimilation would undercut the strength of Jews in America, he once again came to his earlier conclusion: A Jew's true home was Israel. The world in which he made this argument had changed considerably since Rabbi Hertzberg took up the same set of issues in 1976. This selection begins after Halkin notes that much in life that is most significant lies beyond rational argument.*

[Source: Hillel Halkin, "After Zionism: Reflections on Israel and the Diaspora," *Commentary*, June 1997, pp. 27-28, 29-30, 30-31.]

That is certainly true of Zionism itself. The rationales and ideological justifications given for it in the last 100 years have been innumerable and often contradictory: Zionism as an affirmation of Jewish history, Zionism as a revolt against Jewish history, Zionism as a cure for anti-Semitism, Zionism as a bourgeois Jewish utopia, Zionism as the fulfillment of biblical prophecy, Zionism as the Jewish contribution to the world socialist revolution, Zionism as Jewish *Blut-und-Boden*, Zionism as a philanthropic rescue mission, Zionism as a messianic theodicy. The remarkable thing is that, for the most part, the holders of these different views were able to cooperate and work together in practical matters. But that, as far as I could see, was only because they were all serving the same master: Zionism as the Jewish will to live honorably in our times.

But the Diaspora had a will to live, too. And it, too, had given, and would go on giving, innumerable and contradictory rationales for its existence. What Hitler could not convince it of — what the entire horrendous and inspiring history of the Jewish people in the 20th century could not convince it of — no book or library of books was going to convince it of.

The issue was not debatable. The will to live never runs out of arguments. And so, after a while, I began to change the subject, and my American Jewish friends found me more pleasant company.

I was not alone. If the years before and after *Letters to an American Jewish Friend* was written marked the final realization on both sides that, barring catastrophe, the Diaspora would stay where it was, this realization, in turn, helped end the Zionist era in Israel itself. Or to put it another way, if Zionism was the failed world revolution of the Jewish people, the Diaspora was the counterrevolution; already by the 1970's, far more Israelis were living in America than American Jews in Israel.

Yet one cannot blame just the inertia or even the pull of the Diaspora for the death of Zionism as a motivating force in Israeli life — any more than one can credit the arrival in Israel of a half-million Russian Jews in the early 90's to a Zionist revival. For all its uniqueness, Zionism was but one of the revolutionary ideologies that marched across the stage of modern history; and when, for the first time since the French Revolution, all the other grand causes made their exit, it could not have been expected that Zionism, like an actor who has missed his cue, would remain behind by itself.

Besides, Israelis were weary — just how weary, I failed to realize during my first years of living among them. I was full of new beginnings; they, of war, tension, and economic sacrifice. It was no accident that "post-Zionism," both as a mood and as a political outlook, caught on first among a secular, Ashkenazi elite that had borne the brunt of Israel's struggle for two or more generations, and spread more slowly among those who came to Zionist activism and to Israel later, such as religious Jews and immigrants from Muslim countries. And although Zionism (often in a heavily theologized form) may still live on intensely among some of these elements, and particularly among settlers in the Territories, there too it seems doomed to expire — one can only hope not too tragically — with the passage of time and the advances of the peace process.

I was a first-generation Israeli. It took a second fully to open my eyes. For my two daughters, who were one and four years old when *Letters to an American Jewish Friend* was published, Zionism never had the slightest personal relevance.

In some ways, then, the first letter of my book, with its ecclesiastical metaphor of Zionist faith, strikes me today as undiscerning. But the second, on the disappearing Diaspora, is a different matter; for though nothing may date faster than statistics, those of the 1990's bear out my conclusions far better than did those of the 1970's. When the book first appeared, it was widely criticized for being alarmist. Now the alarm bells are being rung by everyone. One American Jewish sociologist, who regularly turned up for years on the same panels that I did, used to argue that intermarriage was an asset to American Jews, since it increased their numbers via conversions. The last I heard, he considers it a demographic disaster.

True, I missed some things here, too: for one, just how rapid would be the growth of ultra-Orthodoxy, the product of an extremely high birth rate and a low rate of defection to the outside world. If this trend continues, traditional Judaism, particularly its far-right wing, a small portion of the American Jewish community two decades ago, will soon be a major part of it. Few non-Orthodox American Jews seem to be thinking seriously even now about what this portends, although it is entirely consistent with what I predicted in general.

I also failed to take into account the splintering of American Jewry as the center fell out of it. I wrote at a time when one could speak of Orthodox Jews, Conservative Jews, Reform Jews, and nonaffiliated Jews, plus a few minor variants. My imaginary correspondent was active in what was known as the *havurah* movement, a blend of the Conservative summer camp, the traditional Jewish prayer-and-study *minyan,* and the communalism of the counterculture of the 1960's and 70's.

Today in America there are gay Jews, feminist Jews, humanist Jews, eco-Jews, Jews for Jesus, Jews for Buddha, patrilineal Jews, unconverted Gentile Jews, and hyphenated Jews of all kinds, including half-Jews, quarter-Jews, and eighth-Jews who consider themselves semi-Jews or full Jews. And that is only to speak of those who still regard themselves as Jews at all.

The fewer Jews, the more sects of them. Not since Hellenistic times, when rabbinic Judaism battled to assert its authority over a wild array of Jewish gnostics, Jewish Christians, and Jewish pagans, has there been such a proliferation of competing Jewish identities having no confessional, social, biological, or other common denominator.

Even the "civil religion" centered on Israel — to invoke a phrase widely used in the 1970's to describe the one tenet shared by nearly all American Jews — has lost its congregation. Nor did it take Israeli-style post-Zionism for this to happen. American Jews were in any case on their way to realizing that an allegiance to Israel could not permanently confer a sustaining significance on their lives — not only because Israel had failed to provide them with applicable models of Jewish life for emulation, but because no community can exist for long by means of a vicarious identification with another.

Is there a Jewish people at all left in America today, a single collective body whose members, however they may quarrel about other things, mutually recognize each other as Jews and agree on the criteria for doing so? Certainly not in the sense that there was even twenty years ago. . . .

We are told by post-Zionism's celebrants that the death of Zionism is nothing to mourn, for the movement launched by Herzl is passing away at a ripe old age, after a full and achievement-crowned life. Unlike other "isms" of our century, it did not crash in flames to a cataclysmic end or waste away in a revolting spectacle of putrescence. It accomplished what it set out to do, namely, to restore the Jewish people to independence in their land. Having done so, albeit at the cost of bloody conflict with the land's natives and neighbors, it leaves behind a grateful posterity that can lay that conflict to rest and turn to new and more private challenges. "Perhaps nothing enslaves the individual more than the 'high,' elevated meanings a community attaches to a life of devotion to collective goals," writes one leading post-Zionist spokesman, the Israeli political scientist Yaron Ezrahi, in his recently published and much praised book, *Rubber Bullets*. As against this, he continues, post-Zionism represents the victory of "liberal-democratic values," and opens the way to both "Arab-Israeli coexistence and a future Israel as an open and advanced society unthreatened by war." The Arabs, Ezrahi is quite certain, will cooperate.

It sometimes strikes me that, regarding Arab-Israeli coexistence, the difference between the Left and the Right in Israel has nothing to do with their relative perceptiveness. Both are equally guilty of projecting their own minds onto the Arabs. The post-Zionist Left says: "Fighting for land and national honor is primitive; we would never do it, and therefore the Arabs, once their reasonable demands are met, will not either." The paleo-Zionist Right says: "Land and national honor are paramount; we would fight for them, and therefore so will the Arabs." Both pure projections — but the mind of the Right, alas, may be more attuned to the mind of the Arabs. . . .

Zionism failed, too, in creating a new worldwide Jewish identity. Its project of "normalizing" the Jewish people by redefining it in territorial and linguistic rather than religious terms stalled halfway, and in some respects has even lost ground. (It is worth remembering, for comparison's sake, that in Eastern Europe, on the eve of World War II, hundreds of thousands of young Jews spoke fluent Palestinian Hebrew and thought of themselves as part of a Palestinian Jewish nation whose land they had never set foot on.) That is why the future will see not one Jewish people but many, and why absurd quarrels over who is a Jew and what makes a Jew a Jew continue today in both Israel and the Diaspora.

And paradoxically, precisely when Zionism's pessimistic analysis of Diaspora Jewry has proved correct for the second time this century — for while Zionists did not predict the Holocaust, they alone foresaw the likelihood of the economic and political destruction of European Jewry — Zionism no longer exists as an intellectual force to offer American Jews a clear understanding of their situation.

But more than anything, the passing of Zionism leaves behind the question: when nothing is left to sustain the Jews of Israel but simple Israeli patriotism — no sense of being the revolutionary bearers of Jewish history, no higher Jewish mission — will that be enough? There are nations that stood their ground bravely because simple patriotism sufficed, such as England during World War II, and nations that fell because it did not, such as France in the same war. One can only hope that Israel will not have to stand the test.

As I say, I have mellowed; there is no point in being rude, or hurting feelings. I have never thought that living in Israel made me a better Jew, only that it made me a Jew living in a better place. But since this too is nothing Diaspora Jews wish to hear, I have learned to keep my peace.

Still, the old anger persists underneath. How much so, I myself did not realize until one evening not long ago when my wife and I were sitting with friends. The subject arose of the revival of Jewish life in Eastern Europe; a mutual acquaintance of ours is currently there, devoting himself to this cause. I found myself remarking heatedly that Jews living in America were one thing, but deliberately to start Jewish life all over again in a part of the world where Jews had been reviled and massacred for centuries — the only word I could think of for it was shameful.

"Well," someone said with that cheerful Israeli cynicism that passes for humor in these parts, "when we here are all dead from Arab nerve gas, you'll be happy there are Jews in other places."

That was too much for me. "If we're going to be dead here, I'd rather they were dead there, too," I said.

On the way home, my wife remarked, "That was a terrible thing to say. I hope you didn't mean it."

I thought about that. Did I mean it?

Yes. I meant it.

Not literally. I'm not that vengeful. But if Israel should ever go under — and I do not find it inconceivable — I would not want the Diaspora to continue. I would not want there to be any more Jews in the world.

It would be too shameful. That is the only word for it that I can think of.

Fighting Communism: Hot Wars and Cold

Cold War

The religious element was especially prominent in the early days of the Cold War. The Soviet Union, so recently an ally in World War II, now loomed as a great menace because of its leadership of world-wide communism. The radio sermon excerpted below may now sound extreme. In the early 1950s it was not extreme, but rather representative of much that could be heard from other religious voices as well. The talk was broadcast via ABC Radio in early April 1951 on Billy Graham's program, "The Hour of Decision." The parents of Billy Graham's wife had only recently been expelled from China where they had worked as missionaries until the triumph of Mao Tse-Tung's communist forces.

Throughout the entire world at this moment Christianity and communism are battling for the minds of men. In Greenland's icy mountains, along India's coral shores, through the heart of darkest Africa, through the Andes of South America, throughout Europe, America, the islands of the sea, these two giants are battling. The outcome will determine what kind of a world the next generation will live in. . . .

Ladies and gentlemen, for some time I have been stating to this radio audience that communism is far more than just an economic and philosophical interpretation of life. Communism is a fanatical religion that has declared war upon the Christian God. To a striking degree this atheistic philosophy is paralleling and counterfeiting Christianity. I do not even attempt to call myself a student of Bible prophecy. There are many things concerning prophetic utterances in the Bible that I do not understand. In the last few weeks, however, I have been spending much of my time in private study devoted to Bible prophecy. I am

---

[Source: *Christianism vs. Communism* (Minneapolis: Billy Graham Evangelistic Association, 1951), pp. 1, 3-4.]

finding not only interesting but amazing things that bear tremendous light upon the conditions of this very hour. This Bible is not only a Bible recording historical events, but it also pronounces with accuracy the events that are yet to come. There are strong indications that the thirty-eighth and thirty-ninth chapters of Ezekiel are devoted almost entirely to the tremendous rise of Russia in the latter days. There are strong indications in the Bible that in the last days a great sinister anti-Christian movement will arise. At this moment it appears that communism has all the earmarks of this great anti-Christian movement. Communism *could* be only a shadow of a greater movement that is yet to come. However, it carries with it all the indications of anti-Christ. Almost all ministers of the gospel and students of the Bible agree that it is master-minded by Satan himself who is counterfeiting Christianity.

Christianity has a Bible; so does communism in the manifests. Christianity demands repentance from sin; communism demands a confession on the part of new converts concerning their past activities, errors and failures. Christianity demands the acceptance of certain cardinal doctrines as prerequisites for entrance into the Kingdom of God; so does communism. Christianity demands the complete surrender of body, soul, and will to Christ; so does communism demand complete surrender to the philosophy of communism. Christianity demands absolute loyalty; Jesus Christ said, "If a man is to follow me, he must take up his cross and deny himself daily." So does communism demand absolute loyalty to its leadership. Christianity demands the winning of new converts; the Christian is to ever be witnessing for his Lord. So does communism demand that every communist try to win others to the communistic way of life. It is a counterfeit from start to finish. The false doctrine of communism lies across our world like a colossus, so that the members of the communist party surrender themselves body and soul to this ideal.

What a challenge this should be to every Christian: Who is greater — Marx or Christ? We have a leader infinitely more wonderful, infinitely grander than anything communism can produce. Christ said, "If any man will come after me, let him deny himself and take up his cross daily and follow me." The only adequate answer to the communist comes when the Christian takes that literally, believes it and brings his life in full abandon and full surrender to Christ. Humanly speaking, faith can be overcome only by faith, courage by courage, loyalty by loyalty, devotion by devotion. The communist stands as a challenge to the Christian to bring to their leader a greater fight, a greater loyalty, a greater devotion, a greater discipline, a more glorious self-denial than anything that communism can show.

Vietnam

While pacifism, especially pacifism based on clear religious conviction, has a long history in this nation, never before Vietnam had pacifism engaged so many or become so powerful a countervailing force in the corridors of power. The longer the war continued, the louder the voice of protest became. It was indeed for the whole nation a "crisis of conscience" as Protestant, Jew, and Catholic declared in 1967 (Robert M. Brown, Abraham J. Heschel, and Michael Novak, Vietnam: Crisis of Conscience*). In that same year the United Presbyterian Church voiced its conviction that "There is no moral issue more urgently confronting our Church and nation than the war in Vietnam." And four years before either of these, Pope John XXIII (papacy, 1958-63) had raised hopes not alone of Catholics but of millions besides that "Peace on Earth" (*Pacem in Terris*) might somehow be within the reach of men and women of goodwill. Three excerpts of longer documents follow: (1) Pope John's* Pacem in Terris*; (2) the United Presbyterians' "Declaration of Conscience"; and (3) a segment of the statement by Rabbi Abraham Heschel (1907-73) entitled "Military Victory — A Moral Defeat."*

1.

143. An act of the highest importance performed by the United Nations Organization was the Universal Declaration of Human Rights, approved in the General Assembly of December 10, 1948. In the preamble of that Declaration, the recognition and respect of those rights and respective liberties is proclaimed as a goal to be achieved by all peoples and all countries.

144. We are fully aware that some objections and reservations were raised regarding certain points in the Declaration, and rightly so. There is no doubt, however, that the document represents an important step on the path towards the juridical-political organization of all the peoples of the world. For in it, in most solemn form, the dignity of a human person is acknowledged to all human beings; and as a consequence there is proclaimed, as a fundamental right, the right of every man freely to investigate the truth and to follow the norms of moral good and justice, and also the right to a life worthy of man's dignity, while other rights connected with those mentioned are likewise proclaimed.

[Sources: (1) *Pacem in Terris*, April 11, 1963 (Washington, D.C.: National Catholic Welfare Conference, n. d.), pp. 34, 35-36, 37, 40. (2) United Presbyterian Church, *Vietnam: The Christian, the Gospel, the Church* (Philadelphia: General Assembly of the United Presbyterian Church, U. S. A., 1967), pp. 132, 133-34. (3) A. J. Heschel, in *Vietnam: Crisis of Conscience* (New York: Association Press, 1967), pp. 52-53, 55-56.]

145. It is therefore our ardent desire that the United Nations Organization — in its structure and in its means — may become ever more equal to the magnitude and nobility of its tasks, and may the time come as quickly as possible when every human being will find therein an effective safeguard for the rights which derive directly from his dignity as a person, and which are therefore universal, inviolable and inalienable rights. This is all the more to be hoped for since all human beings, as they take an ever more active part in the public life of their own country, are showing an increasing interest in the affairs of all peoples, and are becoming more consciously aware that they are living members of the whole human family. . . .

151. It is no less clear that today, in traditionally Christian nations, secular institutions, although demonstrating a high degree of scientific and technical perfection, and efficiency in achieving their respective ends, not infrequently are but slightly affected by Christian motivation or inspiration.

152. It is beyond question that in the creation of those institutions many contributed and continue to contribute who were believed to be and who consider themselves Christians; and without doubt, in part at least, they were and are. How does one explain this? It is Our opinion that the explanation is to be found in an inconsistency in their minds between religious belief and their action in the temporal sphere. It is necessary, therefore, that their interior unity be re-established, and that in their temporal activity faith should be present as a beacon to give light, and charity as a force to give life. . . .

157. The doctrinal principles outlined in this document derive from both nature itself and the natural law. In putting these principles into practice it frequently happens that Catholics in many ways cooperate either with Christians separated from this Apostolic See, or with men of no Christian faith whatever, but who are endowed with reason and adorned with a natural uprightness of conduct. *In such relations let the faithful be careful to be always consistent in their actions, so that they may never come to any compromise in matters of religion and morals. At the same time, however, let them be, and show themselves to be, animated by a spirit of understanding and detachment, and disposed to work loyally in the pursuit of objectives which are of their nature good, or conducive to good.* . . .

167. As the humble and unworthy Vicar of Him Whom the Prophet announced as the *Prince of Peace,* We have the duty to expend all Our energies in an effort to protect and strengthen this gift. However, Peace will be but an empty-sounding word unless it is founded on the order which this present document has outlined in confident hope: an order founded on truth, built according to justice, vivified and integrated by charity, and put into practice in freedom.

2.

There is no moral issue more urgently confronting our Church and nation than the war in Vietnam. The hour is late; the Church dare not remain silent. We must declare our conscience.

We share widely-held feelings of sadness that steps were taken in the past which have involved our nation in its present difficulty. Although each step was taken with hope it would be the last, their cumulative result has brought us to an agonizing dilemma. On the one hand, we cannot responsibly withdraw our military forces unilaterally from Vietnam. On the other hand, further escalation seems to us to raise the spectre of World War III and the possibility of a nuclear holocaust.

A. We recognize that our leaders desire an end to the war, and believe that their motives for pursuing the war are those of honorable men. We must nevertheless declare our deep misgivings at the policy of military escalation (further steps being taken during the week of this General Assembly) which leads the world daily closer to the danger of wider war. Acts of escalation tend to commit us to further acts of escalation and may lessen the possibility of settlement by negotiation. . . .

C. We call upon members of every religious faith and communion, and upon all men of good will everywhere, to make common cause with us in an effort to bring about an end to the war. As we do so:

1. *We must continue to affirm the morality of dissent.* Increasing numbers of citizens, including some in high office, are equating dissent with disloyalty.

The enemy can always misunderstand the meaning of dissent. We, however, must affirm unequivocally that the right of dissent is the life-blood of democracy. We also affirm unequivocally that the first mandate under which the Church lives is the mandate, "You shall have no other Gods before me." (Ex. 20:3.) We acknowledge that, "The church which identifies the sovereignty of any one nation or any one way of life with the cause of God denies the Lordship of Christ and betrays its calling." (Confession of 1967.)

We remind ourselves and other citizens addressing themselves to public questions that we must speak in an informed way, and must avoid impugning the loyalty or integrity of those with whom we disagree. We call for candor on the part of policymakers, and the abandonment of cliches and slogans, in order that there may be a frank facing of the extent and limitations of our national interest in Vietnam and Southeast Asia.

2. *We must continue to affirm the morality of restraint.* We recognize that our military actions have been conducted with a high degree of restraint in comparison to the military power we possess. Nevertheless, we are dismayed that as the war gathers momentum this restraint shows signs of erosion. Our people seem willing to accept as normal today what was unthinkable yesterday.

We recoil from rash proposals to use nuclear weapons, or to invade the North. We deplore the increasing willingness at home to justify inhumane acts because the enemy also commits them. We mourn the fact that although we had hoped to be in Vietnam to liberate its people, our use of modern weapons is increasingly destructive both to that people and to their country.

3. *We must break new moral ground in courage and in ecumenical action.* Let men of all faiths pray that our nation will have the moral courage to undertake these steps of redirection.

We support the concern over Vietnam already expressed by many Jewish groups, by Protestant and Orthodox bodies such as the World Council of Churches and the National Council of Churches, and join in the plea of Pope Paul VI that "men must come together and get down to sincere negotiations. Things must be settled now, even at the cost of some loss or inconvenience, for later they may have to be settled at the cost of immense harm and enormous slaughter that cannot even be imagined now."

4. *We must declare our conscience at whatever cost.* We recognize that if our military escalation is not reversed, the time may come when those who dissent because they seek peace will be placed under even greater pressure, and that the possibility of significant influence by the Church on public policy will have disappeared. Should that time come, we urge our corporate Church and our individual church members still to exercise the voice of conscience, so that faithful witness may be rendered to God's reconciliation in Jesus Christ, which is the only ground of peace.

3.

It is weird to wake up one morning and find that we have been placed in an insane asylum. It is even more weird to wake up and find that we have been involved in slaughter and destruction without knowing it.

What is being done by our government is done in our name. Our labor, our wealth, our civic power, our tacit consent are invested in the production and use of the napalm, the bombs, and the mines that explode and bring carnage and ruin to Vietnam.

The thought that I live a life of peace and nonviolence turns out to be an illusion. I have been decent in tiny matters on a tiny scale, but have become vicious on a large scale. In my own eyes my existence appears to be upright, but in the eyes of my victims my very being is a nightmare.

A sense of moral integrity, the equation of America with the pursuit of justice and peace, has long been part of our self-understanding. Indeed, for generations the image of America has been associated with the defense of human rights and the hope for world peace. And now history is sneering at us.

Vietnam war protestor offers a flower to a military police officer
at a demonstration in Arlington, Virginia, October 21, 1967
(Photo by S. Sgt. Albert Simpson, National Archives and Records Administration)

A ghastly darkness has set in over our souls. Will there be an end to dismay, an end to agony?

The encounter of man and God is an encounter within the world. We meet within a situation of shared suffering, of shared responsibility.

This is implied in believing in One God in whose eyes there is no dichotomy of here and there, of me and them. They and I are one; here is there, and there is here. What goes on over there happens even here. Oceans divide us, God's presence unites us, and God is present wherever man is afflicted, and all of humanity is embroiled in every agony wherever it may be.

Though not a native of Vietnam, ignorant of its language and traditions, I am involved in the plight of the Vietnamese. To be human means not to be immune to other people's suffering. People in Vietnam, North and South, have suffered, and all of us are hurt.

Unprepared, perplexed, uninformed, ill-advised, our nation finds herself in a spiritual inferno. Where do we stand? Where do we go from here? For a long time we suppressed anxiety, evaded responsibility. Yet the rivers of tears and blood may turn into a flood of guilt, which no excuse will stem.

The blood we shed in Vietnam makes a mockery of all our proclamations, dedications, celebrations. We have been moving from obscurity to confusion, from ignorance to obfuscation. Many are unaware, some acquiesce, most of us detest this unfathomable war, but are unable to envisage a way of getting out of this maze. Millions of Americans who cannot close their minds to the suffering and sorrow are stricken with anguish, and form a large fellowship living in a state of consternation.

We are killing the Vietnamese because we are suspicious of the Chinese. The aim is to kill the elusive Vietcong, yet to come upon one soldier, it is necessary to put an end to a whole village, to the lives of civilians, men, women, and children.

Is it not true that Communists are fellow human beings first, antagonists second? Politically, the concept of the enemy is becoming obsolete; yesterday's enemy is today's ally. The state of cold war between the United States and Soviet Russia has given place to a quest of friendly understanding.

The absurdity of this war is tacitly admitted by almost everyone. Our presence in Vietnam has become a national nightmare, our actions are forced, we dislike what we do; we do what we hate to do. Is this a way to bring democracy to Vietnam: more explosives, more devastation, more human beings crippled, orphaned, killed? Is it not clear that military victory in Vietnam would be a tragic moral defeat? That military triumph would be a human disaster? . . .

What is it that may save us, that may unite men all over the world? The abhorrence of atrocity, the refusal of the conscience to accommodate to the arrogance of military power. Indeed, it is the power of the human conscience which has in the last twenty years inhibited the use of thermonuclear weapons. Yet the power of the conscience is tenuous and exceedingly vulnerable. Its status is undergoing profound upheavals. We are challenged too frequently, too radically to be able to react adequately.

However, the surrender of conscience destroys first the equilibrium of human existence and then existence itself. In the past, war was regarded as an instrument of politics. Today politics is in the process of becoming an instrument of military technology. How long can total war be avoided?

Militarism is whoredom, voluptuous and vicious, first disliked and then relished. To paraphrase the prophet's words "For the spirit of harlotry is within them, and they know not the Lord" (Hosea 5:4): "Samson with his strong body, had a weak head, or he would not have laid it in a harlot's lap."

Cold War Ended

In the fall of 1989, Richard Pierard, a history professor from Indiana State University, was living in East Berlin as a Fulbright Professor at the

[Source: Richard V. Pierard, "We Are the People — The Revolution in East Germany," *Reformed Journal*, January 1990, pp. 8, 9-10, 11.]

Humboldt University. From that vantage point he witnessed the dramatic events that led to the breach of the Berlin Wall and then its collapse (November 9, 1989). Excerpts from the account he published in early 1990 highlight the events in Germany that pointed to the later collapse of the communist regime in the Soviet Union. An era of tension with "the Soviet bloc," which had gripped the attention of Americans for over a generation, was fast coming to an end. Pierard's account is especially valuable for its recognition of the importance of the East German churches in what occurred.

The straw that broke the camel's back came on October 7-8, the weekend of the 40th anniversary of the founding of the GDR. The chief of state and party boss (General Secretary of the Central Committee of the Socialist Unity Party, the East German Communist party) Erich Honecker had invited the leading lights of the socialist and communist world to the grand birthday party, including Soviet leader Mikhail Gorbachev. On the evening before, 100,000 paraded past the reviewing stand on Unter den Linden in a staged demonstration of support for Honecker's regime. The Free German Youth, the official youth organization, had brought them in by bus and train from all over the country.

I was there — a scant hundred yards from the two leaders and their entourage of luminaries — and saw what really was happening. The teenagers were shouting "Gorby, Gorby," prancing around the boulevard like kids in a Hoosier high-school homecoming parade, and simply having a good time in the big city. Most of them couldn't care less about the big shots assembled there except to get a close-up glimpse of Gorbachev, who for them was a symbol of hope and change.

The next day, October 7, was a national holiday. After the usual military parade, which did not seem to me to have drawn a spectacular crowd, people gathered in the Alexanderplatz area to drink beer, listen to the many bands, browse in the craft stalls, and just enjoy a nice sunny day. Toward evening, some young people began a more or less spontaneous demonstration for democracy. Such things just didn't happen in the GDR, and the police quickly moved and broke it up with an inordinate expenditure of force.

The next evening, 3,000 people jammed into the Victorian brick Gethsemane Church in the Prenzlauer Berg district to pray and to protest the police brutality. It was a moving experience to see the dedication of these Berliners, most of whom were in their teens, 20s, or early 30s. Upon leaving the church, they took to the street carrying lighted candles, and were immediately confronted with another brutal police action. I missed getting caught up in the violence only because by chance I happened to go out the back door, since it was closest to the train station. . . .

As the demonstrations in the other cities grew larger and larger — in Dresden and Leipzig 100,000 and more citizens were taking to the streets — the organization of performing artists in Berlin applied for and received a parade permit for a demonstration on November 4. Krenz realized just how much trouble he was in, and the night before the rally suddenly went on national television and announced that more reforms were to come. These included establishing a court with constitutional review powers; introducing civilian service as an alternative to the mandatory military training program; economic and administrative reforms, including procedures to allow new political organizations like the Neues Forum, which had been banned by the Interior Ministry but continued to function anyway and was attracting considerable media attention; sweeping changes in the educational system, and the retirement of several older figures, including the 82-year-old chief of the Stasi, Erich Mielke. In this, as well as in two earlier major addresses, Krenz pleaded with his fellow citizens not to abandon their country.

The next morning, at least a half-million people thronged the center of Berlin carrying hundreds of banners and signs protesting the SED power monopoly, denouncing the Stalinist tactics of the Stasi, calling for economic and educational reforms, and demanding the resignation of the Krenz government. It was the greatest mass rally in the history of the GDR, and the emotional impact of such a sea of humanity defies description. People waved their signs and cheered the speakers, many of whom were the country's leading writers and dramatists. The Berlin SED party chief was also invited to speak and was greeted with a chorus of catcalls, though most listened respectfully.

What was particularly impressive was how the march and the mass rally were totally peaceful. The police stood by to keep order, but they really had nothing to do. Parade wardens wearing colored sashes that read "no violence" insured that decorum was maintained. Women put flowers in the policemen's lapels, and one person even pinned a Gorby button on a cop.

In 1968 came the "Prague Spring," and perhaps one could speak of the "Berlin Fall" 21 years later. Certainly the weather was a providential factor. Germany experienced one of the warmest and driest Octobers in this century, and that made it easier for people to take to the streets. But what was so noteworthy about the reform movement was its nonviolent character and the key role of the churches. The Marxist-Leninist government in the GDR had never been able to break the church, although it tried in the 1950s, and it eventually had to settle for a way of living whereby the church would function not against or under the system but as a "Church in Socialism." In return for this tacit recognition, the state would allow churches freedom to do as they wished on their own turf. In effect, the church became a sort of conscience for the GDR and also a place where dissent could be expressed. . . .

The opening of the Berlin Wall and the West German border to all who wanted to travel from the GDR has certainly been one of the great human events of our time. As an eyewitness to this tremendous event, I must confess that words cannot convey adequately the feelings I have or the emotions I saw expressed by so many East and West Berliners alike. It was truly a spiritual event.

This was brought home to me in the Sunday service at the small church in the neighborhood in East Berlin where I had been living during these tumultuous times. It was essentially a service of thanksgiving and most members of the congregation offered up their thanks to God in a time of public prayer which the pastor designated for the occasion. The hymn we sang, the 17th-century Lutheran classic "Now Thank We All Our God," was most appropriate.

The events of the past weeks have truly borne witness to God's sovereign power and grace. It has been powerfully demonstrated to the rulers of East Germany that their power is not absolute and that the revolution cannot be turned back.

Top GDR officials publicly acknowledge that a "Chinese solution," although mentioned in passing during the early days of the unrest, cannot be invoked to save communism in their country. The GDR must adapt or it will perish. One thing is clear. The country will never be what it once was — a dreary, quasi-Stalinist state with a beaten-down, resigned populace and a highly inefficient economy that was kept intact by an 800-mile fence, a wall, and the Soviet army. The East German people have seen the future — and it is not old-style communism.

"We are the people" and "We are mature citizens" are the slogans one hears most in the GDR today The SED dictatorship in the name of the people and the working class is finished, and its passing will be mourned by few.

War in the Gulf

Desert Storm, 1991

The legacy of the Vietnam War included great American uneasiness about getting involved in foreign military adventures. That uneasiness was put to a severe test in the summer and fall of 1990, when Iraq under its dictator Saddam Hussein invaded neighboring Kuwait and, as a part of appropriat-

---

[Sources: (1) George Brushaber, "War Cry," *Christianity Today,* Jan. 14, 1991, p. 14. (2) Nancy Gibbs, "A First Thick Shock of War," © 1991 TIME Inc. reprinted by permission. (3) Roger Ruston, "The War of Religions and the Religion of War," in Brian Wicker, ed., *Studying War — No More? From Just War to Just Peace* (Grand Rapids: Eerdmans, 1994), pp. 13-31.]

ing that small nation, took over also its immensely productive oil wells. In re-
sponse President George H. W. Bush mobilized American public opinion and
a multi-national military force, under the aegis of the United Nations, to
liberate Kuwait. As the crisis point drew nearer, Americans seemed to turn as
if by instinct to religion. The three documents that follow exemplify some of
the ways in which religion, as in all earlier American wars, became promi-
nent in this one as well. (1) In an editorial, Christianity Today *urges its*
readers not to lose sight of higher religious realities. (2) In a report, Time
magazine notes how the outbreak of conflict stimulated religious observances
of several sorts. (3) In a retrospective written after the short war had come to
an end (with Iraq pushed out of Kuwait, but Hussein still in power in Iraq),
a British scholar, Roger Ruston, explains how in his view religion had func-
tioned during the conflict.

1. War Cry

On November 19, in Paris, 34 member nations of NATO and the Warsaw Pact
signed the European Security Agreement. After more than 40 years of East-
West confrontation, the danger of the Cold War seems finally to have given way
to peace.

By contrast, that same day in the Persian Gulf region, war came a giant
step closer. Saddam Hussein matched George Bush's military escalation with
his own announcement that he would now send another quarter-million
troops to the Saudi Arabian border. Though we pray it never happens, at press
time war seems imminent.

As the President struggles to make clear his case for direct action, most
Americans agree Iraqi aggression must be resisted. For the U.S. and its allies to
have the power to restore justice and not to do so may actually be immoral,
which is why we sympathize with our President when he draws the line against
Iraqi aggression. But the tremendous cost of human life that comes with war
should lead us, as Francis Schaeffer suggested, to "draw the line only with tears."
As Christians, we need to urge caution against chauvinistic nationalism and
ethnocentric pride. We must guard against the seductive euphoria of war, especially techno-war in a faraway place against a people we don't understand very
well. But beyond that, what is our message to the church? And from the church
to the world?

First, we must acknowledge that two major wars and hundreds of regional conflicts have not improved human nature. Individuals and nations remain locked in the iron grip of sin with all of its cruelty. The next war may protect territorial interests, but only the redeeming and transforming power of
Christ will change hearts on both sides of the battle front.

Second, we must recognize that God is sovereign; his purposes ultimately prevail. His demands are mercy and justice and faithfulness to him. It is righteousness alone that exalts and preserves a nation, not military strength. Even as we are comforted that God expresses his love and mercy through his sovereign might, we must strengthen our resolve to live as he demands.

Third, we must be careful about attaching undue eschatological significance to this crisis (Matt. 24:6-7). However, to live expecting our Lord's return — whether we are at peace or war — is our reassuring privilege and inescapable obligation.

Fourth, we must exercise responsible citizenship. Profound moral and political judgments do not come easily; as we work toward settled convictions of our own about U.S. involvement in the Persian Gulf, we should participate in the public debate and the political process with humility, gentleness, and grace. Regardless of our views, our troops deserve respect and support. They serve because their leaders and their country have called them. We dare not inflict the lasting damage on these military men and women that we did on their counterparts in Vietnam. As we pray for their safety we must be prepared to suffer with those who suffer, and grieve with those who grieve.

Finally, we must call the church to prayer. It is in such times of testing and crisis that the church has often been its most effective in expressing the will and character of God. If the tanks rumble and the rockets fire, Christians everywhere ought to "pray without ceasing" for our leaders, for the safety of our troops, even for the enemy (Jesus died for Saddam, too).

War tears our souls; victory is often hollow. That is when the church's weapons of love, compassion, service, and prayer — bathed in tears — are needed most.

2. First Shock

Deeply ambivalent and suddenly frightened, many Americans sought comfort in religion. Last week produced a surprising portrait of the nation's faith, a tableau of people praying hard, slipping into chapels for special services during lunch breaks, joining candlelight vigils, seeking moral certainty. On Monday night in Washington, one day before the deadline, parishioners gathered at St. Columbia's Episcopal Church. The congregation had been praying especially for one parishioner: Secretary of State Jim Baker. But this night there was a profound sense of despair and futility. "O God the Father, Creator of Heaven and earth, have mercy upon us," went the reading from the *Book of Common Prayer.* "From violence, battle and murder; and from dying suddenly and unprepared, Good Lord, deliver us."

Blocks away, 6,000 people gathered inside the cavernous National Cathe-

dral, sitting on the floor and packing the aisles under the vaulting stone but-
tresses. After the service many worshipers lighted candles and marched silently
through the streets of the capital. The vigil wound past the Iraqi embassy, quiet
and dark except for a single light, and ended in front of the White House. Susan
Meehan, a Quaker, attended on crutches. "Up at the cathedral they told us to
fling our prayers to heaven," she said, "so I'm flinging mine — nonviolently."

On Tuesday the tension reached its peak. Jewish congregations around
the country began a daylong fast. Demonstrators in Boston poured red paint
on the snow, chanting, "No blood for oil." In Los Angeles high school students
performed a skit in which American businessmen plucked dollar bills off the
bodies of young people. In Providence a George Bush doll was burned in an oil
drum. While thousands chanted through the streets, San Francisco's supervisors declared the city a sanctuary for anyone who chose not to participate in the
war.

Tuesday marked what would have been the 62nd birthday of Martin Luther King Jr., and in Atlanta the day echoed with irony and anger. The coincidence of timing troubled black leaders, who are acutely aware of the lack of
support for war within the African-American community. Organizers of commemorative events had invited General Colin Powell, the first black Chairman
of the Joint Chiefs of Staff, to be grand marshal of the celebration, but at the
last minute he declined. He was busy in Washington, he explained. "It's like
planning for Christmas and then having a member of the family die," observed
John Cox, coordinator of events. "You carry on but the spirit is not the same."

3. The Religion of War

In 1991 we were involved in an international war — the Gulf War — in which
religious talk was very much on the surface, on both sides. It began with the political and military leaders, who tried to make it clear — perhaps to God in the
first place, and the rest of the world afterwards — that their cause was God's
cause. This early resort to God is partly due to the fear which human beings
who are supposed to be in control of events experience when they are facing a
situation which they cannot control. The religious anxieties which people have
in war is a sign that their easy peace-time relationship with the divine is under
strain. War — like childbirth — reveals that they do not have the kind of control over the outcome of events which they take for granted when things are going well (or the mastery over nature which modern human beings like to think
they have achieved through the application of science). The rusty old disused
machinery of prayer gets a kick in the hope that it is still connected. When the
outcome remains uncertain and so much depends upon it, including perhaps
their own survival, even political leaders become persons of prayer for a time.

Their prayer is addressed to what the Bible calls the 'God of Battles'. And it is calculated to excite those religious emotions among the population without which it could not be mobilised for the sacrifices ahead.

It is easy to believe that the religious language of leaders is aimed at public opinion rather than at God and that there is some kind of manipulation of base religious emotions going on. However, to dismiss it that easily would be a serious mistake of understanding. It would fail to take seriously the genuine religious content of the situation. Those who use religious language in these circumstances are making the claim that their deepest interests coincide with those of God and his righteousness, and that consequently the most serious of absolutes is at stake and that they have a sacred duty to see that it is upheld.

By the time we were two weeks into the Gulf War in January 1991, the air was as thick with religious language as it was with missiles. When President Bush said, 'We know that this is a just war, and we know that, God willing, this is a war we will win', he was using the common currency of religious language. Saddam Hussein used it even more freely, for instance: 'We are being faithful to the values which God Almighty has inspired in us, for we have no fear from the forces of Satan, the devil that rides on your shoulders'. Of course the American leaders of the coalition were careful to avoid any suggestion that difference of religion entered into the Gulf war in any way. How could they? Being Christian or Muslim was not the issue. *The quasi-religion of sovereign states was the issue.* The integrity of sovereign state borders is a kind of absolute of the modern world order. It is that which allows politicians to excite the popular religious passions which are necessary for going to war. . . .

It has been widely argued that the violation of Kuwait's sovereignty by Iraq was the pretext rather than the ultimate cause of the intervention; that access to oil was the deciding factor, and that the whole elaborate pretence of UN resolutions and solemn recital of just war doctrines was a moral fig leaf for purely material interests. But an association of material interests with religious passions is nothing new in the history of armed conflict. They do not exclude one another. Indeed, religion may be at root an elaborate mechanism for coping with rivalry over material interests within communities. By suppressing rivalry and violence within communities it serves to unite them against outsiders who threaten the interests of the community as a whole. And nothing unites them so closely as blood sacrifice. The sacrifice of young men on the battlefield is the critical event which seals the unity of the community and the justice of the cause, allowing the identification to be made with God's justice.

Iraqi Freedom, 2003

In March 2003 the United States once again led a coalition of nations to war against Iraq. This time the president was George W. Bush, and the coalition embarked on its mission without the sanction of the United Nations. The official purposes of the war included the desire of the American government to depose Saddam Hussein as ruler of Iraq, to destroy what were thought to be Hussein's caches of Weapons of Mass Destruction, and by destroying Hussein to wage war on the forces of world-wide terrorism. "Operation Iraqi Freedom" lasted for slightly more than five weeks, and Hussein was deposed. Conflicting opinion about this Iraq war, including conflicting religious opinions, was sharper than twelve years earlier. The following documents, two from evangelical Protestants and two from Islam spokespersons, illustrate those conflicts. (1) R. Albert Mohler, Jr., president of the Southern Baptist Theological Seminary in Louisville, Kentucky, strongly supports the war. (2) Jim Wallis, editor of Sojourners *magazine in Washington, D.C., opposes it. (3) Shahid Athar, president of the Islamic Medical Association of North America and a professor at Indiana University School of Medicine in Indianapolis offers a balanced assessment. (4) Omar Siddiqui, in the Muslim Student Association's official publication,* MSA Link, *vigorously denounces the war.*

1. Unqualified Support

The day of decision has come, and thousands of brave Americans are fighting on the fields of battle in Iraq, and in the skies over that mournful nation. For the American people, this is another reminder that freedom is costly — and liberty must always be defended against its enemies.

For the Iraqi people, this is the promise of liberation from a tyrannical dictator. As President Bush told the Iraqi people, this military campaign is "directed against the lawless men who rule your country, and not against you."

For all of us, this is a call to prayer. We must pray for the safety and success of our brave men and women in uniform. We must pray for our President, who as Commander in Chief bears such a monumental burden of leadership

---

[Sources: (1) R. Albert Mohler, Jr., "Thoughts and Adventures," 21 March 2003, http://www.sbts.edu/mohler/ThoughtsPrint.php?article=03_21_2003 (27 May 2003). (2) Jim Wallis, "Hearts & Minds," *Sojourners*, May-June 2003, 7-8. (3) Shahid Athar, "Personal Reflections on the Iraq War," http://www.islamfortoday.com/athar20.htm (27 May 2003). (4) Omar Siddiqui, "You Are with Us or You Are Dead," *MSA Link*, Spring 2003, p. 8; http://www.msa-national.org/publications/msalink/Link_Mar03.pdf (27 May 2003).]

and responsibility. And we must pray for the Iraqi people, that civilians would be protected and taste the fruit of liberty.

President Bush has shown remarkable courage and moral clarity in insisting that the dictator of Iraq must be removed. "It is too late for Saddam Hussein to remain in power," the President declared — and now we know just how serious he was.

The President's doctrine of preemptive military action makes moral sense in this post-9/11 world, and his moral vision reminds us of other presidents tested by war. Franklin D. Roosevelt once remarked, "When you see a rattlesnake poised to strike, you do not wait until he has struck before you crush him." Those who oppose this military action must explain why they would leave the rattlesnake in position to strike.

President Dwight D. Eisenhower, who as Supreme Commander led the allies to victory in Europe in World War II, stated the case plainly: "In war there is no substitute for victory." Let us pray that this military campaign will be a victory for world peace.

2. Serious Objections

The American-led war against Iraq has begun. Over the past six months, tens of millions of people, including churches and religious leaders from all over the world, undertook a powerful campaign to stop this war and offered serious alternatives to confront the real threats posed by Saddam Hussein. But now the fighting and killing has begun. As I write, the early American military confidence has run into serious Iraqi resistance and casualties are mounting — both civilian and military. It is not too early to begin to assess the lessons of war.

1. Nobody should be surprised that a vastly superior American fighting force will vanquish a vastly inferior Iraqi army. But one of America's worst characteristics is hoping that success wipes away all the moral questions. In the long run, it won't. War is always ugly, and this one will be too.
2. There are many more civilian casualties in modern warfare than military casualties. Smart bombs are never as perfect as boasted, and not all Iraqis may want to be "liberated" by an American occupation. Above all, we must remember that "collateral damage" is never collateral to the families and loved ones of those killed in war. Don't accept the first reports on casualties from governments (on either side) or "embedded" journalists — many of whom now sound more like cheerleaders than reporters. Be sure that technology does not ultimately usurp theology or morality. Find alternative sources for information. Watch and wait for the real story.
3. Humanitarian aid must never be co-opted by the military as "force en-

hancement" (as U.S. Secretary of Defense Donald Rumsfeld now terms it). Assistance to the victims of war must never become another arm of military power. Instead it is the painful task to be taken on after the destruction caused by war. Many predict that the aftermath of this war could be far more dangerous and costly, in human terms, than the military campaign. Listen to the non-governmental relief organizations as we move forward.

4. If an evil, dangerous, and unpopular regime does collapse quickly, that is not an endorsement of war as the answer but a sign that a better way to resolve the threat might well have been possible. The best wisdom of most church leaders, Nobel Peace laureates, and a majority of international political figures and diplomats around the world was that alternatives to a full-scale military assault on Iraq were not adequately tested. This was not a war of last resort.

*   *   *

8. Dissent in a time of war is not only Christian, it is also patriotic. A long and honorable record of opposition to war in church tradition and American history puts dissent in the mainstream of Christian life and American citizenship. Rather than acquiesce to the war, prayerful and thoughtful dissent is more important than ever.

9. The churches have demonstrated the most remarkable unity in our history in opposition to a war, even before the war with Iraq started. The American churches didn't just say "no" to war, but offered compelling and credible alternatives. These alternatives were seriously considered by many political leaders around the world, but not by our own government. An American president who increasingly uses the language of Christian faith refused even to meet with American church leaders for discernment and prayer as he made momentous decisions to go to war. The American churches are now in deep solidarity with the worldwide body of Christ and may have to choose between their Christian alliances and the demands and policies of their own government. We must learn to be Christians first and Americans second.

10. The onset of war with Iraq does not demonstrate the failure of the peace movement, but rather the failure of democracy. Tens of millions of people around the world have become engaged in active citizenship against the policies of pre-emptive war for resolving the greatest threats to peace and security. It is time to build on that movement, rather than withdraw from collective action. We must learn the differences between grief and despair, between lamenting and languishing, between hope and hostility. We are stronger now, not weaker. Our action has just begun.

3. Islamic Assessment

As I write this article, whether I like it or not, whether protestors and the United Nations approve of it or not, the Iraq War is on. The "shock and awe" mission is on and thousands of bombs are dropping on Baghdad as our soldiers are struggling to make their way through the desert. The extent of civilian casualty will never be told to us but what I can see from the pictures on the TV screen, the whole city is in flames. We will never be told the total civilian casualties of the war or the sufferings of people and our brave soldiers.

The question I ask myself is "Which side do I belong to?" Is it a war against Islam and Muslims by the Christian invaders and their reluctant arm-twisted allies, or is it a war of liberation of the oppressed Iraqi people? Is it a war of blood for oil by the only super power which is now seen as an imperial power?

One of my African-American Christian patients thought this was a war by Anglo-Saxon powers for the domination of the rest of the world. One e-mail suggested that it is the Christian fundamentalists who voted for Mr. Bush and pushed him to war for Armageddon as they think Jesus will return in Iraq only after Iraq has been Christianized. So, there is no limit to the imagination.

One of the most thought provoking e-mails that I got was from my friend Mr. Courtnay Weldon, who wrote "for the last 12 years or so, all of the wars in which the USA has been involved, have been for the sake of Muslims". He gave the example of the Russian invasion of Afghanistan, the ethnic cleansing in Bosnia and Kosovo by the Serbs, the Iraqi invasion of Kuwait, the Taliban's oppression of Afghan people and now Iraq. I told him, this is true, but also for the last 12 years, the most people who have died in such wars or were made refugees worldwide, Muslims too. I ask him now "will the self-proclaimed liberators of the oppressed Muslims now go to Palestine, Kashmir or Chechnya too to liberate them from oppressors?"

As a man of religion, I am opposed to a war unless it is in defense when attacked. All 19 of the hijackers were Saudis. Iraq had never attacked the USA. Therefore, in the opinion of millions of protestors all over the world, it was not justified to go to war. If the theory of presence of weapons of mass destruction is valid, then all nations have the right to attack other nations including us, on the basis of that theory, as we have more weapons of mass destruction than anyone else.

At the same time, I am reminded of Prophet Mohammad's two sayings, "If you see wrong doing, stop it by hand (force), if you can not, then by tongue and if you can not do even that, then at least feel bad in your heart". The other saying is "Help your brother when he is right and when he is wrong". Companions were amazed and asked "How can we help a brother when he is wrong"? Prophet Mohammad said "you stop him from doing wrong, that is his help".

The crimes of Saddam Hussein are well known. The brutal dictator who gassed and killed his own people deserves no mercy. Thus, applying the sayings of the prophet together, Saddam had to be removed, unfortunately at a very high price of civilian casualties.

The sayings of Prophet Mohammad need to be confirmed by the Quran which says about the cry of the oppressed people: "O God, bring us forth from this town of which the people are oppressors, Oh, give us from Thy presence some protecting friend! Oh, give us from Thy presence some defender" (Quran 4:75).

Will President Bush and the allied forces behind him be that liberator and defender? Only history will prove that. For now, as a Muslim-American, I am praying for both the Iraqi people as well as our soldiers, for God's protection for all those innocent people who are in harm's way. . . .

One of the best e-mails of support that I got after September 11th 2001 was from a chaplain in California who wrote, "We Americans should stop singing God Bless America. This is a selfish notion to ask for God's blessing just for our selves only. We should sing God Bless the World". I say Amen to this.

4. Islamic Opposition

We can be sure to count among the casualties of an American bombfest in Baghdad not just Iraqi civilians, but our own consciences and any sense of the rule of law. But this should not come as any surprise. Immediately after the 9/11 tragedy, in his September 20th "Attack on America" Address, to a Joint Session of Congress and the American People, U.S. President George Bush declared his vision of the post 9/11 world:

> "*Americans are asking: Why do they hate us? They hate what we see right here in this chamber — a democratically elected government. Their leaders are self-appointed. They hate our freedoms — our freedom of religion, our free-dom of speech, our freedom to vote and assemble and disagree with each other. . . . These terrorists kill not merely to end lives but to disrupt and end our way of life. . . . This is the world's fight. This is civilization's fight. This is the fight of all who believe in progress and pluralism, tolerance and freedom.*"

Two themes stand out from this excerpt. The attacks on the World Trade Centers are characterized as (a) an attack on freedom and fundamental rights and (b) an attack on civilization and a way of life. The former can be associated with popular conceptions of democracy and human rights, the latter can be seen as more expansive to encompass the broader idea of culture and tradition. Post 9/11, popular discourse has been saturated with references to an impending clash between the western and non-western world. This has been politicized as a battle between good and the "axis of evil", between democracy and terror, between the love for freedom and blind hatred.

The American government's argument is predicated on a basic line of reasoning that emerged post 9/11:

> *9/11 must be avenged. Terrorists caused 9/11. Terrorists hate America. America is Good. Terrorists are Evil. People who hate America are terrorists and are thus Evil.*

Weaved within this reasoning is a trigger-happy foreign policy. An "us" versus "them" obsession creates a chilling justification for Bush's new war:

> *Iraq is not America. Therefore, Iraq is Evil. Therefore, Iraq supports terrorists. Therefore, Iraq had some part to play in 9/11. Therefore, Iraq must be bombed to avenge 9/11.*

Forget that former UN Inspectors, respected diplomats and world leaders have repeatedly put their reputations and lives on the line to defy claims that Iraq has weapons of mass destruction or the capability to produce them. Forget that international law explicitly outlaws the use of aggressive or pre-emptive force. The post 9/11 reasoning ignores all of this, and reduces the world into a "you are with us or you are dead" equation. What are the costs?

To acquiesce to this is to allow for the murder of innocent peoples, and an American led witch hunt of every nation in the world that does not reflect its image of what a good, America obeying world should look like. This should frighten us, because it is more of an assault on our way of life than any amount of 9/11's could ever be. We are being told that our governments have the right to kill with impunity, when they feel fit. We are being told that when our governments say something is evil, we should believe them because they say so, as if "evil" is some kind of buzz-word that justifies the means to achieve any ends. We are being told that our governments can overthrow and replace the leadership of other peoples at whim, but that similar violent protest is 'barbaric' and 'hooliganism' when it suddenly appears in our midst, as in the streets of Seattle or Quebec City. Are we some different breed of human that the basic norms and reasoning we apply to the rest of the world do not apply to us?

The hypocrisy is so blatant. And democracy is no better off. The bombing of Iraq will only be a beginning. The Salem witch-hunt should have taught us that vengeance, hysteria, and disdain for human life all go hand in hand. The words of Denis Halliday, former UN Humanitarian Coordinator for Iraq, should cause us grief: *"We are in the process of destroying an entire society. It is as simple and terrifying as that. It is illegal and immoral."*

2. Society and Its Conflicts, 1950s and 1960s

Communism and the Churches

"Reds and Our Churches"

In 1953 an article appearing in the American Mercury *began with this sentence: "The largest single group supporting the Communist apparatus in the United States today is composed of Protestant clergymen." For openers, that sweeping assertion would be hard to beat. Its author, J. B. Matthews (b. 1894) of Kentucky Methodist background, had in the early 1930s been attracted to communism and to the Soviet Union. By the end of the decade, he had become quite disillusioned with communism and with much else besides. With the zeal of the convert, he now began a new career as vigorous anti-communist and chief investigator for the House of Representatives committee charged with investigating "Un-American Activities." A portion of his inflammatory article follows.*

The largest single group supporting the Communist apparatus in the United States today is composed of Protestant clergymen.

Since the beginning of the First Cold War in April, 1948, the Communist Party of this country has placed more and more reliance upon the ranks of the Protestant clergy to provide the party's subversive apparatus with its agents, stooges, dupes, front men, and fellow-travelers.

Clergymen outnumbered professors two to one in supporting the

---

[Source: J. B. Matthews, "Reds and Our Churches," *American Mercury,* 77 (July, 1953), 3, 4-5, 13.]

Communist-front apparatus of the Kremlin conspiracy. In the May issue of the AMERICAN MERCURY, we pointed out that during the past seventeen years the Communist Party has enlisted the support of at least thirty-five hundred professors — many of them as dues-paying members, many others as fellow-travelers, some as out-and-out espionage agents, some as adherents of the party line in varying degrees, and some as the unwitting dupes of subversion. During the same seventeen-year period, the Communist Party has enlisted the support of at least seven thousand Protestant clergymen in the same categories — party members, fellow-travelers, espionage agents, party-line adherents, and unwitting dupes. . . .

The People's Institute of Applied Religion — a Communist school which is run, sponsored, and subsidized by Protestant clergymen — publishes a handbook which says: "True religion uses the class struggle as the most effective weapon of constructive social change in a class society. It recognizes from its study of our religious heritage that the class struggle, while it is not a permanent weapon of the people, is the historic weapon."

The People's Institute defines salvation, in its handbook, as follows: "Salvation is the result of the collective effort of the workers and other victims of this [the capitalist] world system to save *themselves* from the oppressors."

On the subject of Protestantism, the People's Institute offers the following viewpoint: "Protestant church religion came into being to enhance the rise of capitalism. It proclaimed the divine right of property. It deified [spelled *defied* in the original] the kings of finance, the lords of commerce and the captains of industry. Today this church religion is directed by remote control from the Chamber of Commerce, the National Association of Manufacturers and the offices of cartel imperialists. With these it has economic investments in the capitalist exploits of the whole world."

Any casual student of Communism will recognize the party line in these quotations from the published handbook of the People's Institute of Applied Religion. More about the Communist training school for clergymen presently!

Our next witness is the Director of the Federal Bureau of Investigation. In testimony before the Congressional Committee on Un-American Activities, on March 26, 1947, J. Edgar Hoover — who speaks with the highest authority on the subject of Communism — said: "I confess to a real apprehension so long as Communists are able to secure ministers of the Gospel to promote their evil work and espouse a cause that is alien to the religion of Christ and Judaism." . . .

Preachers, too, are people. As such, they are citizens to be held responsible for their civic and political acts. If professors and government employees are held to strict accountability for collaboration with the Communist-front apparatus, why not clergymen? Do clergymen have their own little Yalu River — their professional status — beyond which they have sanctuary? Why should they be allowed to participate, without investigation and exposure, in the "campaign to disarm and defeat the United States"? The Communist Party counts heavily on this immunity which cowardly politicians would grant to ministers of the Gospel. . . .

Why, one often hears, is it a matter of any great concern that ministers of the Gospel join, sponsor, or otherwise support the Communist-front apparatus? The answer to that question is that the Communist-front apparatus is an integral part of the whole nefarious Communist conspiracy to destroy us; that it is assigned as definite a role as the Communist Party itself, the espionage cells, the Communist training schools, and the Communist press. In the May issue of AMERICAN MERCURY, the multiple uses of the Communist-front apparatus were set forth in some detail. The reader is invited to refer to that discussion in my article on "Communism and the Colleges."

It hardly needs to be said that the vast majority of American Protestant clergymen are loyal to the free institutions of this country, as well as loyal to their solemn trust as ministers of the Gospel. In a sense, this overwhelming majority is embarrassed by the participation of the minority in the activities of the most sinister conspiracy in the history of the world.

The international Communist conspiracy aims at the total obliteration of Judeo-Christian civilization. Communist dogma is diametrically opposed to every tenet of Judeo-Christian theology and philosophy. It is, therefore, nothing short of a monstrous puzzle that some seven thousand Protestant clergymen have been drawn during the past seventeen years into the network of the Kremlin's conspiracy. Could it be that these pro-Communist clergymen have allowed their zeal for social justice to run away with their better judgment and patriotism?

A partial explanation of these thousands of clergymen who have collaborated in one way or another with the Communist-front apparatus may be found in the vogue of the "social gospel" which infected the Protestant theological seminaries more than a generation ago. Many graduates of the "liberalized" Protestant seminaries abandoned religion altogether in favor of the "social gospel."

The Rev. Walter Rauschenbusch,[1] with his *Christianizing the Social Order,* and the Rev. Harry F. Ward,[2] with his *The New Social Order,* pioneered the "social gospel" in the years before World War I, the former a Baptist and the latter a Methodist. In the generation which followed, these two men recruited through their teaching and writings thousands of younger clergymen who began to fancy themselves as modern editions of the Eighth Century Prophets — Amos, Hosea, Isaiah, and Micah. They forgot that these Prophets were as passionately concerned with individual human freedom as they were with social justice.

1. See above, pp. 109-10.
2. See above, pp. 268-70.

"I Protest"

Among the Protestant clergymen who found themselves persistently under attack was Methodist Bishop G. Bromley Oxnam (1891-1963). A highly respected and highly visible Methodist, Oxnam served as president of the Federal Council of Churches from 1944 to 1946 and as president of the World Council of Churches from 1948 to 1954. The Un-American Activities Committee repeatedly released "unevaluated" reports implying that Oxnam either sympathized with the Communist party or allowed himself to be used by it. The same hard choice was offered in those days to many Americans inside the churches and out: confess either to treason or to treasonable stupidity. Oxnam was not summoned to appear before the committee; rather, he demanded to be heard. He protested "against procedures that are in effect the rule of men and not of law; procedures subject to the prejudices, passions and political ambitions of Committeemen; procedures designed less to elicit information than to entrap; procedures that cease to be investigation and become inquisition and intimidation."

. . . So with but fifteen minutes allotted, I turned to what I believed to be the fundamentals.

The room became silent. I said:

When I declare, "I believe in God, the Father Almighty," I affirm the theistic faith and strike at the fundamental fallacy of communism, which is atheism. I thereby reaffirm the basic conviction upon which this republic rests, namely, that all men are created by the Eternal and in His image, beings of infinite worth, members of one family, brothers. We are endowed by the Creator with certain inalienable rights. The State does not confer them; it merely confirms them. They belong to man because he is a son of God. When I say, "I believe in God," I am also saying that moral law is written into the nature of things. There are moral absolutes. Marxism, by definition, rules out moral absolutes. Because I believe the will of God is revealed in the Gospel of Christ, I hold that all historically conditioned political, economic, social, and ecclesiastical systems must be judged by the Gospel, not identified with it, This is to say I reject communism, first, because of its atheism.

There was a puzzled expression upon the faces of some Committeemen. I continued:

[Source: G. B. Oxnam, *I Protest* (New York: Harper & Brothers, 1954), pp. 35-37.]

Bishop G. Bromley Oxnam (1891-1963)
(Methodist Information Service)

When I declare, "I believe in Jesus Christ, His only Son, our Lord," I am affirming faith in a spiritual view of life. By so doing, I repudiate the philosophy of materialism upon which communism is based, and thereby undermine it. I reject the theory of social development that assumes social institutions and even morality are determined by the prevailing mode of production. When I accept the law of love taught by Christ and revealed in His person, I must, of necessity, oppose to the death a theory that justifies dictatorship with its annihilation of freedom. I am not an economist, but have studied sufficiently to be convinced that there are basic fallacies in Marxian economics. Believing as I do that personality is a supreme good and that personality flowers in freedom, I stand for the free man in the free society, seeking the truth that frees. I hold that the free man must discover concrete measures through which the ideals of religion may be translated into the realities of world law and order, economic justice, and racial brotherhood.

As a result of long study and of prayer, I am by conviction pledged to the free way of life and opposed to all forms of totalitarianism, left or right, and to all tendencies toward such practices at home or abroad. Consequently, I have been actively opposed to communism all my life. I have never been a member of the Communist Party. My opposition to communism is a matter of public record in books, numerous articles, addresses, and sermons, and in resolutions I have drafted or sponsored in which powerful religious agencies have been put on record as opposed to communism. It is evidenced likewise in a life of service and the sponsorship of measures designed to make the free society impregnable to communist attack.

Loyalty to my family, my church, and my country are fundamental to me; and when any man or any Committee questions that loyalty, I doubt that I would be worthy of the name American if I took it lying down.

I then proceeded to certain considerations that I stated "I desire to lay before this Committee":

First, this Committee has followed a practice of releasing unverified and unevaluated material designated as "information" to citizens, organizations, and Members of Congress. It accepts no responsibility for the accuracy of the newspaper clippings recorded and so released; and insists that the material does not represent an opinion or a conclusion of the Committee. This material, officially released on official letterheads and signed by an official clerk, carried no disclaimer, in my case, and the recipient understandably assumed it did represent a conclusion. I am here formally to request that this "file" be cleaned up, that the Committee frankly admit its inaccuracies and misrepresentations, and that this matter be brought to a close.

It is alleged that the Committee has "files" on a million individuals, many of whom are among the most respected, patriotic, and devoted citizens of this nation. This is not the proper place to raise question as to the propriety of maintaining such vast "files" at public expense; but it is the proper place, in my case, to request that the practice of releasing unverified and unevaluated material, for which the Committee accepts no responsibility, cease. It can be shown that these reports are the result of inexcusable incompetence or of slanted selection, the result being the same in either case, namely, to question loyalty, to pillory or to intimidate the individual, to damage reputation, and to turn attention from the communist conspirator who pursues his nefarious work in the shadows, while a patriotic citizen is disgraced in public. The preparation and publication of these "files" puts into the hands of irresponsible individuals and agencies a wicked tool. It gives rise to a new and vicious expression of Ku-Kluxism, in which an innocent person may be beaten by unknown assailants who are cloaked in anonymity and at times immunity, whose whips are cleverly constructed lists of so-called subversive organizations and whose floggings appear all too often to be sadistic in spirit rather than patriotic in purpose.

Civil Rights and the Churches

Martin Luther King, Jr. (1929-68)

The modern world is short of prophets, not of men and women who predict but of men and women who pronounce, pronounce with awful clarity the demand that God's justice run down like waters and righteousness as a mighty stream. Martin Luther King, Jr., quoted those words from the prophet Amos as well as many other prophetic voices from Old Testament and New. Thus he sought to stir the conscience even of a nation, to move the ponderous and resistant machinery of government. His cause was civil rights, human freedom, divine justice. King, a Baptist minister in Montgomery, Alabama, gave inspiration to his own black brothers and sisters as he counseled resistance, not violent resistance, but a strong, steady, loving, believing resistance. Right up to the night in April, 1968, when he was assassinated, King never wavered in his own assurance that "We Shall Overcome." Two documents, both King's and both from 1963, reflect the depth and height of emotional intensity at this time. (1) The first comes from a Birmingham jail in April of that year; King had been arrested for leading a protest march in which whites and blacks, Protestants, Catholics, Orthodox, and Jews had all participated. (2) The following August tens of thousands marched to Washington where on the mall near the Washington Monument and beside the Lincoln Memorial King delivered his finest speech.

1.

I think I should indicate why I am here in Birmingham, since you have been influenced by the view which argues against "outsiders coming in."[3] I have the honor of serving as president of the Southern Christian Leadership Conference, an organization operating in every southern state, with headquarters in Atlanta, Georgia. We have some eighty-five affiliated organizations across the South, and one of them is the Alabama Christian Movement for Human Rights. Frequently we share staff, educational and financial resources with our affiliates. Several months ago the affiliate here in Birmingham asked us to be on call

3. This letter was written in response to eight Alabama clergymen who signed a statement protesting the march.

[Sources: (1) M. L. King, Jr., *Why We Can't Wait* (New York: Harper & Row, 1963), pp. 77-79, 81, 83-84. (2) Leon Friedman, ed., *The Civil Rights Reader* (New York: Walker & Co., 1967), pp. 112-13.]

to engage in a nonviolent direct-action program if such were deemed necessary. We readily consented, and when the hour came we lived up to our promise. So I, along with several members of my staff, am here because I was invited here. I am here because I have organizational ties here.

But more basically, I am in Birmingham because injustice is here. Just as the prophets of the eighth century B.C. left their villages and carried their "thus saith the Lord" far beyond the boundaries of their home towns, and just as the Apostle Paul left his village of Tarsus and carried the gospel of Jesus Christ to the far corners of the Greco-Roman world, so am I compelled to carry the gospel of freedom beyond my own home town. Like Paul, I must constantly respond to the Macedonian call for aid.

Moreover, I am cognizant of the interrelatedness of all communities and states. I cannot sit idly by in Atlanta and not be concerned about what happens in Birmingham. Injustice anywhere is a threat to justice everywhere. We are caught in an inescapable network of mutuality, tied in a single garment of destiny. Whatever affects one directly, affects all indirectly. Never again can we afford to live with the narrow, provincial "outside agitator" idea. Anyone who lives inside the United States can never be considered an outsider anywhere within its bounds.

You deplore the demonstrations taking place in Birmingham. But your statement, I am sorry to say, fails to express a similar concern for the conditions that brought about the demonstrations. I am sure that none of you would want to rest content with the superficial kind of social analysis that deals merely with effects and does not grapple with underlying causes. It is unfortunate that demonstrations are taking place in Birmingham, but it is even more unfortunate that the city's white power structure left the Negro community with no alternative. . . .

You may well ask: "Why direct action? Why sit-ins, marches and so forth? Isn't negotiation a better path?" You are quite right in calling for negotiation. Indeed, this is the very purpose of direct action. Nonviolent direct action seeks to create such a crisis and foster such a tension that a community which has constantly refused to negotiate is forced to confront the issue. It seeks so to dramatize the issue that it can no longer be ignored. My citing the creation of tension as part of the work of the nonviolent-resister may sound rather shocking. But I must confess that I am not afraid of the word "tension." I have earnestly opposed violent tension, but there is a type of constructive non-violent tension which is necessary for growth. . . .

We have waited for more than 340 years for our constitutional and God-given rights. The nations of Asia and Africa are moving with jetlike speed toward gaining political independence, but we still creep at horse-and-buggy pace toward gaining a cup of coffee at a lunch counter. Perhaps it is easy for those who have never felt the stinging darts of segregation to say, "Wait." But when you have seen vicious mobs lynch your mothers and fathers at will and drown your sisters and brothers at whim; when you have seen hate-filled policemen curse, kick and even kill your black brothers and sisters; when you see the vast majority of your twenty million Negro brothers smothering in an airtight cage of poverty in the midst of an affluent society; when you suddenly find your tongue twisted and your speech stammering as you seek to explain to your six-year-old daughter why she can't go to the public amusement park that has just been advertised on television, and see tears welling up in her eyes when she is told that Funtown is closed to colored children, and see ominous clouds of inferiority beginning to form in her little mental sky, and see her beginning to distort her personality by developing an unconscious bitterness toward white people; when you have to concoct an answer for a five-year-old son who is asking: "Daddy, why do white people treat colored people so mean?"; when you take a cross-country drive and find it necessary to sleep night after night in the uncomfortable corners of your automobile because no motel will accept you; when you are humiliated day in and day out by nagging signs reading "white" and "colored"; when your first name becomes "nigger," your middle name becomes "boy" (however old you are) and your last name becomes "John," and

Martin Luther King Jr. and the march on Selma, Alabama, in 1965
(Religion News Service)

your wife and mother are never given the respected title "Mrs."; when you are harried by day and haunted by night by the fact that you are a Negro, living constantly at tiptoe stance, never quite knowing what to expect next, and are plagued with inner fears and outer resentments; when you are forever fighting a degenerating sense of "nobodiness" — then you will understand why we find it difficult to wait. There comes a time when the cup of endurance runs over, and men are no longer willing to be plunged into the abyss of despair. I hope, sirs, you can understand our legitimate and unavoidable impatience.

2.

I say to you today, my friends, that in spite of the difficulties and frustrations of the moment I still have a dream. It is a dream deeply rooted in the American dream.

I have a dream that one day this nation will rise up and live out the true meaning of its creed: "We hold these truths to be self-evident; that all men are created equal."

I have a dream that one day on the red hills of Georgia the sons of former slaves and the sons of former slaveowners will be able to sit down together at the table of brotherhood.

I have a dream that one day even the state of Mississippi, a desert state sweltering with the heat of injustice and oppression, will be transformed into an oasis of freedom and justice.

I have a dream that my four little children will one day live in a nation where they will not be judged by the color of their skin but by the content of their character.

I have a dream today.

I have a dream that one day the state of Alabama, whose governor's lips are presently dripping with the words of interposition and nullification, will be transformed into a situation where little black boys and black girls will be able to join hands with little white boys and white girls and walk together as sisters and brothers.

I have a dream today.

I have a dream that one day every valley shall be exalted, every hill and mountain shall be made low, the rough places will be made plains, and the crooked places will be made straight, and the glory of the Lord shall be revealed, and all flesh shall see it together.

This is our hope. This is the faith with which I return to the South. With this faith we will be able to hew out of the mountain of despair a stone of hope. With this faith we will be able to transform the jangling discords of our nation into a beautiful symphony of brotherhood. With this faith we will be able to work together, to pray together, to struggle together, to go to jail together, to stand up for freedom together, knowing that we will be free one day.

This will be the day when all of God's children will be able to sing with new meaning "My country 'tis of thee, sweet land of liberty, of thee I sing. Land where my fathers died, land of the pilgrim's pride, from every mountainside, let freedom ring."

And if America is to be a great nation this must become true. So let freedom ring from the prodigious hilltops of New Hampshire. Let freedom ring from the mighty mountains of New York. Let freedom ring from the heightening Alleghenies of Pennsylvania!

Let freedom ring from the snowcapped Rockies of Colorado!

Let freedom ring from the curvaceous peaks of California!

But not only that; let freedom ring from Stone Mountain of Georgia!

Let freedom ring from Lookout Mountain of Tennessee!

Let freedom ring from every hill and mole hill of Mississippi. From every mountainside, let freedom ring.

When we let freedom ring, when we let it ring from every village and every hamlet, from every state and every city, we will be able to speed up that day when all of God's children, black men and white men, Jews and Gentiles, Protestants and Catholics, will be able to join hands and sing in the words of the old Negro spiritual, "Free at last! free at last! thank God almighty, we are free at last!"

Black Manifesto, 1969

The year after King's death the religious institutions of America found themselves challenged roughly by a group of black leaders identified with the National Black Economic Development Conference (Detroit, April 1969). Under the leadership of James Forman (b. 1928), the Conference adopted a manifesto addressed "To the White Christian Churches and the Synagogues in the United States of America and to All Other Racist Institutions." The rhetoric had grown sharper and the demand for justice had received a price tag: 500 million dollars in reparations "to the black people in this country." This amounts only to about fifteen dollars per black in America and is but "a beginning of the reparations due us as people who have been exploited and degraded, brutalized, killed and persecuted." The concluding section of the manifesto follows.

[Source: R. S. Lecky and H. E. Wright, eds., *Black Manifesto: Religion, Racism, and Reparations* (New York: Sheed & Ward, 1969), pp. 125-26.]

Brothers and sisters, we are no longer shuffling our feet and scratching our heads. We are tall, black and proud.

And we say to the white Christian churches and Jewish synagogues, to the government of this country and to all the white racist imperialists who compose it, there is only one thing left that you can do to further degrade black people and that is to kill us. But we have been dying too long for this country. We have died in every war. We are dying in Vietnam today fighting the wrong enemy.

The new black man wants to live, and to live means that we must not become static or merely believe in self-defense. We must boldly go out and attack the white Western world at its power centers. The white Christian churches are another form of government in this country, and they are used by the government of this country to exploit the people of Latin America, Asia and Africa, but the day is soon coming to an end. Therefore, brothers and sisters, the demands we make upon the white Christian churches and the Jewish synagogues are small demands. They represent fifteen dollars per black person in these United States. We can legitimately demand this from the church power structure. We must demand more from the United States Government.

But to win our demands from the church, which is linked up with the United States Government, we must not forget that it will ultimately be by force and power that we will win.

We are not threatening the churches. We are saying that we know the churches came with the military might of the colonizers and have been sustained by the military might of the colonizers. Hence, if the churches in colonial territories were established by military might, we know deep within our hearts that we must be prepared to use force to get our demands. We are not saying that this is the road we want to take. It is not, but let us be very clear that we are not opposed to force and we are not opposed to violence. We were captured in Africa by violence. We were kept in bondage and political servitude and forced to work as slaves by the military machinery and the Christian Church working hand in hand.

We recognize that in issuing this Manifesto we must prepare for a long-range educational campaign in all communities of this country, but we know that the Christian churches have contributed to our oppression in white America. We do not intend to abuse our black brothers and sisters in black churches who have uncritically accepted Christianity. We want them to understand how the racist white Christian church with its hypocritical declarations and doctrines of brotherhood has abused our trust and faith. An attack on the religious beliefs of black people is not our major objective, even though we know that we were not Christians when we were brought to this country, but that Christianity was used to help enslave us. Our objective in issuing this Manifesto is to force the racist white Christian church to begin the payment of reparations

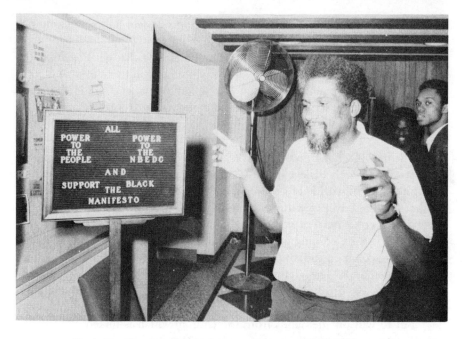

Black Manifesto spokesman James Forman seized office space
belonging to the National Council of Churches and
United Presbyterian Board of Mission, New York City, 1969.
(Religion News Service)

which are due to all black people, not only by the church but also by private
business and the United States government. We see this focus on the Christian
church as an effort around which all black people can unite.

Response to Racism and Manifesto

*Among other things, the Black Manifesto urged that on Sunday, May 4, 1969,
blacks around the country "commence the disruption of the racist churches
and synagogues throughout the United States." This was confrontation of the
most direct sort, with James Forman himself disrupting the services of New
York's Riverside Church. Institutional response to this tactic was uniformly
negative. The Roman Catholic Archdiocese of New York replied that "we do*

[Source: R. S. Lecky and H. E. Wright, eds., *Black Manifesto: Religion, Racism, and Reparations*
(New York: Sheed & Ward, 1969), pp. 141, 142-43.]

not endorse the 'Black Manifesto' and its demands." The Synagogue Council of America declared. "We find the demands and the tactics objectionable on both moral and practical grounds." And Riverside Church let it be known that "we have received from the courts a Civil Restraining Order that could place any individual in contempt of court who interfered with our worship of Almighty God or otherwise sought to render the Riverside Church inoperative." All of the above institutions, however, separated the immediate challenge from the underlying and persisting problem of racism. And all pledged themselves to renewed effort to alleviate that "degradation and hopelessness that still afflict the lives of so many of our fellow citizens." A portion of the Synagogue Council statement (together with the National Jewish Community Relations Advisory Council) follows, the statement being dated May 12, 1969.

Two separate issues have been raised by the "Black Manifesto": one by the substance of the demands, the other by the tactics employed to advance them. We find the demands and the tactics objectionable on both moral and practical grounds.

(1) The Demands

It is evident that much remains to be done if the racial discrimination that has shamed our American past is to be wiped out. We believe that it is entirely in order for our religious and communal institutions — no less than other segments of our society — to be challenged, both from within and from without, to face up to their own shortcomings and responsibilities. The gap between principle and performance is lamentably large; we have fallen short of our responsibilities in working for racial and economic justice.

We submit, on the other hand, that the demands for reparations by the Black Economic Development Conference is not an answer to the inequities and injustices of our society. It is clear that even if these demands were met in full, these inequities and injustices would not be rectified. . . .

What is required is massive government action in the areas of employment, housing, education, health and welfare. To say this is not to shirk personal or organizational responsibility, for such action can come about only if we as citizens declare and press our determination to pay the substantial costs that are involved. . . .

The Synagogue Council of America, through its newly established division of urban affairs, the National Jewish Community Relations Advisory Council and their national constituent agencies are prepared to assist synagogues and communal institutions in the implementation of these goals.

(2) The Tactics

The tactics resorted to by spokesmen for the Black Economic Development Conference in advancing their demands must also receive our serious attention, for these tactics involve disruption of divine services, demands for "ransom," and threats of violence.

We recognize that Americans "can no longer speak of 'violence' and 'extremism' without the terrible knowledge that their most destructive manifestation in American life is to be found in the violence done to the lives, the hopes and aspirations of our Negro citizens" (SCA policy statement March 6, 1968). It is equally true, however, that even in pursuit of desirable ends, violence does not contribute to the fashioning of a better society; violence only breeds more violence and nourishes repression, not justice.

We further express our conviction that the values by which men's actions and goals are judged are not subject to the exigencies of time and certainly not to those of race. The "revolution" in our cities and on our campuses does not create its own morality. The exegesis which enables some religious leaders to suspend biblical injunctions against violence, arson and murder and to invest these with a special grace when committed in the name of the "revolution" has no sanction in Jewish tradition.

If we speak up at this time, it is not only to clarify our position in regard to the demands and the tactics of the Black Economic Development Conference, but to urge that reprehensible actions not be permitted to divert our attention from the hard tasks which require our efforts and resources if our moral and religious professions are to be taken seriously. By implementing the specific actions outlined above, synagogues and communal institutions will give tangible expression of their commitment to the elimination of the poverty, degradation and hopelessness that still afflict the lives of so many of our fellow citizens.

Politics and Religion — 1960s

"A Roman Catholic for President?"

The question of a Catholic president raised memories of 1928 (see above, p. 263) and fears of unknown tomorrows. In both 1928 and 1960, the question

---

[Source: J. C. Bennett, in *Christianity & Crisis* (Mar. 7, 1960), reprinted in W. H. Cowan, ed., *Witness to a Generation* (Indianapolis: Bobbs-Merrill, 1966), pp. 62-63, 64-65.]

sometimes met with reason and careful argument, at other times with passion and prejudice unchecked. A singularly well-informed authority, John C. Bennett (b. 1902), professor and president at Union Theological Seminary in New York City, wrote from the vantage point of one thoroughly versed in Christian ethics. Bennett was also keenly attuned to the rapidly beating pulse of a non-Catholic public facing the direct issue of a Catholic president in the person of John F. Kennedy.

The issue raised by the possibility of a Roman Catholic candidate for the Presidency is the most significant immediate problem that grows out of the confrontation of Roman Catholicism with other religious communities in the United States. There are a great many Protestants of influence who are inclined to say that they would never vote for a Roman Catholic for President. Many of them refuse to say this with finality, but there is a strong trend in this direction. Our guess is that it may be stronger among the clergy and among official Protestant spokesmen than among the laity.

Aside from crude forms of prejudice and a reluctance to accept the fact that this is no longer a Protestant country, there are two considerations behind this position that have some substance. The first is that the traditional teaching of the Catholic Church is at variance with American conceptions of religious liberty and of church-state relations. There is a fear that a Catholic President might be used by a politically powerful Catholic Church to give that church the preferred position to which, according to its tradition, it believes itself entitled.

The other consideration is that there are a few specific issues on which there is a Catholic position, and, short of any basic change in our institutions, the nation's legislation and policy might be deflected by a Catholic President toward these known positions of his church. One example that is not often mentioned is the intransigent view of the problems of the cold war that was expressed in the American Catholic Bishops' statement late in 1959. (We would not vote for any man, Protestant or Catholic, who takes such a view.) On matters of this kind most Catholics are more likely to be affected by the position taken by the authorities of their church than would a Protestant. Even though they may not agree with the bishops, it would be embarrassing to oppose them publicly. Catholic bishops do their debating privately; American Catholicism on the hierarchical level, therefore, gives the impression of a united front that no Protestant churches are able to give.

We want to direct three comments to those who take a negative view concerning a possible Roman Catholic President:

(1) If the American people should make it clear that a Catholic could never be elected President, this would be an affront to 39,500,000 of our fellow citizens, and it would suggest that full participation in American political life is denied to them as Catholics. This would be true even though Catholics are gov-

ernors, senators, congressmen and Supreme Court justices. We believe that this situation would wound our common life and damage our institutions more grievously than it would be possible for a Catholic President to do even if he chose to. We are shocked that so many Protestants seem unwilling to give any weight to this.

(2) We are justified in ascertaining what view of church-state relations and of the basis of religious liberty a particular Catholic candidate holds. We may learn this without grilling him, for his record of public service and its implications would be an open book.

There are two main views of religious liberty that are held among Catholics. The traditional view regards as normative the idea of a Catholic state with the church in a privileged position and with at least a curtailment of the liberties of non-Catholics. This view is an inheritance from an earlier period of history, and many Catholic theologians and ecclesiastical leaders now reject it. They believe in religious liberty for non-Catholics on principle and not merely as a matter of pragmatic adjustment to the American situation.

This more liberal view is not limited to this country; it is held widely in Western Europe. It is one view held in Vatican circles. Those who hold this view believe that Pius XII was at least open to it, and they are even more sure that this is true of his generous-minded successor. . . .

(3) So far as the specific issues on which there is a known Catholic position are concerned, there are very few that come to the desk of the President. More of them are dealt with by mayors and governors, and the Republic has survived many Catholic mayors and governors. And on many issues within the purview of the President, the Catholic community is divided — even, for example, on the appointment of an ambassador to the Vatican. (It was a Baptist who made the latest appointment to the Vatican.) Furthermore, a President is subjected to so many pressures and counter pressures that he is less vulnerable to any one form of pressure than most other public servants.

There is the vexing problem of birth control. As a domestic problem it belongs chiefly to the states, and it is fortunate that many Catholics, while they do not reject their church's position on birth control in terms of morals and theology, do not believe there should be a civil law that imposes the Catholic moral teaching upon non-Catholics. . . .

We should like to add to these considerations a more positive note: a Catholic President who is well instructed in the moral teachings of his church would have certain assets. (It is chiefly in the areas of sex and medicine that the Protestant finds elements of an intolerable legalism in Catholic moral teaching.) If he is of an essentially liberal spirit he may absorb the best in the real humanism of Catholic thought.

A Catholic President might have a better perspective on the issue of social justice than many Protestants. He might be guided by the ethical inhibitions present in Catholic views of the just war so as to resist the temptation to make military necessity paramount in all matters of national strategy. He might have a wiser and more seasoned understanding of the claims of the person in relation to the community than many a one-sided Protestant individualist.

We are not now speaking of any particular Catholic candidate, and there are elements in Catholic moral doctrine that we reject. When these are interpreted by the narrower type of ecclesiastic, we often find them repellent. But Catholic teaching has its better and more humane side, and it is the repository of much wisdom that could stand a Catholic President in good stead.

"It Is My Job to Face It . . ."

"The religious issue," as John F. Kennedy noted, would not go away in the campaign for the presidency in 1960. It was raised as Kennedy sought the nomination of the Democratic party, then raised more widely and vociferously once that nomination was his. Ignoring the issue did not dispose of it. Kennedy therefore concluded that it was his job "to face it frankly and fully." He did so on three occasions: in Washington, D.C., in April before the Society of American Newspaper Editors; in Los Angeles in July after winning the Democratic nomination; and in Houston before the Ministerial Association in September, less than two months before the election. The remarks below are from the first of the three occasions.

I have decided, in view of current press reports, that it would be appropriate to speak with you today about what has widely been called "the religious issue" in American politics.

The phrase covers a multitude of meanings. There is no religious issue in the sense that any of the major candidates differ on the role of religion in our political life. Every Presidential contender, I am certain, is dedicated to the separation of church and state, to the preservation of religious liberty, to an end to religious bigotry, and to the total independence of the officeholder from any form of ecclesiastical dictation.

Nor is there any real issue in the sense that any candidate is exploiting his religious affiliation. No one's candidacy, by itself, raises a religious issue. And I believe it is inaccurate to state that my "candidacy created the issue."

Nor am I appealing, as is too often claimed, to a so-called Catholic vote. Even if such a vote exists — which I doubt — I want to make one thing clear

[Source: Moses Rischin, ed., *Immigration and the American Tradition* (Indianapolis: Bobbs-Merrill, 1976), pp. 414-15, 416-17, 418-19, 420-21.]

again: I want no votes solely on account of my religion. Any voter, Catholic or otherwise, who feels another candidate would be a superior President should support that candidate. I do not want any vote cast for me for such illogical and irrelevant reasons.

Neither do I want anyone to support my candidacy merely to prove that this nation is not bigoted — and that a Catholic can be elected President. I have never suggested that those opposed to me are thereby anti-Catholic. . . .

For the past month and years I have answered almost daily inquiries from the press about the religious issue. I want to take this opportunity to turn the tables — and to raise some questions for your thoughtful consideration.

First: Is the religious issue a legislative issue in this campaign?

There is only one legitimate question underlying all the rest: Would you, as President of the United States, be responsive in any way to ecclesiastical pressures or obligations of any kind that might in any fashion influence or interfere with your conduct of that office in the national interest? I have answered that question many times. My answer was — and is — "No."

Once that question is answered there is no legitimate issue of my religion, but there are, I think, legitimate questions of public policy — of concern to religious groups which no one should feel bigoted about raising, and to which I do not object answering. But I do object to being the only candidate required to answer those questions.

Federal assistance to parochial schools, for example, is a very legitimate issue actually before the Congress. I am opposed to it. I believe it is clearly unconstitutional. I voted against it on the Senate floor this year, when offered by Senator Morse. But interestingly enough, I was the only announced candidate in the Senate who did so. Nevertheless, I have not yet charged my opponents with taking orders from Rome.

An Ambassador to the Vatican could conceivably become a real issue again. I am opposed to it, and said so long ago. But even though it was last proposed by a Baptist President, I know of no other candidate who has been even asked about this matter.

The prospects of any President ever receiving for his signature a bill providing foreign aid funds for birth control are very remote indeed. It is hardly the major issue some have suggested. Nevertheless, I have made it clear that I would neither veto nor sign such a bill on any basis except what I considered to be the public interest, without regard to my private religious views. I have said the same about bills dealing with censorship, divorce, our relations with Spain or any other subject.

These are legitimate inquiries about real questions which the next President may conceivably have to face. But these inquiries ought to be directed equally to all candidates.

Secondly, can we justify analyzing voters as well as candidates strictly in terms of their religion? I think the voters of Wisconsin objected to being categorized simply as either Catholics or Protestants in analyzing their political choices. I think they objected to being accosted by reporters outside of political meetings and asked one question only — their religion — not their occupation or education or philosophy or income — only their religion. . . .

The voters are more than Catholics, Protestants or Jews. They make up their minds for many diverse reasons, good and bad. To submit the candidates to a religious test is unfair — to apply it to the voters themselves is divisive, degrading and wholly unwarranted.

Third and finally: Is there any justification for applying special religious tests to one office only? The Presidency? Little or no attention was paid to my religion when I took the oath as Senator in 1953 — as a Congressman in 1947 — or as a naval officer in 1941. Members of my faith abound in public office at every level except the White House. What is there about the Presidency that justifies this constant emphasis upon a candidate's religion and that of his supporters?

The Presidency is not, after all, the British crown, serving a dual capacity in both church and state. The President is not elected to be protector of the faith — or guardian of the public morals. His attendance at church on Sunday should be his business alone, not a showcase for the nation.

On the other hand, we are in no danger of a one-man Constitutional upheaval. The President, however intent he may be on subverting our institutions, cannot ignore the Congress — or the voters — or the courts. And our highest court, incidentally, has a long history of Catholic justices, none of whom, as far as I know, was ever challenged on the fairness of his ruling on sensitive church-state issues. . . .

If there is bigotry in the country, then so be it — there is bigotry. If that bigotry is too great to permit the fair consideration of a Catholic who has made clear his complete independence and his complete dedication to separation of church and state, then we ought to know it.

But I do not believe this is the case. I believe the American people are more concerned with a man's views and abilities than with the church to which he belongs. I believe that the founding fathers meant it when they provided in Article VI of the Constitution that there should be no religious test for public office — a provision that brought not one dissenting vote, only the comment of Roger Sherman that it was surely unnecessary — "the prevailing liberality being a sufficient security against such tests." And I believe that the American people mean to adhere to those principles today.

But regardless of the political outcome, this issue is here to be faced. It is my job to face it frankly and fully. And it is your job to face it fairly, in perspective and in proportion.

I am confident that the press and the other media of this country will recognize their responsibilities in this area — to refute falsehood, to inform the ignorant, and to concentrate on the issues, the real issues in this hour of the nation's peril.

The Supreme Court has written that as public officials "we are neither Jew nor gentile, neither Catholic nor agnostic. We owe equal attachment to the Constitution and are equally bound by our obligation, whether we derive our citizenship from the earliest or latest immigrants to these shores . . . (for) religion is outside the sphere of political government."

We must all — candidates, press, and voters alike — dedicate ourselves to these principles, for they are the key to a free society.

Moral Responsibility and Religion

The Great Society

Following the assassination of John F. Kennedy in November of 1963, Vice President Lyndon B. Johnson upon assuming the presidency moved quickly in urging Congress to pass major civil rights legislation as a memorial to the fallen leader. Johnson thereafter pressed his war against poverty as an additional step toward what he called "the Great Society." Some churches concluded that it was their responsibility to enlist in that "war," while others saw this emphasis as more the affair of politics or of governmental agencies. A Methodist perspective is provided below.

As a nation, we have the wealth, income, technical know-how and productive capacity to reduce drastically the incidence of poverty in America — serious social, economic, political, and cultural deprivations of individuals and families.

As a nation, we clearly have the capacity to achieve this degree of social justice in our time. What we need is national commitment — a dedication to the task on the part of people, local communities, private organizations (including churches), labor, business, and public authorities at every level of government.

With the passage of Economic Opportunity Act (Public Law 88-452), the Federal Government initiated a national attack on poverty. That government pledged its resources to combat domestic poverty. Under the Act, an Office of

[Source: *Concern* (published by the General Board of Christian Social Concerns of The Methodist Church), Dec. 1, 1965, p. 14.]

Economic Opportunity (OEO) was established to administer national programs. . . .

These OEO programs confront churches with both a challenge and an opportunity. Churches are challenged to commit a substantial portion of their institutional resources to coordinated national, state, and local programs to combat poverty. More important, perhaps, is the unparalleled opportunity the churches now have to demonstrate what love, brotherhood, and human dignity really mean in the context of a responsible society. In imaginative, creative, and sacrificial ways, churches can help establish social, economic, and political relationships which will restore to the poor the satisfaction of belonging to a community in which they can find security and significance. The church will, of course, include the impoverished in all efforts to develop Christian fellowship.

It seems unlikely that churches can either fully meet the challenge or take advantage of the opportunity offered by OEO programs to combat poverty without becoming more involved in formal relations with government, particularly at the local level. Therefore, the General Board of Christian Social Concerns recommends:

1. That national agencies, annual conferences, and local congregations of The Methodist Church cooperate with and supplement the efforts of agencies of government to eradicate poverty, through means such as:
   a. serving as participants in policy-shaping and project-implementation where community anti-poverty programs are under way;
   b. acting as a catalyst in the initiation of anti-poverty programs in communities where such programs have not yet been undertaken;
   c. supporting the involvement of the poor in anti-poverty policy and program development;
   d. working for the strengthening and improvement of the legislative framework for the struggle against poverty.
2. That, if churches find it desirable to enter into contractual relationships with government and to accept public funds, the following principles should govern that relationship:
   a. Churches should seek no self-aggrandisement.
   b. The Methodist Church and its local congregations should seek out other religious and secular institutions in the community with which to cooperate in the development of comprehensive programs.
   c. The decisions to cooperate should rest with the official governing body of the institution, but this body may find it desirable to establish a non-profit organization to implement its purposes. Where such organizations are established, churches should make careful provisions for continuing liaison.
   d. Before entering into any such contractual relationship, the official gov-

erning body of the church or agency should become familiar with the
governmental principles and regulations involved as stated in Public
Law 88-452 and the regulations pertaining thereto.

We believe that The Methodist Church and its congregations should support
the officially stated objectives of the War on Poverty. At the same time, we urge
churches and church-related organizations to give careful and continuing consideration to the possibility that religious principles or the integrity of government may be compromised in such supportive arrangements as may be
evolved. Such a result must be avoided. We urge The Methodist Church and all
of its agencies to maintain a continuing responsibility for assuring that the
stated purposes of the Act are adhered to faithfully at the same time that every
effort is made to insure the greatest possible effect in eradicating poverty.

The Betrayed Society

*On August 9, 1974, for the first time in America's history a president of the
United States resigned from that high office. The word "Watergate" had by
then come to symbolize corruption, cover-up, and abuse of power. Richard M. Nixon, said the House of Representatives Judiciary Committee, "has
acted in a manner contrary to his trust as President and subversive of constitutional government, to the great prejudice of the cause of law and justice
and to the manifest injury of the people of the United States." Words such as
"trust" and "justice" and phrases such as Breach of Faith (Theodore White,
1975) suggested an ethical element, perhaps even a religious element in this
national tragedy. Where the repentance, the atonement, the reconciliation?
Where or what was the moral hidden away in this long national nightmare
(as newly inaugurated President Gerald Ford had called it)? Chair of the
Senate Select Committee to investigate the sorry episode, Sam J. Ervin, Jr.
(1896-1985), in submitting the committee's final report added his own "Meditations." Ervin, Presbyterian layman and "simple country lawyer" (Harvard bachelor of law in 1922), took a long look into the lessons of history and
a deep gaze into the nature of man.*

Unlike the men who were responsible for Teapot Dome, the presidential aides
who perpetrated Watergate were not seduced by the love of money, which is
sometimes thought to be the root of all evil. On the contrary, they were insti-

---

[Source: Sam J. Ervin, Jr., *The Whole Truth: The Watergate Conspiracy* (New York: Random
House, 1980), pp. 310-11, 312.]

gated by a lust for political power, which is at least as corrupting as political power itself.

They gave their allegiance to the President and his policies. They had stood for a time near to him, and had been entrusted by him with great governmental and political power. They enjoyed exercising such power, and longed for its continuance.

They knew that the power they enjoyed would be lost and the policies to which they adhered would be frustrated if the President should be defeated.

As a consequence of these things, they believed the President's reelection to be a most worthy objective, and succumbed to an age-old temptation. They resorted to evil means to promote what they conceived to be a good end.

Their lust for political power blinded them to ethical considerations and legal requirements; to Aristotle's aphorism that the good of man must be the end of politics; and to Grover Cleveland's conviction that a public office is a public trust.

They had forgotten, if they ever knew, that the Constitution is designed to be a law for rulers and people alike at all times and under all circumstances; and that no doctrine involving more pernicious consequences to the commonweal has ever been invented by the wit of man than the notion that any of its provisions can be suspended by the President for any reason whatsoever.

On the contrary, they apparently believed that the President is above the Constitution, and has the autocratic power to suspend its provisions if he decides in his own unreviewable judgment that his action in so doing promotes his own political interests or the welfare of the nation. As one of them testified before the Senate Select Committee, they believed that the President has the autocratic power to suspend the Fourth Amendment whenever he imagines that some indefinable aspect of national security is involved.

I digress to reject this doctrine of the constitutional omnipotence of the President. As long as I have a mind to think, a tongue to speak, and a heart to love my country, I shall deny that the Constitution confers any autocratic power on the President, or authorizes him to convert George Washington's America into Gaius Caesar's Rome.

The lust for political power of the presidential aides who perpetrated Watergate on America blinded them to the laws of God as well as to the laws and ethics of man.

As a consequence, they violated the spiritual law which forbids men to do evil even when they think good will result from it, and ignored these warnings of the King James version of the Bible:

1. "There is nothing covered, that shall not be revealed; neither hid, that shall not be known."

2. "Be not deceived; God is not mocked: For whatsoever a man soweth, that shall he also reap."

I find corroboration for my conclusion that lust for political power produced Watergate in words uttered by the most eloquent and learned of all the Romans, Marcus Tullius Cicero, about 2100 years ago. He said:

"Most men, however, are inclined to forget justice altogether, when once the craving for military power or political honors and glory has taken possession of them. Remember the saying of Ennius, 'When crowns are at stake, no friendship is sacred, no faith shall be kept.'" . . .

Since politics is the art or science of government, no man is fit to participate in politics or to seek or hold public office unless he has two characteristics.

The first of these characteristics is that he must understand and be dedicated to the true purpose of government, which is to promote the good of the people, and entertain the abiding conviction that a public office is a public trust, which must never be abused to secure private advantage.

The second characteristic is that he must possess that intellectual and moral integrity, which is the priceless ingredient in good character.

When all is said, the only sure antidote for future Watergates is understanding of fundamental principles and intellectual and moral integrity in the men and women who achieve or are entrusted with governmental or political power.

3. The Nation and Its Churches

The Ecumenical Age

National Council and World Council

(1) The Federal Council of Churches (see above, pp. 178-80), after nearly one-half century of ecumenical activity, merged with several interdenominational boards in 1950 to form the National Council of Churches of Christ in the U.S.A. Twenty-nine denominations participated in this original structuring, but more would be added. By 1960 the Council, with a membership of about forty million, had reached beyond the limits of Protestantism to include many of the churches within Eastern Orthodoxy. Roman Catholic churches were not affiliated, but dialogue — especially in the 1960s — between Protestants and Catholics, also between Orthodox and Catholics, markedly increased. What follows below is a portion of the National Council's message "To the People of the Nation" on the occasion of the 1950 founding. (2) While the World Council of Churches came into being in 1948 with its First Assembly in Amsterdam, most Americans became conscious of the new organization in 1954 when it held its Second Assembly in the United States, at Evanston, Illinois. A large meeting (the World Council represented more than 150 denominations, again including Eastern Orthodoxy but excluding Roman Catholicism except as observers), the Evanston gathering dramatized the dawning of what did indeed appear to be a new ecumenical age. "The Message" from the Evanston Assembly is presented below.

[Sources: (1) National Council, *Christian Faith in Action: Commemorative Volume* . . . (New York: National Council, 1951), pp. 150, 151-52, 152-53. (2) "The Message" of the World Council, Second Assembly, August 31, 1954, in *Christian Century*, Sept. 22, 1954, pp. 1123-24.]

1.

This Council has been constituted by twenty-nine Churches for the glory of God and the well-being of humanity. It manifests our oneness in Jesus Christ as divine Lord and Saviour; his is the mandate we obey and his the power upon which we rely. It is designed to be an instrument of the Holy Spirit for such ministries of evangelism, education, and relief as are better achieved through Christian cooperation than by the labors of separated groups. It coordinates and continues the work of eight interdenominational agencies ministering in as many fields of Christian usefulness. . . .

The Council has nothing to fear from the times, though it has much to desire of them. Being the servant of One who holds in His hand all the nations, and the isles, as a very little thing, it is free from the apprehensions of those who, taking counsel of men alone, forget that no age is isolated from God's ageless purpose. We call our fellow citizens to Christian faith: this will defend them from groundless social dreads and lift them to concerns worthy and productive.

The Council stands as a guardian of democratic freedom. The revolutionary truth that men are created free follows from the revelation of God in Jesus Christ, and no person who knows that God as Father has given him all the rights of sonship is likely to remain content under a government which deprives him of basic human rights and fundamental freedoms. The nation may expect in the National Council a sturdy ally of the forces of liberty.

The Council stands for liberty with the richest content. It stands for the freedom of men to be as the Lord God meant them to be. It stands for Christian freedom — including the freedom to pursue happiness and with justice and sympathy to create conditions of happiness for others. It therefore stands against the misuse of freedom. The nation may expect from the National Council, in the name of One who suffered death upon a cross, an unrelenting, open-eyed hostility, as studious as it is deeply passionate, to all of man's inhumanity to man.

The Council opposes materialism as an end in itself. It is the foe of every political system that is nourished on materialism, and of every way of living that follows from it. From that smug idealism which is a form of selfishness, the Council prays to be protected; but danger on this hand does not lessen the necessity it feels to fight a constant fight against all kinds of secular materialism which demolish the slowly built edifice of Christian morality and fair dealing.

Through the Council the churches, as they are dedicated to the doing of God's will, must increasingly become a source of spiritual power to the nation. The American Churches, of which the Council is one of the visible symbols, are in their true estate the soul of the nation. When those Churches take their true course, they draw their standards not from the world around but from the guiding mind of Christ. The Church is not the religious phase of the civilization in which it finds itself; it is the living center out of which lasting civiliza-

Official emblem adopted by the National Council of Churches in 1955
(National Council of Churches)

tions take life and form. In this sense the Council will be an organ through which the will of God may become effective as an animating, creative and unifying force within our national society.

The Council gives thanks to God for all those forces which make for harmony in our society. When, for example, science employs its ingenuity to knit the world together in bonds of communication, when business and industry make a like contribution through the life-bringing mutuality of commerce, when the arts depict the beauty and the tragedy of our existence which draw us into unity with one another, when the many professions and occupations recognize themselves as callings to human usefulness, then the Council salutes and supports them. By word and deed and in the name of Christ who gave his life for all mankind it affirms the brotherhood of men and seeks by every rightful means to arrest those forces of division which rend the nation along racial lines and stay its growth toward unity. . . .

We of the National Council of the Churches of Christ in the U.S.A. begin our work in humility as we see the magnitude of the task ahead. We are not unconscious of our own short-comings. Knowing that men too often dream in marble and then build with straw, we whose very human lives are not separate from sin and ignorance can make no boast of past or future excellence.

But this we have done: by God's grace we have forged an implement for cooperation such as America has never seen before. Into it have been poured the thoughts of wise and noble men and women, the prayers and consecration of the faithful, and the longing of all the participating Churches to serve the spiritual needs of all the people. The Council is our Churches in their highest common effort for mankind.

Our hope is in Jesus Christ. In Him we see the solution of the world's ills, for as human hearts are drawn near to him, they are drawn near in sympathy and understanding to each other. The Council itself is a demonstration of his power to unite his followers in joyous cooperation. Let nation and nation, race and race, class and class unite their aims in his broad purposes for man, and out of that unitedness there will arise new strength like that of which we ourselves already feel the first sure intimations.

In this hope we commend you, our fellow citizens, to God's mercy, grace and peace.

2.

To all our fellow Christians, and to our fellow men everywhere, we send greetings in the name of Jesus Christ. We affirm our faith in Jesus Christ as the hope of the world, and desire to share that faith with all men. May God forgive us that by our sin we have often hidden this hope from the world.

In the ferment of our time there are both hopes and fears. It is indeed good to hope for freedom, justice and peace, and it is God's will that we should have these things. But he has made us for a higher end. He has made us for himself, that we might know and love him, worship and serve him. Nothing other than God can ever satisfy the heart of man. Forgetting this, man becomes his own enemy. He seeks justice but creates oppression. He wants peace but drifts toward war. His very mastery of nature threatens him with ruin. Whether he acknowledges it or not, he stands under the judgment of God and in the shadow of death.

Here where we stand, Jesus Christ stood with us. He came to us, true God and true Man, to seek and to save. Though we were the enemies of God, Christ died for us. We crucified him, but God raised him from the dead. He is risen. He has overcome the powers of sin and death. A new life has begun. And in his risen and ascended power he has sent forth into the world a new community, bound together by his Spirit, sharing his divine life, and commissioned to make him known throughout the world. He will come again as judge and King to bring all things to their consummation. Then we shall see him as he is and know as we are known. Together with the whole creation we wait for this with eager hope, knowing that God is faithful and that even now he holds all things in his hand.

This is the hope of God's people in every age, and we commend it afresh today to all who will listen. To accept it is to turn from our ways to God's way. It is to live as forgiven sinners, as children growing in his love. It is to have our citizenship in that Kingdom which all man's sin is impotent to destroy, that realm of love and joy and peace which lies about all men, though unseen. It is to enter with Christ into the suffering and despair of men, sharing with them the great secret of that Kingdom which they do not suspect. It is to know that whatever men may do, Jesus reigns and shall reign.

With this assurance we can face the powers of evil and the threat of death with a good courage. Delivered from fear we are made free to love. For beyond the judgment of men and the judgment of history lies the judgment of the King who died for all men, and who will judge us at the last according to what we have done to the least of his brethren. Thus our Christian hope directs us toward our neighbor. It constrains us to pray daily, "Thy will be done on earth as it is in heaven," and to act as we pray in every area of life. It begets a life of believing prayer and expectant action, looking to Jesus and pressing forward to the day of his return in glory. . . .

Meeting of World Council of Churches in Evanston, Illinois, in 1954
(National Council of Churches)

The forces that separate men from one another are strong. At our meeting here we have missed the presence of Chinese churches which were with us at Amsterdam. There are other lands and churches unrepresented in our council, and we long ardently for their fellowship. But we are thankful that, separated as we are by the deepest political divisions of our time, here at Evanston we are united in Christ. And we rejoice also that, in the bond of prayer and a common hope, we maintain communion with our Christian brethren everywhere. . . .

Consultation on Church Union / Churches Uniting in Christ

The National Council and the World Council represent Christian cooperation and programs of mutual assistance. Neither directly promotes church union or sees this as its primary function. The Consultation on Church Union (COCU), by contrast, emerged in the 1960s as the most ambitious effort in modern America to bring about actual union. Proposed initially by the stated clerk of the Presbyterian Church, U.S.A., Eugene Carson Blake, in Bishop James Pike's Episcopal Cathedral in San Francisco in 1960, the discussions continued thereafter. By the 1990s, somewhat weary participants in COCU agreed that they should think more in terms of "covenants" than of mergers, the former term implying the recognition by all participating denominations of one another's baptism, membership, and clergy. More a working partnership than a superchurch, the COCU movement was reorganized early in the new century under the title Churches Uniting in Christ. The stated purposes of the new organization have been outlined especially with local congregations in mind, and especially for the effort to combat racism in American society.

As many of you as were baptized into Christ have clothed yourselves with Christ. There is no longer Jew or Greek, there is no longer slave or free, there is no longer male and female; for all of you are one in Christ Jesus.

Galatians 3:27-28

After forty years of study and prayer through the Consultation on Church Union (COCU), the nine church members agreed to stop "consulting" and

[Source: "What is CUIC?" http://www.eden.edu/cuic/whatiscuic/whatiscuic.htm (May 27, 2003).]

start living their unity in Christ more fully. On January 20, 2002, these churches inaugurated a new relationship to be known as **Churches Uniting in Christ** (CUIC).

Each communion retains its own identity and decision-making structures, but they also have pledged before God to draw closer in sacred things — including regular sharing of the Lord's Supper and common mission, especially a mission to combat racism together. Each church also committed itself to undertake an intensive dialogue toward the day when ministers are authorized to serve and lead worship, when invited, in each of the communions.

Churches Uniting in Christ is not a new structure. It is an officially recognized invitation to live with one another differently. Christians in the pews know that we belong together because we all belong to the same Lord. Churches Uniting in Christ is a framework for showing to the world what we truly are — the one Body of Jesus Christ.

What could this mean for your congregation?

- Pray for nearby CUIC congregations by name. Make their joys and sufferings your own.
- Include representatives of neighboring CUIC congregations in your baptisms, ordinations, and installations.
- Celebrate the Lord's Supper with other CUIC congregations in your area, at least on special occasions.
- Undertake mission projects with CUIC partners on a regular basis, especially projects aimed at overcoming racism.
- Invite a member of a neighboring CUIC congregation to serve on a board or committee of your church.
- Invite other congregations to participate in your special events, from worship services to ice cream socials.
- Organize shared youth retreats or adult education courses. Teach about the other churches in your own education program.
- Add the words "Member of Churches Uniting in Christ" to your church signboard.

How can your congregation be involved?

- Read in worship a pastoral letter from the heads of the nine churches expressing a commitment to oppose racism together.
- Celebrate the inauguration of CUIC with other participating congregations in your area.

- Take the initiative to promote the kinds of activities listed in this brochure.
- Share your local activities with others by emailing us at llong@eden.edu. We will post your ideas on the website.

The Lausanne Covenant

The numerous Christian groups that have been wary about participating in the National and World Councils sustain a great array of voluntary associations among themselves. One of the most important of these networks is made up of the evangelicals, Pentecostals, moderate fundamentalists, Holiness, and pietistic groups that often work together ad hoc *to promote Christian evangelization. In the summer of 1974 an unusually large (2,700) and representative (from more than 150 countries) gathering of such people took place in Lausanne, Switzerland, for an International Congress on World Evangelization. Leadership and much of the funding for the meeting came from Billy Graham, who with the various activities of his Evangelistic Association had been engaged in world-wide network-building for a quarter of a century. The "Lausanne Covenant" that came from the meeting was an unusually clear statement of traditional evangelical convictions, but now joined to a clear-cut embrace of social concern. Since 1974 this covenant has served as a landmark in world evangelical movements to which growing numbers of Americans are connected through immigration, mission service, development projects, publications, and other means.*

The Lausanne Covenant

Introduction

We, members of the Church of Jesus Christ, from more than 150 nations, participants in the International Congress On World Evangelization at Lausanne, praise God for his great salvation and rejoice in the fellowship he has given us with himself and with each other. We are deeply stirred by what God is doing in our day, moved to penitence by our failures and challenged by the unfinished task of evangelization. We believe the gospel is God's good news for the whole world, and we are determined by his grace to obey Christ's commission to proclaim it to all mankind and to make disciples of every na-

---

[Source: "The Lausanne Covenant," *Christianity Today*, August 16, 1974, pp. 22-23.]

tion. We desire, therefore, to affirm our faith and our resolve, and to make public our covenant.

1. The Purpose of God

We affirm our belief in the one eternal God, Creator and Lord of the world, Father, Son and Holy Spirit, who governs all things according to the purpose of his will. He has been calling out from the world a people for himself, and sending his people back into the world to be his servants and his witnesses, for the extension of his kingdom, the building up of Christ's body, and the glory of his name. We confess with shame that we have often denied our calling and failed in our mission, by becoming conformed to the world or by withdrawing from it. Yet we rejoice that even when borne by earthen vessels the gospel is still a precious treasure. To the task of making that treasure known in the power of the Holy Spirit we desire to dedicate ourselves anew.

2. The Authority and Power of the Bible

We affirm the divine inspiration, truthfulness and authority of both Old and New Testament Scriptures in their entirety as the only written word of God, without error in all that it affirms, and the only infallible rule of faith and practice. We also affirm the power of God's word to accomplish his purpose of salvation. The message of the Bible is addressed to all mankind. For God's revelation in Christ and in Scripture is unchangeable. Through it the Holy Spirit still speaks today. He illumines the minds of God's people in every culture to perceive its truth freshly through their own eyes and thus discloses to the whole church ever more of the many-coloured wisdom of God.

3. The Uniqueness and Universality of Christ

We affirm that there is only one Saviour and only one gospel, although there is a wide diversity of evangelistic approaches. We recognize that all men have some knowledge of God through his general revelation in nature. But we deny that this can save, for men suppress the truth by their unrighteousness. We also reject as derogatory to Christ and the gospel every kind of syncretism and dialogue which implies that Christ speaks equally through all religions and ideologies. Jesus Christ, being himself the only God-man, who gave himself as the only ransom for sinners, is the only mediator between God and man. There is no other name by which we must be saved. All men are perishing because of sin, but God loves all men, not wishing that any should perish but that all should repent. Yet those who reject Christ repudiate the joy of salvation and condemn themselves to eternal separation from God. To proclaim Jesus as "the Saviour of the world" is not to affirm that all men are either automatically or ultimately saved, still less to affirm that all religions offer salvation in Christ. Rather it is to proclaim God's love for a world of sinners and to invite all men to respond to him as Saviour and Lord in the wholehearted personal commitment of repentance and faith. Jesus Christ has been exalted above every other name; we long for the day when every knee shall bow to him and every tongue shall confess him Lord.

4. The Nature of Evangelism

To evangelize is to spread the good news that Jesus Christ died for our sins and was raised from the dead according to the Scriptures, and that as the reigning Lord he now offers the forgiveness of sins and the liberating gift of the Spirit to all who repent and believe. Our Christian presence in the world is indispensable to evangelism, and so is that kind of dialogue whose purpose is to listen sensitively in order to understand. But evangelism itself is the proclamation of the historical, biblical Christ as Saviour and Lord, with a view to persuading people to come to him personally and so be reconciled to God. In issuing the gospel invitation we have no liberty to conceal the cost of discipleship. Jesus still calls all who would follow him to deny themselves, take up their cross, and identify themselves with his new community. The results of evangelism include obedience to Christ, incorporation into his church and responsible service in the world.

5. Christian Social Responsibility

We affirm that God is both the Creator and the Judge of all men. We therefore should share his concern for justice and reconciliation throughout human society and for the liberation of men from every kind of oppression. Because mankind is made in the image of God, every person, regardless of race, religion, colour, culture, class, sex or age, has an intrinsic dignity because of which he should be respected and served, not exploited. Here too we express penitence both for our neglect and for having sometimes regarded evangelism and social concern as mutually exclusive. Although reconciliation with man is not reconciliation with God, nor is social action evangelism, nor is political liberation salvation, nevertheless we affirm that evangelism and socio-political involvement are both part of our Christian duty. For both are necessary expressions of our doctrines of God and man, our love for our neighbour and our obedience to Jesus Christ. The message of salvation implies also a message of judgment upon every form of alienation, oppression and discrimination, and we should not be afraid to denounce evil and injustice wherever they exist. When people receive Christ they are born again into his kingdom and must seek not only to exhibit but also to spread its righteousness in the midst of an unrighteous world. The salvation we claim should be transforming us in the totality of our personal and social responsibilities. Faith without works is dead.

6. The Church and Evangelism

We affirm that Christ sends his redeemed people into tile world as the Father sent him, and that this calls for a similar deep and costly penetration of the world. We need to break out of our ecclesiastical ghettos and permeate non-Christian society. In the church's mission of sacrificial service evangelism is primary. World evangelization requires the whole church to take the whole gospel to the whole world. The church is at the very centre of God's cosmic purpose and is his appointed means of spreading the gospel. But a church which preaches the cross must itself be marked by the cross. It becomes a stumbling block of evangelism when it betrays the gospel or lacks a living faith in God, a genuine love for people, or scrupulous honesty in all things including promotion and finance. The church is the community of God's people rather than an institution, and must not be identified with any particular culture, social or political system, or human ideology.

7. Cooperation in Evangelism

We affirm that the church's visible unity in truth is God's purpose. Evangelism also summons us to unity, because our oneness strengthens our witness, just as our disunity undermines our gospel of reconciliation. We recognize, however, that organizational unity may take many forms and does not necessarily forward evangelism. Yet we who share the same biblical faith should be closely united in fellowship, work and witness. We confess that our testimony has been marred by sinful individualism and needless duplication. We pledge ourselves to seek a deeper unity in truth, worship, holiness and mission. We urge the development of regional and functional cooperation for the furtherance of the church's mission, for strategic planning, for mutual encouragement, and for the sharing of resources and experience.

8. Churches in Evangelistic Partnership

We rejoice that a new missionary era has dawned. The dominant role of western missions is fast disappearing. God is raising up from the younger churches a great new resource for world evangelization, and is thus demonstrating that the responsibility to evangelize belongs to the whole body of Christ. All churches should therefore be asking God and themselves what they should be doing both to reach their own area and to send missionaries to other parts of the world. A reevaluation of our missionary responsibility and role should be continuous. Thus a growing partnership of churches will develop and the universal character of Christ's church will be more clearly exhibited. We also thank God for agencies which labour in Bible translation, theological education, the mass media, Christian literature, evangelism, missions, church renewal and other specialist fields. They too should engage in constant self-examination to evaluate their effectiveness as part of the Church's mission.

9. The Urgency of the Evangelistic Task

More than 2,700 million people, which is more than two-thirds of mankind, have yet to be evangelized. We are ashamed that so many have been neglected; it is a standing rebuke to us and to the whole church. There is now, however, in many parts of the world an unprecedented receptivity to the Lord Jesus Christ. We are convinced that this is the time for churches and para-church agencies to pray earnestly for the salvation of the unreached and to launch new efforts to achieve world evangelization. A reduction of foreign missionaries and money in an evangelized country may sometimes be necessary to facilitate the national church's growth in self-reliance and to release resources for unevangelized areas. Missionaries should flow ever more freely from and to all six continents in a spirit of humble service. The goal should be, by all available means and at the earliest possible time, that every person will have the opportunity to hear, understand, and receive the good news. We cannot hope to attain this goal without sacrifice. All of us are shocked by the poverty of millions and disturbed by the injustices which cause it. Those of us who live in affluent circumstances accept our duty to develop a simple life-style in order to contribute more generously to both relief and evangelism.

10. Evangelism and Culture

The development of strategies for world evangelization calls for imaginative pioneering methods. Under God, the result will be the rise of churches deeply rooted in Christ and closely related to their culture. Culture must always be tested and judged by Scripture. Because man is God's creature, some of his culture is rich in beauty and goodness. Because he has fallen, all of it is tainted with sin and some of it is demonic. The gospel does not presuppose the superiority of any culture to another, but evaluates all cultures according to its own criteria of truth and righteousness. and insists on moral absolutes in every culture. Missions have all too frequently exported with the gospel an alien culture, and churches have sometimes been in bondage to culture rather than to the Scripture. Christ's evangelists must humbly seek to empty themselves of all but their personal authenticity in order to become the servants of others, and churches must seek to transform and enrich culture, all for the glory of God.

11. Education and Leadership

We confess that we have sometimes pursued church growth at the expense of church depth, and divorced evangelism from Christian nurture. We also acknowledge that some of our missions have been too slow to equip and encourage national leaders to assume their rightful responsibilities. Yet we are committed to indigenous principles, and long that every church will have national leaders who manifest a Christian style of leadership in terms not of domination but of service. We recognize that there is a great need to improve theological education, especially for church leaders. In every nation and culture there should be an effective training programme for pastors and laymen in doctrine, discipleship, evangelism, nurture and service. Such training programmes should not rely on any stereotyped methodology but should be developed by creative local initiatives according to biblical standards.

12. Spiritual Conflict

We believe that we are engaged in constant spiritual warfare with the principalities and powers of evil, who are seeking to overthrow the church and frustrate its task of world evangelization. We know our need to equip ourselves with God's armour and to fight this battle with the spiritual weapons of truth and prayer. For we detect the activity of our enemy, not only in false ideologies outside the church, but also inside it in false gospels which twist Scripture and put man in the place of God. We need both watchfulness and discernment to safeguard the biblical gospel. We acknowledge that we ourselves are not immune to worldliness of thought and action, that is, to a surrender to secularism. For example, although careful studies of church growth, both numerical and spiritual, are right and valuable, we have sometimes neglected them. At other times, desirous to ensure a response to the gospel, we have compromised our message, manipulated our hearers through pressure techniques, and become unduly preoccupied with statistics or even dishonest in our use of them. All this is worldly. The church must be in the world; the world must not be in the church.

13. Freedom and Persecution

It is the God-appointed duty of every government to secure conditions of peace, justice and liberty in which the church may obey God, serve the Lord Christ, and preach the gospel without interference. We therefore pray for the leaders of the nations and call upon them to guarantee freedom of thought and conscience, and freedom to practise and propagate religion in accordance with the will of God and as set forth in The Universal Declaration of Human Rights. We also express our deep concern for all who have been unjustly imprisoned, and especially for our brethren who are suffering for their testimony to the Lord Jesus. We promise to pray and work for their freedom. At the same time we refuse to be intimidated by their fate. God helping us, we too will seek to stand against injustice and to remain faithful to the gospel, whatever the cost. We do not forget the warnings of Jesus that persecution is inevitable.

14. The Power of the Holy Spirit

We believe in the power of the Holy Spirit. The Father sent his Spirit to bear witness to his Son; without his witness ours is futile. Conviction of sin, faith in Christ, new birth and Christian growth are all his work. Further, the Holy Spirit is a missionary spirit; thus evangelism should arise spontaneously from a spirit-filled church. A church that is not a missionary church is contradicting itself and quenching the Spirit. Worldwide evangelization will become a realistic possibility only when the Spirit renews the church in truth and wisdom, faith, holiness, love and power. We therefore call upon all Christians to pray for such a visitation of the sovereign Spirit of God that all his fruit may appear in all his people and that all his gifts may enrich the body of Christ. Only then will the whole church become a fit instrument in his hands, that the whole earth may hear his voice.

15. The Return of Christ

We believe that Jesus Christ will return personally and visibly, in power and glory, to consummate his salvation and his judgment. This promise of his coming is a further spur to our evangelism, for we remember his words that the gospel must first be preached to all nations. We believe that the interim period between Christ's ascension and return is to be filled with the mission of the people of God, who have no liberty to stop before the End. We also remember his warning that false Christs and false prophets will arise as precursors of the final Antichrist. We therefore reject as a proud, self-confident dream the notion that man can ever build a utopia on earth. Our Christian confidence is that God will perfect his kingdom, and we look forward with eager anticipation to that day, and to the new heaven and earth in which righteousness will dwell and God will reign for ever. Meanwhile, we rededicate ourselves to the service of Christ and of men in joyful submission to his authority over the whole of our lives.

Conclusion

Therefore in the light of this our faith and our resolve, we enter into a solemn covenant with God and with each other, to pray, to plan and to work together for the evangelization of the whole world. We call upon others to join us. May God help us by his grace and for his glory to be faithful to this our covenant! Amen, Alleluia!

Strife in the Denominations

The Lutheran Church–Missouri Synod

In the 1970s Missouri Lutherans resisted the ecumenical trend moving other Lutherans in America toward that epochal merger that in 1987 created the Evangelical Lutheran Church in America. In 1974 the president and most of the faculty and student body of Concordia Seminary in St. Louis separated themselves from their Synod's control to create their own movement: Evangelical Lutherans in Mission (or ELIM). This group later joined in the 1987 merger noted above. For the Lutheran struggle, as also in the Baptist battles

---

[Sources: (1) James E. Adams, *Preus of Missouri and the Great Lutheran Civil War* (New York: Harper & Row, 1977), pp. 15-16. (2) John H. Tietjen, *Memoirs in Exile* (Minneapolis: Fortress Press, 1990), pp. 209-12. (3) Robert D. Preus, "Foreword," to Kurt E. Marquart, *Anatomy of an Explosion: A Theological Analysis of the Missouri Synod Conflict* (Grand Rapids: Baker, 1977), pp. 3-5.]

noted below, the question often boiled down to "Who is in charge?" and just what Christian liberty permitted or required. But many other matters were caught up in the whirl: institutional autonomy, doctrinal beliefs, academic freedom, pastoral (male) authority, liberty of conscience, and (for some) the relevance of the political agenda of the new Christian right. Three documents follow on the Lutheran situation: (1) James Adams, under the heading of "The Missouri Waltz," offers a personal perspective on the denomination as it had come to exist by the 1970s. (2) John H. Tietjen, formerly president of the besieged Concordia Seminary, in his memoirs reflects on the turbulent days of 1974. (3) Robert Preus, one of the five conservative professors at Concordia Seminary who remained with the denomination, offers a preface to a book that explains things from the side of those conservatives.

1. The Missouri Waltz

Lutheran Church–Missouri Synod faithful were convening at their headquarters city of St. Louis in June 1938. Although epochal proposals on inter-Lutheran ecumenism crowded the agenda, Missourians managed time for traditional concerns. An essay was read reaffirming that women were not to vote in congregational assemblies because the Bible prohibited it. One delegate rose to object mildly to the finality of the synod's position. Conceivably women might some day be delegates at a Missouri convention, he noted.

Synod officer G. Christian Barth could not let that remark pass unchallenged. Here in awesome assembly a deviant word had been uttered. Here might be the seed of theological division. Barth requested a committee "counsel" with the brother. Before the 1938 convention ended, the wayward brother had been won over. He had retracted. The convention agreed to reaffirm the biblical reasons for never allowing women to vote. "Consensus" on doctrine and practice again reigned supreme in Missouri.

The fact that only a few decades ago the Missouri Synod interrupted a national Assembly to counsel one brother for an offhand dissent reveals the synod as more state of mind than church. Missouri had tried always to be one, holy, catholic, and apostolic, but if it couldn't be all those, it could always be one. That was its unique witness. That was the ecclesiastical waltz Missouri could always dance when other churches couldn't.

The fathers of the Missouri Synod pointed to the meaning of the Greek word for synod, a "walking together," as descriptive of their church. Outsiders inevitably saw Missouri more as marching in a lock step of tribal uniformity. But whether genuine consensus or rank conformity, their "walking together" resulted in one of the most successful immigrant churches in American religious history.

From a handful of churches at its founding, the Missouri Synod had become a colossus by the 1970s. With 2.8 million members, it was the second largest Lutheran denomination in the United States, the seventh largest of all Lutheran churches in the world, and the eighth largest religious body in America. Almost 6200 congregations held membership. As much as $325 million annually (with $26 million for annual headquarters budget) had been generated in recent years. Clergy numbered 7600, with 6150 of them active.

Missouri Synod Lutherans were among the few American religious groups to establish their own elementary schools. Second in size only to Catholic schools, that system included 1200 elementary schools with 150,000 pupils and 35 secondary schools. Missouri had 14 junior and four-year colleges, and two large seminaries.

Although the anachronistic name tied it to the single state of Missouri, the synod was international. Yet it had remained predominantly midwestern and urban, with two-thirds of all its members living within a three-hundred-mile radius of Chicago.

2. Exile

As 11:00 a.m. was approaching on Tuesday, February 19, 1974, nearly all the faculty and students of Concordia Seminary gathered in its field house and were sitting on retractable bleacher benches, pulled open on the east side of the gymnasium for the occasion. Gerald Miller, student body president, was standing in front of a microphone set on the center line of the basketball court. The [Seminary] community had gathered for a student vote on whether students would join the faculty in resuming theological education through a seminary in exile. . . .

Each person seated in the bleachers had in hand a one-page document. On one side, printed in full, was the ultimatum of the Board of Control, requiring the faculty to resume classes that day or forfeit salaries, housing, and offices. On the other side was an agenda including a proposal for action that had the unanimous support of the student Coordinating Committee. . . .

For almost two hours the students listened to reports and received answers to questions. Student Dale Kuhn reported on the fruitless forum that had been sponsored by the Synod's Board of Directors the previous weekend. Faculty spokesperson Robert Bertram elaborated on the decision of the faculty to make no response to the [Board of Control's] ultimatum, but to resume teaching off-campus. Paul Lessmann, faculty member responsible for internship and field education programs, responded to student concerns about internships and calls to ministry.

Academic dean John Damm dealt at length with the nature of the proposed seminary in exile and the reasons for it. "Seminex is not a new seminary," Damm explained, as he stood next to Gerald Miller, "not a new institution; it is Concordia Seminary, but in exile. Seminex represents not a departure from synod but a commitment to the synod which has been rapidly departing from the best in its tradition. It is the only way we can see to complete theological education and simultaneously to call the synod back to its own evangelical fountainhead." . . .

Damm stated that in the projected seminary in exile most classes would be held at St. Louis University and Eden Seminary, although some might take place in faculty homes and church basements. Seminex would continue the educational program in which students were enrolled and "will see to it that all qualified students receive the proper theological degree." . . .

Shortly before 11:00 a.m. student James Wind moved adoption of the statement drafted by the student Coordinating Committee, copies of which the students had before them. After rehearsing the reasons for the student moratorium and the decision of the [Board of Control] to terminate the contracts of the faculty, the statement declared, "we find it impossible in good conscience to continue our education under the present seminary Board of Control. Instead, we will continue to pursue our calling as students in preparation for ministry in the Lutheran Church–Missouri Synod under the terminated faculty. . . . We therefore resolve to resume our theological education in exile, trusting in the grace of our Lord Jesus Christ." Around 11:15 the students were ready to vote. A loud and vigorous aye resounded throughout the field house. I heard only a dozen or so nays and abstentions.

After brief instructions about coming events and procedures to follow, faculty and students climbed down from their bleacher seats to participate in a public enactment of exile, whose end result had been prearranged by academic dean John Damm but whose steps along the way had been devised overnight by student leaders. I was surprised when I saw students pick up white wooden crosses about two feet in height as they left the field house on their way to the [Seminary] quadrangle. Many faculty member donned academic robes and hoods and headed in the same direction. . . .

As I arrived at the quadrangle in the center of the campus, surrounded on four sides by Tudor Gothic buildings, I looked on in amazement. Planted in the frozen soil were white wooden crosses, one for each member of the faculty and executive staff, bearing our individual names in black letters. The students were planting their own crosses in the ground next to ours as they moved through the quadrangle. The seminary was turned into a cemetery.

Students and faculty moved from the quadrangle through the archway to the entrance area in the parking lots in front of the statue of Martin Luther. As they did so, they intoned Luther's hymn, "A Mighty Fortress Is Our God." Standing at the top of the entrance steps, faculty member Alfred von Rohr

Sauer read a Scripture lesson from the Book of Lamentations, and Gerald Miller read the students' Seminex resolution. Then students boarded up the entrance to the [Seminary] with two huge frames cut to fit the dimensions of the Gothic archway. Written across the two boards in large white letters on a black surface was the single word: EXILED.

3. Rationale

The story had to be told, the story of a large, confessional church body gradually, almost imperceptibly but seemingly irrevocably, losing its evangelical and confessional character and identity. But then, contrary to all expectations and historical precedent, a reversal of a trend which has dominated modern church history! The lay people and rank and file clergy of the Missouri Synod take a stand. They elect new leaders with a mandate to turn the direction of their synod back to the old ways, to the evangelical orthodoxy they had learned and known so well. They support an investigation of the doctrine of the largest and at the time most prestigious seminary of their synod. They study the issues confronting their church, they review their doctrinal position; and in convention assembled they take the bold unprecedented step of condemning the doctrine taught at that very seminary which was founded by and flourished under the greatest theological leaders the synod had ever known. The majority of the faculty members denounce the action of their church, and at what seems like a propitious time they refuse en masse to carry out their call to teach in the church. Students by the hundreds follow their professors into what was called an exile, but was really more a sort of captivity, led by the prestige and persuasions of their teachers and by the incredibly great pressure of their peers. And for the most part both faculty and students are still lost to the church, lost not because their friends and former brethren have not tried to retrieve them, but because they reject their synod, not merely its leaders and some of its actions, but also its theology. The scars inflicted on their church by their departure are deep, and they will last beyond the lives of any of us.

Yes, this story, so bizarre, so ironic, so tragic, had to be told. But who was to tell it? Some bright graduate student at Seminex (the rump institution founded by the dissident faculty of Concordia Seminary, St. Louis) with a horizon no higher than the confines of the classrooms of St. Louis University, the Jesuit institution that offered Seminex shelter, no broader than the explanations and excuses of Seminex professors for their untoward actions? Or should some historical theologian of Seminex tell the story? But the involvement and the guilt in a decision to leave one's call and attempt to destroy a seminary of one's church hardly lends credibility to any serious and unbiased writing of one's own history. But perhaps some secular or theological pundit — writing for money, of course — and these people seem to be everywhere, pontificating on what has befallen Missouri — could do the job honestly and objectively. I would merely ask, has it been done thus far in the scenarios and the often wild improvisations of the events which have thus far distorted history and discredited our church body?

For a time some of us who were in the minority at Concordia Seminary, St. Louis, thought of pooling our resources, which were vast in terms of experience and hard evidence, to write an account of what really happened. But God kept us all too busy for that, thankfully. For we too would have revealed our prejudices and biases concerning all the events that had occurred throughout the controversy in St. Louis. For a time we looked for an older, perceptive soldier of the cross who might tell the story with sufficient wisdom and perspective not merely to relate, but analyze the events in the light of God's economy and thus teach the reader. But no such person appeared.

Then Prof. Marquart returned to our country, after a long pastorate in Australia, to accept a call at Concordia Theological Seminary in Fort Wayne. He was the ideal person to tell the story. He was uninvolved in the events and so had had little occasion to form prejudices or animosity toward any of the principal actors in the drama. . . . Moreover, and most important, Prof. Marquart is able to rise above personal biases and single dramatic events to the real issues that underlie the whole struggle and brought about the explosion which took place in Missouri — to the doctrinal issues. These are what he speaks of and explains and analyzes in this book. And only when we carefully follow him as he leads us through our past will we understand what really happened. And perhaps, as an adjunct to this learning experience in church history, the history of our own synod, we will by grace become more understanding and forgiving and loving. And again by God's grace some healing and reconciliation can take place.

The Southern Baptist Convention

Since 1979, the Southern Baptist Convention (SBC), which remains by far the nation's largest Protestant denomination, has been embroiled in a series of controversies. While in many local churches, religious life proceeds as be-

---

[Sources: (1) Timothy George, "Toward an Evangelical Future," in *Southern Baptists Observed*, ed. Nancy Tatom Ammerman (1993), pp. 276-77. (2) *2000 Baptist Faith and Message*, http://www.sbc.net/bfm/bfm2000.asp (14 May 2003). (3) Jerry Rankin, "Does It Matter What Missionaries Believe?" http://www.baptist2baptist.net/papers/rankinresponse.asp (28 May 2003). (4) Jim Denison, "Jim Denison writes to Pastors and Baptist Leaders," http://www.bgct.org/bgctroot/officeloader.cfm?contentuuid=6DFE0E3E-EBF6-4EC0-98D43D0FBBDD1E8F&deptid=9 (28 May 2003).]

fore, the cooperative institutions of the denomination have been transformed. Conservatives, who felt that the inerrancy (or errorlessness) of the
Bible was being compromised and who felt that modern American culture
was undermining social righteousness, mobilized at the national level and,
in a series of campaigns extending for more than a decade, took control of
the SBC's superstructure from its previous moderate leadership. That control
extended to the denomination's six seminaries, which include by far the largest institutions of ministerial training in the country. After securing institutional control at the national level by the early 1990s, conservatives have so-
lidified their position in a number of ways. The excerpts below try to provide
flavor for this heartfelt and complicated controversy: (1) Timothy George is a
lifelong Southern Baptist who yet has the luxury in his position as dean of
the interdenominational Beeson Divinity School in Alabama to stay somewhat above the fray. In 1993 he published an assessment that tried to bring
theological resources to bear on the denominational crisis. (2) In 1998 the
SBC revised its basic doctrinal statement, the Baptist Faith and Message, to
include a culturally conservative account of gender relations. That Message
was further revised in 2000. Presented below are some of the new or altered
parts of the Message that emerged from that process. (3) In a 2001 letter that
circulated to Baptist newspapers around the country, Jerry Rankin, President of the denomination's International Mission Board (IMB), explained
why he believed all of the SBC's thousands of missionaries should be required to sign the revised Baptist Faith and Message. (4) Not long after the
IMB implemented such a policy, Jim Denison, chair of the Baptist General
Conference of Texas (a state convention that has objected to several of the
national moves by conservative leaders), responded with his objections.

1. Assessment, 1993

The Controversy in the Southern Baptist Convention is over. This does not
mean that all the fighting has stopped, much less that the belligerents on either
side have suddenly been seized with the spirit of genuine reconciliation. Far
from it. Ecclesiastical wars, like wars fought with real bullets and bombs, leave
lingering scars that only time and a new generation of noncombatants can begin to heal. For this shalom we must wait.

Still, as everyone on all sides now admits, the battle for control of America's largest Protestant denomination has resulted in a decisive shift in direction
for the SBC — called a "take-over" by moderates, and a "turnaround" by conservatives. This process is not likely to be reversed in the foreseeable future, despite continuing skirmishes between incumbents and insurgents, and numerous guerrilla maneuvers played out at all levels of local Baptist politics.

The thesis of this chapter can be stated quite simply: The recent conflict in the SBC is part of the wider struggle of American evangelicals to come to grips with the crisis of modernity and can only properly be understood in that larger context. Of course there are many other aspects of the Controversy that can be and have been studied with much profit: its southern dimension, its economic implications, its demographic makeup, its populist appeal, its political configurations, and so forth. However, when viewed against the background of recent religious history, one fact stands out above all others. For only the second time in this century the veering of a major American denomination away from its historic, evangelical roots toward a more liberal, mainline Protestant posture has been arrested and reversed. Moreover, this change has been as sweeping and dramatic as it was unexpected. It is little wonder, then, that sociologists of religion would seize on a phenomenon that even a close reading of American denominational history would not have prepared one to predict. . . .

Although I shall also touch upon this aspect of the story, I am more interested in the theological forces that gave rise to the Controversy in the first place, and in the profound crisis of identity that its aftermath has posed for Southern Baptists. Moderates, as defenders of the latest Lost Cause, must now decide to either find a place to stand in the new order or seek alternative alignments. For most of them, secession is not an option; but how to function within a fractured family is not at all clear at present. Conservatives have an even greater worry: Can they survive their own success? Can they forge a new consensus that will include most, if not all, Southern Baptists without replicating the very system their movement was launched to correct? The mere replacement of one set of bureaucrats with another doth not a reformation make.

Throughout its long and fractious history, the Church of Jesus Christ has ever been pulled between the poles of identity and adaptability. Where identity has triumphed exclusively, the church has become insular, cloistered, turned in on itself. Where adaptability has reigned as the orthodoxy of the day, the church has become diffuse, assimilated, bereft of transcendence. As Southern Baptists move from an era of conflict toward one of reintegration, this tension will set the bounds in the quest for a new consensus and the recovery of a vision worthy to reclaim.

2. The Baptist Faith and Message, 2000

I. The Scriptures

The Holy Bible was written by men divinely inspired and is God's revelation of Himself to man. It is a perfect treasure of divine instruction. It has God for its author, salvation for its end, and truth, without any mixture of error, for its matter. Therefore, all Scripture is totally true and trustworthy. It reveals the principles by which God judges us, and therefore is, and will remain to the end of the world, the true center of Christian union, and the supreme standard by which all human conduct, creeds, and religious opinions should be tried. All Scripture is a testimony to Christ, who is Himself the focus of divine revelation. . . .

VI. The Church

A New Testament church of the Lord Jesus Christ is an autonomous local congregation of baptized believers, associated by covenant in the faith and fellowship of the gospel; observing the two ordinances of Christ, governed by His laws, exercising the gifts, rights, and privileges invested in them by His Word, and seeking to extend the gospel to the ends of the earth, each congregation operates under the Lordship of Christ through democratic processes. In such a congregation each member is responsible and accountable to Christ as Lord. Its scriptural officers are pastors and deacons. While both men and women are gifted for service in the church, the office of pastor is limited to men as qualified by Scripture.

The New Testament speaks also of the church as the Body of Christ which includes all of the redeemed of all the ages, believers from every tribe, and tongue, and people, and nation. . . .

XV. The Christian and the Social Order

All Christians are under obligation to seek to make the will of Christ supreme in our own lives and in human society. Means and methods used for the improvement of society and the establishment of righteousness among men can be truly and permanently helpful only when they are rooted in the regeneration of the individual by the saving grace of God in Jesus Christ. In the spirit of Christ, Christians should oppose racism, every form of greed, selfishness, and vice, and all forms of sexual immorality, including adultery, homosexuality, and pornography. We should work to provide for the orphaned, the needy, the abused, the aged, the helpless, and the sick. We should speak on behalf of the unborn and contend for the sanctity of all human life from conception to natural death. Every Christian should seek to bring industry, government, and society as a whole under the sway of the principles of righteousness, truth, and brotherly love. In order to promote these ends Christians should be ready to work with all men of good will in any good cause, always being careful to act in the spirit of love without compromising their loyalty to Christ and His truth. . . .

XVIII. The Family

God has ordained the family as the foundational institution of human society. It is composed of persons related to one another by marriage, blood, or adoption.

Marriage is the uniting of one man and one woman in covenant commitment for a lifetime. It is God's unique gift to reveal the union between Christ and His church and to provide for the man and the woman in marriage the framework for intimate companionship, the channel of sexual expression according to biblical standards, and the means for procreation of the human race.

The husband and wife are of equal worth before God, since both are created in God's image. The marriage relationship models the way God relates to His people. A husband is to love his wife as Christ loved the church. He has the God-given responsibility to provide for, to protect, and to lead his family. A wife is to submit herself graciously to the servant leadership of her husband even as the church willingly submits to the headship of Christ. She, being in the image of God as is her husband and thus equal to him, has the God-given responsibility to respect her husband and to serve as his helper in managing the household and nurturing the next generation.

Children, from the moment of conception, are a blessing and heritage from the Lord. Parents are to demonstrate to their children God's pattern for marriage. Parents are to teach their children spiritual and moral values and to lead them, through consistent lifestyle example and loving discipline, to make choices based on biblical truth. Children are to honor and obey their parents.

3. Does It Matter What Missionaries Believe?

Does it matter what missionaries believe? Should missionaries sent out by a denominational agency have any accountability to the churches that support them?

Since the New Hampshire Baptist Confession of 1833, Baptists have drafted documents of belief that distinguish them from other Christians. The Baptist Faith and Message, like other confessions of faith, imposes no theological creed on individuals and churches. It does represent the common faith shared by Southern Baptists who choose to affiliate in associations and conventions.

Some people are predisposed against the Southern Baptist Convention's adherence to historic fundamentals of faith based on the authority of God's infallible Word. They have criticized the International Mission Board for asking missionaries to reassure Southern Baptists that they affirm the Baptist Faith and Message. They seem to view the request as something unprecedented in Southern Baptist missions history.

Even in the 19th century, before the BF&M was written, trustees of the Foreign Mission Board required missionary candidates to affirm a doctrinal statement to assure Southern Baptists their beliefs were consistent with the generally held doctrines that distinguished the convention. Since 1970, under the leadership of Dr. Baker James Cauthen, and later under Dr. Keith Parks, every Southern Baptist missionary appointed by what was then the Foreign Mission Board signed a statement that he or she had read and was in agreement with the Baptist Faith and Message. Since the 2000 BF&M was adopted, more than 1,500 new missionaries have been approved and sent out. These missionaries have gone to the uttermost parts of the world without expressing problems with the appropriateness of this requirement or stating that signing this statement of affirmation was imposing a creed.

Critics are implying that missionaries are being coerced into doctrinal conformity and that creedal beliefs are being imposed. On the contrary, missionaries are being asked to sign a statement that their own beliefs are consistent with the current BF&M and that they will carry out their work in accordance with it.

Some overseas personnel may not fully agree with or understand the need for the revisions to the BF&M made in 2000 or for the family article in 1998. The fact that they have the freedom to state their disagreements creates an opportunity to discuss the cultural and societal changes in American churches that made those changes appropriate.

IMB administration and trustees have the utmost confidence in Southern Baptists' overseas missionaries. We know their passion for reaching a lost world and their willingness to sacrifice and devote their lives to God's call. That passion and willingness doesn't come from theological relativism, but out of a conviction based on the authority of God's Word and obedience to the Lordship of Jesus Christ.

All Southern Baptist missionaries on the field have already affirmed their agreement with the Baptist Faith and Message that was current when they were appointed. The reason I have asked them to reaffirm their beliefs in regard to the 2000 BF&M is to remove suspicions that their beliefs and practices could be inconsistent with our common confession of faith and move us forward in reaching a lost world. Southern Baptists rightly expect the missionaries they send out and support to represent the confession of faith our churches have adopted. The administration of our mission entities should provide that assurance.

4. Jim Denison Responds

The day we have prayed wouldn't come — has arrived.

For 23 years Texas Baptists have watched the Southern Baptist Convention become increasingly exclusive, demanding, divided and damaged. We have suffered with Baptist heroes such as Russell Dilday and Keith Parks as they have been maligned and attacked and fired after decades of service. State conventions and local associations have been embroiled in political conflict. The Baptist Faith and Message has been altered to repudiate cherished Baptist beliefs regarding the centrality of Christ in interpreting scripture and the autonomy of the church, and to restrict the traditional Baptist understanding of the priesthood of the believer. . . .

All the while, the first concern of all Texas Baptists has been the missionaries. Baptists joined hands and hearts in 1845 to fulfill the Great Commission through cooperative missions. Setting aside peripheral theological differences, we came together to do missions more effectively. And God gave our efforts his great blessing, as we took the gospel to more people and nations than any missions enterprise in Christian history. At the front of this column of progress have been the missionaries — God-called men and women who sacrificed ambition, security, and often their lives to take God's love to those in desperate spiritual darkness.

So long as the missionaries were supported and protected, many felt that the denominational controversy was not a crisis demanding their attention. Quite bluntly, many considered this conflict to be irrelevant to the life of their local congregation. But now the denominational crisis has struck at the very soul of our Baptist identity and purpose.

As you know, Dr. Jerry Rankin released in January, 2002 a letter to all missionaries related to the International Mission Board of the Southern Baptist Convention. In this letter he states his intention to require all missionaries to state their allegiance to the 2000 Baptist Faith and Message. For the first time in SBC history, the board president is requiring their appointed missionaries to give personal allegiance to a new and twice amended faith statement. This manmade document — when recently changed — established itself dangerously close to equal ground with the Bible.

The selection and screening process that led to their missionary appointment is no longer valid. The faith statement they affirmed during their appointment and that they demonstrate in their lives everyday is no longer good enough. The test for missions service has primarily become their signature on a loyalty oath. Their commitment to the Bible is not enough. Their future in missions service is in serious doubt.

This initiative is tragically wrong in three catastrophic ways. First, it breaks faith with the missionaries. It places their theological integrity under suspicion. It states clearly that they cannot trust the denomination to support the ministry it commissioned them to fulfill. What will be the next litmus test of their theological or denominational loyalty? What will be the next condition for their future support? What will their next amendment to the Baptist Faith and Message say about what missionaries are required to affirm?

Second, it betrays a promise given by Dr. Rankin that this action would not be taken. The Missions Sending Agencies Study Committee of the Baptist General Convention of Texas met with Dr. Rankin and his executive staff during 2000-2001 as part of our study. Committee members specifically asked if a signature of affirmation of the 2000 Baptist Faith and Message would be required of all current missionaries. They were promised that this action would not be taken of current missionaries. All were grateful for such assurance. Our committee is shocked that he chose not to keep his word.

Third, Dr. Rankin's decision defines clearly the future that Texas Baptists might anticipate in missions involvement. If you or the members of your church cannot affirm the 2000 Baptist Faith and Message in its entirety, if you cannot sign this manmade document, you may have no future with the International Mission Board. Our church members cannot answer God's Great Commission call to overseas ministry through the Southern Baptist Convention. You and your members could never serve as IMB trustees without agreeing to this loyalty oath. This is a present-day crisis with catastrophic implications for the future.

And so the denomination controversy of the past 23 years is far from over. In fact, it has reached the most serious level of crisis since it began. The missions enterprise, which first joined Baptists in cooperative ministry 157 years ago, is now under attack. The future of our engagement in global missions is unclear.

Vatican II and Beyond

"Pope John's 'Revolution'"

The lovable and unpredictable Pope John XXIII indicated that he planned to open a few windows at the Vatican and let in some fresh air. To many, the momentous gathering in Rome known as Vatican Council II (1962-65) blew more like a gale. Liturgy was modified, authority distributed, ecumenical overtures extended, the modern world more embraced than shunned — all this and much more. It was a Council whose implications would require working out for the remainder of the century, and no doubt well beyond. Something of the high drama and high hope in this epochal gathering is con-

[Source: X. Rynne, *Letters from Vatican City* (Garden City, N.Y: Doubleday & Co., 1963), pp. 73-77.]

veyed in the following account of the opening session; it is written by "Xavier Rynne," pseudonym for a well-informed, delightfully literate insider.

To anyone who had the good fortune to be standing in front of the bronze doors leading into the papal palace, on the side of St. Peter's Square, at eight o'clock on the morning of Thursday, October 11, 1962, there was suddenly revealed a dazzling spectacle. At that moment, two papal gendarmes, resplendent in parade uniform of white trousers and black topboots, coats, and busbies, slowing swung the great door open, exposing to a portion of the crowd row upon row of bishops, clad in flowing white damask copes and mitres, descending Bernini's majestic *scala regia* from the papal apartments. As brilliant television floodlights were switched on along the stairway, the intense light brought to mind Henry Vaughan's lines:

> I saw Eternity the other night,
> Like a great ring of pure and endless light.

In rows of sixes, an apparently inexhaustible phalanx of prelates filed out of the Vatican palace, swung to their right across St. Peter's Square, then wheeled right again, to mount the ramplike steps leading into the basilica. Every now and then, this white mass was dotted with the black cassock, full beard, and round headdress of an oriental bishop, and with the bulbous gold crown and crossed pectoral reliquaries of a bishop of the Byzantine rite. Toward the end came the scarlet ranks of the Sacred College of Cardinals. Finally, the pope appeared, carried, in deference to the wishes of his entourage, on the *sedia gestatoria,* and looking rather timid, perhaps even frightened — as he always does when first mounting this oriental contraption — but gradually warming to the mild acclamation of the overawed crowd, and gently smiling and quietly weeping as he was carried undulantly forward, blessing the onlookers. At the entrance to the Council hall in the basilica, the procession halted while the pope dismounted and walked the length of the nave to the Confession of St. Peter.

Before the high altar the pope had ordered the substitution of a simpler, more informal style of throne for the unwieldy, pretentious "doctoral" throne, with a red damask backdrop and canopy, that the organizers of the Council had devised. The significance of this was soon made clear by the pope's opening speech, which stressed the Council's pastoral, or ministering, role over the dogmatic, or condemnatory, approach. After the traditional hymn "Veni Creator Spiritus," a solemn mass of the Holy Spirit was celebrated, in which the Epistle and the Gospel were chanted in both Greek and Latin, to signify the unity of both parts of the Church, East and West. The celebrant was the elderly but vigorous Cardinal Tisserant, bearded dean of the College of Cardinals. A touch of Byzantine court ceremonial followed the mass, as the cardinals mounted the steps of the papal throne one by one, with their scarlet mantles trailing behind them, to make their obeisance to the See of Peter. After the bishops' solemn profession of faith in unison, recitation of the litany of the Saints, and more prayers from the Greek rite, Pope John began to deliver his sermon.

In clear and resonant tones that could be distinctly heard throughout the basilica, the pope, after a few introductory remarks, said that he was tired of listening to the prophets of doom among his advisers. "Though burning with zeal," he said, these men "are not endowed with very much sense of discretion

A first meeting between a Roman Catholic pope (John XXIII) and a former president of the Southern Baptist Converstion (Brooks Hays, right), in 1961
(Religion News Service)

or measure." They maintain that "our era, in comparions with past eras, is getting worse, and they behave as though they had learned nothing from history, which is nevertheless the great teacher of life." They were, he said, under the illusion that "at the time of the former Councils, everything was a triumph for the Christian idea and way of life and for proper religious liberty," and he added, "We feel that we must disagree with these prophets of doom, who are always forecasting disaster, as though the end of the world were at hand," and continually warning him, "in the course of our pastoral office," that the modern world is "full of prevarication and ruin." . . .

The pope then proceeded to outline, serenely and optimistically, what he expected of the Council and why he had summoned it. "Divine Providence," he said, "is leading us to a new order of human relations." It was imperative for the Church "to bring herself up to date where required," in order to spread her message "to all men throughout the world." While the Church must "never depart from the sacred patrimony of truth received from the Fathers," she must "ever look to the present, to new conditions and new forms of life introduced into the modern world, which have opened new avenues to the Catholic apostolate."

Then came the phrases, so pregnant with meaning, that either alarmed or gratified his listeners, depending on their theological outlook. The pope said that he had not called the Council to discuss "one article or another of the fundamental doctrine of the Church . . . which is presumed to be well known and familiar to all; for this, a Council was not necessary." Thus were ruled out the hopes of those who had expected the Council to proclaim some new dogma, isolated from the rest of Christian doctrine, in the manner of the previous Ecumenical Council here, in 1869-70, which concentrated on the dogma of papal infallibility. No, said the pope; "the world expects a step forward toward doctrinal penetration and a formation of consciences." This must be "in conformity with authentic doctrine," of course, but it "should be studied and expounded through the methods of research and through the literary forms of modern thought." In other words, doctrine was to be made more intelligible to contemporaries in the light of scholarship in biblical, theological, philosophical, and historical disciplines.

He next touched on a subject that is almost taboo in traditionalist Catholic theological circles, saying, "The substance of the ancient doctrine of the *depositum fidei* is one thing; the way in which it is expressed is another." That is, Catholic doctrine remains the same in substance, but the formulations of it vary and are not to be regarded as unalterable ends in themselves. The task of the Council, he told the assembled prelates, was to find the best formulas for our time, without being too hidebound or showing a too slavish respect for those of a previous age. He further emphasized the pastoral, rather than the doctrinal, note by declaring, "Nowadays, the bride of Christ [the Church] prefers to make use of the medicine of mercy rather than that of severity. She considers that she meets the needs of the present day by demonstrating the validity of her teaching rather than by condemnation." This was an unmistakable disavowal of the inquisitorial and condemnatory approach of the Holy Office. Finally, the pope turned his attention to the problem of Christian unity. "The entire Christian family has not yet fully attained the visible unity in truth" desired by Christ, he said, and the Catholic Church "therefore considers it her duty to work actively so that there may be fulfilled the great mystery of that unity." He said that the key to "the brotherly unity of all" — embracing not only Christians but "those who follow non-Christian religions" — is "the fullness of charity," or love. Thus Pope John put his seal on the methods and goals of Catholic participation in the ecumenical, or worldwide, movement for reunion.

This inaugural address to the Council, carefully worded and balanced, and delivering a bold message of renewal and reform, marked the end of the closed mentality that has characterized not a few Catholic bishops and theologians since the sixteenth century. Whether this message reached all the prelates to whom it was addressed, or will be heeded by all it did reach, is another matter; one does not cease being a prophet of doom overnight. But the Council as a whole received the pope's message gladly.

Liturgical Renewal

The most conspicuous single alteration for which Vatican II was responsible, changing some of the externals of the mass, reached into every Roman Catholic parish and pew. This reform also provoked the sharpest reaction by those who saw the abandonment of Latin and the adoption of innovations as a surrender to mere novelty and fad. Others, exhilarated by the new openness, went too far too fast so that, some years after the Council, the Vatican found it necessary to emphasize the continued separation between priest and laity, between sacred and secular. And in between the opposers and the runaways, the vast majority of Roman Catholics endeavored to understand just what it all meant. Here, the Trappist Thomas Merton (see above, pp. 215-17) with some humor and much good sense hints at both problems and possibilities.

What is meant by liturgical renewal, and what are some of the problems involved? We, the ordinary clergy and laity, the commoners in the "people of God" need to understand this well, because the main job of renewal is ours. Li-

---

[Source: Thomas Merton, *Seasons of Celebration* (New York: Farrar, Straus, & Giroux, 1965), pp. 231-37.]

turgical reform merely from the top down, renewal by juridical *fiat* alone, is not really likely to work. Yet this is apparently the way many are expecting it to "happen."

Those who are passionately dedicated to the liturgical movement may perhaps be attaching too much importance to the fact that certain desirable changes have been, will be, or at any rate always *can* be legislated. But, as we are aware from the civil rights conflict, the mere opening of new ways by law does not mean that one can always travel them in fact. Hence those who are not so enthusiastic about liturgical renewal are perhaps consoling themselves with stoical reflections on the unwillingness and incapacity of most priests and laypeople to make the required changes in such a way as to effect a real and basic renewal of worship.

Changes are certainly being made. There can be no question that now, after nearly a year of the "new Mass," the changes are pointing in the right direction. Obviously the reform has only begun. The "new Mass," as it now stands, seems to represent certain practical compromises that were needed in order that a certain amount of vernacular might be allowed. But it certainly does seem illogical to switch from English to Latin just for the Prayer and then go back to English for the Epistle; or to say "The Lord be with you" now in English and now in Latin. The logic of Liturgical renewal certainly requires that the entire Mass be said in the language of the people, and this must eventually come. . . .

The best thing about the "new Mass" is the real opening up of opportunities for participation. With the altar now facing the people, there is obviously more sense of communication on both sides, and much less danger of the old wool-gathering distractedness which always threatens the man who is merely absorbed in his own routine thoughts and imaginings. Communication being consciously established and maintained, priest and people can more easily become aware that they are together *celebrating* the mystery of our Redemption in the Eucharistic Sacrifice and the Lord's Supper. . . .

Obviously all is not yet perfect. Those who imagined that it was enough to have the texts translated into the vernacular were perhaps unprepared for the problems that might still remain. Our Bible readings are now in English. But what English! A text is being used that was prepared for private reading and study, and its attempts at bright colloquialism do not stand up well under the exigencies of public and solemn celebration. A certain sacred and timeless seriousness is required in our vernacular liturgical texts, or they will rapidly become unbearably trite.

Complaints are made about the hymn singing, and doubtless it is not always up to the standard of Gregorian. But at least it is something that everyone can do. How many parishes were there, before the Council, where *all* the congregation knew how to sing the common of the Mass in Gregorian?

In reaction to Vatican II,
the Catholic Traditionalist Movement
maintained an all-Latin mass in Westbury, New York
(Religion News Service)

There remains very much to be done. We are in a period of transition. Neither misplaced enthusiasms nor resentful non-participation will help the Church now. We must go forward in a spirit of sober and reasonable experimentation, and this means facing the hazards of trial and error. No matter what changes are made, if they are only new gestures performed in the old spirit, they will not constitute a liturgical renewal. It is not the old forms that must go so much as the old spirit. So let us take a quick look at the "old spirit," fully aware that it does not belong only to the past. It is still very much with us, even with some of those who favor progressive ideas. . . .

What difference does it make if the priest says the whole canon out loud if it still means something like this: "I am the priest, you are the laity, and this is a strictly business deal. You have your place and I have mine. I am here to confect valid sacraments for you to receive and you are there because if you were not there I would not be here confecting sacraments. Besides everyone knows that unless I exercise my special office as the only one who can validly make Our Lord sacramentally present, you won't even have a religion. Indeed you will be, for all intents, and purposes, godless. As to who you are or what you think about all this, I couldn't care less. So let's get the whole thing over with so that I can go mind my business and you yours." . . .

According to this outlook, what matters is not that the ceremonies have meaning, or that the sacraments eloquently speak the grace which they signify, or that the order and comeliness of worship should help to manifest the splendor of God's love and of His presence in the midst of His people. All that matters is that the sacraments be valid, the formulas correct, and the gestures rubrically exact. Worship is mechanically efficient, the worshipper gets grace with a minimum of trouble, and all goes smoothly!

This mentality is responsible for a deadly atmosphere of officialism in cult, a pervasive and deadening influence which one is expected to counteract by interior and subjective worship, governed entirely by one's own individual tastes and needs and which, in the last analysis, is one's own responsibility and nobody else's business.

Let me say at once that this private realm of sincerity and personal awareness is not to be scoffed at. Where worship is cold, formal, official and empty of personal communication, what other refuge is left for the worshipper? I am not too sure I think it is a good thing to make him feel guilty about it, unless you have something better to offer here and now, in the concrete and not just on paper or in your own head.

What is required above all is a new spirit of *openness,* in which the priest is open to his people, and they are open to him and one another. This means that the words of the liturgy should be spoken by a person, to persons, and not just uttered abstractly in a sacred void.

It is true, and this is sometimes forgotten, that the words of the Liturgy are sacred and the people are gathered in a "sacred space." "The Lord be with you" is something else again than "Hello gang!" So the whole idea of "renewal" means something else than saying the formulas of prayer in a familiar language and with the intonations of colloquial and rotarian togetherness. It means discovering a *new* sense of sacred space, of community, of oneness in the Spirit, as a result of a communication on a deep level with which we have long ceased to be familiar: it means learning to experience the mystery of oneness in grace. This demands a community presence and awareness that is distinct from our ordinary assemblies: a presence to one another in Christ. A presence also in celebration. It means therefore a sense of mystery. One cannot possibly experience this liturgical presence and oneness if one is not open to the reality of the Spirit in and through all who have been brought together in the worshipping assembly. Yet this sense is not mystical and esoteric. It is based on our natural human affinities for one another as beings with the same needs, the same joys, the same hopes, fears and loves, who have been brought together by the merciful love of Christ. The words, songs, ceremonies, signs, movements of worship are all designed, by their very nature, to open the mind and heart of the participant to this experience of oneness in Christ. But this sacramental consciousness depends first of all on human sympathy, relatedness and on some degree of mutual understanding. Hence the obligation to be at peace with all before going to worship.

Religious Liberty

By general agreement the most "American" of the sixteen documents issued by Vatican II was its final one, the Declaration on Religious Liberty. Also by general agreement its author, advocate, and ever-watchful shepherd was John Courtney Murray (1904-67), Jesuit theologian and professor at Woodstock Seminary in Maryland. As Murray himself noted regarding the Declaration: "It was, of course, the most controversial document of the whole Council, largely because it raised with sharp emphasis . . . the issue of the development of doctrine. The notion of development, not the notion of religious freedom, was the real sticking-point for many of those who opposed the Declaration even to the end." And development there had emphatically been: from a Church privileged, powerful, and often intolerant to an institution now saying that its only civil right was to enjoy a "full measure of freedom." As Murray commented, the Declaration on Religious Liberty is "the Church's final farewell to the sacred society."

Declaration on Religious Liberty: On the Right of the Person and of Communities to Social and Civil Freedom in Matters Religious

1. A sense of the dignity of the human person has been impressing itself more and more deeply on the consciousness of contemporary man. And the demand is increasingly made that men should act on their own judgment, enjoying and making use of a responsible freedom, not driven by coercion but motivated by a sense of duty. The demand is also made that constitutional limits should be set to the powers of government, in order that there may be no encroachment on the rightful freedom of the person and of associations.

This demand for freedom in human society chiefly regards the quest for the values proper to the human spirit. It regards, in the first place, the free exercise of religion in society.

This Vatican Synod takes careful note of these desires in the minds of men. It proposes to declare them to be greatly in accord with truth and justice. To this end, it searches into the sacred tradition and doctrine of the Church — the treasury out of which the Church continually brings forth new things that are in harmony with the things that are old.

First, this sacred Synod professes its belief that God himself has made known to mankind the way in which men are to serve Him, and thus be saved

---

[Source: *Declaration on Religious Liberty,* Dec. 7, 1965 (Washington, D.C.: National Catholic Welfare Conference, n. d.), pp. 1-5, 11-12.]

in Christ and come to blessedness. We believe that this one true religion subsists in the catholic and apostolic Church, to which the Lord Jesus committed the duty of spreading it abroad among all men. Thus He spoke to the apostles: "Go, therefore, and make disciples of all nations, baptizing them in the name of the Father, and of the Son, and of the Holy Spirit, teaching them to observe all that I have commanded you" (Mt. 28:19-20). On their part, all men are bound to seek the truth, especially in what concerns God and His Church, and to embrace the truth they come to know, and to hold fast to it.

This sacred Synod likewise professes its belief that it is upon the human conscience that these obligations fall and exert their binding force. The truth cannot impose itself except by virtue of its own truth, as it makes its entrance into the mind at once quietly and with power. Religious freedom, in turn, which men demand as necessary to fulfill their duty to worship God, has to do with immunity from coercion in civil society. Therefore, it leaves untouched traditional Catholic doctrine on the moral duty of men and societies toward the true religion and toward the one Church of Christ.

Over and above all this, in taking up the matter of religious freedom this sacred Synod intends to develop the doctrine of recent Popes on the inviolable rights of the human person and on the constitutional order of society.

2. This Vatican Synod declares that the human person has a right to religious freedom. This freedom means that all men are to be immune from coercion on the part of individuals or of social groups and of any human power, In such wise that in matters religious no one is to be forced to act in a manner contrary to his own beliefs. Nor is anyone to be restrained from acting in accordance with his own beliefs, whether privately or publicly, whether alone or in association with others, within due limits.

The Synod further declares that the right to religious freedom has its foundation in the very dignity of the human person, as this dignity is known through the revealed Word of God and by reason itself. This right of the human person to religious freedom is to be recognized in the constitutional law whereby society is governed. Thus it is to become a civil right.

It is in accordance with their dignity as persons — that is, beings endowed with reason and free will and therefore privileged to bear personal responsibility — that all men should be at once impelled by nature and also bound by a moral obligation to seek the truth, especially religious truth. They are also bound to adhere to the truth, once it is known, and to order their whole lives in accord with the demands of truth.

However, men cannot discharge these obligations in a manner in keeping with their own nature unless they enjoy immunity from external coercion as well as psychological freedom. Therefore, the right to religious freedom has its foundation, not in the subjective disposition of the person, but in his very nature. In consequence, the right to this immunity continues to exist even in those who do not live up to their obligation of seeking the truth and adhering to it. Nor is the exercise of this right to be impeded, provided that the just requirements of public order are observed.

3. Further light is shed on the subject if one considers that the highest norm of human life is the divine law — eternal, objective, and universal — whereby God orders, directs, and governs the entire universe and all the ways of the human community, by a plan conceived in wisdom and love. Man has been made by God to participate in this law, with the result that, under the gentle disposition of divine Providence, he can come to perceive ever increasingly the unchanging truth. Hence every man has the duty, and therefore the right, to seek the truth in matters religious, in order that he may with prudence form for himself right and true judgments of conscience, with the use of all suitable means.

Truth, however, is to be sought after in a manner proper to the dignity of the human person and his social nature. The inquiry is to be free, carried on with the

John Courtney Murray, S.J. (1904-67), guiding hand behind the
Declaration on Religious Liberty proclaimed by Vatican II
(Woodstock College)

aid of teaching or instruction, communication, and dialogue. In the course of these, men explain to one another the truth they have discovered, or think they have discovered, in order thus to assist one another in the quest for truth. Moreover, as the truth is discovered, it is by a personal assent that men are to adhere to it.

On his part, man perceives and acknowledges the imperatives of the divine law through the mediation of conscience. In all his activity a man is bound to follow his conscience faithfully, in order that he may come to God, for whom he was created. It follows that he is not to be forced to act in a manner contrary to his conscience. Nor, on the other hand, is he to be restrained from acting in accordance with his conscience, especially in matters religious.

For, of its very nature, the exercise of religion consists before all else in those internal, voluntary, and free acts whereby man sets the course of his life directly toward God. No merely human power can either command or prohibit acts of this kind.

However, the social nature of man itself requires that he should give external expression to his internal acts of religion; that he should participate with others in matters religious; that he should profess his religion in community. Injury, therefore, is done to the human person and to the very order established by God for human life, if the free exercise of religion is denied in society when the just requirements of public order do not so require.

There is a further consideration. The religious acts whereby men, in private and in public and out of a sense of personal conviction, direct their lives to God transcend by their very nature the order of terrestrial and temporal affairs. Government, therefore, ought indeed to take account of the religious life of the people and show it favor, since the function of government is to make provision for the common welfare. However, it would clearly transgress the limits set to its power were it to presume to direct or inhibit acts that are religious. . . .

12. The Church therefore is being faithful to the truth of the gospel, and is following the way of Christ and the apostles when she recognizes, and gives support to, the principle of religious freedom as befitting the dignity of man and as being in accord with divine revelation. Throughout the ages, the Church has kept safe and handed on the doctrine received from the Master and from the apostles. In the life of the People of God as it has made its pilgrim way through the vicissitudes of human history, there have at times appeared ways of acting which were less in accord with the spirit of the gospel and even opposed to it. Nevertheless, the doctrine of the Church that no one is to be coerced into faith has always stood firm.

Thus the leaven of the gospel has long been about its quiet work in the minds of men. To it is due in great measure the fact that in the course of time men have come more widely to recognize their dignity as persons, and the conviction has grown stronger that in religious matters the person in society is to be kept free from all manner of human coercion.

Ecumenism Outlined

Vatican II was itself an ecumenical event, as non-Catholic observers in large numbers were welcomed guests. The publication of the sixteen documents was likewise ecumenical, as Protestant and Catholic publishers jointly issued the Documents of Vatican Council II, *a publication which included non-Catholic responses and commentaries to each of the decrees. Beyond all this, however, was the work of the Council itself in softening the centuries-old culpability of the Jews for the crucifixion of Christ, in opening new lines of communication with Protestants and the Orthodox, and in condemning all "discrimination against men or harassment of them because of their race, color, condition of life, or religion." As the Jesuit editor of this aforementioned volume said of the Decree on Ecumenism, the most remarkable fact about it is that it is there at all. And, W. M. Abbott added, "the focus is more on a 'pilgrim' Church moving toward Christ than on a movement of 'return' to the Roman Catholic Church." In a speech given in 1965 as the deliberations and debates of Vatican II were drawing to a close, editor Abbott summarized the work done by the Council but with emphasis on the work remaining to be done in ecumenical relations by — say — 1990.*

The Decree on Ecumenism signals every one of us to ecumenical work. Ecumenism, therefore, is not simply a matter one may take or leave; it is to be a central concern for all Catholics, according to their abilities. It will take time to achieve the massive scale of involvement, but the traditionally obedient Catholic people of the United States can be counted on to move in that direction. Some Catholic groups have already moved, on a national scale, and they are already sensitive to criticism. An article in AMERICA recently suggested that the National Council of Catholic Women was not carrying out some of its projects ecumenically enough. There was an immediate and indignant reply.

The Decree on Ecumenism states: "But their primary duty is to make a careful and honest appraisal of whatever needs to be renewed and done in the Catholic household itself, in order that its life may bear witness more clearly and faithfully to the teachings and institutions which have been handed down from Christ through the Apostles." The decree doesn't say this is the work of bishops only, or priests, or theologians. It says it is the work of "Catholics," and many Catholics have started on this work with zest.

The Decree on Ecumenism stipulates that "the manner and order in which Catholic belief is expressed should in no way become an obstacle to dia-

[Source: W. M. Abbott, S.J., "The Ecumenical Movement in America: 1990," *Catholic Mind*, Oct., 1965, pp. 26-28.]

logue with our brethren." The decree follows its own advice and avoids such terms as heretic, schismatic, non-Catholic. It does not even use the word Protestant but constantly uses Pope John's expression "separated brethren" and "our brethren." This pattern of courtesy has already spread widely and will continue to commend itself.

The Decree on Ecumenism has brought to an end that polemical approach that used to characterize so much of Catholicism. The Decree orders that seminarians should master a theology that has been worked out in the ecumenical way "and not polemically." As a result, the formation of the laity and of religious will be sure to develop ecumenically, for, as the Decree observes, "it is the formation which priests receive upon which so largely depends the necessary instruction and spiritual formation of the faithful and of religious." With such a development, the ecumenical environment will be secure.

The ecumenical spirit is not merely one of "glossing things over." The Decree on Ecumenism stresses that ecumenical dialogue must present doctrine "in its entirety," and that nothing is so foreign to the spirit of ecumenism as "a false irenicism which harms the purity of Catholic doctrine and obscures its assured genuine meaning." American Catholics are well enough educated to appreciate the whole view that the decree takes. The ecumenical movement in this country is thus assured of good health and sound structure. Projects of research will from time to time produce results that will, at least temporarily, amaze and disturb "comfortable" minds, but in general the educational work of the bishops and religious orders will not have been in vain.

In spite of some prophets of doom, it can be said that the grass-roots ecumenical movement should be the biggest and best injection of vitality that the individual churches have had since they were founded. The necessity to engage in dialogue — to explain one's faith to another — will force many people to learn their faith as they never have before. . . .

The Decree on Ecumenism humbly begs pardon of God "and of our separated brethren" for sins of Catholics in the past against them. The Declaration on Non-Christians, now ready for the final vote at the next session of the Council, admits there has been hatred and persecution of the Jews by Catholics and deplores it. In the years ahead there will be more and more frank discussion of this sad history. Our textbooks will have more of it, and our press will have more of it. The faults of churchmen and laity will be faced. Those who found it hard to take criticism of Catholic education will find it hard to take this future dialogue, too. But it must all come out in the dialogue. If it doesn't, the Jews especially will regard our dialogue with them as a fraud, and we shall not reach them. . . .

American Catholics, like most American people, are doers, not just hearers, readers, talkers. They will not be satisfied with an annual ecumenical breakfast or supper. In the Decree on Ecumenism they have a mandate for much more. They are already looking for common study-club work, regular neighborhood dialogue sessions, and common witness, especially in social work. They are consoled to learn from the Decree on Ecumenism what they had often suspected was true: they can learn a great deal from, and can be inspired in many cases by, their separated brethren. They have been excited by the prospect of a common Bible. They know, as the Decree on Ecumenism says, that "in the dialogue itself, the Sacred Word is a precious instrument in the mighty hand of God for attaining to that unity which the Saviour holds out to all men."

It is risky to attempt to express the divine plans in a timetable, but it seems safe enough to say that by 1990 our Catholic people will be much closer to Holy Scripture — and, thanks to the vernacular, so will our priests. Without Bible study, the ecumenical movement will not go very far. But Bible study is much more than just begun among our people. We shall have a common Bible long before 1990. In the publication, last June, of a Catholic edition of the Revised Standard Version (imprimatur of Archbishop Gray, of Edinburgh; introduction by Cardinal Meyer of Chicago) we have a common Bible for all practical purposes as far as the New Testament is concerned (the Old Testament should come in another year). In the years ahead we can and will work out a common biblical theology. The common Bible will give the ecumenical movement a great psychological boost. With a common biblical theology we shall be on the verge of the Christian union we seek.

Ecumenism Practiced

The most spectacular result from the new ecumenical principles outlined in the preceding document by W. M. Abbott were the discussions that took place between Lutherans and Catholics over the doctrine of justification. For both Lutherans and Catholics, this word signifies the process by which the holy God considers sinners as freed from their guilt and standing as righteous before God. But since the Reformation of the sixteenth century, Lutherans and Catholics had consistently condemned each other for teaching this doctrine falsely. Lutherans complained that Catholics stressed too much what people did to redeem themselves. Catholics complained that Lutherans stressed so much what God did in justification that there remained no reason for ever doing good deeds. Thus, it marked a great advance in modern ecumenical relations when on October 31, 1999, representatives of the Catholic Church and the Lutheran World Federation signed a "Joint Declaration on the Doc-

[Source: *Justification by Faith: Lutherans and Catholics in Dialogue*, VII, ed. H. George Anderson, T. Austin Murphy, and Joseph A. Burgess (Minneapolis: Fortress, 1985), pp. 15-16, 73-74.]

*trine of Justification" in Augsburg, Germany (where in 1530 the Lutherans
had written the renowned Augsburg Confession that defined their understanding of justification). A lot remained to separate Catholics and Lutherans (along with most other Protestants), like how to regard the pope or the
Virgin Mary. But an unprecedented step had occurred. For Americans, it is
significant that one of the first agreements between Catholics and Lutherans
in a particular nation about this long-contested doctrine had taken place in
the United States. The excerpts presented below come from that agreement
from 1984.*

Introduction

§1. Since 1965 a theological dialogue between Lutherans and Roman Catholics
in the United States has been taking place concerning doctrines that have
united or separated their churches from one another since the sixteenth century. The degree of consensus or convergence that exists on the Nicene Creed,
Baptism, the Eucharist, the Ministry, Papal Primacy, and Teaching Authority
and Infallibility has been expressed in summaries and joint statements that
have become important for relations between our churches and for wider ecumenical discussions.

§2. The question of justification by faith, which is at the heart of the divisions inherited from the sixteenth century, has not yet, however, been directly
addressed in the United States dialogue, although its implications for other topics have been noted in previous documents. . . . The present relationship between the Catholic and Lutheran traditions calls for a greater clarity about the
way to understand and speak of justification than has yet been achieved in official discussions, for the good news of God's justifying action in Jesus Christ
stands at the center of Christian faith and life.

§3. The present statement is a response to this need. It is based on discussions since 1978 of position papers drawing on a considerable body of biblical,
historical, theological, and ecumenical literature. It seeks to indicate how historic disagreements in the interpretation of the biblical doctrine of justification
have developed and to what extent they can now be overcome. It attempts to remove obstacles to joint proclamation of the message of justification and includes a declaration proclaiming our common faith. For justification is above
all a reality to be proclaimed in word and sacrament.

§4. We emphatically agree that the good news of what God has done for
us in Jesus Christ is the source and center of all Christian life and of the existence and work of the church. In view of this agreement, we have found it helpful to keep in mind in our reflections an affirmation which both Catholics and
Lutherans can wholeheartedly accept: our entire hope of justification and sal-

vation rests on Christ Jesus and on the gospel whereby the good news of God's merciful action in Christ is made known; we do not place our ultimate trust in anything other than God's promise and saving work in Christ. This excludes ultimate reliance on our faith, virtues, or merits, even though we acknowledge God working in these by grace alone (sola gratia). In brief, hope and trust for salvation are gifts of the Holy Spirit and finally rest solely on God in Christ. Agreement on this Christological affirmation does not necessarily involve full agreement between Catholics and Lutherans on justification by faith, but it does raise the question, as we shall see, whether the remaining differences on this doctrine need be church-dividing. Our intent in presenting this statement is to help our churches see how and why they can and should increasingly proclaim together the one, undivided gospel of God's saving mercy in Jesus Christ. . . .

Declaration

§ 161. Thus we can make together, in fidelity to the gospel we share, the following declaration:

> We believe that God's creative graciousness is offered to us and to everyone for healing and reconciliation so that through the Word made flesh, Jesus Christ, "who was put to death for our transgressions and raised for our justification" (Rom. 4:25), we are all called to pass from the alienation and oppression of sin to freedom and fellowship with God in the Holy Spirit. It is not through our own initiative that we respond to this call, but only through an undeserved gift which is granted and made known in faith, and which comes to fruition in our love of God and neighbor, as we are led by the Spirit in faith to bear witness to the divine gift in all aspects of our lives. This faith gives us hope for ourselves and for all humanity and gives us confidence that salvation in Christ will always be proclaimed as the gospel, the good news for which the world is searching.

§162. This gospel frees us in God's sight from slavery to sin and self (Rom. 6:6). We are willing to be judged by it in all our thoughts and actions, our philosophies and projects, our theologies and religious practices. Since there is no aspect of the Christian community or of its life in the world that is not challenged by this gospel, there is none that cannot be renewed or reformed in its light or by its power.

§163. We have encountered this gospel in our churches' sacraments and liturgies, in their preaching and teaching, in their doctrines and exhortations. Yet we also recognize that in both our churches the gospel has not always been proclaimed, that it has been blunted by reinterpretation, that it has been transformed by various means into self-satisfying systems of commands and prohibitions.

§164. We are grateful at this time to be able to confess together what our Catholic and Lutheran ancestors tried to affirm as they responded in different ways to the biblical message of justification. A fundamental consensus on the gospel is necessary to give credibility to our previous agreed statements on baptism, on the Eucharist, and on forms of church authority. We believe that we have reached such a consensus.

§ 165. We submit this statement to our churches for study, with the hope that it will serve them as they face the need to make appropriate decisions for the purpose of confessing their faith as one. We also trust that Christian believers of all traditions may find in it an invitation to new hope and new love in the grace that is offered to humanity by God through his Word, Jesus Christ, in the Holy Spirit.

Eastern Orthodoxy and American Culture

Ethnicity and Religion

In America's religious history, ethnicity has often determined patterns of settlement, ecclesiastical ties, seating at worship, and the language of theology. Much of this ethnic stamp had worn away by the middle of the twentieth century, but not among the Eastern Orthodox who were, by and large, recent arrivals. For these new Americans, ethnicity continued to determine social fellowship, marital choice, burial ground, and which foreign newspaper to read. The Greek Orthodox, for example, were still Greek even while they were Americans, with one eye turned toward their adopted land and the other cast toward "home." Two documents from Prelate Archbishop Iakovos (he was elevated to that office in 1959) show this ambivalence, as the Greek Orthodox Archdiocese of North and South America (with about two million members) stays very much Greek in the first document, and struggles to be very much American in the second.

[Sources: Demetrios J. Constantelos, ed., *Encyclicals and Documents of the Greek Orthodox Archdiocese of North and South America* (Thessalonika: Patriarchal Institute for Patristic Studies, 1976), (1) pp. 1173-74; (2) p. 1181.]

1.

October 15, 1964

My dearly beloved in the Lord,

A quarter of a century has now elapsed since that historic day of October 28, 1940, when the heroic Greek people, instead of bowing to the barbarity of invasion, determinedly opposed force, as they had often done in the past, and gained a victory of the greatest moral stature, to the glory of themselves and the entire civilized world.

That historic day, since known as the day of "OXI", when Greece said "No!" to the invader, shines forth resplendent from year to year with new radiance, and illumines the venerable but too often forgotten biblical truth that "not by bread alone can man live".

The abundance of bread and material comforts, and the reality or promise thereof, tend to choke within and around us the meaning and intent of the concepts of freedom and justice, and the protection of the weak of this earth by the strong.

Our present age, which is undoubtedly an era of great conquests in the fields of science and technology and space, is also a period of a pernicious degeneration of man, who has strayed from this faith in God and from the spiritual and ethical values which enriched and beautified even the most difficult and distressing times of years gone by.

We cannot help coming to such grievous conclusions, even unwillingly, when we see the unjustified apathy that has become the policy of even the most liberty-loving nations towards the decade-long struggle for self-determination by the Greeks of Cyprus, and towards the pressures and humiliations likewise endured, most recently during the past decade, by the Greeks of Turkey.

In view of all this, the 1964 observance of the unparalleled resistance of the Greek people, which was crowned by the "No!" they answered to force, and by the "Yes!" history will record to their courage, should be celebrated with a total awakening of our consciences and hearts. This is especially necessary today, when compromise is imposed upon as the best solution to the weightiest of problems, as in the issue of whether or not justice will prevail.

2.

Statement by His Eminence Archbishop Iakovos, Primate of the Greek Orthodox Church of North and South America, on the occasion of the Memorial Service for Rev. James Reed [sic][4] in Selma, Alabama on Monday, March 16, 1965:

4. Actually, James J. Reeb who was attacked in Selma, Alabama on March 10, 1965, a few

Greek Orthodox church in Belmont, California
(winner of an architectural award in 1963)
(National Council of Churches)

I came to this Memorial Service because I believe this is an appropriate occasion not only to dedicate myself as well as our Greek Orthodox Communicants to the noble cause for which our friend, the Reverend James Reed gave his life; but also in order to show our willingness to continue this fight against prejudice, bias and persecution.

In this God-given cause, I feel sure that I have the full and understanding support of our Greek Orthodox faithful of America. For our Greek Orthodox Church and our people fully understand from our heritage and our tradition such sacrificial involvements. Our Church has never hesitated to fight, when it felt it must, for the rights of mankind; and many of our Churchmen have been in the forefront of these battles time and time again.

The great poet John Milton said in the closing lines of *Samson Agonistes:*

---

hours after his participation in a protest march led by Martin Luther King, Jr. A graduate of Princeton Theological Seminary, a Presbyterian then Unitarian minister, Reeb died in a Birmingham hospital on March 12, at the age of thirty-eight. Both President Lyndon Johnson and Vice President Hubert Humphrey expressed the nation's deep regret to Reeb's widow and four children then living in Boston.

All is best, though oft we doubt,
What the invisible dispose of highest wisdom brings about.

I would like to believe that these words have deep relevance to the meaning of the tragic and violent death of the Rev. James Reed. The ways of God are not always revealed to us, but certainly His choice of this dedicated minister to be the victim of racial hatred and the hero of this struggle to gain unalienable constitutional rights for those American brethren of ours who are denied them, and to die, so to speak, on this battlefield for human dignity and equality, was not accidental or haphazard.

Let us seek out in this tragedy a divine lesson for all of us. The Rev. Reed felt he could not be outside the arena of this bitter struggle — and we too must feel that we cannot. Let his martyrdom be an inspiration and a reminder to us that there are times when we must risk everything, including life itself, for those basic American ideals of Freedom, Justice and Equality, without which this land cannot survive.

Our hope and prayer, then, is that we may be given strength to let God know by our acts and deeds, and not only by our words, that like the late Rev. James Reed, we too are the espousers and the fighters in a struggle for which we must be prepared to risk our all.

Elusive Unity

The other ecumenical difficulty besetting Orthodoxy is division within. There is in America no single "Orthodox Church." The two largest ethnic-national groups are Russian and Greek, but in addition to these there are, among others, Albanian, Bulgarian, Rumanian, Serbian, Syrian, and Ukrainian groups. Even the single bloc of Russian Orthodoxy has been further plagued by the awkwardness of a Patriarch of Moscow who for many decades was under the eye of a very un-Orthodox government. The largest of three Russian groups in the United States, the Orthodox Church in America, with about one million members, is no longer under Moscow's authority. One of its recent leaders, Metropolitan Ireney (1970-1981) was a leader in pressing toward the ecumenical goal of "One Orthodox Church" for all America. Orthodoxy, Metropolitan Ireney and his bishops contended, can never really develop in this country until the several autonomous churches

---

[Source: Constance J. Tarasu, ed., *Orthodox America, 1794-1976* (Syosset, N.Y.: Orthodox Church in America, 1975), p. 277.]

overcome their "many trials, divisions, and canonical disturbances" to be-
come one. The following call for unity was issued in 1970.

Message to All Orthodox Christians in America

In the Name of the Father and of the Son and of the Holy Spirit. Amen.

We the Bishops, clergy and laity of the Orthodox Church in America, united in Our Lord and Saviour Jesus Christ at our All-American Church Council, address this message to all our brothers in the Orthodox Faith in America.

The grace and the mercy of God be with you. Time has come for us to fulfill Christ's prayer, "that all may be one . . . that the world may believe that Thou hast sent me" (John 17:21). Our witness to the truth of our Orthodox Faith on this continent, where we Orthodox are a minority, lies in our perfect and total unity. How can the world accept and believe our claim to be the One, Holy, Catholic and Apostolic Church, of having kept in its fulness the Orthodox faith, if we ourselves are divided? We have the same Faith, the same Tradition, the same hope, the same mission. We should then constitute one Church, visibly, organically, fully. Such is the requirement of our Orthodox Faith and we know that always and everywhere the Orthodox Church has existed and exists as one Church. There can, therefore, be no excuse for our jurisdictional divisions, alienation from one another, and parochialism. The removal of such divisions and the organic unity of all Orthodox in America is the goal of our Church and we invite you to become a part of the unity.

But we also know and fully acknowledge that we have come from different backgrounds and have been nourished by various traditions within the same and unique Orthodox Tradition. We firmly believe that this variety constitutes the richness of American Orthodoxy and that whatever is true, noble, inspiring and Christian in our various customs and practices ought to be fully preserved and, if possible, shared. Therefore, although we insist that the One Orthodox Church here must be the home of all, we equally stress that there must be no loss of our respective national and cultural heritages and certainly no domination of any group by any other but a full equality, total trust and truly Christian brotherhood. As we send you the peace and love of our First Council as the Orthodox Church in America, we assure you that we understand ourselves first and foremost as the servants of the full unity of the Church in the freedom, love and mutual respect of all churches and dioceses of our Orthodox Church in the World and in this blessed land of America.

Glory to our Lord Jesus Christ, with the Father and the Holy Spirit, unto ages of ages. Amen.

At the Start of a New Century

St. Vladimir's Seminary in Crestwood, New York, is the intellectual heart of the Orthodox Church in America. On September 14, 2002, St. Vladimir's inaugurated the distinguished historian, John Erickson, as its new dean. That occasion provided Erickson with a chance to reflect on the place of Orthodoxy in the modern world, including its place in the United States of America.

How is Orthodoxy to respond to this changing world? A first and most obvious answer is that we must uphold "the faith once delivered to the saints" (Jude 1:3), that we look to Jesus Christ, "the same yesterday, today and tomorrow" (Heb 13:8), that we remain steadfast in the Tradition which has sustained Orthodox Christians throughout the ages. This is easy to say — and it is true. But it is harder to say precisely *how* we should demonstrate this fidelity here and now. We often take pride in our historic patrimony, in the treasures of our glorious past, and sometimes this tempts us simply to repeat select passages from the Scriptures, the canons, the lives of saints and the writings of the Church Fathers. But we should not let our love of the past and our nostalgia for the past cause us to forget another obvious and important truth: that Christ sent his followers into the world to "make disciples of all nations" (Mt 28:19), to proclaim the Word in each new cultural context. Orthodox theology in the future must remain faithful to Tradition, but for this very reason it must also be committed to mission — and this means that we must take seriously the world in which we live now. Dull repetition is not enough. In the future, Orthodox theology must address a host of questions that would have been unimaginable even a generation ago. It must faithfully proclaim the Word of God, but in ways that will engage all the new words — and the realities behind them — that we encounter and use in daily life today. . . .

We know that over the centuries Orthodoxy has shown a remarkable capacity to adapt to diverse cultures and even to transform and transfigure them. It is unnecessary to review here the accomplishments of SS Cyril and Methodius, St Stephen of Perm, St Innocent of Alaska, St Nicholas of Japan and so many other great missionaries. We *know* that our faith can and should be expressed not just in Greek but also in Aleut and Japanese and Cree — and even English. We *know* that unity of faith is not incompatible with cultural diversity. But sometimes we Orthodox Christians are tempted to identify our faith with a particular culture, possibly even a past culture or an imaginary culture, so that

---

[Source: John H. Erickson, "Orthodox Theology in a Changing World," *St. Vladimir's Theological Quarterly* 46 (2002): 307-08, 310-11.]

it is hard for us to envision the possibility of new and different cultural expressions of Orthodoxy. Sometimes we are so enamored of our great cultural achievements of the past that we despair when faced by a future in which our Orthodox faith — indeed the Christian faith itself — seems to be increasingly marginalized. We are tempted to withdraw into sectarian separation from the world rather than engage it in fresh and creative ways.

We face this temptation in an especially acute way in America today and in other regions of the so-called "diaspora." Will Orthodoxy ever be really at home in America? Will there ever be a truly American expression of Orthodoxy? Much here of course depends on what it means to be Orthodox and what it means to be American — questions that also call for reexamination. In any case, we should not simply give up in despair. Early Christians in the Roman Empire were a persecuted minority in a hostile environment, but they tried to engage and appropriate the best elements in the thought and aspirations of their age. We should do no less. And in addressing the thought and aspirations of our own age, in a critical but constructive way, in the marketplace of ideas and in the public square, perhaps we should also cast a critical glance at our own past achievements. We like to speak of the ways in which historic Orthodoxy has transformed cultures, transfigured cultures, or even "baptized" cultures. But in practice historic Orthodoxy has run the risk of being enslaved by the cultures with which it has become so closely identified — the risk of being too much at home whether in Byzantium or Russia or in some other "Orthodox" culture. And of course Orthodoxy could also become too much at home in America — too comfortable in its recently-won, middle-class, white, Anglophone, suburban respectability. We should remember, as Fr John Meyendorff liked to point out, that the Church does not baptize cultures; it baptizes human beings, one by one. And in baptizing them, it gives them a new homeland, God's heavenly kingdom — a homeland that potentially is open to people of every nation, every language, every culture.

4. Revivalism and Retreat

Postwar Revivalism: Billy Graham

Postwar recovery seemed to include a recovery for organized religion in America: church membership increased, attendance improved, prosperity returned. The 1950s were good years — stable, peaceful, with return to the traditional values of family (the baby boom), of decency (the Eisenhower years), of church (the Billy Graham revivals). Graham (b. 1918), North Carolina native and Baptist evangelist, rose to national prominence in the early fifties, particularly after a successful revival meeting or "crusade" in Los Angeles at the very end of the previous decade. "To me it was like a bolt of lightning out of a clear sky," Graham wrote ten years later of his swift rise to fame. "I was bewildered, challenged and humbled by the sudden avalanche of opportunities that deluged me." In 1960, looking back over that exciting decade and his own large part in it, Graham reflected upon his development and growing confidence.

The lessons of this decade have been staggering. Many of my original concepts and convictions have become more certain; others have been amplified, enlarged and changed.

First, I recognize more clearly today than I did ten years ago the narrow limits assigned to the evangelist. I take as my definition of evangelism the classic one formed by the Archbishop of Canterbury's Committee of 1918: "To evangelize is so to present Christ Jesus in the power of the Holy Spirit that men shall come to put their trust in God through Him, to accept Him as their Savior and serve Him as their King in the fellowship of His Church."

[Source: Billy Graham, "What Ten Years Have Taught Me," *Christian Century,* Feb. 17, 1960, pp. 186, 187, 188, 189.]

One of the best definitions of evangelism is that formulated by representatives of 30 Protestant communions at the 1946 meeting in Columbus, Ohio, of the executive committee of the old Federal Council of Churches. It reads: "Evangelism is the presentation of the good news of God in Jesus Christ so that men are brought through the power of the Holy Spirit to put their trust in God, accept Jesus Christ as their Savior from the guilt and power of sin, to follow and serve Him as their Lord in the fellowship of the church and in the vocations of the common life."

The evangel is the good news that God was in Christ, reconciling the world to himself. The word *evangelism* comes from the word *evangel,* which means "good news" or "gospel." The evangelist is the *keryx,* or the proclaimer of this message. The Scriptures indicate that when Christ gave gifts to his church, one of the gifts was that of the evangelist (Eph. 4:11). Philip was called an evangelist, and Paul told Timothy to do the work of an evangelist. Yet some in the church refuse — to the detriment of the church — to recognize this particular gift that has been given to some men.

The message of the evangelist is "narrow." It does not spread-eagle out into the broad ramifications of a total theology or sociology. Contrary to the opinion of some, the evangelist is not primarily a social reformer, a temperance lecturer or a moralizer. He is simply a *keryx,* a proclaimer of the good news, which in capsule form is "Christ died for our sins according to the Scriptures; . . . was buried, and . . . rose again the third day, according to the Scriptures" (I Cor. 15:3 f.). This terse proclamation stretches over the broad frame of man's basic need. It declares that man is a sinner, that Christ is the only Savior, that Christ lives evermore and that the Scriptures are trustworthy. . . .

A second lesson of the past decade: I have come to face realistically the results of mass evangelism. I am convinced that mass evangelism is not the most ideal method of evangelism. There are many methods that the church can effectively use, and mass evangelism is only one of them. Yet it is an important one.

My associates and I have spent a great deal of time and effort in studying the results of our crusades. Personally I am sick of statistics. How can one translate a reconciled home, a transformed drunkard or a new selfless attitude into a cold statistic? The only reason we keep statistics at all is for the sake of accuracy. If no statistics were kept, the press would exaggerate out of all proportion the number of those who respond to the appeal. For several years we spoke of the responses of the people who came forward in our crusades as "decisions," but we have even stopped doing that, for only God knows how many have made a definite commitment to Christ. Now we simply call them "inquirers" — people whose interest is sufficiently strong to cause them to make further inquiry about the Christian life. But of course each of these persons is dealt with as an earnest seeker of salvation, as indeed most of them turn out to be. . . .

In the third place, my faith in earlier theological concepts has deepened. For example, the years have brought a deepening conviction that the Word of God is quick and powerful and a discerner of the thoughts and intents of the heart.

The church has been effective only when it has spoken with authority. Truth begets its own authenticity; if we allow the truth to become adulterated and weakened by rationalisms it loses its power. At one time I grappled with the problem of the authority of the Scriptures. But the problem resolved itself when I finally said, "Lord, I take the Scriptures as thy revealed Word — by faith!" That ended my doubts. From that day to this the Scriptures have been like a rapier in my hand and I am sure that I would be shorn of any effectiveness I may have if this authority were taken from me. Someone will cry "Bibliolatry," but a soldier need not worship his sword to wield it effectively. I have learned with Jeremiah: "Is not my word like as a fire? saith the Lord; and like a hammer that breaketh the rock in pieces?" (Jer. 23:29). I am convinced that the reason some ministers are cracking up is that they have no authority. I am thankful

Evangelist Billy Graham and presidential candidate
Richard Nixon in Pittsburgh, Pennsylvania, in 1968
(Religion News Service)

that there is a return to biblical preaching in America. The Scriptures are beginning to return to their rightful place as the authority in the church.

A fourth change is to be seen in the fact that during the past ten years my concept of the church has taken on greater dimension. Ten years ago my concept of the church tended to be narrow and provincial, but after a decade of intimate contact with Christians the world over I am now aware that the family of God contains people of various ethnological, cultural, class and denominational differences. I have learned that there can even be minor disagreements of theology, methods and motives but that within the true church there is a mysterious unity that overrides all divisive factors.

In groups which in my ignorant piousness I formerly "frowned upon" I have found men so dedicated to Christ and so in love with the truth that I have felt unworthy to be in their presence. I have learned that although Christians do not always agree, they can disagree agreeably, and that what is most needed in the church today is for us to show an unbelieving world that we love one another. To me the church has become a great, glorious and triumphant organism. It is the body of Christ, and the humblest member is an important part of that body. I have also come to believe that within every visible church there is a group of regenerated, dedicated disciples of Christ.

A fifth change: my belief in the social implications of the gospel has deepened and broadened. I am convinced that faith without works is dead. I have never felt that the accusations against me of having no social concern were valid. Often the message of the evangelist is so personal that his statements on social matters are forgotten or left out when reports are made. It is my conviction that even though evangelism is necessarily confined within narrow limits the evangelist must not hedge on social issues. The cost of discipleship must be made plain from the platform. I have made the strongest possible statements on every social issue of our day. In addition, in our crusades we have tried to set an example. (Naturally, there are some statements that I made a few years ago on sociopolitical affairs that I would like to retract.)

Yet I am more convinced than ever before that we must change men before we can change society. The international problems are only reflections of individual problems. Sin is sin, be it personal or social, and the word repent is inseparably bound up with evangelism. Social sins, after all, are merely a large-scale projection of individual sins and need to be repented of by the offending segment of society. But the task of the evangelist is not merely to reform but to stimulate conversion, for conversion puts man in a position where God can do for him, and through him, what man is incapable of doing for or by himself.

Sixth, I have an increasing confidence in the ultimate triumph of the kingdom of God. I am convinced that history is not wandering aimlessly, but that there is a plan and purpose in what often seems to us hopeless confusion.

God has intervened more than once in history, and there is every reason to believe that he will intervene again. Man may build his towers of Babel, as he always has, and the world may marvel at his genius and his ability to make progress even apart from God, but history shows that ultimately man comes down from his tower in confusion and chaos, disillusioned and frustrated. The Scriptures declare that there is only One whose kingdom shall never end. I believe that when our Lord prayed, "Thy kingdom come, Thy will be done on earth as it is in heaven," he prayed a prayer which is going to be answered. This will come about not by man's efforts within history itself but by a direct, climactic intervention of the sovereign God.

Seventh, the past decade has been a period of ripening tares and ripening wheat. During this interval we have seen a strange paradox that often confused and bewildered me. We have seen a revival of religious interest throughout the United States but an acceleration of crime, divorce and immorality. Within the church there is a new depth of commitment, a new sense of destiny and a spirit of revival, yet in the world there is an intensification of the forces of evil. Crime is on the increase. Fear haunts the council halls of the nations. Wars, hot and cold, are being spawned across the world. Family life is threatened by evil forces. And in many places there is a stark lack of social concern. The tares of evil flourish even in the same field with the growing grain of righteousness. But we forget that Christ said: "In the time of harvest I will say to the reapers, Gather ye first the tares and bind them in bundles and burn them; but gather the wheat into my barn" (Matt. 13:30). The wheat and the tares are destined to grow side by side; when wheat is sown, the Devil sows tares. But a day of separation, an ultimate triumph for truth and righteousness, is coming.

Theological Retreat

Peace and Positive Thoughts

Once the conquest of Hitler's, Hirohito's, and Mussolini's forces was accomplished, religious leaders gave their attention to a conquest of inner turmoil and doubt. Turning from catechism to comfort, popular religion offered assurance that peace can be achieved not only on the battlefield but as well in the recesses of mind and soul, Rabbi Joshua Loth Liebman led off in 1946 with his widely read Peace of Mind, *observing that "it remains only for man*

[Source: F. J. Sheen, *Peace of Soul* (New York: McGraw Hill, 1949), pp. 286-89.]

to hearken to these divine reverberations in his own soul." The Reverend Norman Vincent Peale (see above, pp. 243-45) provided A Guide to Confident Living *in 1948, this to be followed four years later by the spectacularly successful* Power of Positive Thinking. *Dr. Billy Graham also entered the list with his* Peace with God *(1953), declaring therein: "In Christ we are relaxed and at peace in the midst of confusions, bewilderments, and perplexities of this life. The storm rages, but our hearts are at rest." On national television, few if any could compete with the dramatic "presence" of Monsignor Fulton J. Sheen (1895-1979) on the "Catholic Hour" and, in the 1950s, on a program entitled "Is Life Worth Living?" In 1949, Sheen published both* Way to Happiness *and* Peace of Soul. *An excerpt from the latter describes this peace as one of the several effects of conversion.*

The new certitude of the convert, then, is a precious thing and very different from the abandonment of will and intellect some imagine it to be. But the full tale of the benefits from conversion is not ended. We must speak of another christening gift — *peace of soul*. There is a world of difference between peace of mind and peace of soul. Peace of mind is the result of bringing *some* ordering principle to bear on discordant human experiences; this may be achieved by tolerance, or by a gritting of one's teeth in the face of pain; by killing conscience, or denying guilt, or by finding new loves to assuage old griefs. Each of these is an integration, but on a very low level. This kind of peace Our Lord calls false, and He likens it to living under the dominion of Satan: "When a strong man armed keepeth his court, those things are in peace which he possesseth" (Luke 11:21). It is the peace of those who have convinced themselves they are animals; the peace of the stone-deaf whom no word of truth can pierce; the peace of the blind who guard themselves against every ray of heavenly light. It is the false peace of the slothful servant who had the same talent at the end as at the beginning because he ignored the judgment which would demand an account of his stewardship. It is the false peace of the man who built his house on the shifting road, so that it vanished with the floods and the storms. With such false peace of mind, Satan tempts his victims; he makes it seem refined to the refined, sensual to the sensual, and coarse to the coarse.

Conversion brings the soul out of either chaos or this false peace of mind to true peace of soul. "Peace I leave with you, my peace I give unto you: not as the world giveth, do I give unto you. Let not your heart be troubled, nor let it be afraid" (John 14:27). This true peace is born of the tranquillity of order, wherein the senses are subject to the reason, the reason to faith, and the whole personality to the Will of God. The true peace that follows conversion is deepened, not disturbed, by the crosses, checks, and disquietudes of the world, for they are all welcomed as coming from the hands of the Loving Father. This true peace can never come from adjustment to the world, for if the world is wicked, adjustments to wickedness make us worse. It comes only from identification of one's own will with the Will of God.

The peaceful soul does not seek, now, to live morally, but to live for God; morality is only a by-product of the union with Him. This peace unites the soul with his neighbor, prompting him to visit the sick, to feed the hungry and clothe the naked; for by loving another soul one gives to God.

The only real pain the convert now has is his inability to do more for the love of God. It is easy to fulfill the claims of lesser ideals, such as Humanism, and their disciples very quickly become complacent; they are already as virtuous as their code asks them to be. It is very easy to be a good Humanist, but it is very hard to be a true follower of Christ. Yet it is not the memory of *past* sins which creates this pain amid the peace, but present shortcomings: because he loves so much, the convert feels as if he had done nothing. What gift can ever be an expression of this new love? If he could give God the universe, even that would not be enough.

All the energy that was previously wasted in conflict — either in trying to find the purpose of life or in trying alone and futilely to conquer his vices — can now be released to serve a single purpose. Regret, remorse, fears, and the anxieties that flowed from sin now completely vanish in repentance. The convert no longer regrets what he might have been; the Holy Spirit fills his soul with a constant presentiment of what he can become through grace. This spiritual recuperation is accompanied by hope, at no matter what age the change occurs — although the convert always regrets that he waited so long. As St. Augustine said, "Too late, O ancient beauty, have I loved thee." But since grace rejuvenates, it quickens even the old to consecrated service.

And there are many other ways in which peace of soul will manifest itself after conversion: it makes somebodies out of nobodies by giving them a service of Divine Sonship; it roots out anger, resentments, and hate by overcoming sin; it gives the convert faith in other people, whom he now sees as potential sons of God; it improves his health by curing the ills that sprang from a disordered, unhappy, and restless mind; for trials and difficulties, it gives him the aid of Divine power; it brings him at all times a sense of harmony with the universe; it sublimates his passions; it makes him fret less about the spiritual shortcomings of the world because he is engrossed in seeking his own spiritualization; it enables the soul to live in a constant consciousness of God's presence, as the earth, in its flight about the sun, carries its own atmosphere with it. In business, in the home, in household duties, in the factory, all actions are done in the sight of God, all thoughts revolve about His Truths. The unreasoning blame, the false accusations, the jealousies and bitterness of others are borne patiently, as our Lord bore them, so that love might reign and that God might be glorified in the bitter as in the sweet. Dependence on Him becomes strength; one no longer fears to undertake good works, knowing He will supply the means. But above all else, with this deep sense of peace, there is the gift of perseverance, which inspires us never to let down our guard, or to shrink from difficulties, or to be depressed as the soul presses on to its supernal vocation in Christ Jesus, Our Lord.

The Death of God

The 1960s, turbulent and antiauthority in so many ways, made no exception for that normally staid and stodgy discipline of theology. With free speech movements, political protests, anti-Vietnam riots, and televised trials, the "death of God" theology took its place. For a few years, theology was again suitable for public discussion, though the discussion now concerned the futility or marginality of the hoary discipline. As William Hamilton (b. 1924) noted in 1966, the theologian in America today is "a man without faith, without hope, with only the present, with only love to guide him." Hamilton, at that time on the faculty of Colgate Rochester Divinity School, joined with such others as Thomas J. Altizer, Paul Van Buren, A. J. Robinson, Gabriel Vahanian, Richard Rubenstein, and Leslie Dewart to explain this new and somewhat unnerving stance with respect to the current task of theology — or at least of "radical theology." In the excerpt below, Hamilton responds to specific questions about this theology whose object of investigation no longer survives.

Question 1:   What God is referred to in the phrase the "death of God"?

The "death of God," as the radicals use it, does not mean that some ways of thinking or talking about God in traditional Christianity are done for. It means that no ways are possible. The "God" meant in the phrase "death of God" is the God in the phrase "I believe in God the Father Almighty, Maker of heaven and earth." The God whose death is believed in is the Christian God. "Death of God" does not refer to a disappearance of a psychological capacity. Let me put it this way. Faith in God in the classical Christian tradition has always meant this: an act of passionate, personal daring and courage can be made, and when it is made, a real other is made known, over against man, making demands and making Himself known. This is the meaning of faith in God. It is this God of faith, known in this way (as against the God of religion or culture), who is no more.

[Source: J. L. Ice and J. J. Carey, *The Death of God Debate* (Philadelphia: Westminster Press, 1967), pp. 213-15.]

Question 2:   Are radical theologians Christians?

Yes, because the "death of God" is now (mainly but not entirely) being talked about by Christians. Yes, because it is the Christian God that is referred to in the phrase. Yes, because the "death of God" is an affirmation that does not disable or block, but acts as enabling things, making possible Christian allegiance not possible along other lines. But what is the proper definition of a Christian in this context? Two answers can be given. In one sense, the Christian is defined by his choice of comrades. Whom does he seek out? Whose questions and answers are his? Who makes the noises he wishes to make? "Death of God" is a Christian affirmation in this sense. The Christian is also a man in relation to Jesus, and the radical theologian affirming the "death of God" claims to be Christian in this second sense as well.

Question 3:   Would the radical theologians call themselves agnostics, or atheists, or antitheists?

"Atheist" would be the closest. Agnostic suggests maybe, and "death of God" is not a maybe theology. Antitheism suggests an aggressiveness about others' views that the radicals don't have. But if they are atheists, they are atheists with a difference. Perhaps the difference can be put in this way. Traditional atheism believes that there is now no God and that there never has been, beliefs in God of the past being deception, ignorance, fear. Radical theology believes that there was once a time (Bible, sixteenth century, for example) when having a god was appropriate, possible, even necessary. But now is not such a time. There was once, and is not now. The present of the radical is like that of the atheist, but the memories are different. The radical can say yes to the Christian past; the atheist cannot.

Question 4:   Isn't radical theology just another form of humanism?

It is humanism, if humanism means a belief that there are no viable objects of loyalty beyond man, his values, his communities, his life. But it is a Christian humanism.

Question 5:   Why have you insisted on the phrase "death of God"? Just because it gives offense?

It is an offensive phrase, but we have not chosen it to give offense. We have chosen it partly because we wish to relate to the tradition of religious thought in the past century that has made use of it, but primarily because it expresses exactly what we wish to express — the sense of a possession that has been taken away, a possession we do not expect to be made good, to come back. Thus, the traditional words — absence of God, or silence, or disappearance, or eclipse — all live within the world of a loss that is temporary, short-ranged, soon to be removed. And whatever we expect or hope for, the object of hope is not the Christian God.

Religious Humanism

In 1933 a Humanist Manifesto declared that "the quest for the good life is still the central task of mankind." In that quest, old theologies, outworn creeds, and the "outward forms of religion" play little part, or perhaps even an obstructive part — according to this perspective. Yet, it is important that religion survive, for "religions have always been the means for realizing the highest values of life." A generation later an effort to update and rewrite that Manifesto failed, but a personal statement issued in the wake of the Death of God theology retained the characteristic emphases of religious humanism. ". . . It is important to the survival of mankind, and indeed of life itself, that religion does not die with God." This statement came from William S. Fisk, lay president of a Unitarian-Universalist fellowship in Ohio.

But out of his necessity, man created more than gods. He created religion, too; and these are not co-equal. For religion pervaded men's lives, ordered their societies, set the patterns of behavior, set the goals of men's desires. Religion provided, and still provides, a repository for the highest and best of man's thoughts and aspirations. In many forms, this is cloaked in divine sanction as a means of enforcement and promulgation, but basically, all of man's hopes for his future, all of what he has learned on how to live and prosper, all the essence of centuries of trial and error are found in the values of the religions of the world. . . .

Our age has seen what can happen when the great values of religion were brushed aside, and the weakened faith in a man-made God could not support them. The gas chambers at Dachau are evidence enough; the mass removal of dissidents to Siberian work camps adds continuing evidence. The willingness of men to conceive of, and prepare for, a nuclear war in which civilization might well die, is only the final proof.

[Source: W. S. Fisk, "'God Is Dead' — Long Live Religion!" *Religious Humanism*, 1 (Winter, 1967), 12-13.]

Humanist Alternative

Liberal religion, humanistic religion, stands as living evidence of another alternative. We meet in our churches, yet there is no excommunication if we do not attend. We possess, and will defend, firm ideals which have grown out of the great religious traditions; yet we do not believe we will live forever in fire if we fail a few times in living up to those ideals. Nor will most of us defend those ideals on any supernatural or divine basis, for many of us would agree that there is no proof of a God who speaks and acts in the world of men. Yet we meet in a church and we speak of our religion. Is this a clue to the future?

The concept of God may well be powerless in the future, but it is important to the survival of mankind, and indeed of life itself, that religion does not die with God. Let us remember that man created God, and man created religion, in the image of his necessity. Let us hold on firmly to that which is still needed; to the values that man has built, not received as a gift of divine revelation — but built painstakingly over the ages of mistakes. Let us hold on to the great empirical truths from all religious systems. Truths — a strong word, but used in this sense: we believe that they work in improving the relations of man to man, and as long as they work, let us act as if they were true. The Golden Rule is not a revelation from on high, nor is it a one-shot bright idea from some past historic pen. It is a universal axiom which developed in every great religion: treat other men in the way that you want to be treated. Its greatness lies in its simplicity and in its changeability. Each man decides for himself, in his own time and with his own knowledge of things, of science, or whatever, how he wants to be considered, and then applies it to others. These kinds of ideals must not die.

Suggested Reading (Chapter Eleven)

For World War II, there is now a fine general study by Gerald L. Sittser, *A Cautious Patriotism: The American Churches and the Second World War* (1997). Martin E. Marty explains how the religious dynamics of the war years flowed into what followed in *Modern American Religion,* vol. 3: *Under God, Indivisible, 1941-1960* (1996). In an edited volume, William R. Hutchison gathered several perceptive essays that trace the development of the country's once-dominant mainline Protestant churches against many of the important trends of the first two-thirds of the century, *Between the Times: The Travail of the Protestant Establishment in America, 1900-1960* (1989). A sprightly effort to write the religious history of the 1960s and 70s has been published by Mark Oppenheimer as *God and Counterculture: Religion in Nixon's America* (2003).

Pacifism flourished in the 1930s but quickly waned during the years of the war itself. For a treatment by the author of several of the best studies of the subject, see Peter Brock, *Twentieth-Century Pacifism* (1970), and for coverage brought closer to the present, Theron F. Schlabach and Richard T. Hughes, eds., *Proclaim Peace: Christian Pacifism from Unexpected Quarters* (1997).

On the secret development and swift use of the atomic bomb, but also on ferocious modern controversies respecting the 50th anniversary of Hiroshima and Nagasaki, see Kai Bird and Lawrence Lifschultz, eds., *Hiroshima's Shadow: Writings on the Denial of History and the Smithsonian Controversy* (1998), and Martin Harwit, *An Exhibit Denied: Lobbying the History of "Enola Gay."* On specifically religious reactions, useful books from the time include two reports sponsored by the Federal Council of Churches: *Atomic Warfare and the Christian Faith* (1946) and *The Christian Conscience and Weapons of Mass Destruction* (1950).

The literature on the holocaust is vast and now growing even more rapidly after the opening in 1993 of the United States Holocaust Memorial Museum in Washington, D.C. David Novick presents the controversial argument that, for the sake of Judaism and Jews in America, there has been too much attention in *The Holocaust in American Life* (1999). For a sampling of the many serious books reflecting on the religious meaning of this horrific event, see A. Roy Eckardt, *Long Night's Journey Into Day: Life and Faith After the Holocaust* (1982), David P. Gushee, *The Righteous Gentiles of the Holocaust: A Christian Interpretation* (1994), and Joel Marcus, *Jesus and the Holocaust: Reflections on Suffering and Hope* (1997).

The relationship between the Holocaust and Zionism is explored in Jacob Neusner's *Stranger at Home* (1981). Other important treatments of Zionism include Arthur Hertzberg, *The Zionist Idea* (1959), Abraham Heschel, *The Earth Is the Lord's* (1966), Howard Greenstein, *Turning Point: Zionism and Reform Judaism* (1981), and S. Almog, et al., eds., *Zionism and Religion* (1998). For strikingly different kinds of Protestant involvement with the Zionism, Jews, and the state of Israel, see Robert T. Handy, ed., *The Holy Land in American Protestant Life, 1800-1948* (1981), and Yaakov S. Ariel, *Evangelizing the Chosen People: Mission to the Jews in America, 1880-2000* (2000).

On the Cold War in general, a reliable survey is provided by Norman Friedman, *The Fifty-Year War: Conflict and Strategy in the Cold War* (2000), while religious involvement moving well beyond just the United States is the subject of Owen Chadwick, *The Christian Church in the Cold War* (1992).

In the period of the Vietnam War, religious no less than political protest reached new heights. The degree of Roman Catholic resistance to or condemnation of that conflict was especially striking. On that confrontation, these studies are particularly revealing: T. E. Quigley, ed., *American Catholics and Vietnam* (1968), and Robert F. Drinan, S.J., *Vietnam and Armageddon: Peace,*

War, and the Christian Conscience (1970). Daniel Berrigan, one of the most conspicuous dissenters of the period, offered his autobiography in *To Dwell in Peace* (1987). Religious opposition to Vietnam, especially that of "Clergy and Laity Concerned about Vietnam," is carefully explored by Mitchell K. Hall, who made use of FBI files in writing *Because of Their Faith* (1990), and more general treatments of religious protest include M. P. Hamilton, ed., *The Vietnam War: Christian Perspectives* (1967).

On the society-wide fixation on *Christianity and Communism,* there were many noteworthy studies in the period, including books with that title by Henri Chambre, S.J. (1960), from Catholic perspective, and by John C. Bennett from a Protestant angle of vision (1960). The confrontational aspects of these two ideologies in America is described in detail in Ralph L. Roy's *Communism and the Churches* (1960).

For Martin Luther King, Jr., the best source is King himself, who can be read in several readily available paperbacks, or heard on tapes and film that recorded his speeches. Under the general editorship of Claborn Carson, *The Papers of Martin Luther King, Jr.* have been appearing in a well-edited scholarly edition since 1992. Full biographical studies have been offered by, among many others, David J. Garrow, *Bearing the Cross: Martin Luther King, Jr., and the Southern Leadership Conference* (1986), Mervyn A. Warren, *King Came Preaching* (2001), and Marshall Frady, *Martin Luther King, Jr.* (2002). A superb general account with King at the center is offered by Taylor Branch in his two volumes to date of *The King Years: Parting the Waters, 1954-1963* (1988), and *Pillar of Fire, 1963-1965* (1998). See also James Forman, *The Making of Black Revolutionaries* (1972). James Baldwin's *The Fire Next Time* (1962) remains a landmark statement about African-American aspirations for full citizenship. The civil rights struggle, along with other developments, is updated in the essays from two solid collections, Paul E. Johnson, ed., *African American Christianity* (1992), and Timothy E. Fulop and Albert J. Raboteau, eds., *African-American Religion* (1997). And for two outstanding books on different aspects of the civil rights era, see on lived realities in Mississippi over a short period of time, Charles Marsh, *God's Long Summer: Stories of Faith and Civil Rights* (1997), and on clashes between Catholic ethnics and African Americans in many cities over more than a generation, John T. McGreevy, *Parish Boundaries: The Catholic Encounter with Race in the Twentieth-Century Urban North* (1996).

A valuable source on John F. Kennedy has been compiled by N. A. Schneider, *Religious Views of President John F. Kennedy in His Own Words* (1965). Watergate has had almost as many interpreters as perpetrators, but among the best books on this sad subject are Leon Jaworski, *The Right and the Power* (1976), and H. Dale Crockett, *Focus on Watergate: An Examination of the Moral Dilemma of Watergate in the Light of Civil Religion* (1982).

For a comprehensive view of ecumenical developments in the decades after World War II, there is a useful survey edited by Harold E. Fey, *History of the Ecumenical Movement*, Vol. 2, *1948-68* (1970). Robert McAfee Brown's *Ecumenical Revolution* (rev. ed., 1969) traced the fast-breaking developments of the era from the vantage point of a participant. Details on the Consultation of Church Union can best be followed in the Proceedings and Digests of the consultations themselves, or on the website for Churches Uniting in Christ that is listed with the document above. To chart the groups that participated in the Lausanne congress, see John R. W. Stott, ed., *Making Christ Known: Historic Mission Documents from the Lausanne Movement* (1997).

Contrasting partisan accounts of the Lutheran Church–Missouri Synod schism of the 1970s can be read in the books cited above by John Tietjen and Kurt Marquart. A fuller account that benefits from the passage of time and that includes more on the Missouri Synod than just the division is Mary Todd, *Authority Vested: A Story of Liberty and Change in the Lutheran Church — Missouri Synod* (2000). The Southern Baptist conflicts have been well covered in two solid works by the sociologist Nancy Tatom Ammerman, *Baptist Battles* (1990) and, as editor, *Southern Baptists Observed* (1993). Conservatives won the denominational battle, but much of the historical interpretation to the broader public has been offered by those who lean in a moderate direction, including Bill J. Leonard, *God's Last and Only Hope: The Fragmentation of the Southern Baptist Convention* (1990), David T. Morgan, *New Crusades, The New Holy Land: Conflict in the Southern Baptist Convention, 1969-1991* (1996), and Barry Hankins, *Uneasy in Babylon: Southern Baptist Conservatives and American Culture* (2002).

Vatican II was covered by many journalists, none superior to Xavier Rynne whose letters were first published in the *New Yorker* and then in a series of paperbacks. The permanent work of the council appeared in a convenient form under the editorship of Walter M. Abbott, S.J., *Documents of Vatican II* (1966). Since 1995 Orbis Press has been publishing successive volumes of a massive official history under the general editorship of Giuseppe Alberigo. For an official statement of Catholic doctrine, which is fully alert to the documents of the Council, see the *Catechism of the Catholic Church* (1994). John Courtney Murray, S.J., authored the Declaration on Religious Freedom that can be read in the Abbott volume. The best introduction to Murray is his own *We Hold These Truths: Catholic Reflections on the American Proposition* (1960), but there have been several thoughtful secondary accounts, including Robert P. Hunt and Kenneth L. Grasso, eds., *John Courtney Murray and the American Civil Conversation* (1992). Fruits of the ecumenical dialogues sparked by the Second Vatican Council are found in two volumes titled *Growth in Agreement,* the first edited by Harding Meyer and Lukas Vischer in 1984, the second edited by Jeffrey Gros, Harding Meyer, and William G. Rusch in 2000.

On Eastern Orthodoxy in America, some of the most important Orthodox theologians who migrated to this country left provocative reflections, for example, Alexander Schmemann in a series of articles on "Problems of Orthodoxy in America," in the *St. Vladimir's Seminary Quarterly,* vols. 8 and 9 (1964, 1965). For wider ranging history by another Orthodox luminary, see Georges Florovsky, *Aspects of Church History* (1975). The contemporary situation for Orthodox churches is well outlined in a number of books. John H. Erickson's *Orthodox Christians in America* (1999) is a very effective overview; Thomas E. Fitzgerald's *The Orthodox Church* (1995) includes biographical sketches of important leaders along with a continuous narrative; Mark Stokoe's *Orthodox Christians in North America, 1794-1994* (1995), which was written with Leonid Kishkovsky, is more comprehensive; and Frederica Mathewes-Green's *Facing East: A Pilgrim's Journey into the Mysteries of Orthodoxy* (1997) offers a winsome memoir concerning one person's movement into the Orthodox church.

The life and thought of Billy Graham, as is also the case of Martin Luther King, Jr., can be followed in many of his own books. His own autobiography, *Just As I Am* (1997), communicates much about his character and his firm sense of mission, but leaves to others to assess the meaning of the Billy Graham phenomenon. Of many who tried to make that assessment, the best attempt has been offered by William Martin, *A Prophet with Honor: The Billy Graham Story* (1991). Donald B. Meyer's *Positive Thinkers* (1965) affords excellent background for the "peace of mind books" of the postwar era. For the radical theology of the 1960s, there is an important statement by two of its exponents in Thomas J. J. Altizer and William Hamilton, *Radical Theology and the Death of God* (1966). Richard Rubenstein's *After Auschwitz* (1966) raises questions about theodicy (or the justification of God in a world marked by gross evil) that remain at the center of theological discussion in a way that the 1960s' tempest over the supposed Death of God does not.

TWELVE

E Pluribus . . . Unum?

The closer historians get to the present, the harder time they have putting a coherent picture together. So it is that in the decades from the 1970s and following, the American religious picture seems to manifest much more diversity than coherence, much more social strain than social harmony, much more public contention over the expression of religion than private contentment at its practices. If not quite in the stridently confrontational manner of the 1960s, religion since that time has still witnessed scant consensus and a variety blossoming into magnificent if often bewildering diversity. If there was any doubt, however, about the public importance of religion, that doubt was put to rest by the terrorist attacks of September 11, 2001, and the nation-wide reaction to those tragic events. Religion seems to be back into politics to stay. Argument over what kind of religion is best for the public good now takes place much more frequently than over whether it is a good thing or a bad thing for religion to exert an influence in the public realm. Public spectacles of other sorts — from the flamboyance of evangelical television preachers to the painful airing of clerical abuse — have since the 1980s absorbed as much political attention as political religion. And yet, what is most visible about religion may not be what is most important. The cultural historian Leigh Eric Schmidt recently made a profoundly wise statement about the religious tradition that has historically occupied center stage in American history: "Most of the things that count about Christianity cannot be counted, like the warmth or coolness of prayer, the resonance or hollowness of scriptural words, the songs or silences of the saints in heaven, the presences or absences in the sacrament." Schmidt's words are a reminder that, for all the religious traditions, what happens in private may be what endures long after public preoccupations have faded into obscurity.

Pluralism Plus

While religious and cultural variety is as American as apple pie and as old as the kachina doll, few would deny that in the last decades of the twentieth century, such variety reached dizzying heights. Most people no longer needed to be told of such diversity, for its manifestations were seen on city streets, in most suburbs, at the airports, in the media, in many rural areas, and sometimes most poignantly within the family. The fresh burst of Oriental religious practice and proselytizing was especially striking. From the older Vedanta Society (see above, pp. 72-73) and Self-Realization fellowship (founded in 1925), Hinduism has appeared in several more recent manifestations. Beginning in 1959, Transcendental Meditation and its persuasive guru, Maharishi Mahesh Yogi, created a Vedic stream that saturated the West coast, much of the East, and many points in between. In the 1960s and 1970s Hare Krishna, or more properly the International Society of Krishna Consciousness, could hardly escape notice, with its devotees' saffron robes, shaved heads, black topknots, and obtrusive methods of fundraising. In the 1980s and 1990s, the ancient Hindu epic poem, the *Mahabharata,* lent itself to dramatic theatrical presentation, both on stage and television. Beyond Hinduism, India offered to America other religious manifestations, including Jainism, the experiment of Rajneeshpuram, turban-crowned Sikhs. But of all religions from the East, it was Buddhism, especially as it passed from India through the filters of Chinese and Japanese civilizations, that promised to make the most enduring impact on American culture.

From the Near East, Islam likewise has grown rapidly since the landmark emigration act of 1965 opened American shores to fresh streams of immigration. American Muslims have multiplied, not so much as a result of conscious missionary effort, as through the inevitable accompaniment of immigrants, students, and temporarily assigned workers. Black Muslims, to be sure, constituted a special case of indigenous Islamic development, since this movement represented both a rejection of Western racism and an embrace of Near Eastern culture and religion. So swiftly has the emerging Islamic population increased that by the turn of the century, Muslims probably had outstripped Judaism in the number of American adherents. The Gulf War of 1991, but, even more, reaction to September 11, 2001, spurred many Americans to a crash course in Islamic history, cultures, and beliefs. Even as mosques and minarets became recognizable features in many landscapes, more and more Americans began to understand something about the variety of Muslims in the world, and in this nation, as well.

Much of the newer diversity in American religion was due to well-worn practices. In particular, successful promoters, charismatic healers, convincing television personalities, and magnetic pulpiteers continued to gather large followings. Intensely reported incidents of death and violence accompanied a very few of the marginal religious movements — followers of James Jones in Jonestown in 1978, Branch Davidians at Waco in 1993, Heaven's Gate (and Marshall Applewhite's Human Individual Metamorphosis) in 1997. But such moments were rare, and much less representative than the more hum-drum religious experiences of what scholars had come to call "new religious movements."

American religion has also found itself pulled to the margins of both Left and Right. On the "radical left" exist many manifestations of Neopagan and New Age religions, with a bewildering diversity of practices and beliefs. While sharing many similarities with Neopaganism, New Age movements reject notions of magic or witchcraft, preferring to seek power from the crystal and wisdom from direct communication with the ancients. Both movements are ever evolving, deliberately eclectic, and highly personal in their emphasis on the transformation or rebirth of each individual.

As in the past, however, the most enduring feature of American religious pluralism remained home-grown, and usually had something to do with one of the historic Christian or Jewish faiths. Innovations in the traditional churches, in the newer American denominations, and in the hybrids, mergers, and schisms that continue to proliferate in the American landscape have continued to be a constant feature of recent decades. These less spectacular instances of religious particularity remain the most important source of the nation's ongoing experiment in religious freedom.

Liberation/Alienation

In the 1950s and 1960s the struggle for human rights and a decent standard of living was largely a matter of power politics and ecclesiastical pressures. In the 1970s and 1980s theology moved to the forefront, no longer speaking in the assured tones of an unchallenged establishment, but now heeding the causes and the voices of the oppressed. A liberation theology — sometimes inspired by Christianity, sometimes directed against it — contended that poverty, hunger, injustice, and oppression were theological concerns, with dependence, domination, and discrimination crying out for theological solutions. Among African Americans, some sought solutions in the tradition of Israel's ancient prophets, like Amos and Isaiah, or in the tradition of America's own modern-day prophetic figures, like Reinhold Niebuhr or Abraham Joshua Heschel. Others, however, with the Black Muslims most pronounced, regarded the Judeo-Christian heritage as so thoroughly entangled with white domination and Western imperialism as to require that blacks reject "the devil white man" and his exploiting, enslaving religion.

Other minorities also hungered for words and deeds that would mark the end to oppression and open the door to opportunity. Some heard those words from Paul John Paul II in his several visits to the United States, as he went out of his way to encourage Polish Americans, Ukrainian Americans, and — above all — Hispanic Americans. By the end of the century, the Hispanic presence had grown with great speed in the Roman Catholic church. It was not until 1970, when Patrick F. Flores was consecrated, that the American church possessed a Hispanic bishop, but institutional developments soon sped up — with the first National Pastoral Conference in 1972 and then in the 1980s Pastoral Letters devoted to Hispanic concerns, and in the 1990s a wide variety of church programs aimed at incorporating Mexicans, Puerto Ricans, Cubans, Central Americans, and other Latin Catholics into the full life of the church. By that time as well, traditional life was diversifying rapidly for another reason, as more and more Hispanics found a religious home outside of the Catholic Church with various Protestant bodies, especially Pentecostals. This development, which paralleled the growth of Protestant Pentecostalism in Latin America, once more brought into being toward the end of the century what had hardly existed before.

Native Americans, having long since despaired of genuine liberation, fought for the right to practice their own version of sacramental Christianity. The Native American Church, chartered in 1918 in Oklahoma, proposed "to foster and promote religious believers in Almighty God and the customs of the several Tribes throughout the United States in the worship of a Heavenly Father, and to promote morality, sobriety, industry, charity, and right living." Yet the Native American Church was not everywhere encouraged. At last, in 1978, the U.S. Congress passed the Indian Religious Freedom Act that explicitly granted to the Native American population rights that most other Americans had claimed as their own for nearly two hundred years. Even then, however, such rights could still be called into question, as the Supreme Court did in rejecting parts of the 1978 law. The legal tale that followed on that decision continues to the present day.

An even more visible form of liberation took place in connection with the religious activities of women. Church and synagogues repeatedly faced questions of gender equity in liturgy, authority, and theology. In 1972 Reform Judaism ordained its first female rabbi, with Conservative Judaism following suit a decade later. In 1976 the Episcopal Church moved to allow the ordination of women, which precipitated considerable controversy and a small schism. By 1989 the Episcopalians had ordained their first female bishop, Barbara C. Harris. Populist and pietist bodies, like many of the Pentecostal and Holiness denominations, had long supported a female ministry, as had the Quakers. But a movement toward more self-consciously conservative theology among pietists, Baptists, and other evangelical and fundamentalist bodies meant that by 2000 there were fewer opportunities for female public ministry in these groups than forty years before. Among Roman Catholics, precipitate decline in the number of women religious paralleled more vocal women's support for ordination. The

Vatican's consistent refusal to consider female ordination has not stopped agitation for that goal among some Roman Catholics. Yet in all but the activities requiring ordination, Catholic women took on many new responsibilities over the last quarter of the century. In the 1990s and the first years of the new century, concern for the integrity of the priesthood overshadowed the ongoing debate over the public service of Catholic women in the church. Among Catholics, as also almost all other major religious traditions, the closing years of the twentieth century saw an increase also in organization and activity among self-consciously conservative women. These movements represent the *yin* to strongly feminist *yang*, and together they have bestowed more diversity on American religious faith and practice.

Litigation/Division

Prior to World War II, the United States Supreme Court heard very few cases relating to the separation of church and state, or to religion in general. Since the War, however, the Court has found itself constantly enmeshed in often delicate efforts to protect the two sides of the First Amendment's key statement: "Congress shall make no law respecting an establishment of religion, or prohibiting the free exercise thereof." The nation's new religious pluralism was responsible for much of the litigation, since new religious movements and new variations of old movements both could easily push against the unstated, but legally questionable, way that things had always been done. By utilizing the Fourteenth Amendment, which guaranteed national protections for residents of the states, to apply the religious clauses of the First Amendment to all fifty states (and not just to the Federal Congress), the Court multiplied its workload and magnified the nation's problems in the contested arena of church-state relations.

The domain of education proved notably troublesome, as the cases bumbled over each other in rapid succession. In public schools, the issues concerned what could be taught, read, sung, or prayed; in private schools, the issues related chiefly to whether public monies could be applied, directly or indirectly, to salaries, buildings, vocational counseling, academic testing, transport, or special education. Modern litigation commenced with a famous case from New Jersey in 1947, *Everson v. Board of Education*, where the court decided by a 5-4 vote to uphold the right of a school board to reimburse students in religious schools for their transportation. But this decision also spelled out a broad meaning for what it meant for the government to "establish" religion and so legitimated challenges to many traditional statutes and actions that litigants perceived as establishing religion. The next year in *McCollum v. Board of Education*, the court began the modern era for public schools by ruling that when the Champaign, Illinois, school system allowed for voluntary released time reli-

gious instruction of its students, it acted illegally by moving toward the establishment of religion. Through the 1950s and 1960s, strenuous tests for "establishment" continued to dominate Supreme Court decisions, but by the 1990s
concern for the "free exercise" of religion had made a comeback. The result was
that in the first years of the new century, a fair bit of confusion prevailed in how
the courts should, or would, adjudicate the delicate task of insuring government neutrality, but also full protection, for an intensely, but also divisively religious nation.

Disagreements in court, however, have been only one part of a contentious period for the religious traditions, and also within the body politic at
large. In recent decades, the most passionate and deeply divisive social issues
have concerned matters of life and death: faith healing, mercy killing, capital
punishment, fetal research, genetic engineering, contraception, and — above
all — abortion. Two very public documents helped to focus and to fire the public controversy: a papal encyclical, *Humanae Vitae,* in 1968, and a Supreme
Court decision, *Roe v. Wade,* in 1973. On the subject especially of abortion,
nearly everyone had an opinion, and nearly every opinion has been held with
tenacity and unshakable conviction. Those with the strongest opinions have
taken to the streets, the courts, and sometimes the jails. Beginning in the late
1980s, church groups have also debated their stance toward homosexual practice, as well as the ordination of homosexuals, almost as vociferously as they engaged the issue of abortion. Especially for the mainline Protestant denominations, contention over a range of issues concerning homosexuality has
guaranteed that national meetings, scheduled at whatever interval, have been
sure to generate a great deal of heat.

Religion and the Public Order

In the United States, civil and ecclesiastical realms are legally separate. In the actual life of the people, however, spiritual and political values, as well as religious
and political rhetoric, are deeply entangled. That entangling has featured large
in each of the presidential elections since 1976 (Carter vs. Ford), with the volume and breadth of political religion seeming to grow with every four-year cycle. In the 1980s Ronald Reagan became the champion of what was then known
as the New Religious Right. In the 1990s, the Religious Right briefly took shape
as "The Christian Coalition," a creation of television evangelist Pat Robertson.
By the year 2000, formal organizations joining conservative religion and conservative politics had faded in significance, but the link between theological
conservatives and the Republican Party was stronger than ever. By that time as
well, an even stronger link had been forged between church-going African
Americans and the Democratic Party. Historically considered, a political land-

scape into which religion exerted a visible presence resembled earlier phases in the national past, like the decades before the Civil War, more than they resembled the Depression (1930s), World War II (1940s), and the Cold War (1950s-80s), when religion worked more in the political background. One result of the new situation was not just more religious rhetoric in politics, but better religious reasoning, with voices from both the Left and the Right being forced to clearer articulation of why religious convictions should influence public policy, or why they should not. Another result was ever clearer indication that, when it came to voting for president (as well as many other offices), religious adherence (or its absence) had become just about the most reliable predictor of electoral behavior.

In this new religiously charged climate, the religious professions of the nation's presidents received closer scrutiny, and they were also pressed to use more explicitly religious language than had been customary in the twentieth century before the 1970s. For some presidents, this deployment of religious language came easier than for others. But from the election of 1976, when Jimmy Carter's profession to having been "born again" galvanized the media, it became customary for the nation's leaders, and would-be leaders, to speak more frankly about their personal religious faith than was customary anywhere else in the western world.

Traumatic public events have always in American history stimulated public and private prayer, religious reflection, and a more intense consideration of the ways of providence. It was no different after September 11, 2001, when four jet planes were commandeered by Muslim extremists and turned into guided missiles that destroyed the World Trade Towers in New York City and badly damaged the Pentagon in Washington, D.C. (with the fourth plane crashing into the Pennsylvania countryside when passengers fought back in an attempt to take control of the plane from the hi-jackers). Fervent religious speech poured from the nation's pulpits, and it informed many public events. Controversy, of course, followed in the wake of these religious observances as well, but the stark realities of death and life seemed to moderate at least some scruples about the separation of church and state.

Into the New Millennium

For the ongoing practices of religion, it meant little if the United States entered a new millennium in 2000 (or 2001 to the chronologically fastidious). New organizations, some of which flourished spectacularly, joined with the old to guide the religious practices of the people. Thoughtful reflection on tested and true institutions, like the black church, was just as pertinent in the first years of the new millennium/century/decade as it had ever been. Likewise, since much ancient religious wisdom consists in knowing when and where to draw the lines that define appropriate belief and practice, it is not surprising that in the new century, efforts went forward to say when enough was enough. For groups as diverse as Orthodox Jewish students at Yale University or the Lakota Indian nation, efforts at drawing boundary lines revealed much about the surrounding culture as well as the religious groups themselves.

The turn of the millennium was an enthralling news item itself, especially because it was not entirely certain that computers programmed to tabulate years by only the last two relevant digits (i.e., 98 for 1998) would behave themselves when the last two digits turned over to 00. Due to adequate foresight and a lot of money spent on re-jigging the computers, the dreaded Y2K (= "year 2000") problem was a bust. What was not a bust, however, was fascination with the End of Time that was sparked by the end of the millennium. In that fascina-

Bill Clinton bows in prayer shortly before being
sworn in as president, January 20, 1993
(Religion News Service)

tion, prophetic-minded evangelical Christians took the lead, but they were far from alone in thinking that the year 2000 bore a significance for religion as well as for the software industry.

For the Roman Catholic Church, the last years of the former century and the first years of the new were traumatic because of a burgeoning scandal involving priests who had preyed sexually on parishioners, usually young and often male. The sex scandal was bad in itself, though hardly unique to Catholics. Compounding this trauma, however, was a church bureaucracy that reacted very slowly and defensively to the need for priestly discipline and reform. When a simmering crisis exploded into a first-order national scandal during the early 2000s, distraught parishioners, angry outsiders, and the long-silent abused sought answers — in the courts, from the American hierarchy, from the Vatican . . . and from God.

Into the New Century theological reflection went on as it had for centuries and would no doubt continue through uncharted times to come. In America, always a country on the move, religiously as in every other sphere of life, some of the most interesting theological reflection was coming from those who had experienced the most movement. Representatives of such ones, whose statements bring this collection of documents to a close, are the Church of Jesus Christ of Latter-day Saints (the Mormons) and Virgilio Elizondo, one of the most creative of contemporary Hispanic religious thinkers. In the early 1820s there were no Mormons, in the early twenty-first century there are millions at home and abroad. In 1950 there were no nationally recognized Hispanic theologians in the Roman Catholic church; fifty years later there was a multitude. Even the things of the Spirit were changing fast.

1. Pluralism Plus

The Far East and the Near East in America

Buddhism

We have already noted how a somewhat insular nation first heard directly from adherents of other great religions at the World's Parliament of Religions in 1893 (see above, pp. 71-78). Many decades had to pass, however, before such religions as Buddhism and Islam came to be seen as something more substantial than a topic for academic discussion, something more enduring than a passing wave of immigration. Buddhism came in many forms, two of the most visible being from Japan: Zen — monastic, austere, disciplined, and paradoxical; and Jodo Shinshu (or Pure Land) — of the world, accessible, relying on faith more than practice, on experience more than puzzle. (1) The Hsi Lai Temple, located in Hacienda Heights, a suburb of Los Angeles, is the largest Buddhist temple in the western hemisphere. The $30 million complex spans fifteen acres and was completed in 1988. The temple claims 20,000 members and promotes a blend of Buddhist teachings. In addition to a monastery, Hsi Lai operates a university, broadcasts television programs, holds conferences, and facilitates community service projects. The following document comes from the temple's official literature and explains their motivations and goals. (2) For some Americans, especially since the 1960s, Buddhism has offered a means to social activism not found in other major world reli-

---

[Sources: (1) "Hsi Lai Temple, Buddhism Coming to the West (1997)," in Thomas A. Tweed and Stephen Prothero, eds., *Asian Religions in America: A Documentary History* (New York: Oxford, 1999), pp. 331-334. (2) "Bernard Glassman and Rick Fields, 'Recipes for Social Change' (1996)," in Tweed and Prothero, *Asian Religions in America*, pp. 285-288.]

gions. One such example is Bernard Glassman, an ordained Soto Zen priest. Born into a Jewish family in Brooklyn in 1939, Glassman studied at the Zen Center of Los Angeles, then ran the center before founding the Zen Center of New York (ZCNY) in 1979. He opened the Greyston Bakery, which has served as the ZCNY's primary source of income. A serious part of Glassman's work has been an outreach to New York's homeless population, through the Greyston Family Inn. In the following document, Glassman articulates the relationship between Buddhism and food preparation.

1. Buddhism Teaching Coming to the West for the Benefits of All

Hsi Lai Temple, the largest international monastery in the West, was founded by Ven. Master Hsing Yun, the founder of Fo Kuang Shan. Taking ten years of planning and untiring efforts to complete, Hsi Lai Temple follows the architectural design of a traditional Chinese monastery to facilitate the Dharma propagation. Since its inauguration in 1988, monastics and lay devotees have worked jointly to achieve goals in community services, education, charity, and international cultural exchange, etc. The temple has not only been functional in benefiting society, it has also built the bridge between the cultures of the East and the West.

Caring for the World

As a guide to future developments, Ven. Master Hsing Yun offers the following four points:

1. There will be Dharma functions and chanting sessions conducted in English. Translation will be provided at all meetings to facilitate English speaking enthusiasts.
2. To respect groups of all ethnic backgrounds, Hsi Lai Temple will hold various international activities and strive to be the "United Nation for Buddhism."
3. Emphasis will be placed on translating sutras and Dharma lectures. In addition to an expansion in television and radio broadcasting, an audiovisual library will be planned.
4. With the joint efforts of monastics and devotees to spread the Dharma, let the seeds of Buddhism grow, blossom, and bear fruits in the West.

It is the wish of every Fo Kuang Buddhist to "let the Buddha's light shine and the Dharma water forever flow." With everyone's support, let us strive forward.

"Walking meditation" *(kinhin)* of Zen Buddhists in Los Angeles
(Zen Center of Los Angeles)

Charity

According to the sutra, we should "teach generosity to the Poor, give medicine to the sick, protect those who are vulnerable, provide shelter to the homeless, and help those who are without help." Hsi Lai Temple follows the Buddha's compassionate spirit in delivering our concerns to different comers of our society. Besides the annual winter relief programs for the needy, we actively reach out and comfort those in illness or difficulty. In 1996, we have expanded our efforts of delivering "caring kits" and food coupons to the poor and distributing food and necessities to the homeless. We have frequently visited senior citizens in convalescent homes, and provided spiritual guidance to abused children. We have organized community blood pressure screening and "Bone Marrow Drive." We have provided comfort for the dying and terminally ill. We visit the sick and donate emergency relief funds. There are over thousands of such events — all in accordance with the Buddha's spirit of "compassion and loving kindness regardless of karmic bond." Hsi Lai Temple aspires to bring warmth to all sentient beings through the material goods and spiritual encouragement.

2. Who Are You Cooking For?

It's very important to remember that we have to take care of our own life. We have to cook for ourselves before we can really invite guests to join us for dinner. We have to nourish ourselves first.

A sick cook won't make a good meal, and a hungry cook won't wait for the meal to be served. If we don't begin by befriending ourselves, our meal will not taste right, no matter how hard we work, or how many ingredients we have, or how fancy our equipment is.

When we learn how to cook for ourselves, though, we find that our vision or understanding of the self grows and expands. The smell of food cooking and the warmth of the kitchen always invites people in. Even though it may seem as if we're cooking for ourselves, we're always cooking for everybody at the same time. This is because we are all interconnected. We are actually one body.

I sometimes use the analogy of one person with two hands. One hand is Sam, the left. The other is Bill, the right. Each has its own identity. When money arrives in the mail and Sam reaches for it, Bill gets a little jealous. When Bill burns himself on a hot stove, Sam thinks, "I should help him, but if I put the wrong kind of medicine on his hand maybe I'll get sued."

Eventually, they find that they have to work together to get anything done. Sam needs Bill to lift a heavy package, or drive a car, or even to open a can of soup. In this way, they discover that they are a part of one body. They are one interdependent world. There is no more separation. When money comes, a

Above, Higashi Hongwanji
Buddhist Temple in Los
Angeles, one of fifty-one
temples affiliated with
the Buddhist Churches
of America

Right, interior of the Higashi
Hongwanji Buddhist Temple
in Los Angeles

(Photos by Virginia Gaustad)

hand reaches out, and it doesn't matter whether it's left or right. If a hand gets burned, there's no thinking about what to do, the other just automatically helps.

Of course, I don't say, "I have two hands." It's so obvious that I don't even say, "These are my hands." They're just a part of me. I see you and me as separate until I realize that we are both part of one interconnected world as well. Eventually, all there is is one whole universe unfolding, and everything is taking care of everything else.

Self and Other

So the Zen cook cooks for others because he or she sees that the separation between self and other is illusory. This is actually very different from feeding others to help "them" or to do good.

My own interest in feeding others — in what people call social action — has a lot do with what I can learn from people I seem to be helping. By becoming one with them by seeing the world as much as I can through their eyes, I learn what their needs are. At the same time, I broaden and expand my own view of life.

. . . When we decided to build housing for the homeless, we wanted to help folks get off welfare. But when we went out to the welfare motels and talked to people, we found that most people wanted jobs but needed child care first. Working together, we came up with a comprehensive model for the Greyston Family Inn, which included housing, child care, counseling and job training.

The Complete Meal

Most people could see that only a holistic, totally integrated approach could break the cycle of homelessness and poverty. We had to include all the elements and ingredients of a good meal. The biggest and most immediate problem, of course, was to provide some kind of stability, which for the homeless meant permanent housing. In order to do this we formed an entirely independent corporation with its own board of directors called Greyston Family Inn. Calling on some of the wealthy and influential people we met in Westchester, we began to work our way through the maze of red tape and bureaucracies until we finally obtained a grant from the New York State Housing Assistance Program to buy and renovate a deserted building a few blocks from the bakery, at 68 Warburton Avenue.

. . . So we formed a construction company, headed by minority managers and supervisors, that offered on-the-job training to unemployed and homeless people. Then we went to work, completely gutting and reconstructing the building. In this way, the money stayed in the community, and the homeless were involved from the very beginning in building their own homes as well as learning a trade. Finally, in October, two years after we had begun the process, the first eighteen families moved into their own building.

Once the building was complete, we began to add the other ingredients according to plan. Because the homeless were mainly single-parent families, we added a child care center. Because none of the parents had jobs, we added job training as well. We started a tenant's organization, encouraging people to take more and more control of running the building.

. . . So far the results of the program have far exceeded our expectations. One tenant had a job when people began to move into the building — he lost it almost immediately, partly due to the pressures of being reunited with his wife and kids. But within five months, eleven out of twenty-five adults in the building were working. Four were employed as child-care aides in the building, and some were planning to get further training to become assistant teachers and then teachers. One person was working in the bakery, another as the superintendent of the building. And the rest had jobs outside. Six were completing high school equivalency courses. One was studying radiology in college, and three completed a beginning word processing course taught by Greyston Family Inn and were enrolled in a more advanced course in a local education center.

But the greatest change is the change from despair to hopefulness. As one tenant says, "Besides everything else — besides the apartment, child care, and job help — the one thing Greyston offers is encouragement. After you're homeless for a while, once you feel you're alone, it takes its toll on your self-esteem. You look at yourself the same way the public looks at someone who's homeless: as someone who can offer the community nothing."

Islam

Islam came from many nations: Indonesia, Pakistan, Turkey, Iran, Iraq, Egypt, Morocco, Tunisia, Syria, Kuwait, Yemen, and more. The task for Muslim leaders in America was to create an American Islamic community

[Sources: (1) "Religious Accommodations Task Force," *MSA Link,* Spring 2003, 3, http://www.msa-national.org/publications/msalink/Link_Mar03.pdf (27 May 2003). (2) Muqtedar Khan, "A Memo to American Muslims," http://www.islamfortoday.com/khan01.htm (27 May 2003). (3) "We're All Americans . . . But, Which One of Us Is a Muslim?" *Islam in America* Council on American-Islamic Relations Advertisement Series 1 (2003), http://www.americanmuslims.info/ads/0216.pdf (27 May 2003).]

and, especially from the 1990s, to make the American public as a whole more aware about the nature of Islam in the U.S. Efforts to that end increased noticeably after the September 11, 2001 attacks in New York City and Washington, D.C. But even these were more than reactionary efforts since the several million Muslims now in America had long contended that they should be treated as a significant, but misunderstood, segment of the national population. The following documents illustrate these sentiments. (1) The first is a call to action from the Muslim Student Association, the largest Islamic student organization in the country, that appeals to Muslim college students to work for stronger religious accommodation on their campuses. (2) The second represents the views of Muqtedar Khan, Director of International Studies at Adrian College, Michigan, for whom the attacks of September 11, 2001, offered an opportunity to unite strongly pro-American and strongly pro-Muslim opinions. (3) The third comes from an advertisement placed by the Council on American Islamic Relations as part of a year-long campaign in the New York Times.

1. Religious Accommodations Task Force (RAFT)

As college students, on a typical day we pray, eat, sleep and study. Each of these activities can become a trying experience for Muslim students struggling to adhere to the basics of Islam. Where will I pray? What will I eat? Can I sleep in an Islamic setting? Will I be able to take a class on Islam or Arabic?

Over the years, MSAs [Muslim Student Associations] nationwide have worked to help ease these daily struggles for Muslim students at their respective campuses. The Prophet (pbuh) said, ". . . he who finds relief for one who is hard pressed, Allah would make things easy for him in the Hereafter." (Sahih Muslim Book 035, Number 6518). We pray that the leaders of these initiatives will be rewarded with ease in Hereafter. Amen.

The RATF [Religious Accommodations Task Force] of MSA National seeks to research and document religious accommodation successes, compare techniques, and share experiences with those embarking on the diplomatic journey with the university administration. In the past semester, the RATF has provided resources and consultation to over ten schools attempting to establish prayer rooms, a few schools exploring Zabiha food options, and other schools responding to bigoted programs or remarks on campus. Of these schools, we are pleased to announce that Ohio State University, University of Missouri–Kansas City (UMKC), and Cal State Dominguez Hills have recently opened prayer rooms for Muslim students. Additionally, at the MSA Northeast Conference in November, RATF distributed the 2002-2003 Survey of Religious Accommodations.

Right, Muslims gather for the Friday congregational prayer at the Islamic Center of Southern California.

Below, the Islamic Center in Los Angeles serves as host for instructional activities, social events, as well as worship and prayer.

(Photos by Virginia Gaustad)

What does YOUR school have?

For religious accommodations, knowing of similar programs at other schools continues to be a compelling argument. To help ease the struggles of Muslim students nationwide, let us know of existing programs at yours. Look out for the RATF Survey at an MSA Conference near you!

2.

In the name of Allah, the most Benevolent and the Most Merciful. May this memo find you in the shade of Islam enjoying the mercy, the protection and the grace of Allah.

I am writing this memo to you all with the explicit purpose of inviting you to lead the American Muslim community in soul searching, reflection and reassessment.

What happened on September 11th in New York and Washington DC will forever remain a horrible scar on the history of Islam and humanity. No matter how much we condemn it, and point to the Quran and the Sunnah to argue that Islam forbids the killing of innocent people, the fact remains that the perpetrators of this crime against humanity have indicated that their actions are sanctioned by Islamic values.

The fact that even now several Muslim scholars and thousands of Muslims defend the accused is indicative that not all Muslims believe that the attacks are unIslamic. This is truly sad.

Even if it were true that Israel and the US are enemies of the Muslim World, [I] wonder what is preventing them from unleashing their nuclear arsenal against Muslims; a response that mercilessly murders thousands of innocent people, including hundreds of Muslims is absolutely indefensible. If anywhere in your hearts there is any sympathy or understanding with those who committed this act, I invite you to ask yourself this question, would Muhammad (pbuh) sanction such an act?

While encouraging Muslims to struggle against injustice (Al Quran 4:135), Allah also imposes strict rules of engagement. He says in unequivocal terms that to kill an innocent being is like killing entire humanity (Al Quran 5:32). He also encourages Muslims to forgive Jews and Christians if they have committed injustices against us (Al Quran 2:109, 3:159, 5:85).

Muslims, including American Muslims have been practicing hypocrisy on a grand scale. They protest against the discriminatory practices of Israel but are silent against the discriminatory practices in Muslim states. In the Gulf one can see how laws and even salaries are based on ethnic origin. This is racism, but we never hear of Muslims protesting against them at International fora.

The Israeli occupation of Palestine is perhaps central to Muslim griev-
ance against the West. While acknowledging that, I must remind you that Israel
treats its one million Arab citizens with greater respect and dignity than most
Arab nations treat their citizens. Today Palestinian refugees can settle and become citizens of the United States but in spite of all the tall rhetoric of the Arab
world and Quranic injunctions (24:22) no Muslim country except Jordan extends this support to them.

While we loudly and consistently condemn Israel for its ill treatment of
Palestinians we are silent when Muslim regimes abuse the rights of Muslims
and slaughter thousands of them. Remember Saddam and his use of chemical
weapons against Muslims (Kurds)? Remember Pakistani army's excesses
against Muslims (Bengalis)? Remember the Mujahideen of Afghanistan and
their mutual slaughter? Have we ever condemned them for their excesses? Have
we demanded international intervention or retribution against them? Do you
know how the Saudis treat their minority Shias? Have we protested the violation of their rights? But we all are eager to condemn Israel; not because we care
for rights and lives of the Palestinians, we don't. We condemn Israel because we
hate "them".

Muslims love to live in the US but also love to hate it. Many openly claim
that the US is a terrorist state but they continue to live in it. Their decision to
live here is testimony that they would rather live here than anywhere else. As
an Indian Muslim, I know for sure that nowhere on earth, including India, will
I get the same sense of dignity and respect that I have received in the US. No
Muslim country will treat me as well as the US has. If what happened on September 11th had happened in India, the biggest democracy, thousands of Muslims would have been slaughtered in riots on mere suspicion and there would
be another slaughter after confirmation. But in the US, bigotry and xenopho-
bia has been kept in check by media and leaders. In many places hundreds of
Americans have gathered around Islamic centers in symbolic gestures of protection and embrace of American Muslims. In many cities Christian congregations have started wearing hijab to identify with fellow Muslim women. In patience and in tolerance ordinary Americans have demonstrated their
extraordinary virtues.

It is time that we acknowledge that the freedoms we enjoy in the US are
more desirable to us than superficial solidarity with the Muslim World. If you
disagree then prove it by packing your bags and going to whichever Muslim
country you identify with. If you do not leave and do not acknowledge that
you would rather live here than anywhere else, know that you are being hypocritical.

It is time that we faced these hypocritical practices and struggled to transcend them. It is time that American Muslim leaders fought to purify their own
lot.

3.

WE'RE ALL AMERICANS...

BUT, WHICH ONE OF US IS A MUSLIM?

We all are...we're American Muslims. It's impossible to make general assumptions about Muslims because we represent more than one billion people from a vast range of races, nationalities and cultures – from the South Pacific to the Horn of Africa. Only about 18 percent of Muslims live in the Arabic-speaking world. The largest Muslim community is in Indonesia. Substantial parts of Asia and most of Africa have Muslim majority populations, while significant minorities are to be found in the countries of the former Soviet Union, China, North and South America, and Europe.

American Muslims are an equally diverse group of people. We're immigrants from across the globe who came here seeking freedom and opportunity. We're the children of immigrant parents, and descendants of Africans who have called America home for generations. We're converts of varied nationalities and ethnic backgrounds. We're doctors, lawyers, teachers, politicians, civil rights activists, mothers, fathers, students... making our homes and raising our families in communities across America.

What we all have in common is a shared faith and a shared commitment to our nation's safety and prosperity. We're Americans and we're Muslims.

WE'RE AMERICAN MUSLIMS

Number one of fifty-two in the *Islam in America* series.
To learn more about the series, visit www.americanmuslims.info

COUNCIL ON AMERICAN-ISLAMIC RELATIONS

Fatal Movements

Jonestown

Much of American religion in the 1960s and 1970s seemed to be akin to the child's game of "follow the leader." The largest advertisements on the religion pages of major metropolitan dailies testified to the prowess and salesmanship of the preacher-performer, the pied piper of new life-styles, the announcer of millenniums to come, or the midwife of millenniums at hand. Denominations and recognizable institutional affiliations counted for little. In no sense typical of such cults but, on the contrary, atypical in its abnormality and tragedy, the group led by the Reverend James Warren (Jim) Jones (1931-78) shocked the sensibilities of the nation. On November 18, 1978, in far-off Guyana over nine hundred followers of Jones joined him in mass suicide. Jones, from a midwestern and Disciples of Christ background, emerged in California as a messiah to the poor and oppressed, to the empty and confused, to those searching for authority and assurance. As the object of unquestioning trust Jones came to see himself as worthy of such trust, as more than the announcer of divine things but as the very embodiment of the divine. His faithful followed him from northern rural California to San Francisco, and from there to the steamy jungles of Guyana where a Marxist-Christian utopia was to arise from the earth. The darkest side of that grim tragedy was the number of children and young people led to their doom. Two documents follw: (1) a petition to Jim Jones from distraught parents who, months before the tragedy in November, tried to open up lines of communication with their children, and (2) a grim assessment after that dark day by an author who lost her two sisters, Carolyn and Ann, in the disaster; although her book is called In Defense of People's Temple, *Rebecca Moore (b. 1951) retains few illusions.*

1.

We, the undersigned, are the grief-stricken parents and relatives of the hereinafter-designated persons you arranged to be transported to Guyana, South America, at a jungle encampment you call "Jonestown." We are advised

---

[Sources: (1) Kenneth Wooden, *The Children of Jonestown* (New York: McGraw Hill Book Co., 1981), pp. 210-12, 213-14. (2) Rebecca Moore, *In Defense of People's Temple — And Other Essays* (Lewiston, NY: Edwin Mellen Press, 1988), pp. 131-32.]

there are no telephones or exit roads from Jonestown, and that you now have more than 1,000 U.S. citizens living with you there.

We have allowed nine months to pass since you left the United States in June 1977. Although certain of us knew it would do no good to wait before making a group protest, others of us were willing to wait to see whether you would in fact respect the fundamental freedoms and dignity of our children and family members in Jonestown. Sadly, your conduct over the past year has shown such a flagrant and cruel disregard for human rights that we have no choice as responsible people but to make this public accusation and to demand the immediate elimination of these outrageous abuses.

Summary of Violations

We hereby accuse you, Jim Jones, of the following acts violating the human rights of our family members:

1. Making the following threat calculated to cause alarm for the lives of our relatives: "I can say without hesitation that we are devoted to a decision that it is better even to die than to be constantly harassed from one continent to the next."
2. Employing physical intimidation and psychological coercion as part of a mind-programming campaign aimed at destroying family ties, discrediting belief in God, and causing contempt for the United States of America.
3. Prohibiting our relatives from leaving Guyana by confiscating their passports and money and by stationing guards around Jonestown to prevent anyone escaping.
4. Depriving them of their right to privacy, free speech, and freedom of association by:
   a. Prohibiting telephone calls;
   b. Prohibiting individual contacts with "outsiders";
   c. Censoring all incoming and outgoing mail;
   d. Extorting silence from relatives in the U.S. by threats to stop all communication;
   e. Preventing our children from seeing us when we travel to Guyana.

The "1,000 U.S. citizens" you claim to have brought to Guyana include our beloved relatives who are "devoted to a decision that it is better to die." We frankly do not know if you have become so corrupted by power that you would actually allow a collective "decision" to die, or whether your letter is simply a bluff designed to deter investigations into your practices. . . .

We hereby give you the opportunity now to publicly repudiate our inter-

People's Temple leader, Jim Jones, in Georgetown, Guyana, 1978
(Religion News Service)

pretation of your threat. If you refuse to deny the apparent meaning of your letter, we demand that you immediately answer the following questions:

1. When you refer to "a decision that it is better even to die than to be constantly harassed," has this "decision" already been made or is it to be made in the future? If made, when and where? Were our relatives consulted? Did anybody dissent? By what moral or legal justification could you possibly make such a decision on behalf of minor children?
2. When you say you are "devoted" to this decision, does it mean it is irreversible? If irreversible, at what point will the alleged "harassment" have gotten so great as to make death "better"? Would it be an International Human Rights Commission investigation, or an on-premise investigation of your operations by the U.S. Government? Who besides you will decide when that point "to die" is reached?

We know your psychological coercion of the residents of Jonestown to be so "totalitarian" that nobody there, including adults, could possibly make such a decision to die freely and voluntarily. The evidence is that our relatives are in fact hostages, and we hereby serve notice that should any harm befall them, we will hold you and People's Temple church responsible and will employ every legal and diplomatic resource to bring you to justice.

2.

The people in Jonestown had consciences, and knew the difference between right and wrong. In fact, it was their sensitivity to injustice, their anger over privilege and wealth that perverted their good impulses. Their rage turned inward, to self-destruction.

They accepted, little by little, the withdrawal of small freedoms, the use of deception, the madness of Jim Jones. It happened over a period of twenty-five years, not overnight. It's much easier to handle one lie at a time, than a number of lies all at once. This is what happened to the individuals in People's Temple. Their freedom and their judgment eroded a piece at a time. With the conviction of the justice of their cause, the members lost detachment and perspective. They lost their ability to poke fun at themselves, to laugh at their leaders. This is how evil flourishes. Not by deciding to live with a horror, but by accepting small atrocities bit by bit.

It's far easier to dismiss Temple members as a bunch of crazy cultists. "It makes the night less frightening," *Newsweek* columnist Meg Greenfield wrote, "if we can attribute grotesque behavior to ordinary, manageable causes." By distancing ourselves from the people in Jonestown, we forget the fact that, contrary to popular opinion, we are very much like them. When we ignore this, we run the risk of making their mistakes. The irony of history is that People's Temple prominently displayed a quotation by historian George Santayana: "Those who do not remember the past are condemned to repeat it." The handpainted wooden sign formed the backdrop of many press photographs of the bodies.

As we look back, we ask ourselves what we could have done differently. My aunt asked us if we would have kidnapped Carolyn and Annie. Barbara [the mother] says yes, we would have done anything. "If we'd known of the potential suicide," John [the father] wrote me, "we would have done something, probably have returned to Jonestown." John doubts he would have tried kidnapping; however, "my hope was that, in time, the movement and they would change, as movements always change."

But kidnapping, like deprogramming and brainwashing, negates the concept of free will, and refutes the notion that individuals must take responsibility for their actions and their lives. People in Jonestown accepted evil, as they performed good. Perhaps it didn't seem evil to them. They had already made so many compromises, one more didn't matter.

I've talked to many who believe that people mindlessly obeyed Jim Jones, like robots programmed to till the soil, cultivate the gardens and the farms. But robots don't draw pictures. They don't make dolls or plant flowers along the walkways. They don't paint signs or put posters on the walls. They don't argue in community meetings or dance to an electric organ.

No one overturned the vat of poison. Even though it was soon apparent that this was not a rehearsal and that death lay directly ahead, no one rebelled enough to stop it. They had personal responsibility and they chose to die. They were decent people, and they killed themselves and each other.

That's the tragedy of Jonestown. And perhaps its lesson. Decent people do wrong, they do evil, even as they rationalize and explain it. And sometimes their arguments even make sense.

Branch Davidians

In 1990, David Koresh became leader of the Branch Davidians, an apocalyptic sect with origins from the 1930s in the Seventh-Day Adventists. Claiming to be a prophet and angel of God, Koresh based his message heavily on prophetic imagery from the Bible. Among Koresh's claims was the assertion that the end of the world would begin when the U.S. Army attacked the Branch Davidian compound in Waco, Texas. Following Koresh's guidance, the Branch Davidians began amassing firearms, ammunition, and food to prepare for conflict. On February 28, 1993, agents of the Bureau of Alcohol, Tobacco and Firearms (ATF) tried to arrest Koresh on charges of illegal possession of firearms. Gunfire erupted, and while no one is certain who fired first, four ATF agents were killed, 16 were wounded, and an undetermined number of Davidians were killed and wounded. The FBI assumed control of the situation and a standoff between government forces and the Davidians followed for the next 51 days. On April 19, the FBI launched teargas into the compound and the Davidians fired back. Fires, which the FBI claimed the Davidians started, engulfed the compound and by the end of the day 76 Davidians, including David Koresh and more than twenty children, were dead. Not only was this one of the most important news items of the 1990s, but it was also a significant instance of the public examination of religious language. Throughout the standoff, the Davidians used religious terms to explain their aims and purposes, which, however, often left federal negotiators perplexed, or uninterested. In the following assessment, Nancy T. Am-

---

[Source: Nancy T. Ammerman, "Lessons from Waco" (American Sociological Association), *Footnotes* 22:1 (1994): 3.]

merman, a sociologist of religion, reflects on the tragedy. Ammerman was one of ten scholars selected by the Justice and Treasury Departments to make recommendations on how to avoid repeating the mistakes in dealing with the Branch Davidians.

Lessons from Waco

The release of Treasury and Justice Department reports on the Waco tragedy has brought that grim episode again to our minds: the failed raid, the long stand-off, the seemingly incomprehensible Bible-talk from David Koresh, the tales of strange practices inside the group, the final horrible inferno, and followers willing to go back into a burning building rather than be taken away by federal agents.

The events of those days raise many issues about how our government works, as well as many questions about what the Branch Davidians were all about. Having been part of the team of behavioral scientists asked to advise Justice and Treasury about this tragedy, the issues that have come most insistently in my mind have to do with the failure of both government and the general public to understand the nature of groups like the Davidians.

What sociologists and others who have studied religion in American society have to offer in the midst of the current debate are insights that might have led the agents in charge in Waco to act differently. These observations are not intended to absolve the Davidians of guilt, but they are offered here as an alternative way of understanding the dozens, if not hundreds, of non-mainstream religious groups that exist throughout the country.

1. We must understand the pervasiveness of religious experimentation in American history. We simply have been a very religious people. From the days of the first European settlers, there have always been new and dissident religious groups challenging the boundaries of toleration, and the First Amendment to our Constitution guarantees those groups the right to practice their faith. Only when there is clear evidence of criminal wrong-doing can authorities intervene in the free exercise of religion, and then *only with appropriately low levels of intrusiveness.*

2. We must understand that new groups almost always provoke their neighbors. By definition, new religious groups think old ways of doing things are at best obsolete, at worst evil. Their very reason for existing is to call into question the status quo. They defy conventional rules and question conventional authorities. The corollary is that they themselves are likely to perceive the outside world as hostile — and it often is. New groups frequently provoke resistance, in recent years often well-organized through the "Cult Awareness Network."

3. We should also understand that many new religious movements ask for commitments that seem abnormal to most Americans, commitments that mean the disruption of "normal" family and work lives. While it may seem disturbing to outsiders that converts live all of life under a religious authority, it is certainly not illegal (nor particularly unusual, if we look around the world and back in history). No matter how strange such commitments may seem to many, they are widely sought by millions of others.

4. We must also understand that the vast majority of those who make such commitments do so voluntarily. The notion of "cult brain-washing" has been thoroughly discredited by the academic community, and "experts" who propagate such notions in the courts have been discredited by the American Psychological Association and the American Sociological Association. While there may be real psychological needs that lead persons to seek such groups, and while their judgment may indeed by altered by their participation, neither of those facts constitutes coercion.

5. People who deal with new or marginal religious groups must understand the ability of such groups to create an alternative world. The first dictum of sociology is "Situations perceived to be real are real in their consequences." No matter how illogical or unreasonable the beliefs of a group seem to an outsider, they are the real facts that describe the world through the eyes of the insider.

6. People who deal with the leaders of such groups should understand that "charisma" is not just an individual trait, but a property of the constantly-evolving relationship between a leader and followers. So long as the leader's interpretations make sense of the group's experience, that leader is likely to be able to maintain authority. These interpretations are not a fixed text, but a living, changing body of ideas, rules, and practices. Only in subsequent generations are religious prescriptions likely to become written orthodoxies.

7. Finally, authorities who deal with high-commitment groups of any kind must realize that any group under siege is likely to turn inward, bonding to each other and to their leader even more strongly than before. Outside pressure only consolidates the group's view that outsiders are the enemy. And isolation decreases the availability of information that might counter their internal view of the world. In the Waco case, negotiating strategies were constantly undermined by the actions of the tactical teams. Pressure from encroaching tanks, psychological warfare tactics, and the like, only increased the paranoia of the group and further convinced them that the only person they could trust was Koresh.

No one can say whether a better understanding of groups like the Davidians would have changed the outcome in Waco. But decisions based on research evidence that takes human social and religious dynamics into account — something the people in charge at Waco never sought — would certainly seem preferable to decisions based on tactical necessity alone.

Neopaganism: The Circle

Neopaganism sees itself as a revival of ancient pre-Christian religion: the old nature religions of Greece and Rome, of the wandering Teutonic tribes, and of others as well. Beyond that, Neopaganism may be most helpfully identified by what it is not: neither Christian nor Judaic, neither monotheistic nor agnostic, neither Oriental nor humanist. Neopagans usually affirm a polytheistic understanding of the divine, emphasize a basis for religion in nature, center practices and traditions around individual inner spirituality, and claim historic roots dating back thousands of years. Contrary to popular belief, not all neopagans are "anti-Christian" in their teachings. Neopagan groups witnessed substantial increases in numbers and visibility during the latter part of the twentieth century. The great diversity of movements described under this catch-all phrase includes practitioners of the Wiccan tradition or "nature religion" however loosely defined. One of the more visible American neopagan communities over the last three decades has been the Wisconsin-based Circle Sanctuary. It was founded in 1974 and in 1983 purchased a 200-acre nature preserve in southeastern Wisconsin. The Circle publishes Circle Magazine, *a quarterly newspaper, as well as books, tapes, and other products. The following documents (1) detail the goals and purposes of the Circle Sanctuary and (2) describe a sacred neopagan ritual; the latter was written by Sanctuary co-director and high priestess Selena Fox.*

1.

Circle Sanctuary's Purpose and Work

- Promote dialogue, cooperation, and mutually beneficial networking among individuals, groups, and organizations of a wide range of Pagan denominations and paths through Circle Network.
- Provide Pagan individual and group contacts through publications, correspondence, and telephone.
- Publish a quarterly Pagan religious journal, Circle Network News, and other periodicals.

[Sources: (1) "Circle Sanctuary's Purpose and Work," http://www.circlesanctuary.org/aboutcircle/activities.htm (27 May 2003). (2) Selena Fox, "Circle of Goddesses," *Circle Magazine,* Spring 2002, pp. 30-31, http://www.circlesanctuary.org/circle/articles/circlecraft/CircleOfGoddesses.html (27 May 2003).]

- Maintain Circle Sanctuary land, a Pagan religious center and Nature preserve.
- Promote the creation and sharing of Pagan rituals, meditations, music, images, and other sacred art forms.
- Provide Pagan ministerial services including counseling, spiritual healing prayer circles, and psychotherapy, plus conduct worship services as well as weddings, child blessings, funerals, house blessings, and other rites of passages.
- Sponsor the international Pagan Spirit Gathering in June and other religious festivals throughout the year.
- Sponsor Pagan religious educational activities, including workshops, talks, leadership training, and youth programs.
- Publish and distribute Pagan religious books, tapes, and other resources for spiritual development and practice.
- Engage in Pagan religious freedom activist work through the Lady Liberty League.
- Promote understanding and tolerance in mainstream society regarding Paganism through public education and informational media work.
- Engage in academically sound and publishable research as well as assist professors and other researchers at colleges and universities with their Pagan studies research in a variety of disciplines, including psychology, religious studies, sociology, anthropology, archaeology, history, literature, arts, environmental science, and other fields.
- Facilitate academic collaboration and networking through coordination of the Pagan Academic Network, and sponsor the Nature Religions Scholars Network within the American Academy of Religion.
- Engage in historic preservation activities, including maintaining paleo-Indian sites.
- Engage in environmental preservation activities, including prairie restoration, songbird repopulation, wetland protection, and forest management.
- Engage in charity projects and community services, including crisis referrals and food and clothing drives for the homeless and indigent.
- Participate in interfaith dialogue and collaboration, including helping to sponsor conferences such as the Parliament of the World's Religions and serve as a consultant for Harvard's religious Pluralism Project.
- Engage in international and multicultural exchange and cooperation for greater planetary peace and wellness.

2.

Every Goddess is a facet of the Great Goddess, also known as the All-Goddess, or simply, The Goddess. Each particular Goddess form can show a way of communion and union with the Great Goddess. Each Goddess form has Her own cultural roots, symbols, qualities, forms, lore, and style. Each has Her own lessons to teach. Like threads of different colors, sizes, compositions, and textures, Goddess forms combine to weave a multi-colored tapestry that is the Great Goddess.

The ritual below incorporates work with a variety of Goddesses, as well as the All-Goddess. Since group energy is an essential component, it is not suitable as a solitary rite. The ritual works best with small groups, and between five and thirteen participants is ideal. The ritual can aid in group bonding and development, as well as in the spiritual growth of participants. It also helps the participants and the group as a whole deepen connections with the Goddess as Unity as well as in some of Her many forms.

I developed this ritual through my Circle Craft teaching and group facilitation work with women and men in the 1970s. In the 1980s, it was a regular part of the priestess training that I did through Circle Sanctuary. Over the years, I also have facilitated this ritual at various women's spirituality conferences and retreats across North America, and for Goddess spirituality groups composed of all women and those with both men and women. For grammatical convenience, I present the ritual here in its form for a women's Goddess spirituality group. However, by changing pronouns, such as her to her/him, or her to him, this transcript can be adapted for use by groups of women and men and for men's Goddess spirituality groups.

Everyone in a group that is planning to do this rite should have some previous experience with grounding, centering, and energy raising before doing it. Advance preparation specifically for this rite is also important. Each participant needs to select a suitable Goddess form with which to connect. The group needs to plan how it will do the ritual. And, if the group has not had much experience working together before, it is best to precede the Goddess alignment part of the ritual with additional group chanting, drumming/rhythm making, and/or other group attunement activities.

It is important to choose a suitable location in which to do this rite. The site can be either outside or indoors, but it must be a place where loud chanting and other ritual energy work will not disturb others or cause interference by outsiders. An excellent time to do this ritual is on the night of a Full Moon.

The Ritual

To prepare for the ritual, participants need to make their Goddess selections. Pick a Goddess whose energies and qualities you wish to connect with more fully and manifest more strongly in yourself and in your life. For example, to embody and express more compassion, work with Kuan Yin. To feel more sensuous and attractive, pick Venus, Oshun, Erzulie, or Aphrodite. To aid in creative expression and inspiration, choose Brigid, Sarasvati, or the Greek Muse appropriate to your creative work.

Before the ritual, do some research on the Goddess you have selected, even if you have already formed an alignment with Her. Read about what forms She takes and what symbols are associated with Her. Learn about Her qualities and familiarize yourself with Her legendary actions. Once you have done this, reflect on whether or not it still feels right to work with Her. If not, begin the process again until you find a suitable Goddess with which to work.

Participants should gather together at least an hour before the ritual. After exchanging social greetings, discuss plans for the ritual and make final decisions about ritual format and logistics, such as how to create sacred space, what beginning and ending chants to use, and what ritual items are needed.

When everyone is ready, go to the ritual site. Once there, stand or sit in a circle and do a silent centering meditation, while a purifying incense such as sandalwood, rosemary, cedar, mugwort, or sage is passed around. Each participant should cleanse herself with the incense as well as the area around her. When the incense has gone completely around the circle, it should be placed in the center.

The group next makes sounds together to enhance attunement of the participants with each other. This can be chanting an *Aum* together on a single note, singing a favorite All-Goddess chant, doing improvised chanting, making rhythms together with drums and rattles, or some other group music-making agreed upon in the planning session.

Once the group is attuned, it is time to dedicate the place of the rite as sacred space. The group should do this in its customary manner or in the way decided upon during planning. One common method for creating sacred space is by honoring the sacred directions.

Now, all join hands and stand in a circle facing center. Together, visualize a ring of radiant white light encircling the group. Experience this living circle of light as the Great Goddess, the All-Goddess. Sing a chant together, such as: *We are the Circle, We are the Goddess.*

Having connected with the Goddess as a whole, it is time to work with different forms of Her. Each participant in turn comes to the center of the circle and speaks the name of her Goddess and the qualities she wants activated within herself. The group responds to each one by chanting the Goddess name and the qualities in an improvised energy chant. As the group chants to her, the person in the center should call to her mind images of her selected Goddess and should feel herself merging and becoming one with the Goddess. Then, when she senses the energy has built enough, she raises her hands skyward to signal the group to peak the energy. The group releases the energy raised into her and falls silent. The person slowly moves her hands to her heart as she drinks in the energy and feels the power of the Goddess flowing throughout her whole being. When she feels complete with this integration, she steps out of the circle, and another person enters the center.

The energy chanting done for each person can take a variety of forms. The person should express her preferences to the group after she steps into the center. The Goddess name and qualities can be whispered, shouted, and/or sung. Group members can take turns chanting the Goddess name and qualities as the chant builds. The chant is enhanced when done as an affirmation, such as "You are Isis, you are strong, you are caring, you are beautiful." Speaking the person's name as part of these affirmations is especially powerful.

When everyone in the group has taken a turn in the center, it is time to focus on the All-Goddess again. The group joins hands to do a group energy dance. All take two steps inward, while still holding hands, and then several steps backward. This is repeated over and over as a Goddess chant is sung, such as *We are the Goddess, Goddess flows through Us.* When the group senses it is time to end the chant, all move inward. Instead of holding hands, each places her arms around the backs of the women by her side. This group hug formation helps the group as a whole assimilate the power of the ritual, as well as aids individual members in grounding and centering. While in this position, women speak thanks to the Goddesses they worked with, and the group as a whole gives thanks to the All-Goddess by singing a note in unison.

The group then ends the ritual in its customary or planned manner. Divine forces invoked in creating sacred space are thanked. The circle is uncast. The group departs. It is a good idea to share and consume food and juice at the end of the ritual, since this can help in grounding and the return to waking daily consciousness. Doing some form of post-ritual feasting together also can be a time to share and process experiences with other group members.

Participants should take some time out soon after the ritual is over to record their experiences in their personal journals. They also should pay close attention to their dreams and meditations in the days and weeks following this ritual, since they often are vehicles for receiving guidance from the Goddess in one or more of Her many forms.

2. Liberation/Alienation

African-Americans

Liberation Theology

The Third World, the persecuted and oppressed, the hungry and the poor, all found in theology, or at least in some theology, a message of emancipation and liberation. For many of these persons, Christianity had a new relevance, a new dynamism, even a new revolutionary power: For blacks in America, the strongest theological voice was that of James Cone (b. 1938), professor of theology at Union Theological Seminary in New York City. Cone published Black Theology and Black Power *in 1969,* A Black Theology of Liberation *in 1970, and edited (with G. S. Wilmore) an enormously valuable documentary history of* Black Theology *in 1979. In the excerpt below, Cone explains why liberation is at the heart of theology and why black theology may at present be the only theology possible in America.*

Christian theology is a theology of liberation. It is *a rational study of the being of God in the world in light of the existential situation of an oppressed community, relating the forces of liberation to the essence of the gospel, which is Jesus Christ.* This means that its sole reason for existence is to put into ordered speech the meaning of God's activity in the world, so that the community of the oppressed will recognize that their inner thrust for liberation is not only *consistent* with the gospel but *is* the gospel of Jesus Christ. There can be no Christian theology which is not identified unreservedly with those who are humiliated and abused.

[Source: J. H. Cone, *A Black Theology of Liberation* (Philadelphia: J. B. Lippincott, 1970), pp. 17-18, 22-24.]

In fact, theology ceases to be a theology of the gospel when it fails to arise out of the community of the oppressed. For it is impossible to speak of the God of Israelite history, who is the God who revealed himself in Jesus Christ, without recognizing that he is the God *of* and *for* those who labor and are heavy laden.

Unfortunately, American white theology has not been involved in the struggle for black liberation. It has been basically a theology of the white oppressor, giving religious sanction to the genocide of Indians and the enslavement of black people. From the very beginning to the present day, American white theological thought has been "patriotic," either by defining the theological task independently of black suffering (the liberal northern approach) or by defining Christianity as compatible with white racism (the conservative southern approach). In both cases theology becomes a servant of the state, and that can only mean death to black people. It is little wonder that an increasing number of black religionists are finding it difficult to be black and also to be identified with traditional theological thought forms.

The appearance of Black Theology on the American scene then is due exclusively to the failure of white religionists to relate the gospel of Jesus to the pain of being black in a white racist society. It arises from the need of black people to liberate themselves from white oppressors. Black Theology is a theology of liberation because it is a theology which arises from an identification with the oppressed blacks of America, seeking to interpret the gospel of Christ in the light of the black condition. It believes that the liberation of black people *is* God's liberation.

The task of Black Theology then is to analyze the nature of the gospel of Jesus Christ in the light of oppressed black people so they will see the gospel as inseparable from the necessary power to break the chains of oppression. This means that it is a theology of and for the black community, seeking to interpret the religious dimensions of the forces of liberation in that community.

There are two reasons why Black Theology is Christian theology and possibly the only expression of Christian theology in America. First, there can be no theology of the gospel which does not arise from an oppressed community. This is so because God in Christ has revealed himself as a God whose righteousness is inseparable from the weak and helpless in human society. The goal of Black Theology is to interpret God's activity as he is related to the oppressed black community.

Second, Black Theology is Christian theology because it centers on Jesus Christ. There can be no Christian theology which does not have Jesus Christ as its point of departure. Though Black Theology affirms the black condition as the primary datum of reality which must be reckoned with, this does not mean that it denies the absolute revelation of God in Jesus Christ. Rather it affirms it. Unlike white theology, which tends to make the Christ-event an abstract, intellectual idea, Black Theology believes that the black community itself is precisely where Christ is at work. The Christ-event in twentieth-century America is a black-event, that is, an event of liberation taking place in the black community in which black people recognize that it is incumbent upon them to throw off the chains of white oppression by whatever means they regard as suitable. This is what God's revelation means to black and white America, and why Black Theology may be the only possible theology in our time.

Muslim Theology

Black Muslims — or the Nation of Islam — represented not merely a rejection of the white man's theology but of Christianity itself. What was evident initially was not so much an embrace of worldwide Islam as it was a thrusting away of a religion that was seen as only another instrument in the hands of whites for keeping blacks suppressed, dependent, and haunted by a sense of their own inferiority. Malcolm X (1925-65) preached the Black Muslim gospel of the black's inherent and historical superiority, a truth that has been deliberately concealed from him for centuries. In 1963 and after, Malcolm X began to moderate his rhetoric and pull away from the dogmatic certainties handed down by Elijah Muhammad and other leaders in the Black Muslim movement. This moderation was seen as defection, and on February 21, 1965, Malcolm X was assassinated. That violent act robbed the United States of a major voice and a much-needed voice of reconciliation. The document below, however, comes from his earlier phase as loyal spokesman for Black Muslims and for Allah as perceived by that group.

"The true knowledge," reconstructed much more briefly than I received it, was that history had been "whitened" in the white man's history books, and that the black man had been "brainwashed for hundred of years." Original Man was black, in the continent called Africa where the human race had emerged on the planet Earth.

The black man, original man, built great empires and civilizations and cultures while the white man was still living on all fours in caves. "The devil white man," down through history, out of his devilish nature, had pillaged, murdered, raped, and exploited every race of man not white.

Human history's greatest crime was the traffic in black flesh when the devil white man went into Africa and murdered and kidnapped to bring to the West in chains, in slave ships, millions of black men, women, and children who were worked and beaten and tortured as slaves.

[Source: *The Autobiography of Malcolm X* (New York: Grove Press, 1964), pp. 163-64.]

The devil white man cut these black people off from all knowledge of their own kind, and cut them off from any knowledge of their own language, religion, and past culture, until the black man in America was the earth's only race of people who had absolutely no knowledge of his true identity.

Martin Luther King, Jr., and Malcolm X met in Washington, D.C., in 1964; the next year Malcolm X was slain, and three years later, King.
(Religion News Service)

In one generation, the black slave women in America had been raped by the slavemaster white man until there had begun to emerge a homemade, handmade, brainwashed race that was no longer even of its true color, that no longer even knew its true family names. The slavemaster forced his family name upon this rape-mixed face, which the slavemaster began to call "the Negro."

This "Negro" was taught of his native Africa that it was peopled by heathen, black savages, swinging like monkeys from trees. This "Negro" accepted this along with every other teaching of the slavemaster that was designed to make him accept and obey and worship the white man.

And where the religion of every other people on earth taught its believers of a God with whom they could identify, a God who at least looked like one of their own kind, the slavemaster injected his Christian religion into this "Negro." This "Negro" was taught to worship an alien God having the same blond hair, pale skin, and blue eyes as the slavemaster.

This religion taught the "Negro" that black was a curse. It taught him to hate everything black, including himself. It taught him that everything white was good, to be admired, respected, and loved. It brainwashed this "Negro" to think he was superior if his complexion showed more of the white pollution of the slavemaster. The white man's Christian religion further deceived and brainwashed this "Negro" to always turn the other cheek, and grin, and scrape, and bow, and be humble, and to sing, and to pray, and to take whatever was dished out by the devilish white man; and to look for his pie in the sky, and for his heaven in the hereafter, while right here on earth the slavemaster white man enjoyed *his* heaven.

Many a time, I have looked back, trying to assess, just for myself, my first reactions to all this. Every instinct of the ghetto jungle streets, every hustling fox and criminal wolf instinct in me, which would have scoffed at and rejected anything else, was struck numb. It was as though all of that life merely was back there, without any remaining effect, or influence. I remember how, some time later reading the Bible in the Norfolk Prison Colony library, I came upon, then I read, over and over, how Paul on the road to Damascus, upon hearing the voice of Christ, was so smitten that he was knocked off his horse, in a daze. I do not now, and I did not then, liken myself to Paul. But I do understand his experience.

Hispanics

Unity in Pluralism

In 1977 the second National Pastoral Hispanic Conference (Encuentro) met at Trinity College in Washington, D.C. The very fact of such a gathering (the first had been held in 1972) dramatized the growing recognition of this large and largely ignored minority within the Catholic community. But the proceedings themselves were also dramatic as the 850 delegates passed resolutions relating to human rights, education, political responsibility, and the conduct of the Church. The Cuban bishop-in-exile, Eduardo Boza Masvidal (b. 1915), spoke of what Latins had to give to North American culture and vice-versa. In seeking "unity in pluralism" the choice for Hispanics — whether north or south of the border — was not between capitalism and Marxism, but between a prophetic Church and an indifferent one.

The Second National Hispanic Pastoral Encuentro, which has called together representatives from the various Hispanic communities residing in the United States, does not seek to isolate Hispanics from the mainstream, neither does it seek to encourage mistaken ideas of nationalism. Its objective, rather, is to accomplish the opposite: to create unity in pluralism and thereby to bear witness to the marvelous plan by which God made us all brothers, members of the large human family which is subject to His universal fatherhood. However, at the same time, He has made us all different, each with our own physical and spiritual identity.

God, in His infinite wisdom, did not ordain that each of us be a "standard" type, each cut with the same mold, uniform. Rather, He willed that individuals as well as nations retain their own identity, their language, their values, their customs, their history, their qualities and also their defects, that is to say, all those aspects which constitute their own culture. Thus, even among the Hispanic nations, there exists a great deal of diversity. This diversity neither destroys, nor does it go contrary to the unity which God intended for mankind, because unity is different from uniformity. It is compatible with diversity in the same manner that each member of a family has his own personality. This in no way destroys the unity of the family. Yet no member can take upon himself the right of absorbing another so as to make of the other a replica of himself.

Great enrichment is possible whenever two cultures come together in a

[Source: E. R. Masvidal, in *Proceedings of the Segundo Encuentro Nacional Hispano de Pastoral* (Washington, D.C.: U.S. Catholic Conference, 1978), pp. 58-59.]

Mariachi band accompanies Requiem Mass for slain Franciscan father Renaldo
Rivera in front of St. Francis Cathedral, Santa Fe, New Mexico, 1982
(Photo by Peggy Gaustad)

spirit of mutual respect, each contributing some of its values. This constitutes a
healthy integration, and both benefit. However, the opposite occurs whenever
one culture absorbs the other, because then the assimilated culture has lost its
own identity and its values. It is no longer itself. It is dead. . . .

I have observed that many Cubans, with whom I am in close personal contact, though I suppose the same to occur among other nationalities, present this dilemma: What must I do: integrate myself into the mainstream or continue to feel Cuban? I believe this "either-or" premise to be false; one must do both things. We must become a part of the country in which we live, love it, feel its problems, give it our best effort. At the same time we must continue to be what we are. We must not lose our own identity.

This unity in pluralism must be lived at many different levels. It must exist, first of all, within the Church. The Church is one and the same throughout the world. Wherever we go, the bishop of that diocese becomes our pastor. We must feel that that local Church is our own. In his letter to the Ephesians, St. Paul enunciates the fundamental reasons for our unity: we all have "but one Lord, one faith, one baptism, one God and Father."

Christ's message is for all peoples, yet each people must live this message within the framework of its own culture. The Second Vatican Council points this out very clearly in its *Decree on the Church's Missionary Activity.* It states: "Particular traditions, together with the individual patrimony of each family of nations, can be illumined by the light of the Gospel and then be taken up into Catholic unity" (*Ad Gentes,* 22).

Secondly, this unity in pluralism must be visible in the Church's attitude toward the exterior world. It must be open to all the peoples of the world, to their anxieties and to their problems. In this same letter to the Ephesians, St. Paul tells us that Christ, by means of His death, tore down the wall of hatred which separated men, that He came to draw close all those who were far away from God. For this reason the Second Vatican Council begins its *Pastoral Constitution on the Church in the Modern World* with these words: "The joys and the hopes, the griefs and the anxieties of the men of this age, especially those who are poor or in any way afflicted, those too are the joys and hopes and the griefs and anxieties of the followers of Christ. Indeed nothing genuinely human fails to raise an echo in their hearts" (*Gaudium et Spes,* 1).

Today, more than ever, Christians must reject the temptation to isolate themselves in closed groups. If Christ called us to be "leaven" we have to be in the midst of all. Nevertheless, we must continue to be different, so that instead of adopting the principles and criteria of the world, we will be able to infuse it with Christian values. Our pluralism is not a confusion of ideas. It is not apathy, neither is it moral relativism. Our criteria and ideas must be very clearly delineated in our minds, even while we respect those held by others. Only in this way will our light shine before all men, so that they in turn will give glory to our Father in heaven.

We must be open to all men, but above all we must be committed to the plight of the poor and oppressed. We must follow the example of Christ, who, while loving all people, showed a preference for the weak and needy. For this reason He said: "Come unto me all you who toil and are laden." At present many of our brothers throughout Latin America and the rest of the world are forced to live in very harsh circumstances. Many are oppressed, many hungry, many unjustly imprisoned, many tortured under dictatorship both of the right and of the left, by regimes which are either Marxist or capitalist. We cannot be indifferent to any of these sorrows. For this reason an open Church is a prophetic Church which denounces evil wherever it exists. We cannot be harsh with one system or ideology and complacent of another, as unfortunately some Christians are today, because our commitment is not to a system but to Christ, to justice and to truth. It is necessary for Christians to refute the false premise which others seek to impose upon them, that one is either a capitalist or a Marxist. We are with the poor and oppressed of the world from the East and West, from North and South. We seek redemption by uniting with Christ for the salvation of the world, which begins in the heart of each man when he seeks liberation from sin. We strive to build a society in which the dignity of man as child of God is respected, as well as his God-given rights; where men are not divided by hatred or class struggle, but united by love; and where the human person will not be oppressed by the state, or by the oligarchies, but rather, we will be builders of our own destiny in a society in which liberty will not be an empty word. . . .

A Pastoral Plan

In 1987 the Roman Catholic bishops in the United States, much concerned about their long neglect of Hispanics and now concerned about the tendency of some of this number to turn away from the Church toward certain Protestant sects, promulgated a "National Pastoral Plan for Hispanic Ministry." Revised in 1989, this plan "takes into account the sociocultural reality of our Hispanic people and suggests a style of pastoral ministry and model of Church in harmony with their faith and culture." Cultural pluralism was explicitly endorsed, always understood of course to co-exist within the frame of a "fundamental unity of doctrine."

10. The historical reality of the Southwest, the proximity of countries of origin, and continuing immigration, all contribute to the maintenance of Hispanic culture and language within the United States. This cultural presence expresses itself in a variety of ways: from the immigrant who experiences "culture shock,"

[Source: *Pastoral Letters of the U.S. Catholic Bishops,* Vol. V (1983-88) (Washington, D.C.: U.S. Catholic Conference, 1989), pp. 565-66.]

to the Hispanic whose roots in the United States go back several generations and who struggles with questions of identity while often being made to feel an alien in his own country.

Despite these differences, certain cultural similarities identify Hispanics as a people. Culture primarily expresses how people live and perceive the world, one another, and God. Culture is the set of values by which a people judge, accept, and live what is considered important within the community.

Some values that make up the Hispanic culture are a "profound respect for the dignity of each *person* . . . deep and reverential love for *family life* . . . a marvelous sense of *community* . . . a loving appreciation of God's gift of *life* . . . and an authentic and consistent *devotion* to Mary. . . ."

Culture for Hispanic Catholics has become a way of living out and transmitting their faith. Many local practices of popular religiosity have become widely accepted cultural expressions. Yet the Hispanic culture, like any other, must continue to be evangelized.

11. The median age among Hispanic people is twenty-five. This plus the continuous flow of immigrants ensures a constant increase in population.

Lack of education and professional training contribute to high unemployment. Neither public nor private education has responded to the urgent needs of this young population. Only 8 percent of Hispanics graduate at the college level.

Families face a variety of problems. Twenty-five percent of the families live below the poverty level, and 28 percent are single-parent families.

Frequent mobility, poor education, a limited economic life, and racial prejudice are some of the factors that result in low participation in political activities.

As a whole, Hispanics are a religious people. Eighty-three percent consider religion important. There is an interest in knowing more about the Bible and a strong presence of popular religious practices.

Despite this, 88 percent are not active in their parishes. On the other hand, the Jehovah's Witnesses, pentecostal groups, and other sects are increasing within the Hispanic community. According to recent studies, the poor, men, and second-generation Hispanics are those who least participate in the life of the Church.

Hispanic Evangelicals

Concern among the American Roman Catholic bishops about the increasing number of Hispanics who are becoming Protestant is well-founded. For reasons spelled out in the report below, an increasing flow of first-generation Hispanic Americans have joined second- and later-generations in finding their religious home in Protestant churches. In this respect the recent history of North America matches that of Latin America, where in some regions substantial gains for Protestant churches have also been witnessed in recent years. This report appeared in the Christian Century *in 1994 under the title "Hispanics Turn Evangelical."*

Hispanic Catholics in North America are abandoning their church at the rate of 60,000 a year, according to Andrew M. Greeley, the Catholic priest, sociologist and novelist. Some remain unchurched, but many have found a place in the pews of evangelical congregations. Twenty-five years ago North America was home to fewer than 100,000 Hispanic Protestants. Today there are slightly more than 5 million. Catholicism, once the over-whelmingly dominant religious tradition among Hispanic Americans, is no longer automatically their Christian community of choice. Many observers believe that this shift signals a change laden with profound implications for U.S. culture, politics and society.

In an indication of their growing numbers and sophistication, 500 Hispanic evangelical leaders gathered in Long Beach, California, in mid-November to launch the Alliance of Evangelical Ministries, known by its Spanish acronym, AMEN. Organizers hope AMEN will streamline their unwieldy, fast-growing religious movement and give it the visibility they think it deserves. Hispanics account for almost all recent growth in evangelical churches, even in pre-dominantly black and Anglo congregations, according to AMEN President Jesse Miranda, a professor of theology at Azusa Pacific College near Los Angeles.

Hispanic Americans come to evangelical churches for a variety of reasons. Some critics say Latinos become Protestants because they have been lured away by what Pope John Paul II has called "rapacious wolves," the mostly Anglo-American evangelical missionaries in Latin America. But others say that to speak of Hispanics leaving the Catholic Church assumes that they were once really in that church. "I think most are really only cultural Catholics," says Jose Cintron, an Hispanic evangelical missionary. "They are nominal Catholics, Catholics in name only."

Given that fleeting attachment to Roman Catholic doctrine, it is no sur-

---

[Source: "Hispanics Turn Evangelical," *Christian Century,* Dec. 14, 1994, pp. 1183-84.]

prise, in Miranda's view, that many immigrants move easily into evangelical churches. "Some [recent immigrants] think Latin America is Catholic and that North America is Protestant," says Miranda. "They identify Protestantism with their new land, so they join Protestant churches."

Like most members of new religious movements, Hispanic evangelicals face serious obstacles. They are divided by theology, class, politics and national origin. Even language is a point of conflict; not all young Hispanics can or want to speak Spanish. The movement's ministers are often "long on enthusiasm but short on education," as one observer put it. The role of women has set conservatives against their liberal evangelical brethren. Also hobbling the movement's growth is widespread poverty and a *cacique* — or boss — mentality that pits church leaders against one another in the competition for status and authority.

If that isn't daunting enough, evangelicals say they also face a dominant Hispanic Catholic culture that shuns them. Alma Arias is one of those who contend that Catholic prejudice is a fact of life for America's Hispanic evangelicals. Born and raised in Guadalajara, Mexico, Arias was 14 when her father led the family from the local Catholic church into a newly established evangelical congregation. Relatives and friends were not pleased. "It was very hard at the beginning," she remembers. "It was very strange. All my friends stopped talking to me." Some former friends called her family *hermanos separados* — separated brothers. Others used less genteel descriptions. Cousins, uncles and aunts told her she had been brain-washed.

Other evangelicals argue that the tension between Hispanic evangelicals and Catholics has more to do with events in Latin America where, they say, a dominant Catholic majority, backed by the power of national governments, is working to eradicate the evangelical movement. "Working with Catholics here [in Chicago] would be like neo-Nazis working with Jews," says Andreas Panasiuk, an Hispanic evangelical born and raised in Argentina and now a Chicago broadcaster. "We have to resolve the tension we have in Latin America before we can work together in the United States."

But Hispanic evangelical leaders in the U.S. are clearly more concerned with building a movement in North America than with healing Catholic-evangelical divisions in Latin America. At their Long Beach conference they discussed the need to educate ministers, implement economic-development programs in their communities and reach out to youth.

An abiding interest in social causes marks a dramatic difference between Hispanic and Anglo evangelicals. Anglos tend to emphasize the personal relationship between each believer and Jesus, and to discount — often as Catholic heresy — any emphasis on good works as a means of salvation. But Hispanics say, an approach that de-emphasizes good works neglects the realities of their communities in the U.S.

"The needs of the Hispanic churches are more liberal, perhaps, than those of the Anglo churches," says Miranda. In his view some Hispanic evangelicals are uneasy about being associated with their more conservative Anglo counterparts. "They don't even want us to call ourselves 'evangelicals,' but *evangelicos*" — the Spanish version of the same word. Miranda dismisses the works-and-faith split as an Anglo phenomenon. "Ours is a civic spirituality, demonstrating divine grace on Sunday and good works on Monday," he said at the founding of AMEN.

Miranda believes that the growth line of Hispanic evangelicals will flatten out or possibly decline "as immigration slows" sometime in the next two to three years — but not before Hispanic evangelicals number some 14 million, nearly three times their current number.

Native Americans

Indian Religious Freedom Act, 1978

By means of a Joint Resolution, the United States Congress on August 11, 1978, offered to the country's native inhabitants the fundamental guarantees of religious freedom that most other citizens had enjoyed since the adoption of the First Amendment to the Constitution in 1791. Such a resolution was needed because Federal policy had been anything but "clear, comprehensive, and consistent," and because violation of sacred places and prohibition of sacred rituals had become commonplace.

Whereas the freedom of religion for all people is an inherent right, fundamental to the democratic structure of the United States and is guaranteed by the First Amendment of the United States Constitution;

Whereas the United States has traditionally rejected the concept of a government denying individuals the right to practice their religion and, as a result, has benefited from a rich variety of religious heritages in this country;

Whereas the religious practices of the American Indian (as well as Native Alaskan and Hawaiian) are an integral part of their culture, tradition and heritage, such practices forming the basis of Indian identity and value systems;

[Source: *U.S. Statutes at Large* (Washington, D.C.: Government Printing Office, 1980), p. 469.]

Whereas the traditional American Indian religions, as an integral part of Indian life, are indispensable and irreplaceable;

Whereas the lack of a clear, comprehensive, and consistent Federal policy has often resulted in the abridgment of religious freedom for traditional American Indians;

Whereas such religious infringements result from the lack of knowledge or the insensitive and inflexible enforcement of Federal policies and regulations premised on a variety of laws;

Whereas such laws were designed for such worthwhile purposes as conservation and preservation of natural species and resources but were never intended to relate to Indian religious practices and, therefore, were passed without consideration of their effect on traditional American Indian religions;

Whereas such laws and policies often deny American Indians access to sacred sites required in their religions, including cemeteries;

Whereas such laws at times prohibit the use and possession of sacred objects necessary to the exercise of religious rites and ceremonies;

Whereas traditional American Indian ceremonies have been intruded upon, interfered with, and in a few instances banned: Now, therefore, be it

Resolved by the Senate and House of Representatives of the United States of America in Congress assembled, That henceforth it shall be the policy of the United States to protect and preserve for American Indians their inherent right of freedom to believe, express, and exercise the traditional religions of the American Indian, Eskimo, Aleut, and Native Hawaiians, including but not limited to access to sites, use and possession of sacred objects, and the freedom to worship through ceremonials and traditional rites.

Ecclesiastical Support

In response to the congressional action of 1978, many churches in the American Northwest in 1987 expressed both their support for this resolution as well as their own apology for the fact that it was even necessary. Catholics, Baptists, Methodists, Presbyterians, Episcopalians, and others joined in a statement addressed to the "Tribal Councils and Traditional Spiritual Leaders of the Indian and Eskimo Peoples of the Pacific Northwest."

[Source: Matthew Fox, *The Coming of the Cosmic Christ* (San Francisco: Harper & Row, 1988), Appendix B, pp. 247-49.]

Dear Brothers and Sisters,

This is a formal apology on behalf of our churches for their long-standing participation in the destruction of traditional Native American spiritual practices. We call upon our people for recognition of and respect for your traditional ways of life and for protection of your sacred places and ceremonial objects. We have frequently been unconscious and insensitive and have not come to your aid when you have been victimized by unjust Federal policies and practices. In many other circumstances we reflected the rampant racism and prejudice of the dominant culture with which we too willingly identified. During the 200th Anniversary year of the United States Constitution we, as leaders of our churches in the Pacific Northwest, extend our apology. We ask for your forgiveness and blessing.

As the Creator continues to renew the earth, the plants, the animals and all living things, we call upon the people of our denominations and fellowships to a commitment of mutual support in your efforts to reclaim and protect the

Blackfoot Indian father Ksistaki-Poka, the first Native American to be ordained as a Roman Catholic priest, here blesses fellow tribesmen along with Flathead and Coeur D'Alene Indians.
(Religion News Service)

legacy of your own traditional spiritual teachings. To that end we pledge our support and assistance in upholding the American Religious Freedom Act (P.L. 95-134, 1978) and within that legal precedent affirm the following:

1) The rights of the Native Peoples to practice and participate in traditional ceremonies and rituals with the same protection offered all religions under the Constitution.
2) Access to and protection of sacred sites and public lands for ceremonial purposes.
3) The use of religious symbols (feathers, tobacco, sweet grass, bones, etc.) for use in traditional ceremonies and rituals.

The spiritual power of the land and the ancient wisdom of your indigenous religions can be, we believe, great gifts to the Christian churches. We offer our commitment to support you in the righting of previous wrongs: To protect your peoples' efforts to enhance Native spiritual teachings; to encourage the members of our churches to stand in solidarity with you on these important religious issues; to provide advocacy and mediation, when appropriate, for ongoing negotiations with State agencies and Federal officials regarding these matters.

May the promises of this day go on public record with all the congregations of our communions and be communicated to the Native American Peoples of the Pacific Northwest. May the God of Abraham and Sarah, and the Spirit who lives in both the cedar and Salmon People be honored and celebrated.

Women

Judaism

If civil rights dominated the 1950s and 1960s, women's rights and feminist movements dominated the 1970s. Religion of course did not, could not remain aloof to this "liberation," anymore than it had to those already considered. Questions arose concerning the ordination of women ministers, priests, and rabbis; concerning full participation in the liturgies and on the governing boards of local or national churches, and concerning masculinely loaded

[Source: Blu Greenberg, *On Women and Judaism: A View from Tradition* (Philadelphia: Jewish Publication Society of America, 1981), pp. 21-22, 25-26, 27-29.]

theological and biblical language — "the rhetoric of sexuality." Even in Or-
thodox Judaism, seemingly impervious to the feminist movement (in any
case, impervious to the ordination of women rabbis), the wedge of women's
liberation entered. In the engaging autobiographical account below, one fol-
lows the slowly dawning realization that male domination in Orthodox Ju-
daism had been total.

I was born into a strongly traditional family. With all the structure this entails, it was quite natural to be socialized early into the proper roles. I knew my place and I liked it — the warmth, the rituals, the solid, tight parameters. I never gave a thought as to what responsibilities I did or didn't have as a female growing up in the Orthodox Jewish community. It was just the way things were — the most natural order in the world.

My friends and I shared the same world of expectation. I remember the year of the bar mitzvahs of our eighth-grade male friends. We girls sat up in the women's section of the synagogue and took great pride in "our boys." If we thought about ourselves at all, it was along the lines of "thank God we are fe-males and don't have to go through the public ordeal." Quite remarkably, there never was any envy of what the boys were doing, never a thought of "why not us?" Perhaps it was because we knew that our big moment would come: as proper young ladies growing up in the modern Orthodox community in the 1950s, *our* puberty rite was the Sweet Sixteen.

My short-lived encounter with daily prayer ended when I was fourteen. I had graduated from a local yeshiva in Far Rockaway, New York, and had begun commuting to a girls' yeshiva high school in Brooklyn. This meant getting up an hour earlier to catch the 7:18 Long Island train, so prayer was the first thing to go. I had it down to a science: if I laid out my clothes in exactly the right or-der the night before, I could set the alarm for 6:52, get up, wash, dress, eat the hot breakfast without which, my mother insisted, a person could not face the world each day, and still have time to walk briskly to the train. I would reserve a four-seater in the same car each day. Just as the train started to pull out, my friends who were attending the boys' yeshiva would come dashing down the platform and fling themselves onto the slowly moving train. I knew that they had been up since six o'clock to allow enough time for *shaharit*, the mandatory morning prayers. There they were, a little bleary-eyed, already spent at 7:18, with just a package of Sen-Sen for breakfast. Those were wonderful, funny trips. Though I laughed with the boys each morning, I certainly didn't envy their more rigorous regimen. . . .

After my marriage in the late 1950s, my feelings of contentment and ful-fillment were enhanced rather than diminished. The ways of a traditional Jew-ish woman suited me just fine. All those platitudes about building a faithful Jewish home were not nearly as pleasant as the real thing itself. Moreover, none

Rabbi Sally Priesand (center), ordained as first female rabbi in
the United States, Temple Emanu-El, New York City, 1972
(Religion News Service)

of those obligations ruled out graduate studies and plans for a career. It was a
time of peaceful coexistence between the traditional roles and the initial
stirrings of self-actualization for women. I considered myself very lucky to have
a husband to care for me and I for him — a man, moreover, who encouraged
me to expand my own horizons.

The religious role of a married woman was also perfect in my eyes. I
found the clear division of labor, and its nonnegotiable quality, most satisfying.
It never crossed my mind that experiencing certain *mitzvot*[1] vicariously was
anything less than the real thing. Quite the reverse. When my husband had to
be away on the Sabbath, the act of my reciting the blessings over the wine and
the bread for our small children only served to heighten my sense of loneliness
for him.

The real thing, then, was for him to perform his mitzvot and for me to attend to mine. I wasn't looking for anything more than I had, certainly not in the

1. Commandments, duties.

way of religious obligations or rights. On those bitter cold Sabbath mornings I was absolutely delighted to linger an hour longer in a nice warm bed and play with the kids rather than to have to brave the elements. I could choose to go to the synagogue when I wanted or pray at home when I wanted; for my husband there was no choice.

The *mehitzah*[2] separating men from women in the synagogue served to symbolize the dividing line. Although there were certain things about sitting behind the *mehitzah* that I didn't exactly appreciate, none seemed an attack on my womanhood. Not only did I not perceive the *mehitzah* to be a denigration of women in the synagogue, but I couldn't understand why some Jews felt that way. At some level, to me the *mehitzah* symbolized the ancient, natural, immutable order of male and female. One didn't question such things. . . .

And then came feminism. In 1963, I read Betty Friedan's *Feminine Mystique,* still the classic text of the women's movement. I was a little intimidated by its force and had trouble with what seemed to me a portent of friction between the sexes, but the essential idea, equality of women, was exciting, and mind-boggling, and very just. Still, correct or not, it didn't mean me, nor did it apply to women in Judaism. On that score I was defensive, resistant, and probably just plain frightened. It must have threatened my status quo.

And yet . . . Once I had tasted of the fruit of the tree of knowledge, there was no going back. The basic idea had found a resting spot somewhere inside me. Little by little, and with a good deal of prodding from my husband, I became sensitized to issues and situations that previously had made no impression on me. Some of my complacency was eroded; my placidity churned up. In place of blind acceptance, I slowly began to ask questions, not really sure if I wanted to hear the answers. Because I was so satisfied, because I had no sense of injustice, some of the new thinking, including my own, came to me as a shock. Things that had run right past me before I now had to grab hold of, for a still moment, to examine under the white light of equality.

I began to think not just about the idea, but about myself as a woman — in relation to people, to a place in the larger society, to a career, and finally to Judaism. I did not look back over my past and say it was bad. In fact, I knew it was very good. What I did begin to say was that perhaps it could have been better. Again, it was not a case of closing my eyes and thinking hard. Instead, it was a series of incidents, encounters, a matter of timing; it was also memories and recollections, a review in which isolated incidents began to emerge as part of a pattern. This pattern now had to be tested against a new value framework.

It was almost ten years before I began systematically to apply the new categories to my Jewishness. As I reviewed my education, one fact emerged — a fact so obvious that I was stunned more by my unresponsiveness to it over the

2. Curtain.

years than by the fact itself. It was this: the study of Talmud, which was a primary goal in my family and community, consistently was closed off to me. Beginning with elementary school, the girls studied Israeli folk dancing while the boys studied Talmud. In the yeshiva high school, the girls' branch had no course of study in Talmud; the boys' branch had three hours a day. In Israel, in the Jewish studies seminar, all of the classes were coeducational except Talmud. The girls studied laws and customs on one day and enjoyed a free period the other four days.

And then there was my father. The great love of his life, beyond his family, was not his business; it was his study of the Talmud. Every day, before he left for work, he would spend an hour studying Talmud with a rabbi friend. In fact, he had not missed a day of study in his life, even during family vacations or times of stress. Yet although he reviewed religious texts regularly with his daughters, it was never Talmud. He even would collar my dates, while I was getting ready, for a few minutes of Talmud discussion. That we didn't participate in those years more directly in our father's passion for Talmud study was not a willful denial on his part; he simply was following the hallowed custom. As a result of all this, when I began to study rabbinic literature in graduate school in my late twenties, I realized that my male fellow students all had the edge of fifteen or twenty years of Talmud study behind them.

Gradually, too, I became aware of the power of conditioning and how early in life it takes place. On the last Sabbath that my husband served as rabbi of a congregation, the children and I decided to surprise him. Moshe, then ten and a half, prepared the haftarah reading, David, nine, the *An'im Zemirot* prayer, and J. J., six, the *Adon Olam*. It was a real treat for their father and for the entire congregation; it seemed to the boys as if the whole world was proud of them. On the following Sunday morning, their grandparents visited and gave each of the boys two dollars for doing such a fine job. When the boys told Deborah, then eight, that they each had been given two dollars, she complained that it wasn't fair. At which point Moshe retorted, with the biting honesty of a ten year old: "Well, so what, you can't even do anything in the synagogue!" Click, click, I thought to myself, another woman radicalized.

Oddly enough, until that moment it never had occurred to me that it could or should be otherwise, that perhaps it wasn't "fair" to a little girl. Even more astounding was the fact that with all the weeks of secret practice, all the fuss I had made over the boys beforehand, and all the compliments they received afterward, Deborah never once had complained. It was only the two dollars that finally got to her; to everything else she had already been conditioned . . . to expect nothing.

Mormonism

The Equal Rights Amendment (ERA) proposed that just as the rights of citizens could "not be denied or abridged . . . on account of race, color, or previous condition of servitude," so those rights could not be violated on grounds of gender. The amendment, requiring the endorsement by two-thirds of the states, failed to win ratification in 1982. What it did win was both passionate support and passionate opposition. Many religious bodies endorsed the amendment, some opposed it, and some held themselves aloof. The Church of Jesus Christ of Latter Day Saints through its leadership spoke against the amendment as a threat to traditional family life and moral values. One member of that church, Sonia Johnson, openly and strongly supported ERA. When neither she nor the church authorities backed away from an inevitable confrontation, Sonia Johnson was formally tried and excommunicated in December of 1979. Below, the excommunicated Mormon gives her version of the summons to trial in Virginia before the court presided over by Bishop Jeff Willis.

I read the letter again. This was Wednesday night [Nov. 14, 1979] — late by now. The trial was set for early Saturday morning. Slowly I began to understand the strategy behind it all. They were giving me only two days! Two days to prepare my defense, to prepare myself spiritually, psychologically, two days to find witnesses. *Only two days!* The cruelty of that and the already clear judgment it revealed that had been made about my guilt struck me like a heavy fist in the face. They did not intend to give me a real trial at all! They were not even going to give me a real chance to defend myself. I had been found guilty and now they were only going through the formalities. . . .

Press coverage of the trial had begun.

Thursday, November 15. I tried all day to reach Jeff [Willis]. Judy told me he was on jury duty (ironies never ceased) and could not be reached all day. Frantically, I explained to her that I had only two days before the trial and that I did not even know what the charges were. Would she please help me get in touch with Jeff. Finally, she made an appointment for me with him at 8 P.M. that night at the Sterling Park Ward chapel. One whole precious day wasted. In the end, I drove out to Sterling Park Ward alone, and at 8 P.M. sat for the last time alone with Jeff Willis in that office.

As I recall, the first question I asked him was, "Who is my accuser?" "I am," he answered. "Who is my judge, then?" "I am," he said again. "But how can

---

[Source: Sonia Johnson, *From Housewife to Heretic* (New York: Doubleday & Co., 1981), pp. 276, 278-80.]

you be both my accuser and my judge? For heaven's sake, Jeff, I've been an American too long to feel comfortable with that. I'm accustomed to at least the appearance of due process. If you've decided I'm guilty — and you must have, since you're willing to accuse me — how can you bring an impartial decision?" "Don't worry, Sonia," he assured me. "I will receive the correct decision through

Three Episcopal women ordained in 1974 celebrate the Eucharist
in Riverside Church, New York City.
(Religion News Service)

inspiration from our Heavenly Father. The courts of the church are courts of love." Ignoring the love nonsense, I asked, "How do you expect to be able to hear God's will over the roar of your own conviction that I'm guilty? What exactly do you expect him to do, Jeff? Hit you over the head with a lightning bolt? Knock you down on the road to Langley?"

I was not mollified. I was as prayerful a person as I had ever known (except for my mother), and I knew how hard it is to get answers. I had heard mission presidents say that they could not tell whether or not someone had negroid ancestry no matter how hard they prayed. I very much suspected that Jeff was more influenced by what his superiors told him *they* had heard from God than he was from what he had personally managed to glean. "Wait just a second, God. I have to check it out with the Big Boys." But I was determined not to view the situation as hopeless — though I know now that it was from the beginning.

"What are the charges against me, Jeff? Please write them down so we will each know this is what you said, and so I won't make a mistake when I tell my witnesses what they need to respond to."

He refused to write anything down. That's what comes of working for the CIA — deep distrust as a first response. So I asked him if he would dictate the charges to me. He agreed to do that. Perhaps because they were not in his handwriting, he could forever deny that they had come from him. I cannot imagine why else he refused to write them himself. These are his exact words as I took them down on the night of November 15, 1979:

"You have broken the covenants you made in the temple, specifically:

1. evil speaking of the Lord's anointed;
2. the law of consecration;
3. your general attitude and expression."

I protested. Where have I spoken evil of the Lord's anointed? I asked. In your APA speech, he answered. Show me the place, I demanded. "You call them chauvinistic," he shot back. "That's not evil; that's true!" I replied. "And what's this about the law of consecration?" You promised in the temple to give your time, your talents, all the Lord has blessed you with and all he may yet bless you with to the upbuilding of the church and to the establishment of Zion."

"Jeff, I pay a full tithing and have all my life. I'm the ward organist and spend many extra hours practicing alone and with the choir. I teach the cultural refinement lesson in Relief Society, I am a visiting teacher [in the Relief Society], I attend church, we hold family home evenings, I attend the temple. If you're going to excommunicate everybody in the ward who is doing this much or less, you won't have anybody left in the congregation when you're through!

"And tell me how I'm going to defend myself against your annoyance at my 'general attitude and expression.' What does that even mean? Just because men in the church don't like uppity women, does that mean we should all be

excommunicated?" I thought but held my tongue: "Do we have to have an attitude of hero worship and awe even when our male leaders do little or nothing
to deserve it? Why should we be in awe? Because you're *male?*"

Roman Catholicism

*Rosemary Radford Ruether (b. 1936) has taken a prominent place as both
participant in and observer of the feminist movement and its relationship to
religious institutions. Women, as Ruether noted in 1989, have been confined
to passive and secondary roles throughout the long history of the Judeo-
Christian tradition. Furthermore, "the public theological culture is defined
by men not only in the absence of but against women." Turning to her own
ecclesiastical tradition, Ruether tells "The Roman Catholic Story," the excerpt below concentrating on a 1977 document issued by the Vatican. This
"Declaration" was supposed to clarify if not pacify the issues concerning the
ordination of women in the Roman Catholic Church. As Rosemary Ruether
explains, it neither clarified nor pacified.*

On January 27, 1977, . . . the Vatican released the hastily assembled *Declaration
on the Question of the Admission of Women to the Ministerial Priesthood.* The
declaration states that the exclusion of women was founded on Christ's intent
and is basic to the Church's understanding of priesthood, and that therefore it
cannot be changed. This statement makes a rather amazing effort to separate
the tradition of exclusion of women from priesthood from concepts of
women's natural inferiority and status of subjection. It is clear that the latter rationale no longer works. But it is also clear that the entire tradition of the exclusion of women from priesthood has, in fact, been based on exactly these underpinnings. The declaration denies this. It asserts that, following Jesus, the
Church has always believed in the equality of women with men in the natural
order. Exclusion from priesthood is not based on any such concept of inferiority or subjection, but rather on some mysterious sacramental bond between
Christ, maleness and priesthood.

   Needless to say, such a construction of the tradition of exclusion of
women from priesthood will not bear examination. A declaration that declares
its hands tied, unable to change any tradition so long established, actually goes
about its business by sweeping away a two-thousand-year tradition and pre-

---

[Source: Rosemary Radford Ruether, "Entering the Sanctuary: The Roman Catholic Story," in
Rosemary Radford Ruether and Eleanor McLaughlin, eds., *Women of Spirit: Female Leadership
in the Jewish and Christian Tradition* (New York: Simon and Schuster, 1979), pp. 379-82.]

tending that it never existed! It asserts its fidelity to "tradition" by a sweeping denial of what has been an integral aspect of this entire tradition.

The attempt of the declaration to replace the traditional basis of exclusion with a theological construct that links maleness, Christ and priesthood astonished those who had previously had little interest in the subject. One might say that if the Vatican lost its credibility for "infallibility" in matters of morals with the birth-control controversy, it lost its credibility for "infallibility" in matters of faith with the declaration on the admission of women to the priesthood.

From far and wide came cries of dismay. Those committed to women's ordination quickly released carefully worded statements which unequivocally rejected the authority of the declaration and pointed out its historical errors and its theological untenability. But strong criticism came from quarters not previously involved in the issue. Almost the entire faculty of the Jesuit School of Theology in Berkeley (twenty-three members) sent a statement directly to the Pope pointing out the historical, Scriptural and theological untenability of the statement. Even the venerable German theologian Karl Rahner issued a statement indicating the theological unacceptability of the declaration. Never has an official Vatican declaration been so roundly rejected and even ridiculed by both theological authorities and the general populace. The Catholic liberal press took mischievous delight in reporting that according to a Gallup poll, support for the ordination of women among American Catholics actually rose, in the two months following the release of the declaration, from twenty-nine percent to forty-one percent, the sharpest upsurge of support for this idea ever to take place among Catholics. Although Gallup had been reporting a gradual rise in support for women's ordination among Catholics, the progress had been slow, a percentage point or two a year. The phenomenal rise of support from mid-January to mid-March of 1977 could only have reflected the reaction to the Vatican statement. One might surmise that many Catholics were simply indifferent to the issue or supposed the Church had some good reason. But once brought face to face with the crudities of the declaration, many persons were galvanized into an opinion for the first time!

It is hard to know where this movement will go in the immediate and long-range future. One more impasse among several within recent years between public opinion in the Church and hierarchical power appears to have developed. The hierarchy loses credibility, but still holds the power. No democratic structures exist, similar to those in the American Episcopal Church, which might gradually develop a winning parliamentary battle for votes that could change a historical practice. It is likely that a long seedtime must set in. A growing practice of ministry shared by men and women will develop on local congregational levels. A certain educational process will go on between women and ordained males on the injustice of the restrictions placed on their female

In 1989 the Episcopal Church ordained its first female bishop, the Reverend Barbara
Harris (center); she is flanked by her bishop in Boston, David E. Johnson (left),
and the Presiding Bishop of the Episcopal Church, Edmond L. Browning
(Religion News Service)

colleagues. Laity will become used to seeing women minister in a number of
adjunct roles and wonder why not sacraments. Perhaps there will be discussions and conferences around this in local churches. House prayer groups may
just go ahead and authorize women to celebrate. Struggles between bishops and
liberal congregations will take place.

Eventually more bishops will be consecrated who wonder at the absurdity
of the exclusion (with a growing example of women in full sacramental ministry in other churches). After that it is up to the Holy Spirit to suddenly shake
the power structure anew (as in the days of John XXIII) in ways that no one can
anticipate. In any case those who are committed to such a change in Roman Ca-

tholicism know that they are committed for the long haul. For it is not possible to imagine the admission of women to the Catholic priesthood without, at the same time, modifying certain fundamental notions about hierarchy, theology, Church and authority. This, even more than women, may be what the hierarchy fears.

Conservatives

In the decade of the 1990s, wider-ranging research greatly expanded aware-
ness of diversity among religious women. Not surprisingly, when scholars
probed sympathetically into religious movements, they found that simple
stereotypes like "radical feminists" or "reactionary conservatives" rarely
matched reality. One of the most interesting of these projects was conducted
by Christel Manning, who for a period of several years during the 1990s be-
came a participant observer at several houses of worship while carrying out
extensive interviews with female members of a conservative Protestant con-
gregation, a conservative Catholic parish, and a synagogue of conservative
Orthodox Jews. Her research pointed to the contrasts that America's chang-
ing culture was creating between day-to-day women's lives and the roles for
women outlined by traditional religious experiences. The complexity she
found in attitudes among her subjects toward feminism represented the more
general complexity she discovered through her research.

I have a feminist friend who cannot understand why I wanted to spend two years getting to know women in conservative religious communities. "How could you stand it?" she asked me. "Women like that are actively trying to un-ravel all the progress the movement has made for us — and for them." When I tell her that many of the women I talked to integrate feminist values into their lives, she is unimpressed. "Then who do you suppose votes for Pat Robertson?" she retorts, "and who sends membership checks to Concerned Women for America [an anti-feminist lobby group]?" She has a point. Though ordinary women in conservative Christian and Orthodox Jewish communities are much more open to feminist values than the statements of their leaders would have us believe, they do support those leaders. Indeed, a survey of the women in this study would reveal that the majority agree with their leaders' opposition to the feminist movement.

[Source: Christel Manning, *God Gave Us the Right: Conservative Catholic, Evangelical Protestant, and Orthodox Jewish Women Grapple with Feminism* (New Brunswick: Rutgers University Press, 1999), pp. 167-68, 192-95.]

That does not mean, however, that these women are actively involved in antifeminist politics, or that all of them support the kind of cross-denominational conservative alliance promoted by Robertson or Concerned Women for America (CWA). My friend's comment reveals her lack of exposure to real-life conservative Christian and Orthodox Jewish women. If she spent some time talking to and observing the behavior of these women, she would realize that there is considerable variation among the three communities, both in the degree and the nature of their opposition to the feminist movement. More importantly, my friend ignores the fact that many secular (and liberal Christian and Jewish) women are critical of that movement and, even if they do not actively oppose it, do little to support it. Women in conservative religious communities, as it turns out, are just as ambivalent about the feminist movement as secular American women.

Like secular women, Evangelical, conservative Catholic, and Orthodox Jewish women are not well informed about the feminist movement. They equate it ideologically with liberal feminism, which downplays gender differences and rejects differential treatment of men and women, and politically with the National Organization for Women, which supports complete gender equality, reproductive choice, and gay rights. There seems to be little awareness outside of academia of the diversity within feminism and the fact that some versions of it are quite compatible with religious traditionalism. Given this narrow definition of feminism, women in conservative religious communities resemble secular women in their assessment of the movement's impact. I asked all of the women how they feel about the women's movement and whether they think that feminism has had a positive or negative impact, both on American society generally and on their religious community in particular. Based on their responses to these two questions, women in all three traditions can be grouped into two categories: *profeminists,* who believe that this movement has been good for America and their church or synagogue, and *antifeminists,* who do not. . . .

The relationship of conservative Christian and Orthodox Jewish women to the feminist movement is far more complex than one would expect. Both the religious right and feminist leaders like to think that women in conservative religious communities actively oppose the feminist movement and that this is a significant reason why they joined a conservative tradition. In reality, however, the women I studied were deeply ambivalent about the movement. Not only did all three communities contain both pro- and antifeminists, but upon close examination there is not much difference between the two categories: antifeminists do not want to live without the changes the movement has wrought, and profeminists are still critical of many aspects of the movement. Moreover, the women who fall into each category are not necessarily those one might expect. Many working women, for example, are antifeminists, while a number of homemakers are profeminist.

Conservative Christian and Orthodox Jewish women's ambivalence about the feminist movement resembles the feelings of many American women, especially younger ones. As Elizabeth Fox-Genovese . . . has pointed out, "Polls show that women's issues — equal pay for equal work, sexual harassment, day care, and shared responsibility in marriage — have mass support." Yet "only about a third of American women are willing to call themselves feminists," and the proportion of college women is "fewer than one in five." Her research demonstrates that secular women express many of the same criticisms of feminism as the religious women in my study. Supporters of the feminist movement complain, with some justification, that many of these women take their improved status for granted and notice only the supposed downsides of feminism: its failure to acknowledge and appreciate real gender differences, its devaluation of motherhood and homemaking, and its extremist leaders. Feminist activists also point out that they have continued to promote the kinds of changes that all American women (including those in this study) care about, for example, legislation that would allow both male and female workers to spend more time with their children. Unfortunately, such "family friendly" activism does not get as much media attention as feminist efforts to secure abortion and lesbian rights, issues that religious conservatives oppose and even liberal and secular women have mixed feelings about. Until feminist leaders convince them otherwise, many American women, like the religious women in this study, will not feel represented by the feminist movement.

Ironically, women in conservative religious communities — antifeminists in particular — actually resemble some of the most radical secular feminists today. Debra Kaufman . . . has noted the similarities between radical feminists and the newly Orthodox Jewish women she had studied, and I believe her observations are applicable to conservative Christians as well. Both radical feminists and religious conservatives celebrate gender differences. For both groups, "women represent a special source of strength, knowledge, and power." Just as radical feminists believe that "men see the world from a dualistic viewpoint, rationally attempting to analyze and exploit nature, while women trust their intuitive mode of knowing," conservative Christian and Orthodox Jewish women "claim that there are natural differences between the sexes, and that women's superior moral sensitivities arise from their greater intimacy with the everyday physical world." Finally, religiously conservative women, like radical feminists, have argued that this is a man's world that should be reformed according to women's values. . . .

Many women in this study understood only too well that the American economic system is centered around the needs of men. Women had to deny their reproductive nature in order to compete with men in the marketplace on male terms, either by having abortions or by not giving their children the care that they deserved. The women in this study *were* politicized by this understanding. Not only did most of them support increasing the number of women in politics, but they were adamant about electing candidates that cared about women's issues. To them, caring about women's issues meant supporting a woman's inherent desire to nurture her child rather than abort it. It meant restructuring the workplace in such a way as to allow women to have a career *and* care for their children. While radical feminists seek to free women from the burdens of reproduction (through contraception, abortion, and perhaps in the future through technology), conservative religious women want society to affirm and support their reproductive nature by freeing both men and women from inflexible work arrangements. Their political standpoint clearly differs from that of radical feminists, but they are politicized just the same.

Their deep ambivalence about the feminist movement is common to all three groups in this study. However, there are also important differences. There are far more antifeminists at Victory church and St. Joseph's than at Beth Israel. Among antifeminists, Evangelicals are upset that feminism discourages male responsibility, making men into homosexuals, while Catholics feel feminism discourages female responsibility, causing more women to have abortions. Jewish antifeminists, by contrast, are more concerned with the impact of feminism on Orthodox Judaism than either of those issues. Among profeminists, both Jews and Catholics express some doubts over whether their religious communities should accommodate feminism, the former because they fear for the survival of Jewish tradition, the latter because they fear further division in their church. By contrast, it was a profeminist Evangelical who insisted that feminism originated in her community and that it is, or should be, her church's mission to spread feminist values to the rest of society.

3. Litigation/Division

Education

Prayer and Meditation: *Wallace* v. *Jaffree,* 1985

In 1962 and 1963 the U.S. Supreme Court upset a lot of tradition and a great many people. In cases decided in those years, the Court agreed (with only a single dissent) that prayer and Bible reading — as acts of worship — were unconstitutional in the public schools. The uproar was both instantaneous and continuous as diverse groups lobbied Congress to "do something," such as remove such matters from the Court's authority or pass a Constitutional Amendment that would render the Court's verdict null and void. Or some reasoned that, if audible prayer were not allowed, perhaps silent prayer would be. In a case that originated in Alabama, the Court in 1985 decided that even a prescribed period of silent prayer constituted an act of worship inappropriate to a public educational institution. (1) Justice John Paul Stevens, speaking for the majority, retained the Court's tradition of the previous quarter-century or more. (2) But there were two dissenters, with Justice (later Chief Justice) William Rehnquist strongly protesting against the strict separationist path defended most vigorously by Thomas Jefferson and James Madison.

[Sources: R. T. Miller and R. B. Flowers, *Toward Benevolent Neutrality* (Waco, Texas: Baylor University Press, 1987), (1) p. 436; (2) p. 452.]

1.

Just as the right to speak and the right to refrain from speaking are complementary components of a broader concept of individual freedom of mind, so also the individual's freedom to choose his own creed is the counterpart of his right to refrain from accepting the creed established by the majority. At one time it was thought that this right merely proscribed the preference of one Christian sect over another, but would not require equal respect for the conscience of the infidel, the atheist, or the adherent of a non-Christian faith such as Mohammedism or Judaism. But when the underlying principle has been examined in the crucible of litigation, the Court has unambiguously concluded that the individual freedom of conscience protected by the First Amendment embraces the right to select any religious faith or none at all. This conclusion derives support not only from the interest in respecting the individual's freedom of conscience, but also from the conviction that religious beliefs worthy of respect are the product of free and voluntary choice by the faithful, and from recognition of the fact that the political interest in forestalling intolerance extends beyond intolerance among Christian sects — or even intolerance among "religions" — to encompass intolerance of the disbeliever and the uncertain. As *Justice JACKSON* eloquently stated in *Board of Education* v. *Barnette:* "If there is any fixed star in our constitutional constellation, it is that no official, high or petty, can prescribe what shall be orthodox in politics, nationalism, religion, or other matters of opinion or force citizens to confess by word or act their faith therein." The State of Alabama, no less than the Congress of the United States, must respect that basic truth.

2.

The Framers intended the Establishment Clause to prohibit the designation of any church as a "national" one. The Clause was also designed to stop the Federal Government from asserting a preference for one religious denomination or sect over others. Given the "incorporation" of the Establishment Clause as against the States via the Fourteenth Amendment in *Everson,* States are prohibited as well from establishing a religion or discriminating between sects. As its history abundantly shows, however, nothing in the Establishment Clause requires government to be strictly neutral between religion and irreligion, nor does that Clause prohibit Congress or the States from pursuing legitimate secular ends through nondiscriminatory sectarian means.

The Court strikes down the Alabama statute in *Wallace* v. *Jaffree* because the State wished to "endorse prayer as a favored practice." It would come as much of a shock to those who drafted the Bill of Rights as it will to a large number of thoughtful Americans today to learn that the Constitution, as construed by the majority, prohibits the Alabama Legislature from "endorsing" prayer. George Washington himself, at the request of the very Congress which passed the Bill of Rights, proclaimed a day of "public thanksgiving and prayer, to be observed by acknowledging with grateful hearts the many and signal favors of Almighty God." History must judge whether it was the father of his country in 1789, or a majority of the Court today, which has strayed from the meaning of the Establishment Clause.

A Conservative Court and Separation: *Lee* v. *Weisman,* 1992

After Presidents Ronald Reagan and George Bush had appointed a majority of justices to the Supreme Court, many citizens expected a notable shift in the Court's opinions regarding prayer in the public schools. The opportunity for such a shift occurred when the Court agreed to hear a case arising from Providence, Rhode Island, where prayers were offered at the graduation ceremonies. The tradition of strict separation, begun in 1962, would in 1992 be modified or abandoned — so many assumed. By a 5 to 4 vote, however, the Court upheld the earlier rulings. (1) Justice Anthony M. Kennedy wrote the majority opinion, a portion of which is given below. (2) Justice Antonin Scalia's dissenting opinion is also excerpted below.

1.

. . . The lessons of the First Amendment are as urgent in the modern world as in the 18th century when it was written. One timeless lesson is that if citizens are subjected to state-sponsored religious exercises, the State disavows its own duty to guard and respect that sphere of inviolable conscience and belief which is the mark of a free people. To compromise that principle today would be to deny our own tradition and forfeit our standing to urge others to secure the protections of that tradition for themselves.

The importance of the event [of graduation] is the point the school district and the United States rely upon to argue that a formal prayer ought to be permitted, but it becomes one of the principal reasons why their argument must fail. Their contention, one of considerable force were it not for the constitutional constraints applied to state action, is that the prayers are an essential

---

[Source: *The New York Times,* June 25, 1992, p. B11.]

part of these ceremonies because for many persons an occasion of this significance lacks meaning if there is no recognition, however brief, that human
achievements cannot be understood apart from their spiritual essence. We
think the Government's position that this interest suffices to force students to
choose between compliance or forfeiture demonstrates fundamental inconsistency in its argumentation. It fails to acknowledge that what for many of
Deborah's classmates and their parents was a spiritual imperative was for Daniel [the father] and Deborah [the daughter] Weisman religious conformance
compelled by the State. While in some societies the wishes of the majority
might prevail, the establishment clause of the First Amendment is addressed to
this contingency and rejects the balance urged upon us. The Constitution forbids the State to exact religious conformity from a student as the price of attending her own high school graduation.

2.

In holding that the establishment clause prohibits invocations and benedic-
tions at public-school graduation ceremonies, the Court, with nary a mention
that it is doing so, lays waste a tradition that is as old as public-school graduation ceremonies themselves, and that is a component of an even more long-
standing American tradition of nonsectarian prayer to God at public celebrations generally. . . . Today's opinion shows more forcefully than volumes of argumentation why our Nation's protection, that fortress which is our Constitution, cannot possibly rest upon the changeable philosophical predilections of
the justices of this Court, but must have deep foundations in the historic practices of our people.

*   *   *

One can believe in the effectiveness of such public worship, or one can depre-
cate and deride it. But the long-standing American tradition of prayer at official
ceremonies displays with unmistakable clarity that the establishment clause
does not forbid the government to accommodate it.

The narrow context of the present case involves a community's celebration of one of the milestones in its young citizens' lives, and it is a bold step for
this Court to banish from that occasion, and from thousands of similar celebrations throughout this land, the expression of gratitude to God that a majority
of the community wishes to make.

Equal Access as "Free Exercise": *Rosenberger* v. *University of Virginia*, 1995

This case arose after a religious student group at the University of Virginia tried to get the University to cover the printing costs for its publication. The University refused because it did not want to "establish" religion by providing public funds for religious purposes. When the student group could not get the university to reconsider its decision, it sued in court with the argument that, since the university provided funds for the publication of other students' publications, it was discriminating illegally against this group by withholding funds. They argued in particular that the Constitution's guarantee of free-speech and the free exercise of religion deserved to take precedent over broad application of the First Amendment's establishment clause's prohibitions. The decision of the Supreme Court in favor of the students and to allow the funding was narrow (5-4), but did continue the trend visible since the 1980s of allowing more accommodation between non-coercive religious practice and public space. The excerpts below include portions of Justice Kennedy's opinion for the majority, Justice Thomas's concurring opinion, and the opinion of the four dissenting justices.

Justice Kennedy delivered the opinion of the Court.

The University of Virginia, an instrumentality of the Commonwealth for which it is named and thus bound by the First and Fourteenth Amendments, authorizes the payment of outside contractors for the printing costs of a variety of student publications. It withheld any authorization for payments on behalf of petitioners for the sole reason that their student paper "primarily promotes or manifests a particular belie[f] in or about a deity or an ultimate reality." That the paper did promote or manifest views within the defined exclusion seems plain enough. The challenge is to the University's regulation and its denial of authorization, the case raising issues under the Speech and Establishment Clauses of the First Amendment. . . .

Petitioners' organization, Wide Awake Productions (WAP), qualified as a CIO [Contracted Independent Orgamization]. Formed by petitioner Ronald Rosenberger and other undergraduates in 1990, WAP was established "[t]o publish a magazine of philosophical and religious expression," "[t]o facilitate

[Source: John F. Wilson and Donald L. Drakeman, eds., *Church and State in American History: Key Documents, Decisions, and Commentary from the Past Three Centuries*, 3rd ed. (Boulder, CO: Westview, 2003), pp. 256-58, 259-63.]

discussion which fosters an atmosphere of sensitivity to and tolerance of Christian viewpoints," and "[t]o provide a unifying focus for Christians of multicultural backgrounds." WAP publishes Wide Awake: A Christian Perspective at the University of Virginia. The paper's Christian viewpoint was evident from the first issue, in which its editors wrote that the journal "offers a Christian perspective on both personal and community issues, especially those relevant to college students at the University of Virginia." The editors committed the paper to a two-fold mission: "to challenge Christians to live, in word and deed, according to the faith they proclaim and to encourage students to consider what a personal relationship with Jesus Christ means." The first issue had articles about racism, crisis pregnancy, stress, prayer, C. S. Lewis' ideas about evil and free will, and reviews of religious music. In the next two issues, Wide Awake featured stories about homosexuality, Christian missionary work, and eating disorders, as well as music reviews and interviews with University professors. Each page of Wide Awake, and the end of each article or review, is marked by a cross. The advertisements carried in Wide Awake also reveal the Christian perspective of the journal. For the most part, the advertisers are churches, centers for Christian study, or Christian bookstores. By June 1992, WAP had distributed about 5,000 copies of Wide Awake to University students, free of charge.

WAP had acquired CIO status soon after it was organized. This is an important consideration in this case, for had it been a "religious organization," WAP would not have been accorded CIO status. As defined by the Guidelines, a "religious organization" is "an organization whose purpose is to practice a devotion to an acknowledged ultimate reality or deity,". . . At no stage in this controversy has the University contended that WAP is such an organization.

A few months after being given CIO status, WAP requested the SAF to pay its printer $5,862 for the costs of printing its newspaper. The Appropriations Committee of the Student Council denied WAP's request on the ground that Wide Awake was a "religious activity" within the meaning of the Guidelines, *i.e.,* that the newspaper "promote[d] or manifest[ed] a particular belie[f] in or about a deity or an ultimate reality." It made its determination after examining the first issue. WAP appealed the denial to the full Student Council, contending that WAP met all the applicable Guidelines and that denial of SAF support on the basis of the magazine's religious perspective violated the Constitution. The appeal was denied without further comment, and WAP appealed to the next level, the Student Activities Committee. In a letter signed by the Dean of Students, the committee sustained the denial of funding.

Having no further recourse within the University structure, WAP, Wide Awake, and three of its editors and members filed suit. . . . They alleged that refusal to authorize payment of the printing costs of the publication, solely on the basis of its religious editorial viewpoint, violated their rights to freedom of speech and press, to the free exercise of religion, and to equal protection of the law. . . .

It is axiomatic that the government may not regulate speech based on its substantive content or the message it conveys. . . . Other principles follow from this precept. In the realm of private speech or expression, government regulation may not favor one speaker over another. . . . Discrimination against speech because of its message is presumed to be unconstitutional. . . . These rules informed our determination that the government offends the First Amendment when it imposes financial burdens on certain speakers based on the content of their expression. . . . When the government targets not subject matter but particular views taken by speakers on a subject, the violation of the First Amendment is all the more blatant. . . . Viewpoint discrimination is thus an egregious form of content discrimination. The government must abstain from regulating speech when the specific motivating ideology or the opinion or perspective of the speaker is the rationale for the restriction. . . .

A central lesson of our decisions is that a significant factor in upholding governmental programs in the face of Establishment Clause attack is their neutrality towards religion. . . . We have held that the guarantee of neutrality is respected, not offended, when the government, following neutral criteria and evenhanded policies, extends benefits to recipients whose ideologies and viewpoints, including religious ones, are broad and diverse. . . . More than once have we rejected the position that the Establishment Clause even justifies, much less requires, a refusal to extend free speech rights to religious speakers who participate in broad-reaching government programs neutral in design. . . .

The governmental program here is neutral toward religion. There is no suggestion that the University created it to advance religion or adopted some ingenious device with the purpose of aiding a religious cause. The object of the SAF is to open a forum for speech and to support various student enterprises, including the publication of newspapers, in recognition of the diversity and creativity of student life. The University's SAF Guidelines have a separate classification for, and do not make third-party payments on behalf of, "religious organizations," which are those "whose purpose is to practice a devotion to an acknowledged ultimate reality or deity." The category of support here is for "student news, information, opinion, entertainment, or academic communications media groups," of which Wide Awake was 1 of 15 in the 1990 school year. WAP did not seek a subsidy because of its Christian editorial viewpoint; it sought funding as a student journal, which it was. . . .

To obey the Establishment Clause, it was not necessary for the University to deny eligibility to student publications because of their viewpoint. The neutrality commanded of the State by the separate Clauses of the First Amendment was compromised by the University's course of action. The viewpoint discrimination inherent in the University's regulation required public officials to scan and interpret student publications to discern their underlying philosophic assumptions respecting religious theory and belief. That course of action was a denial of the right of free speech and would risk fostering a pervasive bias or hostility to religion, which could undermine the very neutrality the Establishment Clause requires. There is no Establishment Clause violation in the University's honoring its duties under the Free Speech Clause. . . .

Justice Thomas, concurring.

I write separately to express my disagreement with the historical analysis put forward by the dissent. Although the dissent starts down the right path in consulting the original meaning of the Establishment Clause, its misleading application of history yields a principle that is inconsistent with our Nation's long tradition of allowing religious adherents to participate on equal terms in neutral government programs.

Even assuming that the Virginia debate on the so-called "Assessment Controversy" was indicative of the principles embodied in the Establishment Clause, this incident hardly compels the dissent's conclusion that government must actively discriminate against religion. The dissent's historical discussion glosses over the fundamental characteristic of the Virginia assessment bill that sparked the controversy: The assessment was to be imposed for the support of clergy in the performance of their function of teaching religion. . . .

James Madison's Memorial and Remonstrance Against Religious Assessments (hereinafter Madison's Remonstrance) must be understood in this context. Contrary to the dissent's suggestion, Madison's objection to the assessment bill did not rest on the premise that religious entities may never participate on equal terms in neutral government programs. Nor did Madison embrace the argument that forms the linchpin of the dissent: that monetary subsidies are constitutionally different from other neutral benefits programs. Instead, Madison's comments are more consistent with the neutrality principle that the dissent inexplicably discards. . . .

Legal commentators have disagreed about the historical lesson to take from the Assessment Controversy. For some, the experience in Virginia is consistent with the view that the Framers saw the Establishment Clause simply as a prohibition on governmental preferences for some religious faiths over others. . . . Other commentators have rejected this view, concluding that the Establishment Clause forbids not only government preferences for some religious sects over others, but also government preferences for religion over irreligion. . . .

I find much to commend the former view. . . . The funding provided by the Virginia assessment was to be extended only to Christian sects, and the Remonstrance seized on this defect. . . .

In addition . . . , "Madison's arguments all speak, in some way, to the same intolerance, bigotry, unenlightenment, and persecution that had generally resulted from previous exclusive religious establishments.". . . The conclusion that Madison saw the principle of nonestablishment as barring governmental preferences for *particular* religious faiths seems especially clear in light of statements he made in the more-relevant context of the House debates on the First Amendment. . . . (Madison's views "as reflected by actions on the floor of the House in 1789, [indicate] that he saw the [First] Amendment as designed to prohibit the establishment of a national religion, and perhaps to prevent discrimination among sects," but not "as requiring neutrality on the part of government between religion and irreligion"). Moreover, even if more extreme notions of the separation of church and state can be attributed to Madison, many of them clearly stem from "arguments reflecting the concepts of natural law, natural rights, and the social contract between government and a civil society," . . . rather than the principle of nonestablishment in the Constitution. In any event, the views of one man do not establish the original understanding of the First Amendment.

But resolution of this debate is not necessary to decide this case. Under any understanding of the Assessment Controversy, the history cited by the dissent cannot support the conclusion that the Establishment Clause "categorically condemn[s] state programs directly aiding religious activity" when that aid is part of a neutral program available to a wide array of beneficiaries. . . . Even if Madison believed that the principle of nonestablishment of religion precluded government financial support for religion *per se* (in the sense of government benefits specifically targeting religion), there is no indication that at the time of the framing he took the dissent's extreme view that the government must discriminate against religious adherents by excluding them from more generally available financial subsidies. . . .

The historical evidence of government support for religious entities through property tax exemptions is also overwhelming. As the dissent concedes, property tax exemptions for religious bodies "have been in place for over 200 years without disruption to the interests represented by the Establishment Clause." . . . In my view, the dissent's acceptance of this tradition puts to rest the notion that the Establishment Clause bars monetary aid to religious groups even when the aid is equally available to other groups. A tax exemption in many cases is economically and functionally indistinguishable from a direct monetary subsidy. In one instance, the government relieves religious entities (along with others) of a generally applicable tax; in the other, it relieves religious entities (along with others) of some or all of the burden of that tax by returning it in the form of a cash subsidy. Whether the benefit is provided at the front or back end of the taxation process, the financial aid to religious groups is undeniable. The analysis under the Establishment Clause must also be the same. . . .

Though our Establishment Clause jurisprudence is in hopeless disarray, this case provides an opportunity to reaffirm one basic principle that has enjoyed an uncharacteristic degree of consensus: The Clause does not compel the exclusion of religious groups from government benefits programs that are generally available to a broad class of participants. . . .

Justice Souter, with whom Justice Stevens, Justice Ginsburg, and Justice Breyer join, dissenting.

The Court today, for the first time, approves direct funding of core religious activities by an arm of the State. It does so, however, only after erroneous treatment of some familiar principles of law implementing the First Amendment's Establishment and Speech Clauses, and by viewing the very funds in question as beyond the reach of the Establishment Clause's funding restrictions as such. Because there is no warrant for distinguishing among public funding sources for purposes of applying the First Amendment's prohibition of religious establishment, I would hold that the University's refusal to support petitioners' religious activities is compelled by the Establishment Clause. . . .

* * *

The Court's difficulties will be all the more clear after a closer look at Wide Awake than the majority opinion affords. The character of the magazine is candidly disclosed on the opening page of the first issue, where the editor-in-chief announces Wide Awake's mission in a letter to the readership signed, "Love in Christ": it is "to challenge Christians to live, in word and deed, according to the faith they proclaim and to encourage students to consider what a personal relationship with Jesus Christ means." . . .

Using public funds for the direct subsidization of preaching the word is categorically forbidden under the Establishment Clause, and if the Clause was meant to accomplish nothing else, it was meant to bar this use of public money. Evidence on the subject antedates even the Bill of Rights itself, as may be seen in the writings of Madison, whose authority on questions about the meaning of the Establishment Clause is well settled. . . . Four years before the First Congress proposed the First Amendment, Madison gave his opinion on the legitimacy of using public funds for religious purposes, in the Memorial and Remonstrance Against Religious Assessments, which played the central role in ensuring the defeat of the Virginia tax assessment bill in 1786 and framed the debate upon which the Religion Clauses stand:

> "Who does not see that . . . the same authority which can force a citizen to contribute three pence only of his property for the support of any one establishment, may force him to conform to any other establishment in all cases whatsoever?" . . .

Madison wrote against a background in which nearly every Colony had exacted a tax for church support, . . . the practice having become "so commonplace as to shock the freedom-loving colonials into a feeling of abhorrence." . . . Madison's Remonstrance captured the colonists' "conviction that individual religious liberty could be achieved best under a government which was stripped of all power to tax, to support, or otherwise to assist any or all religions, or to interfere with the beliefs of any religious individual or group." Their sentiment as expressed by Madison in Virginia, led not only to the defeat of Virginia's tax assessment bill, but also directly to passage of the Virginia Bill for Establishing Religious Freedom, written by Thomas Jefferson. That bill's preamble declared that "to compel a man to furnish contributions of money for the propagation of opinions which he disbelieves, is sinful and tyrannical." Jefferson, A Bill for Establishing Religious Freedom, . . . and its text provided "[t]hat no man shall be compelled to frequent or support any religious worship, place, or ministry whatsoever. . . ." We have "previously recognized that the provisions of the First Amendment, in the drafting and adoption of which Madison and Jefferson played such leading roles, had the same objective and were intended to provide the same protection against governmental intrusion on religious liberty as the Virginia statute." . . .

The principle against direct funding with public money is patently violated by the contested use of today's student activity fee. Like today's taxes generally, the fee is Madison's threepence. The University exercises the power of the State to compel a student to pay it, . . . and the use of any part of it for the direct support of religious activity thus strikes at what we have repeatedly held to be the heart of the prohibition on establishment. . . .

The Court, accordingly, has never before upheld direct state funding of the sort of proselytizing published in Wide Awake and, in fact has categorically condemned state programs directly aiding religious activity. . . .

Even when the Court has upheld aid to an institution performing both secular and sectarian functions, it has always made a searching enquiry to ensure that the institution kept the secular activities separate from its sectarian ones, with any direct aid flowing only to the former and never the latter. . . .

Reasonable minds may differ over whether the Court reached the correct result in each of these cases, but their common principle has never been questioned or repudiated. "Although Establishment Clause jurisprudence is characterized by few absolutes, the Clause does absolutely prohibit government-financed . . . indoctrination into the beliefs of a particular religious faith." . . .

The Court is ordering an instrumentality of the State to support religious evangelism with direct funding. This is a flat violation of the Establishment Clause.

Religious Freedom Restoration

Religious Freedom Constrained

In 1978 efforts to grant Native Americans the same religious rights that the Constitution had granted to other Americans finally seemed to have carried the day (see above, pp. 620-21, on the Indian Religious Freedom Act). In 1990, however, in a case coming out of the Pacific Northwest (Oregon Employment Division v. Smith), the U.S. Supreme Court rendered an opinion that made the Religious Freedom Act sound hollow indeed. In its majority opinion, the Court agreed to the dismissal from state employment of two persons who admitted using peyote as part of the official ritual of the Native American Church. What was even more unnerving about the majority opinion, however, was that its author, Justice Antonin Scalia, seemed determined to overthrow three decades of religious liberty guarantees for all Americans. The decision drew a vigorous dissent (written by Justice Harry Blackmun), but an equally vigorous separate opinion by Justice Sandra Day O'Connor. Even though Justice O'Connor agreed with the decision of the majority, she found the grounds upon which that decision was reached wholly unacceptable, even frightening. A portion of her concurring opinion is excerpted below.

Although I agree with the result the Court reaches in this case, I cannot join its opinion. In my view, today's holding dramatically departs from well-settled First Amendment jurisprudence, appears unnecessary to resolve the question presented, and is incompatible with our Nation's fundamental commitment to individual religious liberty.

The Court today extracts from our long history of free exercise precedents the single categorical rule that "if prohibiting the exercise of religion . . . is . . . merely the incidental effect of a generally applicable and otherwise valid provision, the First Amendment has not been offended." *Ante,* at 1599-1600 (citations omitted). Indeed, the Court holds that where the law is a generally applicable criminal prohibition, our usual free exercise jurisprudence does not even apply. *Ante,* at 1603. To reach this sweeping result, however, the Court must not only give a strained reading of the First Amendment but must also disregard our consistent application of free exercise doctrine to cases involving generally applicable regulations that burden religious con-

---

[Source: *U.S. Supreme Court Reporter,* Vol. 110 (St. Paul, Minn.: West Publishing Co., 1990), pp. 1606, 1607, 1608, 1613.]

duct. . . . Because the First Amendment does not distinguish between religious belief and religious conduct, conduct motivated by sincere religious belief, like the belief itself, must therefore be at least presumptively protected by the Free Exercise Clause.

The Court today, however, interprets the Clause to permit the government to prohibit, without justification, conduct mandated by an individual's religious beliefs, so long as that prohibition is generally applicable. *Ante,* at 1599. But a law that prohibits certain conduct — conduct that happens to be an act of worship for someone — manifestly does prohibit that person's free exercise of his religion. A person who is barred from engaging in religiously motivated conduct is barred from freely exercising his religion. Moreover, that person is barred from freely exercising his religion regardless of whether the law prohibits the conduct only when engaged in for religious reasons, only by members of that religion, or by all persons. It is difficult to deny that a law that prohibits religiously motivated conduct, even if the law is generally applicable, does not at least implicate First Amendment concerns.

The Court responds that generally applicable laws are "one large step" removed from laws aimed at specific religious practices. *Ante,* at 1599. The First Amendment, however, does not distinguish between laws that are generally applicable and laws that target particular religious practices. Indeed, few States would be so naive as to enact a law directly prohibiting or burdening a religious practice as such. Our free exercise cases have all concerned generally applicable laws that had the effect of significantly burdening a religious practice. If the First Amendment is to have any vitality, it ought not be construed to cover only the extreme and hypothetical situation in which a State directly targets a religious practice. . . .

Finally, the Court today suggests that the disfavoring of minority religions is an "unavoidable consequence" under our system of government and that accommodation of such religions must be left to the political process. *Ante,* at 1606. In my view, however, the First Amendment was enacted precisely to protect the rights of those whose religious practices are not shared by the majority and may be viewed with hostility. The history of our free exercise doctrine amply demonstrates the harsh impact majoritarian rule has had on unpopular or emerging religious groups such as the Jehovah's Witnesses and the Amish. Indeed, the words of Justice Jackson in *West Virginia Board of Education* v. *Barnett* . . . are apt:

"The very purpose of a Bill of Rights was to withdraw certain subjects from the vicissitudes of political controversy, to place them beyond the reach of majorities and officials and to establish them as legal principles to be applied by the courts. One's right to life, liberty, and property, to free speech, a free press, freedom of worship and assembly, and other fundamental rights may not be submitted to vote; they depend on the outcome of no elections."

Religious Freedom Restoration Act, 1993

As a result of the Oregon Employment Division v. Smith decision, many interested parties concluded that religious liberty itself was threatened. In an unprecedented union of interests, a large number of religious liberals and conservatives representing a wide variety of traditions came together to form the Coalition for the Free Exercise of Religion. They lobbied together in Congress for the Religious Freedom Restoration Act, which in October 1993 passed the U.S. House unanimously and the Senate by a vote of 97 to 3. President Bill Clinton signed the bill into law in November 1993.

This Act may be cited as the 'Religious Freedom Restoration Act of 1993'.

SEC. 2. CONGRESSIONAL FINDINGS AND DECLARATION OF PURPOSES.
(a) **Findings:** The Congress finds that —
  (1) the framers of the Constitution, recognizing free exercise of religion as an unalienable right, secured its protection in the First Amendment to the Constitution;
  (2) laws 'neutral' toward religion may burden religious exercise as surely as laws intended to interfere with religious exercise;
  (3) governments should not substantially burden religious exercise without compelling justification;
  (4) in Employment Division v. Smith, 494 U.S. 872 (1990) the Supreme Court virtually eliminated the requirement that the government justify burdens on religious exercise imposed by laws neutral toward religion; and
  (5) the compelling interest test as set forth in prior Federal court rulings is a workable test for striking sensible balances between religious liberty and competing prior governmental interests. . . .

SEC. 3. FREE EXERCISE OF RELIGION PROTECTED.
(a) **In General:** Government shall not substantially burden a person's exercise of religion even if the burden results from a rule of general applicability, except as provided in subsection (b).
(b) **Exception:** Government may substantially burden a person's exercise of religion only if it demonstrates that application of the burden to the person —
  (1) is in furtherance of a compelling governmental interest; and
  (2) is the least restrictive means of furthering that compelling governmental interest.

[Source: *Religious Freedom Restoration Act of 1993*, http://www.welcomehome.org/rainbow/nfs-regs/rfra-act.html (April 14, 2003).]

(c) **Judicial Relief:** A person whose religious exercise has been burdened in vio-
    lation of this section may assert that violation as a claim or defense in a ju-
    dicial proceeding and obtain appropriate relief against a government.
    Standing to assert a claim or defense under this section shall be governed by
    the general rules of standing under article III of the Constitution. . . .

SEC. 5. DEFINITIONS.
    As used in this Act —
1. the term 'government' includes a branch, department, agency, instrumentality, and official (or other person acting under color of law) of the
   United States, a State, or a subdivision of a State;
2. the term 'State' includes the District of Columbia, the Commonwealth
   of Puerto Rico, and each territory and possession of the United States;
3. the term 'demonstrates' means meets the burdens of going forward with
   the evidence and of persuasion; and
4. the term 'exercise of religion' means the exercise of religion under the
   First Amendment to the Constitution.

SEC. 6. APPLICABILITY.
(a) **In General.** — This Act applies to all Federal and State law, and the imple-
    mentation of that law, whether statutory or otherwise, and whether
    adopted before or after the enactment of this Act.
(b) **Rule of Construction.** — Federal statutory law adopted after the date of the
    enactment of this Act is subject to this Act unless such law explicitly ex-
    cludes such application by reference to this Act.
(c) **Religious Belief Unaffected.** — Nothing in this Act shall be construed to
    authorize any government to burden any religious belief.

SEC. 7. ESTABLISHMENT CLAUSE UNAFFECTED.
    Nothing in this Act shall be construed to affect, interpret, or in any way ad-
dress that portion of the First Amendment prohibiting laws respecting the
establishment of religion (referred to in this section as the 'Establishment
Clause'). Granting government funding, benefits, or exemptions, to the extent permissible under the Establishment Clause, shall not constitute a violation of this Act. As used in this section, the term 'granting', used with respect to government funding, benefits, or exemptions, does not include the
denial of government funding, benefits, or exemptions.

Judicial Setback: *City of Boerne* v. *Flores*, 1997

With the passage of the Religious Freedom Restoration Act (RFRA), issues of religion and state were now mixed with questions about whether the Supreme Court or the Congress was the authoritative interpreter of the Constitution. Hence, it was not surprising that the Court found an early occasion to declare the 1993 Act unconstitutional. The occasion was an effort by Archbishop Patricio Flores of San Antonio to obtain a building permit to enlarge a Catholic Church in the city of Boerne, Texas. When that request was denied, Archbishop Flores filed suit in federal court on the basis of the RFRA: the city was illegally impinging on the Constitution's guarantee of religious liberty. But a federal court disagreed, ruled in favor of the city, and declared the RFRA unconstitutional. The matter went to the Supreme Court, which in 1997 by a 6-3 decision agreed in declaring the RFRA unconstitutional. A number of states filed friend of the court briefs supporting Boerne. The following document is a summary of that decision made by the Legal Information Institute of Cornell University.

Respondent, the Catholic Archbishop of San Antonio, applied for a building permit to enlarge a church in Boerne, Texas. When local zoning authorities denied the permit, relying on an ordinance governing historic preservation in a district which, they argued, included the church, the Archbishop brought this suit challenging the permit denial under, *inter alia,* the Religious Freedom Restoration Act of 1993 (RFRA). The District Court concluded that by enacting RFRA Congress exceeded the scope of its enforcement power under §5 of the Fourteenth Amendment. The court certified its order for interlocutory appeal, and the Fifth Circuit reversed, finding RFRA to be constitutional.

Held: RFRA exceeds Congress' power.

(a) Congress enacted RFRA in direct response to *Employment Div., Dept. of Human Resources of Ore.* v. *Smith,* 4.94 U.S. 872, in which the Court upheld against a free exercise challenge a state law of general applicability criminalizing peyote use, as applied to deny unemployment benefits to Native American Church members who lost their jobs because of such use. In so ruling, the Court declined to apply the balancing test of *Sherbert* v. *Verner,* 374 U.S. 398, which asks whether the law at issue substantially burdens a religious practice and, if so, whether the burden is justified by a compelling government interest. RFRA

[Source: Syllabus: *City of Boerne v. Flores, Archbishop of San Antonio,* 25 June 1997, http://supct.law.cornell.edu/supct/html/95-2074.ZS.html (May 14, 2003).]

prohibits "[g]overnment" from "substantially burden[ing]" a person's exercise of religion even if the burden results from a rule of general applicability unless the government can demonstrate the burden "(1) is in furtherance of a compelling governmental interest; and (2) is the least restrictive means of furthering that . . . interest." 42 U.S.C. §2000bb+1. RFRA's mandate applies to any branch of Federal or State Government, to all officials, and to other persons acting under color of law. §2000bb-2(l). Its universal coverage includes "all Federal and State law, and the implementation of that law, whether statutory or otherwise, and whether adopted before or after [RFRA's enactment]." §2000bb-3(a). . . .

(c) RFRA is not a proper exercise of Congress' §5 enforcement power because it contradicts vital principles necessary to maintain separation of powers and the federal-state balance. An instructive comparison may be drawn between RFRA and the Voting Rights Act of 1965, provisions of which were upheld in *Katzenbach, supra,* and subsequent voting rights cases. In contrast to the record of widespread and persisting racial discrimination which confronted Congress and the Judiciary in those cases, RFRA's legislative record lacks examples of any instances of generally applicable laws passed because of religious bigotry in the past 40 years. Rather, the emphasis of the RFRA hearings was on laws like the one at issue that place incidental burdens on religion. It is difficult to maintain that such laws are based on animus or hostility to the burdened religious practices or that they indicate some widespread pattern of religious discrimination in this country. RFRA's most serious shortcoming, however, lies in the fact that it is so out of proportion to a supposed remedial or preventive object that it cannot be understood as responsive to, or designed to prevent, unconstitutional behavior. It appears, instead, to attempt a substantive change in constitutional protections, proscribing state conduct that the Fourteenth Amendment itself does not prohibit. Its sweeping coverage ensures its intrusion at every level of government, displacing laws and prohibiting official actions of almost every description and regardless of subject matter. Its restrictions apply to every government agency and official, §2000bb+2(l), and to all statutory or other law, whether adopted before or after its enactment, §2000bb+3(a). It has no termination date or termination mechanism. Any law is subject to challenge at any time by any individual who claims a substantial burden on his or her free exercise of religion. Such a claim will often be difficult to contest. See *Smith, supra,* at 887. Requiring a State to demonstrate a compelling interest and show that it has adopted the least restrictive means of achieving that interest is the most demanding test known to constitutional law. 494 U.S., at 888. Furthermore, the least restrictive means requirement was not used in the pre-*Smith* jurisprudence RFRA purported to codify. All told, RFRA is a considerable congressional intrusion into the States' traditional prerogatives and general authority to regulate for the health and welfare of their citizens, and is not designed to identify and counteract state laws likely to be unconstitutional because of their treatment of religion.

Contraception and Abortion

Contraception: *Humanae Vitae*

If Vatican II can be styled as Pope John's revolution, Humanae Vitae *(1968) may be regarded as Pope Paul's counterrevolution. This important encyclical, contrary to wide expectations, reaffirmed the historic opposition of the Roman Catholic Church to any form of birth control except that of the "natural" rhythm method and, of course, abstinence. The papal letter stated that "every action which either in anticipation of the conjugal act, or in development of its natural consequences, purposes to render procreation impossible" is absolutely prohibited. ". . . Each and every marriage act must remain open to the transmission of life." Before* Humanae Vitae *was issued, surveys conducted among America's Catholics showed that the Church's teaching on contraception was a most troublesome one for the faithful and that, further, it was being widely ignored. The encyclical proved more of a shock because it had been widely rumored that the papal commission advising Pope Paul VI would recommend some modification in the long-standing condemnation of all artificial means of birth control. Thus, when* Humanae Vitae *was proclaimed on July 29, 1968, it provoked protests, outcries, and defiance. More was at stake than a single moral teaching: the whole question of papal authority came under urgent and critical review. Two statements follow: (1) Roman Catholic theologians at the Catholic University of America, one day after the encyclical was published, issued a declaration which spoke of the "defects" in* Humanae Vitae; *(2) Protestant theologian and leading ecumenist Robert McAfee Brown (b. 1920) was invited by Charles E. Curran, then professor of moral theology at Catholic University, to offer "a Protestant reaction" to the papal pronouncement.*

[Sources: (1) Charles E. Curran and Robert E. Hunt, *Dissent In and For the Church: Theologians and Humanae Vitae* (New York: Sheed & Ward, 1969), pp. 24-26. (2) Charles E. Curran, ed., *Contraception: Authority and Dissent* (New York: Herder and Herder, 1969), pp. 193-94, 201-7.]

1.

1. As Roman Catholic theologians we respectfully acknowledge a distinct role of hierarchical *magisterium* (teaching authority) in the Church of Christ. At the same time, Christian tradition assigns theologians the special responsibility of evaluating and interpreting pronouncements of the magisterium in the light of the total theological data operative in each question or statement. We offer these initial comments on Pope Paul VI's Encyclical on the Regulation of Birth.

2. The Encyclical is not an infallible teaching. History shows that a number of statements of similar or even greater authoritative weight have subsequently been proved inadequate or even erroneous. Past authoritative statements on religious liberty, interest-taking, the right to silence, and the ends of marriage have all been corrected at a later date.

3. Many positive values concerning marriage are expressed in Paul VI's Encyclical. However, we take exception to the ecclesiology implied and the methodology used by Paul VI in the writing and promulgation of the document: they are incompatible with the Church's authentic self-awareness as expressed in and suggested by the acts of the Second Vatican Council itself. The Encyclical consistently assumes that the Church is identical with the hierarchical office. No real importance is afforded the witness of the life of the Church in its totality; the special witness of many Catholic couples is neglected; it fails to acknowledge the witness of the separated Christian churches and ecclesial communities; it is insensitive to the witness of many men of good will; it pays insufficient attention to the ethical import of modern science.

4. Furthermore, the Encyclical betrays a narrow and positivistic notion of papal authority, as illustrated by the rejection of the majority view presented by the Commission established to consider the question, as well as by the rejection of the conclusion of a large part of the international Catholic theological community.

5. Likewise, we take exception to some of the specific ethical conclusions contained in the Encyclical. They are based on an inadequate concept of natural law: the multiple forms of natural law theory are ignored and the fact that competent philosophers come to different conclusions on this very question are disregarded. Even the minority report of the papal commission noted grave difficulty in attempting to present conclusive proof of the immorality of artificial contraception based on natural law.

6. Other defects include: overemphasis on the biological aspects of conjugal relations as ethically normative; undue stress on sexual acts and on the faculty of sex viewed in itself, apart from the person and the couple; a static worldview which downplays the historical and evolutionary character of humanity in its finite existence, as described in Vatican II's *Pastoral Constitution on the Church in the Modern World;* unfounded assumptions about 'the evil

consequences of methods of artificial birth control'; indifference to Vatican II's assertion that prolonged sexual abstinence may cause 'faithfulness to be imperiled and its quality of fruitfulness to be ruined'; an almost total disregard for the dignity of millions of human beings brought into the world without the slightest possibility of being fed and educated decently.

7. In actual fact, the Encyclical demonstrates no development over the teaching of Pius XI's *Casti Connubii* [1930] whose conclusions have been called into question for grave and serious reasons. These reasons, given a muffled voice at Vatican II, have not been adequately handled by the mere repetition of past teaching.

8. It is common teaching in the Church that Catholics may dissent from authoritative, noninfallible teachings of the magisterium when sufficient reasons for so doing exist.

9. Therefore, as Roman Catholic theologians, conscious of our duty and our limitations, we conclude that spouses may responsibly decide according to their conscience that artificial contraception in some circumstances is permissible and indeed necessary to preserve and foster the values and sacredness of marriage.

10. It is our conviction also that true commitment to the mystery of Christ and the Church requires a candid statement of mind at this time by all Catholic theologians.

2.

In recent years it has been the rule of ecumenical encounter not to engage in vigorous criticism of the "other" side. The proper ecumenical stance has been to concentrate on the failings of our own confessional family and to appreciate the good qualities of our ecumenical counterparts. On the whole, this is a good principle. But to assume in relation to *Humanae Vitae* a judicious silence, when so much is at stake, not only for ecumenism but for the whole family of man, is no way to contribute to the ecumenical future. If my own denomination, or the World Council of Churches, made a mistake as monumental as I feel *Humanae Vitae* to be, I would want every Catholic who would to join the chorus of criticism, so that we might collectively forestall the repetition of such an error in the future. So the ecumenically responsible thing to do is not to say, "Wasn't *Populorum Progressio* forward looking?", but to ask, "How can the harm of *Humanae Vitae* be undone?"

Ecumenical responsibility demands personal honesty, and it is therefore only fair to forewarn readers at the start that the underlying presupposition of the following pages is that *Humanae Vitae* is a tragedy for the Catholic Church and for the contemporary world. It is not only its content that upsets me, although I think it objectively wrong on almost every score, from its lack of contact with the modern world to its limited understanding of the psychology of marriage and its faulty understanding of the place of sexual intercourse in that relationship. It is also the manner of its issuance that upsets me; it not only fails to produce convincing arguments to support its thesis and to go counter to the overwhelming majority opinion of the papal commission that was presumably to guide its final content, but it also flies in the face of collegial principle that I thought had been established by Vatican II and implies, possibly by intent, that papal authority is once again to be understood along the most reactionary lines of nineteenth-century Catholic thought.

It grieves me to write such words, for I know that to many Catholics they will seem shrill and lacking in the ecumenical charity all of us have been trying to establish. But if our goal is to speak the truth in love, we must remember that sometimes in the name of love we are forced to speak in terms that initially hurt. And if out of hurt can come healing, then perhaps out of the total episode of *Humanae Vitae* — both its presentation and reception — some good may yet come. . . .

An article in *Observatore Romano,* that bastion of orthodoxy, appearing in late August 1968, suggested that Catholics should accept the teaching of *Humanae Vitae* unquestioningly, since the Pope knows best, just as a patient unquestioningly accepts the diagnosis of a doctor because of the doctor's superior wisdom, or a foot soldier unhesitatingly carries out the command of his superior officer because of the officer's greater knowledge of military tactics. Even on the basis of these very dubious analogies it could be argued that a doctor might diagnose wrongly, and a military tactician make an unwise decision. So too, pressing the analogy, might a pope be incorrect. Conservatives as well as progressives have conceded that the encyclical is not infallible. Since the opposite of infallibility is fallibility, it might be presumed that one could question the conclusions of a fallible document, and that, of course, is precisely what the dissenters have done.

But the ecclesiastical authorities have questioned this right. They have demanded ecclesiastical loyalty oaths from those who dared to differ, and have begun engaging in punitive measures against those who do not fall into line. This, I assume, is because papal encyclicals up to now have enjoyed a kind of "practical infallibility," so that although one might have inward doubts, he did not voice them, lest scandal be caused to the faithful.

At all events, earlier papal encyclicals have been accorded a high degree of authority. But this has not been true of *Humanae Vitae.* From the moment of its release it has been the object of strong dissent by many of the most able Catholic theologians of our time, as well as priests and laymen. The authority of the pope, in other words, has been seriously questioned.

The type of questioning, I believe, is of an order different from past questioning. When the dogma of the assumption was promulgated in 1950, for example, many Catholics said that they questioned the "opportuneness" of the definition, but not that they questioned its substantive truth. Today, the disaffection over *Humanae Vitae* is not merely with the "opportuneness" but with the substantive claims. The Pope, so say the Catholic dissenters, is wrong, Rome has spoken, but the case is *not* closed. On the contrary, it remains open, and hundreds of theologians have said in effect that although the Pope has denied to Catholics the right to use contraceptives, Catholics can for good and sufficient reasons use them anyhow.

What does this do to the notion of papal authority? It obviously compromises it in very serious terms, and means that drastic overhauling of traditional views of authority is urgent, with no guarantee provided that the overhauling will be rapid enough to overtake the disintegrating process. . . .

I see no way in which this crisis of authority can be resolved without great damage to the Roman Catholic Church. The priests, theologians, and lay people are not going to accept *Humanae Vitae* with the dutiful docility the curia expects, and the Pope is not about to admit that he was wrong. (A papacy that cannot yet be quite sure if a mistake was made about Galileo will be in no hurry to acknowledge that a mistake has been made about birth control.) In the past, of course, such an *impasse* was solved by time. Catholics can now look at *Unam Sanctam* [1302] and dismiss it as time-bound, and they can employ the same procedure with the *Syllabus of Errors* [1864] or Pius IX's characterization of the notion of religious liberty as a "nightmare." In these and dozens of other instances, there has been time for the church to adjust. With *Humanae Vitae* there is not. For not only does it appear in an age of instant communication, but it appears in an age where, if its teachings were widely followed, many well-informed people believe that the consequences in terms of population explosion could well destroy man's future.

Can one then do no more than throw up his hands in dismay? I believe there are other options and that the most important one centers around the pressing of the very principle the encyclical appears to have bypassed, the principle of collegiality. Heiko Oberman, a Protestant observer at Vatican II, stated that while it had affirmed the collegiality of the bishops, it might take Vatican III to affirm the collegiality of the pope. The crisis of authority in the church today indicates that even more than this will be needed, and that it will be needed considerably sooner than Vatican IV. What will be needed is an extension of the principle of collegiality to include the collegiality of the whole people of God, for example the drawing into the highest councils and decisions of the church of the priests, theologians and laity. Such an extension could be justified on the controversy over birth control alone, for it is clear that the wisdom of the laity in this matter has exceeded the wisdom of the bishops, the bishop of Rome included. (Joseph Noonan has a cartoon in the *National Cath-*

olic Reporter, August 21, 1968, p. 4, which shows a woman saying, "I keep asking myself 'Do I really have a better understanding of the matter than the Pope?' And I keep answering 'Yes.'")

The church could learn from the experience of the reception of *Humanae Vitae* that the full exercise of teaching authority cannot rest with the bishop of Rome alone, nor even with the college of bishops alone, but must include the priests, theologians, and laity as well. Informally, the principle has long been acknowledged: the teaching of the church must correspond to the *sensus fidelium.* But the *sensus fidelium* in recent years has been highly elusive, particularly to inhabitants of Vatican City, to be intuited perhaps but never validated by a head count. Surely now, however, some kind of structure must emerge by means of which subsequent articulations of the Catholic faith can take account of the charisms that Vatican II insisted were not the exclusive prerogative of the hierarchy. The reception of *Humanae Vitae* is a grim reminder that when the hierarchy speaks without "consulting the faithful in matters of doctrine," it paints itself into awkward corners.

Abortion: The Courts, 1973, 1989, 1992

In the 1970s and well beyond, no issue divided American society more sharply than did abortion. What might appear to some to be a very private matter in fact became a noisy, clamorous, public question as opposing armies took to the streets — and to the courts. In 1973 the Supreme Court at last agreed to hear a case on abortion, all earlier cases having been dismissed as moot since no pregnancy ever lasted long enough for a case to make its way to the highest court. The lengthy decision in Roe v. Wade, *written by Justice Harry Blackmun (and supported by a 7 to 2 vote), presented a virtual history of abortion attitudes and practices throughout the world. (1) Only a small portion of that opinion is given below: one segment from the introduction, and another from the conclusion.*

This 1973 case did not settle the public debate, but only gave it greater focus and intensity. Now the question was posed in terms of either overturning Roe v. Wade *or sustaining it. All eyes centered on the Court once again in 1989 as a Missouri law promised to return to the states all jurisdiction in the explosive area of abortion. With several separate opinions in the case of*

[Sources: (1) *U.S. Supreme Court Reporter,* Vol. 93 (St. Paul, Minn.: West Publishing Co., 1974), pp. 708-9, 732. (2) *Supreme Court Reporter,* Vol. 188 (St. Paul, Minn.: West Publishing Co., 1989), p. 3067. (3) *Supreme Court Reporter,* Vol. 188 (St. Paul, Minn.: West Publishing Co., 1989), pp. 3065-67. (4) *The New York Times,* June 30, 1992, pp. A16-A17. (5) *The New York Times,* June 30, 1992, pp. A16-A17.]

Webster *v.* Reproductive Services, *the Court upheld the constitutionality of the Missouri statute. Two vigorous dissents were entered, the first (2) by Justice Harry Blackmun who argued passionately that the Court had gone too far, and the second (3) by Justice Antonin Scalia who argued just as passionately that the Court had not gone far enough.*

Public attention was riveted once again in 1992 as a Pennsylvania case, Planned Parenthood *v.* Casey, *made its way to the Supreme Court. Narrowly, the question was whether Pennsylvania's restrictions on obtaining an abortion were constitutional; broadly, the question that loomed large was whether, after nineteen years,* Roe *v.* Wade *would be overturned. Most court-watchers thought that it would. By a 5 to 4 vote, however, the Court decreed that while states could make abortion more difficult, they could not absolutely prohibit it. No "undue burden" could be placed upon the woman seeking an abortion.*

The Court divided even more than the 5 to 4 vote indicates, as there were justices who concurred in part and dissented in part. The two more liberal justices, Harry A. Blackmun and John Paul Stevens, would have preferred to dismiss all of Pennsylvania's restrictions. The four more conservative justices (William H. Rehnquist, Antonin Scalia, Byron R. White, and Clarence Thomas) would have preferred to see Roe *overturned completely. A center group of justices (Sandra Day O'Connor, Anthony M. Kennedy, and David H. Souter) made the difference in sustaining the central holding in* Roe.

(4) Justices O'Connor, Kennedy, and Souter, writing for the majority and especially for the "center," explain their position in the excerpt below. (5) Chief Justice Rehnquist, for the dissenters, argues that too much weight was given to the force of an earlier decision ("stare decisis") and to the pressure of public opinion.

1. *Roe* v. *Wade* (Blackmun)

We forthwith acknowledge our awareness of the sensitive and emotional nature of the abortion controversy, of the vigorous opposing views, even among physicians, and of the deep and seemingly absolute convictions that the subject inspires. One's philosophy, one's experiences, one's exposure to the raw edges of human existence, one's religious training, one's attitudes toward life and family and their values, and the moral standards one establishes and seeks to observe, are all likely to influence and to color one's thinking and conclusions about abortion.

In addition, population growth, pollution, poverty, and racial overtones tend to complicate and not to simplify the problem.

Our task, of course, is to resolve the issue by constitutional measurement, free of emotion and of predilection. We seek earnestly to do this, and, because we do, we have inquired into, and in this opinion place some emphasis upon, medical and medical-legal history and what that history reveals about man's attitude toward the abortion procedure over the centuries. We bear in mind, too, Mr. Justice Holmes' admonition . . . :

"[The Constitution] is made for people of fundamentally differing views, and the accident of our finding certain opinions natural and familiar, or novel, and even shocking, ought not to conclude our judgment upon the question whether statutes embodying them conflict with the Constitution of the United States."

*   *   *

To summarize and to repeat:

1. A state criminal abortion statute of the current Texas type, that excepts from criminality only a *life-saving* procedure on behalf of the mother, without regard to pregnancy stage and without recognition of the other interests involved, is violative of the Due Process Clause of the Fourteenth Amendment.

(a) For the stage prior to approximately the end of the first trimester, the abortion decision and its effectuation must be left to the medical judgment of the pregnant woman's attending physician.

(b) For the stage subsequent to approximately the end of the first trimester, the State, in promoting its interest in the health of the mother, may, if it chooses, regulate the abortion procedure in ways that are reasonably related to maternal health.

(c) For the stage subsequent to viability, the State in promoting its interest in the potentiality of human life may, if it chooses, regulate, and even proscribe, abortion except where it is necessary, in appropriate medical judgment, for the preservation of the life or health of the mother.

2. *Webster* v. *Reproductive Services* (Blackmun, dissenting)

Today, *Roe* v. *Wade*, 410 U.S. 113 (1973), and the fundamental constitutional right of women to decide whether to terminate a pregnancy, survive but are not secure. Although the Court extricates itself from this case without making a single, even incremental, change in the law of abortion, the plurality and JUSTICE SCALIA would overrule *Roe* (the first silently, the other explicitly) and would return to the States virtually unfettered authority to control the quintessentially intimate, personal, and life-directing decision whether to carry a fetus to term. Although today, no less than yesterday, the Constitution and the decisions of this Court prohibit a State from enacting laws that inhibit women from the meaningful exercise of that right, a plurality of this Court implicitly invites every state legislature to enact more and more restrictive abortion regulations in order to provoke more and more test cases, in the hope that sometime down the line the Court will return the law of procreative freedom to the severe limitations that generally prevailed in this country before January 22, 1973. Never in my memory has a plurality announced a judgment of this Court that so foments disregard for the law and for our standing decisions.

Nor in my memory has a plurality gone about its business in such a deceptive fashion. At every level of its review, from its effort to read the real meaning out of the Missouri statute, to its intended evisceration of precedents and its deafening silence about the constitutional protections that it would jettison, the plurality obscures the portent of its analysis. With feigned restraint, the plurality announces that its analysis leaves *Roe* "undisturbed," albeit "modif[ied] and narrow[ed]." But this disclaimer is totally meaningless. The plurality opinion is filled with winks, and nods, and knowing glances to those who would do away with *Roe* explicitly, but turns a stone face to anyone in search of what the plurality conceives as the scope of a woman's right under the Due Process Clause to terminate a pregnancy free from the coercive and brooding influence of the State. The simple truth is that *Roe* would not survive the plurality's analysis, and that the plurality provides no substitute for *Roe's* protective umbrella.

I fear for the future. I fear for the liberty and equality of the millions of women who have lived and come of age in the 16 years since *Roe* was decided. I fear for the integrity of, and public esteem for, this Court.

I dissent.

3. *Webster* v. *Reproductive Services* (Scalia, dissenting)

The real question, then, is whether there are valid reasons to go beyond the most stingy possible holding today. It seems to me there are not only valid but compelling ones. Ordinarily, speaking no more broadly than is absolutely required avoids throwing settled law into confusion; doing so today preserves a chaos that is evident to anyone who can read and count. Alone sufficient to justify a broad holding is the fact that our retaining control, through *Roe*, of what I believe to be, and many of our citizens recognize to be, a political issue, continuously distorts the public perception of the role of this Court. We can now look forward to at least another Term with carts full of mail from the public, and streets full of demonstrators, urging us — their unelected and life-tenured judges who have been awarded those extraordinary, undemocratic characteristics precisely in order that we might follow the law despite the popular will — to follow the popular will. Indeed, I expect we can look forward to even more of that than before, given our indecisive decision today. And if these reasons for taking the unexceptional course of reaching a broader holding are not enough, then consider the nature of the constitutional question we avoid: In most cases, we do no harm by not speaking more broadly than the decision requires. Anyone affected by the conduct that the avoided holding would have prohibited will be able to challenge it himself, and have his day in court to make the argument. Not so with respect to the harm that many States believed, pre-*Roe,* and many may continue to believe, is caused by largely unrestricted abortion. That will continue to occur if the States have the constitutional power to prohibit it, and would do so, but we skillfully avoid telling them so. Perhaps those abortions cannot constitutionally be proscribed. That is surely an arguable question, the question that reconsideration of *Roe* v. *Wade* entails. But what is not at all arguable, it seems to me, is that we should decide now and not insist that we be run into a corner before we grudgingly yield up our judgment. The only sound reason for the latter course is to prevent a change in the law — but to think that desirable begs the question to be decided.

It was an arguable question today whether § 188.029 of the Missouri law contravened this Court's understanding of *Roe* v. *Wade,* and I would have examined *Roe* rather than examining the contravention. Given the Court's newly contracted abstemiousness, what will it take, one must wonder, to permit us to reach that fundamental question? The result of our vote today is that we will not reconsider that prior opinion, even if most of the Justices think it is wrong, unless we have before us a statute that in fact contradicts it — and even then (under our newly discovered "no-broader-than-necessary" requirement) only minor problematical aspects of *Roe* will be reconsidered, unless one expects State legislatures to adopt provisions whose compliance with *Roe* cannot even be argued with a straight face. It thus appears that the mansion of constitutionalized abortion-law, constructed overnight in *Roe* v. *Wade,* must be disassembled door-jamb by door-jamb, and never entirely brought down, no matter how wrong it may be.

Of the four courses we might have chosen today — to reaffirm *Roe,* to overrule it explicitly, to overrule it *sub silentio,* or to avoid the question — the last is the least responsible.

4. *Planned Parenthood* v. *Casey* (O'Connor, Kennedy, and Souter)

Men and women of good conscience can disagree, and we suppose some always shall disagree, about the profound moral and spiritual implications of terminating a pregnancy, even in its earliest stages. Some of us as individuals find abortion offensive to our most basic principles of morality, but that cannot control our decision. Our obligation is to define the liberty of all, not to mandate our own moral code. The underlying constitutional issue is whether the state can resolve these philosophical questions in such a definitive way that a woman lacks all choice in the matter, except perhaps in those rare circumstances in which the pregnancy is itself a danger to her own life or health, or is the result of rape or incest.

*   *   *

When this Court reexamines a prior holding, its judgment is customarily informed by a series of prudential and pragmatic considerations designed to test the consistency of overruling a prior decision with the ideal of the rule of law, and to gauge the respective costs of reaffirming and overruling a prior case. Thus, for example, we may ask whether the rule has proved to be intolerable simply in defying practical workability, whether the rule is subject to a kind of reliance that would lend a special hardship to the consequences of overruling and add inequity to the cost of repudiation, whether related principles of law have so far developed as to have left the old rule no more than a remnant of abandoned doctrine, or whether facts have so changed or come to be seen so differently, as to have robbed the old rule of significant application or justification.

So in this case, we may inquire whether Roe's central rule has been found unworkable; whether the rule's limitation on state power could be removed without serious inequity to those who have relied upon it or significant damage to the stability of the society governed by the rule in question; whether the law's growth in the intervening years has left Roe's central rule a doctrinal anachronism discounted by society; and whether Roe's premises of fact have so far changed in the ensuing two decades as to render its central holding somehow irrelevant or unjustifiable in dealing with the issue it addressed.

Although Roe has engendered opposition, it has in no sense proven "unworkable," representing as it does a simple limitation beyond which a state law is unenforceable.

5. *Planned Parenthood* v. *Casey* (Rehnquist, dissenting)

There is also a suggestion in the joint opinion that the propriety of overruling a "divisive" decision depends in part on whether "most people" would now agree that it should be overruled. Either the demise of opposition or its progression to substantial popular agreement apparently is required to allow the Court to reconsider a divisive opinion. How such agreement would be ascertained, short of a public opinion poll, the joint opinion does not say. But surely even the suggestion is totally at war with the idea of "legitimacy" in whose name it is invoked.

The Judicial Branch derives its legitimacy, not from following public opinion, but from deciding by its best lights whether legislative enactments of the popular branches of Government comport with the Constitution. The doctrine of *stare decisis* is an adjunct of this duty, and should be no more subject to the vagaries of public opinion than is the basic judicial task.

There are other reasons why the joint opinion's discussion of legitimacy is unconvincing as well. In assuming that the Court is perceived as "surrender[ing] to political pressure" when it overrules a controversial decision, the joint opinion forgets that there are two sides to any controversy. The joint opinion asserts that, in order to protect its legitimacy, the Court must refrain from overruling a controversial decision lest it be viewed as favoring those who oppose the decision. But a decision to adhere to prior precedent is subject to the same criticism, for in such a case one can easily argue that the Court is responding to those who have demonstrated in favor of the original decision.

The decision in *Roe* has engendered large demonstrations, including repeated marches on this Court and on Congress, both in opposition to and in support of that decision. A decision either way on *Roe* can therefore be perceived as favoring one group or the other. But this perceived dilemma arises only if one assumes, as the joint opinion does, that the Court should make its decisions with a view toward speculative public perceptions.

Abortion: The Churches, 1984, 1985, 1987, 1996

For a great many people, abortion remained an issue that was fundamentally moral and religious. The churches as official bodies have taken note of it, even as individuals with religiously informed consciences have spoken to the question. Four statements follow. (1) In 1984 some Roman Catholic priests and nuns (27 in all) took out a full-page advertisement in the New York Times *to call for free discussion of the question. (2) The following year, the U.S. Catholic Conference, in response to the earlier advertisement, indicated that the issue within the Church was settled. (3) In 1987, the United Church of Christ (of Congregational heritage) upheld the right of safe and legal abortions. (4) And in 1996 the Southern Baptist Convention registered its firm opposition to partial-birth abortion.*

[Sources: (1) J. Gordon Melton, ed., *The Churches Speak Out: Abortion* (Detroit: Gale Research, 1989), pp. 15-16. (2) J. Gordon Melton, ed., *The Churches Speak Out: Abortion* (Detroit: Gale Research, 1989), pp. 17-18. (3) J. Gordon Melton, ed., *The Churches Speak Out: Abortion* (Detroit: Gale Research, 1989), pp. 159-60. (4) http://www.sbc.net/resolutions/resprintfriendly.asp?ID=26

1.

Catholic Statement on Pluralism and Abortion (1984)

A Diversity of Opinions Regarding Abortion Exists Among Committed Catholics.

Continued confusion and polarization within the Catholic community on the subject of abortion prompt us to issue this statement.

Statements of recent Popes and of the Catholic hierarchy have condemned the direct termination of pre-natal life as morally wrong in all instances. There is the mistaken belief in American society that this is the only legitimate Catholic position. In fact, a diversity of opinions regarding abortion exists among committed Catholics:

- A large number of Catholic theologians hold that even direct abortion, though tragic, can sometimes be a moral choice.
- According to data compiled by the National Opinion Research Center, only 11% of Catholics surveyed disapprove of abortion in all circumstances.

These opinions have been formed by:

- Familiarity with the actual experiences that lead women to make a decision for abortion;
- A recognition that there is no common and constant teaching on ensoulment in Church doctrine, nor has abortion always been treated as murder in canonical history;
- An adherence to principles of moral theology, such as probabilism, religious liberty, and the centrality of informed conscience; and
- An awareness of the acceptance of abortion as a moral choice by official statements and respected theologians of other faith groups.

Therefore, it is necessary that the Catholic community encourage candid and respectful discussion on this diversity of opinion within the Church, and that Catholic youth and families be educated on the complexity of the issues of responsible sexuality and human reproduction.

Further, Catholics — especially priests, religious, theologians, and legislators — who publicly dissent from hierarchical statements and explore areas of moral and legal freedom on the abortion question should not be penalized by their religious superiors, church employers, or bishops.

Finally, while recognizing and supporting the legitimate role of the hierarchy in providing Catholics with moral guidance on political and social issues and in seeking legislative remedies to social injustices, we believe that Catholics should not seek the kind of legislation that curtails the legitimate exercise of the freedom of religion and conscience or discriminates against poor women.

In the belief that responsible moral decisions can only be made in an atmosphere of freedom from fear or coercion, we, the undersigned, call upon all Catholics to affirm this statement.

2.

Much has been made lately of statements by persons who, emphasizing that they are Catholics, assert that they are not bound by what the church says about abortion. In reply, we wish to make a very simple point: The church's teaching in this matter is binding not only because the church says so, but because this teaching expresses the objective demands placed on all of us by the inherent dignity of human life. A Catholic who chooses to dissent from this teaching, or to support dissent from it, is dissenting not only from church law but from a

Antiabortion protest, Washington, D.C., 1978
(Religion News Service)

higher law which the church seeks to observe and teach. Such dissent can in no way be seen as legitimate alternative teaching.

Through the Respect Life Program, which begins on the first Sunday of October, the church recommits itself at every level to the Christian message of unconditional love for all human beings. This program addresses a broad range of issues involving the sanctity and dignity of human life, while giving special attention to the current situation of virtually unrestricted abortion. It provides resources and suggests programs to enable parishes, schools and church-related organizations to contribute to the church's long-range effort. We urge all Catholics to participate in this effort by finding out how they can help make the Respect Life Program a success in their area.

Respect for life requires us to speak a firm no to all that threatens or diminishes life both before and after birth. We must say no unequivocally to abortion, to euthanasia, to nuclear war, to degrading poverty and to many other violations of human dignity. But these noes express the church's positive attitude of love for all human life as a precious gift of the Creator. Every Catholic has the awesome responsibility of understanding this message more clearly and communicating it to others, so that all God's children may have life and have it more abundantly.

3.

United Church of Christ
Sexuality and Abortion: A Faithful Response (1987)

WHEREAS, Scripture teaches that all human life is precious in God's sight and teaches the importance of personal moral freedom, and

WHEREAS, previous General Synods, beginning in 1971, have considered the theological and ethical implications of abortion, and have supported its legal availability, while recognizing its moral ambiguity and urging that alternatives to abortion always be fully and carefully considered, and

WHEREAS, women and men must make decisions about unplanned or unwanted pregnancies that involve their physical, emotional, and spiritual well-being, and

WHEREAS, the United States leads nearly all other developed nations of the world in pregnancy, abortion, and childbearing rates for teenagers, and

WHEREAS, access to birth control is being jeopardized by decreases in Federal funding for human services, including family planning programs, and certain groups continue their efforts to reverse the Roe

vs. Wade decision of 1973, which affirms the right to choose a safe
and legal abortion, and

WHEREAS, abortion is a social justice issue, both for parents dealing
with pregnancy and parenting under highly stressed circumstances,
as well as for our society as a whole, and

WHEREAS, previous General Synods have called upon the church to provide programs of counseling and education about the meaning and
nature of human life, sexuality, responsible parenthood, population
control, and family life.

THEREFORE, BE IT RESOLVED, that the Sixteenth General Synod:

1. Affirms the sacredness of all of life, and the need to protect and defend
   human life in particular;
2. Encourages persons facing unplanned pregnancies to consider giving
   birth and parenting the child or releasing the child for adoption before
   considering abortion;
3. Upholds the right of men and women to have access to adequately funded
   family planning services, and to safe, legal abortions as one option among
   others;
4. Affirms the need for adequately funded support systems, including health
   and day care services, for those who choose to raise children;
5. Urges that resources on human sexuality being prepared by the Board for
   Homeland Ministries be used widely in the churches, and that the Resolutions of previous General Synods on sexuality issues be distributed and
   studied as part of these resources;
6. Urges the United Church of Christ, at all levels, to provide support, resources, and information to persons facing unplanned pregnancies, including counseling of persons who choose to have abortions;
7. Urges the United Church of Christ, at all levels, to provide educational resources and programs to persons, especially young persons, to help reduce the incidence of unplanned and unwanted pregnancies, and to encourage responsible approaches to sexual behaviour;
8. Urges pastors, members, local churches, conferences, and instrumentalities to oppose actively legislation and amendments which seek to revoke
   or limit access to safe and legal abortions.

4.

Southern Baptist Convention Resolution on the Partial-Birth Abortion Ban (1996)

WHEREAS, The Southern Baptist Convention has consistently and over-whelmingly adopted resolutions affirming the declarations of Scripture that all human life is a sacred gift from our sovereign God and therefore that all abortions, except in those very rare cases where the life of the mother is clearly in danger, are wrong, and

WHEREAS, A specific technique known as partial-birth abortion is a particularly grisly procedure wherein a doctor uses forceps and hands to deliver an intact baby, feet first, until only the head remains in the birth canal, whereafter the doctor pierces the base of the baby's skull with surgical scissors, whereafter he or she then inserts a canula into the incision and suctions out the brain of the baby so the head collapses; and

WHEREAS, The Congress of the United States has passed legislation which would make this inhumane procedure, which the American Catholic cardinals have correctly characterized as more akin to infanticide than abortion, illegal except to save the life of the mother; and

WHEREAS, The President of the United States vetoed this legislation and offered as justification for his action that he had prayed about the matter and determined that he could not sign the legislation unless it contained an exception for cases where there might be serious health consequences to the mother and

WHEREAS, The mother's health exception has been completely discredited as a catch-all loophole which has been demonstrated to include any reason the mother so desires; and

WHEREAS, The Bible is the perfect revelation of God's will, including His perfect moral will for those whom He has created in His very own image; and

WHEREAS, It is impossible to conclude that God, who is perfect and unchanging in all His attributes, and whose laws are perfect and immutable, would reveal to any person, through prayer, that which is contrary to His Word; and

WHEREAS, Abortion in general, and partial-birth abortion in particular, continues as a blight upon our culture and surely deserves God's judgment; Now, therefore,

BE IT RESOLVED, That we, the messengers to the Southern Baptist Convention, meeting in session June 11-13, 1996, in New Orleans, Louisiana, do commend those members of Congress who voted to support legislation which would have abolished partial-birth abortions; and

BE IT FURTHER RESOLVED, That we express our strong disapproval of the votes of those members of Congress who stood in opposition to this legislation; and

BE IT FURTHER RESOLVED, That we express our strong disapproval of President Clinton's veto of this legislation; and

BE IT FURTHER RESOLVED, That we express our disapproval of the President's suggestion that God would reveal to him in prayer that any abortion method, particularly one so barbarous in technique and so cruel in effect, would ever have God's approval; and

BE IT FURTHER RESOLVED, That we, the messengers to the Southern Baptist Convention, in a genuine spirit of love do admonish and encourage President Clinton, himself a Southern Baptist, to reverse his shameful decision to veto this legislation and sign it into law; or in the alternative of such failure to reverse his action, we call upon every member of Congress to vote to override the President's veto; and

BE IT FINALLY RESOLVED, That we pray for our nation, upon whom the blight of abortion remains, that we might come to recognize the sanctity of innocent, unborn babies and that we might seek civil justice for these innocent victims of a cruelty so harsh that we are surely accountable for our failure to intervene on their behalf.

Homosexuality and the Churches

One of the most divisive arenas in the American churches from the late 1980s onward has been constituted by debates about homosexuality: Could homo-

---

[Sources: (1) Reconciling Ministries Network, "Why Become a Reconciling Congregation," http://www.rmnetwork.org/papers/resource3.pdf (30 May 2003). (2) The Confessing Movement, "Tract Number Three: Our Doctrinal Standards and Sexuality," http://www.confessingumc.org/tract3.html (30 May 2003).]

sexual practice be "natural" and therefore accepted? Were ancient prohibitions in all the major religious traditions to be maintained? Could nonpracticing homosexuals be ordained? Could practicing homosexuals be ordained? What were obligations, regardless of convictions about homosexual orientation and practice, for welcoming homosexuals as worthy humans in themselves? Where most conservative denominations spoke out against homosexual practice and the ordination of homosexuals, all of the mainline Protestant denominations found themselves embroiled in seemingly endless controversy. The Roman Catholic Church underwent its own traumas on the subject as reports of homosexual orientation and practice among the priesthood kept coming in the early years of the new century. There were also parallel controversies among the different Jewish groups. The documents that follow come from the United Methodist Church, but they illustrate tensions found very widely in American religious bodies. (1) Reconciling Ministries Network, a strongly inclusive voice among Methodists, was founded in the early 1980s, and by 2003 spoke for more than 180 local congregations, 25 campus ministries, and 19 other ministries. This essay explains the organization's mission and goals. (2) In the year 2000, three conservative voices in the United Methodist Church — the Confessing Movement, Good News, and the Institute on Religion and Democracy — joined together as the Coalition for United Methodist Accountability. Its defining document included an outline of views on this controversial subject.

1. Why Become a Reconciling Congregation?

The essence of the Gospel of Jesus Christ is that all people are welcome in the family of God. Signs on churches abound, proclaiming that "everyone" is welcome. But how often is that really true? In any particular church, who might not be welcome?

This paper acknowledges that even congregations with welcoming signs wonder why they should become a Reconciling Congregation — why they should extend a specific invitation to those who are lesbian or gay or establish specific ministries for lesbian and gay people and their families. Some believe that their congregation has no lesbian or gay members and, therefore, "it's not an issue here." Others may say that sexual orientation is a private matter, not something to make an issue of. Others may point out that their congregation already has lesbian and gay members, so "obviously, they feel welcome." Still others will insist that the church shouldn't single out a particular group. . . .

Imagine being afraid to visit a church, having to wonder if you would be ostracized or condemned on your first visit. This is exactly what many lesbian and gay people fear when they contemplate attending church, and the fear only grows if they risk becoming active in a church community, as many do. "They accept me now, but what if they find out? Will they reject me and all I've given to the congregation?"

Within the lesbian/gay/bisexual community, the widely-held assumption is that they are not welcome in churches. . . .

Many lesbian and gay people choose not to put themselves through this ordeal. They have cut themselves off from churches and all the pain churches have brought into their lives. Those who seek to maintain a Christian spirituality often seek alternative communities — either a publicly-identified accepting community, like the Metropolitan Community Church, or other spirituality groups.

Again, imagine visiting a home and being told to leave because of your appearance, your dress, or your speech. Would you return without a personal invitation and assurance that you would be fully welcomed? Probably not. Nor can you expect lesbian, gay, and bisexual people to take the risk of trusting that they are welcome in your congregation, without your congregation taking the first step — to make a public declaration that they are welcome. . . .

Some people say, "This is really a personal, private matter. Why make it a public issue?" Some may worry about how their friends and the general public will react when they find out that your congregation welcomes lesbian and gay people. "Will this become a 'gay' church?" "Will they think I'm one of them?" "Will it compromise our community ministry?"

While such fears are understandable, the suggested alternative — not to make this concern public — contradicts the very nature of our Christian faith and ministry. When we choose to join a local church, we make a statement: that our faith in Jesus Christ is more than a personal, private concern. Our faith is to be lived and nurtured in our relationships with other members of our chosen community. Our faith is to be exemplified in our congregation's public ministry to the larger community. Simply erecting a church building and hanging a sign out front makes our congregational life a public matter.

Certainly the core of the New Testament record is that God calls us to witness publicly to God's saving act in the life and death of Jesus Christ. Jesus' ministry was carried out in the public sphere. But immediately after Jesus' death, his followers hid together behind locked doors. Even though they had personally experienced Jesus' power to transform human lives, they were afraid to go public. Because of real dangers, it seemed much easier to form a private club. But God didn't let it stop there. God appeared in the resurrected Jesus Christ and bestowed the gift of the Comforter, the Holy Spirit, to guide and sustain them in their public ministry. We — no less than the disciples — are called to a public ministry as well.

Unfortunately, rather than enable public ministries with lesbian, gay, and bisexual people, the Bible and Christian tradition are often used to obstruct such ministries. People point to a few passages in the Levitical Code and Paul's letters as "proof" that the Bible condemns homosexuality. They claim that becoming a Reconciling Congregation contradicts the Bible, or that openness to gay/lesbian people compromises the Bible's authority.

Such claims do a great injustice to our Biblical heritage and to the Gospel of Jesus Christ. They reduce the Bible to little more than a listing of rules and laws written for people who lived two to three thousand years ago. The writers' ancient world-views are inextricably woven into their writings — world-views that in many ways contradict our current understanding. In the ancient world, for example, the earth was thought to be flat and assumed to be the center of the universe. Demons and evil spirits were believed to be visibly at work in the world. Women were considered passive receptacles for human reproduction and relegated to secondary social status. Slavery was considered an acceptable human institution.

Surely the purpose of the Bible is not to require us to live within the rules and laws of an ancient culture. Jesus proclaimed a gospel of grace rather than a life bound by laws. He offered a glimpse of a God who offers salvation to people regardless of who they are or what they have done. The parable of the Prodigal Son in Luke captures this radically new understanding of God. The loving and

Religious leaders join in song at a meeting opposing California's Proposition 22, which would define marriage as strictly heterosexual.
(Photo by Ted Parks, Religion News Service)

forgiving father openly welcomes his lost and wandering son, with no strings attached. Similarly, God's grace is not conditional; it is freely given.

This is the Biblical heritage we claim as Christians. We are not required to live within a culture-bound code of law to attain righteousness. The vibrant collection of Biblical stories teach us about God acting in history and people responding in faith. Thus, we are called to ethical living because of God's love and forgiveness, and we seek to reflect God's love in our relationships with other people and in our stewardship of creation.

This is the Gospel you claim in deciding to become a Reconciling Congregation — a gospel that welcomes everyone into the Body of Christ and recognizes that the experience of acceptance can and does transform human lives. The loving parent of the prodigal son did not say, "I love you — if you do this" or "welcome home — but you should change." Similarly, by placing no conditions on admission to the family of God, a Reconciling Congregation manifests Jesus' gospel of grace.

2.

AT ISSUE: **What does the scriptural confession of Jesus Christ as Son, Savior, and Lord, as interpreted according to United Methodist Doctrinal Standards, require of us regarding the recurring debates on sexuality and Christian Marriage?**

As the one and only Lord of all, Jesus Christ reigns over creation and history, and hence over every aspect of human existence, including human sexuality.

During his earthly ministry Jesus taught: "Have you not read that the one who made them at the beginning 'made them male and female,' and said 'For this reason a man shall leave his father and mother and be joined to his wife, and the two shall become one flesh'? so they are no longer two, but one flesh. Therefore, what God has joined together, let no one separate" (Matthew 19:4-6 NRSV). This is basic Christian truth regarding human sexuality. Marriage is an enduring covenant between one man and one woman. Marriage, according to Christian teaching, is a bond with a solemn promise of mutual commitment. Marriage is able to provide a living environment for the welcoming and raising of children, the most precious gifts that come from human sexuality.

The moral relativism of our time rebels against Jesus Christ's gracious rule over human sexuality. This relativism and rebellion have found their way into the United Methodist Church. There are those in the Church who understand marriage as a short-term contract, who desire to legitimize homosexual practice, and who care little about protecting the unborn child and mother. In some quarters of our denomination, premarital sex, extramarital sex, and serial marriage are silently tolerated. A confusion has arisen in our Church between the Lordship of Christ and the reigning cultural virtue of tolerance. The Confessing Movement challenges the misuse of the principle of tolerance to set aside the authority of Scripture and Church's teaching on human sexuality.

Scripture and Sexual Relativism

One result of the confusion over tolerance is that the Church is continually being pressured to make decisions which abandon the normative teaching of scripture with regard to homosexual conduct. The argument is frequently made now that the biblical prohibitions against same-sex acts are irrelevant because they are part of a pre-modern cultural context. But the normative moral force of biblical texts on sexual behavior cannot be explained away by reference to changing cultural contexts. While every sacred text is written, delivered, and shaped within some cultural context, its moral force is not reducible to that context.

For example, many advocates for a Christian acceptance of homosexual behavior argue that the prohibitions in Leviticus against same-sex acts are part of the Jewish law from which the gospel has released Christians. But Paul clearly did not believe that such sexual behavior was a part of the ritual purity code of Levitical law that was transcended by Christ's sacrifice on the cross. The Mosaic moral tradition still exercised normative guidance for Christians. Paul wrote, "Shall we sin because we are not under law but under grace? By no means!" (Rom. 6:15). He understood that grace did not do away with morality; it provided the energizing power for it. "Do we, then, nullify the law by this faith? Not at all! Rather, we uphold the law." (Rom. 3:31).

Those who would legitimize homosexual acts within the Church often base their arguments upon a re-interpretation of Romans 1, arguing that it is not applicable to contemporary understandings of homosexuality. Yet many responsible biblical scholars, as well as the Church at large have not been convinced by these new interpretations. Indeed, Paul's profound analysis of sin in that text rests on a powerful analogy between homosexual behavior and idolatry. Homosexual behavior denies our identity as male and female, just as idolatry denies our identity as creatures of God. John Wesley himself called attention to this analogy (*Notes Upon the New Testament*, p. 522), arguing that just as idolatry brings dishonor to God, so homosexual behavior brings dishonor to the body created for the union of male and female in marriage.

Another argument which is put forward to justify the "blessing" or "marriage" of same-sex partners is the claim that people of homosexual orientation would be denied full personhood or integrated identity if they were denied sexual gratification. To accede to such a claim would amount to a denial of the possibility of celibacy. It would dishonor the life and ministry of generations of Christian singles, and worst of all, it would deny the integrity and full personhood of the Incarnate Lord himself.

The normative character of scripture which our United Methodist doctrinal standards uphold requires that we challenge the current attempts to render the sexual ethics of the Bible as ambiguous and culture-bound. Confessing United Methodists believe that our Church's requirement for "celibacy in singleness and fidelity in marriage" is a valid biblical principle which should be defended. . . .

We commend the following principles for delegates to the General Conference to consider in the continuing debate over sexuality:

1. On the principle of continuity and congruity of precedent with our previous decisions on sexuality, we urge the General Conference of 1996 to continue to hold fast to the Disciplinary language and balance of the five points indicated above.

2. Classic Christian teaching grounds sexual behavior and marriage in the creation story. Therefore, to "bless" committed same-sex unions as if they were valid holy matrimony would be a departure from the biblical understanding of marriage. Such liaisons must not receive the Church's blessing. This should be clearly set forth in our Discipline.

3. Our Discipline should strongly affirm for all persons (laity and clergy) the church's standard of sexual morality: "fidelity in marriage and celibacy in singleness."

4. Religion and the Public Order

Religious Dimensions of Political Life

Religious Belief and Public Morality

In the campaign of 1984 (which Ronald Reagan won handily), the Democratic ticket consisted of Walter Mondale (Presbyterian) as the presidential nominee and Geraldine Ferraro (Roman Catholic) as the vice-presidential nominee. As the first women to be nominated by either major party for so high an office, Geraldine Ferraro was bound to be noticed. She also won notice, however, in her effort to distinguish between her private views on abortion and her public responsibilities in that arena. In this effort she tangled with her archbishop in New York, John J. O'Connor, and in an attempt to clarify a murky issue, Governor Mario Cuomo (b. 1932) stepped in. In a major address delivered to the Department of Theology at Notre Dame University, September 13, 1984 — with the heated presidential campaign still underway — Governor Cuomo spoke to the delicate balance between private religious views and public moral responsibilities.

I speak here as a politician. And also as a Catholic, a lay person baptized and raised in the pre-Vatican II Church, educated in Catholic schools, attached to the Church first by birth, then by choice, now by love. An old-fashioned Catholic who sins, regrets, struggles, worries, gets confused, and most of the time feels better after confession. The Catholic Church is my spiritual home. My heart is there, and my hope.

[Source: Mario M. Cuomo, "Religious Belief and Public Morality," *New York Review of Books,* October 25, 1984, p. 32.]

There is, of course, more to being a Catholic than having a sense of spiritual and emotional resonance. Catholicism is a religion of the head as well as the heart, and to be a Catholic is to say "I believe" to the essential core of dogma that distinguishes our faith. The acceptance of this faith requires a lifelong struggle to understand it more fully and to live it more truly, to translate truth into experience, to practice as well as to believe. That's not easy: applying religious belief to everyday life often presents difficult challenges.

It's always been that way. It certainly is today. The America of the late twentieth century is a consumer society, filled with endless distractions, where faith is more often dismissed than challenged, where the ethnic and other loyalties that once fastened us to our religion seem to be weakening.

In addition to all the weaknesses, dilemmas, and temptations that impede every pilgrim's progress, the Catholic who holds political office in a pluralistic democracy — who is elected to serve Jews and Moslems, atheists and Protestants, as well as Catholics — bears special responsibility. He or she undertakes to help create conditions under which *all* can live with a maximum of dignity and with a reasonable degree of freedom; where everyone who chooses may hold beliefs different from specifically Catholic ones — sometimes contradictory to them; where the laws protect people's right to divorce, to use birth control, and even to choose abortion.

In fact, Catholic public officials take an oath to preserve the Constitution that guarantees this freedom. And they do so gladly. Not because they love what others do with their freedom, but because they realize that in guaranteeing freedom for all, they guarantee *our* right to be Catholics; *our* right to pray, to use the sacraments, to refuse birth control devices, to reject abortion, not to divorce and remarry if we believe it to be wrong.

The Catholic public official lives the political truth most Catholics, throughout most of American history, have accepted and insisted on: the truth that to assure our freedom we must allow others the same freedom, even if occasionally it produces conduct by them that we would hold to be sinful.

I protect my right to be a Catholic by preserving your right to believe as a Jew, a Protestant, or nonbeliever, or an anything else you choose. We know that the price of seeking to force our beliefs on others is that they might someday force theirs on us. This freedom is the fundamental strength of our unique experiment in government. In the complex interplay of forces and considerations that go into the making of our laws and policies, its preservation must be a pervasive and dominant concern.

But insistence on freedom is easier to accept as a general proposition than in its application to specific situations. There are other valid general principles firmly embedded in our Constitution, which, operating at the same time, create interesting and occasionally troubling problems. Thus the same amendment of the Constitution that forbids the establishment of a state church affirms my legal right to argue that my religious belief would serve well as an article of our universal public morality. I may use the prescribed processes of government — the legislative and executive and judicial processes — to convince my fellow citizens — Jews and Protestants and Buddhists and non-believers — that what I propose is as beneficial to them as I believe it is for me; that it is not just parochial or narrowly sectarian but fulfills a human desire for order, peace, justice, kindness, love, any of the values most of us agree are desirable even apart from their specific religious base or content.

I am free to argue for a government policy for a nuclear freeze not just to avoid sin but because I think my democracy should regard it as a desirable goal. I can, if I wish, argue that the state should not fund the use of contraceptive devices not because the pope demands it but because I think that the whole community — for the good of the whole community — should not sever sex from an openness to the creation of life.

And surely I can, if so inclined, demand some kind of law against abortion not because my bishops say it is wrong but because I think that the whole community, regardless of its religious beliefs, should agree on the importance of protecting life — including life in the womb, which is at the very least potentially human and should not be extinguished casually.

No law prevents us from advocating any of these things: I am free to do so. So are the bishops. And so is Reverend Falwell. In fact, the Constitution guarantees my right to try. And theirs. And his.

But should I? Is it helpful? Is it essential to human dignity? Does it promote harmony and understanding? Or does it divide us so fundamentally that it threatens our ability to function as a pluralistic community? When should I argue to make my religious value your morality? My rule of conduct your limitation? What are the rules and policies that should influence the exercise of this right to argue and promote?

I believe that I have a salvific mission as a Catholic. Does that mean that I am in conscience required to do everything I can as governor to translate *all* my religious values into the laws and regulations of the State of New York or the United States? Or be branded a hypocrite if I don't?

As a Catholic, I respect the teaching authority of the bishops. But must I agree with everything in the bishops' pastoral letter on peace and fight to include it in party platforms? And will I have to do the same for the forthcoming pastoral on economics even if I am an unrepentant supply-sider? Must I, having heard the pope renew the Church's ban on birth control devices, veto the funding of contraceptive programs for non-Catholics or dissenting Catholics in my state?

I accept the Church's teaching on abortion. Must I insist that you do? By law? By denying you Medicaid funding? By a constitutional amendment? If so, which one? Would that be the best way to avoid abortions or prevent them?

These are only some of the questions for Catholics. People with other religious beliefs face similar problems.

Let me try some answers. Almost all Americans accept some religious values as a part of our public life. We are a religious people, many of us descended from ancestors who came here expressly to live their religious faith free from coercion or repression. But we are also a people of many religions, with no established church, who hold different beliefs on many matters.

Our public morality, then — the moral standards we maintain for everyone, not just the ones we insist on in our private lives — depends on a consensus view of right and wrong. The values derived from religious belief will not — and should not — be accepted as part of the public morality unless they are shared by the pluralistic community at large, by consensus.

A Reformulated "Christian America"?

When in 1990 the periodical First Things *was launched, it brought a bold new voice to the discussion of religion and American politics. For some liberals, the voice was all too loud and insistent, for some conservatives it represented just what was needed. The editor of* First Things, *Richard John Neuhaus, had been a Lutheran minister and an active opponent of the Vietnam War. Over time he left behind his one-time allies on the American political Left, and he also joined the Roman Catholic Church. In* First Things *Neuhaus tries to draw Protestants, Catholics, the Orthodox, and Jews into dialogue concerning the moral foundations required for a democracy to function. In an essay from December 2000, from which the following excerpts are drawn, he assesses the process by which notions of the United States's unusual relationship with God dropped from the discourse of the nation's political and intellect elites (however much it remains alive among less elite audiences). And he attempts a case for the value of a reformulated notion of "Christian America."*

Civil Religion or Public Philosophy

Traditional language about "Christian America" — which once served both liberal and conservative purposes, as those terms are used today — was vigorously attacked by the school of "Christian realism" associated with Reinhold Niebuhr

[Source: Richard John Neuhaus, "Civil Religion or Public Philosophy," *First Things*, Dec. 2000, pp. 69-73.]

and his brother, H. Richard Niebuhr. From the late 1930s through the 1960s, Reinhold in particular assumed a "prophetic" mode in debunking any idea of the "chosenness" of America. This was part and parcel of his attack on the idea of moral progress. . . . In the regnant liberalism of the time, three ideas came together: the idea of moral progress, the idea of American chosenness, and the idea of a socialist utopia. This made for a heady mix that Niebuhr condemned as a snare and delusion. He employed his impressive polemical powers against the notion that history can be understood in terms of a conflict between "the children of light and the children of darkness." With almost mantra-like repetition, he underscored the "ironies" and "ambiguities" of history.

The Niebuhrs did their job well, perhaps too well in some quarters. While a Niebuhrian sensibility of skepticism toward historical delusions is to be cultivated, it was essentially a corrective against the excesses of the "Redeemer Nation" theme. In mainline Protestantism and in the liberal culture more generally, that skepticism was employed in a polemic against what was perceived as an anti-Communist crusade during the Cold War years. From the 1950s through the end of Soviet Communism in 1991, that crusade was portrayed as a contest between "the free world" and "godless communism." In other words, the children of light against the children of darkness. The attempt to check that exaggeration, an exaggeration frequently freighted with hubris and self-righteousness, reinforced an attitude aptly described as anti-anticommunism. In this view, the great evil was not communism but anticommunism, a cause presumably discredited by the excesses of Senator Joseph McCarthy. The anti-anticommunism that McCarthy did so much to abet lived on long after his censure by the Senate and his pitiful death in 1957. . . .

Prior to what many perceive as the anti-American turn of what is comprehensively (perhaps too comprehensively) called The Sixties, the idea of Christian America had been sharply modified, and in some ways replaced by, the idea of an American "civil religion." This was influentially set forth in Will Herberg's book of 1955, *Protestant, Catholic, Jew: An Essay in American Religious Sociology.* Herberg, a Jew and a great admirer of Reinhold Niebuhr, spoke of the American way of life as "the characteristic American religion, undergirding life and overarching American society despite indubitable differences of religion, section, culture, and class." During those years and up to this day, a statement presumably made by President Dwight D. Eisenhower in 1954 is frequently quoted: "Our government makes no sense unless it is founded on a deeply felt religious faith — and I don't care what it is." While it has never been documented that the statement, first cited in the *Christian Century,* was ever made by Eisenhower, the sentiment fit perfectly Herberg's thesis. As Sydney Ahlstrom wrote in his monumental *A Religious History of the American People,* "The postwar form of civil religion debased the older tradition which had reverenced [America] as a bearer of transcendent values and summoned citizens to stewardship of a sacred trust."

Now even that debased form of the American Way of Life as a civil religion has little currency in our public discourse. Beginning in the late 1960s, sociologist Robert N. Bellah and others tried to revive the civil religion argument, adapting it to the stringent critique of America favored by the left, but their efforts never caught on beyond students of religion in the academy. By the 1970s the doctrine, assuming dogmatic status, had been firmly established that America is a secular society. At least it appeared to be firmly established. When in 1984 I published *The Naked Public Square: Religion and Democracy in America,* it was generally viewed as a provocative — some thought eccentric and even dangerous — challenge to what "everybody knew" about the secularity of America. Still today there are those who contend that the dangerous argument of that book is that the naked public square should be replaced by the sacred public square. My argument then and now, however, is that the naked public square — meaning public life stripped of religion and religiously grounded morality — should give way not to a sacred public square but to a civil public square. . . .

The reconstructed public philosophy that is required could provide a secure foundation for the civil public square. The civil public square is one in which different convictions about the common good are engaged within the bond of civility. The "common good" is — and we can never tire of making this point — unavoidably a moral concept, and that means the religiously grounded moral convictions of the American people cannot be excluded from the public square. Given the role of religion in American culture, both historically and at present, a religion-free public square is a formula for the end of democracy. To exclude the deepest convictions of the people from the deliberation of how we ought to order our life together is tantamount to excluding the people from that deliberation, and that is the end of democracy. We need not be delayed here by the old debate, still pressed by many conservatives, over whether our constitutional order is that of a democracy or a republic. Suffice it that the Constitution itself, as unanimously asserted by the Founders, is that of a republic, but it rests on the democratic premise that political sovereignty rests with the people. The Declaration of Independence declares that "just government is derived from the consent of the governed." As the political sovereign, the people are authorized to name a sovereignty that they acknowledge to be higher than their own; for instance, "the laws of Nature and of Nature's God." This is not, as some claim, a formula for theocracy. It is an exercise of democratic authority through republican or representative means by which the people place a check upon their own power by designating the higher authority to which they hold themselves accountable.

The civil public square requires something not entirely unlike Herberg's civil religion. The problem with calling it a civil religion is that most Americans think they already have a religion and are not interested in exchanging it for another. For this reason among others, it is better to say that the civil public square requires a public philosophy attuned to the Judeo-Christian moral tradition. A Judeo-Christian moral tradition is not a Judeo-Christian religion. A moral tradition is part of religion but by no means the whole of it; nor, especially in Christianity, is it the most important part. But it is a necessary part. Sustaining the Judeo-Christian moral tradition in public requires that Americans who are Christians recognize that tradition as theirs, and recognize that it is necessarily dependent upon Judaism, both historically and at present. Here, too, it becomes apparent that cultivating the Jewish-Christian relationship is much more than a matter of interfaith politesse; it is essential to reconstituting the moral basis of our common life.

Civil religion, when it is untethered from biblical religion, can become a rival religion. Some Christian thinkers would go further and say that civil religion is by definition a rival religion. Such was surely the case with, for example, the religion of America's "manifest destiny" mentioned earlier in this series on Christian America. In that instance, Christians succumb to a notion of the "Redeemer Nation" that is disengaged from, and becomes a competitor to, their Redeemer. The perennial attempts, commonly called "Wilsonian," to assert some grand national purpose within the world-historical scheme of things are usually Christian in inspiration but end by aspiring to take the place of Christianity. If I am right in thinking that Henry Luce of *Time* was premature, that it is the twenty-first century that is "the American century," it is certain that America will be safe neither for itself nor for the world without a guiding public philosophy. And it is, I believe, equally certain that any public philosophy that might be constructed, will not be democratically sustainable unless it engages in a fresh way the idea of Christian America.

Religion and the Ballot, 1996

Innovative research by a number of political scientists has shown how central religious convictions and practices have become for presidential and other elections in contemporary American life. The report that follows on the 1996 presidential election suggests that, even more than income or gender, which have always been recognized as important determinants of electoral behavior, religion may have played an even larger role. The 1996 presidential election pitted the incumbent Democrat, Bill Clinton, against the Republican challenge of Senator Robert Dole and a third-party effort by businessman Ross Perot.

[Source: John Green, Lyman Kellstedt, James Guth, and Corwin Smidt, "Who Elected Clinton: A Collision of Values," *First Things*, Aug./Sept. 1997, pp. 35, 37-38.]

If you believe the conventional wisdom, the 1996 elections were "valueless." And indeed, moral concerns played a very modest role in the campaign. Religious conservatives complained about voters' indifference toward abortion and President Clinton's evident character flaws, while religious liberals lamented public apathy toward social injustice and Speaker Gingrich's ethical lapses. These complaints fit nicely with the most common explanation of the electoral results, namely, that "the economy did it." Prosperity led self-interest to trump all other values; personal gain, present or prospective, skewed the country's moral compass. In this view, the absence of all but material concerns ensured that the elections were seen as valueless — they resolved little. A chastened Democrat renewed his lease on the White House, humbled Republicans retained their grip on Congress, and a majority of voters stayed home on election day. It was as though the nation had experienced a pervasive hardening of the heart and deliberately chose to settle for half a loaf.

There is much to be said for this portrayal of the 1996 campaign, but like most conventional wisdom, its insights are overstated. In reality, the 1996 elections reflected not the absence of values but rather a clash of values. The campaign revealed both the death throes of an old political order and the birth pangs of a new one. These changes are creating new electoral alignments, altering the framework through which short-term economic forces are interpreted politically, and perhaps setting the stage for an eventual resolution of the current impasse.

A good way to illustrate this transition is to look at the 1996 presidential and congressional vote of the most important religious traditions. Religious traditions are critical repositories of cultural values and intimately connected to national politics. . . .

The GOP is still largely an alliance of white Protestants, but increasingly also a party of religious traditionalists. All the white Protestant categories gave Dole substantial, if not always majority, support. Among white Protestants and Catholics, however, traditionalists were by far the most Republican in both presidential and congressional voting. Similarly, the GOP did well among smaller traditionalist contingents, such as Mormons. (The mixed results for the Other Christian category reflects its diversity, including groups as different as Jehovah's Witnesses and Greek Orthodox.)

The 1996 vote clearly shows the transformation of the New Deal political alignments. The ancient cores of the Democratic and Republican parties — white Catholics and white mainline Protestants — have become swing constituencies, divided between modernists and traditionalists. Meanwhile, the growing numbers of nonwhites have moved to the center of the Democratic coalition, joined, at least for the moment, by the expanding secular population. White evangelicals, especially the most traditionalist, have become the core of the GOP electorate. Although white traditionalists tend to be outnumbered, the electoral scales are balanced somewhat by their greater turnout: ethnic and racial minorities, white modernists, and seculars voted less frequently.

What do our results reveal about the nature of voting coalitions? Dole received 37 percent of his votes from evangelicals and only 22 percent from the former mainstay of the Republican Party, mainline Protestants. More important, however, was that over half the Dole vote came from the three traditionalist groups within evangelical and mainline Protestantism and Roman Catholicism, plus the religiously conservative Mormons. When modernist evangelicals are added to the mix almost two-thirds of the tenuous GOP coalition is accounted for.

The Clinton vote, in contrast, was strongest among minorities, the two secular groups, and religious modernists. Together, these groups accounted for close to 80 percent of the votes received by the President. Yet the Democratic coalition is fragile. The minorities are closer to traditionalists on social issues, but closer to modernists on economic matters. Finally, the Perot vote came substantially from the two secular groups (45 percent) while religious modernists made up another 25 percent of the Perot constituency.

The table results are quite potent. Statistical controls for income, gender, region, education, and age do not appreciably alter these patterns, although each has its own influence on the vote. As one might expect, the rich supported the GOP, and the gender gap benefited the Democrats. But, in fact, these religious categories were twice as powerful in predicting the vote as the next strongest demographic variables.

Religion and the Ballot, 2000

Once again in the year 2000, the nation's presidential election was a thoroughly religious affair. Especially the Republican standard-bearer George W. Bush, the Democratic candidate Al Gore, and the Democrats' vice presidential candidate Joseph Lieberman (the first Jew to be nominated by a major party for such high office) referred to religious matters frequently during the campaign. Expert analysis of who voted for whom and why once again reveals striking religious polarity, as well as striking religious prominence, in determining the results.

From the time that George W. Bush declared Jesus his favorite political philosopher to the day Joseph Lieberman joined the Democratic ticket quoting the

---

[Source: James L. Guth, John C. Green, Corwin E. Smidt, and Lyman A. Kellstedt, "Partisan Religion," *Christian Century*, March 21-28, 2001, pp. 18, 20.]

book of Chronicles, religion was in the limelight during the 2000 presidential campaign. And when it was all over, Bush entered office amidst a flurry of worship services, clerical blessings and religious consultations.

Bush's triumph in the primaries was a tribute both to his unprecedented fund raising among Republican business elites and the surprising loyalty of religious conservatives. The dramatic failure of John McCain's attack on Christian Right leaders — calculated to split off traditionalist Catholics and more moderate religious voters — and the collapse of Pat Buchanan's third-party appeal to evangelicals underscored Christian conservatives' commitment to the GOP establishment.

On the Democratic side, religious factors also permeated the nominating process. From the start, Al Gore stressed his own religious credentials, recalling his sometimes-neglected Southern Baptist roots, his flirtation with seminary education, and his internal guidepost, "What would Jesus do?" Coupled with his frequent visits to African-American churches, Gore's combination of traditional and progressive language was designed to solidify key elements in the Democratic religious coalition.

Although both Bush and Gore sought to expand their religious coalitions, especially after the primaries, the Republican and Democratic National Conventions confirmed the sharp differences in the parties' religious profiles. Although Christian conservatives were less visible at the GOP meeting than in 1992 or 1996, they were clearly entrenched in the party machinery. In fact, John S. Jackson III's quadrennial survey found that 29 percent of all GOP delegates came from white evangelical denominations — almost identical to the 1996 figure. Mainline Protestants clung to a diminishing plurality with 33 percent, a pale reflection of their historic dominance. Catholics made up another 20 percent of those present, all other religious groups combined for just 12 percent, and secular delegates accounted for only 5 percent.

The Democrats came from very different religious locations. Only 7 percent belonged to evangelical churches, 19 percent were mainline Protestants, and 23 percent were white Catholics. About half represented religious minorities: Jews (8 percent), black Protestants (15 percent), Hispanic Catholics (8 percent), and other religions (7 percent). Secular activists counted for 14 percent. In almost every religious tradition, Democrats were distinctly less observant than their GOP counterparts. While 55 percent of the Republicans reported attending religious services once a week or more, over half the Democrats claimed to attend only "several times a year," "seldom" or "never.". . .

On Election Day, evangelical Protestants were by far the most solidly Republican subgroup, producing a 75 percent majority for Bush. Indeed, regular church-attending evangelicals gave him a whopping 84 percent, compared to a more modest 55 percent among less-regular adherents. Mainline Protestants still occupied quite a few Republican pews, but were less faithful than their evangelical brethren, giving Bush only 59 percent, with weekly attendees outdoing less observant co-parishioners, 66 to 57 percent. Catholics of European background were closely divided, giving a 51-49 majority to Al Gore, but regular mass attendees were much more supportive of Bush (57 percent) than were other Catholics (41 percent). Thus, in all the major white Christian traditions, regular churchgoers — predominantly traditionalists — have become distinctively more Republican than those less involved in religious institutions.

The Democratic religious coalition was quite different. In addition to capturing less observant Catholics, Gore overwhelmed Bush among the Democrats' traditional minority religious groups: black Protestants (96 percent), Hindus, Buddhists and Muslims (80 percent), Hispanic Catholics (76 percent), Jews (77 percent), other Christians, such as the Orthodox (72 percent), Hispanic Protestants (67 percent) and, finally, secular voters (65 percent).

These coalitional differences are even more impressive when considering the proportion of a candidate's vote drawn from each religious group. Fully one-third of Bush's vote came from weekly church attendees among evangelical Protestants. Add another 10 percent from among observant mainliners, 12 percent from mass-attending Catholics and 3 percent from devout Mormons, and we find that almost 60 percent of the Republican constituency consisted of traditionalist Christians and their allies. On the other side, the bulk of the Democratic coalition was composed of black Protestants and secular voters (19 percent each), Jews, Hispanic Catholics and other religious minorities (15 percent), less observant evangelical and mainline Protestants (15 percent combined) and less committed white Catholics (11 percent). These patterns were replicated in House races, as well as in voters' party identification.

The strength of these patterns certainly suggests that the campaign played its customary role in solidifying each party's religious coalition. On the Republican side, Bush made big gains among evangelical Protestants over the summer, smaller improvements among mainliners and white Catholics, but lost ground among black Protestants, Jews and other religious minorities. Fifty-nine percent of evangelicals said they felt very close or close to Bush by Election Day, compared to only 37 percent of mainline Protestants and white Catholics. Among all three groups, naturally, the religiously observant were most positive about the Republican nominee.

Conversely, Gore improved his position among black Protestants, less observant Catholics and most religious minorities — the core of his electoral coalition. Sixty-seven percent of black Protestants felt very close or close to Gore, as did 37 percent of secular voters. Gore's choice of Joe Lieberman as his running mate may have delayed defections of observant evangelicals, mainliners and white Catholics. In all these Republican-leaning groups Lieberman was actually more popular than the vice president — but in the end his nomination probably won few converts. Indeed, Democratic losses among white Protestants may have cost Gore his home state of Tennessee and, perhaps, the election.

Unlike many other features of the presidential campaign, these religious underpinnings are not likely to disappear soon. Rather, they reflect a new religious order in American politics, where the historic loyalties of the nation's diverse religious traditions are either reinforced or attenuated by divisions between traditionalists and progressives. As in the past, Republicans and Democrats have strong religious constituencies, and both seek to attract religious groups less firmly aligned without antagonizing those core constituencies. In 2000, this new religious order produced partisan parity. This means that any future electoral shifts among religious groups, or the emergence of new religious forces, will be a matter of vital political significance.

Presidents

Jimmy Carter

Jimmy Carter (b. 1924), former governor of Georgia, served as president of the United States from 1977 to 1981. Carter's religious background as a Southern Baptist deacon and Sunday School teacher was influential in his presidential tenure in many ways, perhaps most visible in his efforts at bringing about reconciliation between Egypt and Israel in the Middle East and in promoting the cause of international human rights. Excerpts from the memoir below explain how Carter with his wife Rosalynn dealt with disappointment when his bid for re-election was defeated in 1980 and they returned to Georgia. Their involvement with Habitat for Humanity was a new venture, but one that sustained lines of development that went back to his Baptist youth.

All of us wonder about our real purpose in life. For a few, this question can become a profound source of anxiety. When we have inner turmoil that needs healing, uncertainty about the meaning of life can grow into an obsession with self-pity or depression. For many people, the best solution is to think of something we can do for someone else.

The Bible says that God will wipe away our tears (Revelation 21:4). Wiping away someone else's tears is sometimes necessary to help us dispel our

---

[Source: Jimmy Carter, *Living Faith* (2nd ed., New York: Random House, 1998), pp. 161-68.]

own. No matter what we seek in life, we are more likely to find it if we are not self-centered but concentrate on something or someone outside ourselves.

In many ways, Rosalynn and I were devastated after my defeat for reelection as president in 1980. We had really wanted another four years in the White House and had many plans for ourselves and our nation. Now all these hopes were shattered. And, at the age of fifty-six, I was too young to consider retirement. . . .

When my term in office expired, we moved with Amy back to Plains, where she enrolled in the public school and we became, once again, full and active members of our local church. As we repaired our house and grounds, put a floor in the attic to store possessions accumulated during the past nine years of public service and campaigning, became reacquainted with our farms and woodlands, and settled our urgent business affairs, we also tried to inventory what we might have to invest in a productive future life. We would build The Carter Center and write our memoirs. We also became involved with another interesting and challenging project: Habitat for Humanity.

Working with Habitat for Humanity has changed our attitude about how we can relate to those who really need help. In building homes with "God's people in need," we follow a few simple rules. Volunteers work side by side with families who have been living in subhuman dwellings. The future homeowners are chosen and most other decisions made by a committee formed within the local community. There is no charity involved, if "free handouts" is the meaning of charity. The homeowners must contribute about 500 hours of work on their own and neighbors' houses, and they must also repay the full price of their homes, to which they will then have clear title. This is possible because the houses built by Habitat are relatively inexpensive: much of the construction work is done by volunteers, and Habitat's policy is not to charge interest. This makes monthly payments possible from a very low income, even from a welfare check. . . .

Habitat for Humanity was founded by Millard and Linda Fuller. Millard is a dynamic and charismatic lawyer; he and Linda are two of our closest friends. . . .

As a young lawyer and entrepreneur, Millard continued to be innovative and enthusiastic, and he was soon a millionaire, with so much money coming in from his business ventures that he gave up his law practice. One day, much to Millard's shock, Linda told him that she was leaving him and going to New York for marriage counseling because he was neglecting his family and seemed interested only in getting rich. Millard followed her and begged her to come back to him. Finally, in desperation, he declared that he would give away all his money and join Linda in any work that they could share.

He kept his promise, and they soon settled on the bi-racial Koinonia Farm. There, for five years, the Fullers joined in building houses for destitute

The first pontiff to visit the nation's capital, Pope John Paul II met with President
Jimmy Carter to discuss issues of peace and war, and of human rights, in 1979.
(Religion News Service)

black families. Then they and their four children spent three years in Zaire as
missionaries supported by several Christian denominations and continued to
develop the idea of organizing Habitat for Humanity.

The Fullers say that Habitat uses the "theology of the hammer" or the
"economics of Jesus." By the time this book is published, Habitat will have completed homes for more than 50,000 needy families in about 1,500 communities
in the United States and in forty-five foreign countries.

Now Rosalynn and I send out a large number of fundraising letters for Habitat, spend occasional days on projects near our home, and join with others for a week each year to build a number of complete homes. To date, we have done this in more than a dozen communities, including New York City; Tijuana, Mexico; the Cheyenne River Sioux reservation in South Dakota; Liberty City in Miami; Philadelphia; Chicago; Winnipeg, Manitoba; Atlanta; Charlotte, North Carolina; and the Watts area in Los Angeles. In 1996, our project site was near Budapest in Hungary, and we plan to be in the Appalachian Mountain region in Kentucky in 1997.

Rosalynn and I enjoy vacations, and we could go to Hawaii or on a Caribbean cruise every summer for about the same amount it costs us to travel to one of the Habitat building sites. But when I look back on the last twelve years or so, I see that some of my most memorable and gratifying experiences were when I joined other volunteers and worked to exhaustion building a house alongside the family who would live there. These exhilarating occasions have been rare in my life, but I have learned that the opportunities are always there, for any of us.

It is difficult to describe the emotions of our Habitat workdays. We see extraordinary commitments and lives changed among formerly forgotten people. On our first project, a nineteen-apartment dwelling in Lower Manhattan, one of our homeowners, a former chef named Roosevelt, was sleeping on the street when we met him. He worked with us on this large and difficult project, and when it was finished he lived on the first floor. Because of his fine character and good work, he became the building superintendent. One day while we were installing the roof, I finished a cold drink and began to crumple the aluminum can. Roosevelt startled me by shouting, "Don't bend the can!" I discovered that this was part of his livelihood; he supported himself and began making his monthly payments by collecting empty cans and bottles. . . .

A Habitat family in Olympia, Washington, had been living in an abandoned automobile. One of their children was an eight-year-old boy, who was very excited about getting a new house. When the family was chosen, he jumped up and down and shouted, "We won! We won! We won!" After the Habitat home was finished and the family moved in, the little boy attended a different school. He had always been in the "slow learners'" class, but when he moved his records were lost and he was put in a regular class by mistake. No one noticed the error, and at the end of the first half year, his lowest grade was a B. Now he is still learning with the smartest students. This is what having a decent home for the first time in life can do.

Ronald Reagan

Ronald Reagan (b. 1911), former governor of California, served as president of the United States from 1981 to 1989. Reagan had church experience as a youth with the Disciples of Christ, but was not known as an active church participant during his years as an actor in California. From his time as California governor, he began to develop more connections with religious groups and eventually proved to be an effective communicator with religious rhetoric and symbols. On March 8, 1983, he delivered what would become a famous speech to the annual meeting of the National Association of Evangelicals. In the context of explaining his opposition to the idea of a freeze on nuclear weapons, he articulated his convictions about the Soviet Union as an "evil empire." That conviction would continue to fuel his dealings with the U.S.S.R. and, despite the doubts of many Americans and more Europeans, eventually play a large part in the internal collapse of the Soviet empire.

Those of you in the National Association of Evangelicals are known for your spiritual and humanitarian work. And I would be especially remiss if I didn't discharge right now one personal debt of gratitude. Thank you for your prayers. Nancy and I have felt their presence many times in many ways. And believe me, for us they've made all the difference. The other day in the East Room of the White House at a meeting there, someone asked me whether I was aware of all the people out there who were praying for the president and I had to say, "Yes, I am. I've felt it. I believe in intercessory prayer." But I couldn't help but say to that questioner after he'd asked the question that — or at least say to them that if sometimes when he was praying he got a busy signal it was just me in there ahead of him. . . .

During my first press conference as president, in answer to a direct question, I pointed out that, as good Marxists-Leninists, the Soviet leaders have openly and publicly declared that the only morality they recognize is that which will further their cause, which is world revolution. I think I should point out, I was only quoting Lenin, their guiding spirit, who said in 1920 that they repudiate all morality that proceeds from supernatural ideas — that is their name for religion — or ideas that are outside class conceptions. Morality is entirely subordinate to the interests of class war. And everything is moral that is necessary for the annihilation of the old, exploiting social order and for uniting the proletariat.

Well, I think the refusal of many influential people to accept this elementary fact of Soviet doctrine illustrates a historical reluctance to see totalitarian

---

[Source: Ronald Reagan, Speech on March 8, 1983, Appendix III, in *Winning the New Civil War*, by Robert P. Dugan, Jr. (Portland, OR: Multnomah, 1991), pp. 215, 222-26.]

powers for what they are. We saw this phenomenon in the 1930s. We see it too often today. This does not mean we should isolate ourselves and refuse to seek an understanding with them. I intend to do everything I can to persuade them of our peaceful intent, to remind them that it was the West that refused to use its nuclear monopoly in the '40s and '50s for territorial gain and which now proposes 50 percent cuts in strategic ballistic missiles and the elimination of an entire class of land-based intermediate range nuclear missiles.

At the same time, however, they must be made to understand we will never compromise our principles and standards. We will never give away our freedom. We will never abandon our belief in God. And we will never stop searching for a genuine peace, but we can assure none of these things America stands for through the so-called nuclear freeze solutions proposed by some.

The truth is that a freeze now would be a very dangerous fraud, for that is merely the illusion of peace. The reality is that we must find peace through strength.

I would agree to a freeze only if we could freeze the Soviets' global desires. A freeze at current levels of weapons would remove any incentive for the Soviets to negotiate seriously in Geneva, and virtually end our chances to achieve the major arms reductions which we have proposed. Instead, they would achieve their objectives through the freeze. A freeze would reward the Soviet Union for its enormous and unparalleled military buildup. It would prevent the essential and long overdue modernization of United States and allied defenses and would leave our aging forces increasingly vulnerable. And an honest freeze would require extensive prior negotiations on the systems and numbers to be limited and on the measures to ensure effective verification and compliance. And the kind of freeze that has been suggested would be virtually impossible to verify. Such a major effort would divert us completely from our current negotiations on achieving substantial reductions. . . .

Yes, let us pray for the salvation of all of those who live in that totalitarian darkness — pray they will discover the joy of knowing God. But until they do, let us be aware that while they preach the supremacy of the state, declare its omnipotence over individual man, and predict its eventual domination of all peoples on the earth — they are the focus of evil in the modern world. . . . [I]f history teaches anything, it teaches that simple-minded appeasement or wishful thinking about our adversaries is folly. It means the betrayal of our past, the squandering of our freedom.

So, I urge you to speak out against those who would place the United States in a position of military and moral inferiority. You know, I've always believed that old Screwtape reserved his best efforts for those of you in the church. So, in your discussions of the nuclear freeze proposals, I urge you to beware the temptation of pride — the temptation [to] blithely declar[e] yourselves above it all and label both sides equally at fault, to ignore the facts of history and the aggressive impulses of an evil empire, to simply call the arms race a giant misunderstanding and thereby remove yourself from the struggle between right and wrong and good and evil.

I ask you to resist the attempts of those who would have you withhold your support for our efforts, this administration's efforts, to keep America strong and free, while we negotiate real and verifiable reductions in the world's nuclear arsenals and one day, with God's help, their total elimination. . . .

I believe we shall rise to the challenge. I believe that communism is another sad, bizarre chapter in human history whose last pages even now are being written. I believe this because the source of our strength in the quest for human freedom is not material but spiritual. And because it knows no limitation, it must terrify and ultimately triumph over those who would enslave their fellow man. For in the words of Isaiah: "He giveth power to the faint; and to them that have no might he increaseth strength. . . . But they that wait upon the Lord shall renew their strength; they shall mount up with wings as eagles; they shall run and not be weary. . . ."

Yes, change your world. One of our founding fathers, Thomas Paine, said, "We have it within our power to begin the world over again." We can do it by doing together what no one church could do by itself. God bless you and thank you very much.

Bill Clinton

Bill Clinton (b. 1946), former governor of Arkansas, served as president of the United States from 1993 to 2001. During his tenure he was the focus of unusually ardent criticism from some sectors of the conservative religious world, both for his policies and his personal life. Clinton had been a consistent church-goer since his youth, either in congregations of the Southern Baptist Convention or in Methodist churches, which was the denomination of his wife Hillary. Clinton's personal religious experiences were one of the focal points of a lengthy public discussion in which Clinton participated at Willow Creek Church in suburban Chicago (see below, pp. 714-16) in August 2000, near the end of his presidential term. His questioner was Bill Hybels, the senior pastor at Willow Creek.

QUESTION: All right, these folks all know that you and I have been meeting for many years. I'd just like to ask you, how would you characterize for these people what our meetings are like?

[Source: "Text: President Clinton's Speech at Ministers' Leadership Conference," http://www.washingtonpost.com/wp-srv/onpolitics/elections/clinton081000.htm (29 May 2003).]

CLINTON: Well, first of all, they all have certain things in common, and there's — then they're different from time to time. They all include you asking me point-blank about the state of my spiritual life, and if you think I give you an evasive answer, then you do pointed follow-up questions.

Then — and they all end with a prayer, most of the times we both pray. Before we came out here we both prayed. I prayed that you wouldn't give him too tough a time for asking me to come here today.

And then we talk about things. We talk about, you know, what's going on, what's going on in the office. You ask about the other people that work for me and how they're doing. You — if there's some particular issue in the news, we talked about that, or particularly if there's a big development involving war or peace, we talk about that.

And you've given me the opportunity to ask you questions about what you do. I mean, I was fascinated about how Willow Creek was born and grew, and how you got into this business that I think is so important in trying to build up the strength of local churches throughout the country and throughout the world. And I've learned about what — how I do my work, by talking to you about how you do yours, and I hope that the reverse is true on occasion.

But basically, they've been spiritual conversations, conversations between two friends. There're some things that are always the same, and then they change, based on what's going on. . . .

QUESTION: Something spiritual came into focus for you when you were just a young boy, about 10 years old. Tell us about that.

CLINTON: Well, really it had a lot to do with how I wound up in public life, I think. I became a Christian in 1955, when I was 9, at the Park Place Baptist Church in Hot Springs, Arkansas. The minister's name was James Fitzgerald. He was a great, good man.

QUESTION: Now, did you, like, hear a sermon and then bow and pray?

CLINTON: No, I was — I had been a regular churchgoer ever since I was about 6, you know, but, yes, I was — I loved this man, he was — I haven't seen him since — I haven't seen him in 45 years, but I have a very vivid memory of exactly what he looked like and the way he talked, and he touched my heart, he convinced me that I needed to acknowledge that I was a sinner and that I needed to accept Christ in my heart, and I did.

But, I mean, I was 9 years old. I had a sort of a — and I was trying to figure out what it all meant, you know?

So then when I was about 11 years old, maybe 12, the whole state was in an uproar — I guess I was 12, I think it was September of 1958. Billy Graham was coming to Little Rock to do a crusade in War Memorial Stadium, which is where the Arkansas Razorbacks play their football games when they're playing in Little Rock, and Billy Graham was the only person that could get a bigger crowd than the football team.

So the schools in Little Rock had just been closed in the Little Rock integration crisis. Some of you who are older will remember it, perhaps if you're younger you read about it, but in 1957 it was the first big crisis of the school integration movement, and the governor closed the schools, called out the National Guard to keep nine black children out of the schools and then closed them for a year and all the kids had to go somewhere else to school. And the White Citizens Council was basically dominating the politics of the town.

So Billy Graham, you know, who schedules these crusades years in advance, I mean he didn't plan all this, all of a sudden he's supposed to step in the middle of this. And my Sunday school teacher was going to take me and a bunch of kids over to hear him, I never will forget it.

And the White Citizens Council and other — a lot of the business people in Little Rock were worried about some, sort of, great encounter, because the racial tensions were very high, and they asked Billy Graham to agree to give this crusade to a segregated audience. And he said that if they insisted on that he would not come; that we were all children of God, he wanted to lead everyone to Christ. He wouldn't do it.

And it really touched me, because my grandparents, who had no education particularly and were very modest people, were among the few white people I knew who supported school integration.

And all of a sudden to have Billy Graham validating this, based on his Christian witness, had a profound impact on me. And it got me to thinking at that early age about the relationship between your faith and your work, which of course has been one of the most hotly debated issues in Christianity for 2,000 years now, "What does the book of James really mean?" and all that.

But I mean, I really — I can't tell you what it meant. And for a long time after that, I would send a little bit of my allowance money to Billy Graham. You know, I'm still on somebody's list somewhere . . . for giving next to no money, but it was a pretty good chunk of what I had.

And he came back to Arkansas 30 years later to do another crusade. And I took him by to see my pastor, who was dying at the time and who had been his friend for decades. And we relived that moment. I've never forgotten that and I never will. It's just like it happened yesterday to me. Even now I can hardly talk about it.

QUESTION: Now you and Hillary have been churchgoers all the time in your public service, and some people think that's just as an act. How would you respond?

CLINTON: Well, at least it's a consistent act.

(LAUGHTER)

(APPLAUSE)

CLINTON: Well, I think I have given evidence that I need to be in church.

(LAUGHTER)

CLINTON: I mean, to me it's a — you know, I don't talk about it a lot, I've never sought to politicize it, but it's very interesting. You know, I started off and I went to church with great regularity until I graduated from college — high school, and like a lot of people, when I went to college my attendance became more sporadic.

And actually — and Hillary had been very active in her local Methodist church in Park Ridge, which is not too far from here, when she was growing up.

And I remember, when I was elected and governor, I had my dedicatory service in the church — this is 1979 — in the church in Little Rock, of which I'm still a member, Emanuel Baptist Church.

And Hillary said to me, "You know, we should start going to church again on a regular basis. We ought to do it, and you should join the choir. It would do you good to think about something besides politics."

And because I had a — but I couldn't — so I talked to the choir director and because I was governor I was out three or four nights a week, I couldn't go to practice, but I'd been in music all my life so I was a good sight-reader so they let me sing anyway.

So from 1980 till the year I became president I got to sing in my church choir every Sunday and it meant a lot to me. And then after we came here, we both — because we wanted to go together and with our daughter, we both started going to the Methodist church, I said, here in Washington, Foundry Methodist Church that Dr. Wogaman is the pastor of, and you know him, of course.

And we've gone pretty regularly for seven and a half years now. So I've been doing this a long time. I don't do it for anybody else. I do it for me. It helps me to go. It helps me the same way it helps me to spend an hour talking to you. I'm sitting there in church, just like everybody else, except needing it maybe more, and it's one of the best hours of the week for me. I just let everything else go, take my Bible, read, listen and sing.

I don't know, why does anybody go? It means something to me. It's a way of not only validating my faith but deepening it and basically replenishing it.

One of the things I like about my observant Jewish friends, and you've seen a lot about this in the last few days with all the publicity over Senator Lieberman becoming the vice-presidential nominee, is that they take a whole day — and I mean they really take the day, they don't just go to service for an hour — I mean, for a day, they shut down, and shut the whole world out, and think about what's most important in life.

And anyway in a very small way, that's what my church attendance does for me.

George W. Bush

George W. Bush (b. 1946), former governor of Texas, was elected president in a cliff-hanging decision over Al Gore in November 2000. Bush had partici-pated in religious activities as part of his early family life, but did not become religiously serious until in younger middle age a crisis related to over-indulgence in alcohol moved him to join his wife Laura's Methodist church and to begin religious practices himself. Especially after the terrorist attacks of September 11, 2001, religious rhetoric was regularly interwoven into his public pronouncements, as was the case in this statement that he released af-ter the explosion of the Columbia Space Shuttle on February 1, 2003.

This day has brought terrible news and great sadness to our country. At 9 o'clock this morning, Mission Control in Houston lost contact with our space shuttle Columbia. A short time later, debris was seen falling from the skies above Texas. The Columbia is lost. There are no survivors.

On board was a crew of seven: Col. Rick Husband; Lt. Col. Michael An-derson; Cmdr. Laurel Clark; Capt. David Brown; Cmdr. William McCool; Dr. Kalpana Chawla; and Ilan Ramon, a colonel in the Israeli Air Force.

These men and women assumed great risk in the service to all humanity.

In an age when space flight has come to seem almost routine, it is easy to overlook the dangers of travel by rocket and the difficulties of navigating the fierce outer atmosphere of the Earth. These astronauts knew the dangers, and they faced them willingly, knowing they had a high and noble purpose in life.

Because of their courage and daring and idealism, we will miss them all the more.

All Americans today are thinking as well of the families of these men and women who have been given this sudden shock and grief. You're not alone. Our entire nation grieves with you. And those you loved will always have the respect and gratitude of this country.

The cause in which they died will continue. Mankind is led into the dark-

[Source: "Bush Remarks on Shuttle: 'Destruction and Tragedy,'" *New York Times*, Feb. 2, 2003, p. 32.]

ness beyond our world by the inspiration of discovery and the longing to understand. Our journey into space will go on.

In the skies today we saw destruction and tragedy. Yet farther than we can see there is comfort and hope. In the words of the prophet Isaiah, "Lift your eyes and look to the heavens: Who created all these? He who brings out the starry hosts one by one, and calls them each by name. Because of his great power and mighty strength, not one of them is missing."

The same Creator who names the stars also knows the names of the seven souls we mourn today.

The crew of the shuttle Columbia did not return safely to Earth. Yet we can pray that all are safely home. May God bless the grieving families, and may God continue to bless America.

September 11, 2001

On September 11, 2001, citizens throughout the country were rocked by news that four commercial airplanes had been hijacked and that then two were crashed into New York City's Twin Towers of the World Trade Center and one into the Pentagon in Washington, D.C. The Twin Towers were leveled and a significant part of the Pentagon was destroyed; over 3,000 Americans died. Nineteen Saudi Arabian Muslims linked to the Al Qaeda terrorist network were said to have conspired to organize the attack. Undoubtedly, the event shook the country as it had not been shaken since the Vietnam War. Part of the massive national response was a turn to religion for guidance, solace, and support. (1) Billy Graham was the main speaker at a memorial service in the National Cathedral in Washington, D.C., held on September 14. (2) Jerry Falwell and Pat Robertson, leaders of Christian conservative forces, blamed the attacks on the American Civil Liberties Union, homosexuals, and others whom they considered deviant — as reported in the Christianity Today *article excerpted below. (3) Kyabje Gelek Rinpoche, a Buddhist Lama,*

[Sources: (1) "Billy Graham's Message: National Day of Prayer and Remembrance," ttp:// www.billygraham.org/newsevents/ndprbgmessage.asp (17 Sept. 2001). (2) Ted Olsen, "As the World Prays, Falwell and Robertson Blame ACLU, Gays, and Others for 'Deserved' Attack," *Christianity Today Weblog*, http://www.christianitytoday.com/ct/2001/137/52.0.html (27 May 2003). (3) Kyabje Gelek Rinpoche, "On Love and Compassion in the Wake of the Terrorist Attacks," http://www.imdiversity.com/villages/asian/Article_Detail.asp?Article_ID=7994 (27 May 2003). (4) Shahid Athar, "The Future of American Muslims after September 11," http:// www.islamfortoday.com/athar09.htm (27 May 2003).]

spoke in Chicago about renouncing anger and hatred. (4) Shahid Athar,
president of the Islamic Medical Association of North America, called upon
Muslims to denounce the attacks while yet standing firm in their faith.

1. Billy Graham

President and Mrs. Bush, I want to say a personal word on behalf of many people. Thank you, Mr. President, for calling this Day of Prayer and Remembrance. We needed it at this time.

We come together today to affirm our conviction that God cares for us, whatever our ethnic, religious or political background may be.

The Bible says that He is "the God of all comfort, who comforts us in all our troubles."

No matter how hard we try words simply cannot express the horror, the shock, and the revulsion we all feel over what took place in this nation on Tuesday morning. September 11 will go down in our history as a day to remember.

Today we say to those who masterminded this cruel plot, and to those who carried it out, that the spirit of this nation will not be defeated by their twisted and diabolical schemes. Some day those responsible will be brought to justice, as President Bush and our Congress have so forcefully stated.

But today we especially come together in this service to confess our need of God. We've always needed God from the very beginning of this nation but today we need Him especially. We're facing a new kind of enemy. We're involved in a new kind of warfare and we need the help of the Spirit of God. The Bible's words are our hope: "God is our refuge and strength, an ever present help in trouble. Therefore we will not fear, though the earth give way and the mountains fall into the heart of the sea" (Psalm 46:1, 2, NIV).

But how do we understand something like this? Why does God allow evil like this to take place? Perhaps that is what you are asking now. You may even be angry at God. I want to assure you that God understands those feelings that you may have.

We've seen so much on our television, and hear on our radio, stories that bring tears to our eyes and make us all feel a sense of anger. But God can be trusted, even when life seems at its darkest.

But what are some of the lessons we can learn?

First, we are reminded of the mystery and reality of evil.

I have been asked on hundreds of times in my life why God allows tragedy and suffering. I have to confess that I really do not know the answer totally, even to my own satisfaction. I have to accept, by faith, that God is sovereign, and He is a God of love and mercy and compassion in the midst of suffering. The Bible says God is not the author of evil. It speaks of evil as a "mystery." In 2 Thessalonians 2:7 it talks about the mystery of iniquity. The Old Testament prophet Jeremiah said, "The heart is deceitful above all things and beyond cure. Who can understand it?" He asked that question, "Who can understand it?" And that is one reason we each need God in our lives.

The lesson of this event is not only about the mystery of iniquity and evil, but secondly, it is a lesson about our need for each other.

What an example New York and Washington have been to the world these past few days! None of us will ever forget the pictures of our courageous firefighters and police, many of whom have lost friends and colleagues, or the hundreds of people attending or standing patiently in line to donate blood. A tragedy like this could have torn this country apart, but instead it has united us and we have become a family. So those perpetrators who took this on to tear us apart, it has worked the other way. It has backlashed, it has backfired. We are more united than ever before. I think this was exemplified in a very moving way when the members of our Congress stood shoulder to shoulder the other day and sang, "God Bless America."

Finally, difficult as it may be for us to see right now — this event can give a message of hope — hope for the present, and hope for the future.

So-called "terror evangelists" spread their message on Wall Street after the New York Stock Exchange opened for the first time since the September 11, 2001, terrorist attack.
(Photo by Scott Lituchy, Religion News Service)

Yes, there is hope. There is hope for the present because I believe the stage has already been set for a new spirit in our nation.

One of the things we desperately need is a spiritual renewal in this country. We need a spiritual revival in America. And God has told us in His Word, time after time, that we are to repent of our sins and we're to turn to Him and He will bless us in a new way.

There is also hope for the future because of God's promises. As a Christian, I have hope not just for this life, but for heaven and the life to come. And many of those people who died this past week are in heaven right now and they wouldn't want to come back. It's so glorious and so wonderful. And that's the hope for all of us who put our faith in God. I pray that you will have this hope in your heart. . . .

2. Falwell and Robertson

Will secularist groups and strict separationists complain about today's state-sponsored prayer services? Probably not. But they might want to respond to Jerry Falwell's comments 45 minutes into Thursday morning's *700 Club* broadcast regarding the terrorist attack: "The ACLU has got to take a lot of blame for this. . . . I really believe that the pagans, and the abortionists, and the feminists, and the gays and the lesbians who are actively trying to make that an alternative lifestyle, the ACLU, People for the American Way — all of them who have tried to secularize America — I point the finger in their face and say, 'You helped this happen.'" Falwell's rationale is that the secularization of America has provoked God "to lift the curtain and allow the enemies of America to give us probably what we deserve."

700 Club host Pat Robertson, who said he "totally concurs" with Falwell's assessment, has been preaching a similar message for days. "It [terrorism] is happening because God Almighty is lifting his protection from us," he said in a statement quoted by the Associated Press. "We have a court that has essentially stuck its finger in God's eye. . . . We have insulted God at the highest level of our government. Then, we say, 'Why does this happen?'"

Folks, this is what the National Religious Broadcasters was talking about when it issued suggested guidelines earlier this week for covering the tragedy: "Millions of people are at their television sets looking for answers. This is not the time to run 'Christian TV as usual' — we need to provide answers to people filled with questions."

An ACLU spokeswoman tells both *The Washington Post* and *The New York Times* that it "will not dignify the Falwell-Robertson remarks with a comment," but the White House has not such qualms. An unnamed official there called the remarks "inappropriate," adding, "The president does not share those views." . . .

3. Kyabje Gelek Rinpoche

We say we would like to destroy Osama bin Laden. But we have to destroy our own Osama bin Laden. Your hatred, my hatred, is our own Osama bin Laden hiding in the mountains of our heart. We need a surgical operation to take him out of our heart, our brain. As citizens of the U.S., as persons with compassion and caring, we have to put in our two cents, do whatever we can to reduce hatred, to eradicate it, and to save life, not destroy it because hatred will not help us, it can only hurt us. The recent attacks are a vivid example of how hatred can hurt even innocent people.

I couldn't help thinking that day, how many children were waiting for their parents to come home. A young kid goes to school in the morning, comes home for dinner, then sits there waiting for a father or mother to come home, and they don't. The consequences of the September 11th attacks will be felt for some time. The mental and physical pain, the depression, sadness, they are all the result of hatred: past, present and future hatred.

What does that knowledge do to our mind? It can lead to compassion, or it can lead to hatred. If you think about the victims, you are going to develop compassion. People who were seen on television cheering in the streets had no thought about how this really hurt people, and of how they themselves would be affected by the attacks. They thought: a plane, an explosion, a fire, boom, and America is taught a lesson. That's all. That is ignorance. The real essence of any true spiritual path is Overcoming negative emotions. Our leaders tell us retaliation is necessary for this to not happen again. That may be true. But what kind of retaliation? Is it going to build more hatred, or will it contribute to nonviolence? This situation puts us to the test. How good are we on love and compassion?

Where are we on hatred? It is a test for each and every one of us, particularly those of us who are open-minded and seek to develop love and compassion. That is spiritual practice. We're not talking about politics here, we're talking about spirituality. Judge yourself. Let's judge ourselves, first, individually. How good are you? I, personally, have my disgrace. I was angered by these events. One thing I learned from my friend, the late poet Allen Ginsberg, was to be open. My friends know I hide nothing. So, I admit, I was angry that day. That Tuesday night, I gave a teaching at which I said I was angry. I couldn't get the image of that second plane hitting the second tower out of my head. In the evening when I heard that there had been explosions in Kabul I caught myself thinking, "Good. I hope it was surgical." That is the effect of anger.

Some of you might become sad or depressed instead of angry. Don't do that. You'd be hurting yourself. I don't want to say anger is OK, but it is natural for it to rise. Look at me. I was angry, though as a Tibetan reincarnate lama I have been in the love-compassion business for sixty years. For those who don't have that much experience in the business of love-compassion, it's OK. We just cannot say that we shouldn't be angry. Not right now. Not for a while. Nobody should feel guilty about being angry. Every day of your life, anger, jealousy, and hatred will arise. Disappointment will arise. They are all OK because we are human beings. We have feelings. But despite objections I am repeating what I said that night, on September 11th. It doesn't mean we give our anger free rein, or that we let it run out of control like a wild horse. We must put the bit in our anger's mouth and hold the reins tightly and direct that anger, making sure it doesn't become hatred.

That's what is happening, unfortunately. How ignorant it is when somebody shoots a Sikh in a gas station or when a pilot throws an Indian man off a plane before he will fly it. That is fear and hatred combined. It's wonderful to be waving the American flag, but we have to be really careful. There is only one legislator who voted against the war resolution, and she now has to be surrounded by bodyguards because she voted no.

Freedom and individual rights. They can be destroyed from inside as well as outside. If we forfeit our individual liberties, the terrorists will have really succeeded. It is very good to have a national feeling, and unite, but democracy doesn't always have one single view on which everyone agrees. We don't all think alike which is what makes us a democracy. We don't have everybody agreeing with one single view in Great Britain, or even in India. So the effect of the 911 attack is a real emergency. For life, for death, for politics, freedom, the economy, all of it. Each and every one of us has a responsibility to help ourselves, our children, to keep our way of life, to keep our nation, to keep our freedom. Then, of course, how do we do it? And how do we support those who died? How do we heal ourselves? The emotion of anger is going to be felt, no matter how old you are. Even if you pretend not to be angry, it will bother you. Video games fool us. Because on TV or video games you see a bomb, you see fire, and you don't see any blood or anybody getting killed. In Somalia, 8 people got killed, and you saw them being dragged through the streets.

We don't want to develop more hatred on top of hatred. So we have to take care of our own situation first. We have to clear our own head. We have to stop hatred, otherwise it will go from hatred to more hatred. We have to transform hatred into compassion. . . .

4. Shahid Athar

On September 11th, Islam in the USA was also attacked. About 500 Muslims died in the WTC tragedy and the rest of them became hostage to the fear, intimidation and insecurity about their future. All the progress they had made in the growth of Islam in the USA for the last 50 years seems to be reversed and some immigrant Muslims even started to question whether they should go back to the country they came from. Of course, those American Muslims like my children who were born here have no place to go. This is their home.

The response of many American Muslims to the tragedy of September 11th is in two extremes. At one extreme is the group most visible on the Internet, still working on the conspiracy theory, that is this evil act was done by the work of Mossad, the CIA, the Pentagon, the Militia or the remote control devices blowing up the World Trade Center, completely denying the possibility that it could have been the evil act and plot by Muslim terrorists. This group did not say enough to the fellow Americans that this act was an attack on humanity and not just on America, an attack on innocent civilians and even on the peaceful religion of Islam. Thus, suffering from Stockholm Syndrome, this group became a manifestation of the disease, identifying themselves with the cause of terrorists and even trying to justify their actions.

On the other extreme is the group of Muslim leaders, who after recovering from the shock of September 11th, suffered from unwarranted guilt complex and became apologetic. After visits by the FBI, they realized that they must make a politically correct statement now in order to save American Islam. They had to change their tone of speech and writing, and even retracted and regretted their statements given before September 11th against the "super power". Now, some of them are telling the same American Muslim audience, "if you do not like the West, go back to your own country".

Another prominent writer wrote, "the Muslims are hypocrites of grand scale, in opposing the oppression by Israel, Serbia and Hindu but when the same acts are done by Al Qaeeda and other Muslim terrorist groups they look the other way". True, but apples and oranges cannot be compared. Two wrongs do not make one right and there is no trade off, i.e. we must choose between two types of terrorists, two groups of oppressors and accept state terrorism over the group or individual terrorists. Another group of Muslims find someone else to blame rather than accept responsibility. Not too long ago, I was on a public forum at a Town Hall meeting. My other counterpart speaker was an Afghan origin Professor who put all the blame of the recent trouble with the Taliban on Pakistan in creating, training and sponsoring Taliban terrorism. Those who are true students of Taliban history know this is not true fact. Talibans were created and strengthened with the help of CIA and the American government. The American media never acknowledged the help given to mujahideens by Pakistan in fighting Russian aggression on Afghanistan. We do not realize that if there was no Pakistan, Russians would have won their "great game" in very little time and conquered Afghanistan. It was Pakistan who gave sanctuary to mujahideens and helped them with everything that they had to re-arm and re-group themselves to go back to Afghanistan and fight.

The American Talibans, the likes of Robertson and Falwell, never a fan of these Muslim leaders in the past, are now out to discredit them even more. . . .

Thus, the average middle class, Mosque going Muslims who run grocery stores, are office workers or students, are totally confused at what they should do or say. Should they side with the terrorists overseas or with the super power who is bombing the innocent civilians in hospitals and houses there in order to free the whole world of these terrorists? How can we present Islam to those who stereotype, profile and even call us their enemy? On record are close to 1,000 cases of such hate crimes since September 11th. Is the FBI our friend or our foe? Will our children get admission to schools of flight training, biomedical research and nuclear physics or will we ever feel comfortable flying as a passenger in an airplane? Will our women in hijab be able to go shopping without any fear? The joy of being a Muslim in America is gone, at least for now. All the progress we have made in the last 30 years is being reversed. We have to start all over again. How can we live our faith while we work with those who defame it? We American Muslims are going through the most difficult time in our history in this country. These are difficult questions and I have no simple solution to offer. My advice is to the mainstream ordinary American Muslims and not to our leadership. I hope and pray we regain our bruised self esteem. Many of us, especially those from overseas, tend to live in the past and not in the present. While our bodies are here, our hearts and minds were left behind somewhere else. We need to bring our hearts to the land we have adopted as our home now.

I suggest to myself and all ordinary American Muslims to wake up and take charge of our religion, as we have to take charge of our families, our health and our lives. We should learn Islam for ourselves as a religion of love, peace and tolerance and prove it by our individual actions. If we want to be counted as American Muslims, we must take all the concerns of Americans, whether terrorism, Anthrax, drugs, violence or even pollution as our own concerns. We must show Islam by our actions, not by speeches, videotapes and pamphlets. We must denounce all those who use religion for their political gain and denounce political powers who wish to abase religion of Islam. Thus, we as ambassadors of Islam, must be careful in what we say and to whom we lend our ears and even our money. We must reclaim our faith from the terrorists who hijacked it and also from the leadership who apologize for them. We did not do anything wrong so we should not have low esteem. God has chosen Islam for us and we are thankful for it. As for the question being asked "are you with us or with the terrorists?", we say "we are neither with the terrorists nor with those intent to terrorize us. We are here to stay, vote and participate in the American process and we are neither going back nor can we be interned. Make no mistake!"

5. Into the New Millennium

Institutional Religion

Promise Keepers

From its beginning in 1991, the Promise Keepers movement has challenged men to assert themselves as leaders in their marriages and families. Drawing on evangelical traditions but intentionally targeted ecumenically, Promise Keepers holds conferences where those who attend are urged to live as "men of integrity." Opponents of the organization have suggested that the Promise Keepers perpetuate outmoded views of gender roles and encourage men to become authoritarian at home. Scholars who carry out research find, by contrast, that most wives and daughters approve of their husbands and fathers attending. By the mid 1990s, Promise Keepers were filling stadiums around the country for conferences, their annual budget had soared to over $65 million, and the movement had received support from such evangelical leaders as Bill Bright of Campus Crusade for Christ and James Dobson of Focus on the Family. By 2000, the appeal of the organization had declined and the Promise Keepers were forced to cut back their staff and budget, but the movement remains one of the most significant recent developments for mass audiences. The following "Seven Promises of a Promise Keeper" comes from an early statement of the movement's goals.

1. A Promise Keeper is committed to honoring Jesus Christ through worship, prayer, and obedience to God's Word in the power of the Holy Spirit.

Excerpted from "Seize the Moment" by Randy Phillips, in the book *Seven Promises of a Promise Keeper*, originally edited and published by Focus on the Family. Copyright 1994, Promise Keepers.

The Promise Keepers conference at RFK Stadium
in Washington, D.C., May 24, 1996
(Photo by Carl Bower, Religion News Service)

2. A Promise Keeper is committed to pursuing vital relationships with a few other men, understanding that he needs brothers to help him keep his promises.

3. A Promise Keeper is committed to practicing spiritual, moral, ethical, and sexual purity.

4. A Promise Keeper is committed to building strong marriages and families through love, protection, and biblical values.

5. A Promise Keeper is committed to supporting the mission of the church by honoring and praying for his pastor, and by actively giving his time and resources.

6. A Promise Keeper is committed to reaching beyond any racial and denominational barriers to demonstrate the power of biblical unity.

7. A Promise Keeper is committed to influencing his world, being obedient to the Great Commandment (see Mark 12:30, 31) and the Great Commission (see Matt. 28:19-20).

The Black Church

In 2003 Juan Williams, a correspondent for National Public Radio who had earlier worked on the Washington Post *for over twenty years, published a reflective memoir concerning his own experience in black churches,* This Far by Faith: Stories from the African American Religious Experience. *In a subsequent interview for the* Christian Century, *Williams explained at some length why he had written the book, what he took to be the enduring legacies of black church life, and also what he now understood to be the greatest challenges facing African American spiritual life.*

What led you to write *This Far by Faith?*

I am an immigrant to the U.S. I was born in Panama and my mother brought me and my sister and brother to Brooklyn in 1958 when I was four years old. So the black experience in this country was new to me as a child. I started exploring the neighborhood, meeting new people — it all had a sense of wonder for me.

One of the first things I remember noticing was the power and diversity of the church. Even as a boy I was puzzled by the intensity of religion among the black people around me.

In Brooklyn you could go to the street corner and there would be a Black Muslim guy selling newspapers and telling you that you have to straighten up,

---

[Source: Interview with Juan Williams, *Christian Century,* May 31, 2003, pp. 45-46, 48-49.]

do away with the religion of the slave master, be a strong man, be yourself, understand your roots. And you could see farther down the street a Catholic church with kids going to Catholic school, many of whom were my friends, and they were very studiously involved with the Latin mass and the rosary. There weren't many black priests, but people found sustenance and a home in the Catholic church.

Of course, there was the Baptist church. It seemed like everybody from the Baptist church came from the South. There was a real geographical connection there. You could get good inexpensive food at the Baptist church — southern cooking on Saturday and Sunday. They would feed the kids for free. There also was the African Methodist Episcopal church with its grand traditions and sense of dignity and history.

And then there was my Episcopal church. My father, who is from Jamaica, was Anglican, and that church was extraordinarily supportive of my family, helped my sister and brother in everything from clothes to spending money as they went off to college. A lot of immigrants from the Caribbean attended that church for the same reasons my family did — it was their anchor in a new land.

The black church in all this variety seemed omnipresent in my corner of Brooklyn. There was a powerful faith in action that you couldn't avoid. People were going to church not only on Sunday but also on Tuesday and Wednesday nights for some auxiliary board meeting, women's meeting or youth group. The black community was defined at the center by the black churches. At the heart, *This Far by Faith* is an attempt to understand that childhood immigrant experience of marvel at the church's powerful position in the black community.

Your book goes beyond sociological description to state openly that the story about the struggle for justice and freedom in black America is also the story of faith. . . .

When I was younger I thought that the church was mostly about class and economics. People at the lower end of the economic scale needed the comfort of the church. As I've grown older I've come to understand the centrality of religious experience for black people as an armament against — I don't want to be too dramatic — the assaults of the broader society and as a wellspring of resolve to fight for your rights. If the broader society was saying to you that because of the color of your skin we don't think you're smart, we don't think you're capable of holding anything but a menial job, the church was offering the contrary and subversive message to black people that, whatever anyone else might say, God is with me. God believes in me. God loves me. I am God's child. . . .

Is Afrocentric identity, which is stressed in some black churches, consistent with the integrationist agenda that you're describing?

. . . Today more and more black people are saying that their identity is not going to be that of some bug-eyed comic or gangster rapper that white America likes to gawk at. So who am I? What is my identity and what is my relationship to God and to my faith and my true purpose in life? Those questions are essential to black identity, especially when the dominant culture sends such strong messages about who you are. The attempt to develop a positive basis for black identity in America — an identity that is not driven by historical deformations — is completely understandable.

Where I see myself departing from the aims of Afrocentric identity, in the churches or elsewhere, is when the attempt to form identity becomes simply a reactionary impulse — and often an angry one — to white America. It is simplistic to present black identity as a contradictive stand to whatever white people say is reality. If white people support the war, then we oppose the war. If white people are pro-Bush, then we're anti-Bush. If white people are supporting X, we support Y. Mere contradiction becomes black identity.

You're giving a whole lot of power to white people if you define yourself as the opposite of whatever they assert. You're not opening doors to who you are in terms of a broader culture and broader society; you're narrowing who you are. You become simply a representation of the white person's shadow. On a personal basis I would find that offensive because it would limit me.

But there's still so much anger among African-Americans about what is perceived as the failure of the integrationist experiment that the market is huge for identity politics. Since 1954 and the *Brown v. Board of Education* decision there have been improvements in black life, but no one can kid himself about the inequities that still exist.

Are we correct in detecting a touch of sadness at the end of your book — sadness that the energy and power the black church exerted at the height of the civil rights movement has diminished?

What probably comes through most at the end of the book is a sense of the loss of focus. Beginning in slave days the church focused on the idea of supporting and educating black people and advocating equality. But there was always the deeper purpose that flows out of the common cup that says: here is a vision for God's purpose for us as a people. In too many churches, that's gone.

Much of what I see happening in African-American religious life today is self-indulgent. The gospel of prosperity that's preached in many African-American churches is not about sacrifice for the greater good of the African-American community. And it's not about any example of sacrifice that arises from the example of Christ. It's a get-rich theology. That's tragic when you think of all the African-Americans who suffered tremendously and sacrificed their lives for the greater good of black Americans.

A consequence of the church's lack of focus is the absence of young people. Black middle-class kids aren't interested in the church for a lot of the same reasons that white middle-class kids aren't interested. They don't see the church as relevant today. They don't see the church undertaking high-risk challenges. I don't think young people see discipline and self-sacrifice in mainstream black churches anymore. It's telling that the fastest-growing faiths tend to be Pentecostal fundamentalist groups that offer very clear lines of instruction.

But if the mainstream black churches were true to their heritage, they would stand up and take risks by speaking out against schools of poor quality even though some people in the pews may be running those schools or teaching in them. They should have the courage to say that we have homosexuals in our congregation, that we know people here have sex outside of marriage, and that we are concerned about our members, including heterosexual women, becoming infected with AIDS. And we're worried that so many of us have such stressful lives that we do drugs. This truth is not heard in many black churches.

When young people see that kind of timidity concerning social issues, combined with an obvious concern about money, or growing the congregation or developing megachurches, they become cynical about the church. If the only identity young people can take from church is another version of the culture of materialism, then I hope they stay cynical. That's not where a sense of community comes from. That's not where I get my sense of purpose for life. The church should be a witness to Christ's example. Social timidity and an obsession with money do not reflect Christ's example. . . .

My hope is that the riches of black Christian experience will not be squandered. I hope subsequent generations will tap into this rich identity to say, "Here is where I belong, and this is who I am." I hope that the stories I tell show that being African-American is not simply about being a counterculture, or having a counterexperience to white people. African-American religious experience offers us a strong unifying vision that has been the basis for the freedom struggle, for political organizing, for resilient personal identity and for education. It has given our lives meaning and helped create an American community of greater equality, purpose and opportunity. I hope the book, in a small way, helps the black church claim its proud heritage and put that wealth of experience to good purpose within the black community and the broader society.

Willow Creek

Willow Creek Community Church was founded in the mid 1970s. Within a generation it had grown to become one of the largest churches in America.

[Source: Adelle M. Banks, "A Conversation with Willow Creek's Bill Hybels." © 1997 Religion News Service. Used by permission.]

Through the vision of its founding pastor, Bill Hybels, Willow Creek targeted its outreach to the circumstances of suburban Chicago; the message came out of classical evangelical Christianity but was tailored to the conditions of a busier, more mobile, less rooted modern culture. Much of the planning that went into Willow Creek, for example, was intentionally designed to make people as comfortable about attending church as about visiting the mall or going to see a movie. Willow Creek has used marketing techniques effectively to determine what makes church attractive. Its services are marked by a high degree of professionalism with much of the music composed on site and with drama put to use to underscore the message preached at services. Willow Creek's main worship center was designed to be as neutral as possible; there are no crosses or other religious images in their main auditorium. Casual dress is the norm. By 2003 about 17,500 people were regularly attending weekend services, and the church claimed about 7,500 members. Willow Creek had also become a model for a "megachurch movement" in which techniques that had worked effectively in suburban Chicago were exported to other locations in the U.S. and overseas.. In the following interview, Bill Hybels explains his approach to ministry.

Do you think that most people are seeking God if they don't already believe they've found him?

I think there comes a time in almost every person's life when he or she has one of those late-night, ceiling-staring sessions in which the person asks, "Is this all there is? Is this the totality of what life is all about? Is there life beyond the grave? Do I have a soul?" And then the journey begins.

How would you describe Willow Creek's theology . . .?

It would be the classic historic Christian theology. . . . We would fall right in line with the Billy Graham Evangelistic Association or Wheaton College or any of these classic evangelical institutions. Our statements of faith would probably be almost identical. . . .

Do you think [that megachurches] will remain a viable form of evangelical Christianity?

I think the general tendency is going to be for local churches to grow larger, especially in suburban and urban areas. However, I think there's always going to be the need for vital small churches in rural areas. I don't see that as changing much in the next 15 years. I don't see that there are going to be many churches beyond the 7,000 to 10,000 range, simply because of the complexity required to grow a church beyond that size and the logistics.

But you think there will be more churches in the 2,000 to 7,000 range?

Whereas it used to be that churches between 1,000 and let's say 3,000 or 4,000 were quite rare, they're becoming very common, and I'm quite enthusiastic about that because these kinds of churches tend to be able to provide all of the ministries that families require these days while still being somewhat manageable in scale.

How would you describe your church's approach to women in leadership roles in the church?

We encourage women to identify and develop and use their spiritual gifts. We don't restrict any office or position in the church on the basis of gender.

I understand there has been some kind of position paper [within Willow Creek] on this in the last year or so.

It's a working document right now. . . . It gives a biblical defense for encouraging women to identify and use their spiritual gifts in the church without restriction on the basis of gender. . . .

How might [this move on the part of Willow Creek] affect the evangelical world in general?

I think it will affect it positively. In far too many churches, women grow up feeling like second-class citizens. Many of these women yearn to put on a uniform and get in the game. . . .

Given the fact that your church is independent, do you think denominationalism is on its way out?

I think there are signs of the decline of denominationalism almost everywhere you turn. Now, I wouldn't go quite so far as to say the day of the denomination is over, because certain denominations are awakening to the fact that the people in denominational leadership exist to serve local church pastors instead of vice versa. Right now the Willow Creek Association, which is a fellowship of a couple of thousand churches around the world, is working with dozens of the leaders of these denominations to try to assist them in serving the leadership teams in the congregations of their local churches. In certain denominations — one of which would be the Christian Reformed Church, another the Evangelical Free Church — we've seen spectacular effects from that change in mind-set. These are very exciting prospects.

Drawing Boundaries

Lakota Nation

As in the sixteenth and seventeenth centuries, so also in the twenty-first century, American Indians have constantly had to struggle against an encroaching white culture. As Native Americans pursued legal battles in the late twentieth century to secure full religious freedom, they also took steps against letting their traditions and practices be co-opted by non-Indians seeking a "New Age" religious experience. In 1993, some 500 Lakota representing more than 40 tribes in the U.S. and Canada came together for the Fifth Lakota Summit. At that meeting, they produced a "Declaration of War Against Exploiters of Lakota Spirituality," a document that called for an end to the defilement of Native American religious practice by non-Indians.

WHEREAS we are the conveners of an ongoing series of comprehensive forums on the abuse and exploitation of Lakota spirituality; and

WHEREAS we represent the recognized traditional spiritual leaders, traditional elders, and grassroots advocates of the Lakota people; and

WHEREAS for too long we have suffered the unspeakable indignity of having our most precious Lakota ceremonies and spiritual practices desecrated, mocked and abused by non-Indian "wannabes," hucksters, cultists, commercial profiteers and self-styled "New Age shamans" and their followers; and

WHEREAS with horror and outrage we see this disgraceful expropriation of our sacred Lakota traditions has reached epidemic proportions in urban areas throughout the country; and

WHEREAS our precious Sacred Pipe is being desecrated through the sale of pipestone pipes at flea markets, powwows, and "New Age" retail stores; and

WHEREAS pseudo-religious corporations have been formed to charge people money for admission into phony "sweatlodges" and "vision quest" programs; and

---

[Source: "Declaration of War Against Exploiters of Lakota Spirituality," 1993, http://puffin.creighton.edu/lakota/war.html (29 May 2003).]

WHEREAS sacrilegious "sundances" for non-Indians are being conducted by charlatans and cult leaders who promote abominable and obscene imitations of our sacred Lakota sundance rites; and

WHEREAS non-Indians have organized themselves into imitation "tribes," assigning themselves make-believe "Indian names" to facilitate their wholesale expropriation and commercialization of our Lakota traditions; and

WHEREAS academic disciplines have sprung up at colleges and universities institutionalizing the sacrilegious imitation of our spiritual practices by students and instructors under the guise of educational programs in "shamanism"; and

WHEREAS non-Indian charlatans and "wannabes" are selling books that promote the systematic colonization of our Lakota spirituality; and

WHEREAS the television and film industry continues to saturate the entertainment media with vulgar, sensationalist and grossly distorted representations of Lakota spirituality and culture which reinforce the public's negative stereotyping of Indian people and which gravely impair the self-esteem of our children; and

WHEREAS individuals and groups involved in "the New Age Movement," in "the men's movement," in "neo-paganism" cults and in "shamanism" workshops all have exploited the spiritual traditions of our Lakota people by imitating our ceremonial ways and by mixing such imitation rituals with non-Indian occult practices in an offensive and harmful pseudo-religious hodgepodge; and

WHEREAS the absurd public posturing of this scandalous assortment of psuedo-Indian charlatans, "wannabes," commercial profiteers, cultists and "New Age shamans" comprises a momentous obstacle in the struggle of traditional Lakota people for an adequate public appraisal of the legitimate political, legal and spiritual needs of real Lakota people; and

WHEREAS this exponential exploitation of our Lakota spiritual traditions requires that we take immediate action to defend our most precious Lakota spirituality from further contamination, desecration and abuse;

THEREFORE WE RESOLVE AS FOLLOWS:

1. We hereby and henceforth declare war against all persons who persist in exploiting, abusing and misrepresenting the sacred traditions and spiritual practices of our Lakota, Dakota and Nakota people.

2. We call upon all our Lakota, Dakota and Nakota brothers and sisters from reservations, reserves, and traditional communities in the United States and Canada to actively and vocally oppose this alarming take-over and systematic destruction of our sacred traditions.

3. We urge our people to coordinate with their tribal members living in urban areas to identify instances in which our sacred traditions are being abused, and then to resist this abuse, utilizing whatever specific tactics are necessary and sufficient — for example demonstrations, boycotts, press conferences, and acts of direct intervention.

4. We especially urge all our Lakota, Dakota, and Nakota people to take action to prevent our own people from contributing to and enabling the abuse of our sacred ceremonies and spiritual practices by outsiders; for, as we all know, there are certain ones among our own people who are prostituting our spiritual ways for their own selfish gain, with no regard for the spiritual well-being of the people as a whole.

5. We assert a posture of zero-tolerance for any "white man's shaman" who rises from within our own communities to "authorize" the expropriation of our ceremonial ways by non-Indians; all such "plastic medicine men" are enemies of the Lakota, Dakota and Nakota people.

6. We urge traditional people, tribal leaders, and governing councils of all other Indian nations, to join us in calling for an immediate end to this rampant exploitation of our respective American Indian sacred traditions by issuing statements denouncing such abuse; for it is not the Lakota, Dakota and Nakota people alone whose spiritual practices are being systematically violated by non-Indians.

7. We urge all our Indian brothers and sisters to act decisively and boldly in our present campaign to end the destruction of our sacred traditions, keeping in mind our highest duty as Indian people: to preserve the purity of our precious traditions for our future generations, so that our children and our children's children will survive and prosper in the sacred manner intended for each of our respective peoples by our Creator.

Wilmer Stampede Mesteth; (Oglala Lakota); Traditional Spiritual Leader & Lakota Culture Instructor; Oglala Lakota College, Pine Ridge, South Dakota

Darrell Standing Elk; (Sicangu Lakota); President, Center for the SPIRIT, San Francisco, California, & Pine Ridge, South Dakota

Phyllis Swift Hawk; (Kul Wicasa Lakota); Tiospaye Wounspe Waokiye; Wanblee, South Dakota

Jewish Students at Yale

In 1997, a group of five Orthodox Jews at Yale University challenged the school's policy that required students to live in campus housing for their first two years in residence, or be charged a $7,000 fee. According to the students, the co-ed Yale dorms — with their promotion of "safe sex," their provision of free condoms, and their general attitude toward sexuality — amounted to a gross affront to Jewish morals. The university refused the students' request by arguing its policy was part of the educational process that encouraged people of different backgrounds to learn to live together. In 1998, a U.S. District court ruled against the "Yale Five," and the decision was upheld in 2001. Nonetheless, the incident showed one of the ways that in a very pluralistic America the particular traditions of individual religious groups remained important enough to inspire litigation. The article in the New York Times Magazine, *which is excerpted below, understood that tense relationship.*

As Batsheva Greer was leaving a class several months ago, she mentioned to a fellow Yale freshman that she needed to make a telephone call. The classmate invited Batsheva to use the phone in her dormitory room. And the offer filled Batsheva with distress.

She quailed at the thought of insulting the woman by spurning her offer. To most Yale students, nothing could be more prosaic than strolling into one of the residential colleges, where most of them live, eat and even attend classes. But to Batsheva, those same dormitories represent immorality itself, an arena of coed bathrooms, safe-sex manuals and free condoms, a threat to her very soul.

"That's all right." Batsheva told her classmate. "I've got to be going now." She had grown used to giving such polite, if abrupt, demurrals. Only rarely, with a classmate who understood the depth of her Orthodox Judaism, would Batsheva answer candidly, "I can't go up, and I know you'll understand."

The line that Batsheva Greer would not cross to enter a friend's dorm runs through a Federal lawsuit in which she and three other Orthodox students have charged Yale with religious discrimination for requiring all freshmen and sophomores to live on campus. The line divides Jew from Jew, and separates two irreconcilable worldviews: should the sacred accommodate the secular or the other way around? . . .

Through all this hurly-burly moves Batsheva Greer, a 19-year-old history major with delicate features, wire-rim glasses and a presence so gentle that she

---

[Source: Samuel G. Freedman, "Yeshivish at Yale," *New York Times Magazine*, May 24, 1998, pp. 32-35.]

doesn't seem to displace any air when she enters a room. Her rabbi father has watched her wince at gossip, even the favorable kind. "She is," Daniel Greer explains with pride, "the least likely revolutionary."

His use of "revolutionary," though, is correct. Batsheva's timidity coexists with a steely resolve, one shaped partly by her family and partly by an Orthodox Jewish education in America and Israel. "It's not like I was debating the issue," she says of her decision to join the lawsuit. "It was definite in my mind. There was just no question that I would be sacrificing my religious upbringing to live on campus. My personal feelings about being in the spotlight are irrelevant."

Her primary worry, in fact, is that Yale might settle the case out of court, returning the money that each student has paid for the dorm rooms in which they never spent a single night. That would deprive the plaintiffs of their opportunity to triumph on principle, both legal and moral. "You never think people will have such low regard for religion," she says of Yale officials. "Anyone can see we're serious about this."

For a university that had a Jewish quota until the early 1960's, Yale has changed markedly to address the sensitivities of observant Jews. The university now has a Jewish president, a Jewish dean of undergraduates and a student body estimated to be as much as one-quarter Jewish. Yale allows students to use their meal plan in the kosher cafeteria of a privately financed Jewish center. It provides old-fashioned keys to Orthodox students so they will not violate the Sabbath by using electronic card-keys to enter their dorms. It supplied Batsheva Greer with a female tutor in a music course so she would not broach religious law by singing for a man.

But Yale has traditionally insisted that virtually all students, Orthodox Jews included, must live in the residential colleges their first two years. The university argues that living on campus means living in the real world, with all of its complexities and challenges. "We believe the undergraduate experience is more than just the classroom," says Richard Levin, Yale's president. "And we believe these aren't just dormitories, but communities. This university has been committed to offering an encounter with difference as part of its educational mission. These students want the education, but they don't want the encounter."

In their way, the Yale Five seek nothing less than to reverse the course of Jewish history in America. Ever since Jews began immigrating here in great numbers, the impulse toward assimilation has driven the debate about how a Jew should engage America. Jewish immigrants eagerly embraced secular education, as the New York University historian Hasia Diner points out, neither trying to shape it in their image, as 19th-century Protestants had, nor establishing a countersystem of parochial schools like their Irish-Catholic contemporaries. On American soil, the Reform and Conservative branches of Judaism far outpaced Orthodoxy in membership. The image of the Old World father studying Talmud became one of anachronism, if not outright ridicule.

Only with the rise of Modern Orthodoxy in the postwar years did American Jews begin to develop a system of religious day-schools. Yeshiva University, the intellectual capital of Modern Orthodoxy, espoused a code of *Torah Umadda,* Jewish learning with worldly knowledge. It was thought that a dynamic encounter with America could confirm Jewish piety rather than erode it.

Both Rabbi Greer, Batsheva's father, and Nathan Lewin, the constitutional lawyer representing the Yale students, grew up in New York in such a climate. And their memories of Modern Orthodoxy are of a faith insecure in its adoptive land. Lewin recalls being instructed, as an elementary school student at the Ramaz School in the 1940's, to remove his yarmulke when waiting outdoors during fire drills.

In recent years, Orthodoxy has increasingly split into factions of Modern and *haredi* (also known as ultra-Orthodox). So named for a word describing a Jew's imperative to "tremble" before God, the haredi embrace the technical aspects of modernity — including higher education when it serves a practical purpose — while rejecting the cultural ones.

The sociologist Chaim Waxman of Rutgers University contends that the last decade has seen "the haredization of American Orthodox Jewry." Just last year, a spokesman for the ultra-Orthodox group Agudath Israel denounced the Yeshiva University president, Norman Lamm, as a "hater of God" for supporting religious pluralism in Israel. The very term "Modern Orthodox" has become so pejorative — it is to observant Jews what "liberal" is to Democrats — that even its practitioners prefer to call themselves "centrist" or "traditional."

Elisha Hack, one of the Yale plaintiffs, eschews both "Modern" and "haredi" for a term that might well describe all the plaintiffs. "There is an expression floating around — 'yeshivish,'" says Hack, a 20-year-old freshman from New Haven. "It doesn't exist in a dictionary. It's 'yeshiva' made into an adjective. And it connotes a level of observance, a way of thought, a type of dress."

So just as Elisha wears a plain white shirt and a dark suit, just as he flourishes *tzitzis,* the fringes that remind a Jewish man of his 613 religious obligations, he likens the Yale residential colleges to Sodom and Gomorrah.

Rachel Wohlgelernter felt so strongly that, in order to circumvent the requirement to live on campus, she underwent a civil marriage last September, three months before the religious wedding she had long planned. "I could not place myself in an environment potentially harmful to my spiritual well-being," says Wohlgelernter, a 21-year-old psychology major from Los Angeles.

Fairly or not, then, a dormitory address at Yale has emerged as the signifier of an Orthodox Jew's readiness to engage the larger society. Some of the most indignant letters to *The Yale Daily News* opposing the Yale Five have come from other Jewish students, blaming the plaintiffs for everything from misrepresenting Judaism to ruining the admission chances of future Orthodox applicants. The Orthodox rabbi in charge of the campus's kosher cafeteria has criticized the students for taking their complaints to court. While the president of the Union of Orthodox Jewish Congregations has supported the Yale Five for their desire "to live a moral life," its public-affairs chairman called the lawsuit "a serious mistake."

Steven Bayme, director of Jewish Communal Affairs for the American Jewish Committee, considers the lawsuit a statement of self-assurance. "The assumption 40 years ago that Orthodoxy was something you have to apologize for has receded," he says. "Yet the fact these five students are making it a matter of principle that they won't live in the dorm is troubling. They're making a bold statement that attending Yale is strictly utilitarian. They're saying, basically, there are things we can learn from Yale, but its values are decrepit."

Y2K and Beyond

The beginning of the new millennium in 2000 was marked by The Crisis That Did Not Happen. Fears that computer glitches stemming from programs specifying only the last two digits of calendrical years would lead to world-wide chaos melted away as January 1, 2000, came and went without major upset. Yet the excitement in some religious communities over the prospect of a major computing meltdown fueled the urge for apocalyptic speculation that has never been far away in American religious history. (1) Three evangelical authors cooperated in 1999 to produce a "New Millennium Manual" that tried to rein in some of the wilder speculations. (2) But even if the Y2K (= Year Two Thousand) problem fizzled, apocalyptic fascination continued very strong. A prime illustration, as well as promoter, of that fascination has been the Left Behind series of novels by Tim Lahaye and Jerry B. Jenkins. These novels, which have been appearing since 1995, dramatize the eschatology of dispensational premillennialism in the same way that Hal Lindsey's phenomenal best seller, The Late Great Planet Earth, *did during the 1970s. By 2003, sales of the various novels making up the* Left Behind

---

[Sources: (1) Robert G. Clouse, Robert N. Hosack, and Richard V. Pierard, *The New Millennium Manual: A Once and Future Guide* (Grand Rapids: Baker, 1999), pp. 187-88. (2) Tim LaHaye and Jerry B. Jenkins, *Left Behind: A Novel of the Earth's Last Days* (Wheaton, IL: Tyndale, 1995), pp. 16-19.]

series totaled over 50 million. The excerpt below details the experiences of Rayford Steele, a pilot, and Hattie Durham, a flight attendant, when they realize that the Christian believers have been "raptured," or taken up into heaven as the first step in the dispensational scenario pointing toward the end of the world.

1. And You Thought You Had a Year 2000 Problem

A few years ago if one spoke about "the Year 2000 Problem" in prophetic circles it probably would have been interpreted as the problem one would encounter if he or she predicted Christ would return during that year and he didn't. Now we are all readily aware of the computer glitch that has been variously dubbed the Year 2000 Problem, Y2K, or the Millennium Bug — what *Newsweek* has called "the greatest technological problem in the history of mankind." The problem began with the software designers' answer to saving memory. They chose a two-digit format for dates, for example 99 instead of 1999. This worked well but didn't allow for the issues raised by the year 2000. Thus, at the onset of that year uncorrected computers could read 00 as 1900 rather than 2000, malfunction, and cause the loss of billions of dollars of time-sensitive information. Much discussion has taken place regarding who is taking this forecast seriously and who will be adequately prepared (i.e., year 2000 compliant). As they say, only time will tell.

The problem dovetails with long-held prophetic beliefs that associate powerful computers with the Beast of the Apocalypse. Thus, date setters and millennial entrepreneurs did not miss their opportunity to weigh in on the apocalyptic implications of the computer crisis.

An advertisement for Grant Jeffrey's *The Millennium Meltdown* claimed that "at midnight on December 31, 1999, millions of computers throughout the world will begin to crash." This technological failure and resulting crisis "*may* [emphasis ours] set the stage for the coming world government that was prophesied to arise in the last days." For those who did not care for this approach, Jeffrey also offered a fictionalized forecast of the Y2K phenomenon. His *Flee the Darkness*, coauthored by Angela Hunt, was also released in the fall of 1998.

Another Y2K "consumer advocate," as he is described, Michael Hyatt, also offered two takes on the crisis. One was a novel, *Y2K: The Day the World Shuts Down*, offering a fictional account of the crisis, and the other, *The Millennium Bug Personal Survival Kit: Everything You and Your Family Must Know to Get from One Side of the Crisis to the Other*, included audio tapes and a resource manual and offered (we assume) a nonfictional account of the crisis. The survival guide was offered for a limited time price of $89 (a 50% savings) with a "100% Satisfaction Guarantee." If things turn out to be as bad as Hyatt forecasts and the kit helps one to survive, then it will be money well spent. However, if the crisis does not reach apocalyptic proportions, one wonders how long the publisher will offer the "complete, no-questions-asked refund."

Not to be outdone in missing the latest prophetic bandwagon, Hal Lindsey and Cliff Ford released a video in late 1998, *Facing Millennial Midnight: The Y2K Crisis Confronting America and the World,* which promised the answers to "what will ultimately happen, and why" in regards to the Year 2000 crisis.

Now a technological apocalypse is before us. And we were just wondering if our VCRs would still be working.

2. Left Behind

She pulled his head down so she could speak directly into his ear. Despite her weeping, she was plainly fighting to make herself understood. "I've been everywhere. I'm telling you, dozens of people are missing."

"Hattie, it's still dark. We'll find —"

"I'm not crazy! See for yourself! All over the plane, people have disappeared."

"It's a joke. They're hiding, trying to —"

"Ray! Their shoes, their socks, their clothes, everything was left behind. These people are gone!"

Hattie slipped from his grasp and knelt whimpering in the corner. Rayford wanted to comfort her, to enlist her help, or to get Chris to go with him through the plane. More than anything he wanted to believe the woman was crazy. She knew better than to put him on. It was obvious she really believed people had disappeared.

He had been daydreaming in the cockpit. Was he asleep now? He bit his lip hard and winced at the pain. So he was wide awake. He stepped into first class, where an elderly woman sat stunned in the predawn haze, her husband's sweater and trousers in her hands. "What in the world?" she said. "Harold?"

Rayford scanned the rest of first class. Most passengers were still asleep, including a young man by the window, his laptop computer on the tray table. But indeed several seats were empty. As Rayford's eyes grew accustomed to the low light, he strode quickly to the stairway. He started down, but the woman called to him.

"Sir, my husband —"

Rayford put a finger to his lips and whispered, "I know. We'll find him. I'll be right back."

What nonsense! he thought as he descended, aware of Hattie right behind him. *"We'll find him"?*

Hattie grabbed his shoulder and he slowed. "Should I turn on the cabin lights?"

A still from the film *Left Behind: The Movie,* based on the
best-selling novel by Tim LaHaye and Jerry B. Jenkins
(Religion News Service)

"No," he whispered. "The less people know right now, the better."

Rayford wanted to be strong, to have answers, to be an example to his
crew, to Hattie. But when he reached the lower level he knew the rest of the
flight would be chaotic. He was as scared as anyone on board. As he scanned the
seats, he nearly panicked. He backed into a secluded spot behind the bulkhead
and slapped himself hard on the cheek.

This was no joke, no trick, no dream. Something was terribly wrong, and
there was no place to run. There would be enough confusion and terror without his losing control. Nothing had prepared him for this, and he would be the
one everybody would look to. But for what? What was he supposed to do?

First one, then another cried out when they realized their seatmates were
missing but that their clothes were still there. They cried, they screamed, they
leaped from their seats. Hattie grabbed Rayford from behind and wrapped her
hands so tight around his chest that he could hardly breathe. "Rayford, what is
this?"

He pulled her hands apart and turned to face her. "Hattie, listen. I don't
know any more than you do. But we've got to calm these people and get on the
ground. I'll make some kind of an announcement, and you and your people
keep everybody in their seats. OK?"

She nodded but she didn't look OK at all. As he edged past her to hurry back to the cockpit, he heard her scream. *So much for calming the passengers,* he thought as he whirled to see her on her knees in the aisle. She lifted a blazer, shirt and tie still intact. Trousers lay at her feet. Hattie frantically turned the blazer to the low light and read the name tag. "Tony!" she wailed. "Tony's gone!"

Rayford snatched the clothes from her and tossed them behind the bulkhead. He lifted Hattie by her elbows and pulled her out of sight. "Hattie, we're hours from touchdown. We can't have a planeload of hysterical people. I'm going to make an announcement, but you have to do your job. Can you?"

She nodded, her eyes vacant. He forced her to look at him. "Will you?" he said.

She nodded again. "Rayford, are we going to die?"

"No," he said. "That I'm sure of."

But he wasn't sure of anything. How could he know? He'd rather have faced an engine fire or even an uncontrolled dive. A crash into the ocean had to be better than this. How would he keep people calm in such a nightmare?

By now keeping the cabin lights off was doing more harm than good, and he was glad to be able to give Hattie a specific assignment. "I don't know what I'm going to say," he said, "but get the lights on so we can make an accurate record of who's here and who's gone, and then get more of those foreign visitor declaration forms."

"For what?"

"Just do it. Have them ready."

Rayford didn't know if he had done the right thing by leaving Hattie in charge of the passengers and crew. As he raced up the stairs, he caught sight of another attendant backing out of a galleyway, screaming. By now poor Christopher in the cockpit was the only one on the plane unaware of what was happening. Worse, Rayford had told Hattie he didn't know what was happening any more than she did.

The terrifying truth was that he knew all too well. Irene had been right. He and most of his passengers, had been left behind.

Trauma within Catholicism

Crisis

Instances of clerical sexual abuse are, unfortunately, hardly new in any of the religious traditions. The difference with the Catholic cases that began to attract public attention toward the end of the old century was that the abuse seemed not only suspiciously widespread, but also that it seemed to be covered up. When reporters from the Boston Globe *began to probe into the details surrounding the actions, but also the reassignment, of one of the abusers in the Boston archdiocese, they turned up what they thought was a disconcerting pattern. As they phrased it in the opening paragraph of the book that is also excerpted below: This is "the story of a large number of Catholic priests who abused both the trust given them and the children in their care . . . the story of the bishops and the cardinals who hired, promoted, protected, and thanked these priests, despite overwhelming evidence of their abusive behavior." In response, many (and not just defensive Catholics) pointed out that the church had been moving since the early 1990s to remedy abuses. But Catholics were also in the lead appealing for more thorough shepherding from the bishops, as shepherds of their flocks. The excerpts that follow are from the book published by* Boston Globe *reporters; they describe the last days of Boston's once-powerful Cardinal Law.*

One December morning, Friday the 13th, Cardinal Bernard Francis Law sat down at the Vatican with Pope John Paul II and told him he was ready to resign.

A year of revelations had taken an extraordinary toll on the man who was once mentioned as a possible pope. The story that began with [abusive priest] John J. Geoghan had come to include so many characters that few people could keep track. More than one hundred accused priests. An estimated five hundred men and women suing the archdiocese. A possible price tag of $100 million.

The steady drip of revelations, fueled in part by victims' lawyers who succeeded in forcing the Church to turn over its files on abusive priests, was simply too much for Boston Catholics to stomach. By early December 2002, newly released documents had shown allegations that a priest had terrorized and beaten his housekeeper, another had traded cocaine for sex, and a third had enticed young girls by claiming to be "the second coming of Christ." The clamor for Law's resignation was deafening, from Voice of the Faithful and throughout the

---

[Source: The Investigative Staff of the *Boston Globe, Betrayal: The Crisis in the Catholic Church* (Boston: Little, Brown, 2003), pp. 205-07, 215-16.]

archdiocese. But the loudest voices came from the most unexpected quarter: fifty-eight priests, who signed a letter saying it was time for Law to quit.

As the furor intensified, Law traveled to Washington for a meeting with the pope's apostolic nuncio, Archbishop Gabriel Montalvo, who was the Vatican's top emissary to the United States. Law told Montalvo it was time.

"It came to be ever more clear to me that the most effective way that I might serve the Church at this moment is to resign," Law explained a few days later.

From Washington, he had flown on to Rome, and within a few days it was over. An eighteen-year-career as Archbishop of Boston ended with a terse legalistic statement from the Vatican that made no reference to priests, children, or the crisis in the Church. In a perfunctory list of the pope's activities that day, the Holy See declared that the pope "accepted the resignation from the pastoral care of the archdiocese of Boston, U.S.A. presented by Cardinal Bernard Francis Law, in accordance with Canon 401, para. 2, of the Code of Canon Law."

Over the course of a year that Law had described as a "nightmare," the crisis had reached down into the pews and up to the papacy, ultimately forcing the Church to rethink its whole approach to abusive priests in an effort to protect children and placate an angry public.

Laypeople and clergy struggled to deal with the fallout. As the intensity of the crisis waned, the Church woke up with a hangover: fewer people at Mass and less money in the collection basket.

The crisis seeped deep into American popular culture, transforming how Catholicism was viewed and treated. Catholic priest jokes became a staple of late-night television and were traded even at Catholic social gatherings. Abusive priest and abused altar boy costumes were featured at Halloween parties. At a fall football game between Columbia and Fordham, the Columbia announcer taunted his Jesuit-educated rivals with a crude joke about clergy sexual abuse. By November, a network television drama, *The Practice,* had featured a protagonist who leaves the Catholic Church over the crisis. The most popular movie in Mexico, *El Crimen del Padre Amaro,* was a tawdry melodrama about a handsome priest who has an affair with his housekeeper and her daughter. And despite objections from the Vatican, the top prize at the Venice Film Festival went to a Scottish film, *The Magdalene Sisters,* about abusive nuns in Ireland.

Although incidents of abuse by priests were reported throughout the Catholic world, the scandal resonated most deeply in English-speaking developed countries, such as the United States, Canada, Britain, and Ireland. In the Republic of Ireland, one of the most Catholic countries in Europe, the Church's attempt to reform itself and minimize the scandal with a handpicked blue-ribbon commission was overwhelmed by public outrage, especially after a documentary on the state-run broadcast service showed the extent of the problem and the Church's cover-up in Dublin. The Irish government, which had once afforded the Catholic Church a "special position" in the country's 1937 constitution, decided the Church was incapable of policing itself and set up its own inquiry. . . .

By the time Law quit, Church officials were trying to cast the most positive light on the situation, suggesting that, at last, the Church could move on.

"Let us all pray that this is another step, along with the new U.S. Bishops' Charter for the Protection of Children and Young People, that will advance the healing from this tragic chapter in the history of the Catholic Church in America," said Archbishop Harry J. Flynn of Saint Paul and Minneapolis.

And Cardinal William H. Keeler of Baltimore declared, "I join Cardinal Law in praying that this will be an act of purification for our Church, allowing us to begin healing and reconciliation. Many people have suffered. Trust has been betrayed. Yet, now is not the time to turn away. It is time for us to come together to answer scandal with witness and service, rededicating ourselves to lifting up Christ's call to holiness and hope."

But victims were unsatisfied, saying they wanted to see other bishops ousted and even taken to court. Two days after Law resigned, a handful of protesters showed up at Boston's Cathedral of the Holy Cross. "Law's gone — the fight goes on," read one sign. "Let the dominos fall," read another. One quoted Winston Churchill: "This is not the end. It is not even the beginning of the end. But it is, perhaps, the end of the beginning."

"This was just the tip of the iceberg," said Kathy Dwyer of Braintree, Massachusetts, one of the protesters. "We've got a lot more to take care of."

A somber Cardinal Law made one final appearance in 2002, speaking for about three minutes to a group of reporters hastily summoned to a church library near his house. As a deafening roar of camera shutters tracked his every expression, Law said he could never have imagined a story that would end this way. He said he planned to take a vacation, go on retreat to a monastery, and then move someplace outside the Archdiocese of Boston.

"The course of events in recent months has certainly been different than anything I, or others, would have predicted on the occasion of my installation more than eighteen years ago," he said. "To all those who have suffered from my shortcomings and from my mistakes, I once again apologize, and from them, I beg forgiveness."

Voice of the Faithful

One of the strongest responses to the Catholic crisis was mounted by Voice of the Faithful, an organization of laity, mentioned in the Boston Globe *report, that sought a constructive, Catholic response to the entire situation. It was a body, soon grown very large with many local units throughout the U.S. and abroad, that often sounded like a traditionally Catholic organization. But in purest American fashion, it also represented the mobilization of lay people to form an ad hoc voluntary movement in response to an ad hoc crisis. Among its many purposes, the organization urges prayer for the church; specifically, it requests its members to pray each day at noon, "Jesus, Lord and Brother, help us with our faithfulness. Please hear our voice, and let our voice be heard. Amen." The three documents that follow are (1) an account of the establishment of the group by one of its founding members, Peggie Thorp; (2) a message sent in 2002 to Pope John Paul II; and (3) a statement from April 2003 to clarify the organization's purposes.*

1. The Voice of the Faithful Story

When the faithful speak, the faithful listen. And so it has been these months of our fleeting infancy and explosive growth. From 25 people gathered on a January Monday evening at St. John Evangelist church in Wellesley, Massachusetts, to standing-room-only crowds exceeding 700 all spring, to tens of thousands of members today throughout the world, the group that has become Voice of the Faithful has shared our outrage, pain, deep love of Church, and commitment to act. Mainstream Catholics are talking as never before — to each other and to Church leadership.

The realization that clergy sexual abuse had infected the Catholic priesthood might have driven us far from our Church. Instead, Voice placed the victims first in our mission statement.

The understanding that the great majority of fine priests would suffer by association might have been lost. Instead, Voice placed priests second in our mission statement.

The discovery of a costly cover-up engineered by Church officials and born of abuse of power might have alienated all. Instead, Voice placed structural change third in our mission statement.

Here marked the end of "pay, pray, and obey" Catholicism. And here

---

[Source: The three documents are from the Voice of the Faithful website, http://www.votf.org (5 June 2003).]

marked the beginning of what Catholic priest and author Henri Nouwen noted of lives lived in hope — they are lives of "prayer, community, and resistance."

This crisis has brought faithful Catholics all over the world to their feet — first by ones and twos, and now by the tens of thousands. Over 4,000 of us met for the first time at our convention, "Response of the Faithful," on July 20th in Boston. Our mission is nourished by each other as we continue a Spirit-driven dialogue toward a stronger Catholic Church. Good heart and discerning minds are determined that the voice of the laity will never be silent again.

Our God-given gifts are everywhere evident, materializing, it has seemed, at the very moment of need. We have traveled far with friends and one-time strangers — from folding and unfolding hundreds of chairs to Web site design, management and enhancement; from hours of listening to hours of organizing; from endless questions to workable answers; from 37 supporters on our month-old Web site to over 25,000 today. How fortunate is our Church! Rainer Maria Rilke's poem has fresh resonance — "All will come again into its strength . . . lest we remain unused."

2. Response of the Faithful: A Declaration to the Pope

We the Faithful, in order to form a more perfect Church, gather in Boston on this 20th day of July 2002, to affirm the role of the laity in the constant renewal of the Catholic Church, as proclaimed in *Lumen Gentium* and other documents of the Second Vatican Council. Sharing actively in Christ's priestly, prophetic, and kingly functions in the fulfillment of our lay apostolate, we meet to express our opinion on those things that concern the good of the Church.

We acknowledge with grief and anger the profound suffering of untold numbers of boys and girls, men and women, who have been sexually abused by our clergy. We honor those heroic survivors who have come forward to tell the terrible truth.

We support the decisions of the American bishops in Dallas and commit to work for the full and immediate implementation of the Charter approved there. We petition the Holy Father to support this Charter and to hold account-able any bishop who reassigned an abusive priest or concealed his crimes, and any member of the Curia who participated in these practices.

We dedicate our apostolate to building up a Church in which these crimes and the abuse of power that made them possible will not happen again.

Therefore we affirm the mission of the Voice of the Faithful:

To provide a prayerful voice, attentive to the Spirit, through which the Faithful can actively participate in the governance and guidance of the Catholic Church.

We unite around three goals: To support those who have been abused; to support priests of integrity; and to shape structural change within the Church.

In accordance with our mission and goals, we commit individually and collectively to realize fully the renewal of the Church and the role of the laity envisioned by the Second Vatican Council. We do so as loving members of the Catholic Church, The People of God, called to fulfill the mission of Christ in the Church and in the world.

3. Voice of the Faithful: Statement on Who We Are

Voice of the Faithful, Inc. is an organization composed of Catholics striving to be faithful to the teachings of Our Lord and Savior, Jesus Christ. Joining VOTF is not a break with the Church but a commitment to strengthen and renew it. The following affirmations are not meant to be a complete statement on who we are. They are primarily a response to those who misunderstand us, including members of our Church's hierarchy and lay Catholics who misinterpret our mission and goals.

The Executive Committee of Voice of the Faithful recommended this Statement for action by the VOTF Representative Council, which remanded it on April 26, 2003 to Parish Voice affiliates for discussion and comment in preparation for further action by the Representative Council. The Statement was also reviewed by Rev. Ladislas Orsy, S.J., an advisor to Voice of the Faithful on canon law and theological matters.

- We are faithful Catholics in communion with the universal Catholic Church.
- We love and support our Church and believe what it professes.
- We accept the teaching authority of our Church, including the traditional role of the bishops and the Pope.
- We will work with our bishops, clergy, and other members to strengthen unity and human moral integrity in our Church.
- We believe that sexual abuse by clergy and the response of bishops, protecting abusers and forsaking the abused, have caused great human suffering and damaged the moral authority of our Church.
- We believe that the laity has the graced dignity, intelligence, responsibility and obligation to cooperate in Church governance in a meaningful way according to the norm law (cf. Canon 129) to correct the profound flaws that have been revealed in the human institutional life of our Church.
- We believe that the council documents of Vatican II illuminate the pathway for lay involvement in the Church.
- We urge that the openness and mutual respect advocated by Pope John

Paul II in *Ut Unum Sint* ("That All May Be One") be the model for meaningful dialog among bishop and laity.

Theology in the New Century

Mormons

*Among the many religious proclamations expressly made to greet the dawn-
ing of the new millennium, a formal "Testimony of the Apostles" of "The
Church of Jesus Christ of Latter-day Saints" was among the most interesting.
This testimony concerning "The Living Christ" marked yet another step by
the Mormons toward main traditions of the nation's Christian churches. It is
a significant document both for what it says, and for how it says it. That is,
frank use is made of the Mormon Scriptures and of the words of the Mormon
prophet, Joseph Smith. But those particular elements are employed to demonstrate how close Mormons stand to the Christian traditions rather than to
itemize the particulars of Mormon belief that set them apart for others. In
these terms, this testimony was an important historical, as well as theological, statement.*

As we commemorate the birth of Jesus Christ two millennia ago, we offer our
testimony of the reality of His matchless life and the infinite virtue of His great
atoning sacrifice. None other has had so profound an influence upon all who
have lived and will yet live upon the earth.

He was the Great Jehovah of the Old Testament, the Messiah of the New.
Under the direction of His Father, He was the creator of the earth. "All things
were made by him; and without him was not any thing made that was made"
(John 1:3). Though sinless, He was baptized to fulfill all righteousness. He
"went about doing good" (Acts 10:38), yet was despised for it. His gospel was a
message of peace and goodwill. He entreated all to follow His example. He
walked the roads of Palestine, healing the sick, causing the blind to see, and
raising the dead. He taught the truths of eternity, the reality of our premortal
existence, the purpose of our life on earth, and the potential for the sons and
daughters of God in the life to come.

He instituted the sacrament as a reminder of His great atoning sacrifice.

[Source: "The Living Christ: The Testimony of the Apostles, the Church of Jesus Christ of
Latter-day Saints." LDS Home Page, http://www.ids.org/library/the_liv_chr.html (7 Apr. 2000).]

He was arrested and condemned on spurious charges, convicted to satisfy a mob, and sentenced to die on Calvary's cross. He gave His life to atone for the sins of all mankind. His was a great vicarious gift in behalf of all who would ever live upon the earth.

We solemnly testify that His life, which is central to all human history, neither began in Bethlehem nor concluded on Calvary. He was the Firstborn of the Father, the Only Begotten Son in the flesh, the Redeemer of the world.

He rose from the grave to "become the firstfruits of them that slept" (1 Corinthians 15:20). As Risen Lord, He visited among those He had loved in life. He also ministered among His "other sheep" (John 10:16) in ancient America. In the modern world, He and His Father appeared to the boy Joseph Smith, ushering in the long-promised "dispensation of the fulness of times" (Ephesians 1:10).

Of the Living Christ, the Prophet Joseph wrote: "His eyes were as a flame of fire; the hair of his head was white like the pure snow; his countenance shone above the brightness of the sun; and his voice was as the sound of the rushing of great waters, even the voice of Jehovah, saying:

"I am the first and the last; I am he who liveth, I am he who was slain; I am your advocate with the Father" (D&C [Doctrine and Covenants] 110:3-4).

Of Him the Prophet also declared: "And now, after the many testimonies which have been given of him, this is the testimony, last of all, which we give of him: That he lives!

"For we saw him, even on the right hand of God; and we heard the voice bearing record that he is the Only Begotten of the Father —

"That by him, and through him, and of him, the worlds are and were created, and the inhabitants thereof are begotten sons and daughters unto God" (D&C 76:22-24).

We declare in words of solemnity that His priesthood and His Church have been restored upon the earth — "built upon the foundation of . . . apostles and prophets, Jesus Christ himself being the chief comer stone" (Ephesians 2:20).

We testify that He will someday return to earth. "And the glory of the Lord shall be revealed, and all flesh shall see it together" (Isaiah 40:5). He will rule as King of Kings and reign as Lord of Lords, and every knee shall bend and every tongue shall speak in worship before Him. Each of us will stand to be judged of Him according to our works and the desires of our hearts.

We bear testimony, as His duly ordained Apostles — that Jesus is the Living Christ, the immortal Son of God. He is the great King Immanuel, who stands today on the right hand of His Father. He is the light, the life, and the hope of the world. His way is the path that leads to happiness in this life and eternal life in the world to come. God be thanked for the matchless gift of His divine Son.

Mestizaje

Virgilio Elizondo served from 1972 to 1987 as the founding president of the Mexican American Cultural Center in San Antonio. He is an American of Mexican ancestry who has served as a Catholic priest in his native San Antonio. This meditation, first published in 1988 and then revised in 1998, speaks of the privilege of living between worlds, in mestizaje. *At the start of a new century, Elizondo's experience, as a person astride various cultures who finds inspiration and encouragement in his church community, is coming closer and closer to the norm in American religious experience.*

During my boyhood days there were no questions whatsoever about my identity or belonging. We grew up at home wherever we went — playgrounds, school, church. The whole atmosphere was Mexican and there was no doubt in our minds about the pride of being Mexican. Radio stations provided us with good Mexican music and the local Mexican theaters kept us in contact with the dances, folklore, romance, and daily life of Mexico. The poverty of Mexico, which was always evident in the movies, was completely surpassed by the natural simplicity, ingenuity, graciousness, and joy of the Mexican people. The United States was so efficient, but Mexico was so human. The contrasts were clear. We might be living outside the political boundaries of Mexico, but Mexico was not outside of us. We continued to interiorize it with great pride.

Como México no hay dos — there is nothing else like Mexico. Being Mexican was the greatest gift of God's grace. We loved it, lived it, and celebrated it. In many ways, we felt sorry for the people who were not so lucky as to be Mexican. In those early years I never thought of myself as a native-born U.S. citizen of Mexican descent. My U.S. identity was quite secondary to my Mexican identity. Yet I was happy living in the United States. We belonged to this land called the United States and this land belonged to us. In those early days, I never experienced being Mexican as not belonging. This was my home. I was born here and I belonged here.

Little did I think in those early years that the foundations of a new identity were already being formed within me. I was living a new identity that had not yet been defined and that would take many years to emerge. The new identity was beginning to emerge, not as a theory of evolution or as a political ideology of one type or another. It was rather a life lived not just by me, but by thousands of others who were living a similar experience. We were the first of the new human group that was beginning to emerge.

[Source: "A Galilean Christology," in *The Future Is Mestizo*, rev. ed. (University Press of Colorado, 2000).

The paradise existence of the neighborhood came to a halt the first day I went to a Catholic grade school operated by German nuns in what had been a German parish. There the pastor still told Mexicans to go away because it wasn't their church. My parents had sent me there because it was the nearest Catholic school. Mexicans were tolerated but not very welcome.

The next few years would be a real purgatory. The new language was completely foreign to me and everything was strange. The food in the cafeteria was horrible — sauerkraut and other foods that I only remember as weird. We were not allowed to speak Spanish and were punished when we got caught doing so. The sisters and lay teachers were strict disciplinarians. I don't think I ever saw them smile but I remember well them hitting us frequently with a ruler or a stick. They were the exact opposite of the Mexican sisters around our home who were always happy, joking, and smiling and formed us carefully through counsels, suggestions, and rewards. In one system we were punished for bad things we did while in the other we were rewarded for our good accomplishments.

Mass was so different. Everything was orderly and stern. People seemed to be in pain, and even afraid of being there. It was a church of discipline, but it was not one of joy. In fact, joy seemed to be out of place. Mass was recited, not celebrated. People went because they had to, not because they wanted to. It seemed like a totally different religion.

It was hard going to school in a language that was almost completely unknown and in surroundings that were so foreign and alienating. Things did not make sense. I used to get very bored. The school hours seemed eternal; the clock appeared not even to move during those horribly unintelligible hours. My parents had to force me to study and it was very difficult for me even to make passing grades. Going to school was so different that it was like crossing the border every day, like going to another country to go to school, even though it was only a few blocks from our home.

It was during these days that I first started to get a feeling of being a foreigner in the very country in which I had been born and raised. Guilt started to develop within me: why wasn't I like the other children who spoke English and ate sandwiches rather than *tortillas*? I started to feel different and mixed-up about who I was. But the mixture and the bad feelings came to a quick end every day at three o'clock when school was dismissed and I returned home. It was the beginning of life in two countries that were worlds apart.

I wanted to become what I felt I had to be, for it was my parents, whose authority and wisdom I never questioned, who had sent me to that school. Yet it meant not so much developing myself as ceasing to be who I was in order to become another person. Those three years in primary school were awful. I was afraid to mix with the kids and often felt better going off by myself. The teachers were constantly getting after me for daydreaming. That was my natural escape mechanism or, better yet, my instinct to survive. The dreams were my spontaneous efforts to create an existence of my own, thus refusing to accept the existence that was being imposed on me.

As I look into the past and try to understand it from my present perspective many years later, I re-experience the original pain, sadness, embarrassment, ambiguity, frustration, and the sense of seeking refuge by being alone. Yet I can also see that it was already the beginning of the formation of the consciousness of a new existence — of a new *mestizaje* ("the process through which two totally different peoples mix biologically and culturally so that a new people begins to emerge"). The daily border crossing was having its effect on me. I didn't know what it meant. I didn't even know why it had to be. But that constant crossing became the most ordinary thing in my life. In spite of the contradictions at school, there was never any serious doubt in my mind that my original home experience in a Mexican neighborhood was the core of my existence and identity; there my belonging was never questioned. There I did not seek to go off by myself but was developing into quite an outgoing person. . . .

Yet this certitude of being Mexican began to be questioned whenever we visited our relatives in Mexico. Even though they loved us and we loved to visit them, in many ways they would let us know that we were *pochos* — Mexicans from the United States. To this day, it is not uncommon to hear someone in Mexico say about a Mexican American's Spanish, "For a *norteamericano,* your Spanish is not so bad." Yet it is not uncommon for an Anglo American from the United States to say about a Mexican American speaking perfect English, "For a Mexican American your English is pretty good." Whether in Mexico or the United States we are always the distant and different "other." The core of our existence is to be "other" or to "not be" in relation to those who are. Yet being called *pocho* in Mexico was not insulting, for we were fully accepted. There was always rejoicing when our families visited us in San Antonio or when we visited them in Mexico. *Pocho* was simply a reality. Even though the United States was our home, it was in Mexico that we felt more and more at home. The label marked distance and difference but not separation or rejection.

This was an experience totally different from being called "Meskins," "Greasers," or "wetbacks" in the United States. The titles were used to remind us that we were different — meaning that we were backward, ignorant, inferior, scum. We were not wanted in the United States, merely tolerated and exploited. Our people were consistently subjected to multiple injustices. The movies depicted us as treacherous bandits or drunken fools and our women as wanting nothing better in life than to go to bed with one of the white masters. Anglo-American society had no doubts that it alone was the Master Race! Indians, Mexican "half-breeds," and Blacks were inferior and therefore to be kept down for the good of humanity. . . .

The Galilean identity of Jesus and of his first followers is one of the constants of the New Testament. As I started exploring the socio-cultural imagery of Galilee I became more intrigued. It was a borderland, the great border region between the Greeks and the Jews of Judea. People of all nationalities came along the caravan routes on their way to and from Egypt. There was abundant agriculture and commerce and a flourishing Greek society. The Jews were in the minority and were forced to mix with their Gentile neighbors. It was a land of great mixture and of an ongoing *mestizaje* — similar to our own Southwest of the United States. The Galilean Jews spoke with a very marked accent and most likely mixed their language quite readily with the Greek of the dominant culture and the Latin of the Roman Empire. Peter could deny Jesus, but there was no way he could deny he was a Galilean. The moment he opened his mouth he revealed his Galilean identity.

The more I discovered about Galilee, the more I felt at home there and the more Jesus truly became my flesh-and-blood brother. He was not just a religious icon, but a living partner in the human struggle for life. He too had lived the experience of human distance and ridicule. Being a Jew in Galilee was very much like being a Mexican American in Texas. As the Jews in Galilee were too Jewish to be accepted by the Gentile population and too contaminated with pagan ways to be accepted by the pure-minded Jews of Jerusalem, so have the Mexican Americans in the Southwest been rejected by two groups. . . .

In his *mestizo* existence Jesus breaks the barriers of separation, as does every *mestizo*, and already begins to live a new unity. That is both the threat and the greatness of a *mestizo* existence. *Mestizos* may struggle to become one or the other of the great traditions out of which they are born, but even if they were to succeed, that would be a mere return to the previous divisions of society. We usher in new life for the betterment of everyone when we freely and consciously assume the great traditions flowing through our veins and transcend them, not by denying either but by synthesizing them into something new.

The *mestizo* is the biblical stone, rejected by the builders of this world, that God has chosen to be the cornerstone of a new creation, not chosen for honor and privilege, but for a sacred mission. Having been marginated and misunderstood, we know the suffering of separation by our own experiences; we know that this type of existence is wrong and it must change. But change does not mean that we now take over and impose our ways upon all. This would simply be a new conquest, a new domination, and nothing would really change. The *mestizo* affirms both the identities received while offering something new to both. Being an insider-outsider and an outsider-insider to two worlds at the same time, we have the unique privilege of seeing and appreciating both worlds. It is from this position that we begin to combine the elements of both to form something new.

In the *mestizaje* and mission of Jesus our own *mestizaje* is transformed and redeemed. What appears to be a curse to some now appears for what it truly is — a blessing. What humanly speaking is the basis of margination and rejection is now discovered to be the basis of divine election. What appeared to be at the furthest outposts of the frontiers of nationality and race, now is recognized as the cradle of a new humanity.

Suggested Reading (Chapter Twelve)

For an insightful historical overview of the fact of religious diversity in American history and of various reactions to that diversity, see William R. Hutchison, *Religious Pluralism in America: The Contentious History of a Founding Ideal* (2003). Diana Eck has provided a guide to much of what is happening in religious America that is new, non-European, and non-Christian in *A New Religious America: How a "Christian Country" Has Now Become the World's Most Religiously Diverse Nation* (2001). On the many new configurations since the immigration act of 1965 made it possible for more foreign nationals to arrive in the United States, R. Stephen Warner has been a leader in sorting out a complex reality — see, with Judith G. Witner, eds., *Gatherings in Diaspora: Religious Connections and the New Immigration* (1998), and with Ho Young Kim and Kwang Chung Kim, eds., *Korean Americans and Their Religions* (2001). Among earlier accounts that charted the boom in new religions as it was taking place, helpful orientation was provided by George Baker, ed., *Understanding the New Religions* (1978), I. I. Zaretsky and M. P. Leone, eds., *Religious Movements in Contemporary America* (1974), and Robert S. Ellwood, Jr., *Religious and Spiritual Groups in Contemporary America* (1973). Along with the books suggested in chapter 7 for Buddhism, see also the broad and helpful survey provided by Gurinder Singh Mann, Paul David Numrich, and Raymond B. Williams in *Buddhists, Hindus, and Sikhs in America* (2001). As a reminder concerning the large number of Christians among the new immigrants, see Raymond B. Williams, *Christian Pluralism in the United States: The Indian Immigrant Experience* (1996), and Jeffrey M. Burns, Ellen Skerrett, and Joseph M. White, eds., *Keeping Faith: European and Asian Catholic Immigrants* (2000). For the presence of Islam in America helpful surveys are provided by Frederick Denny, *Muslims in America* (2000), Jane I. Smith, *Islam in America* (1999), and Asma Gull Hasan, *American Muslims: The New Generation* (2000).

The presence of violence in a few of the new religious movements is the subject of Catherine Lowman Wessinger, *How the Millennium Comes Violently: From Jonestown to Heaven's Gate* (2000). Bill Hoffmann and Cathy Burke offer instant analysis for one of these incidents in *Heaven's Gate: Culture Suicide in San Diego* (1997), while the passage of time has given more perspective to Mary

McCormic Maage, *Hearing the Voices of Jonestown* (1998), and Stuart A. Wright, ed., *Armageddon in Waco: Critical Perspectives on the Branch Davidian Conflict* (1995).

Besides the readings suggested in chapter 9 for the religions of nature, see also the helpful surveys provided by Margot Adler, *Drawing Down the Moon: Witches, Druids, Goddess-Worshippers, and Other Pagans in America Today* (1986), and Ronald Hutton, *The Triumph of the Moon: A History of Modern Pagan Witchcraft* (1999). A useful collection of information has also been gathered by James R. Lewis, ed., *Witchcraft Today: An Encyclopedia of Wiccan and Neopagan Traditions* (1999).

The applications of Liberation Theology, for which the heyday was in the 1970s and 1980s, were outlined in Dale Richeson and Brian Mahan, *The Challenge of Liberation Theology* (1981). Paul E. Sigmund's *Liberation Theology at the Crossroads: Democracy or Revolution?* (1990) offers a helpful perspective taking in all of the Western hemisphere. Documents of the movement are gathered together in Alfred T. Hennelly, S.J., ed., *Liberation Theology: A Documentary History* (1990).

For religious nationalism among African Americans in the 1960s and 1970s helpful guidance is offered for, respectively, specific and general subjects in Peter Goldman, *The Death and Life of Malcolm X* (1972), and Albert B. Cleage, *Black Christian Nationalism* (1972). The premier theologian of black liberation, James H. Cone, provided many important reports along the way, including *For My People: Black Theology and the Black Church* (1984), as well as a summary retrospective, *Risks of Faith: The Emergence of a Black Theology of Liberation, 1968-1998* (1999). The broader contexts of African American religious history are expertly supplied by Albert J. Raboteau, *Canaan Land: A Religious History of African Americans* (2001), and Milton C. Sernett, ed., *Afro-American Religious History: A Documentary Witness* (2nd ed., 1999).

Developments in Hispanic Catholic life have been very well served by the excellent collection of documents offered by Timothy Matovina and Gerald E. Poyo, *Presente! U.S. Latino Catholics from Colonial Origins to the Present* (2000), and by a 3-vol. set of pioneering investigations that appeared from the University of Notre Dame Press in 1994: Jay P. Dolan and Allan Figueroa Deck, eds., *Hispanic Catholic Culture in the United States;* Dolan and Gilberto M. Hinojosa, eds., *Mexican Americans and the Catholic Church, 1900-1965;* and Dolan and Jaime R. Vidal, eds., *Puerto Rican Catholics in the United States, 1900-1965*. Other studies that treat this ever-more-important region of American religious life include Ana María Díaz-Stevens, *Oxcart Catholicism on Fifth Avenue: The Impact of the Puerto Rican Migration upon the Archdiocese of New York* (1993), and Susan Ferriss and Ricardo Sandoval, *The Fight in the Fields: César Chavez and the Farmworkers Movement* (1997). A reminder of how rapidly Hispanic Protestant communions have also developed is provided by Manuel Ortiz, *His-*

panic Challenge: Opportunities Confronting the Church (1993), and Edwin J. Hernandez, ed., *Protestantes/Protestants* (1999).

For the religious history of Native Americans, there is a fine general study from Joel W. Martin, *The Land Looks After Us: A History of Native American Religion* (2001). Philip J. Deloria's *Playing Indian* (1998) is especially interesting as a book by the son of Vine Deloria, distinguished scholar and advocate whose many books on Native American culture and religion included *Custer Died For Your Sins: An Indian Manifesto* (1969). For other recent accounts in which religion plays a part, see John D. Loftin, *Religion and Hopi Life in the Twentieth Century* (1991), Ward Churchill, *Indians 'R' Us: Culture and Genocide in Native North America* (1994), and Ian Frazier, *On the Rez* (2000). For the surprisingly expansive and varied development of Christian traditions among Indian cultures, Michael D. McNally offers a sharply focused study in *Ojibwe Singers: Hymns, Grief, and a Native Culture in Motion* (2000), and Marie Therese Archambault, Mark Thiel, and Christopher Vecsey provide a broader interpretation through the documents they edited in *The Crossing of Two Roads: Being Catholic and Native in the United States* (2003).

Feminism and connections to religion have received a full press. From Mary Daly came one of the most thorough applications of feminist reasoning to religious questions, *The Church and the Second Sex, with the Feminist PostChristian Introduction and New Archaic Afterwords by the Author* (1985). The broader contexts in which such religious stories have unfolded is offered by Nancy F. Cott, et al., *Roots of Bitterness: Documents of the Social History of American Women* (2nd ed., 1996). Many of the books suggested with chapter 7 are as relevant for the contemporary history of religious women as for earlier eras. Books that treat more recent developments include an extensive survey of public responsibilities — Catherine Wessinger, ed., *Religious Institutions and Women's Leadership: New Roles Inside the Mainstream* (1996); a useful investigation of trajectories among Jews — Joyce Anther, *The Journey Home: How Jewish Women Shaped Modern America* (1997); a pioneering study of Hispanic women — Jeanette Rodriguez, *Our Lady of Guadalupe: Faith and Empowerment among Mexican American Women* (1994); a wide-ranging collection of documents for Catholics — Paula M. Kane, James J. Kenneally, and Karen Kennelly, eds., *Gender Identities in American Catholicism* (2001); and several helpful books on women in conservative religious movements — Marie R. Griffith, *God's Daughters: Evangelical Women and the Power of Submission* (1997), Brenda E. Brasher, *Godly Women: Fundamentalism and Female Power* (1998), and Christel Manning, *God Gave Us the Right: Conservative Catholic, Evangelical Protestant, and Orthodox Jewish Women Grapple with Feminism* (1999).

Contentions, disputes, and litigation on issues of religion and public life continue to expand at a great pace, as do the books on the subject. An excellent set of documents is offered by John F. Wilson and Donald L. Drakeman, eds.,

Church and State in American History: Key Documents, Decisions, and Commentary From the Past Three Centuries (3rd ed., 2003), and there is an authoritative brief overview from Edwin S. Gaustad in *Church and State in America* (1999). The most important books of an earlier era were probably those like Anson Phelps Stokes, *Church and State in the United States* (1950), which provided ammunition for those who wanted to separate religion and public life as much as possible. More recently, the literary tide has turned in the other direction with strongly-argued presentations of the case for more religion in public life (though not a church establishment) from Richard John Neuhaus, *The Naked Public Square* (1984), Stephen L. Carter, *The Culture of Disbelief: How American Law and Politics Trivialize Religious Devotion* (1993), and Philip Hamburger, *Separation of Church and State* (2002). Against such volumes, the banner of separation is upheld by books like Isaac Kramnick and R. Laurence Moore, *The Godless Constitution: The Case Against Religious Correctness* (1996). In 1999 the *William and Mary Quarterly* devoted an extensive "forum" to the challenge provided by James H. Hutson that Thomas Jefferson's famous description of "a wall of separation between church and state" (in a letter to the Baptists of Danbury, Conn., in 1802) was intended as a political expedient of the moment rather than a general principle for all of American life: Hutson's article and the responses of several historians are found in vol. 46 (Oct. 1999): 775-824. For outstanding accounts of the general subject, see John R. Witte, Jr., *Religion and the American Constitutional Experiment: Essential Rights and Liberties* (2000) with a survey from the founding era, and John T. Noonan, *The Lustre of Our Country: The American Experience of Religious Freedom* (1997) with a discerning meditation on the uniqueness of what has taken place in the United States. Contributions to a complex subject from individual religious traditions are provided by Jonathan D. Sarna and David G. Dalin, eds., *Religion and State in the American Jewish Experience* (1997), and David J. O'Brien, *Public Catholicism* (1997).

The intersections of biology with theology have been well handled by John T. Noonan, ed., *The Morality of Abortion* (1970), and Paul Ramsey, *Ethics at the Edges of Life* (1978). More recent expressions on abortion and the law are surveyed in *The Church Speaks on Abortion: Official Statements from Religious Bodies and Ecumenical Organizations* (1989), and Elizabeth Adell Cook, *Between Two Absolutes: Public Opinion and the Politics of Abortion* (1992). On questions of whether the churches should accept practicing homosexuals and ordain actively gay clergy, it is hard to find dispassionate analysis, though it was attempted in Saul M. Olyan and Martha C. Nussbaum, eds., *Sexual Orientation and Human Rights in American Religious Discourse* (1998). Progressive viewpoints are represented in Kathy Rudy, *Sex and the Church: Gender, Homosexuality, and the Transformation of Christian Ethics* (1999), and traditional viewpoints in Robert A. J. Gagnon, *The Bible and Homosexual Practice: Texts and Hermeneutics* (2001).

Popular and academic treatments of religion and politics continue to abound as more and more religious proposals, and counter-proposals, are made with respect to issues in public life. Historical background is provided by Garry Wills, *Under God: Religion and American Politics* (1990), and Mark A. Noll, ed., *Religion and American Politics* (1990). Thought-provoking analyses from the standpoint of political theory have come from Michael Lienesch, *Redeeming America: Piety and Politics in the New Christian Right* (1993), and Michael J. Perry, *Under God?* (2003). Efforts to chart the rise and influence of Christian conservative politics have been ongoing since the 1980s. Some of the notable attempts include Steve Bruce, *The Rise and Fall of the New Christian Right . . . 1978-1988* (1988), Michael Cromartie, ed., *No Longer Exiles: The Religious New Right in American Politics* (1993), and Steve Bruce, Peter Kivisto, and William H. Swatos, Jr., *The Rapture of Politics: The Christian Right as the United States Approaches the Year 2000* (1995). Expert analysis of relationships between voting and religious adherence is provided by John C. Green, James L. Guth, Corwin E. Smidt, and Lyman A. Kellstedt, *Religion and the Culture Wars: Dispatches from the Front* (1996), and on more general aspects in American political behavior in Corwin E. Smidt, ed., *In God We Trust?* (2001). There is also an informative survey of presidential religion (through Ronald Reagan) in Richard V. Pierard and Robert D. Linder, *Civil Religion and the Presidency* (1988).

Books on the terrorist attacks of September 11, 2001, now appear at a great pace. One of the first general accounts that included awareness of religious dimensions at work was James F. Hoge, Jr. and Gideon Rose, eds., *How Did This Happen? Terrorism and the New War* (2001). Among thought-provoking early assessments were meditations by the new Archbishop of Canterbury, Rowan Williams, *Writing in the Dust: After September 11* (2002), and by a collection of editors, ministers, and educators in Lane T. Dennis, ed., *A Reason for Hope in Times of Tragedy* (2001).

The deep background of American apocalyptic beliefs is the theme of Paul S. Boyer, *When Time Shall Be No More: Prophecy Belief in Modern American Culture* (1992), while specific attention to fears, hopes, and perplexities related to the year 2000 were well treated in Robert G. Clouse, Robert N. Hosack, and Richard V. Pierard, *The New Millennium Manual* (1999).

On the crisis in the Roman Catholic Church related to priests abusing children and young people, the investigative staff of the *Boston Globe*, which did so much to break the story, has provided a summary book, *Betrayal: The Crisis in the Catholic Church* (rev., 2003). The Catholic sex crisis, quite naturally, has also generated a number of works on the Catholic church more generally. Among these, the most notable include Garry Wills' critical volume, *Papal Sins: Structures of Deceit* (2000); an appeal for reform that nonetheless affirms the basic shape of the church from George Weigel, *The Courage to Be Catholic: Cri-*

sis, Reform, and the Future of the Church (2003); and a book on the question of whether the passage of time has fully erased the historic American prejudice against Rome, Philip Jenkins, *The New Anti-Catholicism: The Last Acceptable Prejudice* (2003). A book that does not address the current situation directly, but which is now essential for all considerations of the place of Catholic communities, beliefs, and practices in American life is John T. McGreevy, *Catholicism and American Freedom: A History* (2003).

Especially at the start of a new century, it is difficult to find an angle of vision in which to chart with confidence the many-splendored varieties of American religion. Two books that brought their analysis into the 1980s, but that also offered helpful roadmaps for much that came later, are Robert T. Handy, *Christian America: Protestant Hopes and Historical Realities* (2nd ed., 1984), and Robert Wuthnow, *The Restructuring of America* (1988). Wuthnow's *Christianity in the 21st Century* (1993) is also a discerning guide. Theology in the twenty-first century will doubtless move on from preoccupations of the twentieth. For hints as to what the new century might look like, see Mary Bednarowski, *New Religions and the Theological Imagination in America* (1989), Arturo J. Bañuelos, ed., *Mestizo Christianity: Theology from the Latino Perspective* (1995), and Gabriel Fackre, "The Revival of Systematic Theology: An Overview," *Interpretation* 49 (July 1995): 229-41.

Interpretations abound that seek to find in the histories of large, important religious traditions some indication of what lies ahead. They include, among those not already mentioned with previous chapters, for Catholics — Mary Jo Weaver and R. Scott Appleby, eds., *Being Right: Conservative Catholics in America* (1995), Patrick Carey, *The Roman Catholics in America* (1996), and Michael Zoller, *Washington and Rome: Catholicism in American Culture* (1999); for Protestants as a whole — Randall Balmer, *Grant Us Courage: Travels along the Mainline of American Protestantism* (1996), and Donald E. Miller, *Reinventing American Protestantism: Christianity in the New Millennium* (1997); for evangelical Protestants — Christian Smith, *American Evangelicalism: Embattled and Thriving* (1998), Mark A. Noll, *American Evangelical Christianity* (2001), and D. G. Hart, *That Old-Time Religion in Modern America: Evangelical Protestantism in the Twentieth Century* (2002); and for Jews — Murray Herbert Danzger, *Returning to Tradition: The Contemporary Revival of Orthodox Judaism* (1989), Elliott Abrams, *Faith or Fear: How Jews Can Survive in a Christian America* (1997), and Samuel G. Freedman, *Jew vs. Jew: The Struggle for the Soul of American Jewry* (2000).

Even broader orientation from the end-of-the-century for the organization of religion at, respectively, the national and the local levels, is offered by Robert Bruce Mullin and Russell E. Richey, eds., *Reimagining Denominationalism* (1994), and James P. Wind and James W. Lewis, eds., *American Congregations,* 2 vols. (1994). For a marvelous guide to the churches as of the year 2000, in every county of the United States, see Dale E. Jones, et al., *Religious Congrega-tions and Membership in the United States 2000* (2002). And as a final reminder that religion always takes place in space and across time, the indispensable book is Edwin Scott Gaustad and Philip L. Barlow, *New Historical Atlas of Religion in America* (2001).

Index

Abbelen, P. M., 17, 18-20

Abbot, Ezra, 353

Abbott, Lyman, 62-63, 125-26, 128, 340

Abbott, W. M., S.J., 547-49

Abortion, 531, 580, 636, 637, 660-72, 676, 679, 680, 681, 704, 743; relation of, to social justice, 661, 668, 670, 672; religious responses to laws on, 666-72, 743

Acres of Diamonds (Conwell), 242-43

Adams, James E., 523n., 524-25

Adler, Alfred, 196

Adler, Mortimer J., 438

Adrian College, 591

Afghanistan, 481, 59, 705, 707

Africa, 491, 495, 590, 595, 610, 612; missionary effort in, 145-46, 155-58, 161, 162, 165, 190. *See also* Algeria; Egypt; Somalia, Zaire

African Americans, 195, 208, 257, 476, 688, 689; denominational affiliation of, 79-80, 157-58, 294, 442, 633, 711-12; education of, 79, 713, 714; identity issues among, 158, 492-92, 495, 610-12, 712-14; missionaries sponsored by, 79-80, 155-58, 190; and religion, 1, 495, 571, 577, 608-12, 711-14, 741; status of, in society, 79-80; struggle of, 1, 571, 712, 714 (*see also* Civil Rights movement; Ku Klux Klan; Racism); voting patterns, 688, 689

African Methodist Episcopal Church, 79, 712

Agnew, Spiro T., 442

Ahlstrom, Sydney, 683

AIDS, 714

Alabama, 493, 529, 638, 639. *See also* Birmingham; Montgomery; Selma

Alabama Christian Movement for Human Rights, 490

Alaska, 3, 50-58, 85-86, 87, 620; Russian presence in, 51, 52, 557

Aleuts, 53-56, 57-58, 557, 621

Algeria, 453

Ali, Ameer, 76

Alliance of Evangelical Ministries (AMEN), 618, 620

Al Qaeda, 701, 707

Altizer, Thomas J. J., 566, 573

Ambrose, St., 155

American Academy of Religion, 604

American Bankers Association, 270

American Baptist Home Mission Society, 79

American Civil Liberties Union, 701, 704

American Council for Judaism, 456

American Evangelical Alliance, 93

American Federation of Labor, 89

American Jewish Committee, 723

American Liberty League, 270

American Mercury, 484-86

American Protective Association, 197, 252-54, 256

American Psychological Association, 602

American School for Oriental Research, 372

American Seminary for Foreign Missions, 152-54

American Sociological Association, 602

Amish, 650

Ammerman, Nancy T., 572, 600-602

Amsterdam, 509, 513

Anabaptists, 83

Anderson, Michael, 700

Angels, 9, 327, 339, 342, 369

Anne de Beaupré, St., 249

Anthony, Susan B., 43

Anti-Catholicism, 13-14, 21-23, 28, 42, 68, 196-97, 252-61, 263, 266-67, 300, 323-24, 441, 498-500, 501, 502, 503, 744-45

Antichrist, 523; Communism as, 464; Pope as, 253

Antin, Mary, 13

Anti-Saloon League, 91-92, 185-86, 188

Anti-Semitism: in America, 84, 256-63, 269, 721; considered implicit in Higher Criticism, 412, 414-15; in Europe and elsewhere, 26, 27, 31, 413, 452-54, 459; renounced by Vatican II, 547, 548. *See also* Holocaust

Apocalypse, speculation on, 600, 723, 724, 744. *See also* Prophecy, biblical

Applewhite, Marshall, 577

Aquinas, St. Thomas, 307, 341, 426-30, 438

Architecture, ecclesiastical, 52, 54, 58, 60, 293, 554, 588, 614, 618

Arias, Alma, 619

Aristotle, 315, 316, 427, 507

Arkansas, 266-67, 696, 697, 697. *See also* Little Rock

Armageddon, 447, 481, 570

Armed forces, 87, 176-77. *See also* Conscientious objection *and under* Men, ministry to

Arnold, Sir Edwin, 74

Asch, Sholem, 202-3

Asia, 491, 590, 595; impact of, on Western civilization, 195; impact on, of the West, 145, 165, 167, 495. *See also* Afghanistan; Burma; China; Immigration, Asian; India; Japan; Near East; Southeast Asia; Sri Lanka

Association against the Prohibition Amendment, 264-65

Athanasius, St., 81, 155, 343

Athar, Shahid, 478, 481-82, 701n., 702, 706-8

Atheism, 72, 305, 463, 567, 638

Atlanta, Ga., 197, 476, 491, 693

Atomic power, potential of: for destruction (*see* Nuclear war); for good, 447-48

Augustine, St., 155, 341, 430, 565

Auschwitz, 449-50, 452

Australia, 272, 528

Austria, 161, 255, 453

Azusa Pacific College, 618

B'nai B'rith, 129

Bacon, Benjamin W., 353-56, 360, 364

Baker, James, 475

Baldwin, James, 571

Balkans, 255, 481, 707

Baltimore, Md., 22, 69, 88, 253, 272, 730

Banks, Adelle M., 714n., 715-16

Baptist, R. D., 155n., 157-58

Baptist Faith and Message (SBC, 2000), 528n., 529, 530-33, 534-35

Baptists, 78, 82, 91, 136, 195, 532, 578, 621-23, 743; African American, 79-80, 155-58, 490, 712; Asian American, 10-12; individuals, 129, 164, 222, 242, 348, 404, 486, 490, 500, 502, 559, 688, 690, 697. *See also* American Baptist Home Mission Society; Anabaptists; Baptist World Alliance; National Baptist Convention; Seventh-Day Baptists; Southern Baptist Convention

Baptist World Alliance, 222

Baranov, Aleksandr A., 53

Barrows, John Henry, 4

Barth, G. Christian, 524

Barth, Karl, 428

Barton, Bruce, 298

Bayme, Steven, 723

Beecher, Henry Ward, 62, 86, 125

Beecher, Lyman, 222

Beeson Divinity School, 529

Belgium, 132

Bell, L. Nelson, 463

Bellah, Robert N., 684

Benedict, St., Rule of, 217

Ben-Hur, 193, 204

Bennett, John C., 498n., 499-501, 571

Bergson, Henri, 320n., 431

Bernini, Giovanni, 536

Berrigan, Daniel, 571

Bertram, Robert, 525

Bible, 81, 82, 348; authority of, 39, 305, 331, 333, 337, 349, 353, 358, 365-69, 376, 405, 412, 433-34, 443, 517, 530-31, 550, 671, 676, 677, 709, 711, 743; and culture, 202-3, 298, 377, 437, 675; dissemination of, 143, 194, 437; expositions of, 31, 238, 288-90, 313; inerrancy of, 305, 363, 369, 371, 376, 529, 530-31; liturgical reading of, 9, 58, 527, 540; personal reading and study of, 13, 82, 138, 172-73, 194, 206-10, 280, 284, 288, 289, 348, 363, 417-18, 463, 549, 617; principles of interpreting, 13, 15, 25, 209, 333-35, 348-49, 358-64, 366, 370-72, 374-77, 416, 675, 677; in public schools, 13, 15, 24-29, 345, 347, 638 (*see also* Scopes trial); scholarly study of, 2, 245, 305, 306, 319, 321, 353-86, 400, 407, 412-18, 420-21, 437 (*see also* Woman's Bible); use of: in argument, 27, 28, 35, 37-

39, 43-46, 105-6, 110, 125-26, 155, 157, 164,
189, 207-9, 228-29, 231, 238-39, 244, 284-85,
292-96, 327, 329, 332, 427, 428, 507, 519, 551,
563, 564, 615-16, 674-77, 702-3, 734-35 (*see
also* Bible: citations and allusions); in political rhetoric, 687-88, 701; in sermons,
102-3, 155, 157-58, 221-26 passim, 283, 463-
64
Bible, citations and allusions: on church
unity, 178, 514, 556; on divine judgment,
125-26, 284, 289, 290-91; on duty to society, 102-3, 105, 117, 167, 179, 490, 493; on
evangelistic responsibility, 23, 52, 71, 143,
156-57, 163, 222-23, 544, 557, 711; on government, 277; on Jesus in relation to the
prophets, 114-16; on personal morality,
110, 117, 163, 207-8, 223-25, 464, 467, 698;
on Scripture, 209, 364, 365, 366-67, 369,
374, 561; on sin and holiness, 292-96, 312,
313-14; on things to come, 41, 284-85, 290-
91, 475; on wealth, 106, 110, 270; on
women, 38, 71; incidental, 9, 41, 79-80, 119,
158, 198, 215, 226, 232, 235, 241, 287-88, 306,
331, 335, 398, 403, 404, 406, 428, 470, 477,
553, 690. *See also* Bible: use of.
Bible, parts of: Hebrew Bible, 366, 417; Torah, 2, 29, 32, 32, 307, 359, 384, 407-8, 409;
Genesis, 289, 334, 341-42, 345, 348-49, 353,
358-60, 375, 412, 415-16, 449; Leviticus, 675,
677; Deuteronomy, 372, 373-74; Esther,
God not named in, 28; Psalms, 9, 194, 366,
367, 387-88, 413; Prophets, 112, 114-16, 283,
316, 366, 384, 464, 486, 490, 491, 577;
Apocrypha, 25, 380; New Testament: origins of, 81, 356-68, 372; relation to Old, 37-
38, 114-16, 361, 366-67. *See also* Prophecy,
biblical
Bible, translation(s) of, 2, 25, 46, 166, 305,
353, 377-90, 437, 520, 549, 560 (*see also* Inclusive language); Septuagint, 81, 366, 384;
Targums, 384; Old Latin version, 155;
Jerome's Psalters, 375; King James Version,
25, 82, 377, 380, 386-87, 388-89, 507; Campbell's New Testament, 380; English Revised Version, 377; American Standard
Version, 353, 377, 380-81; *Holy Scriptures
according to the Masoretic Text* (tr. M.
Margolis, 1917), 383; *New Testament: An
American Translation* (*see* Goodspeed, Edgar J.); Confraternity Edition, 380, 540;
Jehovah's Witnesses New Testament, 380;
Revised Standard Version, 377-78, 379,
380-82, 386n., 387, 389, 549; New Ameri-

can Bible, 381; Living Bible, 386n., 387,
390; New International Version, 377n.,
384-86, 387-88; Tanakh, 377n., 383-84, 386-
87, 388
Bill of Rights, 650. *See also* Constitution,
U.S.: First Amendment *and* Fourth
Amendment
bin Laden, Osama, 705
Birmingham, Ala., 490-91, 554n.
Bishop, Jim, 298
Black, J. Sutherland, 372
Black Manifesto, 494-98
Blackmun, Harry, 649, 660, 661-63
Black Muslims, 576, 577, 610-12, 711
Black Theology, 608-10, 741
Blackwell, Antoinette Brown, 35-37, 85
Blake, Eugene Carson, 442, 514
Blavatsky, H. P., 227-29
Blayney, Benjamin, 380
"Blue Laws," 34, 219
Boe, Eugene, 6, 7n., 9-10
Boisen, Anton T., 247-50
Bonaventure, St., 207, 216
Book of Common Prayer (Episcopal), 82, 475
Books of Hours, 209
Booth, Catherine, 168
Booth, William, 168-69
Booth-Tucker, Frederick, 168-71
Boston, Mass., 88, 104, 149, 152, 234, 245, 319,
379, 554n., 633, 728, 739, 732
Boston Globe, 728-30, 731, 744
Boston University, 348
Bowers, Henry Francis, 252
Brady, John, 50-52
Brain-washing, 602, 619
Branch Davidians, 577, 600-602, 741
Brandeis University, 412
Brandon, Joseph R., 27-28
Brandt, John L., 252-54
Brawley, V. M., 79
Breyer, Stephen G., 647
Briand-Kellogg Peace Pact, 89, 448
Briggs, Charles A., 355, 364, 368-69, 372, 437
Bright, Bill, 709
Britain, 133, 161, 254-55, 257, 272
Brooklyn, N.Y., 62, 125, 197, 278, 327, 585, 624,
711-12
Brothers Karamazov, The. *See* Dostoyevsky
Brougham, Henry (Lord), 44
Brown, Arthur J., 64, 66-67
Brown, David, 700
Brown, Robert McAfee, 300, 465, 572, 655,
657-60

Browning, Edmond L., 633
Brownson, Henry F., 253
Brown University, 164
Brown v. *Board of Education,* 713
Brushaber, George, 473n., 474-75
Bryan, Mary Baird (Mrs. W. J.), 351
Bryan, William Jennings, 305, 343, 346-48, 350-52
Buchanan, Pat, 688
Buchman, Frank, 90, 138, 140-41, 189
Buck, Pearl S., 190
Buddha, 73-76, 231, 326, 346, 460
Buddhism, 58-60, 73-76, 86, 227, 315, 316, 325, 701-2, 705-6, 740; impact in U.S., 1, 3, 576, 584-90; photographs, 75, 215, 586, 588; and social activism, 584-85, 587; voting patterns, 689; individual adherents, 59, 73, 74-76, 584n., 585, 587, 589-90, 701, 705-6; mentioned, 4, 72
Buffalo, N.Y., 272
Burke, W. M., 185-86, 188
Burma, 144
Bush, George H. W., 474, 476, 477, 640
Bush, George W., 478, 480, 481, 482, 687, 688-89, 700-701, 702, 704, 712
Bush, Laura, 700, 702
Business Men's Revival (1857), 67
Butler, Joseph, 420

Caesar, G. Julius, 507
California, 85, 455, 554, 591, 596, 617; Russian missionaries in, 53, 56, 57; mentioned, 136, 185, 312, 482, 694. *See also* Los Angeles; San Francisco
Calvin, John, 338-40, 393
Camp meetings, 198
Campbell, Alexander, 380
Campus Crusade for Christ, 709
Canada, 162, 220, 263, 265, 455, 483, 693, 719, 729
Cannibalism, 147
Capetown (South Africa), 379
Capital and labor. *See* Labor relations
Capitalism, criticism of, 268-71, 485
Capital punishment, 580
Capone, Al, 99
Carlyle, Thomas, 414
Carnegie, Andrew, 133-34
Carnegie Endowment for International Peace, 133
Carroll, H. K., 5, 78
Carter, Jimmy, 580, 581, 690-93
Catherine II, of Russia, 7

Catholic Biblical Association, 373
Catholic Church Extension Society, 149
Catholic Foreign Missionary Society of America, 152-54
Catholic Traditionalist Movement, 541
Catholic University of America, 180, 306, 381, 391, 655-57
Catholic Women's League, 42, 43
Catholic Worker Movement, 272-74, 300
Catholicism. *See* Roman Catholicism
Cawthen, B. J., 533
Caylor, H. E., 379
Censorship, 644-45
Censuses, religious, 5, 78, 157-58, 183. *See also* Statistical decline
Central Conference of American Rabbis, 112-14, 408-11
Central Intelligence Agency, 630, 707
Chak, Fung, 10-12
Chanel, Roy O., 101
Channing, William Ellery, 83
Chapman, John 427
Charismatic movement, 198, 286, 294-96, 301
Charity. *See* Love; Needy, ministry to the
Charter League (Kansas City), 98, 101-2
Chavez, César, 741
Chawla, Kalpana, 700
Chesterton, G. K., 427, 431
Cheyne, T. K., 372, 413
Chicago, Ill.: Christian social work in, 171, 272, 693; Hispanics in, 619; mentioned, 4, 43, 71, 77, 87, 90, 99, 149, 197, 217, 234
Children, abuse of, 120, 127, 596, 600, 728-33; child labor, 118, 120, 410
Chile, 153
China: immigration from, 10-13, 58; missions in, 11, 70, 144, 157, 165, 190; People's Republic of, 470, 473; mentioned, 463, 514, 595
China Bible School 145
Christian Century, 194-95, 446, 509n., 559n., 618-20, 683, 711-14, 715-16
Christian Coalition, 580
Christian living, 434, 630. *See also* Discipleship, cost of; Legalism; Perfectionism
Christian Reformed Church, 8, 716
Christian Science, 196, 234-37, 239, 249, 300
Christian socialism, 89, 117, 121-22
Christianity Today, 432, 442, 473n., 474-75, 701, 704
Chrysostom, St. John, 81
Church: doctrine concerning, 209, 312-13, 405, 434, 531, 562; failings of, 421-22, 495,

512, 516-22 passim, 548, 551-52; relation to the world, 117, 119, 389-90, 510, 517, 519, 522, 615. *See also* Culture, religion and; Protestantism, divisions in

Church and state: relationships of, 432, 472, 499-500, 504-6, 600-601, 730, 742-43; separation of, 13, 16, 22, 23, 24, 25, 26-27, 82, 86, 176, 261, 346, 501-4, 579-80, 638-48, 743. *See also* "Blue Laws"; Politics; Tax exemption; Vatican, diplomatic relations with

Church attendance, 8, 9, 12, 20, 55, 58, 78, 168, 171, 175, 220, 630, 688-90, 708, 712, 715, 729, 737; by U.S. presidents, 503, 696-700 passim. *See also* Welcoming

Churches Uniting in Christ, 442, 514-16, 572

Church finance, 157, 225, 280, 729

Churchill, Winston, 730

Church of England, 82, 315, 321, 377, 380, 559

Church of God in Christ, 294

Church of Jesus Christ of Latter-Day Saints, 78, 85, 346; missions, 158-62; movement toward mainstream, 583, 734-35; voting patterns, 686, 687, 689; women in, 628-31

Church Peace Union, 89, 132-34, 137

Cicero, M. Tullius, 508

Cincinnati, Ohio, 24-27, 87, 100, 358

Cintron, José, 618

Circle Sanctuary, 603-7

Cities. *See* City government; Social reform; Urbanization

City government, 93-96; corruption in, 98-102, 120, 264. *See also* Urban reform

City of Boerne vs. *Flores*, 653-55

Civil disobedience, 163

Civil religion, 26, 27, 33-34, 393, 441, 443, 461, 476-77, 566, 581, 639-41, 682-85, 702-4, 743, 744. *See also* Nationalism, as a quasi-religion

Civil Rights movement, 1, 439, 441, 490-98, 540, 571, 595, 623, 713; the Churches and, 490, 494-98, 553-55

Civil War: 63; aftermath of, 1, 2, 79, 84; mentioned, 172, 174, 198, 252, 439

Clark, Duncan, 379

Clark, Laurel, 700

Clarke, E. H., 35-36

Cleveland, Grover, 507

Cleveland, Ohio, 40, 87

Clifford, W. K., 309-10, 311

Clinton, Bill, 582, 651, 671, 672, 685, 686, 687, 696-700

Clinton, Hillary Rodham, 696, 698-99

Cloud of Unknowing, The, 215

Clouse, Robert G., 723n., 724-25

Coalition for the Free Exercise of Religion, 651

Coalition for United Methodist Accountability. *See* Confessing Movement

Coffin, Henry S., 225-26

Cold War, 440-41, 462-63, 470-73, 474, 484, 499, 570, 581, 683

Coleman, William H., 278-80

Colgate Rochester Divinity School, 566. *See also* Rochester Seminary

College of New Jersey. *See* Princeton University

Colonialism. *See* Imperialism

Columbia space shuttle, 700

Columbia University, 317, 729

Columbus, Ohio, 407, 560; reform in, 94-96

"Columbus Platform," 407, 408-11

Commission on Social Justice (1928), 112-14

Committee on Bible Translation, 384-86

Communion. *See* Eucharist

Communism: 269, 274, 275, 433, 462-63, 683; the churches and, 431, 439, 441, 470, 484-89, 570, 571

Community, sense of, 17, 505, 617, 714. *See also* Ethnic identity

Concerned Women for America, 634, 635

Concordia Seminary (St. Louis), 523-24, 525-28

Concordia Theological Seminary (Fort Wayne), 528

Cone, James, 608-10, 741

Confessing Movement (United Methodist), 672n., 673, 676-78

Confucianism, 4, 12, 58, 325

Confucius, 231, 326, 346

Congregationalism: 78, 82, 136, 442; preaching and, 195, 221; social gospel and, 94, 102-4; women in, 35-37; individual adherents, 4, 21, 35, 62, 102, 165, 221, 278. *See also* United Church of Christ

Congress, U.S., 270-71, 482, 578, 651-62, 653-55, 666, 671, 672, 686, 702, 703

Connecticut, 416, 743. *See also* New Haven

Conscience, 320n., 468, 470, 669. *See also* Conscientious objection; Dissent; Religious liberty

Conscientious objection, 25, 135, 136, 162

Conservatives, religious, 391, 619, 634-37, 673, 676-78, 686-87, 688, 689, 742, 745. *See also* Fundamentalists; Judaism: Conservative *and* Orthodox; National Association of Evangelicals; Neo-Fundamentalism

Constantine (Emperor), 119

Constitution, U.S., 23, 393, 507, 641, 652, 653, 662, 665, 666, 684, 743; Article VI, 261, 266, 268, 503; guarantees in, 2, 491, 663; oath to defend, 264, 265, 680; threatened, 13, 14, 260, 270-71; mentioned, 27, 32, 116, 255, 504

Constitution, U.S., First Amendment: establishment clause, 24, 25, 26, 64-65, 346, 347, 579-80, 639-40, 642, 644-48, 652, 680 (*see also* Church and state: separation of); freedom of religion, 26, 34, 261, 345, 482, 499-500, 501, 580, 601, 620-23, 638-41, 642, 643, 648, 649-52, 653-54; freedom of speech, 345, 482, 639, 642-45, 647, 681

Constitution, U.S., Fourth Amendment, 507

Constitution, U.S., Fourteenth Amendment, 579, 639, 642, 643, 653, 654, 662

Constitution, U.S., Eighteenth Amendment, 91, 99, 186, 263, 264-65

Constitution, U.S. *See also* Equal Rights Amendment

Consultation on Church Union, 442, 514, 572. *See also* Churches Uniting in Christ

Contemplative life, 214-17

Contraception, 500, 502, 580, 632, 637, 655-60, 669, 680, 681

Conversion, 248, 283, 560, 612, 697. *See also* Roman Catholicism: conversion to

Conway, Katherine E., 40

Conwell, Russell H., 196, 242-43, 300

Cooper, John H., 161

Cornell University, 653

Coué, Émile, 249

Coughlin, Charles E., 268n., 269, 270-71, 300

Council on American-Islamic Relations, 590n., 591, 595

Councils, Ecumenical, 81, 538. *See also* Vatican I; Vatican II

Cousins, Norman, 448, 449

Cowper, William, 46

Cox, John, 476

Creation, doctrine of, 315, 318, 334-35, 338-43

Creation Science Research Center, 543

Creationism, 436

Creeds: Apostles', 357; Augsburg Confession, 550; Nicene, 550; other, 404-6, 510-12, 517, 530-32, 715, 734-35. *See also* Dogma

Crime, 88, 99, 265-66, 442, 563; in relation to First Amendment rights, 649-50; hate crimes, 708; reduction in, following revival, 280

Cuba, 4, 63, 66, 613, 615

Cultural Awareness Network, 601

Culture, religion and, 392, 433, 439, 511, 520-21, 557-58. *See also* Church, relation to the world; Dogma, development of

Cuomo, Mario, 679-82

Curran, Charles E., 655

Cyprian, St., 68, 155

Cyprus, 553

Cyril, St. (Constantine), 557

Czechoslovakia, 472

Dabney, Robert L., 35, 37-39

Da Gama, Vasco, 155

Dalai Lama, 215

Dallas, Tex., 222, 732

Daly, Mary, 742

Damm, John, 525-26

Dante, 83, 329

Darrow, Clarence S., 343, 344-46

Darwin, Charles, 310, 337, 435

Darwinism, 229. *See also* Evolution

Day, Dorothy, 272-74, 300

Dayton, Tenn., 304, 343ff.

Death of God theology, 444, 566-69, 573

Declaration of Conscience, 465, 467-68

Declaration of Independence, 23, 493, 684

Declaration of Principles (1885), 29

Declaration on Non-Christian Religions (Vatican II), 548

Declaration on Religious Liberty (Vatican II), 543-46

Decree on Ecumenism (Vatican II), 547-49

Deism, 338, 420

Deloria, Vine, 742

Democracy, 95, 96, 467, 482, 510, 684, 706; failure of, 480; in church government, 531

Democratic Party, 1, 264, 268, 270, 395, 441, 501, 581, 679, 685, 686-90

Demonstrations, 471-72, 476, 483, 490, 492, 660, 663-64, 666, 668, 719. *See also* Nonviolent protest

Demosthenes, 329

Denison, Jim, 528n., 529, 533-35

Denmark, 159

Denominationalism, 745; decline of, 716

DePauw University, 223

Depression. *See* Great Depression

Deshon, George, 206n., 207-9

De Smet, Pierre Jean, S.J., 3, 47-50

Detroit, Mich., 275, 494

Devotional exercises, 194, 206-11. *See also* Meditation

Dewart, Leslie, 566

Dewey, George (Admiral), 63, 65

Dewey, John, 317-19, 435, 436

Dharma, 76, 585

Dharmapala, H., 73-76

Diaspora, Jewish, 452-56, 458, 459, 460, 462

Dilday, Russell, 534

Diner, Hasia, 721

Discipleship, cost of, 102-4, 148, 518, 562

Disciples of Christ, 78, 134, 136, 252, 442, 459, 460-63, 596, 694

Dispensationalism, 288-91, 301, 723

Dissent, 174, 467, 480; status of, in Roman Catholicism, 655n., 657, 658, 667, 668-69. *See also* Civil disobedience; Nonviolent protest

Diversity, 78-83, 86, 107-8, 197, 613-15, 690, 711-12; ethnic mingling, 4, 413-14. *See also* Ecumenical activity; Immigration; Pluralism; Protestantism, divisions in; *and specific ethnic and religious labels*

Divorce: increase in, 563, 676-77; legislation on, 502, 680

Dixon, Thomas, 4

Dobson, James, 709

Dogma: authority of, 532-33, 538-39, 676, 680; development of, 30-31, 305, 357-58, 360, 361, 363-64, 367-69, 397-99, 409, 538, 543, 544, 659; necessity of, 309, 313-14, 357-58; rejection of, 83, 214, 230, 309, 312, 318, 335, 357, 402-3, 404-5, 566, 568. *See also* Creeds

Dole, Robert, 685, 686, 687

Dostoyevsky, Fyodor, 274

Douglas, Lloyd C. *See Robe, The*

Draper, John W., 322-24, 330

Dream, American, 493

Dresden (Germany), 450

Dreyfus, Alfred, 452

Driver, S. R., 372, 373-74

Drugs: among African Americans, 714; in China trade, 144-45

Druids, 147

Due process, 629, 662, 663

Duhm, Bernard, 413, 415

Duns Scotus, John, 216

Dutch immigrants, 6, 7-8, 9, 254-55, 257

Dwyer, Kathy, 730

Eastern Orthodoxy, 58, 81, 256, 443-44, 552-58, 572-73; ecumenical interests, 4, 444, 509, 553-55; internal division, 555-56; social activism, 431, 490; Vatican overtures to, 536, 537, 547; voting patterns, 686, 689. *See also* Russian Orthodoxy.

Ecumenical activity, 8, 42, 80-83, 91-92, 101, 144, 172, 174-76, 190, 391, 439, 442, 468, 516-23, 547-52, 651, 657, 659, 711, 743. *See also* Ecumenical movement

Ecumenical movement, 178-80, 442, 509-16, 539, 571-72. *See also* Federal Council of Churches; Inter-faith activity; National Council of Churches; World Council of Churches

Eddy, Mary Baker, 234-37, 300

Eden Seminary, 526

Edinburgh, 549

Education: importance of religion in, 15-17, 28; Judaism and, 24-29, 411, 417, 454, 624, 721-23; missions and, 144, 166; Roman Catholicism and, 13-17, 22, 25, 42, 66, 67, 180, 306, 332, 391, 401, 438, 548. *See also* African Americans: education of; Church and state: separation of; Prayer: in schools; Women: education for

Education: public schools, 13; Christianization of, sought by KKK, 260; critiques of, 13-15; racial discrimination in, 441, 617, 714, 737-38 (*see also Brown v. Board of Education*; Segregation); religion and, 13-15, 16, 24-29, 579-80, 638-48 (*see also* Scopes trial); temperance instruction in, 40

Education: private schools, church-related, 25, 502, 579. *See also* Lutheran Church–Missouri Synod: schools of

Edwards, Jonathan, 419, 420, 436

Egypt, 151, 165, 690

Eichenberg, Fritz, 273

Eisenhower, Dwight D., 479, 559, 683

Elections. *See under* Politics

Elizondo, Virgilio, 583, 736-40

Elliott, Charlotte, 211

Ellis Island (N.Y.), 21

Ellwood, Robert S., 227, 299

Ely, Richard T., 89, 119-20, 188

Emerson, Ralph Waldo, 346

Emmanuel Movement, 245-47

Emmons, Grover C., 209

Encyclicals. *See under* Popes

England. *See* Britain

English language: changes in, 209, 378, 383-85 (*see also* Johnson, Samuel); spread of, 71, 151

Enlightenment, the, 303

Episcopalians, 78, 136, 195, 442, 475, 578, 621-

23, 629, 632, 633, 712; National Cathedral, 475-76, 701; individuals, 104, 119, 245, 364, 442, 514, 633. *See also* Church of England

Equal Rights Amendment, 628

Erickson, John H., 557-58, 573

Ervin, Sam J., Jr., 506-8

Eschatology. *See* Kingdom of God; Last things

Ethnic identity, 84, 578, 741-42; assimilation without loss of, 493, 553-55, 556, 557-58, 613-16 (*see also* Mestizaje); problems concerning, 17-20, 443-44, 460-62, 481, 573, 614, 720-23 (*see also* African Americans: identity issues among); sympathetic response of churches to, 594, 621-23; threatened, 64-65, 712-14. *See also* Racism

Ethnic identity, preservation of: for African Americans, 158, 711-12; for Chinese immigrants, 10, 12-13; for Eastern Orthodox, 552-53; for Hispanics, 614, 617; for Jews, 33, 34, 455, 624-26, 627, 722; for Muslims, 708; for Native Americans, 578, 620-21, 649, 717-19, 742; for Scandinavians, 9, 17

Eucharist, 274, 282, 515, 540, 550, 552

Europe, 106, 462, 595 (*see also individual countries*); missions to, 159, 160-62

Eusebius, 81

Evangelical and Reformed Church, 275, 419. *See also* United Church of Christ.

Evangelical Association, 78

Evangelical Awakening, 165-66

Evangelical Free Church, 716

Evangelical Lutheran Church in America, 443, 523

Evangelical Lutherans in Mission, 523

Evangelical theology. *See* Neo-Fundamentalism.

Evangelical United Brethren. *See* Evangelical Association; United Brethren.

Evangelism, 168-69, 222-23, 226, 279, 281, 510, 560, 562, 575, 674; defined, 143, 518, 559-60; prerequisite to social change, 140-41, 166-67, 169, 172, 223, 226, 249, 562, 616. *See also* Missionary effort; Revivalism

Evans, Hiram Wesley, 257-59, 262

Evans, Warren Felt, 230-32, 234, 237

Evanston, Ill., 442, 509

Everson v. *Board of Education*, 579, 639

Evolution, controversy concerning, 283, 304-5, 327-29, 334-35, 336-52, 399, 415-16, 435, 436. *See also* Darwin; Darwinism

Excommunication, 117, 161, 237, 370, 456, 628-31

Experience: as ground for belief, 398; religious, 212-17, 294-98, 308, 313, 321, 436, 518, 546, 711, 715, 737. *See also* Conversion

Ezrahi, Yaron, 461

Faber, Frederick W., 352

Fackenheim, Emil L., 449-52, 458

Fackenheim, Rose, 450

Fagley, Richard N., 446-49

Faith, 308-11, 320, 335-36, 406, 418, 430, 551. *See also* Justification, doctrine of

Falwell, Jerry, 681, 701, 704, 707

Family, 37, 121-22, 220, 617, 661, 670; importance to society, 88, 186; threatened, 38-39, 97-98, 120, 179-180, 276, 628. *See also* Home; Marriage; Women: in the work force

Faunce, W. H. P., 164-65

Federal Bureau of Investigation, 485, 571, 600, 707, 708

Federal Council of Churches, 91, 137, 178-80, 181, 190, 250, 442, 446, 487, 560, 570. *See also* National Council of Churches

Feminist movement, 39, 43, 44-45, 623, 626-27, 631, 634-37, 704. *See also* Women

Fetal tissue research, 580

Fichte, Johann Gottlieb, 366

Fiction, 4, 84, 88, 102-4, 183, 193-4, 199-206, 298, 723-24, 725-27

Fillmore, Charles, 237-39, 242, 300

Fillmore, Myrtle, 237, 242

Finland, 161

Finney, Charles G., 183, 300

First Things, 682-87

Fish, Hamilton, 6

Fisk, William S., 568-69

Fitzgerald, James, 697

Flores, Patricio F., 578, 653

Florida. *See* Miami

Flynn, Harry J., 730

Focus on the Family, 709

Fo Kuang Shan, 585

Food, religious observances concerning, 584n., 585, 587, 589, 591, 712, 721, 723

Ford, Clifford, 725

Ford, Gerald, 506, 580

Fordham University, 729

Foreign aid, 502. *See also* Humanitarian aid

Foreign policy, 92, 455, 457, 483

Forman, James, 494, 496, 571

Fort Wayne, Ind., 528

Fosdick, Harry Emerson, 126, 128, 130-31, 360-64, 438

Foursquare Gospel, International Church of the, 286-88, 301
Fox, Matthew, 621n.
Fox, Selena, 603
Fox-Genovese, Elizabeth, 636
France, 151, 161, 174, 321, 392, 427, 429, 431, 441, 452, 453, 462
Francis of Assisi, St., 212, 342
Freedom: Christian, defined, 430; of conscience, 401, 552, 669; constitutional, 594, 597; to love, 513; from oppression, 410, 466, 479, 481, 488, 493-94, 510, 553; threatened, 270, 706. *See also* Constitution, U.S.: First Amendment; Human rights; Religious liberty
Free Tabernacle (Brooklyn), 327
French Revolution, 414, 459
Freud, Sigmund, 196
Friedan, Betty, 626
Friends, Society of, 43, 45, 78, 83, 135, 136, 211, 476, 578
Froebel, Friedrich W. A., 220
Fuller, Linda, 691-92
Fuller, Millard, 691-92
Fundamentalism, 85, 306-7, 401, 437; Christian and Muslim compared, 707; criticism of, 417, 420, 423-24, 434-35, 481; mentioned, 318, 412, 432, 433. *See also* Dispensationalism; Lutheran Church–Missouri Synod; Neo-Fundamentalism; Southern Baptist Convention

Galileo, 235, 659
Gallup Poll. *See* Opinion surveys
Galpin, Mr. (interpreter), 48
Gambling, 218
Garis, R. L., 252n., 254-56
Gay rights, 635, 636. *See also* Homosexuality
Genetic engineering, 580
Geoghan, John J., 728
George, Henry, 117
George, Timothy, 528n., 529-30
Georgia, 333, 493, 494, 690, 691. *See also* Atlanta
Germany: East (DDR), 470-73; immigration from, 9, 18-20, 84, 254, 257, 392 (*see also* Prussia); and Jehovah's Witnesses, 162-64; and Jews, 453, 455 (*see also* Holocaust); missions to, 161; and theological study, 225, 364, 422, 550; and world affairs, 126-27, 133, 187, 440
Gestefeld, Ursula, 237
Gethsemani Abbey, 216

Gibbons, James (Cardinal), 17-18, 21n., 22, 23, 65, 88-89, 104-9, 152, 154, 330-32, 437
Gibbs, Nancy, 473n., 475-76
Gilson, Etienne, 426n., 427, 429-32, 438
Gingrich, Newt, 686
Ginsberg, Allen, 705
Ginsburg, Ruth Bader, 647
Gladden, Washington, 88, 94-96, 109, 188
Gladstone, William E., 220, 341-42
Glassman, Bernard, 584n., 585, 587-90
Glazer, Nathan, 457-58
Glossolalia, 198, 294-96
God: concepts of, 55, 236-37, 315-16; and evil, 573, 702-3; humanization of, 231; as Judge, 421, 512, 531, 704; love of, 237, 409, 564, 702; as "Mother," 237; to be obeyed rather than men, 163, 468; sovereignty of, 421, 475, 702. *See also* Death of God theology; Justice: of God
"God Bless America," 482, 701, 703
Goddess worship, 605-7, 741
Goethe, J. W. von, 403
Goodspeed, Edgar J., 377, 378-80
Gorbachev, Mikhail, 471, 472
Gore, Albert, 687, 688, 689-90
Gotti, Girolamo (Cardinal), 153
Government, purpose of, 508, 522
Graham, Billy, 300, 442, 444, 463-64, 516, 559-63, 564, 573, 697-98, 701, 702-4, 715
Grant, Bruce, 379
Grant, Heber J., 161
Gray, G. Charles, 101
Gray, Gordon Joseph (Cardinal), 549
Great Depression, 197, 268, 300, 581
"Great Society," The, 442, 504-6
Greatest Story Ever Told, The, 199-201
Greece, 161, 553; immigration from, 255, 552
Greek Orthodox Archdiocese of North and South America, 552-55
Greeley, Andrew M., 618
Green, John C., 685-90, 744
Greenberg, Blu, 623n., 624-27
Greene, Graham, 431
Greenfield, Meg, 599
Greer, Batsheva, 720-21
Greer, Daniel, 721
Greyston Family Inn (New York), 585, 589-90
Grinnell College, 121
Gulf War, 473-77, 576
Gutenberg Bible, 379
Guth, James L., 685-90, 744
Guyana, 596-97

Habitat for Humanity, 690, 691-93

Hack, Elisha, 722

Halakah, 29

Halkin, Hillel, 458-63

Halliday, Denis, 483

Hamilton, William, 566-68, 573

Hammurabi, Code of, 414

Hare Krishna, 576

Harper, William Rainey, 355

Harrell, Costen J., 211

Harris, Barbara C., 578, 633

Harvard University, 165, 193, 312, 314, 319, 344, 353, 356, 364, 432, 437, 441, 506, 604

Hasidism, 299, 438

Hastings, James, 372

Haughery, Margaret Gaffney, 42

Haverford College, 211

Hawaii, 3, 58-60, 73, 87, 620, 621

Hay, John, 61

Hayes, Rutherford B., 1

Haymarket Riot, 88

Hays, Brooks, 537

Healing, 196, 230, 231-37, 240-42, 245-51, 286, 297-98, 300, 301, 565, 576, 580. *See also* Medical missions

Heaven, 9, 122, 274, 329, 408, 441, 591, 704

Heaven's Gate, 577, 740. *See also* Y2K problem

Hebrew Union College, 306, 358

Hecker, Isaac, 391-94, 437

Hell, 83, 408

Hemphill (Rev. Mr.), 24, 27-28

Henry, Carl F. H., 432-35, 438

Herberg, Will, 443, 683, 684

Heresy, 83, 305, 372

Heresy trials, 364, 368-69

Herron, George D., 89, 121-22

Hertzberg, Arthur, 452n., 454-56, 457, 458

Herzl, Theodor, 440, 452-54, 461

Heschel, Abraham J., 299, 465, 468-70

Higher criticism. *See* Bible, scholarly study of

Hillis, N. D., 125, 128

Hiltner, Seward, 196, 250-51

Hinduism, 4, 71-73, 147-48, 227, 426, 740; shortcomings of, 69-70, 707; voting patterns, 689; individual adherents, 72-73; mentioned, 76, 170, 325

Hiroshima, 440, 446-49, 450, 570

Hispanic Ministry, National Pastoral Plan for, 616-17

Hispanics, 274, 578, 583, 613-20; identity issues among, 613-16, 617, 736-40; religion and, 617, 737; religious affiliations of: Roman Catholic, 81, 578, 583, 613-17, 618, 653, 741; other, 578, 617-20, 741-42; voting patterns, 688, 689; women, 742

History, 221-22, 284-85, 288-91, 324-26, 349, 416, 431-32, 448, 599, 683. *See also* Dispensationalism; Memory

Hitler, Adolf, 162, 422, 446, 459

Hocking, William E., 165-67

Holiness Movement, 198, 291-93, 294, 301; churches identified with, 516, 578

Holland, 8, 78, 161. *See also* Amsterdam; Dutch immigrants

Holmes, Ernest S., 239-42

Holmes, John Haynes, 128-29

Holmes, Oliver Wendell (Chief Justice), 662

Holocaust, 440, 449-52, 568, 570, 573

Holy Cross, Order of the, 341

Holy Roman and Universal Inquisition. *See* Inquisition

Holy Spirit: power of, 245, 279, 280, 517, 522, 633, 674, 709; role in inspiring Scripture, 207-8, 363-64, 365-66, 369; role in sanctification, 292; as source of spiritual gifts, 294, 551 (*see also* Glossolalia)

Home, 179-80, 184, 299; as center of Jewish religious life, 26, 31, 218, 411, 624-26; lack of, in slums, 103, 169; ministries to strengthen, 42; role in spiritual formation, 15-16, 98, 140, 218-19, 226, 532; Sunday a day for, 220. *See also* Family

Homeless, the: in cities, 169, 693 (*see also* Housing, substandard); outreach to, 41, 169, 585, 587, 589-90. *See also* Habitat for Humanity

Homer, 329

Homosexuality, 531, 580, 637, 643, 701, 704, 714, 743; churches and, 672-78

Honecker, Erich, 471

Hoover, Herbert C., 263, 266, 267

Hoover, J. Edgar, 485

Hope, 493, 511, 568, 590, 703-4; Messianic, 115-16

Hopkins, Emma C., 237

Hosack, Robert N., 723n., 724-25

House Committee on Un-American Activities, 484, 487-89

Housing, substandard, 88, 97-98, 103, 120, 691. *See also* Habitat for Humanity; Homeless

Houston, Tex., 501, 700

Hsi Lai Temple, 584-85, 587

Hsing Yun, 585

Huestis, Charles H., 219n., 220
Hughes, John, 2, 13-15
Huguenots, 257, 333
Human beings: brotherhood of, 42, 78, 88, 105, 113, 137, 227-28, 410, 449, 469, 487, 488, 493, 505, 539, 613; dignity of, 110, 112, 113, 175, 270, 465-66, 505, 518, 543, 544, 546, 597, 616, 617, 657, 668, 669, 673, 677, 680, 712; divine image in, 409, 435; divinity of, 195, 208, 231-33, 408; equality of, 113; faith in self-sufficiency of, 446-47; moral responsibility of, 312-14, 567; need for God, 405, 512; unity of, as vision for future, 30, 539, 613
Human Individual Metamorphosis, 577
Humanism, 427, 433, 444, 565, 568-69; Christian, 428, 567
Humanist Manifesto, 568-69
Humanitarian aid, 133-34, 479-80, 483
Human rights, 62, 113-14, 465, 468, 487, 491, 510, 544, 597-98, 616, 620, 646, 692. *See also* Religious liberty; Universal Declaration of Human Rights
Humboldt University, 471
Hume, David, 316, 334, 420
Humphrey, Hubert, 554n.
Hungary, 161, 255, 693
Hunt, Angela, 724
Hunter, George W., 347
Huntington, De Witt Clinton, 291-93
Huntington, Frederic Dan, 88, 104-6
Husband, Rick, 700
Hussein, Saddam, 473-482 passim, 594
Huxley, Thomas, 309, 327-28, 330, 336
Hyatt, Michael, 724-25
Hybels, Bill, 696-98, 715-16
Hymns, 9, 12, 29, 51, 82, 180, 186, 279, 307, 352, 473, 526, 536, 540, 742
Hypnosis, 195, 249

Iakovos (Archbishop), 552-55
Iceland, 161
Idaho, 10-12, 48
Idealism, philosophical, 303, 312-14, 402, 433, 438
Illinois, 93, 580, 696. *See also* Chicago; Evanston; Peoria
Immigration, 504; Act of 1965, 740; attitudes toward, 196-97, 252, 154-63, 300; Asian, 1, 2, 3, 10-13, 58-59, 84, 740; Caribbean, 712; European, 2-3, 32-35, 740; Hispanic, 578, 616-17, 620, 711. *See also* Ethnic identity *and under specific nationalities*

Immigration Restriction League, 197, 252
Immortality, 329, 332, 405, 408
Imperialism, 4, 22, 61-67, 144-45, 155, 156, 276, 439, 481, 485, 495, 577
In His Steps, 88, 102-4
Inclusive language, 378, 385-86, 734, 735
Independent, The, 80, 245
Index of Prohibited Books, 341, 371
India, 165, 594, 706; contribution of, to religion, 73, 74, 147-48, 227; immigration from, 740; missions in, 69, 71, 144, 157, 161
Indian Religious Freedom Act, 578, 620-21, 623, 649
Indiana, 118. *See also* Fort Wayne
Indiana State University, 470
Indiana University, 478
Individualism, 269, 501
Indonesia, 165, 590, 595
Industrial revolution, 88, 94
Innocent of Alaska, St., 557
Inquisition, 370-71, 401, 539. *See also* Index of Prohibited Books
Inter-faith activities, 176-77, 178, 181, 215, 391, 621-23, 682. *See also* World Parliament of Religions
International Congress on World Evangelization, 442, 572. *See also* Lausanne Covenant
International New Thought Alliance, 195
International Society of Krishna Consciousness, 576
Iowa, 197, 252
Iraq, 473-74, 477, 590; invasion of (2003), 478-83
Ireland, John (Archbishop), 64-66, 253, 254, 391-94, 395-97
Ireland, relations of, with Roman Catholic church, 729-30
Ireney (Metropolitan), 555-56
Irish: contributions of, to Christianity, 18; immigration, 9, 17-20, 97, 176, 254-55, 257, 259, 392, 721
Irving, Washington, 76-77
Irwin, William A., 378, 380-82
Isaacs, Abram S., 24, 28-29
Isidore the Farmer, St., 81
Islam, 4-5, 155-56, 316, 325, 408, 458, 584, 595, 639; beliefs, 76-78, 315, 593, 707, 708; practice of, in U.S., 576; variety within, 576, 593; women in, 708. *See also* Black Muslims; Koran; Mohammed; Muslims
Islamic Medical Association of North America, 478, 702

Israel, State of, 410, 440, 454, 455, 456, 457-63, 570, 593-94, 690, 700, 707. *See also* Zionism

Italy: 161, 440; immigration from, 20, 255

Jackson, John S., III, 688
Jackson, Robert H., 639, 650
Jackson, Sheldon, 3, 50-51
Jainism, 72, 576
Jamaica, 512
James, Henry, Sr., 195
James, William, 193, 299, 308-11, 312, 314, 432, 436
Japan, 3, 58-60, 86, 144, 151, 154, 165, 258, 440, 557, 584. *See also* Hiroshima
Japanese Americans, 439
Jefferson, Thomas, 87, 267, 268, 638, 648, 743
Jeffrey, Grant, 724
Jehovah's Witnesses, 162-64, 198, 284-85, 301, 378, 380, 617, 650, 686
Jenkins, Jerry B., 723, 725-27
Jerome, St., 375
Jesuits, 47-50, 253, 254, 431, 527, 547
Jesuit School of Theology (Berkeley), 632
Jesus, 193, 567; birth of, 199-20; confessed as Lord, 467, 488, 510, 511, 518, 533, 676, 731; human and divine, 231, 431, 434, 512, 734-35; as a Jew, 261, 263; as king, 116, 156, 143, 513, 735 (*see also* Kingdom of God); lives of, 193, 199-203, 298; as Logos, 426; marginalized as Galilean, 738-39; as moral example, 83, 102-4, 135, 136, 405, 434, 488, 615-16, 713, 714, 734; as prophet, 114-16; self-identification of, with the suffering, 609-10, 615-16; teachings of, 132, 136, 197, 203, 228, 267, 269-70, 275, 326, 348, 350, 361, 488, 734
Jewish Publication Society, 378, 383-84, 387
Jewish Theological Seminary of America, 412
Jewish Welfare Board, 176-77
Joan of Arc, St., 171
Jodo-Shinshu, 58-60, 584
John of the Cross, St., 215, 216
Johns Hopkins University, 119, 401
Johnson, David E., 633
Johnson, Lyndon B., 440, 441, 504
Johnson, Samuel, 380
Johnson, Sonia, 628-31
Johnston, H. H., 145-46
Jones, E. Stanley, 147-48, 190
Jones, James Warren, 577, 596-600
Jones, Rufus, 194, 211-14, 299
Jones, Sam, 197, 281-82, 300

Jonestown, 577, 596-600, 740-41
Judaism: 2, 4, 24-34, 72, 84, 177, 181-83, 189, 210, 256, 261, 305, 306-7, 325, 378, 383-84, 407-13, 416, 437, 438, 457, 576, 639, 682, 722-23, 745; conversion to, 460; diversity in, 2, 177, 306, 438, 460-61, 673, 721, 745; growth of, in U.S., 2, 78; "Jews for Jesus," 460, 570; mysticism in, 299; relation to state, 743; social concerns, 90, 112-14, 176-77, 189, 410-11, 441, 450, 465, 468-70, 476, 490, 495, 497-98; voting patterns, 688, 689; women in, 4, 85, 217-19, 578, 623-27, 634-37, 742; individuals, 29, 98, 128, 176, 202, 217, 257, 358, 412, 449, 452, 454, 457, 458, 585, 623-37, 683, 687, 689, 699. *See also* Anti-Semitism; Bible, parts of: Torah; B'nai B'rith; Education: Judaism and; Halakah; Holocaust; Israel; Zionism; Zohar
Judaism, divisions of: cooperation among, 29, 177, 383 (*see also* Synagogue Council of America); Conservative, 29, 31-32, 84. 306-7, 412-18, 438, 460, 578, 721-22; Orthodox, 29, 32-34, 84, 217, 307, 407, 412, 414, 460, 582, 624-27, 634-37, 720-23, 742, 745; Reform, 29-31, 84, 112, 306, 358, 406-11, 438, 578, 721-22
Jung, Carl G., 196
Justice, 468; coupled with love, 30, 87, 88, 105, 111, 405, 466, 630; in distribution of wealth, 112, 113, 117, 120, 122; as eschatological hope, 30, 105, 405, 408, 410, 512; essential to peace, 466; of God, 407, 477, 518; as religious imperative, 12, 105, 112, 126, 277, 408, 475, 510, 518-19, 553, 593; social justice, 88, 111-12, 179, 270, 408, 410-11, 486, 488, 491, 500-501, 504, 522. *See also* Commission on Social Justice; Labor relations; National Union for Social Justice
Justification, doctrine of, 549-52
Justinian, 315

Kansas, 455. *See also* Topeka
Kansas City, Mo.: 237, 591; reform in, 98-102
Kastrometinoff, George, 51
Katzenbach. See South Carolina v. Katzenbach
Kaufman, Debra, 636
Kayserling, Meyer, 414
Keeler, William H. (Cardinal), 730
Kellogg. *See* Briand-Kellogg
Kellstedt, Lyman A., 685-90, 744
Kennedy, Anthony M., 640-41, 661, 664-65

Kennedy, John F., 441-42, 499, 501-4, 571

Kentucky, 97, 216n., 484, 693. *See also* Louisville

Khan, Muqtedar, 590n., 591, 593-94

Kierkegaard, Søren, 425, 449

King, Martin Luther, Jr., 441, 476, 490-94, 554n., 571, 611

Kingdom of God: achieved through social change, 114, 119, 410, 411, 419, 523; extended through missions, 142-43, 162, 163-64, 517; inclusiveness of, 83; a present condition, 513

Kingsley, Charles, 44

Klooster, Lucy, 6, 7-8

Knights of Columbus, 176, 177, 190

Knights of Labor, 89, 107-9, 189

"Know Nothing" principle, 260

Koinonia Farm, 691-92

Koran, 78, 346, 482, 593, 594

Korean immigration, 740

Koresh, David, 600, 601, 602

Krenz, Egon, 472

Ksistaki-Poka, Fr. (Blackfoot priest), 622

Kuhn, Dale, 525

Ku Klux Klan, 197, 256-63, 266-67, 300, 489

Kulp, Edmund, 101

Kuwait, 473-74, 477, 481, 590

Labor relations, 88-89, 104-14, 117-18, 123-24, 140, 179, 224, 410, 741

LaHaye, Tim, 723, 725-27

Laity: ministry of, 9-10, 79-80, 175-76, 181, 527; role of, 82, 711; status of, in Roman Catholicism, 254, 539-42, 547-49, 579, 659-60, 731-34

Lamm, Norman, 722

Land reform, 117-18

Language, 19, 55-56, 58, 376, 591, 619, 737, 738; gender implications in, 605, 623-24 (*see also* Inclusive language); "God talk," 423; vernacular, in worship, 12, 20, 411, 539-40, 557, 585 (*see also* Catholic Iraditionalist Movement). *See also* English language; Rhetoric; Translation

Lao-tzu, 325

Last things, 284-91 passim, 583; Judgment, 156-57; Second Coming, 197-98, 284-85, 286, 290, 475, 522-23, 724, 725-27, 735. *See also* Antichrist; Apocalypse, speculation on; Armageddon; Kingdom of God; Millennialism; Prophecy, biblical

Latin America, 144, 152, 495, 578, 616, 618, 619. *See also* Chile, Cuba, Mexico, Puerto Rico

Latourette, Kenneth Scott, 90, 189

Lausanne Covenant, 516-23

Law, Bernard Francis (Cardinal), 728-29, 730

Lazia, John, 99

Le Conte, Joseph, 333-36, 436

Lee, Ann, 35

Lee v. Weisman, 640-41

Legalism, 432, 434, 676

Lenin, V. I., 694

Lessman, Paul, 525

Levin, Richard, 721

Lewes, G. H., 336

Lewin, Nathan, 722

Lewis, C. S., 643

Lewis, Sinclair, 183

Liberalism, theological, 318, 401-4, 419, 424, 435, 438, 486. *See also* Modernism; "Religious Humanism"

Liberation Theology, 577, 608-10, 741

Lieberman, Joseph, 687-88, 689-90, 699

Liebman, Joshua Loth, 563

Life, sacredness of, 128, 137, 669. *See also* Abortion

Life-style, simplicity in, 520

Lindsey, Hal, 723, 725

Liquor trade: abroad, 144, 155, 156, 157; in U.S., 183-84, 186. *See also* Temperance movement

Little Rock, Ark., 697-98, 699

Liturgical renewal (Roman Catholic), 539-42

Loisy, Alfred F., 370

Long, Huey, 300

Lord's Prayer, 24, 29, 42, 211, 379-80

Los Angeles, Calif., 239, 286, 476, 501, 559, 584, 585, 693, 722; photographs, 586, 589, 592

Louisiana. *See* New Orleans

Louisville, Ky., 364, 478

Lourdes, 249

Love: as attitude toward the poor, 169, 171; as central ethical principle, 73, 105, 235, 350-51, 405, 433, 466, 488, 539, 551, 705-6; as a command rejected in practice, 228-29; as divine attribute, 237, 409; as eschatological hope, 30, 277; as motivation for service, 235, 272-74; speaking the truth in, 658. *See also* Justice: coupled with love

Luce, Clare Boothe, 437

Luce, Henry, 685

Lund, Anthon H., 160

Luther, Martin, 393, 526

Lutheran Church–Missouri Synod: internal strife, 442-43, 523-28, 572; schools of, 525
Lutherans, 5, 6, 9-10, 78, 82, 138, 195, 204, 252, 442-43, 572, 682. *See also* Evangelical Lutheran Church in America; Lutheran World Federation
Lutheran World Federation, 549-52
Lyman, Francis M., 159, 160-62
Lyon, Warren H., 161

Macarius (Hieromonk), 53-55
McCain, John, 688
McCarthy, Joseph, 441, 683
McCollum v. *Board of Education*, 579-80
McComb, Samuel, 245
McConnell, Francis J., 223-25
McCool, William, 700
McCosh, James, 336-37, 338, 436
McElroy, Henry J., 100-101, 102
Macfarland, Charles S., 91, 178-80
McGlynn, Edward, 89, 117-18
Machen, J. Gresham, 401-4, 437
MacIntyre, Alasdair C., 438
McKinley, William, 63, 65
McNamara, Robert S., 440
McPherson, Aimee Semple, 198, 286-88, 301
McQuaid, Bernard J., 391, 394-96
Madison, James, 638, 645-46, 647-48
Mahabharata, 575
Malcolm X, 610-12, 741
Manifesto Against War, 137
Manning, Christel, 634-37, 742
Manning, Henry Edward (Cardinal), 253
Marginalization, 736-40. *See also* Prejudice; Racism
Maritain, Jacques, 426n., 427-29, 431, 432, 438
Markow, Mischa, 162
Marquart, Kurt E., 523n., 528, 572
Marriage, 38, 44, 180, 532, 624-26, 636, 656, 657, 658, 676-78, 709, 711; threatened, 38-39, 180. *See also* Divorce
Martineau, James, 83
Marty, Martin E., 188, 301, 436, 569
Martyrdom, 276, 555, 611
Marx, Karl, 106, 464
Marxism, 111-12, 197, 487, 488, 596, 613, 616, 694; rejection of, 111-12, 113. *See also* Communism
Mary, St. (Virgin), 199-201, 550; Assumption of, 659; devotion to, 42, 617
Maryknoll. *See* Catholic Foreign Missionary Society of America
Maryknoll Sisters, 190

Maryland, 543. *See also* Baltimore
Mason, C. H., 204-96
Masonic Order, 107, 268
Massachusetts, 234, 348, 441, 730, 731. *See also* Boston
Masvidal, Eduardo Boza, 613-16
Mather, Cotton, 247
Mather, Kirtley F., 343-44, 348-49
Mathews, Shailer, 404-6
Matter, unreality of, 232, 236, 239, 249
Matthews, J. B., 484-86
Mayerberg, Samuel S., 98-102
Media, 636, 707; responsibility of, 503-4, 594, 704
Media, films, 726, 729, 738
Media, newspapers: African American-owned, 80; help or hindrance to reform, 40, 100, 101, 221, 264; religious advertising in, 596; reporting on religion, 379-80
Media, radio, 564, 585
Media, television, 729; Buddhist, 585; evangelical, 575, 576, 580, 704
Medicaid, 681
Medical missions, 145, 166, 463
Meditation, 148, 194, 210, 220, 607, 638; Buddhist, 75, 586. *See also* Contemplative life; Devotional exercises; Transcendental Meditation
Meehan, Susan, 476
Meer de Walcheren, Petrus van der *(Le paradis blanc)*, 216
Megachurches, 714, 715-16
Memory, 490-50, 451-52
Men, ministry to, 171, 172-74, 184; in armed forces, 172, 176-77. *See also* Knights of Columbus
Mennonites, 6-7
Merton, Thomas, 214n., 215-17, 299, 539-42
Mesmer, Friedrich, 195
Mestizaje, 736-40
Methodist Episcopal Church, 135, 147, 223
Methodist Episcopal Church, South, 135-36
Methodists: 8, 12, 69-71, 78, 82-83, 91, 195, 198, 209n., 291, 621-23, 673-78; African American churches, 79, 712; ecumenism and, 82-83, 442; Prohibition and, 263-66; social responsibility and, 486, 504-6, 621; individuals, 5, 142, 147, 209, 220, 223, 230, 243, 252, 268, 281, 291, 297, 322, 484, 486, 487, 696, 699, 700
Methodius, St., 557
Metropolitan Community Church, 674
Mexican American Cultural Center, 736

Mexican War, 439

Mexico, 274, 392, 619, 693, 729

Meyendorff, John, 558

Meyer, Albert Gregory (Cardinal), 549

Miami, Fla., 693

Michigan, 6, 7-8. *See also* Detroit.

Mielke, Erich, 472

Migrant labor, 741

Militarism, 129-30, 470, 495. *See* Nuclear weapons

Millennialism, 197-98, 284-91

Millennium, turn of. *See also* Y2K problem

Miller, Gerald, 525, 526, 527

Milton, John, 21, 554-55

Milwaukee, Wis., 17

Mind, power of, 228, 230-42, 243-45, 246, 249, 291, 311

Minneapolis, Minn., 64, 730

Minnesota, 6, 9-10, 392, 396. *See also* Minneapolis; St. Paul

Minor v. *Board of Education,* 24-27

Miracles, 320, 327, 372, 394, 407, 413, 435

Miranda, Jesse, 618-19, 620

Miranda, Julian, 17n., 20

Missionary effort: Buddhist, 73, 76, 584-90; Orthodox, 52-58, 557; Protestant, 3, 4, 10-12, 64-67, 79-80, 83, 85, 90, 142-48, 155-64, 189-90, 442, 463, 516-23, 529, 532-33, 534-35, 618, 643; Roman Catholic, 18, 23, 47-50, 82, 90, 148-54, 181, 190, 253-54, 538, 615, 622

Missionary movement, 67-71, 86, 90, 142-67, 189-90; evaluation of, 90, 144-46, 164-67, 190, 520-21; with indigenous churches as goal, 144, 520-21. *See also* Medical missions

Missionary Review of the World, 67-69

Mississippi, 493, 525, 660, 663, 664

Missouri. *See* Kansas City; St. Louis

Modernism, 306-7, 319-21, 391-418, 433, 435, 437-38, 442

Mohammed, 76-77, 231, 321, 326, 481-82, 591, 593

Mohler, R. Albert, Jr., 478-79

Monasticism. *See* Contemplative life

Mondale, Walter F., 679

Monopolies, 96, 107, 109, 113, 121

Monotheism, 221, 408, 409, 467, 469

Montalvo, Gabriel, 729

Montgomery, Ala., 490

Moody, Dwight L., 51, 183, 197-98, 207, 278-80, 281, 300-301

Moore, Edward C., 356-58, 360

Moore, Rebecca, 596, 599, 600

Morality: absolutes in, 487; dependence of, on religion, 15; determined by ends, 694; empirically derived, 569; legislative imposition of, 194, 500, 681-82 (*see also* Abortion; "Blue Laws"; Prohibition); not attainable by human effort alone, 312-14, 405; principles underlying, 667; relativism in, affirmed, 569, rejected, 615, 676; sexual, 531, 670, 678, 711, 714, 720 (*see also* Contraception; Divorce; Homosexuality; Pornography; Sexual abuse)

Moral Re-Armament, 90, 138-41, 189

Moravians, 83

Morgan, G. Campbell, 198, 221-22

Morgenstern, Julian, 358, 360

Mormons. *See* Church of Jesus Christ of Latter-Day Saints

Morris, C. S., 155-57

Morse, Wayne, 502

Moses, 326, 407, 416

Mott, John R., 142-43, 144, 190

Mott, Lucretia, 43, 45, 85

Muhammad, Elijah, 610

Mullan-Gage Act (N.Y.), 263

Mulry, Thomas M., 174-76

Muncie, George W., 298

Murray, John Courtney, S.J., 432, 543-46, 572

Music, in worship, 12, 411, 540, 606-7, 614, 715

Muslims: extremists, 581, 701, 707; missionaries to, 68; prejudice against, 76, 77, 591, 595; in U.S., 1, 576, 590-95, 689, 706-8, 740; and U.S. foreign policy, 477, 481; individuals, 76-78, 478, 481-83, 590n., 591, 701n., 702, 706-8. *See also* Islam

Muslim Student Association, 478, 590n., 591, 593

Myers, Joseph, 101

Mystery, 227, 295, 324

Mysticism, 299, 319, 320; nature of, 212-14

Nagasaki, 446, 447

National Association of Evangelicals, 694

National Association of Manufacturers, 270, 485

National Baptist Convention, 155

National Black Economic Development Conference, 494

National Camp Meeting for the Promotion of Christian Holiness, 198

National Catholic War Council, 91, 124, 180

National Catholic Welfare Council [Conference], 91, 123, 180-81, 370n., 376n.

National Conference of Christians and Jews, 181

National Council of Catholic Women, 547

National Council of Churches, 442, 444, 468, 496, 509, 510-12, 514, 516

National Council of Jewish Women, 217

Nationalism, as a quasi-religion, 456, 457-58, 461, 467, 477

National Jewish Community Relations Advisory Council, 497-98

National Organization of Women, 635

National Origins Act (1924), 252

National Pastoral Hispanic Conference, 578, 613-16

National Public Radio, 711

National Religious Broadcasters, 704

National Study Conference on the Churches and World Peace, 137

National Union for Social Justice, 269, 270-71

Native American Church, 578, 649, 653

Native Americans, 85, 324, 578; cemeteries of, 604, 621; government policy regarding, 47-48, 85, 609, 620-21, 622, 623, 649-52, 742; missions to, 47-50, 85; religion of, 299, 620-23, 717-19, 742 (*see also* Native American Church); tribes: Blackfoot, 622; Coeur D'Alene, 622; Dakota, 718-19; Flathead, 622; Hunkpapas, 47-50; Lakota, 582, 717-19; Nakota, 718-19; Nez Perce, 48; Ojibwe, 85, 742; Sioux, 47-50, 693. *See also* Alaska

Nativism. *See* Immigration, attitudes toward

NATO. *See* North Atlantic Treaty Organization

Natural law, 466, 656, 684

Natural theology, 315-16, 397, 432, 433

Nazarene, The, 202-3

Nazism, 449-52

Near East, 144, 204. *See also* Israel; Palestine; Palestinians

Needy, ministry to the, 41, 42, 83, 82, 90-91, 102-4, 117, 134, 168-71, 172-73, 174-76, 190, 272-74, 300, 410, 510, 585, 587, 589-90, 591, 698; attitude of love and respect urged in, 90, 169, 175, 505, 691. *See also* Habitat for Humanity; Humanitarian aid; Medical missions

Neo-Fundamentalism, 307, 432-35, 437, 438, 478, 516, 745

Neo-Orthodoxy, 307, 419-26, 433, 438

Neopaganism, 577, 603-7, 704, 741

Neo-Thomism, 307, 426-32, 438

Netherlands. *See* Holland.

Neuhaus, Richard John, 682-85, 743

New Age, 299, 577, 717, 718

"New Christian Right," 524, 744

New Deal, 686

New England, 9, 82, 196-97

New Hampshire Baptist Confession (1833), 532

New Haven, Conn., 176

New Jersey, 295, 579

Newman, John Henry (Cardinal), 253

New Mexico, 81. *See also* Santa Fe

New Orleans, La., 42, 672

Newport, R.I., 33

New Religious Right, 580

New Scofield Reference Bible, 288

Newspapers. *See under* Media

New Thought, 195-96, 230-42, 299, 444

New York (state), 14, 263-66, 267, 347, 455, 541, 589, 679, 681. *See also* Buffalo; New York; Oswego; Rochester

New York (N.Y.): ethnic diversity in, 413, 741; government of, 263-66; Jews in, 33, 189, 210, 413-14, 625, 722; photographs of, 33, 210; port of entry, 8; and Prohibition, 263-66; responses to poverty in, 91, 118, 174-75, 272, 585, 693; site of Sept. 11 attack, 581, 591, 593, 701, 703; visited by Archbishop Ireland, 395; mentioned, 8, 13, 67, 77, 87, 89, 117, 128, 133, 138, 181, 221, 225, 243, 257, 327, 364, 368, 372, 412, 422, 497-98, 499, 608, 629. *See also* Brooklyn; Ellis Island

New York University, 322, 721

Nicholas of Japan, St., 557

Niebuhr, H. Richard, 419-22, 438, 683

Niebuhr, Reinhold, 197, 275-77, 300, 419, 422, 577, 682-83

Nixon, Richard M., 442, 506, 507, 561, 569

Nobel Peace Prize, 480

Nonviolent protest, 491. *See also* Demonstrations; Dissent

Noonan, Joseph, 659-60

North Atlantic Treaty Organization, 474

North Carolina, 559, 693

Northwestern University, 119

Norway, 6, 9-10, 159

Nouwen, Henri, 732

Novak, Michael, 465

Nuclear war, 447-49, 467, 568, 70, 669; role of religion in averting, 448-49. *See also* Hiroshima

Nuclear weapons, 448, 483, 570; restrictions on, 681, 694-96

Oberlin College and Seminary, 36, 380
Oberman, Heiko, 659
O'Connell, William H., 149, 150-51
O'Connor, John J. (Cardinal), 679
O'Connor, Sandra Day, 649-50, 661, 664-65
Office of Economic Opportunity, 504-6
Ohio, 93, 137, 263-66. *See also* Cincinnati,
Cleveland, Columbus
Oklahoma, 263, 297
Olcott, Henry S., 227
Olsen, Ted, 701n., 704
Ong, Walter J., S.J., 431-32
Opinion surveys, 137, 194-95, 444, 591, 632,
667, 688
Optimism: considered dangerous, 120
Oregon, 10-12, 56
Oregon Employment Division v. *Smith*, 649-
50, 651, 653
Origen, 81
Orsy, Ladislas, S.J., 733
Orthodox Church in America, 555, 557-58
Oswego, N.Y., 356
Oursler, Fulton, 199-201
Overpopulation, 661, 670
Ovid, 321
Oxford Group Movement. *See* Moral Re-
Armament
Oxnam, G. Bromley, 487-89

Pace, E. J. (cartoonist), 328, 362
Pacifism, 7n., 133, 138, 272, 465, 570. *See also*
Peace movements
Page, Kirby, 134-37, 189
Paine, Thomas, 46, 696
Palestine, 161. *See also* Zionism
Palestinians, 450, 461, 594
Panasink, Andreas, 619
Pantheism, 228, 312
Paradis blanc, Le. See Meer de Walcheren,
Petrus van der
Pasteur, Louis, 226
Patrick, St., 392
Paul, St., 313, 491, 560, 612, 677
Paulist Fathers, 207, 397
Peace: as hope and goal, 406, 408, 410, 411,
468, 512, 522, 681, 692; as inner state, 406,
428, 513, 542, 563-66, 573
Peace movements, 89-90, 128-41, 189, 411, 480
Peale, Norman Vincent, 196, 243-45, 300, 564
Peirce, Charles S., 308, 436
Pendergast, Thomas J., 98-102
Pennsylvania, 162, 581, 661. *See also* Philadel-
phia; Pittsburgh

Pentecostal Holiness Church, 297
Pentecostalism, 294-98, 301, 442, 516; African
Americans in, 714; Hispanics in, 578, 617;
unitarian tendencies in, 294
People for the American Way, 704
People's Temple. *See* Jonestown
Peoria, Ill., 97
Perfectionism, 198, 291-93
Perot, Ross, 685, 687
Perry, Matthew, 165
Persecution, 26, 27, 31, 83, 115, 155, 158, 159,
162-64, 260-61, 300, 452, 522, 548, 558, 645-
46. *See also* Martyrdom
Petzholdt, Alexander, 7
Peyote, 649, 653
Philadelphia, Pa., 67, 221, 242, 272, 273, 379,
407, 693
Philippines, 4, 61, 63, 64-67, 87, 151
Phillips, Randy, 709, 711
Philosophy, religion and, 303, 308-21, 334,
397-98, 426, 427-30, 433, 436
Pieper, Francis, 5
Pierard, Richard V., 470-73, 723n., 724-25, 744
Pierson, A. T., 67-69, 86
Pike, James A., 442, 514
Pittsburgh, Pa., 406, 561
"Pittsburgh Platform," 406-8
Planned Parenthood v. *Casey*, 661, 664-66
Pledge of Allegiance, 441
Plummer, Alfred, 372
Pluralism: of religions, 3, 58-59, 90, 576-77,
579, 584-607, 680, 682, 740; within a reli-
gious group, 613-17, 667. *See also* World
Parliament of Religions
Poetry, religious, 59-60, 536, 555. *See also*
Hymns
Poland, 161, 455; immigration from, 9, 202,
255, 578
Political realism. *See* Niebuhr, Reinhold.
Politics: corruption in, 95, 96, 98-102, 107,
120, 179, 185, 264, 270-71, 439, 442, 507-8
(*see also* Watergate); elections, 261, 498-
502, 581, 685-90; legislative process, 344-
46, 347; qualifications for, 508; refusal to
be involved in, 163, 394-96; as a religious
calling, 120; role of religious institutions
and individuals in, 85, 92, 94-96, 174, 185-
88, 254, 395-96, 466, 467-68, 480, 497, 505,
518, 531, 577, 580-81, 638, 670, 671-72, 681,
684, 714, 744. *See also* Public officials, religious orientation of; Urban reform
Polynesia, 165, 595
Polytheism, 324, 603

Popes: Benedict XV, 111; John XXIII, 443, 465-66, 535, 536-39, 548, 633, 655; John Paul II, 578, 618, 692, 728, 731, 732, 733-34; Leo XIII, 111-12, 123-24, 175, 253, 370, 375; Paul VI, 468, 632, 655-56; Pius IX, 111, 443; Pius X, 149-50, 154, 320, 370-72, 373, 396-401, 443; Pius XI, 657; Pius XII, 373, 374-77, 500

Popes, encyclicals and other statements issued by, 124; *Casti connubii*, 657; *Divino afflante Spiritu*, 372n., 373, 374-77; *Graves de communi*, 111; *Humanae vitae*, 580, 655-60; *Lamentibili sane exitu*, 370-72; *Longinqua oceani*, 253; *Pacem in terris*, 465-66; *Pascendi dominici gregis*, 306, 320, 370, 396-400, 443; *Populorum progressio*, 657; *Providentissimus Deus*, 370, 375; *Rerum novarum*, 111-12, 124; *Syllabus of Errors*, 443; *Testem benevolentiae*, 306, 370; *Unam sanctam*, 659; *Ut unum sint*, 734

Pornography, 531

Poverty: amid affluence, 492; alleviation of (*see* Labor relations; Needy, ministry to the; Social reform; War on Poverty); extent of, 169, 520; undesirable effects of, 97-98, 104, 256, 498, 617, 619, 669; voluntary, 272-74, 713 (*see also* Life-style, simplicity in)

Powderly, Terence, 107

Powell, Colin, 476

Powell, John Wesley, 324-26, 436

Power: abuse of, 731; corrupting effect of, 88, 506-7, 597, 731

Pragmatism, 303, 308, 435, 436

Prayer, 186, 279, 515, 522, 575, 582, 592, 624, 694, 695, 697, 711; nature of, 211-12, 405, 411; as personal devotion, 13, 172, 194, 210-12, 216, 488; prayer groups, 138, 173; prayer for guidance, 671, 732; in schools, 579, 638-41; in times of national crisis, 475, 476-77, 478-79, 702, 704. *See also* Lord's Prayer

Preaching, 37, 40, 55, 91, 102, 119-20, 143, 155n., 194-95, 220, 275, 279, 280, 299, 327, 403, 433, 434, 551, 561-62, 576; examples, 103-4, 157-58, 183-85, 221-26, 242-43, 281-84, 463-64

Prejudice, 10, 499, 503, 554, 594, 617, 619, 650, 654, 712-13, 722, 738, 739. *See also* Anti-Catholicism; Anti-Semitism; Muslims: prejudice against; Racism

Presbyterians: 8, 78, 82, 91, 136, 299, 442, 443; 621-23; biblical criticism and, 364, 368-69; missions and, 48, 50-52, 64, 66-67, 144; national policy and, 64, 66-67, 136; preaching and, 37, 195, 225-26; individuals, 35, 64, 119, 131, 225, 336, 338, 401, 442, 506, 514, 554n., 679. *See also* United Presbyterian Church, U.S.A.

Presidents, and religion, 501, 685, 687, 690-701, 744. *See also* Public officials, religious orientation of

Preus, Robert D., 523n., 524, 527-28

Price, Thomas F., 152-54

Priesand, Sally, 625

Princeton Theological Seminary, 250, 401, 436, 554n.

Princeton University, 336, 337, 338

Prison reform, 83

Private religion, 9, 193-95, 199-206, 298-99, 542, 545-46

Process theology, 315-16

Proctor, Redfield, 63

Progress: of civilization, 164-65, 259, 323, 324-26, 450 (*see also* Optimism); in doctrine, 30, 221, 370, 408 (*see also* Dogma: development of); of morality, 683

Prohibition, 91-92, 186, 188, 263-66. *See also* Temperance movement

Prohibition Amendment. *See* Constitution, U.S.: Eighteenth Amendment

Prohibition Party, 186

Promise Keepers, 709-11

Prophecy, biblical, 284-86, 288, 290-91, 301, 463-64, 475, 744; and Zionism, 459. *See also* Heaven's Gate; Last things

Prosperity, personal. *See* Wealth

Protestantism, divisions in, 5, 80-83, 86, 144, 178-79, 277, 306, 519, 523-35, 572, 672-73, 686-90 passim. *See also* Ecumenical movement

Providence, R.I., 476

Providence, divine, 9, 10, 12, 18, 31, 144, 151, 332, 338, 374, 392, 407, 427, 433, 538, 545

Prussia, 7

Psychic powers. *See* Mind, power of

Psychology, religion and, 196, 227-28, 245-51, 300, 318, 402. *See also* Mind, power of

Public officials, religious orientation of: influence on electorate, 441-42, 498-99, 502-3, 685-90; influence on policy decisions, 499-502, 504, 661, 679, 680-82, 690

Public order, religion and, 679-708. *See also* Civil religion; Public officials, religious orientation of

Puerto Rico, 61, 65, 66, 87, 151, 274; immigration from, 274, 741

Pullman Strike, 88
Purcell, John Baptist, 47

Quakers. *See* Friends, Society of
Quigley, James Edward, 90, 149-50
Quimby, Phineas P., 230, 234, 237

Racism, 254-59, 262, 494-98, 577, 609; alleviation of, 144, 493; avoidance of, 172, 174, 585, 594, 691-92, 711; discrimination based on, 256, 450, 491-93, 498, 593-94, 609, 610-12, 617, 654, 661, 706, 713, 717-19, 738, 742 (*see also* Education, racial discrimination in); opposition to, 189, 227, 260-61, 498, 515, 531, 555, 711-12. *See also* Civil Rights movement; Ethnic identity; Holocaust; Ku Klux Klan; Liberation theology; Marginalization; Prejudice; Reparations; Segregation
Rackman, Emanuel, 29n., 32-34
Radio. *See under* Media
Rahner, Karl, 632
Ramon, Ilan, 700
Rankin, Jerry, 528n., 529, 532-33, 534-35
Rationalism, 27, 32, 37, 83, 319, 320-21, 365, 398, 429-30
Raulston, John T., 347
Rauschenbusch, Walter, 89, 109-10, 114-16, 188-89, 419, 486
Reagan, Nancy, 694
Reagan, Ronald, 566, 580, 640, 679, 694-96
Reconciling Ministries Network, 672n., 673-76
Red Cross, 129, 276
Reeb, James J., 553-55
Reformation, Protestant, 82, 122, 305, 353, 356, 357, 358, 549
Reformed churches, 78, 82; Dutch, 7-8, 243. *See also* Huguenots
Rehnquist, William, 638, 639-40, 661, 665-66
Released time, 579-80
Religions: comparative study of, 227, 325-26, 569; compared: from Christian perspective, 12, 334, 426, 517-18, 539, 548; from Jewish perspective, 407, 408; unity of all, 227-29, 230. *See also* Pluralism
Religious Freedom Restoration Act, 651-55
"Religious Humanism," 444, 568-69
Religious liberty, 25, 82, 83, 522, 543-46, 604, 656, 667, 668, 680, 717. *See also* Constitution, U.S.: First Amendment
Religious Science, Church of, 196, 239-42
Renewal, spiritual, 140, 276, 445, 520, 539,

704. *See also* Liturgical renewal; Revivalism
Reparations, 456, 494-98
Republican Party, 1, 186, 265, 267, 270, 395, 580, 685, 686-90
Revelation, divine, 72, 331, 363-66, 374, 409, 419-22, 426, 433-34, 530-31, 543-44, 609
Revivalism, 67, 82, 83, 138, 172, 183, 192, 276, 278-84, 287, 300-301, 439, 444, 559-63, 703, 704. *See also* Evangelical Awakening
Revolutionary War, 63, 439
Rhetoric: of fringe groups, 600, 601; religious, in political speech, 476-77, 480, 580, 581, 687-88, 694, 700
Rhode Island. *See* Newport; Providence
Richter, Jean Paul, 342
Rilke, Rainer Maria, 732
Rinpoche, Kyabje Gelek, 701, 705-6
Ritschl, Albrecht, 320n.
Rivera, Reynaldo, 614
Robe, The, 204-6
Roberts, Oral, 297-98
Robertson, Pat, 580, 634, 635, 701, 704, 707
Robinson, A. J., 566
Rochester, N.Y., 391, 394-95
Rochester Seminary, 109. *See also* Colgate Rochester Divinity School
Roe v. *Wade,* 580, 660-666, 669-70
Roman Catholicism: 13-23, 82, 84, 91, 92, 106, 206-9, 214-17, 257, 299, 357, 498-504, 564, 653, 655-60, 666-69, 679-82, 744-45; authority in, 306, 371, 377, 399-401, 632-34, 655-60, 667-68, 681, 731, 733; biblical concerns and, 25, 207-9, 254, 305, 357, 370-72, 373, 374-77, 380, 381, 400, 437, 540, 549; charismatics in, 295; charitable programs, 42-43, 82, 174-76; conversion to, 199, 272, 437, 682; ecumenical participation, 4, 91-92, 174-76, 509, 527, 536, 537, 547-52, 572, 659; ethnicity in, 17-20, 81, 613-17, 737, 740, 741; government relations, 743; growth in U.S., 1, 2, 21, 78, 91, 196; ethnic diversity in, 17-20, 84, 392, 712, 740; modernism and, 305-6, 319-21, 323, 330-32, 341-43, 370, 391-401, 437, 538-39, 656; sex abuse scandal in, 575, 583, 673, 728-34, 744; and social concern, 84, 88-89, 90, 106-9, 111-12, 122-24, 180-81, 189, 394, 441, 490, 496-97, 500-501, 570-71, 615-16, 621, 669, 681; voting patterns in, 686-89 passim; women in, 20, 40, 42-43, 85, 578-79, 631-34, 637, 660, 742; individual adherents, 263, 266-68, 269, 319, 341, 392-94, 431, 441, 499, 539, 564, 631,

666, 679-82. *See also* Anti-Catholicism; Education: Roman Catholicism and; Liturgical renewal; Missionary effort: Roman Catholic; Popes; Vatican II.

Roman Catholicism, bishops, 583; Hispanic, 578, 653; Pastoral Letters of: (1884), 13, 15-17; (1919), 131-32, 180-81; (1920), 111-12; (1959), 499; (1983), 681; (1987), 616-17; individual bishops, 13-15, 17-18, 61-62, 64-66, 90, 97-98, 106-9, 149-51, 330-32, 391, 392-96, 613-16, 653; in U.S., 22-23, 111, 123-24, 131, 180, 391, 394-96, 499, 578, 583, 616-17, 618, 671, 681, 728, 730, 732, 733. *See also* United States Catholic Conference

Romania, 453

Rome, 536, 729

Roosevelt, Franklin D., 122, 479

Roosevelt, Theodore, 121

Rosenberger v. *University of Virginia*, 641-48

Royce, Josiah, 303-4, 312-14, 315, 436

Rubenstein, Richard, 566, 573

Ruether, Rosemary Radford, 85, 631-34

Rumsfeld, Donald, 480

Russell, Bertrand, 315

Russell, Charles Taze, 284

Russia, 3, 6-7, 161, 162, 227, 255, 440, 441, 450, 453, 455, 456, 459, 471, 484, 568, 595, 694-96, 707. *See also* Cold War

Russian America. *See* Alaska

Russian American Company, 51, 56-57

Russian Orthodoxy, 3, 51, 52-58, 85-86, 443, 558; ecumenical interest, 555-56

Ruston, Roger, 473n., 476-78

Rutgers University, 722

Rutherford, Joseph Franklin, 162-63

Ryan, John A., 89, 122-24, 189, 331

Rynne, Xavier (pseud.), 535n., 536-39, 572

Sabbath, observance of, 32, 34, 194, 217-19, 299, 411, 699-700, 721. *See also* Sunday, observance of

Sacred Congregation de Propaganda Fide, 19, 149, 154

St. Louis, Mo., 87, 272, 303, 523, 524

St. Louis University, 431, 526, 527

St. Paul, Minn., 391

St. Petersburg, Fla., 258

St. Vladimir's Seminary, 557

Saloons, 99, 101, 103, 120, 171, 179, 265-66. *See also* Anti-Saloon League; Temperance movement

Salvation, 119, 148, 166, 281-82, 290, 312, 313, 485, 518-19, 543-44

Salvation Army 83, 90, 166, 168-71, 172, 190, 283

San Antonio, Tex., 736, 738

Sanctification. *See* Perfectionism

San Francisco, Calif.: Chinatown, 12-13; Orthodox missions in, 56, 57, 58; photograph, 236; mentioned, 24, 87, 514, 596, 719

Sankey, Ira D., 51, 278-80

Santa Fe, N.Mex., 614

Santayana, George, 304, 312, 319-21, 599

Sarna, Nahum, 412, 415-18, 437

Saturday Evening Post, 183-84

Scalia, Antonin, 640, 641, 649, 661, 663-64

Scandinavia: immigrants from, 9, 254-55; missions to, 159, 161

Schaeffer, Francis, 474

Schaff, Philip, 80-83, 86, 372

Schechter, Solomon, 2, 29, 31-32, 412-15

Schleiermacher, Friedrich, 420, 425

Schmemann, Alexander, 573

Schmidt, Leigh Eric, 575

Schouw, Martin van der, 8

Schut, C., 153

Schuyler, Eugene, 6-7

Science: criticism of, 271, 305, 350; place of faith in, 309; recent developments in, 432; religion and, 230, 235, 304-5, 317-18, 322-52, 359, 398, 402-3, 404, 407, 432, 433, 435, 436-37, 511. *See also* Atomic power; Fetal tissue research; Genetic engineering; Psychology, religion and

Scofield, Cyrus I., 288-91

Scofield Reference Bible, 198, 288. *See also New Scofield Reference Bible*

Scopes, John Thomas, 343, 352n.

Scopes trial, 304-5, 343-52, 436

Scottish Realism, 303

Seattle, Wash., 272, 483

"Second blessing," 293, 294

Segregation, 450, 453, 491-92, 698. *See also* Education: racial discrimination in

Selma, Ala., 492, 553

Seminex, 525-27

Sept. 11, 2001, 479, 481, 482, 483, 575, 576, 581, 591, 593, 594, 700, 701-8, 744

Sermons. *See* Preaching

Seven Storey Mountain, 215

Seventh-Day Adventists, 217, 300, 600. *See also* White, Ellen G.

Seventh-Day Baptists, 217

Sexual abuse. *See* Roman Catholicism: sex abuse scandal in

Sheen, Fulton J., 563n., 564-66

Sheldon, Charles M., 88, 102-4
Sherbert v. *Verner*, 653
Sherman, Roger, 503
Sherrill, C. O., 100
Sherwood, J. M., 67
Shinto, 4, 58
Siddiqui, Omar, 478, 482-83
Sikhs, 576, 706, 740
Silverman, Joseph, 257, 260-61, 263
Sisters of Charity and Mercy, 91, 190
Six Day War (1967), 440, 456, 457
Skanchy, Anthon L., 159
Skehan, Patrick, 381
Slavery, 83, 144, 155, 156, 259, 277, 410, 456, 493, 495, 609, 610-12, 675, 712, 713
Smidt, Corwin E., 685-90, 744
Smith, Alfred E., 197, 263-68, 300, 441
Smith, George M., 372
Smith, Joseph, 158, 734, 735
Smith, Joseph Fielding, 160
Smith, Timothy (U.S. Consul), 6, 7
Snow, Erastus, 159
Social concern. *See* Needy, ministry to the; Social reform; Sympathy; *and under* Buddhism; Congregationalism; Eastern Orthodoxy; Judaism; Methodists; Roman Catholicism
Social Gospel, 88-89, 90, 91, 94, 102-4, 109-10, 114-22, 166, 167, 174, 179, 188-89, 435, 486. *See also* Evangelism: prerequisite to social change; Kingdom of God; Labor relations; Needy, ministry to the; Social reform
Socialism, 271, 454, 459, 683. *See also* Christian socialism; Communism.
Socialist Party, 121
Social reform, 12, 21, 42, 88-89, 95-96, 103-4, 120, 167, 168, 174, 179, 180, 189, 190, 226, 496-98; grounded in religious principle, 41, 111, 112-24, 275-77, 405, 408, 410-11, 435, 485, 493-94, 518-19, 531, 562, 563, 565, 577, 608-10, 615-16, 617, 619, 698; responses to racism, 599, 621-23. *See also* Abortion; Family; Justice, social; Kingdom of God; Labor relations; Peace movements; Politics: role of religious institutions and individuals in; Racism: alleviation of, avoidance of, *and* opposition to; Social Gospel; Temperance movement; Urban reform
Society of American Newspaper Editors, 501
Society of Biblical Literature, 372, 437
Society of Jesus. *See* Jesuits.
Society of St. Vincent de Paul, 91, 174-76, 190
Socinians, 83

Socrates, 403
Sojourners, 478, 479-80
Solomon, Hannah G., 217-19, 220
Somalia, 706
Sorbonne, 319
Soul, created *ex nihilo*, 338-39
Souter, David H., 647-48, 661, 664-65
South Carolina v. *Katzenbach*, 654
South Dakota, 693, 719
Southeast Asia, 144, 167. *See also* Vietnam War
Southern Baptist Convention, 222, 442-43, 523-24, 528-35, 537, 572, 666, 671-72, 696. *See also* Baptist Faith and Message; Southern Baptist Theological Seminary
Southern Baptist Theological Seminary, 364-68, 478
Southern Christian Leadership Conference, 490
Soviet Union. *See* Russia
Space exploration, 700-701
Spain, 319, 502; Civil War, 274; Muslim legacy in, 77
Spalding, John Lancaster, 4, 61-62, 86, 88, 97-98
Spanish-American War, 4, 61-63, 86, 87, 89, 439
Speaking in tongues. *See* Glossolalia
Speer, Robert E., 131, 132, 144-46, 190
Spencer, Herbert, 336
Spinoza, Baruch (Benedict), 312, 415
Sri Lanka, 73
Stade, Bernhard, 415
Stampede Mesteth, Wilmer, 719
Standing Elk, Darrell, 719
Stanley, David S., 47-50
Stanton, Elizabeth Cady, 43-46, 85
Statistical decline, 439, 444-45
Stephen of Perm, St., 557
Stevens, John Paul, 638-39, 647, 661
Stoicism, 277
Strong, James, 372
Strong, Josiah, 21-23, 84, 88, 93-94
Student Volunteer Movement for Foreign Missions, 142
Sullivan, W. L., 396n., 397, 400-401
Sunday, Billy, 91, 183-85, 190, 197, 207, 282-84, 300
Sunday, observance of, 120, 179, 194, 204, 219-20, 228-29. *See also* Church attendance
Sunday School, 13, 40, 41, 175, 348, 355, 361, 690, 697

Supreme Court, U.S., 441, 504, 578, 579-80, 638-50, 651, 653-55, 660-66, 704
Sutras, 585
Sweden, 159
Swedenborg, Emmanuel, 195, 230
Swift Hawk, Phyllis, 719
Switzerland, 161, 162, 442, 516, 695
Sympathy, toward the unfortunate, 475, 594, 615, 616, 621-23, 703
Synagogue Council of America, 91, 181-83, 497-98

Tacitus, 127
Taft, Alphonso, 24-27
Taft, William Howard, 24, 63, 66
Talmage, T. DeWitt, 327-29
Tax exemption, for religious institutions, 646, 652
Taylor, Kenneth, 387, 390
Teapot Dome scandal, 506
Television. *See under* Media
Teller, Chester Jacob, 176-77
Temperance movement, 39-41, 85, 179, 183-86, 188, 190. *See also* Prohibition
Tennessee, 304, 344-48, 350, 351, 352n., 690
Teresa of Avila, St., 216
Terrorism, 478, 482-83, 704, 707. *See also* Sept. 11, 2001
Texas, 529, 533-35, 577, 600, 662, 700. *See also* Dallas; Houston; San Antonio
Thatcher, Mr. (songleader), 279
Thayer, J. H., 372
Theology: role of, 423-26; retreat of, 439, 563-69, 573; in 21st century, 734-40, 745. *See also* Dogma
Theosophical Society, 227-29
Thorp, Peggie, 731-32
Tibet, 215, 705
Tietjen, John H., 523n., 524, 525-27, 572
Tilden, Samuel J., 1
Tillich, Paul, 422-26, 438
Tisserant, Eugène (Cardinal), 536
Tolerance, 83, 604, 638, 639, 677, 708
Toomy, Alice T., 39n., 40, 42-43
Topeka, Kan., 86
Toy, Crawford Howell, 364-68
Transcendental Meditation, 576
Translation, nature of, 381-82
Trappist order, 215, 539
Traynor, W. J. H., 252
Trine, Ralph Waldo, 232-33
Trinity College, 613
Truett, George W., 222-23

Truth, 30, 284, 334, 337, 365, 410; all is from God, 331; power of, 544, 561; sought by free inquiry, 318, 330-31, 366, 423, 545-46; speaking, in love, 658; suffering for, 235. *See also* Dharma
Turkey, 165, 255, 553, 590

Ukrainian immigrants, 578
Underhill, Evelyn, 299
Union Theological Seminary, 128, 138, 225, 355, 364, 372, 422, 499, 608
Unitarians, 83, 128, 554n. *See also under* Pentecostalism
Unitarian-Universalists, 568
United Brethren, 78
United Church of Christ, 275, 666, 669-70. *See also* Congregationalism; Evangelical and Reformed Church
United Nations, 465-66, 474, 477, 478, 481, 483
United Presbyterian Church, U.S.A., 465, 467-68, 496
United States Catholic Conference, 666, 668-69
United States Chamber of Commerce, 270, 485
Unity School of Christianity, 196, 237-39, 242, 300
Universal Declaration of Human Rights, 465-66, 522
Universalists, 83, 136
University of California (Berkeley), 333
University of Chicago, 250, 355, 377, 378, 404
University of the City of New York, 327
University of Durham, 372
University of Edinburgh, 225
University of Notre Dame, 341, 679
University of Oxford, 319, 372
University of Pennsylvania, 322
University of South Carolina, 333
University of Toronto, 449
University of Virginia. *See Rosenberger* v. *University of Virginia*
University of Wisconsin, 119
Upper Room, The, 209-11
Urbanization, 87, 88, 93, 97, 103, 168
Urban reform, 88, 93-104, 120, 391. *See also* Social reform
Utah, 158, 349

Vahanian, Gabriel, 666
Van Buren, Paul, 666
Vandals, 155

Van Dusen, Henry P., 138-39
Van Dyke, Henry, 4
Vatican, diplomatic relations with, 500, 502, 729
Vatican Council I, 443, 538
Vatican Council II, 443, 444, 535-39, 543-49, 572, 615, 655, 656-57, 658-59, 679, 732, 733; responses to, 539-42
Vaughan, Henry, 536
Vaughan, Herbert (Cardinal), 152
Vedanta Society, 72, 576
Vedas, 72-73
Veniaminov, John, 3, 53-56
Vermont, 291
Vietnam War, 440, 473, 475, 495, 701; protest movement, 450, 456, 469, 566, 682; religious responses to, 465, 467-70, 570-71
Violence, rejected as a method, 411, 498, 705. *See also* Nonviolent protest; War
Virginia, 293, 628, 645, 647-48
Visual art, religion and, 207, 299, 411
Vivekananda, Swami, 72-73
Vocation, 37, 112, 223-25, 511
Voice of the Faithful, 728, 731-34
Voluntarism, 691
Voting Rights Act, 654

Waldensians, 83
Wallace, Lew. *See* Ben-Hur
Wallace v. *Jaffree*, 638-40
Wallis, Martha, 68
Wallis, Jim, 478, 479-80
Walsh, James A., 152-54
War, 89, 135-37, 176-77, 350, 439-40, 448, 474, 476, 706, 712, 713; abolition of, 134; approved, 63, 89, 125-27; condemned, 128-31, 133, 134; conduct of, 467-68; "just war" question, 128-29, 144, 441, 477, 480, 501; lessons of, 131-32; voted against, 706. *See also specific wars by name and* Armed forces; Conscientious objection; Militarism; Nuclear war; Peace movements
War on Poverty, 504-6
Ward, Harry F., 268-70, 486
Warfield, B. B., 338-40, 436
Warren, Earl, 441
Warsaw Pact, 474
Washington, 10-12. *See also* Seattle
Washington, D.C., 475-76, 490, 570; photographs, 611, 668, 709; site of Sept. 11 attack, 581, 591, 701, 703; mentioned, 180, 478, 501, 613, 699, 729
Washington, George, 23, 33, 507, 640

Washington Disarmament Conference, 89
Watch Tower Society, 284-85
Watergate, 442, 506-8, 571
Watts, Evelyn, 431
Waxman, Chaim, 722
Wealth: dangers of, 103, 106, 270; proposed as a goal, 242-43, 713; renounced, 73 (*see also* Poverty, voluntary); responsible use of, 103, 113, 243, 630, 693, 703; as temptation, 506. *See also* Church finance; Justice: in distribution of wealth
Webb, Mohammed, 76-78
Websites, xxix-xxx, 516, 732
Webster v. *Reproductive Services*, 661, 662-64
Welcoming, church's failure in, 280, 673-76
Weldon, Courtnay, 481
Wellhausen, Julius, 413, 415
Wellington, duke of, 71
Wesley, John, 83, 198, 291, 420, 436, 677
West, American, 3, 47-50, 85, 87, 255
Western Reserve University, 93
West Virginia Board of Education v. *Barnette*, 639, 650
Wheaton College, 715
White, Ellen G., 35, 300
White, Theodore, 506
White Citizens Council, 698
Whitefield, George, 83, 420
Whitehead, Alfred North, 193, 304, 314-16, 436
Wicca, 603, 741
Wilder, Royal G., 67
Wilkins, Ernest, 380
Willard, Frances E., 39-41, 85
Willebrandt, Mabel Walker, 263-66, 267
Williams, Juan, 711-14
Williams, Rowan, 744
Willis, Jeff, 628-31
Willow Creek Association, 716
Willow Creek Community Church, 696, 697, 714-16
Wilmore, G. S., 708
Wilson, Woodrow, 128, 129-30, 187, 685
Wind, James, 526
Winder, John R., 160
Wisconsin, 503, 603. *See also* Milwaukee
Wise, Isaac Mayer, 29-31, 407
Wise, Stephen, 128, 129-30
Wogaman, Philip, 699
Wohlgelernter, Rachel, 722
Woman's Bible, The, 44-45
Women, 85, 267, 619, 675, 679, 708, 742; biblical scholarship of, 2, 43-45; denied vote

or office in churches, 524, 531, 578-79, 623-
27, 628, 630-32, 660; education for, 35-37,
626-27; emancipation of, 2-3, 35-37, 42-46,
623; equality for, with submission, 532,
631; ministry and ordination of, 2, 4, 35,
37-39, 45-46, 85, 168, 171, 195, 578-79, 623,
625, 629, 632-34, 716, 742; reforming activity of, 2, 39-43, 85, 186; sensitivity of, 636;
in Salvation Army, 168, 171; suffrage
movement, 43, 187; support for foreign
missions, 69-71, 86; voting patterns of,
687; in the work force, 98, 120. *See also*
Abortion; Inclusive language
Women's Christian Temperance Union, 39-
41, 42, 186
Women's Missionary Friend, 69
Woodstock Seminary, 543
Worcester, Elwood, 245-47
Wordsworth, Christopher (Bishop), 366
Work, dignity of, 112, 120, 217, 220. *See also*
Vocation
World, religion and. *See* Church, relation to
the world
World Council of Churches, 142, 442, 444,
468, 487, 509, 512-14, 516, 657
World government, 448, 483. *See also* United
Nations
World Parliament of Religions, 4-5, 71-78,
80, 86, 584, 604
World's Student Christian Federation, 142
World War I, 89-90, 91, 125-32, 144, 162, 172,
176-77, 180, 189, 271, 305, 455

World War II, 383, 439-40, 441, 446-52, 462,
463, 479, 503, 563, 569, 581
Worldwide Church of God, 217
World Zionist Organization, 454
Worship, styles of, 58, 83, 280, 294, 299, 325,
326, 443. *See also* Bible: liturgical reading
of; Church attendance; Language; Liturgical renewal; Music
"WWJD," 102, 688

Xavier, St. Francis, 151

Yale University, 225, 275, 317, 353, 419, 437,
582, 720-23
Yeshiva University, 29, 414, 722
Yogi, Maharishi Mahesh, 576
Young, Brigham, 159
Young Men's Buddhist Association, 59
Young Men's Christian Association, 12, 90,
130, 138, 172-74, 177
Young Men's Hebrew Association, 176
Young Women's Christian Association, 12, 90
Young Women's Hebrew Association, 176
Y2K problem, 582, 723, 724-25

Zahm, John Augustine, 341-43, 436
Zaire, 692
Zen Buddhism, 75, 299, 584, 585, 586
Zinzendorf, Nikolaus Ludwig (Count), 83
Zionism, 407, 410, 452-63, 570
Zohar, 413
Zoroastrianism, 72, 227, 231, 325